Research Methods
in Practice

For my husband, Howard, thank you for everything,
and to my father who taught me analytical thinking from an early age
(DKR)

For Ada, Alina, and Lucia, my best buddies in life,
and to my parents who each in their own way made me a researcher
(GGV)

Research Methods
in **Practice**

Strategies for Description and Causation

Dahlia K. Remler • Gregg G. Van Ryzin
Baruch College,
City University of New York

Rutgers University

Los Angeles | London | New Delhi
Singapore | Washington DC

For information:

SAGE Publications, Inc.
2455 Teller Road
Thousand Oaks, California 91320
E-mail: order@sagepub.com

SAGE Publications Ltd.
1 Oliver's Yard
55 City Road
London EC1Y 1SP
United Kingdom

SAGE Publications India Pvt. Ltd.
B 1/I 1 Mohan Cooperative Industrial Area
Mathura Road, New Delhi 110 044
India

SAGE Publications Asia-Pacific Pte. Ltd.
33 Pekin Street #02-01
Far East Square
Singapore 048763

Printed in the United States of America

Library of Congress Cataloging-in-Publication Data

Remler, Dahlia K.
Research methods in practice: strategies for description and causation/Dahlia K. Remler, Gregg G. Van Ryzin.
  p. cm.
Includes bibliographical references and index.
ISBN 978-1-4129-6467-8 (pbk. : alk. paper)
  1. Research—Methodology—Study and teaching (Graduate) I. Van Ryzin, Gregg G. (Gregg Gerard), 1961- II. Title.
LB2369.R46 2011
001.4'2—dc22   2009047307

Printed on acid-free paper.

10 11 12 13 14 10 9 8 7 6 5 4 3 2 1

Acquiring Editor:	Vicki Knight
Associate Editor:	Lauren Habib
Editorial Assistant:	Ashley Dodd
Production Editor:	Karen Wiley
Copy Editor:	QuADS Prepress (P) Ltd.
Proofreader:	Jenifer Kooiman
Indexer:	Molly Hall
Typesetter:	C&M Digitals (P) Ltd.
Cover Designer:	Candice Harman
Marketing Manager:	Stephanie Adams
Cover Art:	Hanna Mandelbaum (HannaJanePaints.com)

Brief Contents

Detailed Contents

Preface

This book began on a Saturday morning in the spring of 2004, when Dahlia came to visit one of Gregg's executive master of public administration classes. It was a chance simply to observe, get feedback, and share ideas about how to teach research methods. We had each taught this kind of course for years in different programs, but this opportunity arose because we were about to become members of the same faculty in the fall.

We are rather different from each other. Dahlia is an economist with a keen interest in economic theory and causal research. Gregg is a psychologist by training with a background in survey research and program evaluation. Dahlia works on issues related to health and health care. Gregg works on issues related to urban services and public opinion. Our teaching and writing styles—even our personalities—are quite different.

But we hit it off immediately. We realized that our differences in training and experience complemented and reinforced each other. We discovered that we both had a deep commitment to trying to teach research methods well—with clarity, rigor, and purpose. We shared a strong belief that research methods matter—not just to those who plan to become researchers—but to decision makers and practitioners preparing to tackle some of society's toughest problems. We also shared a belief in the value of interdisciplinary research. And we were both increasingly disappointed in the books available to assign to our students.

The standard research methods books we were using had a strong sociology flavor, yet our students came from diverse fields and had more policy-related interests. We wanted a more interdisciplinary approach and more examples of applied social and policy research across various substantive areas (such as public management, education, criminal justice, public health, and other areas).

Some of the standard books were initially published several decades ago, and—although new editions were coming out—they seemed to us to be a bit old-fashioned. Research methods and statistics have advanced very rapidly over the past few decades—not only technologically but intellectually—with important influences coming from economics, psychology, political science, epidemiology, statistics, and various other disciplines. We wanted a book that better reflected current thinking.

We also found that the books we were using did not cover causation sufficiently—despite the fact that causal research is essential to understanding the origins of social problems and the effectiveness of proposed solutions. When books did discuss causation, they focused heavily on experiments rather than the observational studies (with control variables), quasi experiments, and natural experiments that modern social and policy researchers mostly depend on to examine causal questions in the real world. We wanted a book that would help students think seriously about causation and recognize and assess the actual research strategies used most often to try to get at it.

Finally, we wanted a book that covered not just the abstract concepts of the scientific method but that gave a feel for the realistic trade-offs, uncertainties, habits, and also excitement that constitute the research experience. To do so, the book we envisioned would contain plenty of in-depth, real-world examples of a wide range of studies that would serve to not only illustrate key methods and ideas but also demonstrate the value of research to public policy and practice. Research is not perfect—often far from it. Still, we believe that it provides the best hope we have for truly improving the world we live in.

By the end of that morning (probably it was the early afternoon by the time we finished our coffee and discussion), we decided to begin writing our own research methods textbook. We started gradually, using a few draft chapters as supplements to the standard textbooks we were using. As we wrote and taught with our emerging book, we found new ways to explain key ideas, experimented with the best order of topics, dug up interesting examples, and worked to clarify and simplify the often confusing terminology of research methods. As the full book took shape, we had many discussions and debates about ideas and worked long hours revising and rearranging the chapters into a logical, clear, and coherent whole. We both learned a tremendous amount in the process of writing this book, and we hope that the book helps students and others learn a great deal as well.

A Note to Instructors: How the Book Is Organized—and Why

We organized the book broadly around what we see as the two main kinds of research: strategies for description (Chapters 4 to 9) and strategies to get at causation (Chapters 10 to 13). Descriptive research questions ask about *what is*—the characteristics and patterns that exist in the social world. Causal research questions ask about *what if*—how things in the social world would be different if we made a change. Both are essential in most basic and applied fields, yet it is critical for students to recognize this distinction when doing or assessing studies (and not, for example, assume that a descriptive study demonstrates causation).

Before getting into the details of descriptive and causal research, students need some foundational concepts and tools (Chapters 1 to 3). These include the nature of research and of the scientific method, and, importantly, the foundational role of theory, the tool of path models, and core concepts (such as variables and relationships) that appear in almost all forms of research. We also cover qualitative research (Chapter 3) as foundational because it often serves as an exploratory method and because it helps generate theory and indentify causal processes. Introducing qualitative methods early also allows later, more quantitative chapters to incorporate and integrate the qualitative perspective so that we can present a mixed-methods approach to most topics.

Although we tried to keep the order of topics fairly traditional, similar to other research methods books and courses, we have situated some chapters differently and introduced novel ones. We put the chapter on qualitative research early in the book for the reasons just mentioned. We cover sources of secondary data (Chapter 6) before primary data (Chapter 7), because many students are more likely to work with secondary data (in their classes and in their careers) and because of the burgeoning availability of secondary data on the Internet. We placed the chapters on statistical analysis at the end of Part II (Strategies for Description) because the tools of statistical analysis (including statistical inference) are largely descriptive—statistics alone do not establish causation—and because students need certain statistical tools as background for some of the most widely used strategies for causation (such as control variables). Compared with most research methods textbooks, our book covers multiple regression extensively, but through intuition and examples, not technical material. Although we envision most students who use this book as having had some prior coursework in basic statistics, the book is nonmathematical and written to be accessible to those without prior coursework in statistics.

In Part III on strategies for causation, we have a somewhat novel chapter at the start focused on the issue of causation itself (Chapter 10)—what it is, why it is important, and how to begin identifying it. We have found that probing these questions in depth provides motivation and background for learning the logic and methods of various real-world causal research strategies. Instead of presenting randomized experiments right away, the "gold standard" for determining causation, we first cover observational studies with control variables (Chapter 11). We do this because such studies are the most numerous in social and policy research and thus the ones students are most likely to encounter in their studies and in their careers. But more important, understanding the limits of observational studies with control variables illuminates the need for and logic of randomized experiments. Following the chapter on randomized experiments (Chapter 12), we have another somewhat novel chapter on natural and quasi experiments (Chapter 13) that covers a variety of real-world strategies that emulate the advantages of experimental research for answering causal questions. Natural and quasi experiments, along with observational studies, represent the vast majority of research used to inform policy and practice. The order of chapters in Part III aims to facilitate understanding of these types of studies.

We recognize, to be sure, that different instructors and programs have different styles and requirements. So to the extent possible (in a linear medium such as a book), we have tried to allow the chapters to be used in a different order. Some instructors may wish to combine, or omit, selected chapters, for example, the multivariate chapter (Chapter 9). But we have put much thought and a good deal of class testing into this book, and we encourage instructors to at least consider the logic of presentation suggested by our table of contents.

Finally, we recognize that we have not succeeded at perfecting the presentation of such a complex and important subject as research methods. Writing a book like this is a humbling experience. We would be immensely grateful for any feedback on the book from both instructors and students.

Acknowledgments

W e would like to thank those who read and commented on individual chapters, the detailed outline or in some cases, the entire book:

Philip Alberti, *New York City Department of Health and Mental Hygiene*

Howard Alper, *New York City Department of Health and Mental Hygiene*

Deborah Balk, *Baruch College and The Graduate Center, City University of New York*

Martin Frankel, *Baruch College and The Graduate Center, City University of New York*

Tod Joyce, *Baruch College and The Graduate Center, City University of New York*

Sanders Korenman, *Baruch College and The Graduate Center, City University of New York*

Cheryl Merzel, *Lehman College and The Graduate Center, City University of New York*

Matthew Neidell, *Columbia University*

Suzanne Piotrowski, *Rutgers University, Newark*

Pauline Rothstein, *New York University*

Alan Sadovnik, *Rutgers University, Newark*

Dorothy Schipps, *Baruch College, City University of New York*

Arloc Sherman, *Center on Budget and Policy Priorities*

Robert C. Smith, *Baruch College and The Graduate Center, City University of New York*

Jeanne Teresi, *Columbia University and Research Division, Hebrew Home at Riverdale*

We would also like to thank Sage's outside reviewers who read and commented on the initial proposal and on drafts of the various chapters:

Adam Atherly, *Emory University*

Anthony Bertelli, *University of Southern California*

David Daniel Bogumil, *California State University, Northridge*

Amita Chudgar, *Michigan State University*

Douglas Jackson-Smith, *Utah State University*

Stephen S. Owen, *Radford University*

Chester Robinson, *Tennessee State University*

Craig Tollini, *Western Illinois University*

Marc D. Weiner, *Bloustein Center for Survey Research, Rutgers University*

The students who read draft chapters of the book in our various classes gave us comments, as well as the opportunity to directly observe what aspects of the chapters did and did not work. Their feedback was critical to the book, and we thank them. We thank Hanna Mandelbaum (HannaJanePaints.com) for creating the original cover art entitled "Interrelated", which represents the idea of complex causal relationships so well.

We thank profusely our editor at Sage, Vicki Knight. She saw potential in our book at an early stage, provided valuable encouragement and criticism as the book took shape, and shared with us her extensive experience in the craft and business of textbook publishing. She is also a joy to work with. We thank Lauren Habib at Sage, who helped us a great deal with the book, our production editors Sarah Quesenberry and Karen Wiley, our copy editor Rajasree Ghosh of QuADS Prepress (P) Ltd, and our marketing editor Stephanie Adams.

Finally, we are grateful to our professors, mentors, colleagues, and students who have furthered our thinking and learning about research methods over the years. Dahlia would particularly like to thank Deborah Balk, Gregory Colman, Allison Cuellar, David Cutler, Sherry Glied, Claudia Goldin, Jessica Greene, Michael Grossman, Katherine M. Harris, Ted Joyce, Lawrence F. Katz, Sanders Korenman, Joseph Newhouse, and Katherine Swartz. Gregg would particularly like to thank Frank Andrews, Steve Dietz, Donna Eisenhower, Martin Frankel, Steven Immerwahr, Robert Kaestner, Sanders Korenman, Rom Litwin, John Mollenkopf, Doug Muzzio, Leanne Rivlin, Susan Saegert, Ann Schnare, Carroll Seron, and Gary Winkel.

About the Authors

Dahlia K. Remler is Associate Professor at the School of Public Affairs, Baruch College, and the Department of Economics, Graduate Center, both of the City University of New York. She is also a Faculty Research Fellow at the National Bureau of Economic Research.

Dahlia has been in an unusual mix of disciplinary and interdisciplinary settings. She received a BS in electrical engineering from the University of California at Berkeley, a DPhil in physical chemistry from Oxford University—while a Marshall Scholar—and a PhD in economics from Harvard University. During the Clinton administration's health care reform efforts, Dahlia held a fellowship at the Brookings Institution to finish her dissertation on health care cost containment. She then held a postdoctoral research fellowship at Harvard Medical School, followed by assistant professorships at Tulane's and Columbia's Schools of Public Health, prior to joining the faculty at Baruch. She enjoys comparing and contrasting how different disciplines see the same issues.

Dahlia has published widely in a variety of areas in health care policy, including health care cost containment, information technology in health care, cigarette tax regressivity, simulation methods for health insurance take-up, and health insurance and health care markets. She has also recently started working on higher education issues. Her work has appeared in the *Journal of Policy Analysis and Management*, *Health Affairs*, the *Quarterly Journal of Economics*, the *American Journal of Public Health*, *Medical Care Research and Review*, and many other journals.

Dahlia lives with her husband, Howard, in New York City, where they enjoy the city's theaters, restaurants, and parks.

Gregg G. Van Ryzin is Associate Professor at the School of Public Affairs and Administration, Rutgers University. He received his BA in geography from Columbia University and his PhD in psychology from the City University of New York. During his doctoral training, he worked as a planner for a nonprofit housing and community development organization in New York City, and he completed his dissertation on low income housing for the elderly in Detroit. He next worked in Washington, D.C., for ICF Inc. and later Westat, Inc. on surveys and program evaluations for the U.S. Department of Housing and Urban Development and other federal agencies. In 1995, he joined the faculty of the School of Public Affairs, Baruch College, where he directed their Survey Research Unit for 8 years. In that role, he helped develop and direct the New York City Community Health Survey, a large-scale behavioral health survey for the city's health department, and also played a key role in shaping and conducting the city's survey of satisfaction with government services. He recently spent a year in Madrid, collaborating with researchers there on the analysis of surveys about public attitudes toward Spanish government policy and programs. This experience has led to a new interest in international and comparative public opinion about government performance and institutions.

Gregg has published more than 30 scholarly articles on housing and welfare programs, survey and evaluation methods, and citizen satisfaction with public services. His work has appeared in *Evaluation Review*, the *International Review of Administrative Sciences*, the *Journal of Policy Analysis and Management*, the *Journal of Public Administration Research and Theory*, the *Journal of Urban Affairs*, *Public Administration Review*, *Public Performance and Management Review*, *Urban Affairs Review*, and other journals.

Gregg lives in New York City with his wife, Ada (a history professor at NYU), and their daughters Alina and Lucia. They enjoy life in their Greenwich Village neighborhood, escaping on occasion to Spain, Miami, Maine, Cuba, and other interesting places in the world.

PART I

FOUNDATIONS

Objectives: In this chapter, you will learn why research methods matter—not just for those who do research—but for those who apply it to policy and practice. Research provides a fact base for decisions and wins arguments; and sometimes (if you're not careful), research misleads. Knowing research methods also provides a foundation for understanding performance measurement, program evaluation, and the push for evidence-based policy and practice in many fields. You will begin to see how descriptive ("what is") questions differ from causal ("what if") questions. And you will learn what defines research and the scientific method more generally as a way of knowing about the world. This chapter aims to spark your interest in research methods—and to help you approach the rest of the book with an open and informed perspective.

Thousands of studies have looked at global warming.

Source: © 2009 JupiterImages Corporation.

Research in the Real World

1

Do Methods Matter?

We want to do things in our lives and in our work to make a difference in the world—to educate children, treat or prevent sickness, reduce crime and violence, promote the arts, feed the hungry, house the homeless, or improve public services to communities. We share a desire to do something meaningful, to leave our mark in the world. But doing so requires a base of evidence beyond our own personal knowledge and experience—evidence about how things really are, and evidence about how to make things better.

We need such evidence not only to enhance our own understanding and decision making but also to convince others—those with the authority and resources that we need to accomplish our aims, or those with opposing points of view who stand in our way.

Good Evidence Comes From Well-Made Research

The best evidence comes from good research. Good research can appear in the form of a study published in a journal, but it can also be an internal analysis of administrative data, a government or foundation report, a performance measurement brief, a program evaluation, a needs assessment, or a client or employee survey. Government agencies collect and disseminate a great variety of empirical evidence on many important topics, such as health services and outcomes, educational attainment, labor market characteristics, crime victimization and punishment, housing conditions, environmental air and water quality, and so on. (See www.fedstats.gov to get a flavor of all that is available from the U.S. federal government alone.)

Because of the Internet and modern communications technology, we now live and work in a world in which an abundance of studies and statistics swirl all about us and hover within easy grasp—provided we know what to choose, how to make sense of it, and where to apply it.

Good research—just like a good car or a good pair of shoes—must be well designed and well made. But we cannot simply rely on brand names (although knowing that research comes from a respected scientific journal or reputable research institution does provide some assurance). Still, each study is unique, and each has unique strengths and weaknesses. So we need to understand how research is made—that is, research methods or *methodology*.

Methodology refers to the sampling strategies, measurement instruments, comparisons, statistical techniques, and other procedures that produce research evidence. So we need to understand methodology to judge the quality of research. Research methodology is what this book is all about.

May the Best Methodology Win

We also need an understanding of research methodology to attack evidence that hurts our cause or defend evidence that helps it.

Consider the controversy over abstinence-only sex education for teenagers. Some communities feel strongly that teens should be discouraged as much as possible from engaging in sexual activity and that comprehensive sex education (which can involve distributing condoms and instructing teens in their use) sends the wrong signal. Others warn that the abstinence-only approach does little to change the reality of teenagers' lives, leaving them vulnerable to unwanted pregnancy and sexually transmitted diseases (including AIDS).

Sex education in schools has spurred controversy—and research.

Source: © iStockphoto.com/IsaacLKoval.

As is often the case with a controversial public policy issue, both sides can point to studies to bolster their arguments. A review by Douglas Kirby (2007) uncovered 115 studies of various pregnancy prevention programs targeting U.S. teens, including abstinence and comprehensive programs. So neither side can win just by pointing to "*a* study" that supports their position.

Instead, we must struggle over how well made the conflicting studies are—meaning their methodology. If my study is better made, I win the argument. But if your study turns out to be better made, you win. So, although the war may start from a substantive policy or program disagreement such as how best to provide sex education to teens, the battles often rage over research methodology.

Research-Savvy People Rule

Some of you may be training to become researchers or analysts—and so doing research will be (or already is) part of your job. Clearly, knowing research methods is important to you. But many of you are (or plan to be) practitioners, doers—implementing programs, delivering services, managing people, or leading organizations. Why do you need to know research methods? We've already suggested a few reasons: Good research provides a fact base for decisions and wins arguments, and the quality of research often hinges on questions of methodology. But knowing research methods can help your career more directly as well.

We live and work in an "information age" in which the ability to find, understand, and make use of complex sources of information—such as research—represents an important skill. An explosion of data of all kinds—from governments and other institutions as well as data generated by programs and organizations—means that those who know how to handle, analyze, and interpret data have great value to organizations and employers. Agencies and organizations regularly commission research, and so their top leaders or managers must know how to make sense of and apply research findings to improve policies and programs. Funding agencies and legislative bodies demand "evidence-based"—meaning research-based—programs and management reforms. To win grants or funding for your program or agency, you need the ability to demonstrate an understanding of research in your field of policy or practice.

So without a grasp of research methods, you will be at a disadvantage in applying for jobs, advancing into leadership positions, and attracting financial and political support for your program or cause. With a good understanding of research methods, you can do more and go further in your career.

Research, Policy, and Practice

Research has become an essential element of modern public policy and management in the form of performance measurement, program evaluation, and the push for evidence-based policy and practices.

Performance Measurement

The world these days is awash in performance measurement and performance management. The idea is sensible: We should measure how well we're doing and ideally manage to improve it. New York City's COMPSTAT program—a data-driven effort to closely track crime and hold managers accountable for controlling it—is an often-cited example. The mass of data available today, thanks to the information revolution, fuels this trend. Performance measurement has now become a pillar of contemporary policy and practice in the public and nonprofit sectors (Hatry, 2007; de Lancer Julnes & Holzer, 2008; Poister, 2003).

In the following chapters, you will see how logic models can help you figure out what to measure. You will learn what makes for valid and reliable measurements. And you will be introduced to various sources of data to measure outputs and outcomes, including both existing data and original surveys. All this material is critical to understanding and implementing performance measurement and management.

Evaluation Research

Many program evaluations aim to answer the question: Did the program or intervention have an impact? Did it improve or change things? Other program evaluations seek to describe the process of implementing the program. Evaluation research is now a standard requirement of most government or foundation grants and contracts. Most new policy or management initiatives demand some form of evaluation as well. So evaluation research, too, has become a pillar of contemporary public policy and management in the public and nonprofit sectors (Rossi, Lipsey, & Freeman, 2003; Weiss, 1997).

But how can we know if a program or initiative is having its intended effect? Later chapters will introduce you to the basic ideas involved in thinking about cause and effect. They will cover strategies for estimating causal effects, including the use of control variables, randomized field experiments, and various forms of what are called natural and quasi experiments. These are the major strategies for conducting evaluations of program impact.

Evidence-Based Policy and Programs

As suggested earlier, governments and foundations increasingly favor *evidence-based* policies and programs—strategies that have proven their effectiveness with research. It's not enough anymore to have a few heartwarming testimonials or a plan that just looks good on paper. The trend toward evidence-based policy and practice now permeates many fields (Davies, Nutley, & Smith, 2000).

Due to limited resources, policymakers and practitioners must often choose between effective programs. Therefore, comparing the effectiveness of different programs is crucial, as is comparing **cost-effectiveness**—the outcome obtained relative to the cost of the program. Such comparisons require evidence about the magnitude of a program's effect—how large an influence a program has on the outcome.

The chapters that follow will give you tools to identify and assess evidence that backs up your program or initiative. And it will help you understand how to produce good research evidence to support your aims.

Evidence Can Mislead

On top of all that we've mentioned so far about the importance of research methods, it can be embarrassing to be wrong—and sometimes, if you're not careful, evidence can mislead.

Misleading Measurements

"No Child Left Behind" (NCLB) was signed into law in 2002, setting in motion a wave of reform in schools all across the United States that became suddenly preoccupied with high-stakes testing, worried about closing the race gap, and apprehensive about the need to demonstrate extraordinary gains in test scores. NCLB won support in part because of the "Houston Miracle," the fact that this large, diverse city had itself demonstrated remarkable gains in reading and math scores, especially for Black and Hispanic students—at least according to scores on the Texas Assessment of Academic Skills (TAAS). If Houston could do it, so could the rest of the nation.

But scores on another test—the Stanford Achievement Test—taken by the same Houston students during the same school years showed a much different picture, according to an analysis by the *New York Times* (Schemo & Fessenden, 2003). Scores on the Stanford test, which is used nationwide, showed little or no gain overall in Houston and little or no narrowing of the race gap. Several well known experts in education statistics, asked by the *New York Times* to review the discrepancy, concluded that the TAAS had considerably overstated the progress made by Houston students. Standardized tests do not necessarily provide a consistent measure.

Misleading Samples

In response to a recent Supreme Court decision on gun control, A *USA Today* (2008) quick poll asked visitors to its Web site, "How many guns do you own?" About 30,000 people die in the United States each year from gun-related accidents or violence (Centers for Disease Control and Prevention, 2008), so the high rate of gun ownership in the United States is an important public health as well as criminal justice issue. But how high is the rate of gun ownership? A total of 1,987 people responded to the *USA Today* quick poll, and the results showed that fully 89% owned a gun—it seems the United States is awash in guns! But the quick poll relied on a voluntary sample—Web site visitors who found the article online and decided to participate in the poll.

When the General Social Survey (GSS) asked a sample of 1,996 adults if they owned a gun, only 35% reported that they did. Which survey do we believe? It turns out that the GSS uses much better methods—including careful random sampling—to produce its results. The true rate of gun ownership in the United States is certainly much closer to 35% than it is to the strikingly high figure of 89%. The flawed methods of the *USA Today* (2008) quick poll grossly overstated gun ownership in the United States. The solid methods of the GSS get us closer to the truth.

Fluoridated water is associated with weakened bones, but is it a cause?

Source: © iStockphoto.com/ guenter2.

Misleading Correlations

Many cities and towns add fluoride to the water supply because it helps prevent tooth decay in children. Other cities do not add fluoride. Recently, people have begun to worry that ingesting fluoride can have adverse effects on older people, in particular, weakening their bones and leading to debilitating and painful hip and other bone fractures. This fear comes from studies that show that older people living in cities and towns with fluoridated water tend to have higher rates of bone fractures as compared with older people living in cities and towns with untreated water (Jacobsen et al., 1990). In other words, there is a *correlation* between fluoride in the water and bone fractures. Should cities stop the practice of adding fluoride to municipal water supplies?

People living in cities that add fluoride to the water may be different from people living in cities that do not. A study in the United Kingdom (Hillier et al., 2000) used methods to take individual differences in characteristics (age, sex, and body weight) and lifestyle (physical activity, smoking, and drinking alcohol) into account. When they did, the correlation between exposure to fluoridated water and bone fractures disappeared. This study suggests that the original correlation many people worried about was probably due to these other factors—it was a **spurious correlation**. In other words, it would be misleading to interpret the correlation between fluoridated water and bone fractures as a causal relationship—and so we shouldn't change municipal water treatment policy because of it.

What Is Research?

This book is about research methods—but what is *research*? We can define *research* as a social and intellectual activity that involves systematic inquiry aimed at accurately describing and explaining the world. But it helps to get a bit more specific.

Secondary and Primary Research

People often *research* a topic at the library or on the Internet. Such information searches and syntheses are best referred to as **secondary research**—the search for published sources describing the results of research or information provided by others. While secondary research is an important skill that we cover in the last chapter (Chapter 15), it is not the focus of most of what we cover in this book, nor what we mean when we use the word *research*.

Rather, we use the term *research* to refer mostly to original, or **primary research**—the original collection or analysis of data to answer a new research question or to produce new knowledge. In journals, such studies are referred to also as *original contributions*. What gets confusing is that original or primary research can involve **primary data** collection—collecting new *data* to provide a description or explanation of the world. But it can also involve the original analysis of **secondary data**—data collected by others, such as existing government surveys, administrative records, or transcripts. Indeed, much primary research gets done using secondary data.

Unfortunately, the term *data* also can be a bit confusing. If we looked up a few published facts or even a table of statistics online or in the library, we sometimes refer to this as finding "data" on a topic. But in this book, we use the term **data** to refer to largely unprocessed observations—*raw data*, it's sometimes called.

We now turn to some of the key features of research, particularly as it applies to policy and practice.

It Comes in Various Shapes and Sizes

As you will see from the many examples throughout the chapters in this book, research comes in a surprisingly wide variety of shapes and sizes:

- Large-scale studies of broad populations
- Small-scale studies of one locally situated group
- Snapshots in time
- Studies of outcomes or events that occur over many periods of time
- Laboratory simulations
- Naturalistic observations of real-world settings
- Carefully planned manipulations
- Theoretical analyses
- Opportunistic discoveries of unplanned events
- Informal research conducted for the purpose of organizational strategy or management

One of the important points to realize about research, and about researchers, is that inventiveness and creativity are an important part of the process. Good research often involves the imaginative application of new methods, innovative techniques, or clever strategies to learn about the world. It is this creative aspect of research methods that makes the topic so interesting to those familiar with it. We will try to give you a flavor of this variety and creativity in the chapters to come.

It's Never Perfect

Research, like everything else that is human, is not perfect—far from it. Every study has weaknesses, as you will learn in this book. It is important to spot these shortcomings and understand their implications.

But it is also important not to entirely discard a study because it has some methodological or other shortcomings. We don't want to throw the baby out with the bathwater. Every study also has strengths, too—or at least, most studies do. There is often something to be learned from almost any study, and the perfect study is just not possible—especially in social and policy research. A good consumer of research can both spot the weaknesses and recognize the strengths.

It's Uncertain and Contingent

We tend to think of research as providing certain and universal conclusions. But experienced researchers know otherwise—especially those involved in social and policy research. Research evidence includes a large dose of *uncertainty*, often expressed in the form of probability statements or qualified conclusions. Thus, researchers talk about the results "indicating" this or that, "suggesting" that something is true, or showing that an outcome was "likely" due to a presumed cause. In part, this comes from the language of modern statistics, which uses the laws of probability to make inferences about unknown populations or causes. But this way of speaking and writing also reflects the inherent uncertainties involved in making firm statements or conclusions about complex human and public affairs.

Social and policy research is also *contingent*—bounded in space, time, and context. A study that finds evidence for the effectiveness of an education reform in one school district, for example, may not hold true in other districts with different children, teachers, budgets, and administrative structures. A mental health intervention that is shown to be effective with affluent suburban adults may not have the same effect on poor, inner-city adults living much different lives. The motivations found to encourage productivity in one organization may not be the same as the motivations that matter in another organization.

It Aims to Generalize

Generalizability is the ability to take the results of research and apply them in situations other than the exact one in which the research was carried out. Although we just noted that research is often contingent, researchers nevertheless strive at the same time to make their work generalizable. This is quite important: If the research results only apply in the exact setting (time, place, circumstances) in which the study was conducted, then they cannot be used to inform policies or practices in other situations.

For example, suppose a study looks at a policy of requiring copayments for emergency room visits and finds no impact on health outcomes for patients. But say the study is done using data from one insurance plan that covers mostly younger, healthy workers with good incomes. Do the results apply to insurance plans that cover older, less healthy individuals with low incomes? Probably not: Such individuals might well behave differently if required to make copayments for their visits to the emergency room. So the study has limited generalizability. We might even worry that the study is only relevant for that one particular insurance plan and the population it serves, making it of little use to anyone else. While generalizability is always a goal, real-world research is often less generalizable than we would like.

This is not to say that social and policy research has little to offer—on the contrary. But you do need to be realistic and appreciate the limits, as well as the rewards, of research.

Bits and Pieces of a Puzzle

It's also true that a single study is almost never definitive. Rather, empirical evidence on a topic is cumulative. Research produces a *body* of evidence, and researchers talk about arriving at a scientific *consensus* within the bounds of what is likely to be true (or not).

Consider global warming—Is the world really heating up and, if so, is global warming natural or manmade? There have been thousands of individual studies of various aspects of global warming over the years, from tracking the melting of the polar ice caps to observing animal species, mapping storms and rainfall, sampling the level of ozone and other pollutants in the atmosphere, and so on. None of these studies alone definitively proves that human activity is causing the earth to get hotter—indeed, some contradict this hypothesis. To help establish a consensus—particularly given the monumental economic and political costs involved in responding to global warming—the United Nations and the U.S. federal government each established scientific panels to review the research evidence. The UN's Intergovernmental Panel on Climate Change concluded that the earth had probably gotten warmer over the past 100 years and that human activity was "very likely" the cause (Intergovernmental Panel on Climate Change, 2007). The U.S. government's panel also said it was likely that global warming had been caused by human activity (U.S. Global Change Research Program, 2009). But this conclusion took many years of research, and thousands of individual studies—not to mention much political debate—to arrive at. And the process goes on.

The same kind of process of accumulating evidence, engaging in scientific debate, and searching for consensus characterizes most areas of research. Of course, most topics of research do not inspire as many studies or the establishment of large national or multinational scientific panels to search for a consensus. Nevertheless, something similar happens on a smaller, quieter scale in the various journals and research conferences where studies on a topic are published and debated. And consensus is not always, or even often, possible: Too much is unknown, and more research remains to be done.

It Involves Competition and Criticism

The process of research is also one of continual competition and criticism—the continuous testing of the consensus. There are researchers who doubt aspects of the manmade global warming hypothesis, for example, and they are busy conducting and gathering evidence to challenge, or at least refine, the consensus. Conclusions that withstand this kind of competitive onslaught become what we consider to be established knowledge (for the time being).

The formal expression of this critical attitude is the **peer-review** process. Most research journals, as well as research funding programs, use a peer-review process in which the studies or proposals are reviewed and approved (or rejected) by a group of peers—other researchers in the same field—who render a judgment on the methodology and worth of the paper or proposal. This process is usually blind (neither the researcher nor the reviewer know who is who) to rule out favoritism and to encourage reviewers to be honest and forthright in their criticism. You, too, should learn to think in this honest, critical way as you hear or read about research.

It Can Be Quantitative, Qualitative, or a Mix of Both

Much research involves numerical measurement and statistics, but research can also involve language, images, and other forms of expressing meaning that researchers then interpret. The former is referred to as *quantitative* research, the latter *qualitative* research. Qualitative studies involving the interpretation of language can be every bit as rigorous and scientific as quantitative studies—despite the lack of scientific-looking tables and formulas. Numbers do not make a study good or scientific.

These days, social and policy research often uses mixed methods that combine the advantages of both quantitative and qualitative techniques. Because social phenomena are so difficult to pin down, researchers often use multiple methods to confirm a finding, a process referred to as **triangulation**.

Although more of the chapters in this book are devoted to topics typically thought of as part of quantitative research, we discuss the role and contribution of qualitative methods in all the chapters. And we devote an early chapter to qualitative research because we consider it to be foundational. In an important sense, good quantitative research is based on good qualitative research. The two perspectives enhance one another.

Formulating Research Questions

Research answers questions—but what kinds of questions, and where do they come from?

How the World Is—Not How It Should Be

To begin with, it is important to understand that research questions are **positive**—about how the world really is; they are not **normative**—about how we want the world to be. Consider again the debate between those who favor an abstinence-only approach to sex education for teenagers and those wanting comprehensive sex education (including the distribution of condoms). Research is well suited to answering the *positive* question of whether these approaches do, or do not, do anything to reduce the rate of sexual activity and sexually transmitted disease among teenagers. Research does not help much with answering the *normative* question of which approach is the right thing to do, given our moral beliefs or community values.

However, doing research does not mean giving up your values. In fact, you can use research to support or create policies that further your goals and reflect your values. For example, if you care about the homeless, you can choose to study the homeless—who they are, how they became homeless, and what programs are most effective at improving their well-being. Values can legitimately shape what one chooses to study. But researchers try hard not to let their values lead them to suppress or distort their findings to conform to their normative beliefs. Good research gives us a window on reality—even if we do not always like what we see.

Applied and Basic Research

Research questions—particularly those in **applied research**—often come from a practical need to know. For example: How many people are currently unemployed? Would smaller classes improve learning? Does adding police officers reduce crime? The answers to questions in applied research typically have direct implications for policy and practice. Most of the examples in this book focus on applied research.

In contrast, **basic research** is often thought of as the pursuit of knowledge for its own sake, rather than being based on an immediate practical need. Basic research in a given field also tends to focus on more abstract or fundamental processes of nature or society. For example, we might be interested in studying how people make decisions involving uncertainty, how the human body responds to long-term exposure to stress, or how children acquire a language. Basic research also advances policy and practice by providing a solid foundation of knowledge. But the link is less direct.

Questions We Ideally Would Like to Answer, and Those We Really Can

Although practical needs generate pressing questions, research frequently cannot answer exactly the question we might ideally want answered. Often, we must settle for an answer to a related question—an approximation of sorts. But it is better to have an approximate answer than none at all.

For example, suppose we want to describe lab tests among those with diabetes in the United States. Due to the fragmented nature of the U.S. health care system, there is no one source of medical records representative of all people with diabetes in the United States. Instead, a study might be done on people over 65 with diabetes using Medicare data, while another study might get records on younger adults from a private insurer operating in one region of the country. Neither study would generalize to the entire U.S. population of diabetics—far from it. So the best that can be done is to conduct several studies that collectively might help us approximate an answer.

Consider another example: Does divorce have long-term detrimental effects on children, psychologically or educationally? Because we cannot rewind the clock and see what would have happened to these children, had their parents not divorced, this question is hard to answer directly. We could compare differences between those whose parents divorced and those whose parents did not, as in a study by Huurre, Junkkari, and Aro (2005). But because these groups may be different in important ways, this comparison answers a different, but still valuable, question. A study by Gruber (2004) used changes over time in state divorce laws to determine the long-term effects on children of making divorce easier. But this, too, is a slightly different question from our desired question, because we still aren't sure if the detrimental effects on children can be attributed to divorce itself or perhaps some other consequence of the changes in law. And Gruber's study was unable to consider some of the psychological outcomes observed by Huurre and colleagues (2005). Flexibility and compromise are required when translating a policy question into a doable research question.

To make good use of research, it is important to understand what question a study addresses, and how it might differ from the one you ideally want answered. In Chapter 15, we return to the difference between applied policy and practice questions and the often more limited, approximate answers that research can provide. We will look at how those differences shape both research and its effect on policy. Also in Chapter 15, we offer some suggestions on developing your own research question, which similarly involves a trade-off between what you ideally want to answer and what you can answer, given available data and resources.

In the next section, we describe perhaps the most fundamental distinction concerning research questions—the distinction between descriptive and causal questions.

Descriptive and Causal Research

Research sometimes aims simply to describe the world—how things are. At other times, its goal is to provide a causal explanation—how would things be different if we changed something? This basic distinction is fundamental to thinking about and conducting research and provides a roadmap of sorts for the rest of this book.

Description: What Is the World Like?

Concern about autism has been growing for the past two decades, and parents and other advocates have pressed for services to help autistic children and for more research about the disease. In

What is known about autism?

Source: © iStockphoto.com/Tramper2.

evaluating how to react to autism, policymakers and practitioners need to know how many autistic people (and particularly autistic children) there are in the population. They need to know if the rate of autism is growing—and if so, how quickly. They need to know whether autism is more concentrated in certain places or groups in the population. They need to know the severity and forms of autism. In other words, policymakers and practitioners need a good *description* of autism to address the problem.

The goal of **descriptive research** is to paint an accurate picture of the way the world is. Descriptive research includes describing just one variable—such as the rate of autism in the population. It also includes describing **relationships**—how two different variables are related. Relationships are often referred to as associations or correlations. For example, autism rates have been growing—so time and autism are related. Or at least it seems so—researchers worry that perhaps we have simply gotten better over time at identifying those with autism and that this enhanced ability to identify the disease accounts for the upward trend. Autism and geographical region are also related—the disease is more common in California, for example, than in other parts of the United States. But it turns out that this description is also not so certain—perhaps autism is not consistently identified everywhere. Descriptive research can be harder than you might expect.

Before figuring out what to do about a problem like autism, the problem must be described. Knowing the lay of the land is important before deciding where to go. But once practitioners have described the problem, the task of tackling and solving it has just begun. After all, we want to figure out how to make things better—not just sit and watch things happen. In the case of autism, policymakers and practitioners want to figure out how to prevent and hopefully cure, or at least ameliorate, the disease.

Causation: How Would the World Be Different If Something Changed?

The goal of **causal research** is to answer "what if?" questions to find out how to make things happen. Specifically, if we change one thing, will other things (outcomes we care about, such as autism) change? And if they do change, by how much?

For example, what would happen to the severity of the disease if autistic children stopped eating gluten? Would it change at all? If so, by how much? Or what would happen to autism rates if children stopped being vaccinated?[1] More generally, we want to know what factors have caused the growth of autism over time (if indeed the trend is real and not just an artifact of better identification techniques).

Descriptive and causal research are both important in practice, but answering causal questions is especially central to the work of practitioners. Public policies, social programs, and management initiatives aim to do things—to make something happen. So answering questions such as "What will happen if we do X?" is essential.

Causal Research Needs Qualitative Research

Qualitative research is also very important to causal research. We often get ideas about possible causes from case studies or qualitative observations. And qualitative methods do an especially good

---

[1]See the chapter "Vaccines and Autism?" in the book by Arthur Allen (2007), which addresses this controversy.

job of uncovering and documenting causal processes or mechanisms—for example, the precise ways in which a program influences participants.

Quantitative, statistical studies do a good job of demonstrating a connection between two variables, such as a program and an outcome, but have less to contribute to our understanding of what process or mechanism was responsible for how the program influenced the outcome. Good causal research often needs the insight from qualitative research.

Don't Confuse Correlation With Causation

It is easy to confuse correlation, the existence of a relationship, with causation. If more educated mothers are more likely to have autistic children—a correlation—then it is easy to conclude that something about educated mothers causes autism. However, that may not be so. Think about the earlier example of fluoridated water and fractured bones. When researchers, policymakers, or practitioners naively assume that a correlation implies causation, grave errors can be made.

For example, because autism rose over the same period that vaccine use rose, and because autism symptoms start at about the same time that toddlers receive many vaccines, many concluded that vaccines cause autism. Many parents started to reject vaccines, causing some outbreaks of previously suppressed illnesses.

One of the most important skills you will gain from this book is how to distinguish a correlation, the description of a relationship, from evidence of a causal effect. We address this in Chapter 10, our chapter on causation. Another, perhaps even more important, skill is how to judge the quality of evidence of causation and how to do research that provides evidence of whether a causal effect exists and how big it is.

Because distinguishing description from causation is so important, we have organized this book around that distinction. Part II of the book covers strategies for description, while Part III covers strategies for causation. We will stress again and again the distinctions between description and causation and between correlation and causation.

Let's look now more closely at what we call *the scientific method* as one of several ways that we have of knowing about the world.

Epistemology: Ways of Knowing

How much do you weigh? How do you *know* that's how much you weigh? Probably you used a scale and remember the result. You measured your weight—an elementary act of research. How high is Mount Everest? If you know, how do you know? Did you measure it? If you don't know, how might you try to learn how high Mount Everest is? You will probably turn to other sources, perhaps searching the Internet and examining a Web site that you trust (secondary research). But of course, you should consider how the Web site got its information.

We have many ways of knowing—what philosophers of science call **epistemologies**. Sometimes we directly learn something ourselves. But we can't do that about most things in the world. Often, we just accept what some trusted authority says is true. Sometimes, we rely on knowledge that comes from our cultural or religious traditions. We know other things through intuition or common sense.

The Scientific Method

There are many ways of knowing things, but in modern society the **scientific method** is a privileged way of knowing—especially in matters of public policy or professional practice. The research methods presented in this book are based on the scientific method.

Obviously, you cannot directly research everything you need to know on your own. So this book will teach you not only to do research but how to critically assess and make use of the research produced and published by others. It will also help you judge knowledge that comes from authority, tradition, and common sense more effectively by using the standards of the scientific method.

The scientific method can be defined as an approach to acquiring and correcting our knowledge about the world. It has several key characteristics:

- Systematic observation—or *measurement* of various features or behaviors in the world (including qualitative observation).
- Logical explanation—in the form of a *theory* or *model* that makes sense according to basic rules of logic and accepted facts.
- Prediction—in the form of a *hypothesis*, based on a theory, of what we will observe if the theory is true. (This is seen as superior to after-the-fact, or ex post facto, explanations, which are not *falsifiable*.)
- Openness—meaning the methods used to produce evidence are clearly documented and made available for review. This allows for *replication*—repeating the study to see if the results hold (and in what contexts).
- Skepticism—researchers scrutinize and critique each other's work, a process referred to as *peer review*, in search of possible shortcomings or alternative explanations.

In sum, the scientific method is a privileged form of knowing because it is generally transparent, logical, and fact-based. But scientific evidence can be misrepresented or misused, so you still need to question scientific knowledge just as you would question common sense, tradition, or authority.

Induction and Deduction

There are several ways in which researchers employ the scientific method to tackle a problem or curiosity, as illustrated in Figure 1.1. One approach is to begin by doing systematic observation of the world, then develop a logical explanation (theory) to account for what they see—an approach referred to as **induction**. In anthropology, for example, researchers typically observe people in a community for some time before developing an explanatory theory. Qualitative research, described in Chapter 3, is often inductive. Induction also happens in quantitative research when many possible relationships between variables are explored before an explanatory theory emerges from the observed patterns.

The other approach is **deduction**: The researcher moves first toward the development of a logical explanation or theory and next gathers evidence to test the theory. For example, in astronomy,

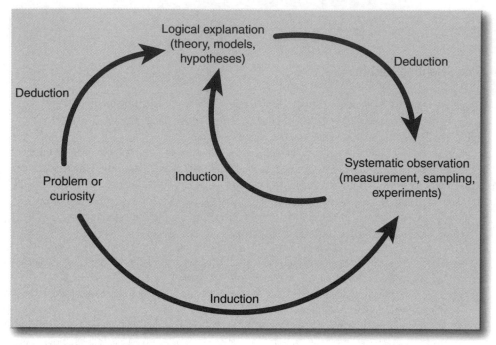

Figure 1.1 Induction and Deduction

researchers might develop a theory that predicts when a planet will appear where in the night sky. They then use telescopes to make observations of the planet and to see if its appearances agree with their prediction. In social research, some researchers called **structuralists** insist that social research must always start with theories and test these with empirical predictions.

Most researchers, however, practice a combination of induction and deduction. They have a theory, gather data to test it, but then also examine the data in other ways to develop new theories.

Proof Requires Fresh Data

While most researchers practice a combination of induction and deduction, even in a single study, the structuralists have a point that applies broadly in research: *Data cannot be used to both develop a theory and definitively confirm it.*[2] Fresh data are required to truly test a theory or support a hypothesis. Think of your favorite detective novel. The detective struggles to come up with a theory of the crime or mystery that fits all the existing clues. Then the detective uses the theory to predict some previously unknown and unsuspected fact—mud on the perpetrator's evening dress, for example. If the prediction indeed matches the fact, the perpetrator's guilt appears much more likely. Prediction provides powerful proof.

---

[2]We cover this issue in more detail in Chapter 8. It is related to issues of statistical power in hypothesis testing.

In social and policy research, some studies strive to generate theory, while others aim to test theories. Research is often an iterative process in which deduction and induction alternate (as Figure 1.1 illustrates).

Truth in Social Science: Controversy and Consensus

The scientific method originated with physical sciences such as astronomy and physics. The discoveries of Newton and Galileo are early examples. Natural and biological scientists were also early users of the method.

The more isolated the study is from real-world complexities, the better the scientific method works. For example, the scientific method works better for physics and biology than for engineering and medicine. Nevertheless, the scientific method is responsible for enormous strides in both engineering and medicine.

Social phenomena are more complex and varied than physical or even biological phenomena due to factors such as human self-awareness, personality, and culture. Social phenomena vary by place and time much more than physical or biological phenomena. So truths in the social and policy sciences, such as how markets work or how children learn, are much grosser approximations of truth than in engineering or medicine—and far from the more universal truths of physics.

Moreover, how we interpret social phenomena is shaped by language and culturally constructed categories. These categories shape our interpretation and even what we observe, and our constructions vary from time to time, from culture to culture, and from political perspective to political perspective. So even when we try to be objective, our interpretations will be at least somewhat conditioned by our categories of subjective experience and judgment.

Because social ideas and facts are constructed, some reject the relevance of the scientific method to the study of society and policy. Indeed, some even reject the idea that an objective truth, even a contingent truth, exists for social phenomena. We acknowledge that all real-world social and policy research will have limitations, based on the researchers' interests and perspectives, and will only get at part of the truth.

But we prefer to take what is probably best described as a **critical pragmatic** point of view in this book. That is, we seek feasible methods and practical knowledge that will help us improve some problem or condition in the world. In doing so, we believe that it is important to try to be objective (as best as we can agree), because that is how we will find the most useful information. When studying social phenomena, the scientific method can serve as an ideal—even if social and policy research does not always live up to this ideal.

Approaching Research From Different Angles

You may encounter research from various angles: as a consumer of research findings in news articles, government reports, or journal articles, as someone who commissions research to satisfy a pressing information need, or as someone who conducts research on your own or as part of a team. This book addresses all these perspectives.

Consuming Research

Research appears in many forms—in journal articles, government papers, foundation or advocacy reports, and various summaries in print and electronic news media. An important goal of this book is to help you become a better consumer of research evidence—to take what's valuable and useful from available research and apply it to the task of solving important problems and improving people's lives. We hope that this book sparks your curiosity about what's out there ("I wonder if someone has done a study about . . ?") and that it gives you the skills and confidence to go directly to the source. There is much to learn from reading an original study (even though it is not always written in a very user-friendly style, something researchers need to work harder at, in our view).

Many of you are members of or will join professional associations—in public administration, education, public health, social work, criminal justice, or other fields. As members, you may receive research journals in your field. Through your association or employer, you also may have online access to relevant research journals. And there is a growing movement toward *open-access* journals—online journals that are freely available to the public. So getting access to original studies in your field is becoming increasingly trouble-free. The only hindrance is your own ability and confidence to read, understand, and apply what's in these research journals. We hope that this book helps you do that.

Often, you'll come across the results of research—not in academic journals or in research reports—but in newspapers, magazines, TV shows, or on the Internet. Some media summaries leave out a lot and some even make mistakes. Journalists have an interest in getting readers' attention and consequently sometimes exaggerate or sensationalize results. Good journalists, however, clearly and accurately explain research—a valuable service to society. The tools that you'll learn in this book will be even more valuable for critically examining journalistic accounts of research. And if you aspire to be a part of the media, this book will give you the tools to describe research accurately to your audience.

Commissioning Research

Policymakers, practitioners, and managers often have important research questions that have not been addressed in prior studies or analyses. So they need to commission research from internal staff or outside consultants.

An understanding of research methods is essential for all phases of this task. You need to adequately frame the initial research question and discuss it with the research team. You need to approve the team's proposal or work plan—how it will sample, measure, and draw analytical conclusions to help answer your question. As the client, you will be called on to make decisions or sign off on changes as the research unfolds (nothing ever goes perfectly as planned). You will be the main reviewer of briefings and draft reports. And most likely, you will participate in the presentation of the final research results in meetings with organizational leaders, in testimony before legislative bodies, or in press conferences with the media.

Who is selected to do the research will, of course, have a critical influence on its quality—so hire or choose your research team wisely. But you, as the client who commissioned and managed the research in the first place, are just as important a part of the process. This book will help you become a better purchaser and manager of research.

Conducting Research

When we think of a researcher, we tend to envision a tweedy professor in a university or a white-coated scientist in a laboratory. If this is your calling, then of course you must know research methods especially well. Indeed, a solid grasp of research methodology can help a new scholar become more productive, succeed at publishing, and participate more fully in his or her field of study.

But not everyone who conducts research these days fits this traditional mold. On the contrary, increasingly, applied research of various kinds is being conducted in large and small government agencies, nonprofit organizations, foundations, advocacy groups, the news media, and a growing industry of consulting firms that support the research needs of public, nonprofit, and business organizations. Some of these applied researchers have PhDs or other doctoral degrees, but many do not. Indeed, there are quite a few master's and even undergraduate programs that provide research and analysis skills sufficient to begin a career as an applied researcher or policy analyst.

Moreover, there are many situations in which practitioners engage in *informal research*. Examples include doing your own survey of employees or clients; making comparisons using performance measures; examining the effectiveness of a new program or management initiative using administrative data; and doing qualitative interviews or focus groups for purposes of internal strategy, marketing, or decision making. These activities are research, too, even though the people doing them do not aim to publish in peer-reviewed journals or release results in fancy research reports. Knowledge of research methods can dramatically improve one's ability to do informal research well.

Ethics of Research

Social and policy research raises important ethical issues because it deals with human beings—their health, living conditions, rights, and well-being. In the chapters to come, we deal with these ethical concerns in the context of particular methods and study types covered in this book. For example, qualitative research presents unique ethical issues that we address in Chapter 3; the use of existing administrative data raises confidentiality concerns that we cover in Chapter 6; and experiments involving human beings require many ethical considerations that we discuss at length in Chapters 10 and 12.

However, there are certain core principles that are worth reviewing here as a preview of what lies ahead. These principles come from an important document known as the Belmont Report (available from the U.S. Department of Health and Human Services at www.hhs.gov/ohrp/humansubjects/guidance/belmont.htm).

- **Respect for persons** dictates that people used as the subjects of research provide informed consent and are not coerced into participating in research.
- **Beneficence** dictates that people who participate in research are not harmed and, indeed, that they should realize some benefit from the research.
- **Justice** requires consideration of equity among subjects and fairness in regard to who becomes a research subject.

The history of applied policy research has some ugly chapters. In the infamous Tuskegee syphilis study, for example, the U.S. Public Health Service recruited poor African American sharecroppers with the disease into a long-term study and then left them untreated for many years—even after penicillin was found to be an effective cure—to study the progression of the disease. The Belmont Report came out of this experience. In Chapter 14, we cover the history and practice of ethics in research in more detail.

Conclusion: The Road Ahead

The ideas and concepts of research methodology come from many different disciplines—sociology, economics, the health sciences, and education, to name a few. As a result, it is less a neatly ordered landscape than a somewhat tangled and overgrown woods. So as you travel the road ahead, we will try to clear away the brush along the way—yet still preserve the variety of ideas and concepts that you will find in the many disciplinary journals and reports of research. It might comfort you to know that even experienced research methodologists, talking across disciplinary boundaries, often do not understand one another because of the many dialects of research methodology. This communication gap is unfortunate, of course, but it is part of the real world of research. Thus, an important skill to have, both as a researcher and a consumer of research, is to be able to see through the tangle of terms and to get a good view of what issue or idea is really at stake.

We begin our journey in the next chapter with an introduction to *theory and models*—the conceptual tools researchers use to think about the world and to begin to figure out how to study it.

EXERCISES

Battleship Research

1.1. You saw in this chapter how research gets used in battles over controversial public policies, such as sex education or global warming. Can you think of other, important policy debates in which opponents use research to support their arguments? How has research methodology played a role in these debates?

Research in the Corner Office

1.2. We made the case in this chapter that the ability to judge and apply research evidence is an important qualification for top management and leadership positions. Identify this kind of position in an organization or agency in your area of policy or practice. In what ways does the person in this job use or commission research? If possible, interview the person.

Following the Trends

1.3. In your area of policy or practice, think of an example for each of the following:
- A performance measure
- A program evaluation
- An evidence-based policy or practice

Misleading Evidence

1.4. We gave a few examples in this chapter of research evidence that sometimes misleads. Can you think of other examples? Think about a misleading measurement, a misleading sample, or a misleading correlation.

Descriptive Versus Causal Research

1.5. The distinction between descriptive and causal questions is a fundamental distinction in research. Think about a current social problem or issue that people are talking about these days. What are some descriptive questions research could help answer? What are some causal questions?

Formulating a Research Question

1.6. Think about a pressing question in your work or community that interests you. What information would help you? How would you use that information? Formulate a research question to provide that information.

Objectives: This chapter introduces you to some of the conceptual building blocks of social and policy research. You will learn how researchers use a theory to explain an outcome of interest—and how they use a model to express a theory. You will understand the parts of a model—variables, relationships, and causal mechanisms. And you will gain practice using path diagrams to think through the logic of a theory. Finally, you will appreciate the usefulness of theories and models for explaining social problems and for designing, implementing, and choosing effective public policies and programs.

The broken windows theory was used to fight crime in New York's subways.

Source: © Danny Lyon/Magnum Photos.

Theory and Models

2

Fighting Crime in New York City[1]

"One unrepaired broken window is a signal that no one cares," wrote James Q. Wilson and George L. Kelling in a 1982 *Atlantic Monthly* article, "and so breaking more windows costs nothing." Thus, going after small, seemingly petty disorders such as vandalism, graffiti, or public drinking may help prevent more serious crime from occurring. "We decided to apply this concept to crime in the subways," recalls William Bratton, then chief of New York City's transit police. "Fare evasion was the biggest broken window in the transit system. We were going to fix that window and see that it didn't get broken again." When Mr. Bratton became commissioner of the city's regular police force in 1993, he began a "quality of life initiative" that took aim at the very "broken windows" Wilson and Kelling wrote about: vandalism, graffiti, panhandling, loitering, and public drinking.

Crime in New York City fell dramatically throughout the 1990s and beyond. Many police chiefs and criminologists credited the "broken windows" theory for New York's success and sought to replicate it in other cities. Others, however, doubted the theory and pointed to other factors—the end of the crack epidemic, demographic change, and the growing economy at the time—for the drop in crime in New York City and other urban areas. Knowing why crime fell in New York City—which theories are true—can help us effectively make crime policy decisions in the future.

This chapter begins by defining theory and models and introducing the basic notions of variables, relationships, and causal mechanisms—the building blocks of theory in social and policy research. After reviewing these ideas, the chapter moves into the subtleties and complexities of thinking about more complex models in the form of path diagrams. This practice with path diagrams will become important later in the book for applying methods demonstrating causation. And the chapter will show that theory, in the form of a logic model, can become a useful tool for planning, managing, and evaluating programs.

---

[1]This example is based on Miller (2001).

What Is a Theory?

The term *theory* in the social sciences sometimes refers to *paradigms* or grand theories of society—such as functionalism, Marxism, critical theory, or postmodernism (e.g., Lemert, 2004). There are also moral theories, religious theories, and philosophical theories. However, we will use the term **theory** as it is more commonly used in social and policy research—as a logical description of how a particular corner or aspect of the world works. Robert K. Merton (1967) called this **middle range theory**. King, Keohane, and Verba (1994) provide a general definition: "A social science theory is a reasoned and precise speculation about the answer to a research question, including a statement about why the proposed answer is correct" (p. 19).

Theory can describe a large-scale occurrence, such as the start of a war between nations, or a relatively small-scale event, such as the ability of a child to sound out a word. A theory is practical because it provides insight on how to change the world. If we know what causes war, perhaps we can find a way to prevent it. If we know what makes a child recognize parts of a word, perhaps we can help children read better. Of course, a theory is not necessarily correct—it must stand up to questioning and empirical testing.

Theories Tell Causal Stories

Inherent in a scientific theory is the notion of *causation*. A theory proposes a causal process or **mechanism** that produces an outcome of interest. According to the broken windows theory, disorder in a neighborhood, such as vandalism and graffiti, *causes* crime because it signals that no one cares, that rules can be broken with impunity. This encourages criminals to act freely. In a sense, a theory provides a causal story of *how* things happen. Of course, proving causation—proving that the story is true—can be difficult. That is what later chapters in this book are all about.

A Cause: One of Many

Our theory says that disorder causes crime, but we really mean that it is *a cause—one of many* causes. The alternative theories suggested earlier—jobs, crack cocaine, and demographic change—are also possible causes, as are the weather, popular culture, and a host of other factors. But the fact that an outcome has many different causes in no way undermines a theory that focuses on just one particular cause. Social phenomena are complex, and we cannot study everything all at the same time.

The many causes and other contingencies involved, however, mean that theories in social and policy research are *probabilistic*—they predict how things are *likely* to turn out, on average. But they do not guarantee a predicted outcome every time. This is because the other causes will be at work, too, in a given setting, often in conflicting and complex ways. So even if our theory remains true, reducing disorder will not necessarily reduce crime the same way in every location—or maybe not at all, in some places. It may lead to a reduction in crime in most precincts, but not all; the strategy may work in New York and Los Angeles, but not Chicago.

Theories Explain Variation

Theories also aim to explain *variation*—the changes or fluctuations in an event or behavior, such as crime. Figure 2.1 shows the variation in the murder rate in New York City from 1980 to 2005, and you can see that it goes up and down. This kind of variation over time is referred to as **longitudinal variation**.

A theory could also explain variation *across* individuals, organizations, or places at the same point in time. For example, we could look at large U.S. cities that are high or low in crime in a given year (say 2005), as in Figure 2.2. This is referred to as **cross-sectional variation**.

Explaining the causes of variation—why crime rises and falls over time, or why some cities have more crime at the same time as others have less—is what theory in social and policy research is mostly about. And if we have a good theory to explain the causes of such variation, perhaps we can find ways to influence it and thus, for example, help lower crime.

Theories Generate Testable Hypotheses

Good theories should have *observable implications* (King et al., 1994). In other words, they should generate **hypotheses**—predictions of what will happen if our theory is correct. The hypotheses can be compared with the facts, making the theory potentially *falsifiable*. A vague statement, a claim that is impossible to verify, or a truism does not qualify as a scientific theory.

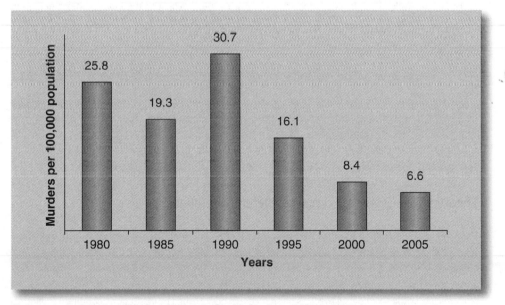

Figure 2.1   Longitudinal Variation: New York City Murder Rate, 1980 to 2005

Source: U.S. Bureau of Justice Statistics (2008).

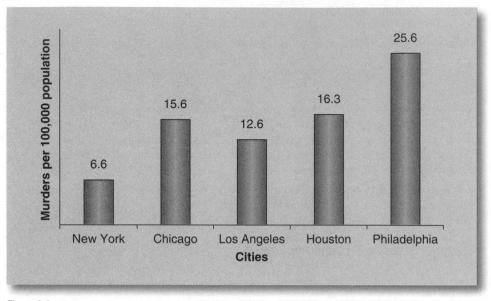

Figure 2.2   Cross-Sectional Variation: Murder Rates in Large U.S. Cities in 2005
Source: U.S. Bureau of Justice Statistics (2008).

In our example of the broken windows theory, we should expect to see *more* crime in neighborhoods with vandalism and graffiti and *less* crime in neighborhoods that do not have these symptoms of disorder. Or better: We would predict that if we took specific steps to reduce vandalism and graffiti in a neighborhood, the rate of more serious crimes would go down. A hypothesis is thus a prediction of what will happen—an observable implication of a theory—that we could compare with facts and data.

So a theory—even if it makes logical sense—is not necessarily true. A theory proposes one possible way that things work. Empirical observations must be made to test this theory against reality—and alternative theories must be tested as well. Only after our theory survives the gauntlet of empirical testing and competition from other theories do we begin to develop confidence that it might truly describe and explain reality.

Theories Take Different Forms in Different Disciplines

The kind of middle-range theories that we use in this book appear across the social sciences. They share the common features of telling causal stories, explaining variation, and generating testable hypotheses. However, theories tend to take different forms in different disciplines. For example, economic theories often center on individuals making rational choices to optimize their well-being (*homo economicus*), while sociological theories often focus on how groups or institutions condition individual behavior. Indeed, the theories of most disciplines have foundational principles or perspectives that establish frameworks for their theories. So if you go further into the theory of any particular discipline, you will need to learn much more about how that discipline develops its theory. Such disciplinary theories provide additional insights, although they can sometimes blind researchers to alternative forms of explanation and understanding.

Where Do Theories Come From?

Theories reflect lived experience, prior research, and even imagination. Often theories come from practitioners, such as police chiefs and patrol officers, who walk their beats and notice patterns of behavior that give them clues as to what might cause a social problem such as crime. Their working theories then become the basis for intervention or reform.

Theory emerges also from attempts to tie together the strands of empirical evidence in a particular field of research, such as criminology. Prior studies may contribute individual pieces of empirical evidence concerning the factors associated with crime, but much is gained when a theory emerges that fits the pieces together into a coherent whole.

Qualitative research, such as participant observation or in-depth interviews (discussed in Chapter 3), is another very important source of theory. Qualitative research provides insight into the processes and influences at work in a particular social setting, such as a high-crime neighborhood. Insights may suggest variables, such as social control, that help prevent crime and that can become the targets of policy intervention.

Induction and Deduction

As we saw in Chapter 1, theories can come from a process of induction—building up theory from scattered pieces of empirical evidence and experience. Theories can also come from a process of deduction—starting from initial ideas or logical principles and then testing these with empirical observations. In practice, theories often come from a mix of both thought processes.

When testing a theory, however, the distinction between induction and deduction is especially important: *You cannot test a theory using the same data or set of facts that inductively produced the theory.*

Testing a theory with the same facts that generated the theory amounts to a sure thing—a test whose answer you know already in advance. It does not permit you to be wrong (it is not *falsifiable*). So you need a new set of data or facts, another study, to test an inductive theory. Because a deductive theory starts first with ideas or logical principles, before collecting data, you do not have the same problem. But, of course, you still need to go out and gather a set of data or facts to test your deductive theory.

Theories, Norms, and Values

Scientific theories are *positive*, not normative—they describe how things are, not how they should be. The broken windows theory does not convey the wishes or dreams of its promoters for how people *ought* to behave, in some ideal sense, or how society should function. Rather, the debates about the correct theory of crime focus on what variables and processes actually *do* produce crime in the real world, in all its often unflattering glory.

But be aware that, in another sense, scientific theories are not value-free. Different theories focus on different causes that imply quite different policy alternatives—get tough with petty criminals, instead of creating economic opportunity in poor neighborhoods, for example. Therefore, the motivations driving the promoters of a theory, like the motivations for much that is human, do involve beliefs and values. But a scientific theory must stand up to the test of empirical observation and competition from other theories.

Theories can be based on underlying assumptions that are not always obvious. For example, psychoanalysts believe that most problems stem from early childhood experiences, and they therefore develop theories consistent with that belief. Economists traditionally believe that individuals behave rationally, and their theories are based on that assumption. Many kinds of implicit assumptions can also shape theories. When you interpret a theory or create your own theory, try to become aware of the underlying assumptions and make them explicit.

Modifiable and Nonmodifiable Variables

As we've noted, there are many causes of a complex outcome such as crime. Many of these we cannot influence, but some we can. For example, perhaps patrol officers have been neglecting vandalism, graffiti, and other acts of disorder in their precincts under the belief that their real job is to focus on more serious felonies, such as robbery, assault, auto theft, and gang violence. With training and leadership, however, the officers could well change their behavior and begin cracking down on petty disorders. Thus, disorder is a **modifiable variable**.

Theories in applied social and policy research tend to develop from an interest in *modifiable variables* because these offer the most useful guidance to policy and practice.

In contrast, other causes of crime may be largely **nonmodifiable**, such as a downturn in the national economy, the weather, popular culture, or an increase in the number of teenagers in the population. It might help to know how these factors influence crime and thus be able to predict when to expect the next jump (or drop) in crime. And basic research in sociology or criminology, for example, might well develop and test theories of how such general cultural, economic, and demographic patterns and trends in society influence crime. But from the point of view of a police department, at least, these remain largely nonmodifiable variables.

What Is a Model?

A **model** serves to articulate and communicate a theory. It is a representation that is specific and clear, in the same way that a miniature model of a building represents clearly and precisely what an architect plans to build. Models may at first seem like unnecessary abstractions, but in fact they help a great deal to make sense of complex phenomena, and they force us to think clearly.

A model is typically either graphical (a picture) or mathematical (an equation). In this book, we will mostly use graphical models to express theory, specifically, **path diagrams** (also called **path models**).

Figure 2.3 is a path diagram that expresses the broken windows theory of crime. It expresses the idea, presented earlier, that seemingly trivial acts of *disorder* trigger more serious *crime*.

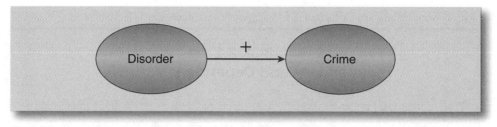

Figure 2.3 Path Model of the "Broken Windows" Theory

Variables and Relationships

A model, such as the path diagram in Figure 2.3 of the broken windows theory, is made up of two components: variables (the ovals) and relationships (the arrows). The plus sign (+) indicates the direction of the relationship, which we have more to say about shortly.

A **variable** is something that can take on different values or assume different attributes—it is something that *varies*. Figures 2.1 and 2.2 demonstrate that the murder rate takes on different values over time and across cities—so it is a variable. Our theory aims to explain this variation, the highs and the lows, by way of another variable—disorder.

The **relationship** between crime and disorder is represented by the arrow pointing from disorder to crime. In a theory, as discussed earlier, we are interested in causal relationships (hence the unidirectional arrow). A **causal relationship** refers to how change in one variable produces or leads to change in another variable. Cracking down on vandalism and graffiti, for example, produces a reduction in more serious crimes (according to the theory).

Independent and Dependent Variables

In the model shown in Figure 2.3, *disorder* is the **independent variable** and *crime* is the **dependent variable**. The independent variable is the *cause*, the dependent variable the *effect*. By convention, the independent variable is symbolized by X, while the dependent variable is symbolized by Y. Just as cause comes before effect, and X comes before Y in the alphabet, the independent variable comes before the dependent variable in the causal order of things. Here is a very helpful little diagram for thinking clearly about the independent and dependent variables:

$$X \rightarrow Y$$

X		Y
"Cause"		"Effect"
Independent		Dependent

Various terms are used by different researchers to describe the independent and the dependent variables, as Box 2.1 explains. For example, in program evaluation and health research, the independent variable is often a *treatment* and the dependent variable an *outcome*.

BOX 2.1
Independent and Dependent Variables

Two of the most fundamental yet often confusing concepts in research are independent variable and dependent variable. It helps to think carefully about the sequence of the variables and to ask yourself which is the presumed "cause" and which the "effect." This basic diagram may help you sort things out:

Symbols:	X	$\longrightarrow$	Y
Meaning:	"Cause"		"Effect"
Name:	**Independent**		**Dependent**
Other names:	Explanatory		Response
	Treatment		Outcome
	Predictor		Predicted
	Regressor		Regressand

As shown, researchers refer to independent and dependent variables by many different names, which is another source of confusion. And in some situations, it is not entirely clear which variable is "cause" and which is "effect," as Chapter 10, on causation, will explain.

Causal Mechanisms

Because theories express causal relationships, change in the independent variable is presumed to *cause* change in the dependent variable. Thus, there must be some notion of how this happens, what researchers call a **causal mechanism**, underlying the relationship. Disorder in a neighborhood signals that no one cares, that rules are not enforced; criminals read these signals and become emboldened to commit crime. This is the causal mechanism in the broken windows theory.

Although it is a critical component of the broken windows theory, notice that this causal mechanism does not appear in Figure 2.3 as such. To provide a full description of the theory, therefore, we need to accompany the path diagram with a statement of the process or mechanism that explains *how* change in the independent variable causes change in the dependent variable.

We will see shortly that we can, in fact, make this causal mechanism more explicit by adding *intervening variables* to the model. Intervening variables represent steps in the causal process leading from the independent to the dependent variable. If these intervening variables can be measured and incorporated in a test of the model, much is gained: We can see not only whether X and Y are related, as predicted by our theory, but whether they are related through the intervening variables that represent the theory's causal mechanism.

BOX 2.2
Equations as Models:
Right-Hand Side and Left-Hand Side Variables

In this book, we mostly use path diagrams for our models. However, models in the form of equations are also used. By convention, as noted previously, Y often symbolizes the dependent variable, and X often symbolizes the independent variable. An equation modeling the relationship will typically look something like this:

$$Y = a + bX,$$

where a and b are specific numbers, such as 5.4 or −9. Notice that the convention with respect to placement of the independent and dependent variables on the page is reversed from the path model: The dependent variable (Y) is on the left, while the independent variable (X) is on the right. Indeed, those who use equations as models frequently refer to independent variables as *right-hand side* variables and dependent variables as *left-hand side* variables.

Direction of a Relationship

As mentioned, the plus or minus sign along the arrow in a model indicates the direction of the relationship. In Figure 2.3, there is a **positive (+) relationship** because *high* values of the independent variable (disorder) are presumed to result in *high* values of the dependent variable (crime). Correspondingly *low* values of the independent variable result in *low* values on the dependent variable. In other words, we would expect cities with low levels of disorder to have low levels of crime and those with high levels of disorder to have high levels of crime. Figure 2.4 illustrates this pattern.

In a **negative (−) relationship**, in contrast, *high* values of the independent variable tend to occur with *low* values of the dependent variable. In other words, the values of the two variables relate in an inverse (opposite) way. For example, we might expect that the level of income in a city and the rate of crime are negatively related: more income in a community, less crimes committed; less income, more crime. In an X-Y graph, a negative relationship is downward sloping (see Figure 2.4).

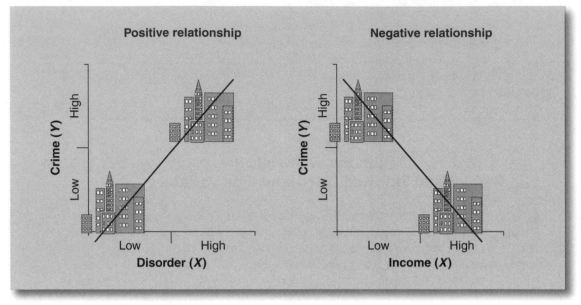

Figure 2.4   Positive and Negative Relationships

Specifying the *direction* of a relationship between the independent and dependent variables is an important part of making a theory precise. Just saying that disorder and crime "are related" in some way is not much of a theory. We need to explain in what way they are related. Specifying the direction of the relationship allows for observable implications—hypotheses that can be tested with data.

Relationship Directions for Nonnumerical Variables

It may be hard to describe the direction of a relationship for some variables—in particular categorical variables that do not have any numerical value, order, or direction (also called nominal variables). For example, suppose a city is divided into four districts or wards—Northside, Southside, Westside, and Eastside—and we have a theory that something unique to each of the districts influences its crime rate. Clearly, we cannot really specify the direction of the relationship between *district* and *crime* as being either positive or negative.

However, a variable that has just two categories—such as having a neighborhood watch group or not having a neighborhood watch group—does have an order to it: Up is having a watch group, Down is not having one. The relationship in this case would be negative (having a watch group means less crime, we might predict). Such variables are called *dummy* (or indicator) variables. Chapter 4 covers the topic of levels of measurement, including categorical, quantitative, and dummy variables. It is sufficient at this point just to be aware that it can be a bit tricky sometimes to show categorical variables in a path diagram.

Naming Variables

Variables must be able to take on different values, so it's best not to think about or name variables in a model in a one-sided or directional manner. Moreover, giving variables a directional name creates confusion when interpreting the model.

For example, say we have a theory that *more* income in a neighborhood causes *less* crime. Good enough—and it works alright to put things this way in a sentence. But often, we are tempted to translate these words directly to a path diagram, like this:

More income → Less crime

At first glance, this might make sense, but we still need to specify the direction of the relationship—an important aspect of the theory, as we've just seen. Is it positive—higher levels of *more income* leading to higher levels of *less crime*? Or is it negative—higher levels of *more income* leading to lower levels of *less crime*? As you can tell, these questions are not at all clear grammatically or logically. Let's try using nondirectional variable names instead, like this:

Income → Crime

This makes the task of specifying the direction of the relationship clearer—even though you may think at first glance that it looks wrong (How does having income cause crime?). But according to our theory, *more* income leads to *less* crime—a negative relationship. So the direction of the relationship should be expressed in the arrow—not in the variable labels. We just need to add a minus sign (–) to the arrow connecting employment to crime to complete the picture.

Income $\overset{-}{\rightarrow}$ Crime

To summarize: When drawing a model, the variable names should be nondirectional, and the direction of the relationship should be indicated by a plus or minus sign on the arrow.

Models With Multiple Causes

To keep things simple, we have been focusing thus far on models that involve a single independent variable—a single cause. This is in part because, as we noted earlier, theory often centers on one independent variable at a time, even though real-world outcomes such as crime may well have many causes. But you should know that, in most social and policy research, models—especially statistical models used for purposes of data analysis—often include multiple causes, multiple independent variables. This is often the situation in multiple regression analysis, for example, perhaps the most widely used statistical technique in social and policy research (a technique we will cover in Chapters 9 and 11).

There are two main reasons to include multiple causes in a model. First, other causes of the outcome may be correlated with the independent variable of interest, and thus it is necessary to separate out the unique effect of the key independent variable from these other causes. We will have much more to say about this topic in Chapter 11, on control variables. Second, in some situations, the theory itself identifies multiple causes of the outcome. For example, we may have a theory that views crime as a complex result of key economic and demographic forces in society.

Causal and Noncausal Relationships

We've been thinking a lot about causal relationships, but it is important to point out that not all relationships in the real world are causal. Any kind of correlation or association is, properly speaking, still a *relationship*—but not necessarily a *causal* relationship.

Variables can be correlated with each other for other reasons, such as the presence of a third, common cause that ties them together—a *spurious* relationship, it is called. For example, in a group of elementary school kids, there is a correlation between shoe size and reading level, but only because shoe size and reading level are influenced by age. Older kids both have bigger feet and read better.

In other cases, variables can be related just by coincidence. For example, you might find that you have more fun on Saturdays with an odd-number calendar date than Saturdays that have an even-number calendar date. Superstitions often get started by people observing chance correlations.

Although causal and noncausal relationships look the same on the statistical surface—patterns of positive, or negative, correlation between variables, as in Figure 2.4—they are fundamentally different.

Children's shoe size and reading level are related because of their age.

Source: © iStockphoto.com/a-wrangler.

Later in this book, we discuss how to distinguish a causal relationship from a mere correlation or just a chance coincidence. For now, simply remember that a straight arrow in a path diagram refers to a causal relationship. We will represent a noncausal relationship in a path diagram by a curved dotted line with no arrowheads at all. (Some choose to represent noncausal relationships using a curved line with arrowheads.)

Unit of Analysis

The variables in a model describe something—people, places, or things. *Income*, for example, is a variable that could describe the income of a person, the combined income of a household, or the median income of a neighborhood, city, or even a nation. The objects or things described by the variables in a model are referred to as the **unit of analysis**. The unit of analysis can also be thought of as the level of aggregation, or disaggregation, of the data that will be used to test the model.

Table 2.1 illustrates what data (perhaps in a spreadsheet) would look like when the unit of analysis is *individuals:* Each row of the spreadsheet is a different individual, and the variable *income* describes these individuals. And Table 2.2 illustrates what the data would look like when the unit of analysis is *cities:* Each row is a different city, and the variable *median income* describes the cities.

Table 2.1   Data With Individual as Unit of Analysis

Person[2]	Income
Joe	44,800
Bill	59,100
Sue	31,500
Ramon	17,200

Table 2.2   Data With City as Unit of Analysis

City	Median Income
New York	39,300
Chicago	38,800
Los Angeles	39,100
Houston	37,400

---

[2]Real data would generally contain an ID number and no names to protect the anonymity of those studied. See the discussion of the ethics of administrative data in Chapter 6.

Same Theory, Different Unit of Analysis

In the case of the broken windows theory, we might use neighborhoods or precincts as the unit of analysis. Neighborhoods can have more or less disorder (vandalism and graffiti), as well as more or less crime. But the unit of analysis could be something larger—a whole city. Cities can have more or less disorder, as well as more or less crime. Or it could be something smaller—a city block. Ultimately, crimes are committed by individuals or small groups of individuals, which are even smaller units of analysis. But as a practical matter, the data in our example of the broken windows theory may be available only for geographic units, such as blocks, precincts, or cities. Table 2.3 shows various units of analysis that might be used to test the theory.

Table 2.3   Different Units of Analysis and Corresponding Variables

Unit of Analysis	Independent Variable	Dependent Variable
Cities	Citywide disorder rate	Citywide crime rate
Neighborhoods	Neighborhood disorder rate	Neighborhood crime rate
Blocks	Block-level disorder rate	Block-level crime rate
Individual persons	Perception of disorder	Decision to commit a crime

When explaining variation over time (longitudinal variation), the unit of analysis must include the time period also. For example, disorder could refer to the level of disorder in a city *in a particular year.* In that case, the unit of analysis would be the *city-year.*

The unit of analysis is important to keep in mind when specifying a theory, interpreting variables, and seeking ways to test the theory. The unit of analysis will also become important later when we cover other topics in the book, such as measurement, sampling, sources and methods of gathering data, and statistical analysis.

Let's turn now to the application of theory and models—in the form of logic models—to the tasks of planning, managing, and evaluating programs.

Logic Models

In many areas of policy and practice these days, you may hear about **logic models** that describe how programs or interventions produce desired outcomes. Logic models (which are also referred to as *program theories, outcome-sequence charts*, or *theories of change*) are increasingly required by government agencies and foundations for program management, funding, and evaluation (W. K. Kellogg Foundation, 2004). As the definition in Box 2.3 makes clear, the idea of a logic model is much like a path diagram—what we have been discussing all along in this chapter, but applied to a particular program or intervention.

BOX 2.3
What Is a Logic Model?

A logic model's purpose is to communicate the underlying "theory" or set of assumptions or hypotheses that program proponents have about why the program will work, or about why it is a good solution to an identified problem. Logic models are typically diagrams, flow sheets, or some other type of visual schematic that conveys relationships between contextual factors and programmatic inputs, processes, and outcomes.

Logic models can come in all shapes and sizes: boxes with connecting lines that are read from left to right (or top to bottom); circular loops with arrows going in or out; or other visual metaphors and devices. What these schemata have in common is that they attempt to show the links in a chain of reasoning about "what causes what," in relationship to the desired outcome or goal. The desired outcome or goal is usually shown as the last link in the model.

Source: Schmitz and Parsons (1999).

Some logic models are focused purely on causal mechanisms—much like the models we have been considering and discussing thus far. But often, logic models include a focus on the implementation of the program as well, including programmatic inputs, activities, and outputs. **Inputs** are the financial, human, and material resources required by the program. **Activities** include training, counseling, marketing, and other tasks that make up the work of implementing the program. And **outputs** are the immediate products of these activities, such as people trained, brochures distributed, or citations issued. Inputs, activities, and outputs lead in turn to **outcomes**. It often helps to further separate these into *short-term* outcomes, *intermediate* outcomes, and *long-term* outcomes. (As you will see shortly, we will also refer to short-term and intermediate outcomes as *intervening variables*.)

Figure 2.5 provides an example from a Centers for Disease Control and Prevention guidebook. It illustrates a logic model for a high blood pressure (HBP) reduction program that emphasizes chronic care management (CCM). The model shows the program's inputs (funding and clinic partners), activities (education and training), and outputs (clinic teams being educated and trained) that in turn set in motion a causal sequence of outcomes. The immediate short-term outcomes are more appropriate treatment of patients and more chronic care management. This leads to the intermediate outcome of more patients who keep their high blood pressure under control and, in turn, the long-term outcome of less heart disease and fewer strokes. Logic models such as this provide both a managerial perspective, showing how program implementation happens, and a causal theory of how the program produces outcomes that matter to funders, policymakers, and society.

When drafting logic models such as these, it is important not to get so immersed in diagramming the details of implementation—inputs, activities, and outputs—that the model fails to clearly articulate how the program produces desired outcomes. After all, doing something about these outcomes

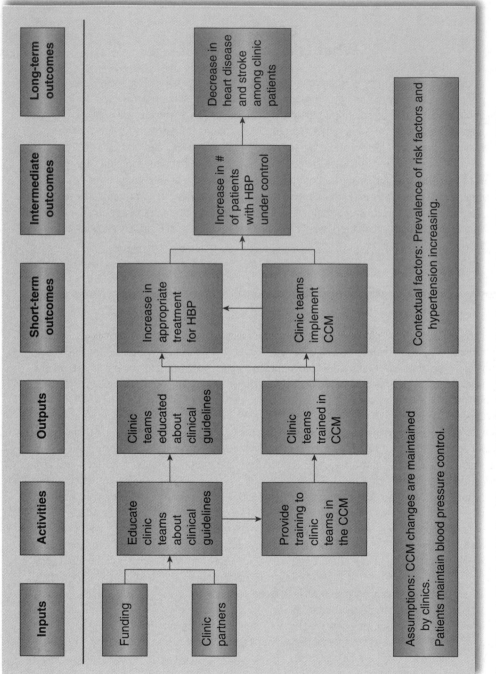

Figure 2.5   Logic Model of High Blood Pressure (HBP) Reduction Program That Emphasizes Chronic Care Management (CCM)

Source: Centers for Disease Control and Prevention (n.d.).

is the whole point of the program. For example, make sure that the logic model includes the ultimate outcome and that the causal mechanism is clear and convincing.

It is helpful to illustrate and practice the idea of a logic model with a more extended example.

Do Smaller Classes Help Kids Learn?

In the fall of 1999, the Jackson, Mississippi, Public Schools (JPS) began the Class-Size Reduction Program, committing $1.8 million in funds to hire 32 new teachers for 26 schools in Grades 1 through 3. According to JPS, "studies indicate that smaller classes reduce discipline problems and increase the time a teacher spends in instruction." Teacher Kescher Love explains, "That's because with fewer students teachers had more time to give to each student. Smaller classes are an important factor." JPS hopes the program will increase the percentage of students passing its third-grade "exit test" (required to move on to fourth grade) as well as improve students' final classroom grades and daily attendance. Initial anecdotal evidence appears encouraging. According to Smith Elementary Principal Gailya Porter, the additional money reduced the average size of her school's third-grade classes to 22 students—well below the state-mandated ceiling of 27 students. "We saw our retentions [the number failing the exit test] in the third grade drop to only four students," Mrs. Porter said (JPS, 2004).

Smaller classes may improve learning in many different ways.

Source: © iStockphoto.com/LeggNet.

You should recognize that underlying Jackson's Class-Size Reduction Program is a theory—a set of assumptions about how reducing the number of students in Grades 1 through 3 will produce improvement in Jackson's third-grade exit tests and other outcomes. Let's build a logic model to express the program's theory, first simply expressing the basic model and then elaborating the causal mechanisms through which it works.

Figure 2.6 shows the simplest model: Class size is related directly to academic achievement, as measured by test scores.[3] It is often a good idea to begin a logic model with just the independent and dependent variables.

But this basic model is incomplete, because it provides only limited information. Suppose, as the anecdotal evidence suggests, that the exit test scores improve after the program's implementation. That's good news for Jackson and its students, of course, but we don't know *how* the program accomplished its success—just that it did (or at least seems to have done so). Perhaps, we could find ways to make the program even more successful if we knew more about how class size influences test scores. But let's suppose that a more systematic evaluation reveals that the program, after all, does little to improve exit test scores—despite the initial, encouraging anecdotes from principals and others. What went wrong? Why isn't the program working as we hoped?

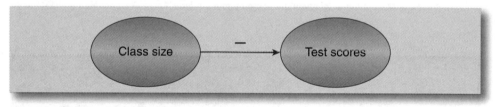

Figure 2.6   Path Model of the Class-Size Reduction Program

Intervening Variables

A more detailed logic model, such as Figure 2.7, might help us unravel the mystery. Recall that JPS pointed to research and the experience of teachers to suggest that smaller class size leads to fewer discipline problems (i.e., more discipline) and, as a result, more time spent on instruction. Smaller class size also may result in more individual attention to students. These factors in turn help students do better on the exit test.

We refer to variables such as individual attention, discipline, and instruction time in Figure 2.7 as **intervening variables**. They *intervene* between the independent and dependent variables along a causal pathway, elucidating the causal mechanism. Intervening variables are also known as **mediators** in some academic disciplines and as *intermediate outcomes* in program evaluation (as we saw earlier).

If the program is not working, we can examine the various paths in Figure 2.7 to find out where things broke down. For example, smaller class size may in fact encourage better discipline and in turn more time spent on instruction, but perhaps the additional instruction time isn't doing anything to

---

[3]There are, of course, many ways to express educational achievement, and test scores may or may not be a good method, but this is not our focus quite yet. See Chapter 4 on measurement for more on this issue.

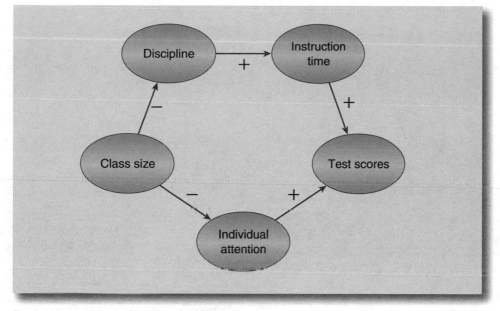

Figure 2.7   Path Model With Intervening Variables

help improve exit test scores. A fresh look at how well the curriculum prepares kids for the exit test may be needed.

You'll notice in the more complex Figure 2.7 that if you follow along the causal pathways, using the rules of multiplication, you will get the original negative relationship specified in the simple, two-variable model shown in Figure 2.6. For example, the pathway class size → discipline → instruction time → test score includes one negative and two positive relationships. Multiplying a negative by a positive and again by another positive results in a negative relationship ($-1 \times 1 \times 1 = -1$). In other words, if class size is negatively related to test scores, then the pathway class size → discipline → instruction time ⟩ test scores should also be negative. This is a good way to check if a logic model is indeed logical and internally consistent.

What About Other Causes?

We've illustrated the presumed *mechanisms* through which class size is expected to affect test scores. This is of particular interest if we want to understand or illustrate the logic of the program, if we need to fine-tune the program, or if we seek to evaluate how the program is working. However, test scores have lots of other causes, and we could flesh out our model further by including them. As you will see in later chapters of this book, some of these other causes may need to be taken into account in order to accurately estimate the true effect of the program. They may be needed as control variables, which we will cover in Part III of the book (particularly, Chapter 11).

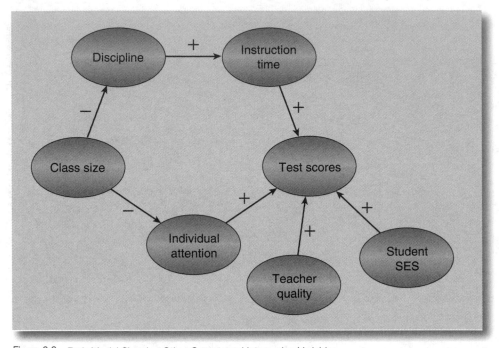

Figure 2.8   Path Model Showing Other Causes and Intervening Variables

For example, say Jackson third graders are increasingly coming from families of lower socioeconomic status (SES), resulting in lower test scores. Since this change in student SES may result in more kids failing the exit tests, scores might come down despite the Class-Size Reduction Program. At the same time, suppose Jackson is also putting an emphasis on recruiting good, experienced third-grade teachers from nearby districts, part of the same push to do better—but quite a different approach than class-size reduction. The new teachers might well be helping more kids pass the exit test, again apart from the effects of the Class-Size Reduction Program.

Figure 2.8 shows these additional factors at work influencing exit test scores along with class-size reduction. Even when concentrating on a single independent variable such as class size, therefore, including other important causes in the model can be valuable in thinking about the program and planning the analysis.

Usefulness of a Logic Model

Logic models serve several useful purposes. To begin with, a good logic model identifies important, sometimes previously unrecognized variables to track. It thus contributes a great deal to the task of establishing relevant performance measures, or performance indicators, to monitor the program. A good logic model helps similarly in the design of a program evaluation, calling attention to important intervening variables to measure as part of the evaluation, in addition to longer-term outcomes.

But a logic model can still be useful by itself even if performance measures and program evaluations are not available, or when planning a program, because it can expose logical weak links in the program theory. To give an example, suppose Westside Hospital proposes a public advertising campaign to increase its volume of heart surgery patients. The basic program theory looks like this:

Marketing program → Patient volume

This seems logical at first glance, but we need to consider how the marketing program will increase the volume of heart surgery patients, the causal mechanism. We can do this by adding intervening variables to the model. Suppose, the theory behind the program is that the marketing campaign will enhance the perceived reputation of Westside in the eyes of prospective patients, these patients will then come to prefer Westside for heart surgery, and thus the volume of patients will increase. Here is the expanded logic model:

Marketing program → Perceived reputation of
Westside → Patients' preference for Westside → Patient volume

This expanded model forces us to consider more explicitly the logic of each link. What about the last link? How important are patient preferences, really, in the decision about where heart surgery takes place? Do patients even get to decide? Perhaps not, as often doctors are the final decision makers. At the very least, the logic model has forced us to think through the logic of the program more carefully.

Tips for Creating a Logic Model

The examples thus far in this chapter have illustrated how to develop a logic model for a program. Now, we lay out several specific tips for doing this yourself. To practice, we will use the example of an AIDS prevention program in China (Box 2.4).

BOX 2.4
China Launches Nationwide AIDS Prevention Program

BEIJING—The Red Cross Society of China (RCSC) launched a three-year nationwide AIDS prevention and care program here on Friday, aiming to reduce vulnerability to HIV and its impact in the country.

The initiative comes in response to an escalating nationwide HIV epidemic, said Yang Xusheng, director of the HIV Prevention Office with the RCSC.

"It's clear the spread of the virus, increasingly through sexual transmission, is being fuelled by a continuing lack of awareness about the disease," Yang said.

(Continued)

(Continued)

The program will try to increase awareness of the disease through various activities, including education and community mobilization that will cover a population of 27 million people through 2010, said Jiang Yiman, RCSC vice president.

He said the program would also provide home-based support and care to 90,000 HIV infected people and their family members.

The program is aimed at preventing further infection of the disease and reducing discrimination to HIV carriers in the society.

Source: China Launches Nationwide AIDS Prevention Program (n.d.).

Tip 1: Start with a single dependent (Y) variable or outcome. Real-world programs often have several outcomes, but it helps to focus on one at a time. The AIDS-prevention program in China, for example, aims both to prevent further infection *and* to care for those who have the disease (and also suffer from discrimination). These different outcomes might well be influenced by different variables, so each may require a somewhat different logic model. Again, it helps to start with one dependent variable at a time.

Tip 2: Next, add a single independent (X) variable representing the program. Many real-world programs have more than one channel or treatment—in effect, more than one independent variable. The AIDS-prevention program in China involves some form of mass-media campaign (such as radio ads and billboards) but also a more grassroots, community-based effort. It is likely that these two channels or treatments operate in much different ways and may even have distinct outcomes (at least distinct intermediate outcomes).

Tip 3: Put the program (the X variable) on the left side of the diagram and the outcome (the Y variable) on the right. Draw the program and the outcome each in one place and one place only in the diagram. For example,

$$\text{Program} \rightarrow \text{AIDS}$$

Tip 4: Be sure to add *intervening variables* to the model—and think carefully about whether the intervening variables represent distinct pathways or instead steps along the same causal pathway. For example, say the community-based component of the AIDS-prevention program involves *distributing condoms* and also holding education sessions to build *knowledge* of the disease. We might at first draw it like this:

$$\text{Program} \rightarrow \text{Knowledge} \rightarrow \text{Access to condoms} \rightarrow \text{AIDS}$$

But that is not correct. Knowledge of AIDS does not *cause* access to condoms (or vice versa). Rather, each is a separate channel or path through which the program influences risk.

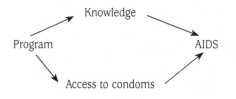

Tip 5: If something is an intervening variable (along the causal pathway), don't draw it as a separate causal pathway. For example, if the program's distribution of condoms increases access to condoms, and this in turn increases the use of condoms, then access and use are not separate causal pathway. In other words, don't draw the diagram like this:

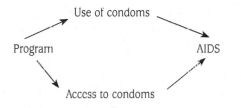

Rather, these intervening variables are steps along the same causal pathway, like this:

Program → Access to condoms → Use of condoms → AIDS

Tip 6: To make your theory really convincing, make sure that you can explain every link in your theory. If a link between one variable and another is not obvious or does not make intuitive sense, then you may need to add intervening variables to explain the connection. You want your model to be fairly self-evident for it to be really convincing to a funder or policymaker.

Tip 7: As explained earlier in this chapter, avoid giving the variable names a direction. For example, don't name the variable "Increased knowledge" but rather just "Knowledge." Express the direction of the relationship between variables by adding + or − signs next to the arrows. Keep in mind that not all variables necessarily will have a direction, particularly some categorical variables.

Tip 8: Finally, be aware that different levels of detail in a logic model are appropriate for different purposes. When you are trying to show the big picture of a complex, multipart program that aims to influence many outcomes, it will be necessary to simplify the logic model and leave out some detail.

We stressed earlier that theories must stand up to empirical evidence. Ideally, each link in your logic model would have empirical evidence backing it. In reality, you are unlikely to be so lucky. It is still important to clearly spell out each important link in your theory, as described in Tip 6, so that its plausibility can be assessed. When possible and appropriate for your audience, describe what evidence exists to support your theory, as well as where evidence is lacking.

Additional Issues in Theory Building

Theories of the Independent Variable

Thus far, our focus has been on theories of what variables drive the dependent variable. However, in later chapters, we will need to focus on theories about what drives the *independent* variable as well. This may seem strange and even contradictory. After all, we defined the independent variable as the cause and the dependent variable as the effect. However, when we start to use empirical evidence, things get more complicated.

For example, people may observe that precincts with lots of disorder are also precincts with lots of crime, and thus conclude that disorder causes crime. However, such observations do not really prove the broken windows theory. Another possible theory, consistent with the evidence, is that disorder and crime are really both symptoms of the same underlying malady—such as social and economic disadvantage. In other words, perhaps *both* disorder and crime are outcomes, caused by another variable, disadvantage, as shown in Figure 2.9. Attacking disorder in hope of reducing crime, therefore, may be a waste of effort.

This is a complex issue that the chapters of Part III will address more fully. Nonetheless, as further motivation for practicing your theory-building skills, keep in mind that figuring out the theory of the independent variable is very important for applying the empirical methods we will learn later in this book for sorting out causal effects.

Moderators

Sometimes a variable in a model is believed to influence—not another variable—but the *relationship* between two other variables. For example, in our class-size model, the effect of instruction

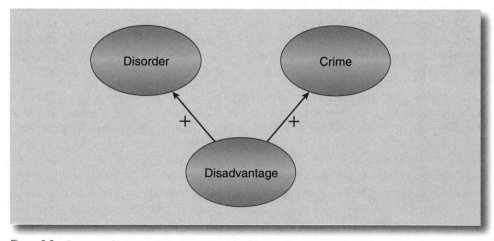

Figure 2.9   Common Cause of the Independent Variable and Dependent Variable

time could depend on how experienced the teacher is. The increase in test scores due to more instruction time could be even higher if there is a more experienced teacher in the room. In this example, teacher experience is said to moderate the effect of instruction time on test scores—thus, teacher experience is a **moderator variable**. In some disciplines, much the same idea is referred to as an **interaction**.

In a path diagram, a moderator variable is depicted by an arrow coming from the moderator and pointing toward the relationship (the middle of the arrow) that it influences, as shown in Figure 2.10. Later chapters will have more to say about how to analyze and interpret moderator (or interaction) effects.

The Aggregation Problem and the Ecological Fallacy

Relationships that hold at one unit of analysis may not hold at more aggregated levels, a phenomenon referred to as the **aggregation problem**. In some cases, the direction of the relationship may even be reversed, a phenomenon referred to as the **ecological fallacy**. Such reversals of direction typically occur when there is some other influential variable that is not included in the analysis.

For example, the term *ecological fallacy* was invented in a study examining the relationship between literacy and immigration at both the state and the individual level in 1930 (Robinson, 1950). Looking across *states*, researchers found a positive correlation between share of the population who are immigrants and the literacy rate. But looking across *individuals*, there was a negative correlation between literacy and immigrant status. Thus, although individual immigrants were less likely to be literate, immigrants moved to states with more literate populations.

Although the aggregation problem and the ecological fallacy matter in some situations, it should be pointed out that quite often, relationships that appear at an individual unit of analysis also hold when the data are aggregated. There is a technical literature about the conditions under which

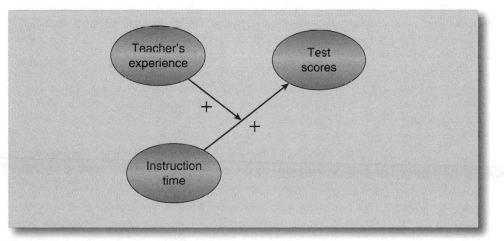

Figure 2.10   Moderator Depicted in a Path Diagram

aggregation is possible (e.g., Blundell & Stoker, 2005). Thus, aggregated data often can and do provide insights into individual behavior.

Hierarchical (Multilevel) Models and Contextual Variables

Some models—called **hierarchical models**, or multilevel models—describe relationships between variables at different units of analysis. For example, a model of student test scores that uses the student as the unit of analysis might also include classroom-level or school-level variables, such as the qualifications of the classroom teacher or the amount of financial resources the school expends per pupil. Higher-level variables such as these are sometimes referred to as **contextual variables**. We discuss this issue a bit more in Chapter 9 on multivariate analysis.

Theoretical Research

Most research is *empirical*, involving evidence, but some research is purely theoretical. That might seem like an oxymoron, and certainly any full investigation of a topic must include empirical evidence. Nonetheless, thinking theoretically is an important part of the greater research endeavor, particularly when mechanisms and relationships are complicated and not obvious.

An example might make the idea of theoretical research clearer. One of us (DR) was interested in understanding why clinical medical care was so much slower to adopt information technology than other sectors of society. That understanding was intended to help develop policies to facilitate and speed up adoption, assuming that it would improve medical care and possibly reduce expenditures. However, theoretical analysis that combined many already established facts revealed surprising advantages for going slowly (Christensen & Remler, 2009). To illustrate just a few of the issues: An electronic medical record is much more valuable if others having compatible systems and providers can communicate. But the rapid pace of technical change and tremendous risks of switching record-keeping systems means that adoption of technology too early could leave providers locked into a poorly performing system that does not communicate well with other systems.

Theoretical research is useful when many facts are already known but it may be unclear how they fit together and what the resulting implications may be. Theoretical research uses existing facts to gain insight, make valuable predictions and recommendations, and suggest hypotheses for future empirical research.

Conclusion: Theories Are Practical

According to Webster's dictionary, the adjective *theoretical* can mean "concerned primarily with theories or hypotheses rather than practical considerations." Many people have a similar association when they hear the word *theory*. Practitioners often think that they do not want to become too theoretical or spend too much time thinking about theory.

We hope that this chapter has convinced you that theories are practical. As we saw, NYPD Commissioner Bratton, not someone you'd necessarily think of as a daydreamer or idler, focused the largest police force in the United States around the broken windows theory. Theories come from police chiefs and criminologists who strive to prevent crime and save property and lives.

We have seen two ways in which a theory is practical. First, theories can help us understand the causes of a social problem or condition we care about. Understanding the causes of crime, for example, helps shed light on what police departments and other institutions in society might do to prevent it. We often welcome theories that help us explain and understand urgent social problems, giving us clues about what programs or interventions are most likely to work.

Second, logic models can help us understand how a program or policy works—how it achieves, or fails to achieve, its intended result or outcome. Such understanding can be used to improve a program or policy if it isn't working well. In other words, it is often not enough to know that a program works or doesn't—we need to know why it works (or doesn't).

For both of these uses of theories, path diagrams are valuable tools. As we move on to later chapters of the book, path diagrams will continue to be essential tools, particularly in Part III, on causation. Once you get used to thinking in terms of using path diagrams, you'll be surprised how useful they can be.

BOX 2.5
Critical Questions to Ask About Theories and Models

- Is the theory about how a single independent variable affects a single outcome (dependent variable)? If so, what are the independent and dependent variables?
- Or is the theory about many causes of an outcome or a few outcomes? If so, what are the outcomes and causes?
- Or is the theory about many relationships, without clear outcomes?
- What is the unit of analysis? Is the theory multilevel?
- Does the theory clearly lay out mechanisms? Are the mechanisms plausible?

EXERCISES

Creating a Path Model

2.1. Create a path diagram model describing the many causes of each of the following outcomes. Put in as many causes and mechanisms as you can think of. Supplement the model with a brief description in words.

- Home energy use by households
- Traffic fatalities

- Youth violence
- Litter

Identifying Independent and Dependent Variables

2.2. Identify the dependent and independent variables implicit in the following quotes:

a. "The key to a good, high-paying job is education."
b. "Oatmeal is an important part of a heart-healthy diet."
c. "Passing out condoms to teenagers just encourages bad behavior."
d. "To reduce youth violence, we need more after-school programs."

Unit of Analysis

2.3. This chapter discussed a class-size reduction program in Jackson, Mississippi. The most basic model of the program looked like this: Class size → Test scores. What are some possible units of analysis for this model? Specify an independent and dependent variable for each of the various units of analysis (as in Table 2.3).

Logic Model of a Program (Project-Length Exercise)

2.4. Consider a policy or social program that actually exists or that you would like to propose. Something that really interests you and that you know something about is best. Prepare a description of the theory of how your program works, such as might go in a grant proposal, only more detailed.

Make sure that you include the following:

a. What are the outcomes (dependent variables) the program is designed to affect? If there are many outcomes, restrict your analysis to one outcome or to a few closely related outcomes.
b. What is the unit of analysis that the variables describe?
c. Describe your program. Be as explicit as possible: Do not use vague generalities.
d. Using a path diagram and a narrative description, describe your theory of how the program is supposed to work. Both the path diagram and the narrative description should make clear the *mechanism(s)* through which the program will affect the outcome. So, if a link is not obvious, break it down into the steps along the way, illustrating the intervening variables. There can be many mechanisms through which a program works. If so, pick only a couple and just note that there are other mechanisms. This section should illustrate to your readers why they should believe that the program will work—will affect the outcome(s). It will also make clear what the weak linkages are.

Objectives: This chapter introduces you to qualitative research—an especially useful approach for generating theory as well as other research purposes. You will learn how qualitative research differs from quantitative research, how these two approaches can be combined, and the role each plays in the research process. You will get a feel for basic types of qualitative studies or methods, including in-depth interviews, focus groups, participant observation, case studies, as well as the analysis of documents and many other forms of existing qualitative data. You will also learn about selecting cases for qualitative research, coding qualitative data, and software for qualitative data analysis. This chapter begins the discussion of qualitative research, but later chapters—although focused on traditionally quantitative topics— provide further details about qualitative research and further illustrations of its usefulness.

Focus groups reveal what drivers think of congestion pricing.

Source: © iStockphoto.com/egdigital.

Qualitative Research

Fighting Malaria in Kenya

The World Health Organization (WHO) estimates that malaria kills nearly 1 million people each year, mostly children living in sub-Saharan Africa (WHO, 2009). Malaria is the fourth leading cause of death for children in developing countries (following birth complications, respiratory infections, and diarrhea, according to the Centers for Disease Control and Prevention [CDC], 2009a). In an effort to combat the disease, which is transmitted from person to person by mosquitoes, governments and private organizations have invested billions in the development and testing of new drugs to treat malaria.

Artemisinin-based combination therapy (ACT) has emerged as an effective approach to treating the disease and saving lives. WHO issued a recommendation that governments use ACT in place of older therapies that are failing because the malaria parasite has grown resistant to them. In response, the Ministry of Health in Kenya supplied ACT and provided training on its use to government health dispensaries in the country, especially those in rural villages threatened by malaria. The ministry expected these steps to lead to the widespread use of ACT to treat malaria patients.

But a follow-up survey of workers in health dispensaries found that far less than half of the patients with malaria were being treated with the new drug therapy. Most of the health workers said that they had received the training and had ACT in stock, but still they were not proving the therapy to sick children in rural Kenya. Why? The answer to this question matters: All the investment in research and development to combat malaria are worth little if frontline health workers cannot, or will not, deliver effective new treatments to sick people.

To find an answer, Kenyan health researcher Beatrice Wasunna and colleagues conducted a series of in-depth qualitative interviews with 36 health workers who had training and supplies of ACT but were not administering the therapy according to official guidelines (Wasunna, Zurovac, Goodman, & Snow, 2008). By in-depth qualitative interviewing we mean that they talked at length with individual health care workers and listened to their explanations, in their own words, for why they were not administering ACT to sick patients.

Malaria is a leading cause of death in developing countries.

Source: © Reuters.

Here is what the findings from the interviews revealed:

- Health workers knew that ACT was expensive medicine, and they feared that the Kenyan government, although it had supplied health dispensaries with an initial stock, would not be able to do so in the future. As one interviewee put it, "We are always sure that we will run short of it in due course. That's why we try to ration" (Wasunna et al., 2008, p. 4). Many said that they reserved their stocks of ACT for the neediest, most deserving patients.

- At about the same time Kenya's drug agency was distributing ACT, the same agency also sent even larger stocks of an older antimalarial drug, amodiaquine. This created much confusion among workers in the local health dispensaries. As one person explained, speaking of his coworkers, "They are asking why the government is still supplying so much of it [amodiaquine], if they are not supposed to use it?"

- The training health workers received on the use of ACT gave inconsistent messages, leaving many with the impression that special testing was mandatory before prescribing ACT. Moreover, the health dispensaries often did not have the microscopes or kits required to do the testing. According to one health worker, "In the first place when we got this [ACT] we were told not to use them unless we get those kits" (p. 5).

- Health workers reported being pressured by patients for the older antimalarial, amodiaquine, because it was more familiar and also because it was simpler to use. "You know the mothers are used to amodiaquine syrup so they usually complain that they have to crush too many [ACT] tablets," explained a health worker.

- Finally, the interviews suggested that most dispensaries were understaffed, with high turnover and lack of supervision. As one health worker describes the problem,

We were told to give quality care, it is one thing saying but another doing. Sometimes you just give quantity care because I'm all alone here. I have 2–3 community health workers and they are not conversant with the new treatment policy . . . If there could be additional health workers, then we can give the patient quality care.

These interview findings suggest possible reasons why health workers in Kenya did not switch to the new therapy—the possible causes of the problem.

Theory, Causes, and Qualitative Research

The Kenyan malaria study illustrates well the nature and value of *qualitative research*. Sometimes the best way to find out an answer to a pressing public policy or management problem is to go directly into the field, observe conditions on the ground, and ask the people involved—in their own words—for their interpretation of what is happening.

Qualitative research is particularly useful and well suited to discovering important variables and relationships, to generating theory and models, and thus uncovering possible causes and causal mechanisms. Glaser and Strauss (1967) coined the term **grounded theory** to refer to this theory-generating aspect of qualitative research. And George and Bennett (2005) employ the notion of *causal process tracing* to explain how good qualitative research uncovers causal mechanisms.

The findings from the in-depth interviews in Kenya, for example, suggested possible causes of the reluctance of health workers to prescribe ACT: lack of trust that ACT supplies would be maintained, continued distribution of older drugs, patients who preferred the older drugs and resisted switching, misunderstandings picked up from the trainings, and lack of staff and resources at the dispensaries. Health officials could use these qualitative findings to come up with a program theory—a logic model—of variables that encourage, or hinder, the use of ACT. Indeed, qualitative studies such as this frequently provide the insights needed to construct the kinds of models we saw in the previous chapter.

It is because of this theory-generating, model-building aspect of qualitative research that we introduce the topic at this point in the book. But qualitative methods are important in their own right as a way of generating research knowledge. In addition, qualitative methods can play an important role in other aspects of research, such as developing measures, pretesting surveys, or following up on experimental findings. We will describe these and other valuable uses of qualitative methods in later chapters.

In this chapter, we focus on the various approaches and methods of qualitative research. We begin by defining qualitative research and contrasting it with quantitative research.

What Is Qualitative Research?

Qualitative research can be defined in terms of the kind of data it produces and in terms of the form of analysis it employs. Some also argue that qualitative research involves a different logic of inquiry as well, a point we will return to shortly. In terms of data, **qualitative research** involves various kinds of *nonnumerical data*, such as interviews (oral communication), written texts or documents, visual images, observations of behavior, case studies, and so on. The malaria study in Kenya, for example, was based on data from in-depth interviews of 36 health workers. The tape recordings and transcripts of these interviews, together with whatever notes or observations the researchers made when they visited the rural health dispensaries, constitute the data for this qualitative study.

In terms of analysis, qualitative research relies on various methods of *interpretation*. Because **qualitative data** are often spoken or written language, or images that have symbolic content, making sense of the data involves interpreting its meaning. Moreover, qualitative analysis relies on the fact that the objects under investigation are human beings and that language provides a unique window into the thoughts, experiences, and motivations of others. This is referred to sometimes as **intersubjectivity**—the notion that language allows us to stand in someone else's shoes, as it were, and see the world from his or her perspective.

Thus, qualitative researchers rely on this human potential for intersubjectivity, achieved through interpretation of language and other symbolic systems (such as body language or images), to explain human behavior. The Kenyan research team listened to the health workers, interpreted their stories, and drew conclusions about why ACT was not being prescribed as intended.

Contrasting Qualitative With Quantitative Research

To understand what distinguishes qualitative research, it helps to contrast it with **quantitative research**. In quantitative research, investigators often observe the world using instruments (including structured questionnaires) that produce quantitative measurements, or numerical data, representing various characteristics, behaviors, or attitudes. They also retrieve data that are already in numerical form, such as prices. Quantitative researchers analyze the numerical data using the tools and techniques of statistics, from simple graphs and tables to sophisticated multivariate techniques.

Quantitative research can investigate characteristics thought of as qualitative, including emotions, beliefs, or other intangible variables. For example, there is a great deal of quantitative research on topics such as happiness, religious beliefs, self-esteem, and trust of other people. What makes these studies quantitative is that they use instruments that produce numerical data, and these data are analyzed using statistics. So it is not the topic of the research that makes it qualitative or quantitative—the distinction lies in the nature of the data and methods of analysis.

Small-n Studies and Purposive Sampling

Quantitative research typically involves probability (random) selection of people or cases and a large sample size, or a "large n" ("n" refers to the "number" of people or cases in the sample). We discuss the ideas and issues of sampling fully in Chapter 5.

Qualitative research, in contrast, most often involves **purposive** or **theoretical sampling** and a "small n." In qualitative research, in other words, people or cases are chosen for a specific purpose, or to generate theory, and the number of people or cases is necessarily limited because of the more intensive, time-consuming character of qualitative data collection and analysis. To this extent, qualitative research involves trading off the generalizability that comes with large, random samples for the ability to do more in-depth (thick) description and to select cases of theoretical importance.

The Kenyan study of malaria, for example, included $n = 36$ qualitative interviews, but it was based on responses from a prior, quantitative survey of $n = 227$ health workers. Many qualitative studies involve even fewer people or cases (a case study of $n = 1$ even). In contrast, many quantitative surveys involve samples of thousands and sometimes even millions. Here is how the Kenyan researchers describe the basis for selecting their sample:

> Four criteria were applied to these health workers to qualify for inclusion in this qualitative study: 1) they must have received training on the new treatment guidelines; 2) they were working at health facilities where [ACT] was in stock on the day of the survey; 3) they were routinely involved in the diagnosis of malaria at their facility; and 4) during the 2006 facility-based assessment they prescribed [ACT] for less than 40% of patients for whom they made a routine diagnosis of malaria. This group was selected deliberately because of their degree of non-adherence, and the lack of other obvious reasons for this. (Wasunna et al., 2008, p. 3)

In this way, the health workers selected for qualitative interviewing were chosen purposively for an important theoretical reason: to find out why health workers with both training and access to ACT were not prescribing the new therapy to their patients with malaria.

The qualitative sampling in this study from Kenya focused on a particular group of theoretical interest. Another qualitative sampling strategy is to select people or cases to produce theoretically interesting *variation*.

Say, for example, you want to study leadership styles in nonprofit organizations, and your initial theory or model suggests that leadership style reflects both the size of the organization and the gender of the director. You would then want variation on both these theoretically key dimensions, as in

Table 3.1. Selecting cases to fill the four cells of this purposive sampling table would help ensure that your study had theoretically interesting variation.

There are many forms of purposive or theoretical sampling for qualitative research. Patton (2002), for example, lists and discusses 16 different strategies, including sampling typical cases, sampling extreme or deviant cases, snowball or chain sampling (also called respondent-driven sampling), sampling cases that both confirm and disconfirm the theory, sampling politically important cases, and so on. We will return to many of these methods in Chapter 5 on sampling.

Table 3.1   Purposive Sampling of Nonprofit Directors

	Female Director	Male Director
Large nonprofit	Case A	Case B
Small nonprofit	Case C	Case D

Focus on Cases Rather Than Variables

As we saw in the previous chapter, theories are mostly about variables and how they are related to one another. This perspective is associated primarily with quantitative research. But qualitative research often does not start with variables. Rather, it focuses on *cases*—individuals, groups, or institutions. We will have more to say about the case study method later in this chapter. A basic motivation for this approach is that by examining cases in their full complexity, the relevant variables can be identified and tested (George & Bennett, 2005). This is another way to appreciate how qualitative research generates theory and helps build models.

Advantages of Qualitative Research

We have already emphasized the theory-generating, model-building advantages of qualitative methods. And we have mentioned how qualitative methods can help us understand or uncover causal processes or causal mechanisms at work in a setting. But there are some other specific situations in which qualitative methods are especially useful:

- Exploratory studies of new or only vaguely understood social or organizational behaviors
- Rapid reconnaissance in situations where time does not permit more structured, quantitative research
- Understanding important individuals, such as leaders of an organization, or unique cases, such as a government agency reacting to a crisis (this is because statistical techniques offer little advantage when only one or a few cases are involved)
- Understanding small groups and group dynamics
- Understanding cultures or subcultures, in large part because cultures are expressed with language and other symbolic systems
- Analyzing visual images or communication
- Analyzing historical or archival texts

Qualitative research has its limitations as well: It is not good for producing precise measurements of variables, estimating characteristics of a large population, calculating the magnitude of relationships between variables, or providing statistical evidence of a cause-effect relationship—although it is good at uncovering possible causes when these are largely unknown, as noted above.

Schools of Thought in Qualitative Research

Because qualitative methods originated from various academic disciplines (anthropology, sociology, clinical psychology, philosophy, and literature), there are various epistemologies or schools of thought in qualitative research. As a result, you may see qualitative researchers describe their work as a phenomenological study, an ethnography, a grounded theory study, and so on. Patton's (2002) comprehensive book on qualitative research methods provides a discussion of these various schools of thought. Table 3.2, which is adapted from Patton's book, provides a useful summary of the foundational questions, disciplinary roots, and key thinkers associated with each of these schools of thought.

We do not have space to explain these various schools of thought here. (See Patton, 2002, for more background on these and other schools of qualitative thought.) But we can make several important points. Qualitative researchers come from different philosophical and epistemological perspectives, often rooted in their disciplinary training. And some schools of qualitative thought argue that qualitative research represents a distinctly different logic of inquiry or epistemology, one that is more humanistic, socially critical, and skeptical of traditional scientific notions of objectivity and causation (Lincoln & Guba, 1985; Patton, 2002). But throughout this book, we approach qualitative methods as an integral part of the scientific tradition, broadly defined, rather than as a separate approach.

In the sections that follow, we take up the discussion of the various methods and sources of data available for conducting qualitative research for policy and practice. So let's now look more closely at some of these—beginning with already existing qualitative data.

Table 3.2 Qualitative Epistemologies or Schools of Thought

School of Thought	Foundational Questions	Disciplinary Roots	Key Thinkers and Writers
Ethnography	What is the culture of this group of people?	Anthropology	Malinowski, M. Mead, Lévi-Strauss, and Geertz
Ethnomethodology	How do people make sense of their everyday lives?	Sociology	Garfinkel
Grounded theory	What theory emerges from a setting and is grounded in the observations made?	Sociology	Glaser and Strauss
Hermeneutics	How can the original intention of the author of a text, or the producer of a cultural artifact, be interpreted and understood?	Theology, philosophy	Gadamer and Ricoeur
Narratology (narrative analysis)	What does this narrative or story reveal about the person or group that created it?	Literature	Foucault, Bal, and Genette

School of Thought	Foundational Questions	Disciplinary Roots	Key Thinkers and Writers
Phenomenology	What is the meaning and structure of the lived experience of a given phenomenon for this person or group?	Philosophy	Husserl, Schutz, and Merleau-Ponty
Semiotics	How do signs (words, symbols) carry and convey meaning in particular contexts?	Linguistics, literature	Barthes
Social constructivism	How have people in this setting constructed their beliefs and views?	Sociology, philosophy	Berger and Luckmann, Searle
Symbolic interactionism	What common set of symbols and understandings give meaning to people's interactions?	Psychology	G. H. Mead, Cooley, Blumer, and Goffman

Source: Adapted from Patton (2002). Used with permission from Sage Publications.

Existing Qualitative Data

Qualitative data can be produced from interviews, focus groups, or other methods of original data collection to be discussed shortly. But a great deal of qualitative data already exist in the form of published and unpublished documents, transcripts, testimonies, tape recordings, official records, correspondence, news articles and reports, and Web logs, as well as a host of cultural artifacts, such as movies, television, music, art, and so on.

For example, Harpster, Adams, and Jarvis (2009) were interested in examining verbal indicators of guilt in 911 calls involving a reported homicide. Using existing tape recordings of 100 calls made to law enforcement agencies across the United States, the researchers looked for indications of the callers' guilt or innocence. They then compared the indications with the callers' actual guilt or innocence, as established by the courts.

One such indication they found is whether the caller began with a plea for help (a sign of innocence) or merely reported the crime without asking for help (a sign of guilt). Consider the following two calls:

Dispatcher: 911, what is your emergency?

Caller: Get an ambulance to 4200 Dryden Road, my friend's been shot!

Dispatcher: 911, what is your emergency?

Caller: I have an infant, he's not breathing.

In the first case, in which the caller asks for help, the person who made the call was innocent. In the second case, in which the father making the call does not ask for help for his child, a later autopsy revealed that he had

Sometimes, people call 911 to report their own crimes.

Source: © iStockphoto.com/Mik122.

in fact shaken his infant son to death. Some of the other key verbal indications of guilt discovered by this study include providing extraneous information, stating conflicting facts, and being inappropriately polite ("Hi, I've been shot and my husband has been shot").

The findings of this qualitative study have important implications for police investigation of suspected homicides. The study also involved statistical analysis, which is not uncommon in qualitative studies that involve coding and content analysis. We will address coding and content analysis a bit later in the chapter.

Archival and Other Written Documents

A great deal of information is written down in various texts and official records stored in physical or electronic archives. Historical research can be thought of as a form of qualitative research based largely on finding and interpreting these archived texts and records. But documents represent an important and widely useful form of existing qualitative data for more contemporary issues and problems as well. Some relevant types of documents include the following:

- Testimonies made at hearings or trials
- Legislative floor debates
- Minutes of meetings held by various types of organizations
- Language contained in laws and regulations
- Mission statements or strategic plans
- Official correspondence from elected officials, government administrators, or businesses
- Notes on clients or patients kept in clinical logs
- Letters of inquiry or complaint sent by customers or citizens

In addition, of course, there are the many published sources—newspapers, magazines, books, journals, professional newsletters, and so on. All these various sources of written material or texts can serve as data for qualitative research.

Visual Media, Popular Culture, and the Internet

Thus far, we have dealt mostly with forms of written or oral language. But qualitative data also come in the form of images such as photographs and videos. Sometimes the images come from published or broadcast sources, such as magazines and newspapers, television, movies, and music videos.

A study by Webb, Jenkins, Browne, Afifi, and Kraus (2007), for example, examined popular movies rated PG-13 to assess the level of exposure to violence that is typical of movies frequented by adolescents. They found that violence permeated nearly 90% of the movies in their sample and that nearly 50% contained acts of lethal violence.

Although plenty of qualitative data already exist, often researchers find that they need to collect their own, original qualitative data. One of the most direct means of doing so is to interview people.

Qualitative Interviews

Interviewing is a basic methodological tool in qualitative research, one that can be used alone or as part of participant observation or case studies (discussed a bit later on). Qualitative interviews involve

open-ended questions that allow people to respond in their own words and that encourage detailed and in-depth answers. In this way, they differ from the highly structured, largely closed-ended (check-the-box) questioning characteristic of most surveys (discussed in Chapter 7). Qualitative interviews can be described as either unstructured or semistructured.

Unstructured Interviews

Unstructured interviews have no predetermined set of questions. An unstructured interview can seem much like an ordinary conversation, but there are important differences. As Robert Weiss (1994) explains in his book *Learning From Strangers:*

> In an ordinary conversation, each participant voices observations, thoughts, feelings. Either participant can set a new topic, either can ask questions. In the qualitative interview the respondent provides information while the interviewer, as a representative of the study, is responsible for directing the respondent to the topics that matter to the study. (p. 8)

Weiss (1994) gives an example from an interview of a 66-year-old woman conducted as part of a study of how people adjust to retirement after a lifetime of work. The topic of the study provides a general framework for the discussion, but much of the interview centers on what the woman has to say about her everyday life and, in particular, her isolation and withdrawal from society. The interviewer's questions are not prescripted but rather arise spontaneously in response to what the woman says during the interview. For example, at one point in the interview, the woman mentions that her daughter recently encouraged her to volunteer. In response, the interviewer asks, "Could you walk me through that conversation with your daughter where she made the suggestion to volunteer?" (p. 6) A fairly long and detailed response follows.

Unstructured interviews are typical of participant observation or ethnographic research in which the researcher is embedded in a setting for an extended period of time, often years. A good example is Robert Smith's (2005) ethnography of Mexican immigrants in New York City. Participation over a long period helps establish the trust needed to conduct in-depth, unstructured interviews of informants, such as recent immigrants, who may be much less forthcoming in more structured, one-shot interviews.

Sometimes, however, qualitative researchers need to conduct interviews that are more structured—semistructured interviews as they are called. But it's important to understand that all qualitative interviewing involves some structure and that, in practice, the distinction is often more one of degree than of kind.

Semistructured Interviews

The study of treating malaria in Kenya involved **semistructured interviews** of workers in local health dispensaries. Here is how Wasunna and colleagues (2008) describe their data collection method:

> Since the study was addressing the sensitive topic of nonadherence to guidelines, individual in-depth interviews (IDIs) were selected as the most appropriate data collection tool to investigate opinions and reasons underlying such behavior. A semi-structured interview guide was developed which allowed for flexibility within the discussions, and explored health worker perceptions about the new treatment policy and reasons underlying their decisions not to

prescribe [ACT]. The influence of perceived severity of illness on prescribing practices was explored through a case vignette methodology in which health workers were asked to respond to a specific case management scenario. (p. 3)

Notice that the in-depth interviews followed a semistructured **interview guide**. A semistructured interview guide is a set of open-ended questions, sometimes accompanied by probes, that help guide or structure the discussion. It helps ensure that each interview covers substantially the same topics, although the guide is meant to be a flexible tool and not a standardized script. Some respondents may have a lot to say about certain topics and less about other topics, and the order in which topics come up during the course of the interview may vary. A good qualitative interviewer does not read from a script.

In the Kenyan study, the researchers also presented a vignette (a short, written description) of a malaria case and asked the health workers how they would respond to the case. Presenting respondents with a vignette, photograph, or other written or visual device can help prompt discussion, as well as vary the pace of an in-depth interview that can last 2 hours or more.

To get a sense of what a semistructured interview guide looks like, let's consider another health study involving rural parents in Canada (Miller, Verhoef, & Cardwell, 2008). These researchers were interested in understanding how rural parents acquired and used health information to make decisions about immunizing their children. Figure 3.1 presents the semistructured interview guide Miller and her colleagues followed in their interviews with parents.

Notice first that there are only 11 questions, yet the interviews likely took at least an hour or two. Semistructured interview guides typically have fewer than 20 questions, sometimes fewer than 10. This is because the questions are intentionally open-ended—meaning they ask for an explanation rather than just brief answers. Asking many "what" or "how" questions tends to help in this regard, for example, "What information did you need and/or want to know?" When a yes/no question is asked, it is followed by an open-ended probe. For example, "Did you use information in the decision? If yes, what role did the information play?" Although it appears simple, it takes time and careful thought to craft a good semistructured interview guide.

1. Could you tell me about the journey/process you went through in making a decision about immunizing your child?

2. Did you use information in the decision? If yes, what role did the information play? Were there other influences in your decision about immunizing?

3. What were the sources of information you used? Where did you look? Please tell me if you found information readily available to you.

4. What information did you need and/or want to know?

5. Did you find information from the sources you used conflicting or confusing? If so, how did you handle it?

6. In your opinion, what makes up good information?

7. Credibility criteria:
   - How did you determine what kind of information was going to be helpful?
   - How did you decide who to believe and trust as sources of information?

- How did you determine they were experts?
- What specifically made the information reliable from your perspective?

8. Health professionals:

- Did you find the information given you by health professionals addressed your concerns/questions adequately? Please explain.
- Did they give consistent information about immunization or were there differences?

9. What is your preference in how you receive information?

10. Do you have any ideas/recommendations of how information can be conveyed to parents more effectively?

11. Do you have any recommendations for health professionals in how they provide and share information to parents about immunization?

Figure 3.1   Semistructured Interview Guide in Miller Immunization Study

Source: Miller et al. (2008).

Asking Truly Open-Ended Questions

Writing questions that are truly open-ended takes practice. Say, for example, we are interested in studying leadership in a nonprofit organization and want to hear from middle managers. We might include in our interview guide a question such as this:

Do you consider your executive director to be a good leader, or not?

Fair enough. But because middle managers tend not to want to talk too much about their executive director, especially if they have something unflattering to say, we might not get much discussion going. "I guess he's okay—better than the last one," we might hear, but that doesn't give us much information or insight. But we can use "what" and "how"to ask the question another way:

Tell me how your executive director is, or is not, a good leader?–or perhaps better:

What makes your executive director a good leader—or what makes him not such a good leader?

These questions are more open-ended—they do not let the respondents off the hook, as it were, so easily. The respondents must explain their answer—*how* is he a good leader (or not), *what* makes him a good leader (or not).

The Power of Probes

Experienced interviewers have a certain touch—getting people to talk, to open up. Think of your favorite TV or radio talk show host—many of them have this skill. Diane Rehm, of American University Radio (WAMU) and National Public Radio, for example, is well-known for her interviewing. (Her in-depth interviews with authors, world leaders, and others can be heard online at http://wamu.org/programs/dr/archives/.) You'll notice several things if you listen carefully: (1) She does not talk much—the air space, as it were, is carefully reserved for the respondent; (2) she uses truly open-ended questions that encourage conversation; and (3) she uses simple probes in a surprisingly effective manner at key moments in the interview. Here are some common probes she and other experienced interviewers tend to use to good effect:

- Say more about that.
- Explain that to me.
- Why is that important to you?
- Tell me what happened.
- Can you give me an example of that?
- What was that like for you?
- Why did that matter to you?
- What made you think of that just now?
- What led up to that?
- What happened next?

This kind of open-ended probing is part of what makes in-depth, qualitative interviewing different from the structured, mostly closed-ended questioning typical of quantitative survey research.

Some Practical Considerations When Doing Interviews

There are a number of practical considerations in doing interviews. To begin with, should the interview be conducted in person, on the telephone, or some other way? In-person interviews are generally favored as they show respect, establish rapport, allow for visuals or hand-outs, and capture body language and voice tone. In-person interviewing sometimes allows the researcher to visit the location where the respondent lives or works, permitting direct observation of the setting. However, sometimes an in-person visit is not practical and so interviewing by telephone, video teleconference, or even e-mail is an option.

Another practical consideration is whether to use audio (or video) recording, or just take notes, and whether recordings should be transcribed. The answers depend on the available resources, the timeline, the sensitivity of the topic, and the importance of capturing exact wording for later analysis and reporting. Most researchers make an audio recording of the interview, provided the respondent agrees and that the recording does not inhibit a candid discussion.

Another decision is whether to interview respondents once (a cross section) or on several occasions over time. Depending on the nature of the research, it may be useful to interview the same respondent on multiple occasions over a period of time. This will allow information about changes or temporal dynamics.

Another decision is how much to tell the respondent in advance about the topics of the interview. For some studies, it may even be helpful to send the outline of topics in advance so that the person can review them and prepare for the interview. Revealing the questions in advance can be necessary sometimes for getting the person to agree to do the interview. But more often, it is sufficient simply to describe the purpose, sponsorship, and general topic of the interview.

Let's turn now to another type of interview—a group interview called a focus group.

Focus Groups

Focus groups are one of most widely used, and widely useful, methods of qualitative research—especially applied research for policy and practice. The method consists essentially of a group interview typically involving 6 to 12 people. The number of participants should be enough to make the discussion lively, but not too many to prevent all from participating. The participants sit around a table, along with a **moderator** who asks questions and guides the group discussion. An audio and sometimes video recording of the discussion is made for later analysis. An assistant moderator sits off to one side and often observers watch the discussion from behind a two-way mirror. Figure 3.2 presents a typical layout of a focus group facility. Although firms rent out specialized focus group facilities that look like this, it is quite possible to hold focus groups in an ordinary conference or meeting room.

Typically a focus group study involves at least 2 or 3 separate focus groups to allow for the possibility of confirming or replicating findings. Some studies can comprise 20 or more separate focus groups, with much depending on the number of subgroups of interest in the study. A school system, for example, may want to hear from parents, students, and teachers to get ideas about a new program or initiative. But the discussion would be less open if we mixed these three subgroups together. Instead, it is preferable to hold separate focus groups of parents only, students only, and teachers only. To feel confident that we have represented the views of each subgroup adequately, however, a study like this would require at least six to nine separate discussions—two to three for each subgroup.

If at all possible, it is best to organize focus groups of people who do not know each other too well, as sometimes prior issues or personal relationships can inhibit or distort the discussion.

What Do People Think of Congestion Pricing?

To get more into the details of the method, let's consider an example. The U.S. Federal Highway Administration commissioned a focus group study of public attitudes toward congestion pricing for the use of roads and highways during peak times (Petrella, Biernbaum, & Lappin, 2007). The study consisted of four focus groups in the northern Virginia suburbs of Washington, D.C. (representing a fast-growing metro area) and four focus groups in the Philadelphia area (representing an older, slow-growth metro area). In each area, two of the four focus groups were made up of the general driving public, while the other two were composed of small business owners and representatives of shipping and transportation companies.

This selection of locations and of different user groups illustrates well the purposive nature of qualitative sampling. Typically, an incentive payment is offered to help ensure that participants will show up as scheduled at the focus group facility and to compensate them for their time. Often focus group participants are recruited by telephone, from lists or from random dialing, but then screened for certain experiences or characteristics.

Moderating a Focus Group

The moderator of these focus groups follows a **moderator's guide** to lead the discussion—a script that looks much like a semistructured interview guide. The discussions open with the general topic of everyday transportation experiences, then begin to focus in more on the question of funding transportation

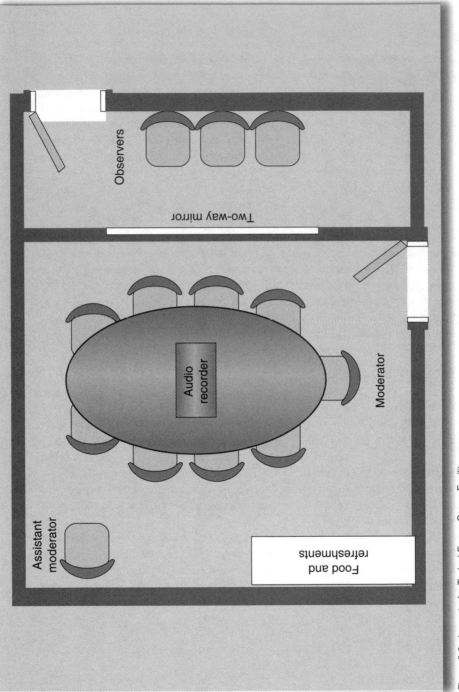

Figure 3.2 Layout of a Typical Focus Group Facility

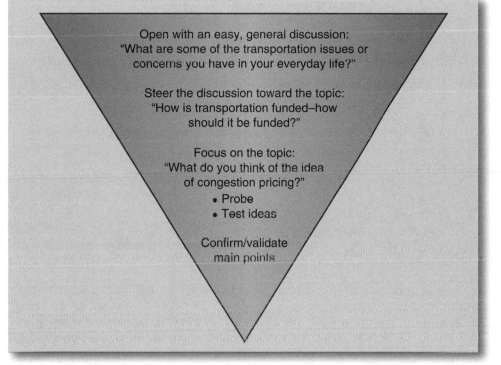

Figure 3.3 General Flow of a Focus Group Discussion

and, specifically, congestion pricing. Figure 3.3 illustrates this focusing-in pattern of the discussion (hence the name focus group).

The discussions are audiotaped (sometimes videotaped as well) for later review and analysis by the research team. If time and resources permit, a full typed transcript of the discussion may be produced for review and analysis, perhaps including coding and content analysis (as described a bit later on). But often the audio recordings alone suffice, with only illustrative quotes transcribed verbatim. The aim is to capture major themes or insights. Here are some themes from the report on congestion pricing (Petrella et al., 2007, p. 8):

- Transportation issues: "Traffic dictates how we live our lives"
- How is transportation funded: general awareness, but short on specifics
- Congestion-based pricing: they get it, for the most part
- People want more information on the program; in particular they want to know what their tax savings would be and how much they would be paying in tolls
- Some would change their travel behavior, or where they live and work
- Environmental benefits not on most people's radar, though potential benefits are acknowledged

Why a Focus Group? Why Not Individual Interviews?

You might be wondering, "What are the reasons for having a focus *group* discussion, as opposed to a series of *individual* interviews?" There are several reasons:

- As a practical matter, the research team can interview 6 to 12 people at one time and place rather than having to schedule and conduct that many individual interviews.
- But more important, individuals in the group cue or prompt each other in ways that a interviewer—even an experienced and well-prepared one—is not able to do in a one-on-one interview. This within-group cuing and prompting can spark an animated discussion and help uncover important issues.
- People will agree or disagree on topics, thus allowing the researcher to see what views are widely shared versus views that are more idiosyncratic. In this way, it helps the researcher better understand the generalizability of qualitative findings.
- Many important issues or topics in social life are influenced by group processes or how others around us view and discuss the matter. Focus groups mimic this social process of knowing or thinking about an issue.

There are reasons not to have focus group discussions as well. The method does not work well for personal or sensitive topics that people do not feel comfortable discussing among a group of strangers. As indicated earlier, focus groups often do not succeed with groups of people who already work together or know each other well (because prior issues and relationships tend to overshadow or distort the discussion). And focus groups do not provide depth on any one individual's experiences.

Telephone and Online Focus Groups

Recruiting participants to show up at a facility at a given time and place can require much effort and inconvenience. Moreover, there are situations in which the potential participants reside in such geographically dispersed locations that they cannot assemble for an in-person discussion. As a result, some studies conduct focus groups by telephone or online.

In a telephone focus group, the respondents use a dial-in conference calling service to connect with each other and the moderator at an agreed on time. As in a regular focus group, the moderator leads the discussion following a semistructured guide, and the discussion is recorded (most conference calling services can do this for a fee). Because of the lack of visual cues and call quality issues with multiple parties on the line, it is often better in a telephone focus group to have fewer participants (4 to 6, rather than 6 to 12). The length of the discussion tends to be shorter as well (about 60 minutes rather than the 90 minutes or more that is typical of in-person focus groups).

Online focus groups are another possibility these days, and indeed a number of market research firms specialize in organizing and conducting focus groups on the Web. Web conferencing services, such as GoToMeeting.com, WebEx.com or Yugma.com, provide Web-based software that can be used to conduct your own online focus group. Using the Web for focus groups is especially suited to situations in which participants need to respond to visual materials, such as ad copy, a video clip, or a PowerPoint show. Obviously, online focus groups work only with participants who have ready access to the Internet and are comfortable with using Web-based communications.

Qualitative Observation

Qualitative research sometimes involves direct observation of behavior. Rather than interview people, the researcher directly observes a setting or behavior and takes notes or records the observations using still or video photography. Capturing the observations in this way allows for later, more careful, review and interpretation.

Take for example a study of hepatitis C prevention by Treloar and colleagues (2008), who videotaped the injecting episodes of drug users in a medically supervised clinic in Sydney, Australia, to study risky practices. An analysis of the videos identified 27 risky practices, such as not washing hands or swabbing the injection site, injecting against the direction of blood flow, and using fingers to stop the bleeding or even licking blood off the injection site. As the authors conclude about their findings:

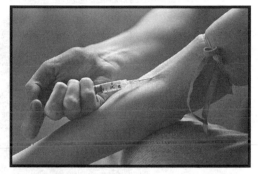

Injection drug users can spread hepatitis C.
Source: © 2009 Jupiterimages Corporation.

> The strength of this study relies on the use of video recordings of injecting episodes . . . It is very difficult to accurately record the behaviours observed in this study using self-report or even during real-time observation: we viewed each video multiple times to accurately record practice. (Treloar et al., 2008, p. 64)

Photography and videography are used in similar ways to study a wide range of behaviors, including classroom interactions in a school or the behavior of suspects and officers during a police interrogation.

Participant Observation and Ethnography

Sometimes to understand a group or social situation, you must join it—that is the essential idea behind **participant observation** (Jorgensen, 1989). The method is associated with **ethnography**, bringing to mind the image of an anthropologist like Margaret Mead living among native people like the Somoans in remote corners of the world (Mead, 1971). But participant observation can be useful for social and policy research in settings closer to home as well.

Why Do the Homeless Refuse Help?

Often homeless individuals with psychiatric problems refuse offers of help despite their desperate need for food, housing, and medical care. Why? Tanya Marie Luhrmann (2008) provided some answers to this question based on more than 1,000 hours of participant observation over 3 years in one Chicago neighborhood. As she describes her method (talking about herself in the third person): "She spent most of her time in the drop-in center but also met with women she knew from the drop-in center in local shelters, parks, and restaurants. These meetings were casual, unscripted, and dominated by the subject's concerns" (p. 15). One of her key findings was that many of the women

Why do some homeless people refuse help?

Source: © iStockphoto.com/skyak.

wanted to avoid the designation of being "crazy" provided by a diagnosis of psychiatric disability, which was often a condition for receiving housing and other benefits.

Notice how the study took many hours and required a fairly long period of involvement of the researcher in the setting. This is typical of ethnographic studies. Such studies are especially well suited to broad, complex, and open-ended research questions (such as why homeless people refuse much-needed assistance). As the research is conducted, important themes and topics emerge.

Notice too how ethnography tends to make use of unstructured interviews, particularly once the trust of participants has been gained. Indeed, the long-term involvement of the researcher in the setting and with the lives of participants greatly facilities access to people and encourages more open, in-depth, and revealing discussions. This is one of the key advantages of ethnography.

Levels on a Participation-Observation Continuum

The researcher may participate in and interact with the setting to a greater or lesser extent. As a result, qualitative researchers often think in terms of a participation-observation continuum of possible roles, following Gold's (1958) original categorization:

Complete participant, in which the researcher takes on a central role in the setting, for example, becoming a teacher in order to study a disadvantaged school.

Participant as observer, in which the researcher spends significant time in the setting, joining in important activities or events, but does not assume an actual role as such. (Luhrmann's 2008 study of homeless people in Chicago is a good example.)

Observer as participant, in which the researcher visits the setting, typically only on one of just a few occasions, to conduct interviews with people and make observations.

Complete observer, in which the research attempts to remain unobtrusive and does not interview or engage with people in the setting, for example, sitting in an emergency room waiting area in order to observe the interactions of patients and staff.

The level of active participation versus unobtrusive observation depends on the setting, the research aims, and the relationship the researcher has with the setting. And there are trade-offs. Participation provides a unique, first-hand perspective many times, but it also risks influencing the very behaviors that you are trying to observe. Participation is also time-consuming and can create ethical dilemmas, as described at the end of the chapter.

Secret Shopping and Audit Studies

In consumer studies, researchers sometimes use a form of participant observation called the **secret (or mystery) shopping** method—playing the role of a customer to experience service quality. But the same approach can be used to evaluate welfare offices, emergency rooms, visitor information centers, 311 help lines, libraries, and so on. For example, a team of field workers might visit library branches to make standard requests for information and assistance, making notes afterward about various aspects of their visit.

A related example is **audit studies**, which have been used to investigate discrimination in employment, housing, and lending (Struyk & Fix, 1993). In an audit study of job discrimination, for example, matched pairs of auditors who are similar in most job-related characteristics (and given the same resume and coaching)—yet differ in race—visit an employer to apply for a job. Discrimination is inferred if there is a systematic difference in job offers. Audit studies are primarily a form of randomized experiment (covered in Chapter 12), but the auditors also observe the setting and how they are treated. Thus, audit studies are—in a very real sense—a form of short-term participant observation.

As the examples of secret shopping and audit studies illustrate, at times, participant observation can involve the observer going underground, as it were, and disguising himself or herself to experience or test the setting. This raises ethical issues that we discuss later in this chapter. But more often in participant observation, including ethnography, the researcher indentifies himself or herself as a researcher, and then proceeds to join the setting to observe and interview people.

Case Study Research

As we mentioned earlier, qualitative research is grounded in the in-depth study of cases, such as people, groups, or organizations. So in one sense, it would seem that most qualitative research could be defined as case study research. But the term **case study** tends to be reserved for research that focuses on a single, complex case.[1] Case studies also typically involve a larger, aggregate-level case—such as an organization, a neighborhood, or a nation-state—rather than an individual person. In clinical research, however, there are case studies of individual patients with a particular condition or disease. And in leadership studies, case studies of individual leaders are not uncommon. Although most case studies involve a single case, you may also come across *comparative case studies* involving two or more cases examined in depth and compared.

Maryland's Gun Violence Act

To get the flavor of a case study, let's consider the following abstract from an article by Frattaroli and Teret (2006) in the journal *Evaluation Review*:

> The Maryland Gun Violence Act, enacted into law in 1996, explicitly authorized courts to order batterers to surrender their firearms through civil protective orders. It also vested law enforcement with the explicit authority to remove guns when responding to a domestic violence complaint. In order to assess how these laws were implemented, we designed a case study and collected data from in-depth, key informant interviews, court observations, and relevant documents. We present findings from this study and recommend how to increase the likelihood that policies designed to separate batterers and guns are implemented in a way that will result in greater protections for victims of domestic violence. (p. 347)

The study found that ambiguities in the language of the law left police officers uncertain about how to carry out the new policies in specific domestic violence situations. And it revealed that leadership commitment to the new policies within police departments influenced how fully and aggressively police officers applied their new authority.

This case study uses many of the qualitative methods discussed earlier—in-depth interviews, participant observation in courtrooms, and the analysis of existing documents. In this sense, the case study is not a different method of qualitative data collection but makes use of several qualitative data collection methods. Moreover, case studies can even involve quantitative methods—a survey of employees within one organization, for example—and frequently a combination of qualitative and quantitative data (mixed methods). The case study uses as many methods as needed to get the fullest possible picture of a particular case.

Note that although the study investigates one law in Maryland, it aims to uncover aspects of implementation that can be applied to similar policies and programs in other places or contexts. The individual case, in other words, provides an opportunity to discover generalizable knowledge. The aim is to gather enough details of the particular case to learn about variables, mechanisms, and patterns that would be relevant to many other cases.

---

[1]Research case studies should not be confused with teaching cases, although both are in-depth analyses of one particular organization or situation. The practice of teaching cases began in business schools but has spread to many public policy schools and other applied programs.

Selecting a Case to Study

Given that a case study often involves just one case, how should we make the selection? There are several approaches. *Paradigmatic* case selection involves selecting a prototypical case that offers the greatest generalizability, revealing what is typical. However, if a researcher's goal is to understand a particular phenomenon in a real-world context, a typical case may not be so useful. For example, if the goal is to understand why public management often breaks down, it might be more useful to study a particularly bad breakdown. That is the rationale for choosing *extreme* cases. Another approach is to choose *critical* cases, cases where the specific intervention or institution is itself particularly important and/or similar to other important cases.

Robert Yin's (2008) book *Case Study Research* explains case selection and provides a good starting point for learning more about case study design and methods.

Qualitative Data Analysis

The raw data from qualitative research typically take the form of field notes, interview transcriptions, video or audio recordings, or documents. **Qualitative data analysis** involves the organization and interpretation of these materials. There are three main steps involved in qualitative data analysis (from Creswell, 2006):

- Preparing and organizing the data
- Reducing and summarizing the data, possibly through a process of coding
- Presenting the data, in narrative form, figures, and/or tables

Simply reading, reviewing, and thinking about the data are an essential aspect of qualitative data analysis. But researchers also employ various strategies and tools to organize and interpret qualitative data. Some of the more specific activities of qualitative data analysis include sketching ideas, making notes or memos, summarizing observations or interviews, creating codes, counting the frequency of codes, reducing codes into themes, relating themes to each other, and relating themes to relevant literature or theory (Creswell, 2006). The specific activities employed in qualitative data analysis vary greatly across researchers and across research topics.

Integration of Analysis and Data Gathering

Qualitative analysis often happens not just at the end of data collection (as with quantitative analysis) but simultaneously with the collection of interviews or other qualitative data. As the researcher conducts interviews or makes observations, patterns and interpretations occur to the researcher, and these influence the course of further data collection. In this way, qualitative analysis is often an integral part of qualitative data collection, as Figure 3.4 illustrates. Notice from this figure that one way to decide how many interviews, focus groups, or observations are "enough" in a qualitative study is that this process of data, analysis, more data, more analysis, and so on reaches a point of *saturation:* Few new questions or issues arise that have not already been discovered.

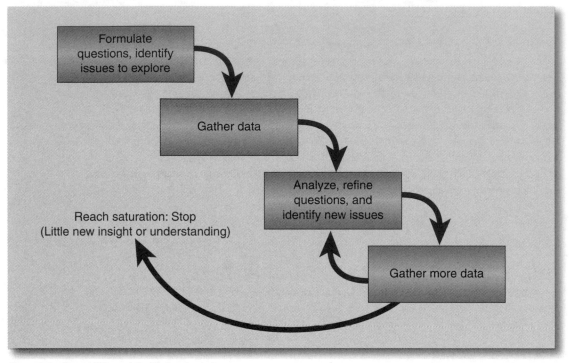

Figure 3.4   General Flow of Qualitative Analysis

The process of analysis and interpretation in qualitative research largely occurs within the mind of the researcher. Therefore, it can be easy to conflate or confuse an objective observation with a subjective interpretation. (This problem, by the way, is not unique to qualitative research and can happen also in more quantitative analysis.) Good qualitative researchers learn to approach their subjects with an open mind, to be transparent in their methods, to look for cases that disprove as well as prove their assumptions, and to support their conclusions with evidence.

Coding and Content Analysis

Sometimes qualitative researchers code their data to make the task of analyzing and interpreting it more systematic. **Coding** refers to a process of tagging the text or other qualitative data using a system of categories, a *coding scheme*—essentially the creation of variables. Coding enables sorting, counting, and other quantitative analysis, but it can also be used without any quantitative analysis—simply as a way to facilitate interpretation of a body of qualitative data. This process of coding and analyzing qualitative data is also referred to as **content analysis**.

To illustrate, recall the earlier example of the study of 911 calls for indications of innocence or guilt. The raw data for this study consisted of 100 recordings of 911 calls made to various police and sheriff departments across the United States to report a homicide. The researchers developed a set of 8 verbal indicators of innocence and 12 verbal indicators of guilt—codes—drawing on theory and prior research. They then examined each call to see if each of the 20 indicators applied or not. So each call had 20 codes, one for each indicator.

Let's try applying some of the categories or codes used in this study. Here are some of the verbal indicators of guilt:

A. Resistance in answering
B. Repetition
C. Conflicting facts
D. Extraneous information
E. Inappropriate politeness
F. Insulting or blaming the victim
G. The "huh?" factor (being caught off guard when asked a simple question)

Now let's consider the transcripts of several calls. For each call, see if you think that any of the codes apply.

Call 1

Dispatcher: Do you know what's wrong with your daughter?

Caller: Not a clue.

Dispatcher: Has she taken any medications?

Caller: She might have, she's very, very sneaky. She threw a huge temper tantrum earlier; she might have taken something.

Call 2

Dispatcher: 911, what's your emergency?

Caller: Hi, I've been shot and my husband has been shot.

Call 3

Dispatcher: 911, what is your emergency?

Caller: I just came home and my wife has fallen down the stairs, she's hurt bad and she's not breathing!

Dispatcher: How many stairs did she fall down?

Caller: Huh?

As you can see, determining which codes apply to a segment of text like this takes some thought. You have to read the call carefully, perhaps reread it a few times, review the available codes, and decide which applies.

As it turns out, Call 1 is an example of Code F, insulting or blaming the victim. Call 2 is an example of Code E, inappropriate politeness (saying "Hi" does not seem quite right when reporting that you and your husband have been shot). And Call 3 is an example of the "huh?" factor, being caught off guard by a simple question. This example involves only short verbal exchanges and a relatively simple coding scheme. The task of coding many long interviews, with a more elaborate coding scheme, can take many, many hours.

The consistency with which codes are applied to the text becomes an important issue in coding and content analysis—sometimes referred to as **intercoder reliability**. We will have more to say about the concept of *reliability* in the next chapter on measurement, but the basic idea is that if you repeat the coding of a particular text, it should result in a consistent category or score. If two coders both assign Code F to Call 1, in other words, this is evidence that the coding of the data is reliable. Even if just one person does all the coding, his or her own consistency in coding should be examined. Researchers sometimes pick interviews or observation to code a second time, just to check their own consistency.

Where Do Codes Come From?

Coding schemes can be developed deductively or inductively, and typically the coding scheme develops and changes as it is used. Codes may be created deductively from just thinking about a topic, from theory, or from prior studies. But codes also arise inductively from reading and interpreting the qualitative data. As such, the coding scheme typically evolves and changes as the analysis proceeds. Codes can be renamed, clarified, collapsed together, split apart, and otherwise reorganized. In an important sense, the development and refinement of a coding scheme itself sheds much light on the interpretation of the data. As we will see next, the task of developing, changing, and refining a coding scheme is greatly facilitated by the use of qualitative analysis software.

To Code or Not to Code?

Not all qualitative research involves coding, and some researchers use coding only as a supplement to more interpretive methods. Coded data can be analyzed quantitatively, but some feel that doing so sacrifices many of the advantages of qualitative research—its rich, thick description and focus on cases, rather than variables. But the decision to code does not mean that other forms of qualitative analysis cannot also be done. And coding can be done purely to better organize qualitative data for later in-depth interpretation, without any intention of doing statistical analysis.

Qualitative Data Analysis Software

With advances in technology, computer software programs have been developed to help with the tasks of qualitative data analysis. Increasingly, qualitative data—including audio and video recordings, photos, and documents—are now readily digitized and can be stored, organized, and analyzed in electronic form. Moreover, the capabilities of qualitative analysis software have improved and now accommodate qualitative data in many different formats, including both text and PDF documents, digital photographs, MP3 and other audio files, and digital video files.

The software includes tools to segment, tag, and categorize the content of these various files so that they can be sorted and analyzed. While software is particularly valuable for coding and content analysis, it can also be valuable purely for data management and organized note-taking.

Some of the more widely used qualitative analysis software programs are Nvivo, Atlas.ti, and Ethnograph. There are some freeware programs as well, including AnSWR and EZ-Text (both provided by the CDC) as well as ELAN and Ethno 2. Figure 3.5 shows a screenshot of Nvivo to give you a flavor of what this kind of software looks like. Qualitative analysis software allows researchers to do many things that are difficult or impossible to do by hand, including the following:

- Store and organize qualitative data in electronic form, including text, images, and audio files
- Search interviews or field notes for key words or phrases
- Create coding categories, as well as flexibly edit or rearrange categories as the analysis proceeds
- Apply codes to segments of text, images, or audio files
- Accommodate multiple coders and provide information on intercoder reliability
- Use codes to retrieve or gather selected segments of text, images, or audio files
- Group or combine codes together into themes
- Track or count the co-occurrence of categories or themes
- Visualize qualitative data as graphs or models

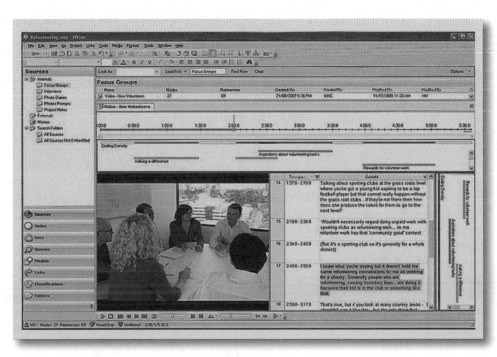

Figure 3.5   Screenshot of Nvivo Qualitative Analysis Software

Source: QSRInternational.com.

Although it provides many efficiencies and new capabilities, qualitative data analysis software is not a substitute for careful, thoughtful interpretation. It is a useful tool, but it does not do the thinking for you. And in some situations, such as a small focus group study or rapid reconnaissance of a situation, it may not be worth the time and effort required to transcribe, code, recode, and analyze the data using software. (For more information and discussion about qualitative data analysis, see Miles & Huberman, 1994.)

The Qualitative-Quantitative Debate

Earlier we defined qualitative research in contrast with quantitative research. As it turns out, much debate has gone on in the social sciences between qualitative and quantitative researchers.

A Brief History of the Debate

The social sciences originated in a more qualitative vein in the early 20th century with, for example, the anthropology of Franz Boas, the psychology of Sigmund Freud, or the sociology of the Chicago School (Ernest Burgess, George Herbert Mead, Robert Park, and Louis Wirth)—all of whom relied on interpretive or case study methods. During World War II, Robert Merton developed the focused interview to study wartime propaganda films, a technique that developed into what we today call *focus group* research (discussed above).

But a movement to model the social sciences on the hard sciences (particularly physics), coupled with rapid advancement in statistics, led to a *quantitative revolution* in various branches of the social sciences. This quantitative turn gathered strength with continuing advances in statistical methods and especially statistical software and computing capabilities. Social science journals of various kinds also proliferated, and the format of many of these journals favored quantitative research.

Qualitative researchers began to push back, pointing out the limitations of quantitative methods. A literature criticizing the quantitative or "positivist" approach emerged, and efforts were made to develop and refine qualitative methods. Books and journals about qualitative methods have since proliferated. Graduate programs in many of the social sciences now offer courses in qualitative methods to balance their courses in quantitative methods. But some disciplines (such as economics) remain predominately quantitative, while others (such as anthropology) remain predominately qualitative.

Some see the qualitative-quantitative divide in the social sciences as fundamental and enduring. Others—especially applied researchers—have come to view the two approaches as more often complementary in practice than conflicting. They recognize that in some situations, qualitative research provides the best approach to answering a pressing policy or practice question. In other situations, quantitative research is needed. Indeed, many researchers today recognize the advantages of *mixed-methods research*—studies that combine qualitative and quantitative approaches (Creswell & Clark, 2006).

Blurring the Lines: How Qualitative and Quantitative Approaches Overlap

Although qualitative and quantitative methods tend to be viewed as distinct categories, in real-world research, they often overlap. Sometimes, the analysis of qualitative interviews or observations, for example, involves *counting* words or behaviors. The use of qualitative analysis software for content analysis, discussed above, can be used in this way. And coded qualitative data can be analyzed quantitatively using a variety of methods. Moreover, quantitative research is often qualitative too: In statistical studies of numerical data, researchers typically include a section labeled "interpretation" in which they bring qualitative judgments or evidence to bear on the meaning of their statistical findings.

Table 3.3 illustrates this overlap between qualitative and quantitative data and analysis (Bernard, 1996). Some studies do involve entirely interpretive analysis of texts or interviews (Box A), and other studies can involve entirely statistical analysis of numerical data (Box D) with very little qualitative interpretation. But many studies fall in Boxes B and C—quantitative studies with substantial elements of qualitative interpretation, or qualitative studies that include statistical analysis of coded or categorized themes, images, or meanings.

Earlier we mentioned that quantitative studies in social and policy research often investigate intangible constructs such as perceptions, emotions, and attitudes—constructs that are essentially qualitative in lived experience. This suggests another way in which qualitative and quantitative methods overlap. Take the example of *social support*—the other people in our lives that are there for us in times of need. We appreciate when we have such support, and feel alone without it, but we experience it qualitatively, not quantitatively, as might happen when we measure our weight or calculate our income. But social scientists have found ways to quantify social support (called a *construct*) by putting numbers to *indicators* of the experience, as illustrated in Figure 3.6. (The scores for family, friends, and significant others are each composed of multiple questions on a questionnaire.) In this way, many of

Table 3.3   Qualitative and Quantitative Data and Analysis

Analysis	Data	
	Qualitative	Quantitative
Qualitative	A Interpretive studies of texts, interviews, images, or qualitative observations	B Interpreting the meaning of numerical findings, or using qualitative evidence to illustrate statistical results
Quantitative	C Turning words or images into numbers—such as word counts or content analysis	D Statistical studies based on surveys or other numerical data

Source: Adapted from Bernard (1996). Used with permission of Sage Publications.

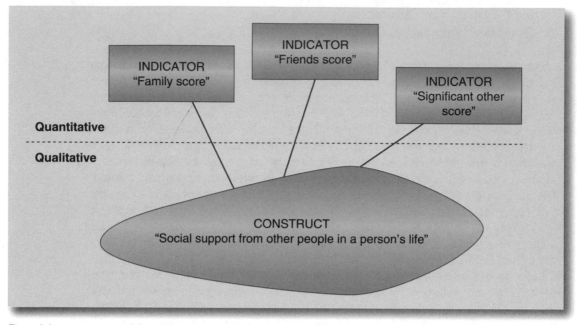

Figure 3.6   Quantitative Indicators of Qualitative Constructs

the measures found in quantitative social and policy research are essentially numerical representations of qualitative experiences. We discuss these issues further in Chapter 4 on measurement.

A Qualitative-Quantitative Research Cycle

It can help to think about qualitative and quantitative approaches as contributing to a cycle of research, as shown in Figure 3.7. When confronted with a new social problem or management challenge, such as a breakdown of morale in a work organization, often the first step is to explore the situation and discover key variables and relationships. Qualitative research is especially well suited to this task. We might decide, for example, to commission a series of in-depth interviews or focus groups to get ideas about what is troubling employees. This initial phase of exploration/discovery also can suggest theories or models to explain what is happening.

Next, it is useful to more systematically measure the key variables and estimate relationships. Based on our initial qualitative findings, for example, we might commission a more structured employee satisfaction survey across the organization, one focused on measuring the key variables uncovered by the initial interviews or focus groups. Data from the survey would then be analyzed statistically, including testing the relevant models.

Finally, the statistical findings may be ambiguous in places, or the data may not fully confirm the model. Moreover, unanticipated relationships between variables may be uncovered by the statistical analysis. In this way, quantitative research too can be exploratory. So we may decide to follow up our survey with more interviews or focus groups, this time with an emphasis on understanding the nature

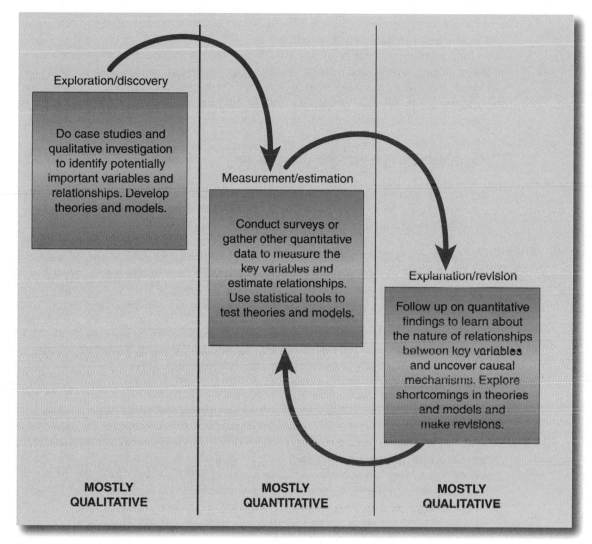

Figure 3.7 Cycles of Research

of relationships evident in our quantitative results. For example, we can explore or seek confirmation of the causal mechanisms—the social, institutional, or psychological processes that produce the statistical relationships we see in our quantitative results.

The same cycle often characterizes academic research as well. For example, a doctoral student doing a dissertation on how public schools handle children with learning disabilities may begin by visiting a few schools, interviewing teachers, parents, and students, and observing the daily classroom routines. These qualitative observations, combined with background literature on the topic, provide a foundation for conducting a survey or gathering existing data (from school records or other sources) for statistical analysis involving many schools. After reviewing the statistical findings, the doctoral student may need to return to a few particularly successful, or unsuccessful, schools to gain a more in-depth understanding of her results.

Large government surveys or program evaluations, even large randomized field experiments, also tend to follow this cycle. Initial qualitative research is used to develop questionnaires, determine site logistics, and carefully design experimental procedures. The survey or experiment is then carried out, producing quantitative data for statistical analysis. But then qualitative follow-up investigation is required to gain a fuller understanding and produce a better interpretation of the quantitative results.

Mixed-Methods Research and Triangulation

The fact that qualitative and quantitative approaches each have unique strengths, as well as limitations, has led many researchers to favor what are call **mixed-methods studies**—studies that explicitly aim to gather both qualitative and quantitative data on a topic of interest (Creswell & Clark, 2006).

For example, the *New York Times* and other large organizations that do public opinion research often conduct follow-up qualitative interviews to accompany their quantitative surveys. In a poll conducted in early April 2009, in the midst of an economic crisis, the *New York Times* found that the percentage who said that the economy was getting worse had surprisingly dropped to 34% from a high of 54% just a few months earlier. The article then quoted from a follow-up interview with a man from Texas:

> Hopefully, the stock market has bottomed out and is on the rise. Once the stock market shapes up, I think the economy will come back, and then jobs will come back and people will start buying automobiles made in America. (Nagourney & Thee-Brenan, 2009)

The quantitative polling results, combined with the qualitative quote, give a fuller picture of the shift in the public's mood at this particular moment in the nation's economic crisis.

Box 3.1 provides another example from an evaluation of transition services for incarcerated youth. In this study, the researchers used quantitative statistical analysis to estimate the relationship between certain characteristics of the youth (such as age of first arrest and number of prior offenses) and recidivism. They also employed qualitative interviews with youth and staff of the transitional living program to gain additional insight on factors that contributed to recidivism. These qualitative interviews suggested that, although the program helped with independent living skills, the youth faced overwhelming challenges on their return to their neighborhoods and peers.

BOX 3.1
Transition Services for Incarcerated Youth:
A Mixed-Methods Evaluation Study

By Abrams, Laura S., Sarah K. Shannon, & Cindy Sangalang. (2008). Transition services for incarcerated youth: A mixed methods evaluation study. *Children and Youth Services Review*, 30(5), 522–535.

Abstract: Despite a considerable overlap between child welfare and juvenile justice populations, the child welfare literature contains sparse information about transition and reentry programs for incarcerated youth. Using mixed methods, this paper explores the benefits and limitations of a six-week transitional living program for incarcerated youth offenders. Logistic regression analysis found that only age at arrest and number of prior offenses predicted the odds of recidivism at one-year post-release. Youth who participated in the transitional living program and dual status youth (those involved in both child welfare and juvenile justice systems) were slightly more likely to recidivate, but these differences were not statistically significant. Qualitative interviews with youth and staff revealed that both groups viewed the transitional living program as having many benefits, particularly independent living skills training. However, follow-up with youth in the community lacked sufficient intensity to handle the types of challenges that emerged. Implications for future research and transition programming with vulnerable youth are discussed.

Ethics in Qualitative Research

Qualitative research raises a variety of unique ethical issues—issues that can sometimes be more difficult to anticipate and handle than those that arise in quantitative research.

Presenting Qualitative Data

Presenting data in the form of extended quotes, photographs, or video recordings can make individuals identifiable. Moreover, in-depth interviewing, case studies, participant observation, and other qualitative methods frequently reveal many details about the people or places in the study. These things can make it hard to provide anonymity or ensure confidentiality, even if only quotes as text are presented. Thus, presenting qualitative evidence without identifying the people or places involved can be a challenge.

Uncovering Sensitive Information

It is difficult to predict or control what information will emerge in a qualitative study. So sensitive information, not necessarily relevant to the research, may be revealed. For example, in a study of subsidized housing one of us (GVR) conducted, an elderly woman being interviewed about her need for subsidized housing began reflecting on her childhood. She then revealed that she had been abused as a young girl and that the experience had complicated many aspects of her adult life, eventually resulting in her need for subsidized housing in old age. This was a study about a housing program—not child abuse. But nevertheless this sensitive information ended up on tape as part of the interview data gathered for the study.

In-depth interviews often uncover sensitive topics, such as corruption in an organization, abuse of power, or private information about the respondent or other people in the setting that can put the researcher in an awkward position. Interviewers may try to head this off, but sometimes the information just spills out. The question then becomes—what to do with this information? Protecting confidentiality can be critical in some cases. But in others, there may be an ethical duty to act. In some other cases, it may be appropriate for the researcher to suggest sources of support or assistance.

Deception in Participant Observation

In some forms of participant observation, the researcher conceals his or her true identity and role as a researcher from participants in a setting. For example, a researcher may spend several hours sitting in an emergency waiting room, pretending to be just another patient, to unobtrusively observe the behavior and interactions of patients and staff. People in this setting may well say things or behave in ways they might not have done otherwise, had they been fully informed that they were being observed as part of a research study.

Informed consent and voluntary participation are key elements of ethical research, but these standards can prove difficult to meet sometimes in participant observation and related forms of qualitative research.

Should Qualitative Research Empower People?

These various ethical quandaries of qualitative research have led some to call for qualitative research to be action oriented, emancipatory, and empowering (Fetterman, Kaftarian, & Wandersman, 1995; McIntyre, 2007; Stringer, 2007). The idea, in brief, is that researchers should not just study people and settings but use their intimate knowledge, along with their authority, to help transform and improve the situation. Although this perspective is not strictly limited to qualitative research, it does arise more in situations where the researcher has intimate knowledge of the setting and a sustained, personal relationship with the people being studied.

Conclusion: Matching Methods to Questions

This chapter has introduced you to qualitative research—an important and widely useful approach to research, especially for generating theory, building models, and uncovering causal processes. You will learn other, more traditionally quantitative methods in the chapters that follow. But we will regularly revisit the qualitative perspective also in these later chapters to emphasize how qualitative and quantitative approaches complement each other and work well in combination.

In closing, it is important to realize that no single approach to research can answer every important policy or practice question. The initial quantitative survey in Kenya, for example, did not reveal *why* some health workers did not provide ACT to all patients. Even if the researchers had followed up with another survey to learn more, they would probably have had to guess at the reasons and causes, possibly missing some important ones. Also, the limited range of responses typical in a quantitative, closed-ended survey would have provided less detail and nuance. So a survey alone would not have fully answered their question about why health workers in the field were not prescribing ACT to their malaria patients.

On the other hand, if the Kenyan study had only relied on a few in-depth interviews, it would not have allowed an estimate of the overall usage of ACT to begin with—possibly leading researchers to miss the very problem the qualitative study helped answer. For getting representative estimates of the extent of a problem, more quantitative methods of measurement and sampling are needed—the topics of the next two chapters. In all research, it is important to match the method to the question, but that is particularly true for choosing between qualitative and quantitative approaches. Often both approaches are needed to provide a complete answer.

BOX 3.2
Critical Questions to Ask About a Qualitative Study

- Why did the researchers choose to use qualitative methods?
- What qualitative method did they use—interviews, focus groups, case studies, textual analysis, mixed methods, or something else?
- Were the methods of data collection and analysis explained clearly and in sufficient detail to understand what was done?
- How were people or cases selected? Were cases chosen theoretically or in a purposive way to further the specific research questions?
- Does the study provide sufficient evidence to support its claims—for example, quotes or results of a more formal content analysis?
- Was the research done in such a way that theories or expectations could potentially be disproven? Does it consider contradictory evidence and alternative explanations?
- Did the researcher clearly distinguish what had been observed from how the observations were interpreted?

EXERCISES

More Qualitative Evidence About Injection Drug Use

3.1. In this chapter, we described a study by Treloar and colleagues (2008) that used video to document risky practices of injection drug users. Below is an abstract from another study using qualitative interviews that provides additional insight on this same topic. Using this abstract, can you come up with a model—including several variables and relationships—of the possible causes of risky injection practices?

We report the findings of an in-depth interview study conducted with 45 female injecting drug users in Britain. Women described experiences of injecting themselves and being injected by others, including instances of bodily harm and pain. Cleanliness when injecting was an issue of particular importance. An interesting division ("line of decency") occurred between opinions on sharing needles versus sharing injecting equipment. Partnership dynamics were important and partners sometimes had a pervasive influence on women's drug use and injecting practices. Narratives of risk showed that some women understood the risk of blood-borne viruses and outlined practical risk-prevention strategies. Some women did not perceive themselves to be at particular risk. Moral opinions were voiced about the risk behavior of others. Notions of risk were highly contextual and depended on a woman's immediate injecting situation. This article reports the inherent complexity resident in women drug users' decisions surrounding their injecting behavior. (Sheard & Tompkins, 2008)

Is It Qualitative or Quantitative?

3.2. Below are short descriptions of studies. For each one, decide if you think it is best described as a qualitative or quantitative study—and explain why.

- Researchers use data from a survey to study the correlation between people's self-reported *happiness* and their belief in *life after death*. They find that 52% of those who believe in life after death are "very happy," compared with only 39% of those who do not believe in life after death.

- As part of a program evaluation, a team of government auditors visit program grantees and interview directors at length about their ability to draw down and expend grant funds on schedule. The interviews reveal that few have expended any funds at all. The directors attribute the problem to excessive delays and complications in executing grant agreements with the agency. The auditors also observe that the directors seem to lack knowledge of the government contracting process.

Should You Use Qualitative or Quantitative Research?

3.3. Below are some research questions. For each one, decide if you think it is best answered by qualitative or quantitative research—and explain why.

- Bullying is an important problem, particularly in middle schools, but not much is known about how students who are the targets of bullying deal with the problem. What strategies do they use to avoid or confront bullies? Who do they turn to for help? How does bullying affect their life inside and outside of school?
- Bullying is an important problem, especially in middle schools, but not much is known about the true extent of the problem. What percentage of kids experience bullying? Are there differences in rates of experienced bullying by gender or race?

Making It Qualitative, Making It Quantitative

3.4. Below are several research topics that might be addressed by either qualitative or quantitative studies. For each one, think of what a qualitative study of the topic might look like. Then think of what a quantitative study of the same topic would look like.

- Teen drug use
- Morale in a work organization
- Teaching effectiveness in elementary school math education
- Police-community relations

Existing Qualitative Data

3.5. Identify a public program, service, or agency of interest to you. What forms of existing qualitative data might there be for studying this program, service, or agency? How would you obtain these data, and what might the data tell you?

Interviewing a Friend

3.6. Conduct an unstructured interview with a classmate, friend, or family member on a simple but fairly interesting topic. Some possibilities could include voting, recycling, exercising, saving money, or commuting. Spend at least 30 minutes doing the interview and try using the power of probes and "what" or "how" questions (as explained in this chapter). Be sure to record the interview or take notes. Write a paragraph or two about what you learned about the topic and the person from the interview.

Planning a Focus Group

3.7. Think of a problem or issue that you are familiar with from work or from your community. Then outline a plan for a focus group study of the issue, including the following:

- The topic of the focus group
- The target population
- How many focus groups to hold—and if there are important subgroups
- Where you would hold the focus groups
- A list of 5 to 7 open-ended questions that would guide the focus group discussion

Observing a Setting

3.8. Identify a simple public setting of interest, such as a park, a post office, a bus stop, or a traffic intersection. Observe the setting for at least 15 minutes, taking occasional notes. Find another similar setting and observe it also for 15 minutes. Write a paragraph or two describing what you observed and learned about the setting.

Developing a Coding Scheme

3.9. StoryCorp.org is a project that records short oral histories from the lives of ordinary people. Find two related stories that interest you, listen to them, and try creating a simple coding scheme that you can use to summarize and compare the stories. You will probably have to listen to the stories several times to fully develop your coding scheme. (The stories are organized by category on StoryCorp.org, which will help you find two stories that are fairly closely related. So they have already done some qualitative coding for you.)

PART II

STRATEGIES FOR DESCRIPTION

Objectives: This chapter will introduce you to the key ideas and issues involved in measurement—the systematic observation and recording of features of the world that matter to us. You will learn how to conceptualize and operationalize a measure and how to think about and assess the validity of a measure. You will learn about measurement error and measurement reliability too. And you will learn about the level of measurement and its implications for data analysis. The trustworthiness of research often hinges on how well the measures used capture the key concepts under investigation. And measurement—in the form of performance measurement—also has become an integral part of public policy and management.

Standardized tests measure some, but not all, dimensions of learning.

Source: © 2009 Jupiterimages Corporation.

Measurement 4

The U.S. Poverty Measure

President Lyndon B. Johnson announced a "War on Poverty" in his 1964 address to Congress "to pursue victory over the most ancient of mankind's enemies." A plethora of new programs targeted the problem of poverty in America, including job training, Head Start preschooling, Medicare and Medicaid, housing assistance programs, and food stamp expansion. The U.S. welfare state assumed its full form during the 1960s, with the War on Poverty as its key mission.

The problem was no one quite knew how to measure poverty. So how was the government to know if its War on Poverty was being won or lost?

In this chapter, we will look at how researchers and practitioners create and carry out measurements—translating concepts that we care about, such as poverty, into recorded observations that can be organized and analyzed. The trustworthiness of research often hinges on how well this translation gets made—how well the measurements capture the key concepts under investigation. And measurement too has become an integral part of delivering public services, evaluating program outcomes, and managing organizations.

What Is Measurement?

Measurement refers to the process of systematically observing some feature or characteristic of the world and then recording it in the form of a number or category. We make observations of the world all the time, but when we make those observations systematic in a form that allows analysis, we've begun doing *measurement*. Once measured, the characteristic can be more effectively organized and understood.

Lyndon B. Johnson launched the War on Poverty.

Source: Arnold Sachs/Hulton Archive/Getty Images.

Think about sitting on a park bench and observing people strolling by. This is observation, certainly, but not measurement. But imagine you were to take out a pad of paper and begin tallying up the passersby in order to count up how many people enter the park? You would then be doing measurement—systematic observation and recording. You might record your tally in categories: children versus adults, for example. Or you might organize your tally into time intervals (every hour, let's say) to see how the number of park-goers rises and falls with the time of day.

Measurement can be as simple as a head count using a pad of paper, or it can be much more operationally complex. To count the number of people in the United States each decade, the Census Bureau engages in years of planning, engages tens of thousands of workers, and spends billions of dollars. (For a history of social measurement, see Duncan, 1984.)

Measurement in Qualitative Research

By most definitions, the term *measurement* implies a process of counting and quantification. And indeed the concepts and methods of measurement in social and policy research come mostly from the quantitative research tradition. However, measurement happens also in qualitative research, in particular, when content analyzing and coding qualitative data (as discussed in the previous chapter). Thus, many of the topics in this chapter apply equally to the process of coding qualitative data. More broadly, the core concepts researchers use to think about measurement—such as conceptualization, validity, and reliability—are relevant to all forms of qualitative observation, whether coded or not. We will return to this point later in the chapter.

Performance Measurement

The need for measurement—like the need to measure poverty—begins often from a practical need to take account of some aspect of the world in order to better understand or influence it. Indeed, **performance measurement**—the use of measurement for administrative purposes or leadership strategy—is increasingly important in many areas of public and nonprofit management these days (as mentioned in Chapter 1). Performance measurement focuses on measuring the activities, outputs, and outcomes of programs or even entire organizations (Hatry, 1999; Holzer & Yang, 2004; Poister, 2003). It can be thought of also as the application of the theory and practice of measurement to professional practice and public accountability. As such, our discussion of key measurement concepts in this chapter has direct application to performance measurement as increasingly practiced in public and nonprofit organizations.

Measurement: The Basic Model and a Road Map

To organize the chapter that follows, it helps to visualize a basic model of measurement (Allen & Yen, 1979), shown in Figure 4.1. Using this model, we can lay out the big picture of measurement and what this chapter will cover.

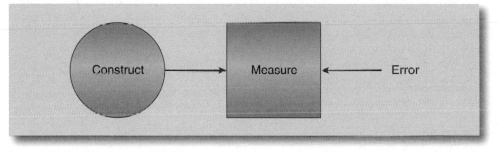

Figure 4.1   Basic Measurement Model

Measurement begins with a **construct** (or **trait**)—the concept or thing that we seek to measure. Clearly and precisely defining our constructs requires careful conceptualization. Next, we must devise or identify an empirical **measure**, or indicator, of the construct. This is the task of operationalization. We will discuss both conceptualization and operationalization in the following pages.

Actual real-world measures almost never fully capture the construct, and they are also influenced by random error that inevitably happens in the measurement processes. The arrow leading from the construct to the observed measure represents the idea of measurement validity—the correspondence with the original concept we want to capture. We will have much to say about the issue of measurement validity as we progress in this chapter. The arrow leading from the random error term to the measure represents the idea of measurement reliability—how much noise, or inconsistency, turns up in our measure. We will cover measurement error and reliability in detail in this chapter as well.

With this basic model of measurement in mind, let's turn to the task of conceptualization—that is, figuring out what it is we want to measure.

Conceptualization

A first—although sometimes overlooked—step in the measurement process is to be clear about what it is you want to measure. How should we define the *construct* (or trait) that we aim to capture through a measurement process? Answering this question is the challenge of **conceptualization**: defining carefully and precisely what it is you seek to measure.

Defining Can Be Difficult

Conceptualization can be fairly straightforward, as when measuring something uncomplicated like the number of people in a park. To be sure, this requires some conceptualization—what constitutes the park boundaries, what period of time to use, what counts as being *in* the park (staying for at least a few minutes, perhaps), and so on. Similarly, outcomes such as births, deaths, body mass (weight), traffic volume, ozone levels, consumer spending, and a host of other constructs that matter in public policy and in research present relatively manageable conceptual challenges, even though they may be technically or logistically difficult to measure.

But other concepts of interest to researchers and policymakers cannot be so directly or unambiguously defined. This often makes it much more difficult to agree on what it is we are trying to measure. Consider the following dialogue about the concept of *poverty:*

What does it mean for a person or a household to be in poverty?

Well, it means that they don't have enough.

But how much is enough and enough of what?

They don't have the necessities: enough to eat, decent housing, and so on.

What's decent housing? Does it include indoor plumbing for toilets and showers?

Definitely!

What about in the 18th century, when even the King of England did not have indoor plumbing? Was he poor?

No. Things were different then. Nobody had that, no matter how rich.

So poverty depends on what other people have.

I guess so.

So if most people become better off and I don't, then I become poor.

That doesn't seem right. It must be that necessities change.

What makes something a necessity?

I don't know, but I know poverty when I see it.

As this dialogue illustrates, coming to agreement on what the concept of poverty means is not so easy. Should we conceive of poverty as an *absolute* standard, such as having just enough food, clothing, and shelter to survive? Or should we conceptualize poverty in more *relative* terms, such as having far less than what others have? Are the necessities of life what most people have? Or are they only what is required to work, maintain basic health, or even just survive?

Ethical Issue: Value Judgments and Politics in Measurement

Another reason that such concepts can be difficult to define conceptually is that they require value judgments. Defining someone as *poor, motivated, reading at grade level, at risk, intelligent,* and so on requires agreement not only about what these concepts mean—but what values or standards ought to be reflected in the acceptable levels we set for these measures. Establishing such standards is more of an ethical or political question than a scientific one.

Differences in conceptualization complicate the task of doing international comparisons of poverty (see Box 4.1)—as well as unemployment, crime, educational achievement, and other important research and policy issues.

BOX 4.1
Is Poverty the Same Thing the World Over?

Mollie Orshansky, the inventor of the U.S. poverty measure, understood that poverty was a controversial and political concept, and so she chose to conceptualize poverty in narrow terms: as having less than the minimum income required by a family to get by. As Orshansky explained, "If it is not possible to state unequivocally 'How much is enough,' it should be possible to assert with confidence how much, on an average, is too little" (quoted in Fisher, 1992). Orshansky's conceptualization is an *absolute* definition of poverty, in the sense that she set an absolute or fixed minimum standard of basic food and other essentials (which, apart from being adjusted for inflation, has remained the same since the 1960s).

This contrasts with the conceptualization of poverty in Europe where they employ a *relative* measure of poverty, defined as some fraction (half) of the typical (median) income of a population. In Europe, in other words, poverty is conceptualized in terms of *having an income that is less than half that of the typical income of others in the society.*

Where Do Conceptualizations Come From?

The notion of poverty extends far back into ancient history. But the need to make the notion into a fleshed-out construct—the need to fully conceptualize it—stems from public policy initiatives and practical programs, such as the War on Poverty. Thus, constructs arise sometimes as a result of public policy initiatives or demands for attention to pressing social problems. As a result, initial conceptualizations of a construct can be found in the language of legislation and regulations, as well as in the language of policy debates. Constructs can also come from management initiatives, such as an agency that decides to improve, let's say, its customer service. Often such management initiatives begin with mission statements or strategic plans that might include a conceptualization of what "customer service" means to the organization. Typically, however, the conceptualizations contained in legislation, mission statements, or other background documents must be refined and specified further to guide measurement.

Importantly, constructs also come from *theory*. As we saw in Chapter 2, theories propose causal stories about how things happen and get expressed typically in models made up of variables and relationships. The variables in a model are constructs. They are specific traits, behaviors, or characteristics that we hope to measure in order to test the theory. So theories—or more precisely theoretical research and writing—serve the important function of identifying and defining constructs to measure. Indeed, clearly defining key constructs—conceptualization—is an important aspect of specifying a theory. And in the case of logic models—the application of theory to program design and evaluation—the activities, outputs, and outcomes in the model are constructs too. As such, logic models similarly serve as tools for identifying and defining important constructs to measure. The exercise of producing a logic model, it should be noted, typically includes a narrative explanation of the logic model, including conceptualizations of key short- and long-term outcomes. But again, these initial conceptualizations sometimes require refinement in the process of developing an actual measure of the construct.

Manifest and Latent Constructs

Some constructs in social and policy research are more directly observable than others. For example, we can pretty well directly observe a child's height and weight, but we cannot so directly observe his or her knowledge of mathematics or language arts. A child's self-esteem is even more hidden. In measurement theory, height and weight are referred to as **manifest constructs** of the child, while self-esteem as well as knowledge of mathematics and language arts are **latent constructs**. It is important conceptually to determine if the construct that you want to measure is a manifest or latent construct.

The field of *psychometrics* deals with the measurement of latent traits or constructs, mostly using scales composed of various manifest indicators, such as answers to questions on a mathematics or language arts test (McIver & Carmines, 1981). We will learn how indicators and scales are used to measure latent constructs later in the chapter.

Dimensions

Some concepts are inherently multifaceted. Consider the concept of health—many would agree it includes being free of pain, able to move easily, not fatigued, mentally alert, and upbeat. Yet these are not necessarily the same things—you could be free of pain but still fatigued or able to move about easily enough but feeling down. Health is complex and multifaceted. As researchers say, the concept of health contains multiple **dimensions** (also referred to as **domains**). To fully define such concepts, one must first describe all their dimensions.

One of the most widely used overall measures of health is the SF-36 (Short Form-36), a 36-item questionnaire developed by the RAND Corporation (2010) for a large study of health outcomes. The SF-36 has the following eight dimensions:

1. Physical functioning (running, lifting, climbing stairs, etc.)

2. Role limitations (not working or getting things done) due to physical functioning

3. Role limitations (not working or getting things done) due to emotional problems

4. Energy/fatigue (feeling worn out or tired)

5. Emotional well-being (feeling down, nervous, or unhappy)

6. Social functioning (health interfering with normal social activities)

7. Pain (severity and interference with functioning)

8. General (self-reported) health

Other health measures have similar, but not identical, dimensions.

Intelligence is perhaps even more abstract than health—and certainly more controversial. It too has been conceptualized as having different dimensions. For example, the extensively used Stanford-Binet measure of intelligence, devised originally in the early 1900s to classify French school children for remedial education, has five dimensions: (1) fluid reasoning, (2) knowledge, (3) quantitative reasoning, (4) visual-spatial processing, and (5) working memory.

In sum, thinking in terms of dimensions can often help structure and clarify the task of conceptualization. And the controversies surrounding a measure can often be understood in terms of the emphasis on, or exclusion of, some dimensions over others.

IQ tests measure multiple dimensions of intelligence.

Source: © iStockphoto.com/wsphotos.

Operationalization

After defining conceptually what to measure, researchers must then figure out *how* to measure it. This is the task of **operationalization**: the specific procedures (operations) a researcher carries out in making and recording a measurement. Let's look at how the U.S. poverty measure is operationalized.

Birth of the U.S. Poverty Measure

At the time President Johnson announced his War on Poverty, Mollie Orshansky was at work in a small office in the Social Security Administration on the development of a practical poverty measure (Fisher, 1992). An economist with prior experience in the Agriculture Department, she conceptualized poverty as an absolute measure—and specifically as "less than the minimum income needed to get by" (see Box 4.1). That still left the problems of defining what it means to "get by" and figuring out what income that would require.

Mollie Orshansky, the inventor of the U.S. poverty measure.
Source: SSA History Archives.

The Agriculture Department had developed a so-called Economy Food Plan to provide basic nutrition when family funds were low. This was the least costly food plan that a family could use and still maintain its health and well-being (if it shopped and cooked wisely). At the time, the Agriculture Department also had survey data on household food expenditures, but the government did not collect information on the various other costs of living (such as housing, clothing, transportation, health care, etc.).

The share of a family's income spent on food had long been considered a useful gauge of economic well-being. (The higher the fraction of income spent on food, the poorer the family.) Orshansky observed that, on average, families in the United States at the time (she was using 1955 data, in fact) spent about one third of their income on food and two thirds on everything else in life. So this became a good, rough guess as to what the other essentials of life must cost.

Thus, a family with income less than three times this basic minimum food expenditure could be classified as *poor.* Further refinements are made to reflect family size, and the poverty threshold gets updated each year to reflect changes in prices. Box 4.2 details this operational definition of the U.S. poverty measure.

BOX 4.2
Operational Definition of Poverty in the United States

It often surprises people to learn how the U.S. government actually operationalizes poverty. Here is how the measurement gets done:

- Establish the baseline poverty threshold (base year is 1966):
  - The cost of an Economy Food Plan devised by the United States Department of Agriculture (USDA)
  - A multiplier (3), based on survey estimates of what typical families spend on food versus other essentials
  - An adjustment for family size

- Update the poverty threshold to present day:
  - An inflation factor (the Consumer Price Index [CPI]) to update the thresholds to current dollars

- Determine whether particular families or individuals are in poverty as well as the poverty rate:
  - Collect current data on the incomes and family size in the U.S. population from one of the established federal surveys (such as the Current Population Survey [CPS]).
  - A family (and all its members) can be classified as "poor" if its income is below the poverty threshold for a family of its size.
  - The percentage of people in poverty can be calculated for the nation, states, or other geographic areas.

Operationalizing poverty involves many details of procedure, data, and calculation. We consider next some other common features of operationalization: instruments; protocols and research personnel; proxies and indicators; and scales and indexes.

Instruments

To operationalize a measure, researchers often use **instruments**—tools that help measure something. For example, in the criminal justice field there is the breathalyzer (for measuring blood alcohol) and the radar gun (for measuring the speed of cars on roadways). In the environmental protection field, there are passive and active air samplers (for measuring air pollutants) and the dosimeter (for measuring noise). In medicine, we find numerous instruments, such as the thermometer, the sphygmometer (for measuring blood pressure), the glucometer (for measuring blood sugar), and so on. When planning or evaluating research, considering the nature (advantages and drawbacks) of the instruments used for measurement is important. In some biomedical studies, even the make and model of the instruments are mentioned in published articles.

Measuring blood pressure with a sphygmometer.

Source: © iStockphoto.com/webphotographer.

Questionnaires Are Instruments

Questionnaires used in surveys of individuals, households, or firms are also thought of by researchers as instruments. Similarly, coding sheets or observation forms used with qualitative data are viewed as instruments as well. And query protocols of computer programs that extract data from computerized databases are also instruments of a kind. Although they are not mechanical or electrical devices that record physical characteristics, questionnaires and coding forms are indeed tools that help researchers operationalize measurements. Thus, they are instruments—and you will find researchers referring to them as such.

Protocols and Personnel

Measurement also involves **protocols** or carefully specified procedures for using the instruments properly. These protocols are an important part of the operationalization of a measure. When measuring a person's height, for example, a medical assistant will ask you to take off your shoes, stand up straight, look forward, and relax your shoulders. Most instruments have protocols like this that guide the person using the instrument to obtain a consistent, accurate reading. Similarly, a questionnaire includes various explanations and instructions that help the respondent answer the questions as completely and accurately as possible.

Often, *technicians*, *interviewers*, or *trained observers* are required to carry out the measurement. These **research personnel** are also a key part of the operationalization of a measurement, and so their selection, training, and supervision become important considerations. In some fields, such as psychological testing in education, only trained and licensed school psychologists can administer the tests or instruments used to measure students. Similarly, some mechanical or electrical instruments can be used only by specially trained people (such as medical technicians) or require licenses or certification. This is because the people using the instruments to carry out the measurement become a critical factor in how well the measurement gets made.

Proxies and Indicators

Sometimes a construct is too difficult or costly to measure directly, or it is not measured in existing data sets available for analysis. In such cases, researchers may operationalize a construct by using a **proxy**—a measure that substitutes for another, unavailable measure. For example, education researchers using existing school records might employ students' class attendance as a proxy for the motivation to learn or reduced-price lunch eligibility as a proxy for the parents' socioeconomic status. Or a criminologist might record the percentage of houses in a neighborhood with bars or gates on the windows as a proxy for the residents' fear of crime.

Proxies have their drawbacks, and sometimes they can mislead. But the clever use of proxies in the hands of a careful researcher can often produce interesting and insightful research findings, despite resource or data limitations.

Proxy Respondents and Proxy Reporting

Sometimes in surveys, respondents report on behalf of someone else in the household or firm. There are a variety of reasons for this. Adults, for example, are often asked to report on behalf of children in the household, as are family members or caretakers on behalf of those without the cognitive or physical abilities to answer for themselves. Or the desired respondent may simply be too difficult to contact. And in some situations, one representative of a firm or agency may be asked to report on behalf of all employees of the organization. For the CPS, the U.S. Bureau of Labor Statistics interviews one respondent in each household yet asks the respondent to report on the working status and earnings of all household members. In all these cases, the respondent is referred to as a **proxy respondent**, and the information gathered on others is **proxy reporting**. In turn, the answers that they provide are *proxies* for the answers the individuals would have provided themselves.

Indicators

We've seen already how some constructs are latent and can be measured only indirectly through various indicators—which are proxies of a kind. But researchers reserve the term *proxy* as such for situations when, as a matter of economy or convenience, they must use a clearly different measure than what might ideally be used. Indicators, in contrast, aim to capture a construct that is not measurable in any other way.

Indicator is a term that comes from psychometrics, and it usually refers to a questionnaire item administered as part of a survey or test. For example, self-esteem is indicated by the extent of agreement with the statement "I feel that I'm a person of worth, at least on an equal basis with others" (Rosenberg, 1965). However, to represent latent constructs such as self-esteem well, researchers use multiple indicators and combine them into a scale or index, as we describe next.

Scales and Indexes

Scales and **indexes** are measures composed of multiple indicators. Also referred to as *composite measures*, they are widely used in social and policy research to operationalize constructs—especially latent constructs. The use of multiple indicators serves several purposes: It ensures fuller coverage of the content of a construct; it better captures the range of intensity or difficulty of the construct; and it helps average out measurement error and thus enhance reliability—issues we'll cover in more detail later in the chapter.

Consider a construct such as *self-esteem*—someone's sense of personal self-worth, which many people believe is a critical factor in problems such as teen pregnancy, drug and alcohol abuse, and dropping out of school. Rosenberg (1965) developed a self-esteem scale that asks respondents to rate their level of agreement with 10 statements (reversed items are flagged with an *):

1. I feel that I'm a person of worth, at least on an equal basis with others.

2. I feel that I have a number of good qualities.

3. *All in all, I am inclined to think I'm a failure.

4. I am able to do things as well as most other people.

5. *I feel I do not have much to be proud of.

6. I take a positive attitude toward myself.

7. On the whole, I am satisfied with myself.

8. *I wish I could have more respect for myself.

9. *I certainly feel useless at times.

10. *At times I think I'm no good at all.

You can see how these statements, the *indicators*, all seem to get at the basic view people have of themselves. Self-esteem is latent, an internal self-perception, but we can infer its intensity or level from a person's pattern of responses to these statements.

Figure 4.2 graphically depicts a measurement model of the Rosenberg self-esteem scale. The arrows leading from the construct to the indicators suggest that a person's manifest scores on the indicators are, in a sense, caused by his or her latent (but real) self-esteem (the construct). The indicators also reflect some amount of measurement error (or noise), perhaps from the way the statement is worded, presented, or interpreted by the respondent. We will explain the idea of measurement error in a later section.

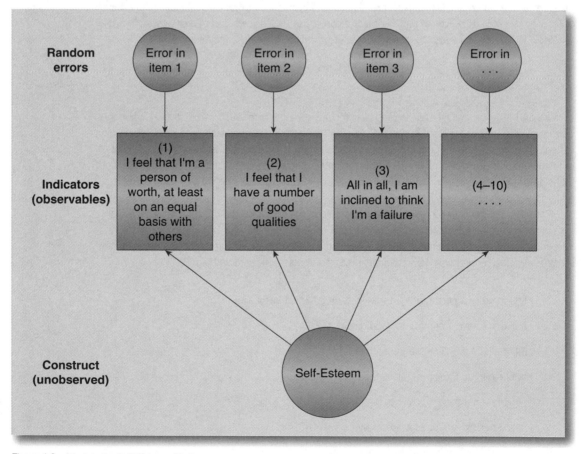

Figure 4.2   Model of a Self-Esteem Scale

The measurement model in Figure 4.2 illustrates how researchers think about scales and indeed measurement more generally. It is the type of model that appears in confirmatory factor analysis and structural equation modeling, advanced statistical techniques used to develop and test scales (discussed briefly in Chapter 9). When looking at data or statistics, all we ever see are the indicators—such as the distributions of responses to questions on a questionnaire. But it is important to realize that researchers think of these indicators as reflecting a mix of the underlying construct as well as some idiosyncratic component, the error or noise that is unrelated to the construct. One of the advantages of multi-item scales, as opposed to single-item measures, is that they permit the underlying construct and error components to be separated statistically.

Is It a Scale or an Index?

Although the terms *scale* and *index* are often used interchangeably in social and policy research, there is a distinction between these terms. In a scale, researchers develop and select items that are correlated with each other. This is important when the items are viewed as reflections of a latent construct. The 10 items of the Rosenberg self-esteem scale, for example, are all highly intercorrelated and thus plausibly reflections of a single, latent construct (Gray-Little, Williams, & Hancock, 1997). Often researchers use the term Likert scale, as discussed in Box 4.3, to refer to this type of scale.

BOX 4.3
What Is a Likert Scale?

Rensis Likert was one of several pioneers of *psychometrics*—the measurement of intangible, psychological traits or attitudes using multi-item scales (McIver & Carmines, 1981). Other notables in this area include Louis L. Thurstone (Thurstone scaling) and Louis Guttman (Guttman scaling). Likert introduced the agree-disagree response format, which became very widely used in scale development and survey research. As a result, some incorrectly refer to all rating scales, regardless of the response format, as Likert scales. And some also refer to a single survey question with an agree-disagree response format as a Likert scale. It is more correct to call an individual question such as this either a "Likert item" or, more simply, just an "agree-disagree" item or question. True Likert scales are composed of multiple agree-disagree items that have been carefully selected and empirically tested. For an introduction to the construction of such scales, see Spector (1992).

In an index, the items are selected for different reasons. For example, the U.S. government's CPI is composed of a market basket of the prices of many different products in the economy. The items that make up the CPI are chosen to represent typical consumption patterns, without regard to whether, for example, milk prices are correlated with gasoline prices. But this distinction between a scale and an index is subtle and often disregarded when the terms are used in research articles and reports.

Validity

We hope that the measurements we use get at the truth—this is the intuitive notion of *measurement validity.* The **validity** of a measure refers to how well the measure actually represents the true construct of interest—the thing we are trying to measure. It turns out to be surprisingly hard to establish whether a measure is valid or not.

Is the U.S. Poverty Measure Valid?

The answer, according to many people, is *no*—but not always for the same reasons (Blank, 2008). To get a feel for the idea, let's look at why different people view the U.S. poverty measure as invalid.

The 1960s-era U.S. poverty threshold is updated by adjusting for inflation using the CPI. It is the same for all parts of the United States, and so it does not reflect local differences in the cost of living—even the striking differences in housing costs across the United States. In 2007, for a family of four (with two adults and two children), the poverty line was about $1,700 a month. Using Orshansky's basic formula, that works out to $567 for food and $1,133 per month for shelter, clothing, transportation, and everything else.

Most people today spend far less than a third of their income on food, because the price of food, adjusted for inflation, has fallen dramatically. But the real price of housing, for example, has increased dramatically. So many contend that the income needed to afford the necessities of life these days is far more than three times the price of a basic food plan.

On the other hand, in the mid-1960s, poor people had only their own incomes with which to purchase necessities. Following the War on Poverty, programs such as food stamps, Medicaid, and public housing provided in-kind benefits. In the 1990s, the Earned Income Tax Credit (EITC) put cash directly in the hands of poor families. The definition of income in the U.S. poverty measure does not count these in-kind benefits or the EITC rebate. So some argue that the official poverty measure overestimates poverty.

While the U.S. poverty measure wasn't a bad attempt in 1966, its validity in today's world is highly questionable. Various revisions and adjustments to the U.S. poverty measure have been studied and proposed, but for political reasons, it has proven very difficult to switch (Blank, 2008). So the validity problems of the official U.S. poverty measure will likely be with us for some time.

There are many approaches to establishing validity and therefore many different types of validity (Carmines & Zeller, 1979). The terminology can get confusing, so we will focus more on the logic and ideas. One class of approaches involves empirical strategies for testing or demonstrating validity, referred to as *criterion-related validity* (Trochim, 2001). The different types will be discussed in the "Criterion-Related Validity" section. But first, we discuss nonempirical, essentially judgmental, assessments of how well a measure represents a construct.

Face Validity

To judge validity, we often look at what is called the **face validity** of the measure: Just based on looking at the measure, on the face of it, how well does the measure get at what we want to measure?

The polygraph—or lie detector—is supposed to measure whether a person is lying or telling the truth. In fact, it measures heart rate, perspiration, and other physiological manifestations of nervousness. The concept of a lie is translated into nervousness, which in turn is translated into the physiological manifestations of nervousness.

On the one hand, this has some face validity—people telling lies are often nervous. On the other hand, it lacks face validity because being nervous and telling a lie are not the same thing and do not always coincide.

Do Self-Reported Measures Have Face Validity?

Many measures work by asking people to report what they did—called **self-reporting**. For example, exit polls ask people how they voted. On the one hand, such measures appear to have face validity because they directly ask what we want to measure. On the other hand, what people do is not the same as what they say they do, so the face validity of such behavioral self-reports can be questioned, especially when they involve sensitive or socially desirable behaviors. Moreover, we will see later on that self-reports of certain subjects have poor criterion related validity.

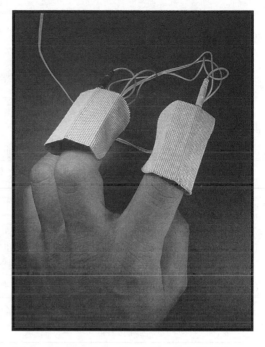

A polygraph attempts to measure if someone is lying.
Source: © iStockphoto.com/MummuMedia.

Content Validity

A good measure should include all the important dimensions of the construct, which is the idea of **content validity**. For example, a measure of suffering, or not suffering, from pain would not be a valid measure of *health* because it would miss so many other dimensions of health, such as illness (which may or may not cause pain), physical limitations, fatigue, emotional well-being, and so on. So even if our measure accurately captured pain, it would lack content validity as a measure of general health.

The content validity of a measure also depends on whether it captures the full range of *variation* in the construct. A measure of pain might be able to differentiate "no" pain and "some" pain, but it might not be able to differentiate between "moderate" pain and "severe" pain.

High-Stakes Educational Tests: Do They Miss Some Dimensions of Educational Achievement?

Standardized educational tests are the subject of much disagreement these days. Some criticize them, saying that they leave out many dimensions of education, focusing only on math and some English language skills. The tests often do not include history or science or a variety of other important topics. Moreover, they are mostly multiple-choice tests that do not gauge students' ability to write an essay or to solve a multifaceted, real-world problem. Such criticisms amount to saying that the content validity of such tests is low, because some dimensions of educational achievement are missed.

Others, however, are strong supporters of standardized tests. They note that empirically the test results predict later academic performance, a form of criterion-related validity known as predictive validity, which we cover shortly. The two views are not inconsistent: Standardized tests could do a good job of capturing some dimensions of education, dimensions that are important for later achievement, while simultaneously missing other dimensions. Few measures capture all dimensions of a complex construct.

Valid for What Purpose?

Because no measure is perfect in all ways, validity should be assessed based on the purpose for which the measure is used. For example, if today's educational tests are viewed as a measure of fundamental skills, they could be valid. But as a measure of all that we might expect from our public schools, many believe that they have limited content validity due to important dimensions being missed.

Consider the concept of happiness, which sometimes gets measured in surveys with the following question:

Taken all together, how would you say things are these days—would you say that you are very happy, pretty happy, or not too happy?

1. *Very happy*
2. *Pretty happy*
3. *Not too happy*

It turns out that this very simple kind of self-reported happiness measure works pretty well—it is valid—for very broad studies of general populations, such as comparing happiness levels across nations or for populations over time (Layard, 2005). But it would not be valid for a clinical diagnosis of depression. For this, psychologists use a much more detailed measure such as the Beck Depression Inventory, a scale that has 21 multiple-choice questions. So the validity of a measure depends on how it is used.

Content validity, face validity, and other nonempirical methods of assessing validity are the first and perhaps the most important forms of validity to assess. But it is hard to prove validity in these ways; it remains primarily a matter of subjective judgment. Sometimes, we would like to have objective ways to test or demonstrate validity.

Criterion-Related Validity

To demonstrate the validity of a measure—to validate it, as researchers sometimes say—it is often necessary to turn to empirical evidence. This is referred to broadly as **criterion-related validity**, and there are various forms of it.

Self-Reported Drug Use: Is It Valid?

Suppose we want to measure people's illegal drug use. This is not too conceptually difficult: We know pretty well what it means to take illegal drugs. Operationally, we might measure this by directly

When asked in surveys, people tend to underreport illegal drug use.

Source: © 2009 Jupiterimages Corporation.

asking people about their drug use—in other words, *self-reported* drug use. This has some face validity but will people tell the truth?

To find out, we need to compare the self-reported measure with some other, more objective measure of drug use. For example, chemical analysis of urine and hair can reveal recent drug use. Using this method in a validity study of steel plant workers in the United States, researchers found that the rate estimated from urine and hair analysis was about 50% higher than self-reported drug use on a questionnaire (Cook, Bernstein, Arrington, & Andrews, 1997).

The National Center for Health Statistics (NCHS) estimates that about 8% of the U.S. population, 12 years of age and older, used illegal drugs in the past month (NCHS, 2007), representing nearly 20 million people. The steelworkers study, however, suggests that this figure could perhaps be much higher.

If a measure agrees with another contemporaneous measure of the same concept, it is said to have **concurrent validity**. Clearly, self-reported drug use has poor concurrent validity. Demonstrations of concurrent validity are only as good as the concurrent measure, however. If hair and urine analysis turn out to be faulty measures of recent drug use, then this validity test does not tell us as much as we might hope.

Does the Measure Predict Behavior?

Another approach is to test how well our measure predicts some future behavior or variable that is a logical consequence of the thing we are trying to measure. So if we want to validate a measure of job satisfaction, for example, we might test to see if those who score low on our measure are more likely to quit their job in 12 months than those who score high on the measure. If so, we can say our measure of job satisfaction has **predictive validity**—it predicts something that logically should follow in the future from the thing we hope we are measuring.

Does Consumer Confidence Predict Economic Activity?

The University of Michigan conducts a monthly survey to measure consumer confidence, officially known as the *Consumer Sentiment Index*. As the name suggests, the index (composed of five survey questions) aims to measure how positive or negative consumers feel about the economy and thus, how likely they will be to spend. Consumer spending constitutes about two thirds of the $13 trillion U.S. economy, and so the Consumer Sentiment Index is a widely watched indicator.

How well does the Michigan index predict actual economic activity? Figure 4.3 shows the pattern over the past several decades, with the periods of economic recession shaded in. The Michigan index trends downward going into recessions and moves back up coming out of recessions. So it seems to

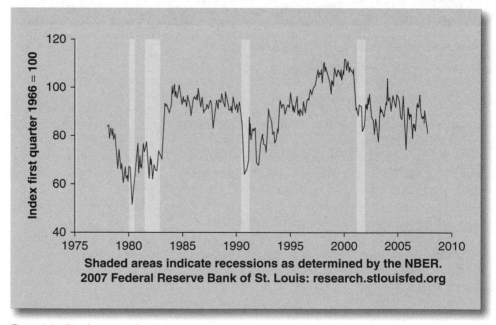

Figure 4.3   The Consumer Sentiment Index

Source: Survey Research Center, University of Michigan.

have predictive validity—it predicts something that a measure of consumer confidence logically should: consumer spending and in turn economic activity.

Are the Relationships Between Variables What We Would Expect?

In many situations, researchers must use other, less direct strategies to assess validity. One such strategy is to make comparisons with other variables that theoretically or logically should be related to our measure of interest. Often, these variables are part of the same survey or other data set, rather than future behaviors. And they are not alternative measures of the same thing, as in concurrent validity. It's helpful to see an example.

The European Social Survey (ESS)—a random sample survey of 40,000 people from more than 30 countries—includes a self-reported measure of health, which asks people to rate their health from $1 = very\ bad$ to $5 = very\ good$. This is interesting and potentially very useful data—but how valid is the ESS measure of health? It is impossibly expensive to obtain current medical records or clinical health exams for so many survey respondents. And we are unlikely to be able to track these individuals into the future to observe their health outcomes. But we do know that older people everywhere suffer more from health problems than do younger people, and the ESS has a measure of age as one of a number of standard demographic variables. So logically we should expect the ESS health measure (if it is a valid measure of health) to be negatively correlated with the ESS age variable (negatively correlated in the sense of more age, less health). Let's calculate the correlation (r) and see what we find:

$$r_{age\text{-}health} = -.36.$$

The result is encouraging: The ESS self-reported measure of health is, indeed, negatively correlated with age as we logically and theoretically expected. And $r = -.36$ is a moderately strong correlation, which also makes sense. The ESS health measure behaves like we expect the construct of health to behave.

The correlation with age confirms that the ESS health measure has what researchers call **convergent validity** because it converges (correlates) with variables we'd expect it to be related to.

Similarly, we can also look to see if the ESS measure of health is *not* related to other measures that it should have little or no logical connection with, such as ideology. This is called **discriminant validity**. Too strong a correlation with other, logically unrelated things indicates that a measure is perhaps capturing something other than what it was intended to measure.

Researchers often consider convergent and discriminant validity together by looking at a correlation matrix as in Table 4.1.

Table 4.1 again shows the moderately strong negative correlation with age, $r = -.36$, suggesting that the ESS measure as convergent validity. But the ESS health measure should *not* be related to many other things, such as political ideology (left-right) or religiosity (how religious people consider themselves to be). Indeed, the other correlations in the first column of the table confirm this. Although the health-ideology (.03) and health-religiosity (−.05) correlations are not exactly zero in the table (because both ideology and religiosity are somewhat related to age, which is related to health), they are very weak. Thus, the ESS self-reported health measure seems to have pretty good discriminant validity as well.

Table 4.1   Correlations From the European Social Survey (ESS)

	Health	Age	Ideology (Left-Right)	Religiosity
Health	1			
Age	−.36	1		
Ideology (left-right)	.03	.07	1	
Religiosity	−.05	.19	.17	1

Both convergent and discriminant validity are forms of **construct validity**—seeing how well our measure corresponds with other variables that are logically or theoretically related to the underlying construct we purport to be measuring. Some examples of construct validity require little theory or logic, as in the simple relationships between health, age, and other variables from the ESS. In other situations, however, researchers rely on more extensive theory and more elaborate models to determine what correlations are expected. In such cases, the tests are also known as **nomological validity**.

But again, the terminology of validity is often confusing and inconsistently applied. Box 4.4 shows the definitions of many of the types of validity, but be aware not all researchers use the terms the same way. What matters most is that you understand what the validity of a measure means—that the measure really captures what it aims to capture—and that you appreciate how various empirical strategies can be used to test validity.

BOX 4.4
The Various (Measurement) Validities

Researchers refer to many different types of validity and not always with consistency. The terms are less important than the big ideas and a feel for what validity means and how it can be demonstrated. However, just in case, here is a fairly complete list of the various validities and their definitions (adapted from Carmines & Zeller, 1979):

Face validity	Does the measure look like it gets at the construct, on the face of it? Does it seem to make sense?
Content validity	Does the measure include all the important dimensions of the construct? Does it capture the full range of the construct?

Criterion-related validity	How well does the measure relate, empirically, to various criteria that can demonstrate its validity?
Concurrent validity	Does the measure concur or agree with other established classifications or test scores?
Predictive validity	Does the measure predict logically related outcomes or behaviors in the future?
Convergent validity	Does the measure correlate with other, closely related measures in the same data set?
Discriminant validity	Is the measure independent of (not correlated with) other measures in the same data set that it does not logically relate to?
Construct validity	Does the measure behave in a statistical model in a way that would be expected, based on theory and prior research?
Nomological validity	Does the measure behave as it should in a system or network of other variables?

Importantly, all these terms refer to the validity of *measures*. The term *validity* is also applied to *studies*—for example, the internal and external validity of a study—as we explain in other chapters.

Limitations of Validity Studies

When researchers and others say a measure has been *validated*, they generally mean that some effort has been made to empirically study the properties or characteristics of a proposed or established measure. Curiously, often so-called validity studies turn out, on closer reading, to be primarily *reliability* studies—studies that look at the test-retest consistency or internal consistency of indicators that make up a measure (as will be discussed shortly).

True validity studies seek to show how well a measure reflects the construct it aims to represent through one or more of the criterion-related validity strategies discussed above, such as concurrent validity, predictive validity, convergent validity, or discriminant validity. Box 4.5 describes a genuine validity study. But a validity study is not an all or nothing proposition—often the evidence is less than completely convincing.

Box 4.5
Example of a Validity Study

By Spencer, E. A., Appleby, P. N., Davey, G. K., & Key, T. J. (2007). Validity of self-reported height and weight. *Public Health Nutrition, 5*(4), 561–565.

Objective: To assess the validity of self-reported height and weight by comparison with measured height and weight in a sample of middle-aged men and women, and to determine the extent of misclassification of body mass index (BMI) arising from differences between self-reported and measured values.

Design: Analysis of self-reported and measured height and weight data from participants in the Oxford cohort of the European Prospective Investigation into Cancer and Nutrition (EPIC–Oxford).

Subjects: Four thousand eight hundred and eight British men and women aged 35–76 years.

Results: Spearman rank correlations between self-reported and measured height, weight and BMI were high ($r < 0.9$, $p > 0.0001$). Height was overestimated by a mean of 1.23 (95% confidence interval (CI) 1.11–1.34) cm in men and 0.60 (0.51–0.70) cm in women; the extent of overestimation was greater in older men and women, shorter men and heavier women. Weight was underestimated by a mean of 1.85 (1.72–1.99) kg in men and 1.40 (1.31–1.49) kg in women; the extent of underestimation was greater in heavier men and women, but did not vary with age or height. Using standard categories of BMI, 22.4% of men and 18.0% of women were classified incorrectly based on self-reported height and weight. After correcting the self-reported values using predictive equations derived from a 10% sample of subjects, misclassification decreased to 15.2% in men and 13.8% in women.

Conclusions: Self-reported height and weight data are valid for identifying relationships in epidemiological studies. In analyses where anthropometric factors are the primary variables of interest, measurements in a representative sample of the study population can be used to improve the accuracy of estimates of height, weight and BMI.

Moreover, many measurements in use in research and public policy have not been empirically validated at all; the researchers or policy analysts simply claim or assume their measures are valid. Often this can be because there is no clear criterion of validity.

And as we have seen, a measure can be valid for one purpose but not another. A simple one-question measure of happiness might be valid for a large social survey but not for clinical diagnosis of depression. Therefore, you can't simply accept the validity of a measure because it was tested in one particular context and with one use in mind. If you intend to use the measure for something else, having a published validity test may not help you.

Validity is obviously an important quality in a measure. We want to know that our measures capture what they were designed to capture. But there is another aspect of a good measure that also matters: *reliability*—or the consistency of the measure. Indeed, discussions of validity and reliability often go hand in hand. But before discussing reliability, it is helpful to first consider the concept of measurement error.

Measurement Error

Error is an inherent part of the measurement process. The old carpenter's adage, "measure twice, cut once," expresses our common understanding that any one measurement of something—even something as simple as a length of wood—is likely to be off the mark, even if only just a touch. Measurement error comes from the imperfections of our instruments (or questionnaires), from the imperfections in our use of the instruments, and from the nature of how people respond to being measured.

Bias

It helps distinguish two forms of measurement error: **systematic measurement error**, or **bias**, and **random measurement error**, or **noise**. Let's consider systematic measurement error or bias first, as

All measurements have errors.

Source: © 2009 Jupiterimages Corporation.

this is what most people have in mind when we think about an "error" in a measurement—although it is often not what researchers and statisticians mean by measurement error.

Say your bathroom scale has not been well calibrated and that, when no one is standing on the scale, the needle rests at +2 pounds instead of zero. Each morning when you weigh yourself, then, the reading will be 2 pounds more than your actual weight. This is a *systematic* error—a 2-pound *bias* (upward) in the measurement of your weight.

Bias is closely related to the idea of validity—although the term typically has a narrower and mostly quantitative meaning. Bias usually refers to a systematic upward or downward distortion in the level of a measurement. Validity, in contrast, refers to the broader definition and meaning of what we aim to measure.

Random Error—Noise

Random measurement error, or *noise*, is a bit more difficult to visualize, but it's a very real and important issue in research. Let's return to our simple example of the bathroom scale. Imagine your scale is a bit old and has a slightly bent needle that doesn't quite rotate as smoothly as it once did. So the needle gets a bit stuck each time it settles, although sometimes it gets stuck above the true mark and sometimes below it. But these errors are random—over many mornings, in the long run, they do not make you appear systematically heavier or lighter than you really are. In other words, the average of these errors over many, repeated measurements (of the same object, you) is zero. This is what researchers mean by random error or noise.

Random error or noise is a very real part of research, as all measurements have some degree of unpredictable or uncontrollable errors that happen in the process of doing the measurement. Mechanical instruments have flaws; questionnaires can be ambiguous or unclear; research workers may use instruments inconsistently; interviewers or observers may mistakenly record an observation; respondents to a survey can get impatient or distracted; the machines, or workers, that enter data into a database can make key-punch errors; and so on. All these things can combine to produce random error or noise in our measurements.

Realize that both types of measurement error—bias and noise—can be present at the same time in a measurement. You can forget to calibrate your bathroom scale, so that it systematically adds 2 pounds to your weight, while at the same time the needle gives inconsistent readings each time you weigh yourself. In fact, often real measurements include some degree of both systematic error (bias) and random error (noise).

Bias and Noise in the U.S. Poverty Measure

As we've already seen, some consider the U.S. poverty measure to be biased downward, that it underestimates the real level of poverty in the U.S. society. The formula for calculating the poverty line (three times the USDA Emergency Food Plan) is out of date, because the cost of food has declined while housing, transportation, health care, and other necessities are more expensive. Others point out that the U.S. poverty measure may be biased upward, that it may overstate poverty because it fails to take into account housing subsidies, food stamps, subsidized child care, tax credits, and other such benefits that were not available in the 1960s. Both are right in many ways—and the debate quickly moves to the broader validity issues involved in measuring a difficult concept such as poverty.

But what about the question of random error, or noise, in the official U.S. poverty measure? To think about this kind of measurement error—the kind of measurement error that researchers and statisticians often have in mind—we need to consider the actual sources of data the U.S. government uses to measure income and family size.

The government, as it turns out, uses several sources of information on household income to calculate poverty. Let's focus on the CPS, the major source of income data for the regular annual poverty estimates that appear most often in the news or research reports. Random measurement error, or noise, comes from the procedures used to carry out this survey.

The CPS is a labor force survey conducted mostly by telephone as well as in-person interviews with more than 75,000 households. (This is the sample size of the Annual Social and Economic Supplement, which provides the data for annual poverty estimates.) A single respondent in each household is asked a series of questions about his or her employment and income as well as the employment and income of other members of the household who are 16 years of age or older. Some 1,500 interviewers are needed to carry out the CPS and, although they receive careful training and supervision and now use computer-assisted interviews, they undoubtedly make occasional mistakes in asking questions and recording answers.

Respondents undoubtedly make mistakes too, as it is difficult to recall and report one's own income flawlessly during a long, live interview. Moreover, respondents to the CPS must report on the income of other members of the household too (proxy reporting), which is even more difficult for people to do without making at least some errors.

The various sources of household income recorded by the CPS are then added up, and total household income is reported—say $21,067 for family with ID number 27031 in the data set. Imputation, methods for filling-in of values when income questions are unanswered or otherwise left blank, provides yet another source of error. Suppose this family has four members, as recorded by the CPS. (However, this number could also involve an error as both respondents may misreport or interviewers may erroneously record the real number of family members.) We then compare the family's income with the poverty line ($20,444 for a family of four) and classify our case with ID number 27031 as "not poor."

You can see how this classification could quite easily be mistaken—it could involve error. And in the CPS, there are undoubtedly many cases that lie close enough to the poverty threshold that random errors in the CPS measurement of income (or family size) could lead to numerous misclassifications—one way or the other (random measurement error).

Error Model of Measurement

The following equation or mathematical model of measurement, which comes from *classical test theory*, can provide another way to think about the issue of errors in measurement.

$$X_i = T_i + B_i + N_i.$$

X stands for the observed value of our variable, for example, the total income of a given family i. The equation alerts us to the fact that the observed or *measured* income of the family—what we come up with from some measurement procedure, such as the CPS, is really a combination of T, the *true* income of the family, plus perhaps some *bias*, B, and certainly at least some *noise*, N. Ideally, we would like B and N to be zero—and thus X to be a pure reflection of T, the true value we are trying to measure. But unfortunately, that is not the case with most real-world measurements. To illustrate, here is a snapshot of a segment of some raw data:

i	X
1	45,737
2	19,074
3	32,911
4	16,987

i again stands for individual, so this table is showing the first four individuals in a data set of many such measurements. X again stands for the variable, in this case household income (in dollars per year). Individual 2, for example, has an annual family income of $19,074.

But notice that we don't directly observe T, B, or N in our data—only X, which reflects some unknown combination of all three of these elements ($X_i = T_i + B_i + N_i$). In practice, the extent of bias B or noise N—in place of the true score T—remains for the most part a matter of judgment and debate. To actually observe B or N, special validity or reliability studies—some discussed earlier—need to be carried out, which brings us to the topic of reliability.

Reliability

Measurement **reliability** refers to the consistency of a measure—and it is directly related to the concept of random error or noise. If our measure has little noise, it will produce few random errors each time we take a measurement. It will be a consistent measure with good reliability. If the measure contains a lot of noise, however, it will be full of random errors and we'll get inconsistent results—even if we measure essentially the same object. It will have poor reliability. Figure 4.4 illustrates good and poor reliability graphically.

A reliable measure is not necessarily a valid one. This is why Figure 4.4 does not include the *construct*—the trait or attribute that we are trying to measure in the first place. Indeed, we can have a very reliable measurement that misleads—such as a bathroom scale that consistently gives the wrong weight. Thus, a measure can have little or no noise but still be seriously biased or reflect something quite different than what we intended to measure.

Why Reliability Matters

But reliability still matters. And it matters in different ways, depending on what purpose we have in mind. There are at least three main ways in which measures get used in research and in practice.

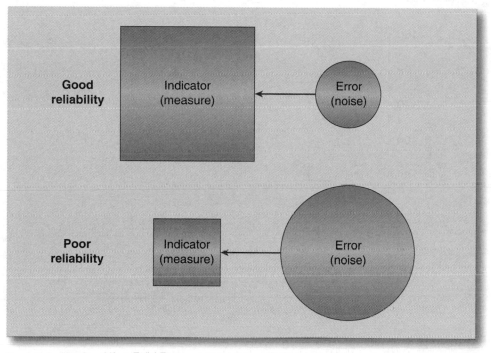

Figure 4.4   Good and Poor Reliability

Calculating Averages

Measures can be used to produce averages (means or proportions) over a group, such as determining the share of U.S. families in poverty. Provided the sample is large enough, a high degree of reliability may be unnecessary because the random measurement errors cancel each other out and thus have little effect on the average. But large random errors do increase the variability of the measure—and in turn confidence intervals (or margins of error) as explained in Chapter 5.

Figure 4.5 shows some made-up data in which the same generic *X variable* is graphed, but each time adding larger random errors to the original variable. But even as the reliability gets worse, and the noise increases, the averages change very little and remain close to 100.

Estimating Relationships

Measures can be used to look at statistical relationships (such as correlations) within a group, for example, the relationship between poverty and crime. In this case, random errors can attenuate, or

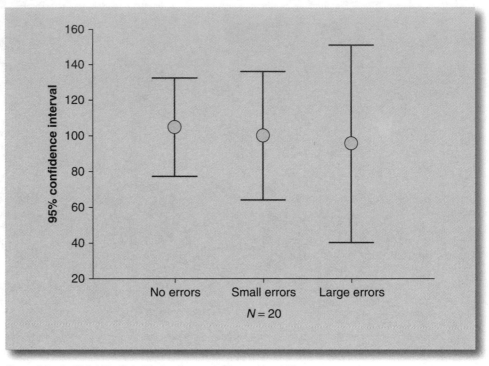

Figure 4.5   As Reliability Gets Worse, Averages Change Very Little

water down, a statistical relationship, making it seem weaker than it really is. This can be a problem because, with unreliable measures, we may overlook a potential causal relationship or falsely conclude that a program had no effect on an outcome.

Figure 4.6 shows three scatterplots of made-up data, with increasingly large random errors added to both the X and Y variables. The slope of the line, which indicates the strength of the relationship, gets flatter as the errors get larger—in other words, the relationship gets weaker.

Classifying Individuals

Measures can be used to target or classify individuals, such as determining if a particular family qualifies for food stamps or a particular child passes a third-grade exit exam. In such cases, reliability matters a great deal because random errors imply the misclassification of individuals. Thus, reliable measures are especially important to ensure fairness in situations such as eligibility determination, psychological diagnoses, and high-stakes testing.

Although we would like always to have good reliability, there are real costs to achieving it.

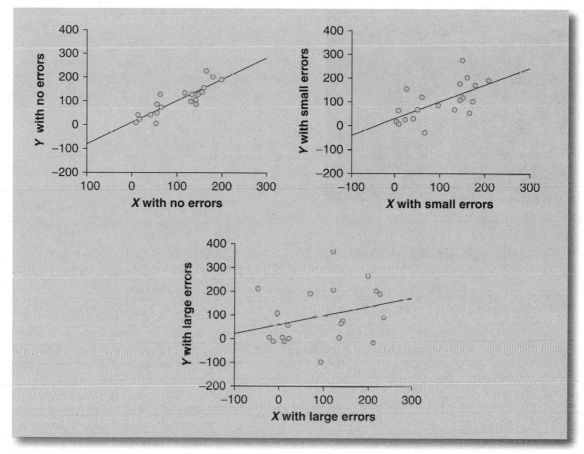

Figure 4.6   As Reliability Gets Worse, Relationships Get Weaker

Many Ways to Tell If a Measure Is Reliable

Reliability is easier in some ways to demonstrate than validity—because we don't have the construct, the "truth," to worry about. We just need to show that a measure consistently gives the same result when applied to the same object or reality. Repeating a measurement and observing its consistency is a good way both to think about and to test reliability. Within that broad basic idea, there are a variety of methods for determining reliability.

Test-Retest Reliability: Measuring the Same Thing Twice

The most common approach to determining reliability is to measure the same thing twice—what researchers call **test-retest reliability**. For example, an education department might hope

Errors can be made in determining eligibility for benefit programs.

Source: © Brian F. Alpert/Hulton Archive/Getty Images.

that its new fifth-grade language arts test is reliable, that it does not contain too much noise or random error. So when developing the test (often under contract to specialized educational testing companies), they will give the test to a group of students and, after a period of time, will retest the same students again. The correlation of the first test results with the second test results provides a gauge of the reliability of the new language arts test.

However, because people learn from taking tests the first time, scores the second time around can reflect this. Test-retest reliability makes a lot of sense for a relatively stable physical characteristic, such as someone's weight on a given morning, but it is more problematic when people can learn or when the intrinsic construct we are measuring changes over time.

Interrater Reliability: How Consistent Are the Research Workers?

As we've seen, often measurements get carried out by people, raters or interviewers, hired and trained to do the measurement. So another type of reliability that we should worry about is how similar the scores of the raters or interviewers are when they measure the same person or object. This is called **interrater reliability**. Obviously, we want the scores to be the same (or at least very similar) and not too dependent on the particular views, personalities, or habits of the research workers.

For example, we could ask four street cleanliness raters, working for a city sanitation department, each to rate the same 20 blocks selected from across a sanitation district. The correlation of the four raters' scores with each other would serve as our gauge of reliability. We could work to improve the habits of those raters whose scores do not match closely with the others.

Reliability of Scales: Split-Half and Internal Reliability

When the measure is a scale or index composed of multiple indicators, such as the SF-36 health scale or the 10-item Rosenberg self-esteem scale, reliability can be gauged through the internal consistency of the various indicators. Do the indicators or items go together—do they paint a consistent picture?

One way to gauge this is to calculate a measure of the **split-half reliability**: Divide the items randomly into two halves, say an SF-18a and an SF-18b, and then look at the correlation between the two halves. Correlations range from 0 to 1, so a higher correlation indicates a more internally reliable scale (see Chapter 8 for more explanation of statistical correlation).

A more sophisticated and more often used measure of internal reliability is **Cronbach's alpha** (named after Lee Cronbach, the educational psychologist who invented it). Cronbach's alpha (sometimes reported as just alpha [α]) is the average of all possible split-half correlations. So it still measures how one half of a test corresponds with the other, but it averages out the variation due to the luck of the draw, as it were, in the split-half method.

Alpha ranges from 0 to 1, with .70 sometimes used as the minimally acceptable level of reliability (Spector, 1992). But as we pointed out earlier, much depends on the purpose of the measure. An alpha just above .70 is not nearly good enough for purposes of psychological diagnosis or high-stakes tests applied to individuals, for example.

The more correlated the responses to the scale items are with each other, the larger the alpha. And the more items we include in the scale, holding constant the degree of correlation, the larger the alpha. So researchers can improve the internal reliability of their scales by selecting items that go well together and by using more items. This is one reason psychological tests have so many items—the Beck Depression Inventory has 21 items, for example—because the more items, the greater the reliability.

In a sense, you can think of internal reliability as similar to interrater reliability—if you imagine that the items or indicators are in sense like "raters" who are rating the same object or concept.

Parallel Forms Reliability: Did Educational Test Scores Really Go Up?

In the United States and around the world, students and schools are being tested like never before. Newspapers and politicians claim success if the score goes up or look for blame if they go down—but are these year-over-year differences real?

For obvious reasons, the questions on educational tests must change each year. But are the two forms of the test really the same? This is a reliability question, sometimes referred to as **parallel forms reliability**. Test scores may go up or down this year for a variety of reasons—the students

Sometimes, using a different test can make scores appear to go up.

Source: © iStockphoto.com/ayzeek.

taking the test each year are a different group of individuals, schools improve or decline, teachers and principals move in and out of the system, and so on. But the test itself changes too.

Unfortunately, too little attention is paid to establishing parallel forms reliability beyond the area of educational testing. Many methods used to establish the effectiveness of programs make use of changes over time in measures, and often the measures themselves change; therefore, better understanding reliability over time is critical.

Validity and Reliability in Qualitative Research

The concepts and techniques of validity and reliability come from the quantitative tradition. But the ideas of validity and reliability apply in many ways to qualitative research as well.

As we mentioned earlier, measurement occurs also in qualitative research, particularly in content analysis and coding. Thus, when creating and applying codes to text or other qualitative data, it is important to think about the validity of the codes—do the codes really capture what we think they do? And it is important to think about the reliability of the coding process—is it being done consistently? It is possible to recode part of the qualitative data, for example, in order to establish what can be called **code-recode reliability**. When several research workers are involved in coding, it is also possible to examine intercoder reliability, which is directly related to interrater reliability. This can be done by having the research workers code the same text and then comparing their consistency.

But not all (or even most) qualitative research involves coding. Still, the fundamental ideas of validity and reliability apply to all types of qualitative observation. Take, for example, the in-depth observation that happens in an ethnographic or participant observation study, such as the one mentioned in Chapter 3 that looked at homeless people in Chicago and why they often refuse help. We still need to think about the extent to which the interpretations derived from participant observation in this study are valid—do they capture the real experiences and motivations of the homeless people studied? And we still need to think about reliability—are the interpretations consistent? Would repeating the participant observation, or would another participant observer, yield similar interpretations and conclusions?

Finally, empirically testing the validity and reliability of qualitative observation presents unique challenges and may not be possible in many qualitative studies. Much the same holds true in many quantitative studies as well. The validity and reliability of measures and observations must be considered as part of all types of research.

Levels of Measurement

Measurements produce *variables* that can be analyzed. For quantitative data, the variables take the form of numbers, but not all numbers have the same meaning. In particular, sometimes numbers represent categories, while at other times they represent actual quantities of something. Thus, researchers distinguish two broad types, or **levels of measurement**:

- **Quantitative variables** in which the numbers refer to actual quantities of something. For example, in a housing survey, we might find a measure of the number of rooms in the housing unit (1, 2, 3, 4 rooms, etc.).

- **Categorical variables** in which the numbers stand for categories. In a housing survey, for example, we might find the type of heating in the housing units recorded as either 1 = *electric*, 2 = *gas*, 3 = *oil*, or 4 = *other*.

The level of measurement is important for the analysis of data. Certain statistical methods require quantitative variables, while other techniques are appropriate for categorical data.

To give a simple example, it would be meaningless to calculate a mean (average) for the type of heating (say 2.3) because the numbers in this measure are really just codes for categories of heating and averaging them tells us nothing. In contrast, it would be useful to find that the mean number of rooms is (say) 4.6 because this number expresses a true quantitative average of something (rooms). In fact, much of the variety and complexity one encounters when learning statistics stems from the fact that different statistical tools get used with different levels of measurement. We will learn more about this in Chapters 8 and 9.

Quantitative Measures

It is perhaps best to begin with quantitative measures or variables, as these are measures in which the numbers refer to real quantities of something. For example, in social research we often measure things such as age (in years), income (in dollars, euros, etc.), hours of work in a typical week, or weight (in pounds or kilograms). When these measurements get recorded in these units, they are quantitative measures or variables.

The **unit of measurement**—the precise meaning of the numbers that appear in a data set—is critical. For example, income in U.S. surveys is often recorded in thousands of dollars, rather than in dollars, so that a value of "26" in the data set means 26,000 dollars of income. If weight appears in the data set as "91," we need to be careful to notice if this means 91 pounds or 91 kilograms. Quantitative data are useless and cannot be interpreted or analyzed unless we know the units of measurement.

Care must be taken to spot measures or variables that may look like they are quantitative, but on closer inspection are not. For example, here is the ESS codebook's description of the measure of household income from the ESS of some 40,000 people living in more than 20 different countries (European Social Survey, n.d.):

HINCTNT: Total household income from all sources

1. *Less than €1,800*

2. *to under €3,600*

3. *to under €6,000*

4. *to under €12,000*

5. *to under €18,000*

6. *to under €24,000*

7. *to under €30,000*

8. *to under €36,000*

9. *to under €60,000*

10. *to under €90,000*

11. *to under €120,000*

12. *€120,000 or more*

Although the measure refers to household income in euros, it records income in 12 broad categories. Often, surveys ask income in this way because respondents are unable, or unwilling (because of privacy concerns), to report their exact income. As a result, this kind of measure of income is categorical, not quantitative.

BOX 4.6
Unit/Level of Measurement/Analysis?

Unfortunately, research terms sometimes sound too much alike and start to blur together in our thinking. Here are the distinctions between three similar-sounding terms:

1. *Level of measurement:* This refers to the distinction between quantitative and categorical variables, to what some call the *ladder of measurement*: nominal, ordinal, interval, and ratio.

2. *Unit of measurement:* This refers to units, such as dollars of income or kilograms of body weight, that define the quantitative variable. If a variable takes the value of 66, for example, the unit of measurement is the answer to the question—66 *what?*

3. *Unit of analysis:* This refers to the objects or things described by the variables. Do the variables in the study describe people, households, neighborhoods, nations, organizations, and so on.

In some discussions of research methods, you'll find quantitative measurements further classified into **interval** and **ratio** measurements. Most quantitative measures you'll come across are in fact ratio measurements—they have a meaningful 0 point, such as €0 of income, or 0 years of work experience or age. (Even though in a real data set, you may not have someone with 0 years of age, a newborn, this variable still has a meaningful 0 point.)

Interval measurements are not as common, but good examples in research are things such as scales or indices that have rather arbitrary units of measurement. For example, the Stanford-Binet IQ test scores used often in educational assessment range in practice from a low of about 50 to a high of about 150, with 100 as the mean (the standard deviation is 16). This is a quantitative measure, but it does not have a true 0 point; thus it is an *interval*-level measurement. However, interval measures still have the feature that the difference between 50 and 60 is the same as the difference between 70 and 80. The size of the interval does have meaning.

For most statistical analyses, the distinction between interval and ratio levels of measurement does not matter much. But the distinction between the quantitative level and the categorical level of measurement does matter.

Categorical Measures

A *categorical* measure or variable is one in which the numerical values in the data set serve to classify the people or objects being measured into categories. There are two kinds of categorical measures or variables:

1. **Nominal:** Measures or variables in which the numbers refer to categories that have no inherent order to them, and so the categories can be arranged in any order.

2. **Ordinal:** Measures or variables in which the numbers refer to categories that do have an inherent order to them, and thus the numbers convey that order.

Let's look at the Global Attitudes Project, a survey organized by the Pew Center that interviewed more than 38,000 people in 44 nations on a wide range of global issues. Consider first the following example of a *nominal* question or measure:

Here is a list of five dangers in the world today. In your opinion, which one of these poses the greatest threat to the world?

1. *Spread of nuclear weapons*

2. *Religious and ethnic hatred*

3. *AIDS and other infectious diseases*

4. *Pollution and other environmental problems*

5. *Growing gap between the rich and poor*

This measure is *nominal* because the numbers 1 to 5 stand for categories that do not have any inherent order to them. In other words, we could easily rearrange the categories, along with their corresponding numeric codes, without really changing the meaning of the measure:

1. *Growing gap between the rich and poor*

2. *Pollution and other environmental problems*

3. *Spread of nuclear weapons*

4. *Religious and ethnic hatred*

5. *AIDS and other infectious diseases*

Again, the codes 1 to 5 just tag the categories and do not imply that the categories follow any particular order.

Ordinal measures, in contrast, are categorical measures that do follow an order. Here is another example from the 44-nation survey of the Global Attitudes Project:

There has been a lot of talk about globalization these days. Do you think that globalization is a very good thing, somewhat good, somewhat bad, or a very bad thing?

1. *Very good*

2. *Somewhat good*

3. *Somewhat bad*

4. *Very bad*

This measure is *ordinal* because the numerical codes 1 to 4 not only represent categories but also express the *order* of the categories, from "very good" to "very bad." We could not, for example, so easily rearrange the categories as we did before:

1. *Very bad*

2. *Somewhat good*

3. *Very good*

4. *Somewhat bad*

This ruins the meaning of things—we need the categories to remain in order. Of course, we could reverse the order, so that 1 = *very bad* and 4 = *very good*, but this simply illustrates again that the categories do, indeed, have an order.

With an ordinal variable, we can't be sure that the distance, say, between *very bad* and *somewhat bad* is the same as that between *somewhat bad* and *somewhat good*. So we need to use caution applying certain statistics—such as means or correlations—that assume a regular, quantitative distance between intervals. Still, in practice, researchers do often treat ordinal measures as if they were quantitative. And researchers have come up with a few ways to convert their categorical measures into quantitative ones.

Turning Categorical Variables Into Quantitative Ones

The desire to convert categorical variables into quantitative ones crops up often in social and policy research. This is due to the fact that (1) categorical measures appear often in surveys, and (2) researchers like to use advanced analytical tools for quantitative data (such as regression, factor analysis, etc.). Various techniques can be used to upgrade the level of measurement.

Dummy Variables

Dummy variables (also called *indicator* variables) are categorical variables that have only two values, 0 and 1. For example, the variable "Employed" indicates if the individual is employed or not; the variable "Female" indicates if the individual is female or male (not female). Dummy variables can be treated sometimes as quantitative variables because they represent a single *unit* of something, such as "employment."

Dummy variables are extremely convenient for analyzing and interpreting data. If a data set has a dummy variable "Employment," the mean of that variable will tell us the share (proportion) of the population that is employed. Dummy variables can also be used for nominal variables with more than two categories, such as "Race"—which might have the categories of White, Black, Hispanic, Asian, and Other. In this case, we convert each category into a separate dummy variable, such as White (1 = *yes*, 0 = *no*), Black (1 = *yes*, 0 = *no*), and so on.

Dummy variables are often used in correlation and regression analysis, especially as independent variables. And dummy variables often get used to represent programs or treatments—specifically whether a person or case is in the treatment group (coded 1) or the control group (coded 0).

Midpoint Approximation

For ordinal measures of an underlying construct that is intrinsically quantitative, such as income, it is possible to approximate a quantitative measure by substituting a midpoint for the original category codes. Returning to the example of the ESS (n.d.), we can recode the income categories to midpoints as shown below:

	Total household income from all sources		Midpoint
1.	Less than €1,800	→	€1,200
2.	€1,800 to less than €3,600	→	€2,700
3.	€3,600 to less than €6,000	→	€4,800
4.	€6,000 to less than €12,000	→	€9,000
5.	€12,000 to less than €18,000	→	€15,000
6.	€18,000 to less than €24,000	→	€21,000
7.	€24,000 to less than €30,000	→	€27,000
8.	€30,000 to less than €36,000	→	€33,000

(Continued)

(Continued)

	Total household income from all sources		Midpoint
9.	€36,000 to less than €60,000	→	€48,000
10.	€60,000 to less than €90,000	→	€75,000
11.	€90,000 to less than €120,000	→	€105,000
12.	€120,000 or more	→	€130,000

The ESS's household income question is essentially ordinal, as the values 1 to 12 in the data set represent income categories, not quantities of euros. But if we recode these values as shown—substituting the midpoints of the income ranges (shown above) for the categories 1 to 12—we can approximate a quantitative measure of income in euros.

Notice that we cannot take the midpoint of the bottom and top categories, and so we have to use our judgment about what value to use.

Multi-Item Scales

Adding up ordinal items or indicators representing a scale, such as the agree-disagree items of Rosenberg's self-esteem scale, produces a composite score that researchers often view as quantitative. Even if the individual items or indicators remain ordinal, the sum of many such indicators produces a fairly continuous set of values that can be treated as a quantitative variable.

Endpoint Scales and Thermometers

Another technique for turning an ordinal measure into at least a semiquantitative measure is to present questions on a 1 to 7 or 1 to 10 scale with only anchoring statements at the ends of the scale, rather than labeling only a few categories. For example, a standard way to ask people about their happiness in life is this question:

Taking all things together, would you say you are . . .

1. *Not too happy*   2. *Pretty happy*   3. *Very happy*

But by adding a few more categories, and only labeling the endpoints, we can ask the question this way:

Taking all things together (on 1–7 scale), would you say you are . . .

Not too happy   *Very happy*

    1   2   3   4   5   6   7

Because the numbers do not have labels, except at the endpoints, some researchers argue that the distance between numbers can be interpreted as equal intervals (of happiness on a 1–7 scale).

Also, the equal spacing of the numbers visually reinforces this meaning. This idea becomes even more apparent with a 10-point scale:

Taking all things together (on a 1–10 scale), would you say you are . . .

Not too happy   *Very happy*

  1   2   3   4   5   6   7   8   9   10

Going still further, survey researchers sometimes use what they call a *feeling thermometer*, an imaginary 0 to 100 quantitative scale to rate political leaders, groups, or institutions in society.

Figure 4.7 presents results from the American National Election Studies showing the public's feelings toward gays and lesbians in the U.S. society.

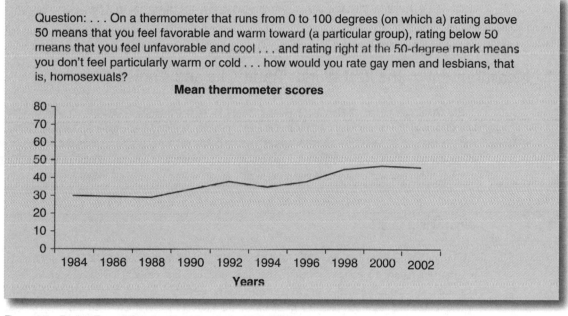

Figure 4.7   Feeling Toward Gays and Lesbians in the United States

This graph shows a gradual "warming" of attitudes toward guys and lesbians in the U.S. society (from 30 to 46 "degrees" over the 18-year period shown), although the thermometer still remains in "cool" territory. Similar feeling thermometers have been used to quantify attitudes toward racial and ethnic groups, political candidates, government institutions, other nations, and so on.

Units of Analysis and Levels of Measurement

We have been thinking mostly in terms of measures of individual people, or sometimes families, but variables can describe larger units of analysis as well. Recall from Chapter 2 that the *unit of analysis* refers to the objects or things described by the measure (people, firms, neighborhoods, etc).

For example, much demographic and policy data get reported and analyzed at various geographic levels, such as cities, counties, or regions. Education data often get reported at the level of schools, not individual students. This matters for the level of measurement because often variables that are categorical at the level of an individual person, student, or household become quantitative at a larger, geographic or organizational unit of analysis.

Let's return to our example of poverty. If we are measuring an individual person or household, using the U.S. government's official poverty measure, we classify them as either "poor" or "not poor." Thus, at the individual level, poverty is a categorical variable. But if we look at poverty at the level of, say, census tracts or counties, then most often we will be dealing with a poverty *rate*, or the *percentage* of people (or households) living in poverty. This percentage might well range from as low as 2, 3, or 4 percent to 20, 30, or 40 percent or more. Thus, at the level of a census tract or county, poverty clearly is a quantitative measure. So to determine the level of measurement, you need to consider the unit of analysis as well.

Measurement in the Real World: Trade-Offs and Choices

In this chapter, we have covered many ideas involved in measurement—the systematic observation and recording of features of the world that matter to us. In an ideal world, we would like to create and use the best possible measures, measures that are highly valid and highly reliable. But in the real world, measurement involves trade-offs and choices. To conclude this chapter, it is helpful to consider some of these real-world trade-offs and choices that we must face when doing measurement.

What Will It Cost?

Everything has its price—including the validity and reliability of measurement. We know, for example, that self-reported measures of health, spending, drug use, and other behaviors are not as valid as more direct, objective methods of measurement, such as clinical exams, obtaining bank records, or taking hair and urine samples. But these other, more direct measurement methods often cost a lot more, and so in practice, we sometimes must settle for self-reported measures that we know are less valid.

Reliability is enhanced by the number of indicators, as we have seen, and the use of multi-item scales produces variables that have a more quantitative level of measurement. But the length of questionnaires or observation forms increases the cost of data collection. Interviewer time, printing and mailing costs, data processing effort, and time in the field—all are affected by the length of our questionnaires or instruments. To economize, we often opt for shorter measures, for example, using one question to measure a construct rather than a scale, even when realizing that the reliability of a single-item measure is less good and that the lower level of measurement may restrict analysis.

Is It Ethical?

Long questionnaires also impose a burden on respondents—raising ethical concerns. We shouldn't ask or expect people to complete hours-long interviews or book-size questionnaires, just because having more indicators gives us more reliability and results in a higher level of measurement.

In an effort to achieve validity, we could always deceive people or violate their privacy. For example, we could ask people for a lock of hair during an in-person interview to take it back to a lab for analysis of drug use. We could make up some harmless excuse for what we're doing ("Hair samples tell us how much healthy sunshine people around here are getting this time of the year"). This would be a more valid measure than asking for self-reported drug use. But tricking people into giving us a hair sample would be unethical.

How Will It Affect the Quality and Rate of Responding?

If an interview or questionnaire is too long, respondents will drop out or fail to respond in the first place. So although from a reliability or level of measurement perspective it might be best to have long, multi-item measures for every construct in a study, the length of an interview or questionnaire affects the response rate and thus the generalizability of the sample. We will learn more about these sampling issues in Chapter 5.

Very long tests, observation forms, or interviews also tend to be completed less carefully than shorter ones. Respondents, observers, or interviewers may engage in *sufficing* behavior—rapidly completing the interview or observation form just to satisfy the researcher but without giving much care to the task. This kind of carelessness in responding or observing introduces new sources of bias and noise into the measurement process—working against our original aims.

Validity-Reliability Trade-Off

Many standardized tests work by giving students a battery of multiple-choice questions, which is good for reliability (the more the items, the more reliable the measure). And it might help in the task of creating a truly quantitative test score. But this may not be the most valid assessment of an ability—such as English language arts. We might like to know if students can read a substantial text, understand it, and then evaluate and react to it in the form of a carefully organized and well-written essay.

In fact, New York State now measures students' English language arts ability by requiring them to spend an entire test day on a single essay, with other days devoted to more traditional multiple-choice questions. Grading these essays, however, is extremely time-consuming and expensive, requiring many extra hours by a team of teachers, and it is difficult to do consistently (think about the *interrater reliability* problem discussed above).

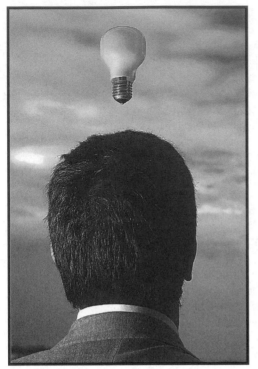

Inventing a measure is tempting, but it has its drawbacks.

Source: © iStockphoto.com/Gimmerton.

Moreover, there is surely random error or noise in using just one essay as an indicator of writing ability. For example, the topic that happens to be chosen for the essay one year is surely more familiar and interesting to some students than to others. Ideally, we would like to have several essays each year to capture students' writing ability across a range of topics. This would help us average out the random errors or noise. But it is not feasible for a school system to administer and grade several days' worth of essay writing—having one long essay to score is difficult enough. Thus, in an effort to get a more valid indicator, such as a long essay, we must sacrifice reliability.

This validity-reliability trade-off is widespread in research. Indeed, it helps explain some of the tension and disagreement between those who favor in-depth, *qualitative* observation and those who prefer more standardized and systematic, but perhaps more superficial, *quantitative* methods of measurement. In a sense, qualitative researchers can be thought of as more focused on validity, while quantitative researchers tend to emphasize reliability.

Use an Established Measure or Invent a New One?

To really get at a construct, it is tempting to create an entirely new and original measure—something that is just right for our particular research or policy goal. But using established measures—measures developed, tested, and applied in previous studies—often provides better assurances of validity and reliability.

Moreover, measures are often used to make comparisons over time, examining trends. Creating a new measure—even if it is more valid—makes it hard to make comparisons across time. This is an issue that is constantly faced by large annual surveys sponsored by governments and other organizations.

For example, the U.S. Bureau of Labor Statistics (BLS) has a long-standing annual survey about employee benefits, including health insurance. However, the form of health insurance has changed dramatically over the past several decades—and it is in the process of further structural changes. Does the BLS try to ask questions about health insurance that allow comparisons over time? Or does it ask questions that create the most valid measures of the type and value of health insurance people have today? Like most agencies, the BLS tries to do some of both, balancing the two concerns.

Incentives to stick with an established measure are part of why we continue to have the flawed U.S. poverty measure. Related political issues, discussed in Chapter 14, are also part of the problem.

Measurement Matters

The topic of measurement, with its sometimes arcane and confusing jargon, can seem to have little practical relevance. We hope that the examples in this chapter have convinced you, however, that this is not the case. Measurement matters—it is how we track critical social and economic problems, inform policy debates, and evaluate outcomes we care about. Measurement also plays a key role in the management of organizations and in the provision of public services. Knowing how to think about and evaluate measurement, therefore, is an important skill whether you are a researcher or a practitioner. But like all skills, it comes mostly with practice. So we encourage you to ask questions about the measures you encounter, to dig beneath the surface. How was the measure defined—conceptualized? How was it operationalized—that is, what are the details of how the measurement was carried out? Does it get at what we think it measures—is it valid? Is the measurement consistent—is it reliable? The more you ask and try to answer these questions, the more skill you will gain in interpreting, doing, and using measurement.

BOX 4.7
Critical Questions to Ask About Measurement

- What is the purpose of the measure—where and how did it originate? (Knowing the history of a measure—such as the U.S. poverty measure—is not only interesting but also provides insight on its usefulness and limitations.)
- What is the conceptual definition of the construct that the measure aims to capture? Are there dimensions to the construct, and if so, what are they? Is there debate, or confusion, about the meaning of the construct?
- How is the measure operationalized? What instruments (including questionnaires), personnel, and protocols (procedures) are used to carry out measurement of the construct? Does the measure involve one item or indicator, or is it a multi-item scale? Is it a proxy measure? Does it involve proxy reporting?
- How valid is the measure? Does it have face validity? Does it capture the dimensions and variation of the construct (content validity)? Is there any empirical evidence about the validity of the measure (criterion-related validity)? If so, what kind of evidence is it (what kind of criterion-related validity is it)—and how convincing is the evidence?
- How reliable is the measure? Is there any evidence for the reliability of the measure? If so, what kind of evidence is it (what kind of reliability test)—and how convincing is the evidence?
- What is the level of measurement of the variable?

EXERCISES

What Does Poverty Mean to You?

4.1. This chapter discussed absolute and relative ways to conceptualize poverty. Which conceptualization do you agree with most? Explain why.

Measuring Consumer Confidence

4.2. Given below are the five questions the University of Michigan uses to compute its Consumer Sentiment Index, based on a random sample of about 500 adults each month. Do you see any dimensions in this measure? Does this measure have good face validity? Does it have good content validity?

a. We are interested in how people are getting along financially these days. Would you say that you (and your family living there) are better off or worse financially than you were a year ago?

b. Looking ahead, do you think that a year from now you (and your family living there) will be better off financially, worse off, or about the same as now?

c. Turning to business conditions in the country as a whole, do you think that during the next 12 months we'll have good times financially or bad times, or what?

d. Looking ahead, which would you say is more likely: that in the country as a whole we'll have continuous good times during the next 5 years or so or that we will have periods of widespread unemployment or depression, or what?

e. About the big things people buy for their homes such as furniture, refrigerators, stoves, televisions, and things like: that generally speaking, do you think now is a good or a bad time for people to buy major household items?

How Clean Are the Trains?

4.3. A mass transit agency is considering two proposed methods for rating the cleanliness of its trains. One proposal is to have raters count the number of pieces of trash in the centermost car of the train that arrives at the end of the line on Wednesday evenings at 8:00 p.m. Another proposal is to have raters ride the train several different times a week, at different locations, and describe its cleanliness in a written report using their own words. Which measure is more reliable? Which measure is more valid?

Is the Vocabulary Test Culturally Biased?

4.4. A *picture vocabulary test* is one way to assess language ability in young school children. Suppose the test asks U.S. children to come up with the vocabulary words for the pictures below:

A   B

How might this test be culturally biased in the context of the United States? What might it be measuring other than language ability? Can you think of some pictures to use that would make the test less culturally biased?

Assessing Performance Measures

4.5. Identify a performance measure that would be useful in your current work, past work, or an area that interests you—or a performance measure that is in fact used in any of those situations. Then, do the following:

- Describe how valid you think the measure is—and why.
- Describe how reliable you think the measure is—and why.
- Given that there are limited resources available, is there a tension between trying to improve both the validity and reliability of the measure? Explain your answer.

Objectives: In this chapter, you will learn about sampling—the selection of people or elements to include in a study. The chapter begins with the idea of generalizability—projecting from one limited study to a larger reality, which is often the aim of sampling. You will then find out about basic sampling concepts, the issues of coverage and nonresponse bias, and the use of volunteers and other nonprobability samples.

Next, you will learn about the theory and methods of random sampling—one of the most important inventions of modern social science and a vital tool for public policy and practice. Finally, you will become familiar with the motivations and methods for more complex forms of random sampling developed to implement the ideas of random sampling in the real world.

Surveying a convenience sample of motorists stuck in a traffic line.

Source: © Hugh Conroy, Whatcom Council of Governments.

Sampling

Gauging the Fallout From Hurricane Katrina

Hurricane Katrina hit the gulf coast of the United States on August 29, 2005, near the city of New Orleans. As most of the world watched in horror, the storm and its aftermath became one of the deadliest and costliest natural disasters in U.S. history. In early September, CBS News conducted a poll of 725 adults nationwide and reported that 77% of the country felt that the federal government's response to the disaster was inadequate, with fully 80% believing that the government did not act as fast as it could have (CBS News, 2005).

At about the same time in early September, a team of public health researchers at an emergency Red Cross shelter in Austin, Texas, set up to accommodate the hordes of evacuees from New Orleans and surrounding areas, questioned 132 shelter residents about their experiences during the disaster. The researchers discovered that it took these survivors 4 full days on average to be evacuated from the city, during which time 63% had sustained injuries, 81% were separated from family members, and 63% reported being directly exposed to corpses. The authors of the study, published in the *American Journal of Public Health,* concluded that "Katrina-related trauma and its psychological sequelae will remain a significant public health issue for years to come" (Mills, Edmondson, & Park, 2007, p. S116).

Both the CBS telephone poll and the emergency shelter study involved **sampling**—the process of selecting people (or elements) for inclusion in a research study. In this chapter, we'll see how the CBS poll of only 725 randomly sampled individuals can represent several hundred million people in the U.S. population. But we'll also consider the many practical difficulties and limitations that often produce bias in telephone polls and other sampling situations. And you'll learn that much useful research gets done with nonrandom samples as well, such as the public health study of evacuees in just one Red Cross shelter in Texas, although there are important limitations as well. Sampling is part of the broader issue of *generalizability*—the extent to which the findings of a study can be projected, or generalized, to other people, situations, or time periods. We begin first with this fundamental notion of generalizability.

Researchers used sampling to understand the effects of Hurricane Katrina.

Source: © David J. Phillip/Corbis.

Generalizability

We often find research interesting or useful—not because of what it uncovers about the people or elements that happen to be in the study—but because of what the findings mean for the larger world we live in.

In the CBS poll, for example, we really don't care that much about what the 725 people in the poll think about the U.S. policy response to Katrina—what matters is what they tell us about the thinking of the whole nation (a few hundred million people). Similarly, with the 132 shelter residents, their experiences are of interest primarily because they shed light on what happened to the tens of thousands of people like them who fled New Orleans. This illustrates the concept of *generalizability*—projecting the results of one study to a much larger reality.

Generalizability is also called **external validity**—the extent to which a study's findings hold true outside of (external to) the particular context of the research (Shadish, Cook, & Campbell, 2002). But because of the many other "validities" in the lexicon of research jargon (measurement validity, internal validity, etc.), we prefer to use the more descriptive term generalizability.

Several factors make a study more or less generalizable.

Population of Interest, Sampling, and Generalizability

Every study has a **population of interest**—the population the study aims to investigate in the first place. The CBS poll aimed to study all U.S. adults, while the shelter study aimed only to study those evacuated from New Orleans. The broader the population of interest, the more generalizable the results. But notice that not all studies necessarily seek to represent a broad national or international population, and indeed, much can be learned from studying more unique or specialized groups.

A related factor affecting generalizability is the time dimension and geographic coverage. If a study is done at one point in time, it may capture some current event or unique coincidence. Public opinion about the government's response to Katrina certainly changed over the days and weeks during which the disaster unfolded and was covered by the news media. But if a study is done over many points in time, the results tend to be more generalizable. Similarly, if a study is done in just one place, it may capture local idiosyncrasies. The Red Cross shelter in the public health study was just one of many such emergency shelters. If a study is done in many places, its results can be more broadly generalized.

A random sample (or **probability sample**), in which participants are chosen randomly from a population, is often much more generalizable than other, nonprobability forms of sampling. Indeed, a small, random sample often beats a much larger nonprobability sample in terms of generalizability. The CBS telephone poll, based on a small random sample, is much more representative than, say, an effort by CBS to have millions of its viewers call the network to express their views.

This kind of **voluntary sample**, in which participants simply volunteer to be part of the study, as well as a **convenience sample**, in which researchers rely on the most readily available participants, will likely produce less representative and therefore less generalizable results. Who are the people in the Red Cross shelter—an example of a convenience sample—supposed to represent? All New Orleans residents? Just those who fled to shelters, rather than to family, friends, or hotels? Just those who fled to the particular shelter studied? It's difficult to know for sure; hence, our ability to generalize is uncertain.

We will learn much more about random (probability) sampling, as well as nonprobability forms of sampling (such as voluntary and convenience sampling), later on in this chapter. Generalizability, however, is not simply a matter of aiming to represent broad populations and employing probability sampling. It is more subtle and complex than this.

Are Experiments More Generalizable?

Many basic biological, psychological, or even economic processes or behaviors can be shown to be fairly universal—highly generalizable, in other words—even when the studies use relatively small samples of volunteers, usually in the context of a controlled experiment. Experiments are used to determine causal relationships—answers to "what if?" questions—and we will have much more to say about them in Chapters 10 and 12.

Consider, for example, the fact that most drug or medical trials—experiments that test the efficacy of treatments we all depend on—come from samples of clinical volunteers. (See, for example, ClinicalTrials.gov for information about ongoing clinical trials in the United States and other countries.) Psychological experiments have discovered important laws of perception, cognition, and behavior using only small numbers of volunteers, often undergraduate psychology majors at one university. Similarly, experimental economists have demonstrated some basic structures of economic behavior (such as altruism and risk aversion) by running small-scale experiments such as the *ultimatum game* or the *prisoners' dilemma*, typically involving only a handful of volunteers.

Of course, not all experiments and causal relationships generalize from idiosyncratic volunteer samples to a broader population. But important and often generalizable findings come from good experimental research done with volunteers or convenience samples. This is because experiments often test well-specified theories, and they do an especially good job at demonstrating causation. We talked about the importance of theory in Chapter 2, and we will explain more about causation in Chapter 10.

Replicating Research and Meta-Analysis

Replication refers to repeating a study with a different sample, in a different place, time period, or policy context, and with a different study design. Replication dramatically enhances the generalizability of small experimental studies done on nonrandom samples. Many of the experimental studies in medicine, psychology, and economics referred to above have been replicated many times. Thus, although a particular study might have limited generalizability on its own, it may fit together with a growing pattern of similar results that accumulate across many related studies. This is why research with small, confined, or highly self-selected samples can still be important—it may be part of a broader field of research that leads, eventually, to generalizable knowledge.

Since replication is critical to generalizability, it is helpful to be able to systematically combine different studies. **Meta-analysis** is a method for pooling together multiple smaller studies to get a much bigger, combined study. Formally, meta-analysis is a set of statistical techniques for integrating the separate effects reported in many studies into a single, more generalizable estimate of the effect of a given treatment, or variable, on an outcome of interest (Lipsey & Wilson, 2001).

For example, meta-analysis was used to join over a dozen studies of the relationship between air pollution and daily mortality in urban areas around the world, showing that airborne particle concentrations are a significant risk factor for mortality (Schwartz, 1994). Another meta-analysis looked at 124 experiments conducted from 1953 to 2002 to test the efficacy of second-generation antipsychotic drugs for treating schizophrenia, finding that only some were more effective than earlier drugs (Davis, Chen, & Glick, 2003). Meta-analysis is applied these days in many areas of research, including health, education, social work, criminal justice, job training and employment, and more.

Is daily mortality linked to air pollution?

Source: © 2009 Jupiterimages Corporation.

Are Relationships More Generalizable?
Health and Happiness in Moldova

Relationships among variables are often more generalizable than descriptive findings such as percentages or means. To illustrate this fact, let's look at some data from the 2000 World Values Survey, one of the largest social surveys of its kind, involving more than 50,000 interviews in nearly 100 different countries. Table 5.1 shows the means of a measure of self-reported health and happiness for all nations in the survey and for the small Eastern European nation of Moldova, the country that happens to have the lowest scores for both health and happiness.

Table 5.1   Health and Happiness Means (World Values Survey)

Means	All Nations ($n = 55,356$)	Moldova ($n = 974$)
Health (0–100 scale)	71.8	50.4
Happiness (0–100 scale)	69.1	50.9

Clearly, the levels of health and happiness in Moldova do not generalize well to other countries—Moldovians rate their health and happiness much lower than the overall average. As it happens, Moldova's per capita gross domestic product (GDP) is less than $3,000 per year, and *The Economist* rated it 99th out of 111 countries on its world quality-of-life index ("Moldova," 2009).

Now let's consider the *relationship* (correlation) between health and happiness—are healthier people happier? Table 5.2 shows for all nations and Moldova the health-to-happiness correlations—indices of the strength (from 0 to 1) and direction (+ or −) of the statistical relationships. (See Chapter 8 for help with interpreting correlations.)

Table 5.2 Correlation of Health and Happiness (World Values Survey)

Correlation	All Nations (*n* = 55,356)	Moldova (*n* = 974)
Health and happiness	.333	.337

The positive .333 correlation for all respondents to the World Values Survey (*n* = 55,356) implies that across the globe, healthier people are, as we might expect, happier—but the relationship is surprisingly similar for just the 974 people surveyed in Moldova. By the way, for the Nigerians in the survey (*n* = 2,021), who perhaps somewhat surprisingly rate their health and happiness among the *highest* of all the nations (86.8 and 85.9, respectively), the correlation of health and happiness is .359, quite similar again to Moldova and to the correlation for all nations. So if we wanted to study the connection between health and happiness, we might do fairly well even with access only to data from the small, landlocked nation of Moldova. The relationship we have discovered seems to be fairly generalizable to many other peoples and parts of the world.

Indeed, one of the reasons why small experiments of volunteers can produce generalizable findings is that experiments—randomized experiments—are designed precisely to produce good evidence of true (unbiased) causal relationships, as we will learn in Chapter 12. And relationships, as we have just seen, tend to be fairly generalizable.

Generalizability of Qualitative Studies

Qualitative research (discussed in Chapter 3) is typically done on small, nonprobability samples and, therefore, is not generalizable in the sense of statistical representativeness. However, qualitative research can produce generalizable theories ("hows" and "whys") without trying to copy the sampling methods of quantitative research (Small, 2005). A qualitative researcher acquires, over a long period of detailed observation, an in-depth familiarity with a group of people or social setting that can allow the researcher to sort out the more universal, generalizable, features of a setting from its more individual, ideographic aspects. But a lot depends on how much time and effort is devoted to qualitative observation as well as the openness and judgment of the researcher (Lamont & White, 2005).

Having considered the foundational issue of generalizability, we can turn now to the more specific concepts and methods of sampling.

Basic Sampling Concepts

As we have said, **sampling** refers to the process of selecting people or *elements* from a population for inclusion in a research study. Researchers do sampling because limited resources or time often prevent them from studying an entire population. Let's begin by looking at some basic sampling concepts (see also Henry, 1990; Kalton, 1983).

Population, Sample, and Inference

When doing sampling, a **sample** is selected from a population of interest—but the word population (or **universe**), as researchers and statisticians use the term, does not necessarily mean the general human population of a society (or the universe of stars and galaxies). For example, environmental scientists monitor the quality of air in urban areas by taking daily *samples* of air, using special monitoring equipment, from the *population* of air surrounding a city (the airshed). Or auditors might take a *sample* of reimbursement records from a *population* of all petty cash reimbursements made by an organization during a given fiscal year. Researchers then use their samples to make *inferences* about the population.

Figure 5.1 illustrates the process of making an **inference** from a sample to a population. Although data are collected on the sample, you must be very clear about the conceptual and operational definition of the population to make a proper inference.

Who Is Included in the Eurozone Unemployment Rate?

For example, Agence France Press (2008) announced the following headline: "Eurozone Unemployment Rate Remains at Record Low 7.2 percent." What is the population this statistic refers to? It takes a little investigating to come up with a precise answer. First, the Eurozone includes the 15 nations that have adopted the euro as their national currency—not all 27 European Union (EU) nations

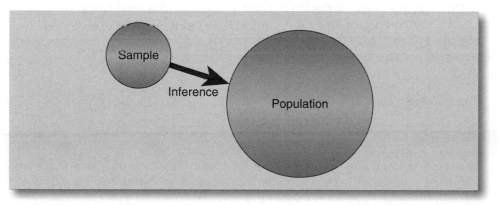

Figure 5.1   Population, Sample, and Inference

(e.g., the United Kingdom and Denmark use their own national currencies, even though they are members of the EU). Moreover, the 7.2% unemployment rate refers to the *labor force*, not to the general population, or even the working-age population. As economists define the labor force, it excludes those who are unavailable to work—for family, health, or other reasons. Even more important, it excludes those who are not actively seeking work because they are discouraged or otherwise don't want or need to work. This latter definition means that the official unemployment rate does not mesh with some individuals' intuitive use of the term *unemployment rate*. In fact, less than half (47%) of the more than 300 million people in the Eurozone remain in the labor force (OECD.Stat Extracts, 2008). So to answer our question, the 7.2% unemployment rate refers just to those in the labor force of the 15 EU nations that use the euro.

Whose Opinions Does an Oklahoma Poll Tell Us About?

Consider another example: What is the population in the following poll reported by the Associated Press (2008)?

TULSA, Okla. (AP)—A recent poll finds Oklahoma voters support pay raises for teachers even if that means no state income tax cuts. The survey of 757 likely voters found 54% say they prefer bringing teacher salaries up to the regional average instead of a merit pay system. Thirty-eight percent prefer developing a merit pay plan. And 57% say they would rather see a teacher pay raise than a cut in state income tax rates.

The population in this poll is "likely voters who live in Oklahoma"—but let's consider what this really means. Of Oklahoma's 3.6 million total "population" (U.S. Census Bureau, 2008), only 2.6 million are eligible to vote by age and citizenship status. And of these, only 926,462 actually *did* vote in the 2006 congressional elections (United States Elections Project, 2008). Likely voters in an election yet to occur are even harder to pin down. Different pollsters use different criteria to determine if someone is a likely voter. Even conceptually, whether or not someone *is* a likely voter depends on *how* likely. So the population in this case is much smaller and more specific than it might at first appear.

These examples illustrate that you must be precise in thinking about the *population* for a particular study and thus what the *sample* and statistics that come from it represent. Many mistakes of inference and interpretation get made by researchers, and often by users of research findings, from not paying careful attention to the precise definition of the population.

Census Versus Sample

When data are collected on the entire population, rather than a sample, this is referred to as a **census**. The U.S. Census and other censuses conducted in various countries around the world attempt to count and assess the characteristics of everyone in the society (the population). This is such a large undertaking in the United States, with its 300 million people, that the government attempts it only once every 10 years. But again, as researchers and statisticians use the term, *census* refers more generally to any study in which you have data on an entire population.

For example, thanks to the convenience of electronic records, auditors may analyze records of *all* petty cash reimbursements by an organization during a fiscal year, not just a sample. If you survey all 800 employees in an organization about their job satisfaction, not just a sample of employees, then you are doing a *census* survey of the population of employees. To take another example, a study titled "Fatal Outcomes from Liposuction: Census Survey of Cosmetic Surgeons" involved contacting all 1,200 actively practicing North American board-certified plastic surgeons to ask about deaths after performing the procedure (Grazer & de Jong, 2000).

With small populations, a census is not difficult to do—and in fact there is little to be gained from sampling. Sometimes, however, a sample is better than a census—even when you can do both—as the case of crime statistics illustrates.

How Many Rapes in the United States?

Rape is one of the major forms of violent crime and a continuing problem in modern societies. According to the FBI's Uniform Crime Reports, there were 94,347 reported cases of forcible rape (including attempted rape) in the United States in 2005. The Uniform Crime Reports are a kind of a *census*—an attempt to count *all* crimes by gathering reports made (usually by victims) to law enforcement agencies across the nation (U.S. Federal Bureau of Investigation, 2008).

The U.S. government also conducts the Crime Victimization Survey (CVS)—a *sample* of the population (12 years of age and older)—to estimate the number of crimes and crime victims in the United States in a given year. According to estimates from the CVS, there were 130,140 rapes or attempted rapes in the United States in 2005 (U.S. Bureau of Justice Statistics, 2008)—35,793 *more* cases of rape than were reported to the FBI.[1]

Why are the two estimates so different, and which is more accurate? Intuitively, one might imagine that the complete census of all reported crimes nationwide and tallied by the FBI would be best. But the FBI's census consists of only *reported* rapes. Many rape victims are afraid, embarrassed, or otherwise unwilling to report rape or attempted rape to the police.

The CVS, on the other hand, asks about crime victimization of various kinds, including rape, in the context of a carefully planned, confidential interview that is conducted in private for research purposes only. Thus, respondents often feel more willing and able to say what happened to them, although it is quite likely that rape gets somewhat underreported to CVS interviewers as well. Still, the reason the U.S. government spends the substantial resources needed to conduct the CVS is that it provides a better estimate of many crimes—even though it is based on just a sample of the U.S. population—than the census of reported crimes gathered each year by the FBI.

Thus, sometimes a sampling approach works better than trying to carry out a population census. So it is often wise to devote more resources—more planning and attention—to getting good data on a small *sample* than to spread resources too thinly on trying for a census of the entire *population*.

---

[1]Although there are some differences in how the FBI and CVS measure or count rape, most of the 35,793 difference is due to the fact that rape often goes unreported to the police and in turn to the FBI. The crime reports suffer from much greater nonresponse bias than the CVS sample does.

Coverage and Nonresponse Bias

Regardless of whether a study is a census or a sample, two major challenges confront most attempts to identify and select people or elements for a study: the issue of finding a sampling frame that adequately covers the population and the problem of contacting and getting people (or organizations) to respond or participate in the study.

Sampling Frames and Coverage Issues

To sample—to obtain study participants—one needs a list or enumeration to sample from. This list is referred to as the **sampling frame**. A membership mailing list serves as a sampling frame for the population of members of a voluntary organization. Local governments will use lists of registered voters, or property tax records, as a sampling frame for the population of community residents. The sampling frame can also be a procedure that enumerates a population, as when exit polls use a visual tally of people leaving a given polling place on Election Day as a sampling frame for selecting respondents to interview.

Ideally, the sampling frame *covers* the entire population of interest, the target population that the study aims to understand. In practice, however, the sampling frame is necessarily something available, concrete, and often limited. **Coverage bias** occurs when the members of the sampling frame are systematically different from the target population in a way that influences the results of the study.

Coverage is a growing problem in telephone surveys. Listed telephone numbers (such as you find in a city's phone book) fail to provide a good sampling frame for most telephone surveys because so many households remain unlisted. And listed households may well be different (older, male, higher-income, longer-time residents, etc.) than unlisted households, resulting in potential coverage bias.

For this reason, another sampling frame based on creating a list of phone numbers from random digits (called **random digit dialing**, or **RDD**) must be used instead. (We will explain more about the details of RDD sampling later on.) However, not all households have traditional landline telephones, as increasing numbers of people rely only on cell phones, and telephone pollsters cannot so easily call cell phones. These households are likely to be younger, unmarried, and more mobile than other households. So there are growing coverage problems and potential coverage bias with the RDD method of sampling as well.

Thus, it is important to investigate the nature of the list or other sampling frame for a study, consider how well it covers the population of interest, and think about the potential for coverage bias.

Nonresponse

Nonresponse and the potential bias it can produce in a study are important factors in most research these days—whether it involves a census or a sample, and whether it is quantitative or qualitative. The **response rate** to a survey or other data collection effort contains two main components:

- **Contact rate**—how successful the researchers are at contacting people or units
- **Cooperation rate**—how willing the contacted people or units are to participate

To arrive at the response rate, these two components are multiplied: Thus, *response rate = contact rate × cooperation rate*. For example, suppose that in a telephone survey, 50% of households on a list answer the phone after several call attempts (contact rate), and 70% of those who answer agree to be interviewed (cooperation rate). So the response rate would be .50 × .70 = .35, or 35%. Be aware that sometimes research reports will call the cooperation rate a "response rate," and the contact rate will be ignored. So it is important to look at the details of what was actually done.

Nonresponse is a growing problem in surveys, particularly telephone surveys such as the national poll about the government's response to Katrina. Most polling organizations won't even reveal their response rates, in large part because they are low and getting lower. In fact, even in well-done telephone surveys these days, the response rate is often less than 50% (sometimes much less), in part because many people screen incoming calls or don't answer their phones (contact rate) and because increasingly, people do not welcome or trust pollsters enough to consent to an interview (cooperation rate).

Nonresponse is an issue in mail surveys also, as letters can be returned because of inaccurate or out-of-date address information (contact rate) and people ignore surveys that they receive in the mail (cooperation rate). Nonresponse is also a growing problem in Internet surveys, as spam filters can trap e-mail messages sent to respondents (contact rate) and many people are suspicious of unfamiliar e-mails or simply disregard them (cooperation rate).

When Does Nonresponse Cause Bias?

The aim of random sampling is to produce unbiased results, but incomplete coverage and nonresponse can produce bias. Much depends, however, on what the study aims to measure and what caused incomplete coverage or nonresponse in the first place. An example will help illustrate.

A poll reported in the *Los Angeles Times* (1991) found that, surprisingly, 73% of Californians in six urban counties reported separating their garbage for recycling, whether required to or not. Telephone polls such as this one often have low response rates, as we have just seen. So let's consider how nonresponse bias may have influenced the result.

Consider two Californians, Joe and Kim. Joe doesn't recycle at all. He has a busy job, values convenience, and does not think recycling is all that important. Kim recycles faithfully, even though she is not required to. She is concerned about pollution, resents wasteful packaging, and is committed to doing whatever she can to help protect the environment. The polling firm calls both Joe and Kim: "Hello. We're taking a poll this evening about recycling your household garbage. Your answers are confidential, and we need only about 15 minutes of your time. Can I get started?" We might predict that, given her commitment to recycling, Kim would probably agree to cooperate.

Some people care a lot about recycling, others less so.
Source: © 2009 Jupiterimages Corporation.

Joe, on the other hand, might not be so interested in talking about his recycling habits. In other words, Kim would have a much higher **propensity to respond** than Joe.

In this example, the *propensity to respond* is directly related to what the survey is trying to measure, recycling behavior. If people, like Kim, who *do* recycle cooperate more than people, like Joe, who *do not* recycle, then the survey estimate—73% of people recycle—will be *biased*. The bias in this case is positive—the number is larger than it would be otherwise, had there been full cooperation (a 100% response rate). We depict this in Figure 5.2. Researchers refer to this as **nonresponse bias** because the nonresponders, the people (like Joe) who refused to be interviewed, have an influence on the results.

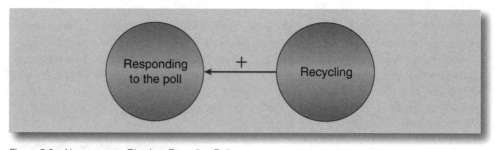

Figure 5.2   Nonresponse Bias in a Recycling Poll

When Propensity to Respond Produces Bias

More generally, we can think of several possible causal models of the propensity to respond (see Groves, 2006), depicted in Figure 5.3. In the models, P represents the propensity to respond, Y represents what we are trying to measure in our survey, and X and Z represent other variables that we will think about shortly.

Consider, first, the *reverse cause* model, which describes the situation in the recycling poll we just discussed. In this case, Y represents recycling behavior and P represents the likelihood that a person participates in the poll. Since Y (recycling) influences P (responding to the poll), the estimate that 73% of Californians recycle is biased.

In the *common cause* model, some other variable Z drives both Y and P. Consider a university with both commuter and residential students that wants to learn about what kinds of clubs students would like. Residential students may be more involved with university life and therefore have a higher propensity of answering a survey. Residential students might also prefer different kinds of clubs. In this case, the survey will overrepresent the preferences of residential students. Again, the survey results will be subject to nonresponse bias. (Applying this example to Figure 5.3, Z represents whether students are residents or commuters, and Y represents type of club preference.)

When Propensity to Respond Does Not Produce Bias

But nonresponse does not necessarily bias the outcome of a study, because the influences Z that affect responding may be distinct from the influences X that affect the outcome. This is the *separate causes* model.

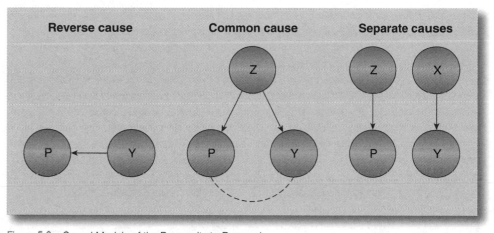

Figure 5.3   Causal Models of the Propensity to Respond

Source: Groves (2006).

Note: In the figures above, P stands for the propensity to respond. Y represents the substantive result or outcome of the study. The letters X and Z represent other variables.

A simple example of this might be an employee satisfaction survey being conducted on a day when a particularly nasty flu bug is going around the office. Having the flu is a causal factor Z that lowers the propensity P to respond to the employee satisfaction survey. But having the flu is not a cause of the outcome Y of job satisfaction, which of course is still caused by many other factors X (such as pay, benefits, promotion opportunities, etc.). In this case, the nonresponse is essentially random and ignorable—it does not bias the results of the study (the measured level of job satisfaction in the organization). Box 5.1 describes the steps needed to assess nonresponse bias in a particular situation.

When Do Coverage Problems Cause Bias?

We have been talking about nonresponse bias, but the same causal models also help us understand when *coverage bias* is a problem.

Earlier, we mentioned the coverage problem with telephone surveys these days, particularly the fact that most telephone surveys leave out younger, unmarried people who use cell phones only. Still, some important public health surveys must rely on telephone sampling frames to estimate health risk behaviors of the population, such as the number of sexual partners. But here, we can sense a potential for bias: If younger, unmarried people have a lower propensity to be included in the sampling

Telephone surveys can miss young people who only use cell phones.

Source: © 2009 Jupiterimages Corporation.

frame, and if these same people also have more sexual partners, then our estimate of this risk factor will be biased. Youth and marital status are a common cause Z of both the propensity P of being in the sampling frame and the outcome Y of the study, the number of sexual partners as a health risk factor. This is the *common cause* model from Figure 5.3.

But again, imperfect coverage does not necessarily produce bias. Say a summer youth program wants to survey families it served last summer about their program preferences this year but has good address information for only half the population served (because of lax and inconsistent key entry of the registration forms submitted by families). These admittedly sloppy administrative practices influence the propensity P to be included in the sampling frame but probably have no effect on the program preferences of families, which is the outcome Y of interest. *Separate causes X*, such as the socioeconomic status of the family, still may influence program preferences, but these factors are unrelated to coverage. Box 5.1 describes the steps needed to assess possible coverage bias in a study.

BOX 5.1
Steps in Assessing Coverage and Nonresponse Bias

- Define carefully the target population of interest.
- To assess *coverage bias*,
  - ○ Identify the sampling frame—who is in the sampling frame but not the target population, and who is in the target population but not the sampling frame?
  - ○ Assess any systematic differences between those in the sampling frame and those in the target population.
  - ○ Determine whether the propensity to be covered is related in any way to what the study is measuring, and if so, how.

- To assess *nonresponse bias,*
  - ○ Identify the nonresponse—who was never contacted or refused to participate?
  - ○ Assess any systematic differences between those who responded and those who did not.
  - ○ Determine whether the propensity to respond is related in any way to what the study is measuring, and if so, how.

Ethics of Nonresponse

When sampling widgets produced on an assembly line, say, to measure production quality, we are free to select individual widgets at will into the sample. But when we sample people for a study, we must tell them first about the study (its purpose and any potential risks) and recognize their right to voluntary participation. We cover the principles and procedures of the ethics of human participation in research further in Chapter 14. But it is important to point out here that, in an important sense, nonresponse and its potential bias are necessary costs of the need to acknowledge and respect the right of voluntary participation in research.

Although it might be possible to reduce nonresponse by deceiving people about a study or coercing them—even physically forcing them—to participate, this would not be acceptable ethically. Yet researchers still do, subtly, push these limits on occasion, for example, by saying an interview will be shorter than it really is or by implying that participation in a study is somehow required by a teacher, employer, or other authority figure (and thus coercing participation). It is for these reasons that ethics committees, known as institutional review boards (IRBs), have been established to watch over researchers and look out for the interests of the people being recruited as research participants.

Nonprobability Sampling

Although random (or probability) sampling provides a kind of "gold standard" in terms of generalizability, we have seen that real-world random sampling can nonetheless be subject to coverage bias and/or nonresponse bias. In fact, for both practical and cost considerations, much research gets done with various forms of nonprobability sampling. These include voluntary sampling, convenience sampling, and purposive sampling.

Voluntary Sampling

In an important sense, as we have just seen, all research involving human participants depends on voluntary participation—a core principle of modern research ethics. But when researchers refer to *voluntary sampling*, they mean that the participants were recruited by putting out an explicit call for volunteers. Here is an example from Craigslist.org, which is often used to recruit volunteers for a study:

Participate in a Research Study

Do you have trouble falling asleep, staying asleep, or getting refreshing sleep?

The Sleep Disorders Center at Rush University Medical Center is conducting a research study on adults with insomnia. If you are 18 years or older and have a sleep complaint you may qualify to participate. The study requires 8 appointments over a 3 month time period. If you qualify, you will receive a thorough sleep evaluation. For more information please call . . .

The people who end up in this study, by responding to the Craigslist ad, are a voluntary sample. Elsewhere on the same Craigslist page, we can also find calls for volunteers to take surveys of various kinds, for example, one seeking Whites to complete a survey on racial attitudes.

The concern with this kind of sampling, however, is a form of nonresponse bias—called **volunteer bias**—that refers to the fact that volunteers may differ from a more representative sample of the population in ways that influence the findings of the study. Thus, the causal models for response and coverage bias (Figure 5.3) apply when thinking about volunteer bias as well. Volunteers for an insomnia study may well suffer from more serious sleep problems, for example, than a more general population of insomniacs. Or Whites who volunteer for a survey on racial attitudes may be more open and accepting of other races than the White population overall. Thus, if the propensity to volunteer is related to the outcome of the study, as it might be in these examples, the results will be biased. Box 5.2 describes the steps to assess possible volunteer bias in a study.

BOX 5.2
Steps in Assessing Volunteer Bias

- Define carefully the target population of interest.
- To assess *volunteer bias*,
  - ○ Identify who volunteers and how they come to volunteer. Who volunteers and who does not volunteer?
  - ○ Assess any systematic differences between volunteers and those in the target population.
  - ○ Determine whether the propensity to be a volunteer is related in any way to what the study is measuring, and if so, how.

Convenience Sampling

Convenience sampling refers to a situation in which a researcher takes advantage of a natural gathering or easy access to people they can recruit into a study. The Katrina-related study of refugees at a Red Cross shelter involved a convenience sample. Recruiting patients in a waiting room for a clinical study, or doing intercept interviews of drivers stuck in traffic, are other examples of convenience sampling. Often, undergraduate psychology majors end up in a university *subject pool*, a convenience sample for purposes of conducting psychological research.

Convenience samples suffer from a form of coverage bias, in the sense that people who happen to be available to a researcher may not cover or represent much of the target population of interest. The refugees of the Austin Red Cross Shelter were a small slice of the hundreds of thousands of evacuees from New Orleans after Katrina struck. But as we noted, much depends on whether the propensity to be included in the sampling frame actually influences the substantive outcome of interest. If not, then results from a convenience sample can still be useful for research.

Sampling Online: Open Web Polls and Internet Access Panels

The Internet has emerged as an increasingly used method in social research, and researchers are struggling with how to sample online. Many organizations put up open Web polls that invite anyone who visits their Web site to answer the questionnaire. Such polls suffer from a high degree of volunteer bias, because those who are most interested and motivated by the topic of the poll are the ones who respond.

How Much Should We Trust Open Web Polls?

An open Web poll on a site called The Internet Party.com (2008) and a Gallup/*USA Today* poll (PollingReport.com, 2008), based on a random telephone sample, asked similar questions about the public's attitude toward the strictness of current U.S. gun laws. Compare the results (The Internet Party's response categories are shown in parentheses):

. . . gun laws in this country (in the United States) should be (are) . . .

	The Internet Party (Open Web poll)	Gallup/USA Today (RDD telephone poll)
More strict (Not restrictive enough)	17%	49%
Less strict (Too restrictive)	66%	11%
Remain as they are (About right)	12%	38%
Don't know (Other)	5%	2%

There are differences in question wording, of course, but these are not likely the reason for the large discrepancy in results. Rather, gun advocates feel strongly about this issue and are motivated to search and respond to the open Web poll, while the general public is less passionate about the topic. Thus, the propensity to respond or volunteer to participate in the open Web poll produces a strong bias in favor of the view held by gun advocates.

How to Create More Trustworthy Internet Surveys

Another approach to sampling in online research is the creation of *Internet access panels,* opt-in e-mail lists (or panels) of people recruited in various ways to participate in Web surveys and other forms of online research. Harris Interactive, Greenfield Online, Zogby International, and many other research firms have established and recruited online panels, some claiming to have millions of members. While these Internet access panels remain composed of volunteers, the motivation to join the panel (financial incentives form part of the recruitment pitch) are not so obviously related to the propensity to respond. Here are the results from Harris Interactive's (2008) panel on the question of whether the public favors stricter, or less strict, gun control laws:

Harris Interactive (Internet Access Panel)	
Stricter	52%
Less strict	22%
Neither	20%
Don't know	7%

These results look much more like the results from the Gallup/*USA Today* poll and seem much less biased than the open Web poll by The Internet Party. It should be noted that Harris Interactive uses weighting (including weighting for the propensity to be online) in an attempt to remove bias. Still, much of the result is likely attributable to the fact that the Internet access panel did not volunteer for the survey based on a passion for gun ownership.

While some studies suggest that Internet access panels can produce results similar to traditional random samples (Braunsberger, Wybenga, & Gates, 2007; Van Ryzin, 2008), other studies caution that substantial bias remains (Malhotra & Krosnick, 2007). Much investigation and debate will continue about the validity of such online methods as people seek to harness the potential of the Internet for social and policy research—and as coverage and response rate problems continue to plague telephone surveys and other, more established, methods.

Purposive Sampling and Qualitative Research

Qualitative research involves sampling as well: What people should we interview in depth or observe unobtrusively in a given setting? What texts or images should we record and include in a content analysis? Sampling for qualitative research may be done randomly, using the various random sampling methods we describe later. But as we saw in Chapter 3, sampling for qualitative research often involves some form of *purposive sampling*—choosing people who have a unique perspective or occupy important roles, or selecting individuals or artifacts to represent theoretical categories or considerations (Patton, 2002). And as we also saw in Chapter 3, qualitative research often involves a small "*n*" or sample size.

For example, after interviewing several people in a neighborhood who oppose the construction of a new housing project, the researcher may purposively seek out supporters of the project to gain a broader perspective. In case study research, investigators typically try to pick a range of sites to visit and observe, for example, small and large schools as well as succeeding and failing schools. As we saw in Chapter 3, they may use a purposive sampling table, such as Table 5.3.

Table 5.3   Purposive Sampling Grid of Schools

	Small	Large
Succeeding	A	B
Failing	C	D

Initially, all possible schools to visit would be arrayed in this way, and then the researchers would choose one school from each category for the case study.

For logistical reasons, having to do with making contacts or gaining access, particularly with hard-to-reach populations (such as homeless families or gang members), qualitative researchers will often use **snowball sampling** or *chain sampling*, in which interviewees are asked to refer people they know to the researcher for inclusion in the sample. Interestingly, some researchers have even developed ways to provide this kind of **respondent-driven sampling** with a statistical foundation (see www .respondentdrivensampling.org).

It is important to point out that qualitative researchers need to worry just as much as quantitative researchers about potential bias due to nonresponse and incomplete coverage, as discussed earlier. The propensity to participate or to be included in a study can be related to (and thus bias) the outcomes of interest, even when those outcomes are observed and recorded qualitatively. Therefore, qualitative researchers must always ask themselves: What kinds of people or cases am I missing in my research? Are there ways in which those in my study systematically differ from those left out—and if so, are the differences important to the findings of my research?

Random (Probability) Sampling

Random sampling (also called **probability sampling**) uses chance to select people (or elements) from the population. Intuitively, it makes sense to do things this way. If we let chance do the selecting, for example, by drawing numbers from a hat, then we can expect that the people (or elements) in the sample will be fairly representative in terms of their characteristics, behaviors, or attitudes relative to the population. In other words, the sample results will be generalizable. Qualitative research can also use random sampling, for example, by selecting schools from each cell in the grid of Table 5.3 using chance so as not to unconsciously influence the findings.

But in addition to this intuitive notion of fairness and representativeness, random sampling provides a foundation for statistical inference—formal methods of assessing the precision of quantitative results from random samples.

The Contribution of Random Sampling

The theory and practice of random sampling is one of the most important inventions of modern social science. It forms the foundation for many of the economic, social, health, environmental, and demographic statistics governments around the world produce and rely on for policy and decision making. For example, major government surveys or surveillance programs based on random sampling give us statistics about the following:

- Unemployment in the labor force (the Current Population Survey, or CPS)
- Crime victimization (the CVS)
- Air quality (ambient air quality surveillance in urban areas)
- Teen smoking and drug use (the Youth Risk Behavior Survey, or YRBS)
- Health status and health care access (the National Health Interview Survey, or NHIS)
- Capital expenditures by businesses (the Annual Capital Expenditures Survey)
- Math and language skills of school children (the National Assessment of Education Progress, or NAEP)
- Housing costs and conditions (the American Housing Survey)
- Age, family structure, and other demographic trends (the American Community Survey)

And random sampling forms the basis of the major social surveys used for much academic research (such as the General Social Survey, the American National Election Studies, the European Social Survey, and the World Values Survey) as well as modern public opinion research reported every day in the media (such as the polls by Gallup, Pew, or Ipsos and the EU's Eurobarometer). Consumer confidence, presidential approval, and public opinion on a range of current policy and political issues all come from random samples.

Random Sampling Versus Randomized Experiments

It is important to note that *random sampling* is something much different from *randomized experiments*, or randomized clinical trials (RCTs), as discussed in Chapter 12.

- *Random sampling* is designed to select elements from a population in order to make statistical inferences about the population.
- *Randomized experiments* assign people or elements to conditions (or treatments) to test causal relationships.

Indeed, most randomized experiments rely on volunteers or convenience samples, not random samples. At the same time, most random sample surveys are purely observational studies (i.e., studies that do not manipulate independent variables to observe their effects on dependent variables) and thus provide only limited evidence of causal relationships. We will learn more about these issues in Part III of this book. In fact, it is rare and difficult to have a study that contains both random sampling and random assignment. One example is the so-called split-ballot experiment in survey research, in which a random sample is selected to be interviewed and then randomly assigned one of two different versions of a question or questionnaire.

Simple Random Sampling

Various forms of random sampling are used in practice—systematic sampling, stratified sampling, cluster sampling, multistage sampling, random digit dialing (for telephone surveys), and so on. These are all forms of random sampling, and we will soon learn more about them.

But for understanding the basic theory and logic of random sampling, it is best to begin with **simple random sampling**—selecting people (or elements) from a population in such a way that each individual has an equal chance, or probability, of selection. Drawing numbers from a hat, marbles from an urn, or ping-pong balls from a lottery machine are examples of simple random sampling. Although simple random sampling forms the basis of statistical theory, the other, more complex, forms of random sampling appear more often in practice.

Let's start with the example of estimating unemployment, which in most countries gets done using monthly or quarterly random sample surveys of the population, such as the United States's CPS (U.S. Department of Labor, 2009). Government labor force surveys use complex forms of random sampling, but for the purpose of learning the logic of sampling, we will simplify things. To estimate

Simple random sampling provides an equal chance of selection.

Source: © iStockphoto.com/Marina Ph.

the unemployment rate this month, let's assume that we select a simple random sample of $n = 400$ individuals from the labor force. Using p to represent the sample proportion, say we get the following results:

$$p = 23 \text{ unemployed}/400 \text{ total in the sample;}$$

$$p = .055.$$

Our sample estimate of the unemployment rate is thus 5.5% based on a simple random sample of $n = 400$ people in the labor force.

Our sample unemployment rate p is unbiased, in the sense that it comes from a simple random sample that gave each individual in the population an equal chance of being selected. But this does not mean that $p = .055$ is equal to the population unemployment rate—the true unemployment rate among the millions of people in the population (the labor force), represented by uppercase P. Our sample p will probably be a bit off the mark, different from the true population parameter P.

To see why, imagine what would happen if we took another random sample of 400 people—will we get exactly 23 who are unemployed, or $p = .055$, again? Probably not. Each random sample, just by the luck of the draw, can vary somewhat from the next sample—and from the population. This is referred to as **sampling variability** or **sampling error**. When examining the results of a given random sample, therefore, we must take this sampling error into consideration. Moreover, we would like some idea of how far off our sample estimate could be from the true unemployment rate in the population.

Theoretical formulas for the precision of an estimate from a sample are based on what happens if we take many repeated samples and examine the distribution of these many estimates—referred to as a *sampling distribution*. In real life, we don't actually take more than one sample, but the math of what would happen if we did determine the formulas used in statistical software to calculate the precision of our estimate, the sampling error.

To understand and be able to predict what factors make an estimate more precise, the next section will go over the idea of sampling distributions and statistical inference. Readers who have had a recent course in statistics and are already familiar with this material—or those who would rather pass over the more mathematical aspects of sampling—can skip the starred (*) sections that follow.

*Sampling Distributions and Statistical Inference

Imagine repeating our given sampling procedure many times, say, drawing up to 1,000 or more samples each of $n = 400$ from the labor force. Each time, we will get a slightly different estimate of the unemployment rate. The **sampling distribution** refers to the distribution of estimates from the many samples. In Figure 5.4, we show sampling distributions with different numbers of samples. By the time we have taken 1,000 samples, a clear pattern emerges: On average, the estimate centers on the true unemployment rate. (Of course, in real life we don't know the true unemployment rate. This is just a computer simulation to illustrate sampling distributions.) Each distinct sample's estimate has its own error—the distance between that estimate and the true unemployment rate. We can see in Figure 5.4 that with a lot of samples, say 1,000, the errors average out to 0.

Moreover, the sampling distribution begins to form a pattern called a **normal distribution** (shown in the lower-right-hand graph in Figure 5.4). The center or mean of the distribution converges on the population parameter *P*. In other words, the average of the many samples converges on the true mark, the parameter of interest. In this example, we happen to know that $P = .05$ (only because this is what we, as textbook authors, set it to when we created the many random samples of $n = 400$ using a computer), meaning that the true unemployment rate in our made-up population is 5%. In practice, *P* is unknown—that is why we draw a sample *p* to estimate it in the first place.

Returning to the shape of the distribution, which is *normal*, we can know certain things about it—if we find out the spread, or standard deviation, of the sampling distribution, also called the **standard error**. The standard error is a measure of the precision of the estimate—how good a job we expect it to do, on average. For a percentage or sample proportion *p*, the spread or standard error (*SE*) of the sampling distribution can be found with this formula:

Standard error of a sample proportion *p*:

$$SE = \sqrt{\frac{P \times (1 - P)}{n}},$$

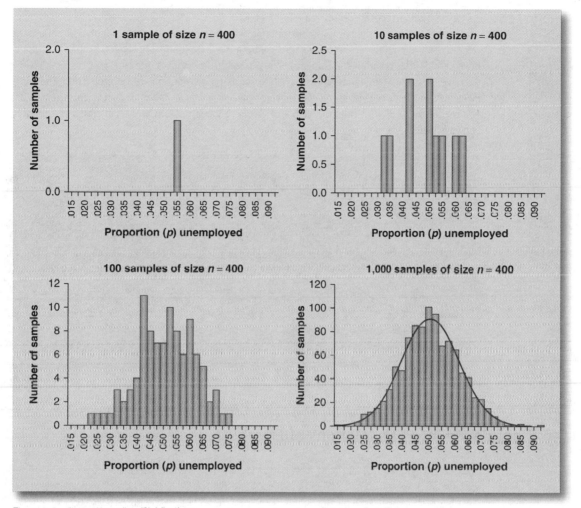

Figure 5.4   Some Sampling Distributions

where *P* is the population proportion (.05 in our example) and *n* is the sample size (400 in our example). So in our example, the standard error *SE* would be the square root of (.05 × .95)/400, which equals 0.011 (or 1.1 %). Remember that the standard error tells us roughly how precise the estimate is.

Now that we've estimated the standard error of the sampling distribution, and we know that its shape is *normal*, we can make use of something called the empirical rule:

- 68 % of the sampling distribution will be within ±1 standard error of the mean.
- 95 % of the distribution will be within ±2 standard errors (1.96 to be exact) of the mean.
- 99.7 %, or nearly all, of the sampling distribution will fall within ±3 standard errors of the mean.

Figure 5.5 illustrates the empirical rule.

Since the mean of the sampling distribution will center on P, the true population parameter, we can use the empirical rule to say some useful things such as, "We have a 95% chance of drawing a sample that is within ± 2 standard errors of the mean—that is, the true proportion P." While we have illustrated the standard error and the sampling distribution with a proportion, the same ideas apply to estimates of many statistics: means, variances, correlation coefficients, and so on. The use of the empirical rule and standard errors to construct confidence intervals is a broadly applicable idea.

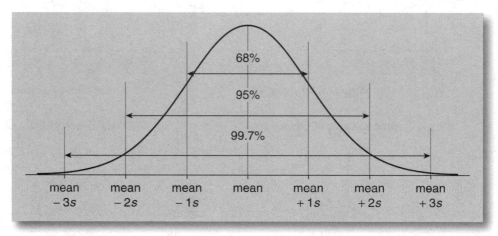

Figure 5.5   The Empirical Rule

Confidence Intervals (Margins of Error)

Because a single random sample is prone to at least some sampling variability (sampling error), as we have seen, we should not read too much accuracy into the result of any one sample. For example, if our sample of $n = 400$ people drawn randomly from the labor force produces a $p = .055$, or a 5.5%, rate of unemployment, we should not assume that this is precisely accurate. A different random sample might result in a somewhat different estimate. As a result, we would do better by constructing an interval or range of possible values for our estimate of the true, unknown population parameter P—the real unemployment rate in the labor force (the population). When you meet someone for the first time, you'd be more often correct guessing that their age falls somewhere in a range of, say, 20 to 30 than estimating that it is exactly 26.

We can use the facts of the sampling distribution—the theoretically generated, long-run pattern of results if we were to repeat our sampling procedure many times—to make a formal statement about the precision of our one sample. We call this statement of statistical sampling precision (really imprecision) a **confidence interval** (CI), or **margin of error**. Pollsters and public opinion researchers tend to talk about margins of error, while scientific journals in health and other fields tend to use the language of confidence intervals. But they are the same thing.

*Calculating a Confidence Interval or Margin of Error

To illustrate confidence intervals, let's return to our earlier example in which we estimated $p = .055$ from a sample of $n = 400$. We'll construct our interval using the standard error SE—usually 2 standard errors (1.96, to be precise) on either side of our sample estimate:

$$p \pm 1.96 \times SE = .055 \pm 1.96(.011)$$

(from our earlier calculation above)

$$= .055 \pm .022.$$

Or equivalently, 5.5% ± 2.2 percentage points.

We can express this either as a ±2.2 percentage point margin of error or as a 95% CI, from 3.3% to 7.7%. (Ideally, the margin of error should be referred to as being in units of *percentage points*, rather than *percent* or %. The reasons are discussed in Chapter 8. This convention, however, is not always observed. The shorter term *"points"* is often, and correctly, substituted for the term percentage points.)

Notice in the formula above that we took a shortcut when calculating the standard error SE. We used the sample p instead of the population P. This is because in practice, the population P is unknown; indeed, it is what we are trying to estimate from our sample p. But since p is a good guess at P, using p to calculate the standard error SE works well enough. In reality today, we don't have to calculate standard errors or confidence intervals—the statistical software does it for us. However, you need to understand enough to interpret standard errors and confidence intervals correctly.

Interpreting Confidence Intervals (Margins of Error)

We calculated that our 5.5% estimate of the unemployment rate has a ±2.2 percentage point margin of error or, in other words, a 95% CI, from 3.3% to 7.7%. Again, these are just two ways of saying the same thing.

But what does this confidence interval (margin of error) really tell us? In the theoretical sampling distribution—the long-run pattern of many hypothetical samples (one of which is our real sample)—95% of the sample proportions theoretically fall within 2 standard errors of the mean (the true population P). So we had a 95% chance of drawing a sample within that range. By constructing the 95% CI around our sample p, we can at least say that we are "95% confident" that the population P (the real unemployment rate in the population) lies somewhere in that interval.

Box 5.3
Relationship Between Various Precision Measures

Smaller standard error → Smaller margin of error → Narrower CI → More precision
Larger standard error → Larger margin of error → Wider CI → Less precision

Interpreting confidence intervals (margins of error) takes practice, so let's try interpreting the accompanying Figure 5.6 from an MSNBC News report (November 1, 2007), specifically the subheadline: "Sixty-seven percent of parents support giving contraceptives to teenagers."

The sample proportion is $p = .67$ (or 67%), but the population P is unknown, because the pollsters interviewed only a sample of 1,004 adults (see the footnote in Figure 5.6), not the millions of adults in the U.S. population. Still, the margin of error of 3.1% (mentioned in the note) tells us that we are 95% confident that P is somewhere in the range of 63.9% to 70.1%. We know this is a 95% CI estimate because that is the standard used by polling organizations, although it's always best to double-check this.

The reported margin of error is subject to some caveats. First caveat: The 3.1% margin of error reported here is based on $p = .5$, or a 50/50 split. For the 67% who support giving birth control to students, using the formula presented earlier, the true margin of error is a little less: 2.9%. Most polls report only the overall margin of error based on a 50/50 split ($p = .5$). They do this, first, because it is a conservative estimate, as we will show when we describe how to calculate the confidence interval for a proportion. They do this, second and more important, because it would be just too confusing to report the actual margins of error for every percentage mentioned in a news article or report. Just looking at the sidebar here, there is technically a different margin of error for the 37%, 30% (twice), 49%, and 46% figures shown.

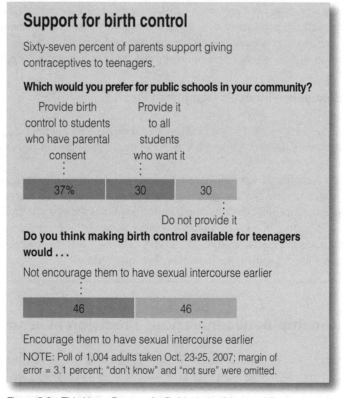

Figure 5.6   This News Report of a Poll Includes Margin of Error

Source: MSNBC News Report (2007).

The second caveat is that the overall margin of error given for a poll such as this does not apply to the percentages reported for subgroups of the sample. For example, the article goes on to say this: "Minorities, older and lower-earning people were likeliest to prefer requiring parental consent, while those favoring no restriction tended to be younger and from cities or suburbs." But these are subgroups of the total $n = 1{,}004$ sample, and the number of respondents in these subgroup is certainly less—perhaps much less—than the total sample size. And as we'll see next, the smaller the sample, the larger the margin of error. So a percentage reported separately for older people or minorities, let's say, would have a much larger margin of error than 3.1%.

Sample Size and Sampling Precision

Confidence intervals and margins of error express sampling precision. And, as a general rule, the larger the sample, the more precise the sample estimate (narrower CIs, smaller margins of error). In our labor survey of unemployment, the 95% CI based on a sample of $n = 400$ was 3.3% to 7.7%—but this is much too wide a guess for purposes of setting economic policy. A 3.3% unemployment rate would suggest that the economy is overheated and prone to inflation, while a 7.7% unemployment rate is much higher and a sign of economic weakness.

A much bigger sample, say $n = 10{,}000$, would help us increase our precision. Using the same formula as before, this much bigger sample would give us a 95% CI estimate of 5.1% to 5.9% unemployment, a better guessing range to work with for setting economic policy, although still wider than one would like. In fact, the CPS, used by the U.S. Bureau of Labor Statistics to track unemployment, employs a monthly sample of about 60,000 households.

The relationship between sample size and sampling precision explains why most government statistics are quite precise for the nation as a whole but much less precise and useful at the state (province) or especially local level. Thus, most cities in the United States don't know their monthly unemployment rate, even while the federal government releases regular data on national unemployment. The same is true for many large federal surveys about health, education, crime, housing, and other policy issues.

*Statistical Explanation of Sampling Size and Precision

Another way to look at the relationship between sample size and precision is to think about the formula for the 95% CI or margin of error: sample proportion $p \pm 1.96 \times SE$, with

$$SE = \frac{\sqrt{p \times (1 - p)}}{\sqrt{n}}.$$

Notice that the sample size n is in the *denominator* of the standard error, so as n increases the standard error SE gets smaller. Bigger samples lead to smaller standard errors, and thus narrower confidence intervals (or smaller margins of error).

Variability and Sampling Precision

But sample size is not the only factor in precision, because much depends on the underlying variability in the data. The more variability in the phenomenon that you are measuring, the wider the confidence interval will be, and the larger the margin of error.

To visualize how this works, imagine trying to estimate the mean income in a community where a severe egalitarianism is enforced: In fact, every single person has identical income. We could get a very accurate picture of the mean income—equal to the income of every individual—simply by measuring a single person's income. In this idealized example, a sample size of only one would give us perfect precision. If we had a little bit of income inequality, we would want a bit more data, but intuitively you can see that a small sample would result in an estimate of mean income very close to the true mean.

Now imagine trying to estimate mean income in a community with great income inequality. A small sample would likely be wildly inaccurate: You might just happen to get a wealthy financier or you might just happen to get a homeless panhandler. Who happened to be in that small sample would make a vast difference in the estimated mean income. To get a really accurate estimate of mean income, you would need a very large sample. Intuitively, when trying to estimate the mean of something, for a given sample size, the more variation in that thing, the less accurate your estimate of the mean will be.

*Statistical Explanation of Variability and Sampling Precision for Means

The role of variability is more easily demonstrated with means, such as mean income, rather than proportions such as the unemployment rate. So we'll continue with mean income as our example to illustrate in statistical form the effect of variability on precision (and return soon to proportions).

The standard error SE of a sample mean is

$$SE = \frac{SD}{\sqrt{n}},$$

where SD is the standard deviation of the sample, which measures the spread or variability of the data. (See Chapter 8 for a review of the standard deviation.) As we saw intuitively, this formula shows that as variability (the numerator) increases, so does the standard error.

Unsurprisingly, as the sample size n increases, the standard error SE gets smaller, just as with a proportion. Indeed, the confidence interval for the sample mean $\bar{x}$ is found with much the same formula as before:

$$\text{Confidence interval} = \bar{x} \pm 1.96 \times SE$$

*Statistical Explanation of Variability and Sampling Precision for Proportions

Now, let us return to the proportion example to see how variability affects the standard error in that case. For our sample of $n = 400$ people in the labor force, the margin of error was 2.1%, yet in the larger poll of $n = 1,004$ U.S. adults, it was 3.1%. How does a bigger sample lead to a larger, not smaller, margin of error in this case? It happens because the 67/33 split in opinion in the poll is more divided (variable) than the 5/95 split for the unemployed versus the employed in our labor market survey. Table 5.4 illustrates how the margin of error depends on *both* the sample size *and* the variability, or split, in the data.

Table 5.4 Margins of Error for Various Values of *p* and *n*

n =	*p* =				
	.055	**.330**	**.500**	**.670**	**.800**
400	.022	.046	.049	.046	.039
1,000	.014	.029	.031	.029	.025
4,000	.007	.015	.015	.015	.012
10,000	.004	.009	.010	.009	.008

Another way to look at this is to think about the formula for the 95% CI or margin of error: sample proportion $p \pm 1.96 \times SE$, with

$$SE = \frac{\sqrt{p \times (1 - p)}}{\sqrt{n}}.$$

We pointed out earlier that the sample size n is in the *denominator* of the standard error, so as n increases, the standard error SE gets smaller. But also notice that $p \times (1 - p)$ is in the *numerator*, and so as p moves farther from an even 50/50 split, this product gets smaller, and thus so, too, will the standard error SE. The closer the split is to 50/50, the more variability there is, and thus the less precise the estimate will be.

What a Margin of Error Does Not Tell You

The margin of error (or confidence interval) only expresses *sampling* or statistical error—not all of the many other kinds of error that can influence research findings. The *New York Times* uses the following standard statement for its polling results to explain this idea:

The New York Times. In addition to sampling error, the practical difficulties of conducting any survey of public opinion may introduce other sources of error into the poll. Variation in the wording and order of questions, for example, may lead to somewhat different results (*New York Times*, 2009).

This statement highlights a form of *measurement error*, such as variations in question wording and question order that influence the results of a survey. But of additional concern with telephone surveys these days is *coverage bias*, as more young people and others switch to cell phones, and *nonresponse bias* due to the declining response rates to telephone surveys, as we saw earlier.

Another kind of error comes from processing and analytical errors. In interviewing situations, the interviewer must enter responses onto a paper form or, increasingly these days, a form on the screen of a computer. There is thus the chance for a writing or key-punch error, just as we all make typos on occasion when using a keyboard. Paper forms that are key-entered by hand, or read by a scanner, provide yet another step in which a processing error can occur. And processing errors can occur when the data get recoded or manipulated statistically for analysis and presentation. There are many steps in the processing and analysis of data and thus many openings for both small and large errors.

The *margin of error* does not tell us anything about how far off the mark we might be due to any of these other important sources of error, which we often must gauge only by subjective judgment.

Two Meanings of the Word Sample

As we have seen, the term *sample* in statistical theory refers to the people or elements selected randomly from a given population—and it implies that you have data on each and every one of those selected. For clarity, we will refer to this as the **true sample**.

But in practice, as we discussed earlier, randomly selecting people does not ensure that they will end up in your sample. You may not be able to contact them, and even if you do, you can't force them to participate. This is the *response rate* problem in surveys that we discussed earlier. Yet researchers typically will call the data they have for analysis the "sample"—when it is only part of the initial, randomly selected, true sample. We prefer to call this data in hand the **observed sample**.

Finding the True Sample Versus the Observed Sample

Let's look at an example of how the word *sample* is used in published research and how it obscures the difference between the true sample and the observed sample. The following abstract comes from an article in *Health Services Research* titled "Understanding Employee Awareness of Health Care Quality Information: How Can Employers Benefit?" (Abraham, Feldman, & Carlin, 2004):

Objective. To analyze the factors associated with employee awareness of employer disseminated quality information on [health care] providers.

Data Sources. Primary data were collected in 2002 on a stratified, *random sample of 1,365 employees* [italics added] in 16 firms that are members of the Buyers Health Care Action Group (BHCAG) located in the Minneapolis–St. Paul region . . .

Data Collection. Employee data were collected by phone survey . . .

Principal Findings. Overall, the level of quality information awareness is low. However, employer communication strategies such as distributing booklets to all employees or making them available on request have a large effect on the probability of quality information awareness.

This is a useful study in a peer-reviewed journal and quite typical of how studies involving random sampling appear in print. But digging into the footnotes of the article, we find that the 1,365 employees who were interviewed, the observed sample, represent just 60% of the true sample of 2,275 employees selected initially at random. In fact, the authors do not even mention the size of the true sample, although it can be inferred from the response rate. This is a fairly good response rate, by the way, so the authors aren't trying to hide anything. Rather, the lack of mention of the size of the true sample illustrates the tendency in published research to blur the distinction between the observed sample and the true sample.

This semantic distinction matters because the response rate—the ratio of the observed sample to the true sample—can be surprisingly low in some kinds of research. For example, the City of Austin, Texas (Valverde & Tajalli, 2006), conducted a citizen survey by mailing questionnaires (in both English and Spanish) to 12,000 households (the true sample), but only 1,601 households ended up returning their completed questionnaires (the observed sample)—a response rate of only 13%. In low-cost telephone surveys, firms may dial dozens and dozens of numbers on average to complete one live interview, with response rates in the single digits (even accounting for all the nonworking or ineligible numbers).

Sampling in Practice

Simple random sampling provides the foundation for statistical sampling theory, but in practice, other methods of sampling must be used for efficiency and logistical reasons. These methods include systematic sampling, stratified sampling, disproportionate sampling, sampling with probabilities proportional to size (PPS), multistage (cluster) sampling, and RDD sampling. But they are all variations of *random* sampling that permit statistical inference, with certain technical modifications to the basic formulas for standard errors. We now describe each of these methods (see also Lohr, 1999).

Systematic Sampling

Systematic sampling involves drawing elements from a list by using intervals—say, every 20th name on the list—beginning at a random start point. It was a common approach to sampling in the age of paper recordkeeping, when lists were stored in file cabinets or in bound ledgers rather than electronic databases. In the current electronic era, simple random sampling is generally performed with random number generators found in ordinary spreadsheet programs. But there are still some practical situations, such as modern day exit polling, in which systematic sampling remains useful.

During an exit poll, research workers are posted outside polling places to talk with a sample of voters, usually just as they exit the polling place. To ensure a random sample, the interviewers use an interval—an Nth, it is sometimes called—to select people as they walk out of the polling place. The Nth is calculated in advance based on past turnout and a desire to end up with, say, 100 interviews by the time the polls close. If in recent elections, the turnout has averaged 4,000 at a given polling place, and assuming a response rate of 50% (about what we might expect for an exit poll), the field workers would need to approach 200 voters in order to successfully complete about 100 exit interviews.

Thus, 4,000/200 is 20, so the sampling interval or Nth would be every 20th voter. To decide whom to interview first, the field worker would pick a random number between 1 and 20, and then approach every 20th person after that.

Systematic sampling can also be used to sample commuters entering train stations, patients in a waiting room, or parents attending school meetings. It is equivalent to simple random sampling in most cases, in terms of the calculation of standard errors, confidence intervals, and related statistics.

Stratified Sampling

Sometimes in sampling situations, it helps first to divide the population into groups—called **strata**. The strata must exhaust the entire population—everyone belongs to one group, and no one is left out. The strata must also be mutually exclusive—so that no one is in more than one group. The population of the United States could be divided into four census regions (Northeast, South, Midwest, West) for stratification purposes. Every state, including Hawaii and Alaska, must be assigned to one region. Individuals must have only one place of residence. Someone who lives half the year in New York and half the year in Florida has to be assigned to just one of those places. In **stratified sampling**, a sample is drawn separately from each group—each stratum.

One motivation for *stratified sampling* is to ensure even coverage across the groups, for example, even coverage across geographic regions. Stratified sampling is often done in proportion to the size of strata. For example, most public opinion polls done of large national populations will treat the regions of the country as strata and draw proportionate random samples separately from each region. Some of these polls involve as few as 400 to 800 interviews, and thus stratified sampling helps ensure that the interviews will be evenly distributed across regions.

Disproportionate Sampling (Oversampling)

Stratified sampling can also be used to oversample selected strata, called **oversampling** or **disproportionate sampling**. The motivation for oversampling is to be able to examine the subgroups separately and to ensure precise results for a small but oversampled subgroup. For example, Native Americans make up a small portion of the U.S. population. To get precise results for Native Americans, a survey might decide to oversample this group. Such sampling is said to be *disproportionate* because the probabilities of selection differ across strata.

In a study that examined the psychological repercussions of the terrorist attack on commuter trains in Madrid in 2004, for example, the investigators (Miguel-Tobal, Cano Vindel, Iruarrízaga, González Ordi, & Galea, 2005) took a random sample of the city's population but oversampled the neighborhoods surrounding the three train stations where the explosions occurred. A proportionate sample of Madrid's population would have resulted in too few interviews for a separate analysis of these three directly affected neighborhoods.

Sometimes when oversampling, the strata cannot be determined in advance, as they can be with geographic areas. For example, in telephone surveys, it is not possible to know in advance the race-ethnicity of the respondent, yet the study may seek to oversample, say, Black respondents (only 13% of the U.S. population), as was the case in a study of attitudes toward the death penalty (Peffley & Hurwitz, 2007). To oversample Blacks, the survey researchers must contact households, select a respondent and identify their race-ethnicity, and then *screen* to get a sufficient sample of the targeted stratum. To get an equal number of Blacks and Whites, for example, every Black respondent will be interviewed, while only about 1 out of 5 randomly chosen Whites will complete a full interview on the phone (the rest will be thanked and the call ended).

*Weighting the Sample

When analyzing data from a disproportionate sample, the strata can be analyzed separately with normal techniques. But to analyze the sample as a whole, that is, with all strata combined, the data must be **weighted**, or else the results will be misleading.

For example, a recent Eurobarometer survey investigated citizen awareness and use of 112, the new European emergency telephone number, based on random samples of $n = 1,500$ people in each of the 27 European Union (EU) countries (European Commission, 2007). This large sample allows for precise analysis of each country individually. But to combine the countries and draw conclusions about the EU as a whole, such as the reported finding that 66% of EU citizens believe that there is not enough information about 112, the sample must be weighted. This is because some EU countries, such as Germany, with more than 80 million people, are very large, while others, such as Luxembourg, with fewer than half a million people, are quite small. Thus, the Luxembourg sample needs to be given a weight of about 1/160 if the German sample gets a weight of 1. Or in other words, the 1,500 people interviewed in Luxembourg end up contributing, after weighting, less than 10 observations to the overall EU average.

*Loss of Precision in Oversampling

Because the 1,500 people in Luxembourg only count toward the European average 1/160th as much as the people in the German sample, the **effective sample size** for the sample as a whole (Europe) is smaller than the total number of observations from all of the European countries. With disproportionate sampling, the effective sample size is always less—and sometimes much less—than it would be had the people or elements been selected using simple random sampling. Thus, disproportionate sampling involves a trade-off: You gain more precision (smaller standard errors) for the individual strata, especially the smaller ones, but at the expense of a loss of precision (larger standard errors) for the sample as a whole, as well as more complexity in analyzing the data.

*Poststratification Weighting

Some studies employ a technique called **poststratification adjustment** or **poststratification weighting**, which is different from but related to stratified sampling. Poststratification weighting involves comparing selected characteristics of the sample, for example, the regional or race-ethnic distribution to the known distribution of the population. If the sample overrepresents one region or race-ethnic group, an adjustment (a weight < 1) is made to bring down this stratum to its proper proportion. If the sample underrepresents a region or group, then a weight > 1 is assigned to bring up its representation.

For example, in many general population surveys, women participate more readily than men, so you may end up with a *sample* percentage female $p = .60$ when the *population* percentage female $P = .50$. A poststratification weight W for females could then be constructed:

$$W = P/p = .50/.60 = .833.$$

The corresponding poststratification weight for males would be $.50/.40 = 1.25$, and thus multiplying the number of females by .833 and the number of males by 1.25 would equalize each group in the sample.

Poststratification weighting tries to accomplish the same thing, after the fact (or *post facto*), that stratified sampling does at the outset of the study. And in practice, both methods can be used together: A stratified sample can be selected at the start and, if varying response rates or other data collection issues result in disproportionate results, poststratification adjustments can be made to bring them into balance.

Sampling With Probabilities Proportional to Size (PPS)

When sampling, researchers at times need to take into account not just the number of elements but their size and relative importance in the population. For example, the Census Bureau's Annual Survey of Manufacturers, a major source of data on the U.S. economy, must consider in its sampling plan the fact that large manufacturers have a much greater impact on the economy than small ones. There are about 350,000 manufacturing establishments in the United States, and the Annual Survey of Manufacturers samples 50,000 of them. About 9,700 of the largest manufacturers are included with certainty, while the remaining sample of medium and smaller manufacturers are sampled with probabilities that are proportional to the size of the establishment (U.S. Census Bureau, 2009a).

PPS sampling is often used as part of a multistage sampling design, in which the first stage of sampling is done with PPS, based on the size of the geographic regions or other clusters that make up the first-stage sampling frame. The next section describes this more complex form of random sampling.

Multistage and Cluster Sampling

Often, there is no comprehensive, national list of households to sample from, and so random sampling from a sampling frame is not possible. In other situations, travel costs make it prohibitively expensive to do in-person interviews of a random sample of a geographically dispersed population. In both cases, **multistage** or **cluster sampling** offers a solution.

Multistage sampling was developed for some of the first major government and social surveys, conducted in person by interviewers who went door to door, and is still in use today. Some surveys that use this method of sampling include the CPS, the General Social Survey, the National Election Studies, the CVS, the American Housing Survey, the National Health Interview Survey, and the Eurobarometer. School-based surveys, such as the National Assessment of Education Progress and the Youth Risk Behavior Survey, use a form of multistage (cluster) sampling of schools.

In multistage sampling, geographic areas (typically counties in the United States) are sampled first, then census blocks (representing clusters of households) within counties, then individual housing units, and finally a randomly selected individual within the household. This kind of sampling is sometimes called *cluster* sampling because the interviewer, rather than just talking with one person in the area before moving on, will typically visit several randomly selected households in the block group. Similarly, with the school-based surveys, counties are selected, then schools, but within schools a whole class (a cluster) will be surveyed.

Figure 5.7 is from the Centers for Disease Control and Prevention (CDC) and illustrates the multistage sampling used in the National Health and Nutrition Examination Survey, a unique survey because it includes physical examinations as well as in-person interviews.

Loss of Precision in Multistage Sampling

Multistage (cluster) samples are complex and, like disproportionate sampling, often involve some loss of sampling precision (larger standard errors) due to the clustering of observations. This is because individuals or households that are clustered together may well be more alike than those sampled independently from across the total population. They share the same neighborhood, economic situation, political culture, and so on. Similarly, students in the same high school class share an educational environment and other characteristics that make them much more alike than a simple random sample of 30 students from the larger population of all high school students.

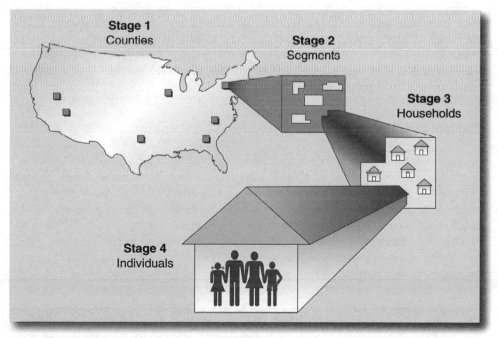

Figure 5.7   Multistage Sampling

Source: Centers for Disease Control and Prevention (2009b).

Statisticians measure this similarity within clusters using the **intraclass correlation**, which ranges from 0 (individuals in the cluster look just like a simple random sample of the population) to 1 (all individuals in the cluster look the same). The intraclass correlation is also referred to as *rho* for "rate of homogeneity." The larger the intraclass correlation, the larger the standard errors are.

Design Effects: Complex Survey Sampling Corrections

As we have discussed, **complex survey sampling**, such as cluster sampling and disproportionate sampling, increases standard errors relative to simple random sampling.

The **design effect** of the sample is one way sampling statisticians take into account the loss of precision due to complex survey sampling. The larger the design effect, the smaller the effective sample. For example, a design effect or *deff* = 2.0 would imply that the clustering and intraclass correlation are such that the multistage sample is only *half* as good as a simple random sample, in terms of its precision. The specific design effect depends on not only the sampling framework but also the specific variable to be corrected, since features such as intraclass correlation differ by variable. See the book by Groves, Fowler, Couper, and Lepkowski (2004) for more discussion of this issue and for more technical details.

Statistical software packages calculate standard errors using the assumption that the data are from a simple random sample, unless specific complex survey sampling commands are used. When analyzing data from complex surveys, correct your standard errors to avoid inferring more precision than is actually the case. This can be done approximately through the use of design effects provided with some complex surveys. Alternatively, it can be done more exactly with complex survey sampling commands in those statistical software packages (such as Stata or SAS) that have such commands (discussed further in Chapter 8). Such corrections are important for the large public use government surveys described in the next chapter, since they generally use complex sampling. Only when design effects are small can such corrections be ignored.

Random Digit Dialing Sampling

In the late 1960s, as the telephone became standard equipment in most households, statisticians developed a method of sampling that gives both listed and unlisted telephone numbers an equal chance of being selected. Named *random digit dialing*, this sampling innovation ushered in a boom in telephone polls and surveys that only now is beginning to reach its limits (as households have begun to screen calls, switch to cell phones, and rely more on the Internet).

RDD works essentially by replacing the digits at the ends of listed residential telephone numbers with random digits. For example, a number such as 212-863-2715, which is in New York City, can be broken up into parts as follows:

Area code	Exchange	Bank
212	863	2715

This is a made-up number, but suppose for the time being that it is a real, listed residential number. RDD sampling replaces selected digits in the bank, say the last two digits, with randomly generated numbers, for example, 20, 71, 03, and so on, to form new phone numbers, like this:

212-863-2720

212-863-2771

212-863-2703

These numbers are then dialed. Some will turn out to be nonworking numbers, fax lines, businesses, and so on. But others will turn out to be residential numbers, including both listed and unlisted numbers, and each such number will have an equal chance of being in the sample (because the numbers were generated randomly). Specialized RDD sampling firms keep up-to-date records of all working area codes and exchanges and generate high-quality RDD samples for use by survey researchers.

Good and Bad RDD Sampling

One of the issues to be alert to in RDD sampling is how much effort the survey organization makes in calling the RDD sample or, alternatively, how many RDD numbers they use up to complete a study. Rigorous, reputable telephone surveyors call the

Good RDD sampling involves multiple calls to each number over several days and at various times.

Source: © 2009 Jupiterimages Corporation.

RDD sample in small batches (called replicates), working each batch thoroughly by calling each number 7 to 10 times or more, on different days of the week and at different times of day, and scheduling callbacks for people who request it. Low-cost or less reputable firms call as many RDD numbers as fast as possible, looking for anyone who happens to be home and is willing to be interviewed, with little effort made to redial numbers or reschedule calls. Such practices exacerbate nonresponse bias by lowering the contact rate.

So just knowing that a survey used "RDD sampling" does not tell you how good or bad the sample really was. You need to look carefully at how much effort was made to contact the sample.

Sampling and Generalizability: A Summary

This chapter has introduced you to sampling—the process of selecting people (or elements) for inclusion in a study—and how it affects generalizability. We saw how random sampling enhances representativeness because it allows the use of statistical theory to project the results of a sample to a well-defined population, within a certain margin of error. But we also saw how small, nonprobability samples can be used in experiments and qualitative research to produce generalizable knowledge, particularly about causation and when supported by strong theory. Ultimately, determining generalizability is a matter of judgment in which many aspects of a study must be taken into consideration.

Still, sampling is a critical factor in the generalizability of any study. Because sampling is such an important and at times complex task, as we saw in parts of this chapter, some people—called sampling statisticians—specialize in sampling design and in statistical techniques for the weighting and analysis of data from complex samples. If you need to do complex sampling, or even if you need to do secondary analysis of data from a complex sample, you may need to consult a sampling statistician for advice.

But sampling happens routinely in many kinds of formal and informal research, and consulting an expert is not always possible. Recruiting people for a focus group, gathering feedback surveys from customers, auditing expenses, and using available data all involve sampling of a kind. We hope that this chapter has given you ideas on how to sample—if the need arises.

Most important, we hope that this chapter has given you the tools to explore nonresponse bias and coverage bias—and their consequences for generalizability—in both quantitative and qualitative studies. Always ask yourself who is missing from the study, whether they are systematically different, and whether those differences could bias the results.

The ideas learned in this chapter, therefore, matter a great deal not only when doing your own research but when using the research of others. For example, knowing how sampling was done, its complexities and limitations, becomes an important part of using secondary data—the topic of Chapter 6.

BOX 5.4
Critical Questions to Ask About Sampling in Studies

- Is it a sample or a census? If a sample, is it a random (probability) sample or a nonprobability sample?
- If it is a nonprobability sample—such as a voluntary, convenience, or purposive sample—how might the type of sampling influence the obtained results?
- What is the sampling frame or method of obtaining sampling units? What population does the sampling frame represent, and how is that different from the target population? How is it different from the ideal study population? What population will the study generalize to? Is there coverage bias for any of the relevant measures?
- Who is likely to respond, and who is not? How might the propensity to respond produce bias in any of the relevant measures?
- What is the level of statistical precision provided by the sample (confidence intervals)? Is the sample size large enough for adequate precision?
- Was simple random sampling used or some form of complex survey sampling used? Why was that method chosen, and does the choice make sense? Was weighting necessary, and if so, was it used? Did the standard errors and other inference measures require correction, and if so, was that done?

EXERCISES

A Charter School's Success Story

5.1. A charter high school surveyed its alumni, from a list it maintains for fund-raising purposes, to find out how well they were doing in the job market. Nearly 50% responded, and the average (mean) salary calculated from the survey was $79,000. Do you think that this estimate is biased? How would the propensity to be covered by the list and the propensity to respond to the survey likely bias the estimate?

Communicating With Parents

5.2. Say you are a principal of a school and want to learn how well parents feel the school communicates with them. You send home a survey with students and then have each teacher follow up with a phone call to parents about how important the survey is. What kinds of nonresponse problems will you have? What bias do you think would result in your measure of school communication? Explain using a path diagram showing the propensity to respond.

Patient Satisfaction

5.3. A clinic wants to survey the satisfaction of its patients. It has few male patients and is particularly interested in determining the satisfaction of male patients and comparing it with that of female patients. What kind of sampling should the clinic use? Explain why and how it should use the data.

Parenting Styles

5.4. A city welfare services department wants to get a good description of parenting styles among parents. It feels that this will help it in assessing "problem" parents and foster parents. For a sampling frame, it gets a list of the parents or guardians of all public school students and their telephone numbers. It plans to sample randomly from that list and conduct a telephone survey.

   a. To what population would this survey generalize if there was a 100% response rate? How does that compare with the population desired? Describe any coverage bias and why it occurs.

   b. What real-world factors will interfere with the generalization to even the study population? Create a path diagram for the propensity to respond that you can use to predict the type and extent of nonresponse bias.

Are We Afraid of the Internet?

5.5. Internet commerce has become vital to the modern economy, yet it remains vulnerable to fear of Internet fraud and identity theft. But how afraid are we, really? A 2007 telephone survey of an RDD sample of 1,000 U.S. adults found that fully 38% did not trust online payments, banks, and other e-commerce providers. Based on what you have read in this chapter about coverage and nonresponse in telephone surveys, how might this estimate be biased?

Eating More Fruits and Vegetables

By Herman, Dena R., Gail G. Harrison, Abdelmonem A. Afifi, & Eloise Jenks. (2008, January). Effect of a targeted subsidy on intake of fruits and vegetables among low-income women in the special supplemental nutrition program for women, infants, and children. *American Journal of Public Health, 98*(1), 98–105.

Objectives. Intake of fruits and vegetables protects against several common chronic diseases, and low income is associated with lower intake. We tested the effectiveness of a subsidy for fruits and vegetables to the Special Supplemental Nutrition Program for Women, Infants, and Children (WIC).

Methods. Women who enrolled for postpartum services ($n = 602$) at 3 WIC sites in Los Angeles were assigned to an intervention (farmers' market or supermarket, both with redeemable food vouchers) or control condition (a minimal nonfood incentive). Interventions were carried out for 6 months, and participants' diets were followed for an additional 6 months.

Results. Intervention participants increased their consumption of fruits and vegetables and sustained the increase 6 months after the intervention was terminated (model adjusted $R^2 = .13$, $p < .001$). Farmers' market participants showed an increase of 1.4 servings per 4186 kJ (1000 kcal) of consumed food ($p < .001$) from baseline to the end of intervention compared with controls, and supermarket participants showed an increase of 0.8 servings per 4186 kJ ($p = .02$).

Conclusions. Participants valued fresh fruits and vegetables, and adding them to the WIC food packages will result in increased fruit and vegetable consumption.

5.6. What kind of sampling do you think this study used—random (probability) sampling or nonprobability sampling—and why? How generalizable are the results?

Sampling as Used in Large Government Surveys

5.7. Identify a large government survey that is important in your field of interest or professional practice—such as the National Assessment of Educational Progress (NAEP), CVS, the CPS, the NHIS, and so on. Find the official Web site for the survey and read about the kind of sampling used in the survey. How large is the sample, and what type of random sampling is it (simple, systematic, multistage, etc.)? Assess the survey's coverage and response rate. Also see if the Web site gives information about survey weights and design effects.

Sampling as It Appears in a Published Journal Article

5.8. Find an original empirical study published in a journal in your field of interest or professional practice. Read the abstract of the article and also the section of the article that describes the sampling and data collection methods. What kind of sampling is it? Why was this type of sampling used? See if coverage and response rates are reported, and discuss the generalizability of the study's findings.

Iraqi Mortality (advanced question)

5.9. A study by Roberts, Lafta, Garfield, Khudhairi, and Burnham (2004) in the journal *Lancet* used cluster sampling techniques to estimate the death toll in Iraq after the U.S. invasion. The stunning estimate of some 100,000 excess deaths in Iraq, likely due to the U.S. invasion, made headlines and sparked controversy around the world. The study was replicated a few years later (Burnham, Lafta, Doocy, & Roberts, 2006), with similar results. Read the original study by Roberts et al. (2004) and answer the following questions:

a. Why did they choose to use cluster sampling? Describe briefly how the sampling worked. Describe the effect that lack of security had on the research design.

b. Discuss the decision to exclude Falluja. Try to use the Falluja example to help explain intuitively why cluster sampling reduced the precision of the results.

c. What effect did using an out-of-date census have on the results? How might migration within Iraq bias the results? How might migration out of Iraq bias the results?

d. What are the pros and cons of a survey such as this compared with methods such as counting deaths at the morgues? Contrast the biases of the two methods.

e. Discuss how politics affects the decision to do (or not do) research such as this as well as decisions about how the research is conducted and how such research is interpreted.

f. What were some of the ethical concerns? How did the researchers address those?

Objectives: In this chapter, you will begin learning about where quantitative data come from—with a focus on secondary or existing data available for social and policy research. You will understand the forms that secondary data can take, including micro and aggregate data, panel data, and time series. And you will become familiar with some of the main sources of secondary data, including administrative record data, published data tables, and public use microdata. With the Internet and the low cost of computing, coupled with the high cost and complexity of primary data collection, the use of secondary data has become increasingly important in many fields. And secondary data are important for practitioners who use reports based on secondary data as a basis for decisions and who can now, because of online data analysis tools, directly access the data on their own.

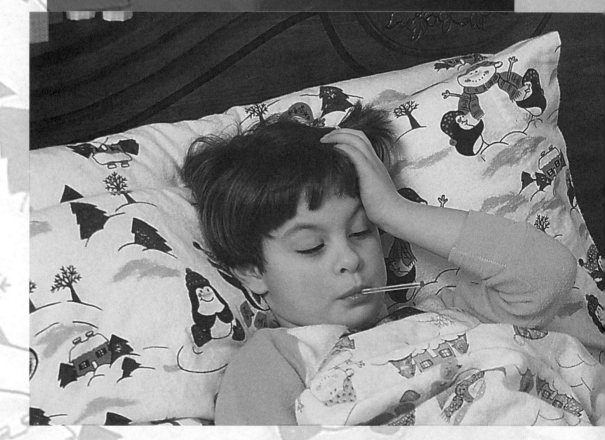

Public health officials use secondary data to monitor flu epidemics.

Source: © 2009 Jupiterimages Corporation.

Secondary Data  6

Tracking the Flu

In January 2008, New York City's health department warned the city's 8 million inhabitants that an influenza epidemic was spreading rapidly across the city. Influenza (the flu) is responsible for several thousand deaths in the city each year, with the elderly and young children most at risk. Certain strains of the flu (such as swine flu or bird flu) can be especially deadly. The health department knew that an epidemic had started because it tracks administrative data from hospital emergency rooms on patients with flu symptoms, it monitors purchases of over-the-counter cold and flu medications at local pharmacies, and it conducts regular sample surveys of the population. In other words, the health department has good *data* to guide its decisions—data that come from various sources and methods.

In this chapter, you will begin discovering sources of *quantitative* data—the most common form of data used in social and policy research. Data are the basic stuff of research—the raw material researchers work with to build an understanding of the world—so it is important to know what they are and where they come from. We begin here with *secondary data*, data that exist already because they were collected as part of a prior administrative or research activity. Low-cost computing and data storage, coupled with the Internet, have made secondary data much more widely available and useful for research. In the next chapter, we will address the topic of collecting your own, *primary data* through surveys or other methods.

What Are Quantitative Data?

Data are facts or pieces of information, and so by **quantitative data**, we mean information that is recorded, coded, and stored in numerical form. (The word *data*, by the way, is plural, not singular.) Often, this information comes from a formal process of *measurement*, as discussed in Chapter 4.

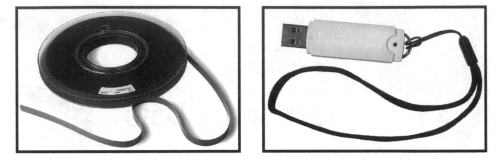

Data Management: Then and Now

Source: 6.02a ©iStockphoto.com/jsolie; 6.02b © 2009 Jupiterimages Corporation.

Numbers provide a convenient and useful form in which to code and store data because they can be easily manipulated by computers—sorted, counted, summarized, and analyzed. The discipline of *statistics* provides a body of concepts and tools for doing this, as covered in Chapters 8 and 9.

Quantitative Data Versus Quantitative Variables

The number of people in emergency rooms with flu symptoms and the dollar amount of purchases of cold and flu medicine are examples of *quantitative variables.* Quantitative variables are also things such as age (in years) or income (in dollars)—any variables in which the numbers represent *quantities* of something (as we saw in Chapter 4). For example, 27 could be used to represent "27 years of age," or 31 might represent "31 thousand dollars of annual income." You can do arithmetic, such as division, on quantitative variables.

Quantitative variables, however, are not the only form of quantitative data. *Categorical variables* can also be recorded as numbers, but the numbers in this case represent *categories* (again, as we saw in Chapter 4). For example, we can record someone's gender as 1 = *male* or 2 = *female.* Or we can record someone's happiness as 1 = *very happy*, 2 = *somewhat happy*, or 3 = *not happy.* Or we can record the region of the country that someone lives in as 1 = *Northeast*, 2 = *Midwest*, 3 = *South*, or 4 = *West.*

Importantly, categorical variables are also a type of quantitative data, because we can use them to sort, count, summarize, and analyze. Indeed, a large body of statistical methods and literature deals with how to analyze categorical variables (Agresti, 2007).

Quantitative Versus Qualitative Research

Quantitative research generally refers to any research involving the statistical analysis of quantitative data—including both quantitative and categorical variables. Quantitative research can be as simple as counting the number of people in an emergency room, or it can involve sophisticated statistical models that examine complex relationships between many different variables.

As explained in Chapter 3, *qualitative research* relies on language, texts, visual images, and other nonnumerical data. Instead of relying on statistical tools to summarize or analyze data, qualitative researchers use various forms of interpretation. But it is also important to recall, from Chapter 3, that there are many areas of overlap—there are qualitative elements in quantitative research, and there is quantification in qualitative research (e.g., as in content analysis). Moreover, many social and policy researchers these days combine both quantitative and qualitative approaches—or *mixed methods*—in their research.

Forms of Quantitative Data

Quantitative data come in various forms or structures. Those who produce data themselves, through surveys or experiments, tend to think of these forms or structures as *research designs*, since as researchers, they *design* the form or structure of the data to suit the context and their research question. But those who use secondary data often think of these more as data *forms* or data *structures* and use the term *research design* instead to refer to what they do, analytically, with the data.

The various forms that quantitative data can take depend both on the level of aggregation (shown in Table 6.1, going across the columns) and on the time dimension (shown in Table 6.1, going down the rows). We will shortly describe both of these distinctions, and the various forms quantitative data can take, in further detail. Real-world examples of these forms of data will appear a bit later in the chapter.

Micro, Aggregate, and Multilevel Data

The term **microdata** refers to data at its most basic level of observation—or *unit of analysis*. For example, student test scores are naturally measured at the level of each individual student. A smaller unit of analysis is not really meaningful. And if one wants to measure student test scores at the level of classrooms or schools, the scores must be aggregated (as discussed shortly). Thus, having a set of scores for individual students would constitute microdata.

But, as suggested, data are often aggregated up to a variety of higher levels, such as classrooms, schools, or districts. Data can be aggregated using a variety of statistical techniques, such as by calculating a mean score for a school, a median score, or the percentage of students in the school who pass a given threshold on the test. The term **aggregate data** refers to data that are summarized at some higher unit of analysis, whether geographic,

Education data can be analyzed at various levels.

Source: © 2009 Jupiterimages Corporation.

Table 6.1   Forms of Data

Time Dimension	Level of Aggregation			
	Microdata	Aggregated (or Ecological) Data	Single Measure (or Completely Aggregated) Data	Multilevel (or Hierarchical) Data
Cross section	Cross-sectional microdata	Cross-sectional data on aggregate units (such as states)	A statistic on one unit (such as a country) at one point in time	Multilevel cross section
Before-after (paired samples)	Before-after microdata	Before-after data on aggregate units	Before-after comparison of one unit	Multilevel before-after data
Panel data (repeated measures or cohort studies)	Panel microdata	Panel aggregate data	Time series	Hierarchical panel data
Pooled cross sections	Pooled cross sections of microdata			Multilevel pooled cross sections

administrative, or some other way of combining or summarizing the microdata. Aggregate data are also referred to in public health and some other fields as ecological data.

Data may be completely aggregated so that there is essentially only a *single* measure—such as the percentage of all students in a country meeting some national standard. Of course, we might find data that are comparable even cross-nationally, so that countries become the unit of analysis. But we may only be interested in studying trends in one country, or the data (such as scores on a national test) may be unique to that country. Alternatively, data can also be intrinsically only one number, such as the U.S. Treasury bill interest rate. There are no separate U.S. T-bill rates for different states or individuals.

Figure 6.1 diagrams the distinction between microdata, aggregated data, and single-measure data.

Data may also combine different levels—so called multilevel (or hierarchical) data. For example, a set of data with scores for individual students could also include some school-level variables, such as whether the school is public or private. Even the average performance of the class or school, an aggregate measure, can become a contextual variable in a multilevel analysis. Looking at Figure 6.1, multilevel analysis can be thought of as drawing connections between variables across levels (such as from a classroom average to an individual test score). Multilevel data are increasingly used in many fields, including education, public health, and criminal justice (Luke, 2004).

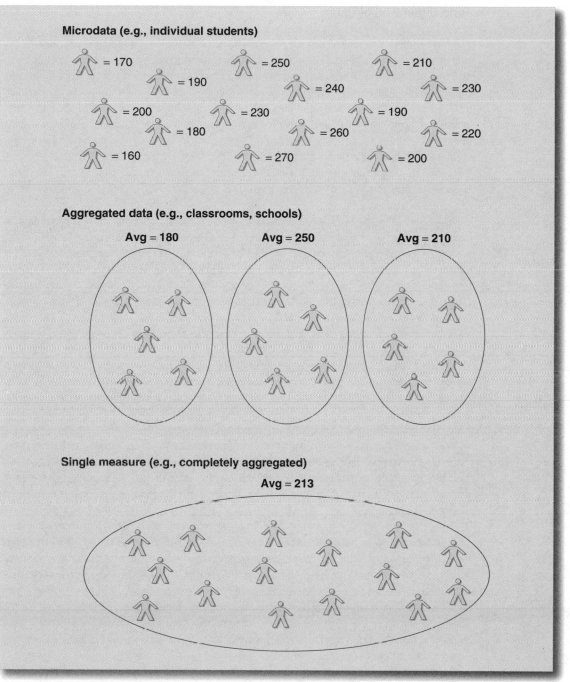

Figure 6.1   Micro and Aggregate Data

Time Dimension of Data

The form of data also reflects the time dimension of data. Many data are **cross-sectional**—they contain measurements taken at a single point in time, such as the test scores of students in a particular year. Surveys are often cross-sectional, a snapshot of public opinion or behavior during one period of time. The Eurobarometer, for example, captures public opinion in the European Union (EU) countries based on a sample of about 30,000 people. Although the Standard Eurobarometer is conducted twice each year, the sample for each survey is still a new cross section of people living in the EU.

In contrast, **longitudinal data** are gathered over time. There are many different types of longitudinal data. For example, we can simply track and compare individuals at two points in time, say, before and after participating in a job training program. This type of longitudinal data is sometimes referred to as *paired-sample* data.

Alternately, there can be *repeated measures* on the same individuals over time—or **panel data**. In health research, this form of data is often referred to as a **prospective cohort**. The Panel Study of Income Dynamics (PSID), for example, has tracked a nationally representative sample of 9,000 U.S. families over time since 1968, with the same families interviewed in each wave of the study. Other important panel studies include the National Educational Longitudinal Study (NELS), the National Longitudinal Survey of Youth (NLSY), the Early Childhood Longitudinal Program (ECLP), the European Community Household Panel (ECHP), and the Framingham Heart Study. Large, long-term panel studies such as these—involving tracking and reinterviewing the same people or households over many years—are very complex, expensive projects to undertake.

In panel data, some variables may be measured repeatedly. For example, blood pressure is measured every 2 years in the Framingham Heart Study, a well-known prospective cohort study, which has followed more than 5,000 men and women from Framingham, Massachusetts, and their descendents since 1948. However, other variables may be long-term outcomes that can only occur once, after some time has elapsed, such as death from heart disease.

The form the data take should be distinguished from how they are analyzed. Some studies make use of time variation in repeated measures, while others do not. Other studies only use longitudinal data to obtain long-term outcomes and do not use the time dimension analytically. The term *repeated measures* is more often used with the former, while the term *cohort study* is more often used with the latter.

Panel data, however, can also be created from aggregated results of surveys or other secondary sources. For example, panel data could consist of repeated measures of trust in European institutions for the member states of the EU, as measured by the Eurobarometer. The natural unit of analysis for trust is still the individual citizen, and the Eurobarometer in microdata form remains cross-sectional. But if the survey results are aggregated to the country level, a panel data set can be created in which trust levels for each country are measured repeatedly over many time periods. In the United States, panel data on the 50 states can be created readily from a wide variety of secondary data reported at the state level over time, such as health indicators, crime rates, economic activity, government expenditures, and so on.

Researchers sometimes combine microdata cross sections from different time periods to form what are known as **pooled cross sections**. Instead of having repeated measures on one group of people, each year (or each period) there is a fresh cross section of people. Many studies pool micro-data cross sections. For example, studies examining the effect of cigarette taxes on individuals' tobacco consumption have used the National Health Interview Survey (NHIS), a very large cross-sectional survey conducted every year in the United States since 1957. The NHIS does not follow the same individuals over time but rather provides a large, representative cross section of individuals each year.

Completely aggregated, or single-measure, data are often longitudinal. One could examine the world population, the world prevalence of AIDS, or the U.S. unemployment rate over time, for example. These are referred to as aggregate **time series** or *historical* data. Demography, macroeconomics, and financial economics often make use of aggregate time-series data. Such studies focus primarily on trends over time and not cross-sectional variation.

Figure 6.2 diagrams the distinction between panel data, pooled cross sections, and time series.

Where Do Quantitative Data Come From?

As the opening example of New York City's health department shows, quantitative data can come from many sources and methods—administrative record-keeping systems, commercial transactions (such as pharmacy purchases), sample surveys, and so on. Indeed, a creative researcher or policy analyst can often find or construct quantitative data in new and surprising ways. For example, the rapid expansion of Web traffic and related transactions has generated a whole new body of data about people's online behavior. Creative researchers also combine and link data from different sources.

For the remainder of this chapter, we will review some major sources of quantitative data—beginning with administrative record data, a natural first place to look for data on many programs and services.

Administrative Records

Administrative records gathered by various government agencies, private firms, and nonprofit organizations in the process of planning and managing programs or services provide an important source of quantitative data for research and policy analysis. These include the following:

- Financial records of income and expenditures
- Employee records
- Records of the production of outputs of goods and services
- Records kept on patients, students, or other clients
- Performance indicators

Typically, administrative data are stored in a management information system (or MIS)—a computer program and related databases that help staff enter, store, sort, and retrieve program data for management or accounting purposes. But many administrative records still reside in paper files.

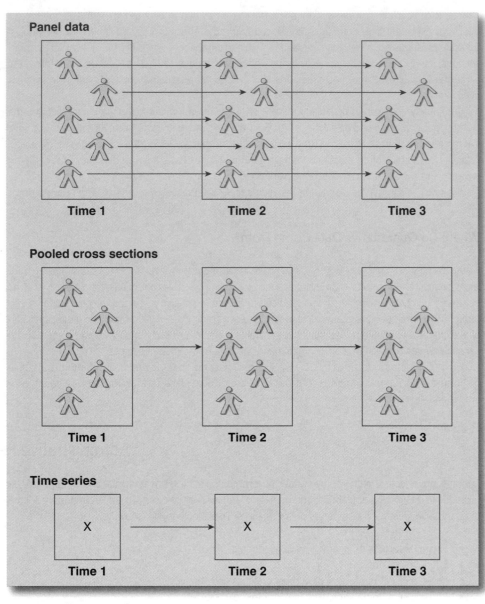

Figure 6.2   Different Forms of Longitudinal Data

Adapting Administrative Data for Research

Although there exist a great deal of administrative data, it is not always easy to adapt these data to research and statistical analysis for several reasons. First, some public and private organizations still rely on paper records. For example, in one study of housing court cases, the motions and outcomes of the eviction cases that were the focus of the study could only be determined by an examination of the paper court records (Seron, Van Ryzin, & Frankel, 2001). Paper records are still the primary form of data storage for much medical care in the United States and other countries (although there is a move now to digitize medical records). To be suitable for quantitative analysis, paper records must be retrieved, coded, and key-punched into a statistical database—a laborious task.

Another potential problem is that the fields, or variables, in the administrative data may need to be cleaned, coded, or reformatted. Even if the data are stored in electronic form, some fields may be in *string* or *alphanumeric* format, and statistical software does not read or handle such nonnumeric data easily. String-formatted data often get entered inconsistently by administrative staff. For example, the type of illness may be entered as "flu," "FLU," "influenza," and so on. Spelling mistakes such as "Influensa" cause further difficulties, although progress is being made with software that finds similar but not identical words. These fields may need to be cleaned and then coded into consistent numeric values, for example, "23" as a code for influenza.

Also, administrative records tend mostly to be organized as **relational databases**, database structures that are composed of various tables of information, such as one for suppliers and another for products, that are linked and work together—as illustrated in Figure 6.3 for a typical business organization.

Statistical software, in contrast, generally requires a **flat-file** layout—a simple two-dimensional layout of rows and columns. In the flat-file format used for cross-sectional statistical data, the rows

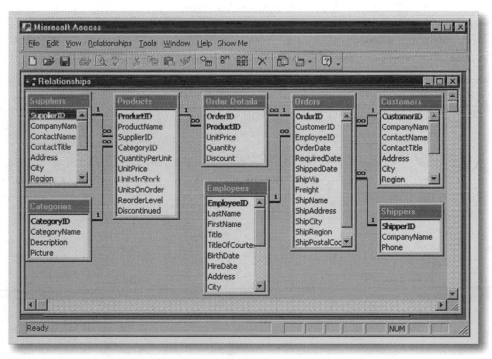

Figure 6.3   A Relational Database for Administrative Data

represent individuals—the *unit of analysis*—and the columns represent *variables*. Figure 6.4 shows a simple example, with individual respondents (the unit of analysis) represented in each row and the variables represented in the columns. Often, the trick for using administrative data in research and analysis lies in converting the data into this flat-file form.

Some more sophisticated forms of data analysis, such as panel data and multilevel data, combine various units of analysis. Relational databases often have all the information necessary for such analyses, but again, this information may not be in the form required by the software.

Cleaning and reformatting administrative data for research is time-consuming and labor intensive, often far more time-consuming than the actual statistical analysis itself.

Vital Statistics, Crime Reports, and Unemployment Claims

Still, some administrative records—such as *vital statistics*—get widely used for demographic and policy research. Health departments require the recording of births and deaths on standardized forms, and these data are gathered and made available to help understand a great deal about the growth and survival of populations.

Another example of administrative record data often used in research are crime reports—particularly the FBI's system of *Uniform Crime Reports*. Crimes get reported by victims and others to local law enforcement agencies, which use this information for their own administrative and strategic purposes. But since 1929, the FBI has encouraged localities to report crimes in a uniform manner to a central system so that these data can be tracked, compared, and analyzed for the United States as a whole.

In the economic domain, the filing of *unemployment claims*—which are administrative records compiled by state unemployment agencies—are closely watched by economists as a measure of the strength or weakness of the labor market.

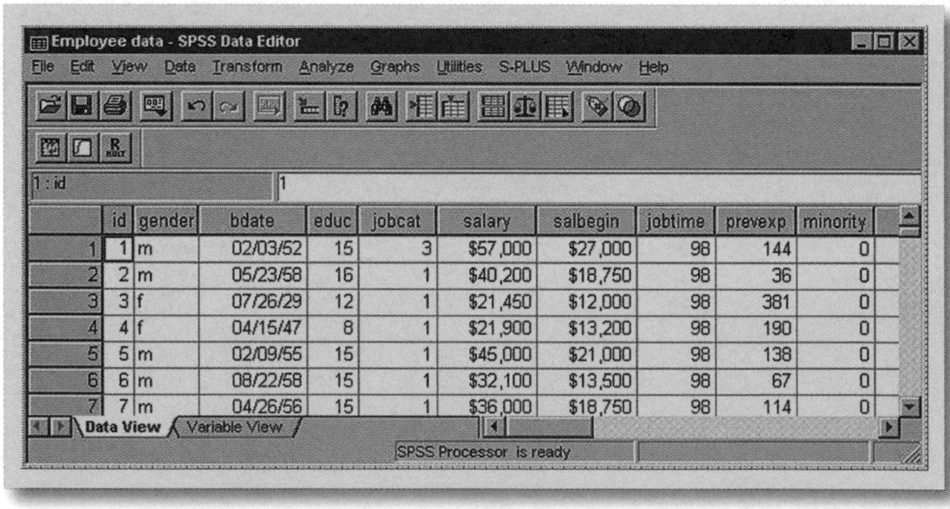

Figure 6.4   Flat-File Database for Statistical Analysis

As more and more administrative data are computerized, and both researchers and administrators become technologically and statistically savvy, administrative data will be relied on increasingly for research and analysis. Insurance claims data, Social Security records, and school records are just a few additional examples.

Ethics of Administrative Record Data

Researchers seeking to use private data from individuals that were obtained for administrative purposes unrelated to research—and sometimes provided by individuals to the government because of a legal obligation or the need to obtain benefits—face important ethical issues. Such data were not collected with informed consent and often contain private information. The government, driven by the public, carefully regulates the use of such records for research.

The Health Insurance Portability and Accountability Act (HIPAA), for example, provides strict regulation on the use and sharing of health insurance and health care records to protect people's privacy. Researchers and policy analysts seeking to obtain such records for statistical analysis must follow strict HIPAA rules and regulations. For more information, see the Web page of the Office of Civil Rights within the U.S. Department of Health and Human Services (www.hhs.gov/ocr/privacy).

A key ethical obligation in research using administrative data is that they be **nonidentifiable**—in other words, the data should not contain information that allows the researcher to figure out the identity of any particular individual. So before being received by a researcher, the data must be stripped of names, Social Security numbers, addresses, or any other information that clearly identifies who an individual is. More general information, such as someone's earnings, occupation, or the city he or she lives in, can be released while still preserving anonymity. However, that information is also limited: It must be impossible for anyone to combine all the variables (such as work history and city and education, etc.) to figure out who someone is. Small area geographic detail, such a postal zip code, is often restricted for this reason.

Researchers often want to match records across confidential data sources. For example, by combining Medicare (U.S. government health insurance for the elderly), Social Security, cancer registry, and death certificate information, researchers can learn about a variety of questions. Iezzoni describes how many different administrative data sets can be combined to learn about the effects of disability (Iezzoni, 2002). For example, by combining all forms of health care paid for by Medicare over several years and linking them to government disability records, much can be learned about the evolution over time of a disability. Obviously, to combine such information requires Social Security numbers and names. To maintain confidentiality, the government will allow researchers to apply to have the government match the data and release them, stripped of all personal identifiers.

With the growth in electronic data and the growing ease of copying and transmitting them, protecting individuals' privacy is an area of growing concern and importance. There have been scandals in many countries about the loss, release, or theft of private data from governmental agencies and private businesses. However, the increasing availability of data also has the potential for helping us learn what lifestyles are most healthy, what educational practices help students learn, and so on. The tremendous potential value of such data suggests that we should try to find appropriate uses of administrative data, but in ways that still protect individuals' privacy.

Published Data Tables

Agencies often aggregate their microdata and make them available in published tables or downloadable spreadsheets. Table 6.2 shows an example of aggregate state-level data on poverty from the U.S. Census Bureau (2009b). The poverty figures are calculated from survey data on individual households, and so the data on these households—their incomes, composition, and other characteristics captured in the survey—are the microdata. Published aggregate data tables are not as detailed as the microdata, but they are easily available, more manageable to work with, and often quite sufficient to address some research questions (such as aggregate panel studies).

Privacy and other concerns can prevent microdata from being made publicly available. But the same data aggregated to the institutional or geographic level—by averaging or reporting percentages in data tables—can be released much more freely and widely.

Where to Find Published Tables

Tables of aggregate data are increasingly available on the Internet from governments and other institutions. The U.S. Census Bureau provides a great deal of aggregate data on states, counties, and cities in the United States, in the *Statistical Abstract of the United States*, the *State and Metropolitan Area Data Book*, and the *County and City Data Book* (available online from the U.S. Census Bureau), as do many other federal statistical agencies (see, e.g., FedStats.gov). The United Nations' Statistics Division, the World Bank, the European Commission's Eurostat, the Organization of Economic Cooperation and Development (OECD), and numerous other international, governmental, and nongovernmental agencies make aggregate data available for public use.

When using aggregate data, it becomes very important to read the notes and documentation of the data carefully so that you understand the variables, the original microdata sources used to construct the variables, the years represented by the data, and any assumptions or calculations that were made in compiling the data. It is also important to carefully and fully cite where and when you downloaded or otherwise obtained your aggregate data (as published data can be updated or corrected over time).

Published Time-Series and Panel Data

Aggregate time series are frequently published online and in printed reports. Table 6.3 shows a time series of both the number and rate of homicides as recorded by the FBI's *Uniform Crime Reports* (as reported in the 2009 *Statistical Abstract*, the U.S. Census Bureau, 2009c). In the layout of longitudinal data such as these, typically, the rows—the unit of analysis—are the time periods (years, quarters, months), and the columns are the variables. Notice that for purposes of publication, the time series is condensed in the early years by presenting homicides only every 5 years (1980, 1985, 1990) instead of annually. If we were interested in homicides for the in-between years, we would need to find another published source for these FBI data. (In fact, the Bureau of Justice Statistics provides online tools for accessing more detailed time-series data on homicides and other crimes in the United States.)

Published data tables can report aggregate time series separately by cities, states, or other, smaller units of aggregation. This results in a form of aggregate panel data. Table 6.2, which shows poverty

Table 6.2   Aggregate Data Table From the U.S. Census Bureau

Table 687. **Individuals and Families Below Poverty Level—Number and Rate by State: 2000 and 2006**

[In thousands (33,311 represents 33,311,000), except as indicated. Represents number and percent below poverty in the past 12 months. The American Community Survey universe includes the household population and the population living in institutions, college dormitories, and other group quarters. Poverty status was determined for all people except institutionalized people, people in military group quarters, people in college dormitories, and unrelated individuals under 15 years old. These groups were excluded from the numerator and denominator when calculating poverty rates. Based on a sample and subject to sampling variability; see Appendix III]

State	Number Below Poverty Level (1,000)				Percent Below Poverty Level			
	Individuals		Families		Individuals		Families	
	2000	2006	2000	2006	2000	2006	2000	2006
United States	33,331	38,757	6,615	7,283	12.2	13.3	9.3	9.8
Alabama	672	742	146	154	15.6	16.6	12.4	12.6
Alaska	55	71	11	13	9.1	10.9	6.8	8.2
Arizona	780	857	150	148	15.6	14.2	11.6	10.1
Arkansas	439	471	96	99	17.0	17.3	13.0	13.1
California	4,520	4,690	832	809	13.7	13.1	10.7	9.7
Colorado	363	556	64	101	8.7	12.0	5.7	8.4
Connecticut	254	280	51	52	7.7	8.3	5.8	5.9
Delaware	70	92	14	16	9.3	11.1	6.7	7.6
District of Columbia	94	108	17	18	17.5	19.6	15.4	16.3
Florida	1,987	2,227	387	417	12.8	12.6	9.3	9.0
Georgia	999	1,334	206	254	12.6	14.7	10.0	11.1
Hawaii	103	116	19	21	8.8	9.3	6.8	7.1
Idaho	144	180	26	36	11.4	12.6	7.7	9.3
Illinois	1,335	1,539	262	286	11.1	12.3	8.6	9.1
Indiana	592	778	113	149	10.1	12.7	7.1	9.0
Iowa	281	316	53	58	10.0	11.0	7.0	7.3

Source: U.S. Census Bureau (2009b, Table 687).

Table 6.3   Time Series Data From the FBI *Uniform Crime Reports*

Table 301. **Homicide Trends: 1980 to 2005**

[Not all agencies which report offense information to the FBI also submit supplemental data on homicides. To account for the total number of homicide victims, the data was weighted to match national and state estimates prepared by the FBI; hence, detail may not equal total. For more information on the methodology, go to <http://www.ojp.usdoj.gov/bjs/homicide/homtrrid.htm#contents>]

Year	Number of Victims						Rate[1]					
	Total	Male	Female	White	Black	Other	Total	Male	Female	White	Black	Other
1980	23,040	17,788	5,232	12,275	9,767	327	10.2	16.2	4.5	6.3	37.7	5.7
1985	18,976	14,079	4,880	10,590	7,891	399	8.0	12.2	4.0	5.2	27.6	5.5
1990	23,438	18,304	5,115	11,279	11,488	400	9.4	15.0	4.0	5.4	37.6	4.2
1993	24,526	18,937	5,550	11,278	12,435	601	9.5	15.0	4.2	5.3	38.7	5.5
1994	25,326	18,294	5,007	10,773	11,856	526	9.0	14.4	3.8	5.0	36.4	4.6
1995	21,606	16,552	5,022	10,376	10,444	581	8.2	12.9	3.7	4.8	31.6	4.9
1996	19,645	15,153	4,469	9,483	9,476	512	7.4	11.7	3.3	4.3	28.3	4.1
1997	18,208	14,057	4,125	8,620	8,842	524	6.8	10.7	3.0	3.9	26.0	4.1
1998	16,974	12,753	4,139	8,389	7,951	393	6.3	9.7	3.0	3.8	23.0	2.9
1999	15,522	11,704	3,800	7,777	7,139	458	5.7	8.8	2.7	3.5	20.5	3.3
2000	15,586	11,818	3,733	7,560	7,425	399	5.5	8.6	2.6	3.3	20.5	2.7
2001	16,037	12,232	3,775	7,884	7,522	424	5.6	8.8	2.6	3.4	20.4	2.8
2002	16,204	12,410	3,764	7,784	7,758	437	5.6	8.8	2.6	3.3	20.8	2.7
2003	16,582	12,804	3,693	7,932	7,893	468	5.7	9.0	2.5	3.4	20.9	2.8
2004	16,137	12,556	3,543	7,944	7,562	417	5.5	8.7	2.4	3.3	19.7	2.4
2005	16,692	13,122	3,545	8,017	7,999	437	5.5	9.0	2.3	3.3	20.6	2.5

[1]Rate is per 100,000 inhabitants.

Source: U.S. Census Bureau (2009c, Table 301).

rates of all 50 U.S. states in 2000 and 2006, provides a basic example—and typically, aggregate panel data of this kind are available for many years. Such aggregated panel data can be analyzed with many valuable statistical techniques to answer important policy questions regarding how outcomes change over time.

Public Use Microdata

As we've said, *microdata* refers to individual-level data on people, households, or firms. **Public use microdata** refers to individual-level data collected and made available to the public. That availability is increasingly widespread. Typically, public use microdata contain information about individual respondents to large social surveys, who can number in the tens of thousands. These surveys are conducted by governmental and nongovernmental organizations. For example, the U.S. Current Population Survey (CPS)—which is publicly available from the Web site of the U.S. Bureau of Labor Statistics—contains data from 60,000 households each month. The CPS can be readily downloaded and used by various researchers and policy analysts (e.g., using the DataFerrett software available at TheDataWeb.org).

Secondary Analysis of Public Use Data: A New Model of Research?

In an important sense, social and policy research are moving increasingly in the direction of relying on these public use microdata sets collected by large, sophisticated statistical agencies and research organizations (Kiecolt & Nathan, 1985). In part, this is because of the growing cost and complexity of gathering social, health, and economic data from individuals and organizations. It also reflects the rapidly expanding ability to transmit and share data and results over the Internet. Even a cursory review of the contents of any major social or policy research journal will convince you of how widespread this model of doing research has become.

Know the Major Surveys in Your Field

Whether you are a practitioner, policy analyst, or researcher, you should become familiar with the major surveys in your field. These surveys often provide much of the fact base for the field as well as being the primary source of information on emerging trends or policy successes and failures. Table 6.4 provides a number of very interesting and important sources of public use microdata in various fields. We encourage you to look over this table and to begin to get familiar with the surveys in your field of interest or practice.

Governments and nongovernmental organizations around the world are increasingly moving in the direction of making their microdata available for public use. Table 6.4 is far from complete, and many other useful surveys exist. More details about many of the surveys, including their strengths and weaknesses, can be found in Kramer, Finegold, and Kuehn (2008).

Some countries collect all their major surveys under one umbrella organization, such as Statistics Canada. Other countries, such as the United States, rely on various statistical agencies representing different

Table 6.4   Selected Major Surveys by Policy Area

Survey Name	Purpose	Sponsor and History	Method	Data Access
Health				
National Health Interview Survey (NHIS)	To assess health status and behaviors, including use of health care	National Center for Health Statistics (NCHS). Began in 1957	Household interview survey of about 35,000 households annually	Public use microdata are available to download from the NCHS
National Health and Nutrition Examination Survey (NHANES)	To measure health and nutritional status, based on physical examinations and laboratory tests	National Center for Health Statistics (NCHS). Began in 1959	Household interview, followed by a mobile examination center. About 9,000 individuals annually	Public use microdata are available to download from the NCHS. Limited access to some parts of the data because of confidentiality
National Health Care Surveys (NHCS)	A family of surveys to track characteristics and practices of various health care provider organizations	National Center for Health Statistics (NCHS). Began in 1973	Organization surveys using various probability sampling methods, depending on the type of organization being surveyed	Public use microdata are available to download from the NCHS
Behavioral Risk Factor Surveillance System (BRFSS)	To understand health behaviors and risks, such as diet, smoking, exercise, and many more	Conducted by state health agencies, under guidance from the Centers for Disease Control and Prevention (CDC). Began in 1984	Telephone interview survey of about 350,000 individuals annually	CDC's Web Enabled Analysis Tool (WEAT) provides online analysis. Public use microdata are available to download
Youth Risk Behavior Survey (YRBS)	To understand health behaviors and risks of the nation's youth	Conducted by the CDC. State and local health agencies conduct their own YRBSs, with guidance from the CDC. Began in 1991	Group-administered survey of a multistage random sample of schools. About 15,000 ninth through twelfth graders surveyed nationally. There are also about 40 state and 20 local YRBSs	CDC's Youth Online provides online data access tools. Public use microdata are available to download

Survey Name	Purpose	Sponsor and History	Method	Data Access
Health				
Medical Expenditure Panel Survey (MEPS)	To learn about U.S. health care use, costs, financing, and health insurance coverage	Conducted by the U.S. Department of Health and Human Services. Agency for Health Research and Quality (AHRQ) annually since 1996. Earlier versions started in 1977	The household component is a probability sample with 2-year panels and follow-up with health care providers. The insurance component is a probability sample of employers	The household component is available for download as public use microdata. The insurance component microdata are not available as public use data sets. All data are available in various aggregate tables. MEPSnet query tool can be used as both to generate statistics
Education				
National Assessment of Educational Progress (NAEP)	To assess what students know and can do in various academic subject areas. Known as "The Nation's Report Card"	U.S. Department of Education, National Center for Educational Statistics (NCES). Began in 1964 (first national assessment in 1969)	School-based, group-administered assessment of a multistage random sample of public and private school students in the United States in grades four, eight, and twelve. About 700,000 students every 2 years.	NAEP Data Explorer provides online data analysis. Public use microdata are available to download
National Educational Longitudinal Study (NELS)	To study policy-relevant educational processes and outcomes by following a sample of students over time	U.S. Department of Education, NCES. Began in 1988	Panel study of a random sample of eighth graders in 1988 who are followed and surveyed every 2 years.	NCES Data Analysis System provides online data analysis. Public use microdata are available to download

Table 6.4 (Continued)

Survey Name	Purpose	Sponsor and History	Method	Data Access
Education				
National Household Education Survey (NHES)	To describe educational experiences in the United States, including adult education, early childhood education, and others	U.S. Department of Education, NCES. Began in 1991	Some surveys are conducted repeatedly, while others are one-time survey of topics of interest	Public use microdata are available for download
National Assessment of Adult Literacy (NAAL)	To describe English literacy of Americans 16 and older	U.S. Department of Education, NCES. 2003 survey designed to be comparable with 1992 survey	Probability sample of both household and prison populations	Public use microdata are not yet available
Labor and employment				
Current Population Survey (CPS)	To describe employment, earnings, and other labor outcomes in the United States	Joint effort of the U.S. Census Bureau and the U.S. Bureau of Labor Statistics (BLS). Begun in 1948	Probability sample of households	Public use microdata and aggregate tables are available for download
Panel Study of Income Dynamics (PSID)	To describe the dynamics of demographic and economic behavior in the United States	Institute for Social Research at the University of Michigan, under contract to various U.S. government agencies, currently the National Science Foundation (NSF). Begun in 1968. Annual until 1997 and biennial thereafter	Panel study, following the same families. Probability sample. Oversample of low-income families	Data center tool enables creation of customized extracts. Entire public use microdata may also be downloaded

Survey Name	Purpose	Sponsor and History	Method	Data Access
Labor and employment				
National Longitudinal Surveys, including the National Longitudinal Surveys of Youth 79 (NLSY 79) and 97 (NLSY 97)	To gather labor market and related information over extended periods of time and across generations. NLSY79 surveyed youth in 1979. NLSY 97 surveyed youth in 1997. Both surveys continue through the present. NLSY79 Children and Young Adults surveys the biological children of women in NLSY79	U.S. Census Bureau, U.S. BLS	Long-term panel surveys	Public use microdata available for download
Criminal justice, housing, public programs, and other policy areas				
National Crime Victimization Survey (NCVS)	To estimate the rate of victimization from various types of crime, including unreported crime	U.S. Department of Justice, Bureau of Justice Statistics. Began in 1973 (redesigned in 1992)	Household interview surveys; multistage probability sample of 76,000 households representing 135,000 individuals	National Archive of Criminal Justice Data (at University of Michigan) provides online data analysis. Public use microdata are available to download
American Housing Survey (AHS)	To assess the condition and cost of the nation's housing units and the characteristics of the occupying households	U.S. Bureau of the Census, with support from the Department of Housing and Urban Development	Household interview and observation survey. Random sample of about 55,300 housing units every 2 years	U.S. Census Bureau AHS Web page provides data tables. Public use microdata are available to download

Table 6.4 (Continued)

Survey Name	Purpose	Sponsor and History	Method	Data Access
Criminal justice, housing, public programs, and other policy areas				
Health and Retirement Survey (HRS)	To understand employment, income, wealth, and health of Americans before and after retirement and how all of these relate to one another	Institute for Social Research at the University of Michigan, under contract to the National Institute on Aging	In-person, very in-depth panel survey conducted every 2 years	Public use microdata available for download. Sensitive data available through application procedure
Survey of Income and Program Participation (SIPP)	To understand income and public program participation in the United States to evaluate the effectiveness of government programs	U.S. Census Bureau. Begun in 1984	2½-year-long panels	DataFerrett application allows the creation of customized data sets and analyses. Full public use data set may be downloaded
Fragile Families and Child Wellbeing Study	To understand the experiences of families at greater risk of breaking up and living in poverty	Shriver National Institute of Child and Human Development, started in 2007	Surveys of parents and in-home assessments	Public use microdata area available for download
Consumer Expenditure Survey (CES)	To provide information on the buying habits of Americans and support the price index calculations	U.S. Census Bureau, U.S. BLS	Probability sample of households. Both in-person interview and expenditure diary collection	Public use microdata and aggregate tables available for download
American Community Survey (ACS)	To provide frequent and geographically detailed demographic information	U.S. Census Bureau. Replaced the long form of the Decennial Census	Based on the Census. Monthly surveys combined to make representative annual survey	Public use microdata subsamples and specifically chosen data tables are available using the DataFerrett

Survey Name	Purpose	Sponsor and History	Method	Data Access
Social and political attitudes (United States)				
General Social Survey (GSS)	To track a wide range of attitudes and behaviors of U.S. adults in many areas of life, such as family, work, community, religion, government, current affairs, and more	National Opinion Research Corporation (NORC) at the University of Chicago, with support from the NSF. Began in 1972	Household interview survey of a multistage random sample of about 4,000 U.S. adults every 2 years	GSS Nesstar at NORC.org provides online data analysis. Public use microdata are available to download
American National Election Studies (ANES)	To measure political attitudes and voting behaviors of the population, before and after U.S. national elections	The University of Michigan and Stanford University, with support from the NSF. Began in 1948 by the University of Michigan. Received NSF support in 1977	Household interview survey of a multistage random sample of about 2,000 individuals every 2 years (during national elections). Interviews conducted with respondents both before and after the election	The ANES Guide to Public Opinion and Electoral Behavior provides data tables online. Public use microdata are available to download. University of California, Berkeley's Survey Documentation and Analysis (SDA) project provides online data analysis
International and comparative surveys				
Eurobarometer	To monitor the evolution of public opinion in the member and candidate states of the EU	European Commission (EC), Public Opinion Section. Began in 1973	Standard Eurobarometer: In-person interviews of about 1,000 individuals per country, conducted twice each year. Flash Eurobarometer: Telephone interviews of a probability sample in each country, with several surveys conducted each year	Summary data tables (PDFs) available on the EC Public Opinion Web site. Public use microdata are available to download from the German Social Science Infrastructure Service (GESIS)

Table 6.4 *(Continued)*

Survey Name	Purpose	Sponsor and History	Method	Data Access
International and comparative surveys				
World Values Survey (WVS)	To study changing social and political values in countries all over the world	A network of social scientists with headquarters in Stockholm, Sweden. Originated at the University of Michigan. Locally funded by participating countries	Each of the over 50 participating countries uses its own method, but all are random samples of the general population. About 1,000 to 2,000 individuals per country	WVS provides an online data analysis tool. Public use microdata are available to download
International Social Survey Program (ISSP)	To coordinate research goals of preexisting social surveys so that they provide a cross-national perspective	A self-funding association of member institutions, with the current secretariat in Tel Aviv, Israel. Began in 1982	Each of the 43 participating countries uses its own method, but all are random samples of the general population. About 1,000 to 2,000 individuals per country	GESIS Data Archive, ZACAT online data analysis tool. Public use microdata are available to download
European Social Survey (ESS)	To study social attitudes and values across European countries	Consortium of European research institutes, currently coordinated by the City University, London, with financial support from the European Science Foundation	Participating countries agree to survey a probability sample of the general population 15+ years of age. About 1,500 individuals in each of over 30 countries every 2 years. Began in 2002	ESS Nesstar provides online data analysis. Public use microdata are available to download
Demographic and Health Surveys (DHS)	Provides technical assistance to more than 200 surveys in 75 countries to provide data on fertility, family planning and maternal and child health	U.S. Agency for International Development (USAID) and other donors. Started in 1984	Representative samples. Methods vary by country	Microdata from most participating countries available for download with registration. Specialized STATcomplier and STATmapper allow creation of multicountry data tables

Survey Name	Purpose	Sponsor and History	Method	Data Access
International and comparative surveys				
Living Standards Measurement Survey (LSMS)	To support household surveys in many countries in order to learn and improve living standards, including employment, health, education, housing and other areas	World Bank, Development Economics Research Group. Begun in 1980	Generally probability samples of households. Methods vary by country	Some, but not all, surveys have public use microdata available for download with registration. LSMS survey finder tool available to help find appropriate surveys
German Socio-Economic Panel (GSOEP)	To understand a wide range of economic and social phenomena	German Institute for Economic Research. Same families studied since 1984. Eastern Germany included since 1990	Probability panel survey of the same families. All household members followed during family breakups	English language version available through Cornell University. Public use microdata available for download
Luxembourg Income Study (LIS)	To learn about cross-national and longitudinal income and wealth patterns, harmonizing and standardizing data across countries	Originated by Luxembourg government. Currently sponsored by social science research foundations of member countries. Begun in 1983	Representative household surveys in member countries. Data harmonized by LIS	Access to microdata is through a job submission system, accepting programs in SAS, SPSS, or Stata

policy areas to manage their own surveys (see FedStats.gov for a directory). Large consulting firms, working under contract, are often involved in much of the actual work of gathering government survey data.

Accessing and Analyzing Public Use Data

Public use data come in various formats, with many sites providing the data already formatted for the most commonly used statistical programs—IBM® SPSS®, SAS, and Stata—or for spreadsheet programs such as Excel. In some cases, the data may come as an ASCII (or text) file, often with SPSS, SAS, or Stata routines to help the user format and label the data. Without either a preformatted datafile or these formatting routines, it can be a time-consuming task to get the data into a usable format.

Importantly, the data come with a **codebook** and related documentation to help you understand how the data were collected, coded, weighted, and so on. It is very important to read this documentation carefully as you begin using the data for your own analysis.

To facilitate quick, convenient analysis and more widespread access, some government statistical agencies and other organizations have created **online data analysis tools**—allowing users to directly analyze data on the Web. A good example is the National Center for Education Statistics' NAEP Data Explorer (see Figure 6.5), which provides online analysis tools for data from the National Assessment of Educational Progress (NAEP)—the "Nation's Report Card" on educational outcomes.

Data Archives

To facilitate access to public use microdata, various institutions around the world have established data archives. These archives store and document data from various surveys and studies, typically in a consistent format and with technology and procedures to manage public access to the data. Here is a list of some major data archives:

- *Inter-University Consortium for Political and Social Research (ICPSR):* Housed at the University of Michigan, the ICPSR is one of the largest and most established social science data archives in the world. See www.icpsr.umich.edu.
- *German Social Science Infrastructure Service (GESIS):* A part of the Leibniz Institute for the Social Sciences with offices in major German cities, GESIS archives data and documentation from various European and international surveys. See www.gesis.org/en/za/index.htm.
- *Roper Center Public Opinion Archive:* Housed at the University of Connecticut, the Roper Center contains a huge collection of public opinion surveys covering many years (requires membership). See www.ropercenter.uconn.edu.
- *Survey Documentation and Analysis (SDA), University of California, Berkeley:* This site provides online access and analysis tools for a number of major social and political surveys. See http://sda.berkeley.edu.
- *Council of European Social Science Data Archives (CESSDA):* An umbrella organization for social science data archives across Europe. See www.nsd.uib.no/cessda/home.html.
- *UK Data Archive (UKDA):* Housed at the University of Essex, this is the largest social science data archive in the United Kingdom and, interestingly, also archives qualitative social science data. See www.data-archive.ac.uk.

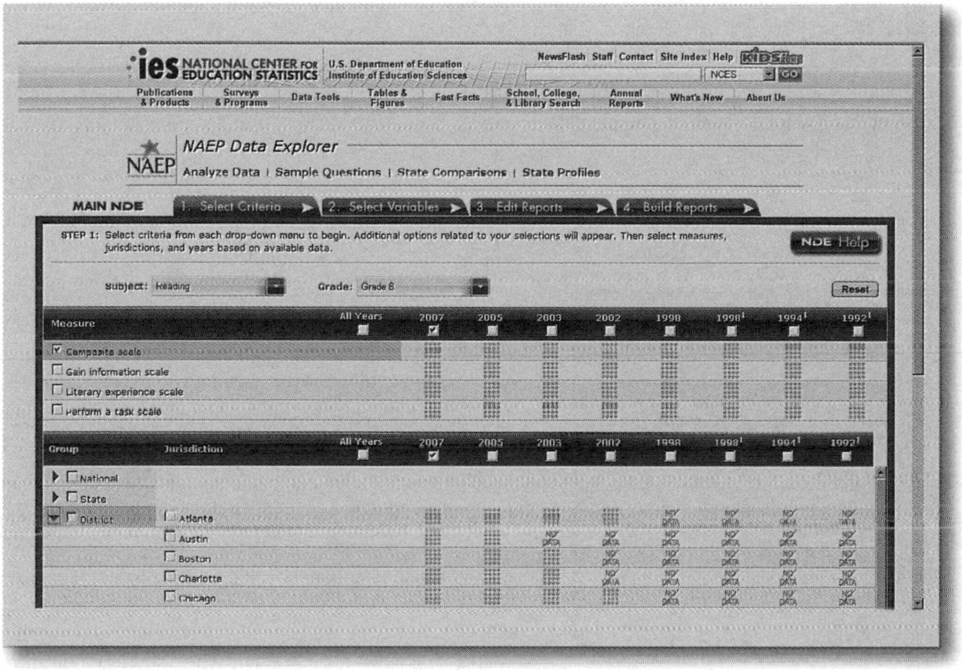

Figure 6.5   Screenshot of the NAEP Data Explorer

Ethics of Public Use Microdata

Public use microdata reveal details about individual survey respondents, and so ethical issues arise in making these data publicly available. Most respondents to such surveys were given initial assurances of privacy and anonymity, yet the surveys capture a great deal of individual-level details that could, potentially, be used to identify individual people or households. For this reason, institutions holding public use microdata do not release much geographic detail and often top-code outlying values for variables such as income and age.

For example, to protect confidentiality, the U.S. Census Bureau releases Public Use Microdata Samples (PUMS) that contain a 1% or 5% random sample of all the forms gathered as part of the decennial U.S. Census or the American Community Survey (which is being carried out regularly and replaces the old Census Long Form as a source of more detailed household characteristics). These random samples contain limited geographic information and other identifiers to help ensure confidentiality.

For researchers who need to know the precise geographic location or other identifying information collected as part of U.S. government surveys, a system of Census Research Data Centers (RDCs) has been established that has secure facilities and strict procedures for working with confidential microdata. (See www.ces.census.gov for more information.)

Linking Data

One way to shape secondary data to fit an information need—and thus to get beyond the problem of being overly driven by the available data—is to link data from various sources. Here are a few ways that this can be done:

- Survey data can be linked with administrative record data (e.g., a health survey can be linked with records of health care use).

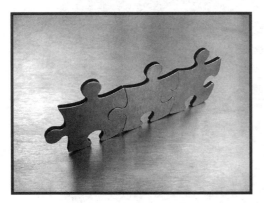

- Survey data can be linked with aggregate data (e.g., a survey of individual households can be linked with data on surrounding community characteristics).
- Linking of data can be done through a geographic information system (GIS), which pinpoints locations of people or events, such as reported crimes and types of land use.
- Quantitative and qualitative data can be linked (e.g., a survey in which researchers followed up on their statistical findings with qualitative focus groups).

Indeed, some of the most interesting and useful research and policy analysis occur when surveys, administrative records, and other sources of data are linked together to produce a broader and more unique set of variables to work with.

Linking data often leads to interesting and useful research.

Source: © 2009 Jupiterimages Corporation.

Some Limitations of Secondary Data

Although secondary data provide a rich and increasingly important resource for research, they have some limitations as well. And, of course, sometimes it is necessary to collect your own, primary data.

Does Data Availability Distort Research?

Some kinds of data are much more available than others. In the United States, for example, individuals older than 65 have government-provided health insurance through Medicare, while those younger than 65 get insurance from a wide variety of other sources, mostly employer-provided plans—and many lack insurance altogether. So it is much more difficult to study health care and health outcomes in the United States for those under 65 years of age. In contrast, because Medicare insurance claims are centralized and available from one source (the government), much more health care research can be—and is—done on the U.S. elderly population. In countries with universal health insurance, however, it is relatively more straightforward to study the health care of all age groups.

This example illustrates that what data are available often determines what study gets done. Some people criticize researchers for being too "data driven"—answering only questions that can be answered with available data, even though those may not be the most important questions. These critics have a point, to be sure. But sometimes, researchers have to take what they can get, and it is arguably better to have the answers to some questions than to none at all. Still the availability of data does mean that some outcomes or topics are much more frequently studied than others.

When to Collect Original Data?

This chapter has stressed the availability and use of existing data—administrative records, aggregate data, and public use microdata—in large part because of the exploding growth and importance of such data in social and policy research. But still, researchers and policy analysts often find that they must collect their own quantitative data for several reasons:

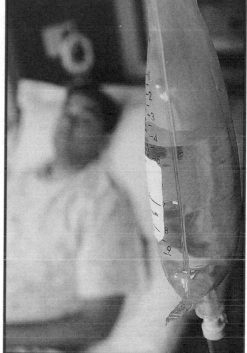

Availability of health insurance claims data shapes health care research.

Source: © 2009 Jupiterimages Corporation.

- Even very large, public use microdata sources often do not provide enough data for small area studies, such as cities or neighborhoods.
- Existing data may not measure the relevant variables of interest—the measures that best meet a specific research objective.
- Existing data may not have the right *combination of variables*, making it difficult to test relationships between variables.
- Existing data may be out of date, conducted too long ago to be useful for present purposes.
- Existing data may not be fully accessible because of privacy and confidentiality concerns, as we have discussed.

The next chapter presents methods of generating your own quantitative data, such as surveys and trained observation.

Conclusion

This chapter has defined quantitative data and introduced you to various sources and methods that provide secondary data for social and policy research. Knowing where data come from or how they are produced matters, even for those who do not do research but rather read it and apply it to public policy and management. Data are the basic material of research, and each source of data has its own advantages and limitations. This chapter has given you a feel for some of the most important sources and forms of data used in contemporary social and policy research. We turn next to the challenge of collecting primary data.

BOX 6.1
Critical Questions to Ask About Secondary Data

- What was the original purpose of the data—why were they collected?
- Are they administrative data, survey data, or some other type of secondary data?
- What form or structure applies to the data? Are they microdata or aggregated? What is the time dimension of the data?
- What variables, or measures, are available in the data? What variables are not available? What kinds of questions can the data help answer?
- Is there an online analysis tool that you can use to produce customized tables or charts from the data?
- Are the microdata available to download for public use, or is their use restricted? In what formats are the data provided?
- Is there a codebook or related documentation of the data? What does the codebook provide in terms of guidelines and technical advice for using the data?

EXERCISES

Secondary Data in the News

6.1. Find a news article about recent results of a national government survey regarding employment, health, education, or other policy area. What is the source of the data for the facts or trends reported in the article? What statistical agency produced the data?

What Form of Data?

6.2. Following are several important sources of secondary data for economic and policy research. For each, identify the form of data it provides: *panel data*, *repeated cross sections*, or *time series*.

   a. The Survey of Income and Program Participation (SIPP)
   b. The Consumer Price Index (CPI)
   c. The Current Population Survey (CPS)

Find a Government Survey

6.3. Pick one of the following policy issues that most interests you:

a. Transportation/commuting patterns

b. How college students pay for their education

c. Food and nutrition habits of the population

d. Demographic characteristics of inmates of state and federal prisons

e. Drug and alcohol use among high school students

f. The victim-offender relationship in violent crimes

g. How countries compare in math and science education

Search the Web and find a large government survey that provides data on this issue. What is the name of the survey, and what agency sponsors it? What specific measures, or variables, does the survey provide for this issue? What kind of analysis of the issue could you do with the data?

Online Data Analysis Tools

6.4. Choose one of the major surveys for policy research from Table 6.4—one that has an online data analysis tool. Locate the online data analysis tool on the survey's Web site, read the relevant instructions, and run an analysis of your choosing. Interpret the results and comment on the usefulness, and limitations, of this kind of online data analysis.

Downloading Microdata

6.5. Choose one of the major surveys for policy research from Table 6.4 and locate its Web site. What options are available for downloading the microdata? What formats do the data come in? Is registration or other permission required to access the data? What available documentation of the data would you also need to download to fully understand and use the microdata?

Objectives: In this chapter, you will learn about collecting primary quantitative data through surveys and observation. You will appreciate the strengths and weaknesses of various survey methods, the steps required in planning and implementing a survey, and the ethical issues involved. And you will be introduced to the method of trained observation, a practical form of gathering data in various public policy and management situations. Knowing about how primary data are collected will help you decide how to collect your own data, should the need arise, as well as give you a better appreciation of the kinds of data that appear in research reports.

Interviewers conduct a telephone survey.

Source: © 2009 Jupiterimages Corporation.

Primary Data Collection

Surveys and Observation

Taking the Nation's Economic Pulse

There was bad economic news in the United States in 2008, a presidential election year. By August, the unemployment rate jumped to 6.1%—a 5-year high—and nonfarm payroll employment was down by some 600,000 jobs from the start of the year (U.S. Department of Labor, 2009). Ominously, consumer sentiment hovered at a 20-year low (Bloomberg Press, 2008), and three out of four U.S. adults believed that the country was heading off on the wrong track (PollingReport.com, 2008). The focus of the battle for the presidency shifted from terrorism and the war in Iraq to the economy.

Our ability to understand the modern economy—and in turn the political and policy responses to its ups and downs—would not be possible without surveys. The monthly unemployment figures are from a government survey of households, and the nonfarm payroll figures come from a different government survey of business establishments. The Consumer Sentiment Index is computed from answers to a telephone survey done by the University of Michigan, and data on public opinion about the direction of the country, presidential approval, and a host of other issues derive from surveys done by various polling organizations.

Surveys form the basis for much of what we know about public health and health care, housing conditions, crime victimization, transportation use, and educational achievement across jurisdictions. And surveys are used by government and nonprofit organizations to understand and manage their

Surveys help us track economic conditions.

Source: ©iStockphoto.com.

employees, assess the needs of the communities they serve, and gather feedback from their clients or customers.

In this chapter, you will be introduced to the various methods and issues involved in survey research—the most important and widely used form of primary data collection in social and policy research. The chapter also introduces another less common but useful method of primary data collection—trained observation.

When Should You Do a Survey?

Surveys involve the collection of information from individuals and organizations by the use of structured questionnaires or interviews. When surveys involve gathering public opinion, they are sometimes called *polls*—but this is just another word for a survey. Surveys often (although not always) focus on a random sample from a much larger population, and so the sampling ideas and issues covered in Chapter 5 are essential in survey research. And the measurement ideas and issues covered in Chapter 4, such as multi-item scales, apply directly to the design and development of questionnaires and related measurement procedures in survey research. But the focus of this section will be on the methods of survey data collection themselves.

Survey research is based on the simple idea that one of the best and most efficient ways to gather data is to ask questions directly of people or organizations. But before doing or commissioning a survey, you should consider the following questions:

Do You Know Enough About the Topic?

To do a survey, you must understand the topic fairly well already to know what specific, structured questions to ask people. But sometimes knowledge of the topic is rudimentary, and thus a more exploratory method—such as focus groups or other qualitative interviewing—should be done first or instead of a more structured survey.

Does the Information Exist Already in Another Source?

The information you seek from a survey may exist already in another source, so asking people or firms to provide it may be unnecessary and a waste of resources and the respondents' time. For example, we would not want to survey big-city police chiefs just to ask them about the local murder rate, the size of their annual budgets, or the number of police officers they employ. These facts are available already from the Bureau of Justice Statistics or publicly available budget documents.

Can People Tell You What You Want to Know?

People or firms may not know the information you want to gather in a survey. For example, if we're interested in how many grams of trans fat people consume in an average day, we might be tempted to ask in a health survey, "Considering all that you eat in a typical day, about how many grams of trans fat do you consume?" But people have only a vague sense of the quantity of food they eat in a day, and they know even less about how much of what they eat is trans fat (or even what trans fat is). To get this kind of detailed information on dietary intake, researchers typically ask people to keep food diaries—or even to save duplicate servings of the food they eat in bags for later laboratory analysis. Surveys are limited to topics that people can knowingly report on.

Will People Provide Truthful Answers?

People or firms may not be willing to provide information, even if they know it. In surveys of employers, we might like to know how many of the firms cheat on their taxes or employ illegal immigrants, but it is unlikely that we will get complete and truthful answers to questions such as these. Similarly, respondents to health surveys are often unwilling to report using drugs or having multiple sexual partners. In most social surveys, it is typical that a fairly large percentage of respondents refuse to provide information on their income.

But often, the situation is not so clear-cut. The information may indeed exist elsewhere, but still it can be gathered in a more timely and consistent way with a survey. People may not know exactly what they eat, but they can still report on their dietary intake in a general way and in broad food categories. If questions are worded carefully and confidentiality is assured, respondents may even admit to some degree of illegal or socially undesirable behavior. But because surveys involve time, effort, and expense—and because they are a burden on respondents—the decision to conduct a survey should be made carefully.

Steps in the Survey Research Process

Before considering the specific methods or approaches to conducting surveys, it is helpful to get a general overview of the survey research process. Typically, a survey involves all or most of the following steps. (For a more in-depth overview of these steps, see Fowler, 2008.)

Identify the Population and Sampling Strategy

The first task is to be clear about whom to survey—the *population*. This is often not as straightforward as it might appear, as Chapter 5, on sampling, pointed out. Careful thought must be given to the geographical or organizational scope of the survey and who is, or is not, eligible to be included in the survey.

Also, thought must be given to who, within the household or organization, should be designated as the respondent. Should it be a randomly selected individual or the most knowledgeable person for the survey topic? When surveying a firm or organization, it is especially important to figure out whom within the organization to interview: the chief executive, the personnel director, a technology or other specialist, or someone else.

Finally, because the population is often large, this step in the process typically involves consideration of a statistical sampling strategy, using one or more of the sampling methods discussed in Chapter 5.

Develop a Questionnaire

Developing a good questionnaire is essential, as much depends on having the right questions for analysis and asking them clearly and carefully. Frequently, it can take a fair amount of time and effort to work out the content of a questionnaire. And typically, all the key users of the survey data are involved in the process. Some exploratory qualitative research, such as *focus groups* with potential respondents, can be valuable at this stage to identify important issues to include in the survey.

A useful first step in drafting a questionnaire is to create an outline of topics or items, without worrying initially about the format or wording of the questions. Once this outline is established, the task of drafting actual survey questions begins. A good approach at this point is to search for questions used in prior surveys, especially well-established surveys done by reputable organizations. This offers the advantage of using questions that have been tested and allows for later comparisons (e.g., for purposes of benchmarking). Some more specific tips on drafting good survey questions are provided later in this chapter.

Pretest Questionnaire and Survey Procedures

Pretesting the questionnaire and survey procedures is a crucial, though often overlooked, step in the survey process. It gets overlooked typically because of time or cost constraints, and thus, it is important at the outset to anticipate pretesting in the schedule and budget for the survey. There are two main types of pretesting:

1. **Cognitive pretesting**, in which the wording and meaning of the questionnaire are probed carefully through a process of debriefing respondents right after completing the questionnaire or interview or by having them "talk aloud" as they complete the questionnaire. *Focus groups* can also be used to debrief a small test group of survey respondents. The point here is to uncover unclear or ambiguous wording or formatting as well as to suggest response categories or even questions that may be missing from the questionnaire.

2. **Field pretesting**, in which the complete survey procedures—the contact procedures, the finalized questionnaire or interview, the technology, and any follow-up procedures—are tested on a small test sample of the population. The idea here is to implement a dress rehearsal for the full-scale survey. If any problems appear, for example, in the delivery of the questionnaire or in the technology used to gather survey responses (such as a computer-assisted script for telephone interviewing or a Web-based questionnaire), they can be detected and corrected before moving ahead with the full survey.

Recruit and Train Interviewers

Because surveys sometimes employ interviewers—to question people in person or on the telephone—the recruitment and training of these research workers is an important consideration. Interviewers need to possess certain personal qualities such as friendliness and trustworthiness and also the ability to appreciate and follow often strict survey procedures. But careful and thorough training of interviewers in proper survey interviewing techniques is also very important.

Such training typically involves at least three components. First, interviewers need training on general survey interviewing ethics and in interviewing techniques such as how to read questions consistently as written, avoid leading respondents or anticipating their answers, and probe for an answer in a neutral way. Second, interviewers must learn the specific questionnaire and the procedures for the particular survey, including any special instructions or vocabulary. And third, interviewers need to practice interviewing, both in mock interview situations and in live interviewing, with oversight and feedback from supervisors. Thorough interviewer training is critical to the overall quality of the survey.

Collect Data

After pretesting and interviewer training, large-scale data collection can begin in earnest. At this step, much depends on the particular survey method, which could involve intercept interviewing, household visits, telephone calling, mailing questionnaires, or e-mailing the survey invitation—all methods we will discuss shortly. The collection of data should be monitored carefully, with daily reporting of response rates and other indicators of how the survey is working in the field. Monitoring of interviewers should be ongoing, with attention to interviewing practices that need improvement or correcting.

It is not uncommon that midcourse adjustments need to be made in the original study design, such as adding more addresses or phone numbers to the sample or even fixing mistakes in the questionnaire that were not noticed in the pretest. Follow-up efforts—such as making extra calls to nonresponders, sending additional mailings or e-mail notices, or revisiting households or firms—are an important part of good data collection, as these efforts help boost the response rate.

Enter and Prepare Data for Analysis

If the questionnaire is computerized, the responses usually get entered and written immediately to an electronic database. But surveys using any kind of paper form require either a process of manual key-entry of the responses or the use of an optical scanner that recognizes the answer choices written on the paper questionnaires. Data entry often involves verification, for example, by double key-entry, to reduce the chance of key-punch errors.

Regardless of how the data reach the electronic database, the format and structure of the database must be checked to make sure that there are no errors, for example, in the alignment or definition of fields or columns in the database. Typically, the database is labeled and formatted for use by statistical software.

It is a good practice to prepare a memorandum describing the data, including how and when the data were collected and the layout of the data file for both current and future users of the survey data.

Analyze Data and Present Findings

The final step in the process is the statistical analysis of the survey data and preparation of a report or other presentation of the findings. Chapters 8 and 9 describe the statistical analysis of data, and Chapter 15 discusses the presentation of research results.

Having some sense of when to consider a survey and the basic steps in the process, we turn next to the actual modes of survey data collection. We focus on the survey methods that are most widely used in social and policy research today. But know that the creativity of good survey researchers—and the ever-expanding possibilities of new technology—can result in variations on these methods and even the innovation of new survey methods. And sometimes, the best approach for a given situation is to combine methods—as in so-called *mixed-mode surveys*—in an effort to contact people and encourage their participation.

Modes of Survey Data Collection

Surveys can be done through *interviews* or through the distribution of *self-administered* questionnaires, and they can be done of individuals, households, or organizations. In this section, we will describe some of the various approaches to survey research—with a focus on both the methodological and practical strengths and weaknesses of different modes. Even when using existing public use survey data, as discussed in Chapter 6, it is helpful to know and appreciate the strengths and weaknesses of the methods used to gather survey data.

Intercept Interview Surveys

One of the simplest modes of survey research is to stop people in public places, *intercept* them, and ask questions. Market researchers often do this in shopping malls, but **intercept interview surveys** have application to social and policy research as well. For example, administrators of parks, museums, and transportation systems often use intercept interview surveys to gather information from users or customers.

Perhaps the most well-known example of an intercept interview survey is the *exit polling* done in the United States and other countries. In exit polling, and in other forms of intercept surveys, respondents are usually selected randomly using *systematic sampling*—as described in Chapter 5. This helps guard against the bias that can arise when interviewers choose respondents based on subjective factors, such as how comfortable they feel approaching the person.

The advantages of intercept interview surveys include the ability to survey people on the spot as they visit facilities, vote, or otherwise gather in public places—indeed, it is often the only practical way to survey populations in such situations. Intercept surveys can also be fairly quick to implement. But

A woman conducts an intercept interview survey.

Source: © iStockphoto.com/wdstock.

Intercept interview surveys are not good for lengthy, more detailed questionnaires—because people stopped on the spot often have limited time and patience. Interviewers can be difficult to supervise, because they must work alone or in pairs in the field, so it can be hard to monitor their work.

Household Interview Surveys

Some of the earliest and most established surveys involve interviews conducted by visiting people in their homes—**household interview surveys**. For example, the American National Election Studies, the General Social Survey, the American Housing Survey, the Crime Victimization Survey, the National Health Interview Survey, and a number of other established government and social surveys rely on household interviews. Most household interview surveys are based on multistage area sampling, as described in Chapter 5.

In the 1940s and 1950s, when some of these surveys began, it was necessary to visit households in person because the telephone was still new and did not reach all households, especially in rural areas (and many more people lived in rural areas back then). But household interviewing also is done when the questionnaire is complex (as in the case of the Crime Victimization Survey), when visual aids are needed (as in the case of the General Social Survey), or when interviewer observations must be made (as in the case of the American Housing Survey). Some surveys, such as the Health and Nutrition Examination Survey, even involve medical examinations, which obviously only can be done in person.

In recent years, household interviewing has been enhanced by the use of laptop computers, referred to as **computer-assisted personal interviewing** (**CAPI**). CAPI provides several advantages. First, complex questionnaires can be navigated more easily, and of course, the data get immediately entered in electronic form. In addition, the computer can be used to present images, including video and sound, if needed. Also, for confidential topics, the computer can be turned toward respondents so that they can read or listen to questions without being observed by the interviewer. This added confidentiality from **computer-assisted self-interviewing** (**CASI**) has been shown to be important in studies in which the survey asks about sensitive topics such as sexual behavior or drug use (Turner et al., 1998).

The household interview survey is often considered to be a gold standard of sorts, as it typically involves rigorous sampling and high response rates. It also helps that some of the most established, reputable surveys use this method. But there are some disadvantages, as well. Household interviews are time-consuming and very expensive to complete. For logistical reasons, the sampling must be clustered, which complicates the statistical analysis and leads to less precision (larger standard errors), as discussed in Chapter 5. Interviews generally cannot be monitored, and thus, there is the risk that some interviewers could make up or falsify interviews (often under pressure to produce completed interviews and achieve high response rates).

Telephone Interview Surveys

Telephone interview surveys today are much more common than in-person household interviews, in large part because they are faster and much less expensive. Most telephone surveys use random digit dialing (RDD), as described in Chapter 5, to select a random sample of households to call, although lists can be used for more specialized populations (such as members of an organization). Many telephone surveys these days use **computer-assisted telephone interviewing** (**CATI**) software that guides the interviewer in asking questions and allows direct entry of the responses into an electronic database. The use of CATI also facilitates monitoring of interviewers and, importantly, the management of the RDD sample, so that numbers can be tried carefully over various times of the day and week and so that callbacks can be scheduled. These days, a well-done telephone survey involves at least 6 to 10 attempts to call each number—some telephone surveys use as many as 15 attempts—spread out over a week or more.

A great many surveys get done by telephone, including the Gallup Poll, the Pew Polls, the major network and newspaper polls, and most other public opinion polls that you see reported in the media. The University of Michigan's widely watched Consumer Sentiment Index is gathered from telephone interviews, as are many consumer product and marketing studies. Various important government surveys also get done by telephone, including large parts of the Current Population Survey (though initial surveys are still completed by in-person household interviews). The Behavioral Risk Factor Surveillance System (BRFSS), organized by the Centers for Disease Control and Prevention (CDC) and carried out by all 50 state health departments in the United States, is one of the world's largest systems of telephone surveys, with more than 350,000 people interviewed each year.

The advantages of telephone surveys lie in their low cost and speed of data collection—indeed, some telephone polls can be completed in a matter of only a few days. But it has been getting harder to reach people by telephone as more and more households screen calls or refuse to cooperate (out of fatigue from telemarketers and fund-raisers). Moreover, increasingly, households do not even have a landline telephone anymore, relying on their cell phones or Internet phones. As a result, the response rate to telephone surveys has been deteriorating steadily. Results from the BRFSS—one of the most carefully conducted and rigorous systems of telephone surveying in the United States—show a decline in response rate from 63% in 1996 to only 50% in 2007 (CDC, 2008). Most other telephone surveys, often using much less rigorous methods than the BRFSS, have much lower response rates.

Mail Self-Administered Surveys

Another widely useful mode of survey research is the **mail self-administered survey**. The method is a mainstay of surveys by government statistical agencies—including the American Community Survey and the decennial U.S. Census—and involves mailing forms to respondents along with instructions to complete and return the forms. Because these forms are *self-administered*, careful attention must be paid to the clarity of the questionnaire layout and instructions. It is also very important to present a clear and compelling cover letter or other request to respondents, as much depends on the respondents' understanding of and feelings toward the survey request.

Based on his work with the U.S. Census Bureau and other survey sponsors, Don Dillman (2007) has pioneered an approach to mail surveys known as the **tailored design method** (formerly the *total*

Many surveys rely on self-administered questionnaires.

Source: © 2009 Jupiterimages Corporation.

design method), or TDM. The TDM emphasizes the importance of all components of the mail survey, from the initial contacting materials, to the survey layout and design, to the timing and tone of the follow-up requests. The method emphasizes multiple contacts using different forms and modes of communication. Although Dillman stresses the need to tailor the approach to each situation, the standard TDM procedure involves the following contacts:

- A brief, prenotice letter telling the respondent to expect the survey. This is sent several days prior to the questionnaire.
- A questionnaire with a cover letter explaining the purpose and sponsorship of the survey.
- A thank-you (reminder) postcard, thanking the participant for responding (or encouraging them to take the time to respond, if they haven't done so already). This is sent about a week after the questionnaire.
- A replacement questionnaire with a second cover letter indicating that the respondent's questionnaire has yet to be received. This is sent 2 to 4 weeks after the initial questionnaire.
- A final contact, such as a telephone call (if possible) or a special delivery mailing (e.g., using the U.S. Postal Service's Priority Mail or Federal Express) emphasizing the importance of responding. This is sent about a week after the last contact.

As you can see, a well-done mail survey requires significant effort and careful planning and is not a one-shot effort. The aim is to achieve an adequate response rate, so that the observed sample (the returned questionnaires) comes close to matching the true sample (the initial mailing list) and the possibility of nonresponse bias is minimized, as Chapter 5, on sampling, discusses.

Well-done mail surveys are not cheap, but they certainly cost much less than household interview surveys and often less than telephone surveys. In addition, mail surveys have the advantage of reaching households that do not have telephones or that rely only on cell phones. And mail surveys have the advantage of being more easily targeted and tied to small geographic areas such as cities or even neighborhoods. This is because in the United States and in most other countries, the postal service maintains very complete records of all residential addresses that can serve as a sampling frame for mail surveys, and these address records contain detailed postal codes that can be used to target cities or neighborhoods.

But there are limitations to mail surveys as well. They require basic literacy, so they may not be suited to countries or communities in which literacy levels are generally low. It can be difficult to control who in a household or organization gets the survey and fills it out. Also, it can be difficult to accommodate multiple languages in a mail survey, as either the questionnaire and cover letter need to be sent initially in multiple languages, or instructions need to be provided for how to obtain a questionnaire in another language (creating an extra hurdle for those respondents seeking to complete the questionnaire in another language). Also, self-administered mail questionnaires are not so good for complex questionnaires with lots of skipping and branching—as people tend to get confused and make mistakes or leave questions blank. Indeed, unanswered or mistakenly answered questions (such as checking multiple responses to a question when only one response is allowed) are much more common on self-administered mail surveys because there is no technological check on the logic of answers, as there is with a computer-assisted telephone interview or Web-based questionnaire. Finally, the data from a mail survey must be entered by hand or by scanning, an imperfect process that can produce data-entry errors if people do not mark their answers clearly.

Group Self-Administered Surveys

Self-administered questionnaires can be distributed in group settings, for example, in schools, workplaces, or community centers—a **group self-administered survey** For such populations, this approach is more practical and cost-effective than mailing individual questionnaires, and it provides the added advantage of having a research worker on hand to provide instructions or assistance to respondents as they complete the questionnaire. Because the survey is administered to groups, the sampling involved is typically some form of multistage, cluster sampling.

Data can be gathered by group self-administered surveys.

Source: © iStockphoto.com/Melhi.

One of the best-known examples of a group self-administered survey is the CDC-sponsored Youth Risk Behavior Survey (YRBS), the source of U.S. national statistics on school violence, tobacco use, drug and alcohol use, sexual behaviors, diet, physical exercise, and other issues vital to the health of the nation's youth. Multistage, cluster sampling is employed to pick schools and, within schools, classrooms to be surveyed (the clusters). The survey is then administered to students in their classroom (or other meeting room) by research workers who provide background and instructions, distribute questionnaires, provide assistance, and collect and safeguard completed questionnaires. Because the YRBS involves minors and asks about sensitive topics, the procedures of obtaining parental permission, avoiding harm or embarrassment, and protecting confidentiality are especially important.

Group administration has clear advantages, since many completed questionnaires can be gathered by a few research workers in a relatively short period of time. And as mentioned, the human presence of these workers to guide and assist respondents is an advantage. However, it can be difficult to arrange to interrupt a school or other organization during its workday, particularly if the survey does not directly serve or benefit the organization's administrators. In group settings, care must be taken to prevent respondents from observing or influencing each other's responses. And because of the clustering inherent in group-administered surveys, the precision of survey estimates is less (the standard errors are greater) than they would be if respondents were sampled individually.

Web or Internet Surveys

In a relatively short time, **Web surveys** have emerged as one of the most important and widely useful alternatives to the more traditional modes of survey data collection discussed thus far. Sometimes referred to as **Internet surveys**, or **online surveys**, Web surveys can take the form of open Web polls posted on a Web site, but they more often involve e-mail messages sent to respondents containing an embedded link to a Web-based questionnaire. With increasing access to computers and the Internet in workplaces and homes, it has become possible to contact and solicit responses from many populations using such e-mail invitations linked to a Web-based questionnaire. Indeed, a whole new industry has sprouted up around the possibilities of Web-based data collection, with companies offering expert services in online research or do-it-yourself software that allows users to design and implement a Web survey from any computer with Internet access.

Web surveys work best for situations in which there is an established e-mail list of the population, such as a membership list for a volunteer group, and the group is accustomed to getting and responding

Web surveys have become important and widely used.

Source: © 2009 Jupiterimages Corporation.

to e-mail communications. Web surveys can also work to capture feedback from regular visitors to a Web site. If the list is large, simple random or systematic sampling may be used—but the low cost of Web surveys often means that it is feasible to attempt a complete *census*.

In an attempt to research a more general cross section of the population, online research companies and organizations have begun creating **Internet access panels**—large e-mail lists of respondents who opt in (sign up) to participate in online surveys on various topics, as discussed in Chapter 5. The strict government regulation of spam (unsolicited e-mail) requires that researchers obtain permission in advance, or use established lists with the permission of the list owner, before sending bulk e-mail invitations to a survey.

Typically, in a Web survey, an e-mail invitation explaining the survey is sent to list members, with an embedded link (a hyperlink) in the message that respondents can click on to go to the Web-based questionnaire. The questionnaire itself may be hosted on the survey researcher's own server or, more likely, on the server of a company that specializes in providing Web survey hosting and software. The respondent then completes the questionnaire, and the data are immediately written and stored in a database on the server. Most Web-based software providers allow for real-time viewing and analysis of responses as they come in. Box 7.1 provides more information on Web survey software.

BOX 7.1
Web Survey Software

Web survey software is evolving as fast as the method of Web survey research itself. A few years ago, Web survey software came only "in a box" to install on your own computer or server. This option still appeals to large businesses or universities, which like to maintain their own servers in house and have dedicated IT departments. But for many individual researchers or smaller organizations, the newer hosted (or ASP [application service provider]) versions of such software better meet their needs. For example, companies such as SurveyMonkey, Zoomerang, LimeService, and many other providers host and maintain the software on their servers so that the researcher only needs access to the Internet to log in, create, send, and analyze a Web survey online. The data can also be exported for offline analysis using standard statistical software. This is a rapidly growing and changing market, with intense competition, so these hosted survey software services keep getting better, easier, and less expensive to use.

There are many advantages to Web surveys, principally, low cost and speed. In fact, the cost of data collection (assuming access to a list of potential respondents) is often just pennies per completed questionnaire. Thousands of survey invitations can be sent at the same time, and often, respondents reply within a few days if not a few hours of receiving the e-mail. In addition, Web surveys can incorporate unique elements—such as intricate skipping and branching patterns, colorful graphics, and multimedia elements—not possible in traditional (paper) self-administered questionnaires. Also, because the responses get written and stored directly to an online database, the cost and complication of manual or mechanical key-entry of the data can be avoided entirely.

However, there are some important limitations to Web surveys. The proliferation of e-mail marketing, spam, and e-mail fraud worldwide has made many people both weary and wary of bulk e-mail messages, particularly messages with embedded links asking people to "click here." Indeed, many people these days simply refuse to respond to such e-mails unless they are from a sender who is known and trusted. E-mail invitations can also appear cheap (which indeed they are), compared with a standard letter or personal phone call, and so respondents feel less obligation to consider a survey request sent by e-mail. Technological issues related to different operating systems, Internet connections, and Web browsers can slow or prevent some respondents from completing Web-based questionnaires.

Establishment (Business or Organization) Surveys

Much of what we have said so far in this chapter assumes a survey targeted to individuals or households, but surveys also are used to gather information from establishments such as business firms or government and nonprofit organizations. Indeed, the U.S. federal government regularly surveys employers, manufacturers, and units of local government. Foundations and government funders often survey the nonprofit organizations, civic groups, or arts organizations that they support. Typically, these surveys involve one of the methods we've discussed already, either in-person interviews, telephone interviews, a mail survey, or a Web survey—and often a combination of methods works best.

Surveying firms or organizations presents distinct challenges that make such surveys different from those directed at individuals or households. Perhaps the biggest difference is in the size and complexity of "the respondent," which in some cases could be an organization with thousands of employees. Key decisions must be made about whom to contact within the organization and where to direct the survey. Although most organizations have a chief executive or president, this person may not always be the appropriate or most knowledgeable respondent for the given topic of the survey. Yet it may be difficult, if not impossible, to identify the appropriate respondent from within various organizations of widely ranging sizes, structures, and job titles. Therefore, it is not uncommon for the survey still to be sent to the chief executive or president—but with instructions to designate the most knowledgeable respondent within the organization to complete the questionnaire.

But getting through to a chief executive requires communicating and dealing with various gatekeepers, which can take a great deal of time and effort. Special contact procedures, especially skillful and mature interviewers, and sustained follow-up are often needed to get through to an organization, ensure that the questionnaire reaches the right hands, and obtain a completed response. Because organizations vary so much, it is often helpful to allow for various modes of responding—by telephone interview, paper form, fax, and so on. The U.S. federal government uses this kind of mixed-mode approach for its surveys of employers and manufacturers.

Panel or Longitudinal Surveys

Another unique form of survey research is **panel surveys** in which the same respondents are tracked and repeatedly surveyed over time, sometimes over many years. Well-known examples of panel surveys include the Panel Study of Income Dynamics (PSID), the National Education Longitudinal Study (NELS), the Medical Expenditure Panel Study (MEPS), the Longitudinal Study of Aging (LSOA), and the British Household Panel Study (BHPS). The NELS, for example, started with a sample of U.S. eighth graders in 1988 and has surveyed these same individuals every 2 years since that time (the NELS panelists are now in their 30s). Typically, panel surveys involve a combination of in-person or telephone interviewing or, sometimes, self-administered questionnaires.

But the real challenge in a panel survey is keeping regular track of respondents over time, particularly as they move, form or dissolve households, or suffer other disruptions in their lives. To accomplish such tracking, researchers typically ask for various point-of-contact information as part of the baseline survey (e.g., close friends or relatives), maintain communications even when survey data are not being collected, and provide financial and symbolic incentives for ongoing participation. But the problem of *panel attrition* is inevitable, as people drop out of the study for various reasons over time. For example, of the more than 18,192 individuals who completed interviews as part of the 1968 baseline to the PSID, only 5,282 were alive and available to be interviewed in 2001—despite the fact that the PSID achieved consistently high response rates, well over 90%, in any one survey year (McGonagle & Schoeni, 2006).

Having discussed the various approaches to survey data collection, we turn next to the important task of crafting a questionnaire.

Crafting a Questionnaire

Researchers, policy analysts, and even administrators sometimes get called on to do surveys—of the communities or clients they serve, the organizations they fund, or the employees they manage. And although writing survey questions might seem at first glance to be a simple task, it can prove difficult to do well. This section provides some general advice on crafting your own questionnaire. For more detailed guidance, you might wish to consult specialized books by Bradburn, Sudman, and Wansink (2004), Converse and Presser (1986), Dillman (2007), or Fowler (1995).

Develop an Outline of Survey Items

It is best to begin not by writing questions but rather by developing a list of survey items or topics. Crafting and formatting survey questions takes time, and it is better to wait on this task until you are certain what pieces of information you need to obtain from the survey. An outline of items or topics is also a useful form in which to solicit input from managers, stakeholders, or others involved in the survey.

If You Could Ask Only One or Two Questions . . .

Sometimes it helps to start not with a wish list of many questions to ask but by imagining that you could only ask your respondents one or two questions. What one or two questions would they be?

What do you most need to know from your survey? This exercise is helpful because it is all too easy to get so immersed in the job of drafting a detailed questionnaire that you lose track of—and even forget to include—the most important questions that initially motivated your survey.

Prepare Mock Tables and Charts of Survey Results

Consider preparing some mock-ups of the final tables and charts you expect to produce or present from your survey. Although starting with the questionnaire seems like a natural first step, it is often better to work backward—to begin with the results you expect to report. In the end, your audience or users of the survey will look at the results—not the questionnaire. This way, you can then check to see if the questionnaire you design actually will produce the data you'll need to fill in your tables or charts.

Look for Prior Surveys on Your Topic

Good questionnaires are often as much the product of borrowing from other surveys as writing from scratch. It is common and considered good practice in survey research to use the exact wording of questions from prior surveys. This is referred to as *replicating* questions or using *standardized* questions. Prior surveys by government agencies and established survey research organizations typically contain questions that have been carefully developed, tested, and proven over time. (In the report about the survey and its results, citations should always be made to the original source(s) of the question wording.) In addition, replicating questions from prior surveys can allow you to compare or benchmark your results, often against national or international norms. So you should certainly review and consider using questions on your topic that come from the major government or social surveys. Of course, if the question you wish to pose has not been previously developed and tested, this option is not available.

Hook Respondents With Your First Few Questions

It is worth mentioning the importance of the first few questions on your questionnaire—as they can make a critical difference to the response rate. If your respondents find the first few questions relevant, interesting, and easy to answer, chances are that they will complete the entire questionnaire. If not, they are likely to stop answering it. To illustrate, consider the two questionnaires shown in Box 7.2.

BOX 7.2
Comparing Opening Questions

QUESTIONNAIRE A

This important survey is about *crime and safety in your community.* Your answers are confidential and will be used only for statistical purposes to better serve you and your neighbors. Thank you in advance for your participation.

(Continued)

(Continued)

1. *About how much income does your household receive annually from all sources? (Please include all income earners in your household, as well as all sources of income—including wages, pensions, and investments.)*

   $___ ___ ___ , ___ ___ ___ .00

2. *Please rank the following priorities for local government, as you see things. (Put a 1 by your first priority, a 2 by your second priority, and so on, until you have numbered all items.)*

   ___ *Balance the local budget*
   ___ *Improve education*
   ___ *Improve community safety*
   ___ *Reduce traffic congestion*
   ___ *Promote jobs and economic development*
   ___ *Protect the natural environment*
   ___ *Other (specify):* _____

QUESTIONNAIRE B

This important survey is about *crime and safety in your community*. Your answers are confidential and will be used only for statistical purposes to better serve you and your neighbors. Thank you in advance for your participation.

1. *How safe do you feel walking alone at night in the neighborhood where you live?*
   a. *Very safe*
   b. *Somewhat safe*
   c. *Somewhat unsafe*
   d. *Very unsafe*

2. *In the last year (12 months), would you say that the safety of your neighborhood has...*
   a. *Gotten better*
   b. *Gotten worse*
   c. *Remained about the same*

Questionnaire A in Box 7.2 opens with a detailed household income question that is not directly related to the announced topic of community safety. It is a personal question and difficult to answer so precisely (indeed, income should often be asked in broad categories to avoid this problem). This is followed by a ranking question that, although it includes community safety, is a complex cognitive task to complete (try doing it yourself, and you'll see). Ranking questions are notoriously difficult for respondents and should be avoided unless absolutely necessary. (Asking respondents instead to *rate* each item separately—say on a scale of 1 to 10—often works much better for these kinds of questions. Later, you can rank the *items* according to their means across all respondents.) With opening questions such as these, Questionnaire A is sure to turn off many would-be respondents.

In contrast, Questionnaire B begins with two relatively simple rating questions that both directly relate to the announced topic of the survey. They are easy and fairly interesting to answer, getting the respondent quickly into the task of completing the questionnaire. If more difficult or personal questions must be asked, these should be put toward the end of the questionnaire. Once respondents have committed to answering initial questions, they are much more likely to answer difficult or sensitive questions later in the questionnaire.

Closed-Ended Versus Open-Ended Questions

Closed-ended questions provide categories for respondents to choose or check, such as those in Questionnaire B in Box 7.2. In contrast, open-ended questions ask respondents to answer in their own words. Novice survey designers often make the mistake of using too many—sometimes way too many—open-ended questions. Consider the questionnaire shown in Box 7.3.

BOX 7.3
Questionnaire Composed of Open-Ended Questions

This important survey is about *crime and safety in your community.* Your answers are confidential and will be used only for statistical purposes to better serve you and your neighbors. Thank you in advance for your participation.

1. *What are the most important priorities for local government, as you see things?*

   _____

   _____

   _____

2. *What community safety issues or problems do you see in your neighborhood?*

   _____

   _____

   _____

3. *What steps would you like local government to take in order to help improve the safety of your neighborhood?*

   _____

   _____

The questionnaire in Box 7.3 asks legitimate questions, and it would be interesting to find out how people answer in their own words. But as respondents, we might view this questionnaire as a bit of a chore, like an essay exam, requiring three minicompositions. Imagine how daunting this questionnaire would begin to seem if it continued on with 10, 15, or 20 such questions—it would become nearly impossible to complete in a reasonable amount of time (without resorting to banal, one-word answers).

Open-ended questions can be quite interesting and useful, but they should be used very sparingly and with a clear awareness of the added burden they place on respondents. It should also be pointed out that analyzing open-ended questions—reading and summarizing perhaps hundreds or even thousands of written responses—takes a great deal of time and effort. Too often, open-ended questions get asked in surveys only to have the answers essentially discarded later because the researcher did not anticipate the time required to read and summarize them. Responses to open-ended survey questions are qualitative data, and full analysis is as time-consuming as any other analysis of qualitative data.

Some Advice on Question Wording

Wording questions well is as much an art as a science, but experienced survey researchers have established some helpful principles. The following list of 18 principles for writing survey questions is provided by Dillman (2007), based on his substantial experience as well as careful empirical study of how people understand and respond to survey questions:

- Choose simple over specialized words (avoid social science or policy jargon).

For example, do not ask, "Do you favor, or oppose, an increase in the excise on tobacco consumption?" Rather, ask, "Do you favor, or oppose, an increase in taxes on cigarettes?"

- Use as few words as possible to pose the question.

Don't ask, "About how much did you pay last month for the electricity that you used in your household for things such as lights, appliances, and so on?"
Rather, it is better to ask, "About how much was your electric bill last month?"

- Use complete sentences to ask questions.

For example, don't ask simply, "Employed?" as a question.
Instead, ask, "Are you currently employed, or not?"

- Avoid vague quantifiers when more precise estimates can be obtained.

For example, don't ask, "Last week, did you use public transportation often, sometimes, rarely, or never?"

Rather, it is more useful to ask, "Last week, did you use public transportation 5 or more days, 2 to 4 days, only 1 day, or not at all?"

- Avoid specificity that exceeds the respondent's potential for having an accurate, ready-made answer.

For example, avoid asking, "Last week, exactly how many trips in total did you make using public transportation? If you used public transportation on one day to go to and from work, that would count as two trips."

Compare this with the previous example, which asked about "days" instead of "trips" and gave ranges instead of asking for an exact count.

- Use equal numbers of positive and negative categories for scaled questions.

For example, don't use *very satisfied/satisfied/somewhat satisfied/dissatisfied* as the categories.

Rather, use a more symmetrical set of response categories such as *very satisfied/somewhat satisfied/somewhat dissatisfied/very dissatisfied*.

- Distinguish undecided from neutral response options by placement at the end of the scale.

For example, in an agree-disagree question, present the response categories as *agree/disagree/unsure*.

This is less confusing than *agree/unsure/disagree*, in which *unsure* could more easily be interpreted as a neutral response.

- Avoid bias from unequal comparisons (make answer choices as neutral and as comparable as possible).

For example, don't ask, "Are you concerned that the government will enact new antiterrorism laws that excessively restrict the average person's civil liberties, or are you not concerned about this problem?"

Instead, make it a more equal comparison: "Which concerns you more right now: that the government will fail to enact strong antiterrorism laws, or that the government will enact new antiterrorism laws that excessively restrict the average person's civil liberties?" (Wording from a CBS News/*New York Times* poll, PollingReport.com, 2009).

- State both sides of attitude scales in the question stem.

For example, don't write, "On a scale of 1 to 10, please indicate how satisfied you are with local public schools. (1 = *very dissatisfied* to 10 = *very satisfied*)."

Rather, put it like this: "On a scale of 1 to 10, please indicate how satisfied, or dissatisfied, you are with local public schools. (1 = *very dissatisfied* to 10 = *very satisfied*)." It's a subtle difference, but it can matter to respondents.

- Eliminate or randomly rotate the order of "check all that apply" question formats to reduce primacy effects (the tendency to choose the first few categories listed).

For example, a "check all that apply" question looks like this:

Please indicate what you consider to be the top priorities for local government these days. (Check all that apply.)

1. *Growing the local economy*

2. *Improving public schools*

3. *Reducing crime*

4. *Expanding public transportation options*

5. *Creating more parks and recreation opportunities*

6. *Reducing traffic congestion*

7. *Preserving the natural environment*

8. *Providing services for the elderly and disabled*

9. *Reducing racial or ethnic tensions in the community*

The first few categories will get more checks than the last few, simply because of their order in the list. This problem can be avoided, however, in Web and telephone surveys that use software that allows randomization, or rotation, of categories (so that the order is not the same for each respondent).

- Develop response categories that are mutually exclusive.

For example, when asking, "How often did you use public transportation last week?" don't use response categories such as *often*, *as much as possible*, *whenever the weather permitted*, or *just a few times.*

- Use cognitive design techniques to improve recall (such as priming respondents by asking for details about a past event or behavior).

For example, we might ask, "During your most recent visit to your doctor, how satisfied were you with the amount of time your doctor spent with you?"

But it might be helpful to first ask, "Was your most recent visit to your doctor for a regular checkup or for some other reason?" This reminds, or primes, the respondent to recall his or her most recent visit. Then ask, "During this visit, how satisfied were you with the amount of time your doctor spent with you?"

- Provide appropriate time referents (typically a short time period for recalling behavior—or ask for an estimation only).

For example, you might be interested in asking, "Do you do any exercise, or not?" But it is very unclear what this means.

Providing a time frame makes this question much more concrete: "In the last 7 days, did you do any exercise, or not?"

- Be sure that each question is technically accurate.

For example, you might ask, "Do you own your home, are you renting, or something else?" But most homeowners in the United States and other countries have a mortgage, so they do not really "own" their homes outright until they pay off their mortgage.

It would be better to ask, "Do you own your home (with or without a mortgage), are you renting, or something else?"

- Choose question wordings that allow essential comparisons to be made with previously collected data.

This refers to the point made earlier in this chapter about the value of using standardized questions from established government and social surveys. For example, if you are interested in measuring the amount of generalized social trust in a community, that is, how much people trust others, you could use a standard question from the General Social Survey: "Generally speaking, would you say that most people can be trusted or that you can't be too careful in dealing with people?"

- Avoid asking respondents to say "yes" to mean "no" (the problem of double negatives).

For example, don't use this kind of awkward phrasing: "Do you support opposition to the proposed highway expansion, or not?"
It is much clearer to ask, "Do you support, or oppose, the proposed highway expansion?"

- Avoid double-barreled questions (questions that actually contain two or more topics or elements about which respondents may have different or even contradictory opinions).

Consider, for example, this question: "Do you agree, or disagree, that the city needs a new high school on the site where the old riverside mill now stands?" Someone may agree with the need for a new school but feel strongly that the old riverside mill should be preserved and not destroyed. For complex issues such as this, it is best to break the issue into parts and ask separate questions.

- Avoid asking respondents to make unnecessary calculations.

For example, don't ask, "What percentage of your income each month do you spend on electricity?"
Instead, ask the income question (annual income is usually easier for respondents), ask the electric bill question (usually a monthly bill), and then do the calculation yourself: (monthly electric bill × 12)/ income.
Dillman (2007) provides a much more detailed discussion and additional examples of each of these principles.

Put Yourself in Your Respondent's Shoes

In the design of a survey, the survey researcher's attitude vis-à-vis respondents sometimes reminds us of the driver and the pedestrian. When driving a car, we tend to view pedestrians as unaware, slow nuisances. But when we are on foot, we see drivers as reckless and arrogant. Well, the same is often true of researchers and respondents.

When asked to respond to a questionnaire, we all appreciate clear instructions, simple and straightforward questions, and short questionnaires. But when designing a survey, we frequently change our perspective—we become drivers—arrogant and uncaring, unwilling to make compromises, demanding detailed responses to overly long, often confusing questions. So when designing a survey, we would advise you to try to think like a respondent, *not* like a researcher. See your survey from the point of view of the real people you will be asking to complete it: Is it worth my time? Is it interesting? Is it clear and simple? Is it short?

Ethics of Survey Research

Survey research raises some unique and important ethical issues centered on contacting people, persuading them to participate, and handling potentially sensitive personal information gathered in surveys.

Informed Consent

Informed consent is a basic principle of research ethics—but it can be a challenge to implement in many survey situations. In most telephone surveys, for example, informing the respondent and obtaining his or her consent must occur in the opening minute or two of the interview. Typically, a statement is read introducing the topic and sponsor of the survey, a statement of confidentiality is given, and the interview begins. The willingness of the respondent to begin the interview is considered then as a form of *tacit consent*. Similarly, in most online surveys, the respondent is told about the survey in an e-mail, and his or her willingness to click through to the Web-based questionnaire serves as tacit consent to participate. And mail surveys, as well, make use of tacit consent. Only in household interview surveys, or group interview surveys, is it possible to obtain a more formal, written consent.

Pushing for a High Response Rate

As discussed in this chapter as well as in Chapter 5, on sampling, achieving a high response rate is critical to the quality of survey data. To obtain a high response rate, researchers make multiple contact attempts, call repeatedly, work to convince people who initially refuse to participate later on, use multiple modes, and provide financial and other incentives. But in practice, these efforts to achieve a high response rate can turn into efforts to pressure or coerce people into responding.

Respondents are sometimes even deceived by researchers regarding the length of the interview or questionnaire, out of a concern that telling them the truth up front will discourage their participation. Although high response rates are a good thing statistically, they do not justify pressuring or misleading respondents.

Overburdening Respondents

As a survey researcher, it is easy to fall into the habit of thinking that respondents should be asked to provide all the information that you might possibly need. The tendency, too often, is to add extra questions—just to be sure. But the burden should fall on the researcher to use discipline and restraint in the design of the survey, not on the respondents to make an extra effort. Moreover, overburdening respondents with excessive, redundant, or unnecessary questions not only harms them—by abusing their time and cooperation—but hurts the reputation of surveys in general and the response rate trends in society at large.

If a great deal of information is needed, or if physical measurements or lengthy tests must also be given, then the timing and format of data collection must accommodate respondents properly. For example, breaks and snacks may be used to reduce the burden on respondents, although, of course, the time burden will still be large.

Protecting Privacy and Confidentiality

In the design of surveys, identifying information or other potentially private information should be asked only if absolutely necessary. For many survey purposes, there is no need to know someone's full name and address, for example. If such identifying information is necessary for implementing the survey, then it should be used only for that purpose and kept separately from the substantive answers to the questionnaire. This can be accomplished by the use of code numbers that link the contact information to the survey responses. It is often best to ask for age, income, level of education, and other personal information in broad categories rather than in detail.

Some of the most interesting new uses of survey data relate to linking individual survey responses to contextual data on the surrounding neighborhood, nearby infrastructure, and the availability of amenities and public services. This is done by *geocoding*, or pinpointing the geographic location, of the surveyed households. But this creates additional privacy and confidentiality concerns, as knowing the precise street and block where a respondent lives is tantamount to knowing the respondent's identity.

Surveying Minors

Surveys of children and youth are important in social and policy research, but special procedures must be followed in conducting such surveys. For example, many institutional review boards or research ethics committees require parental consent, which must be obtained in writing in advance.

Making Survey Data Available for Public Use

Increasingly, large social and government surveys are being made available for public use over the Internet, as we have seen already in Chapter 6. This is a good thing for the advancement of research and informed public policy, as the considerable investment it takes to conduct a survey can be shared with many more researchers and policy analysts than in the past. But this widespread, public availability of individual survey responses—including details on individuals' characteristics, thoughts, and behaviors—raises ethical issues. As a result, public use survey data often contain limited geographic information on respondents and employ *top-coding* to limit the reporting of extreme values for potentially identifying variables such as income, age, or family size. Survey sponsors typically require users of public use survey data to register and to sign confidentiality statements.

Survey data collection is a large and important topic in social and policy research. In this section, we have tried to give a useful overview of the various modes of doing surveys, the design of questionnaires, and the ethical issues involved. Although surveys are the most widely used method of collecting primary quantitative data, they are not the only one. The next section introduces a less well-known but useful method—trained observation.

Trained Observation

Quantitative data can be gathered by simply observing things—and this is the basic idea behind the method of **trained observation**. The method involves carefully *training* research workers to systematically *observe* and record conditions or behaviors, typically using an observation rating form. It has been used by researchers and policy analysts to rate neighborhoods, parks, streets, hospitals, classroom behavior, subways and buses, and public housing communities. It can be a fairly cost-effective method of data collection in that a small team of observers can cover a large number of facilities or locations in a reasonable period of time.

As we have seen in Chapter 3, observation—such as participant observation—is an important part of qualitative data collection. The distinction here is that explicit procedures are developed to quantify the observations by means of systematically coding or rating aspects of the observed situation. But it must be noted that many qualitative researchers code, count, and summarize their observations, in addition to taking notes or otherwise qualitatively recording or interpreting the situation. And quantitative trained observation can also include qualitative information, such as photographs or field notes.

Let's look at some examples of trained quantitative observation.

Observing Social Disorder

Robert Sampson, Stephen Raudenbush, and colleagues at the Project on Human Development in Chicago Neighborhoods drove an SUV slowly down the streets of 80 sampled neighborhoods in Chicago to observe, videotape, and rate neighborhood conditions, with a focus on physical and behavioral indicators of social disorder. These trained observer ratings were then analyzed along with survey data, census data, and crime reports to examine the influence of feelings of collective efficacy on levels of neighborhood crime and disorder (Sampson & Raudenbush, 1999). Here is a description of the various indicators of neighborhood disorder that were observed and recorded from the viewpoint of the project's SUV:

> The researchers collected data on the following areas of interest: land use, residential housing, commercial industrial buildings, drinking establishments, recreational facilities, street conditions, the number of security persons, children, and teenagers visible, traffic, the physical condition of buildings, cigarette and cigars on the street or in the gutter, garbage, litter on the street or sidewalk, empty beer bottles visible on the street, tagging graffiti, graffiti painted over, gang graffiti, abandoned cars, condoms on the sidewalk, needles and syringes on the sidewalk, and political message graffiti. Information was also gathered on adults loitering or congregating, people drinking alcohol, peer groups, gang indicators present, intoxicated people, adults fighting or hostilely arguing, prostitution on the street, and people selling drugs. (Project on Human Development in Chicago Neighborhoods, 2008)

Going back to the "broken windows" theory from Chapter 2, you can see in this example of systematic neighborhood observation how a concept such as "disorder" might actually be measured.

Assessing Street Cleanliness

New York City's street cleanliness scorecard provides a good, applied example of the use of trained observers. Begun in the 1970s, the street cleanliness scorecard produces monthly ratings of street cleanliness for each of 59 community districts in the city. The observers are trained to base their ratings on photographic standards and written definitions, as shown in Figure 7.1.

Scores in Figure 7.1 range from 1.0 (cleanest) to 3.0 (dirtiest), with a score of 1.5 or less defined as "acceptably clean." In 2007, 94% of the city's streets were rated acceptably clean—up from 90% in 2004.

Trained observers can now use handheld computers with software installed to guide their observation and ratings, as happens in the ComNET project to rate street-level neighborhood conditions (Fund for the City of New York, 2008). Importantly, the use of handheld computers can allow observers to capture qualitative data as well, such as digital photographs of conditions, which can be downloaded along with quantitative observer ratings into a centralized database.

The method of trained observation typically begins with the development of a rating form along with procedures and standards, including the use of photographic standards. This development phase can involve substantial pretesting of the observation forms and procedures in the field. *Interrater reliability*—the consistency with which two or more observers rate the same object or condition, as discussed in Chapter 4—must be tested. If lacking, it should be improved through changes to the form, the rating procedures, or the training of the observers. Once the observation form and procedures are well established, actual field work and data collection can begin. Still, observers must be monitored and ongoing checks on interrater reliability must be performed.

| 1.2 | A clean street, except for a few traces of litter. |

| 2.5 | Litter is highly concentrated, there are no gaps in the piles of litter. The litter is a straight line along the curb. |

Figure 7.1   Photos of Street Cleanliness for Use by Trained Observers

Source: The City of New York (2008).

Handheld computers are used by trained observers.

Source: © 2009 Fund for the City of New York. Center on Municipal Government Performance.

Conclusion

Despite the rapid growth of public use data, as discussed in Chapter 6, the need for collecting original data remains. This chapter covered several of the most important methods—including the sometimes overlooked but quite useful method of trained observation. The many varieties of survey research are widely used in primary data collection, including interview surveys by telephone and in person and self-administered surveys by mail and, increasingly, the Internet. Indeed, the use of the Internet for survey research may soon become the most widely used method, if it is not already.

Knowing where data come from or how they are produced matters, even for those who do not do research but rather read it and apply it to public policy or management. Data are the basic material of research, and each source of data has its own advantages and limitations. This chapter has given you a feel for some of the most important sources of primary data and methods of primary quantitative data collection used in contemporary social and policy research.

The next step—to explore and analyze the data using the tools of statistics—is the topic of the next chapter.

BOX 7.4
Critical Questions to
Ask About Primary Data Collection in Studies

- Did the study involve original data collection or not? Why was original data collected (as opposed to, e.g., using secondary or administrative data)?
- If data collection was done through a survey, what kind of survey was it? What modes of survey data collection were used? And what are the strengths and weaknesses of the modes?
- Who conducted the survey? Was it a professional survey firm, and if so, what kind of firm? Or was the survey conducted by the researcher and his or her assistants? How well were the interviewers or survey workers trained and monitored?
- Does the article or report provide the question wording for key variables? If not, how much does this limit your ability to judge the meaning of the results?
- Was the wording of the questions clear and unambiguous? Are any questions potentially leading or biased? Do respondents know the answers to the questions? Are they willing to answer? Were the questions pretested?
- How long was the questionnaire or interview? Were respondents burdened by the length of the questionnaire or interview, and if so, how might this influence the quality of the data?
- (Also refer to the critical questions to ask about sampling and measurement, as these are aspects of original data collection as well.)

EXERCISES

Is a Survey Necessary?

7.1 Below are some variables and samples in social and policy research. For each situation, decide whether or not you think a survey is appropriate—and if not, in what other ways you might obtain the information.

a. To find out the annual budgets of a sample of nonprofit organizations
b. To find out about the job satisfaction of a sample of employees of a large public agency
c. To find out the salaries of a sample of employees of a large public agency
d. To find out how many high school students in a sample use tobacco

What Survey Mode to Use?

7.2. The City of Tampa, Florida, runs a system of senior centers where older citizens of the city can obtain services, information, and opportunities for social interaction. The city government is interested in conducting a user satisfaction survey of the centers' clients. What survey mode would you suggest that the city use? Explain why your suggested approach is better than other alternatives.

Design Your Own Questionnaire

7.3. You are the director of a local art museum and you want to understand the profile of those attending your museum. Design a 5- to 7-item brief questionnaire to gather useful information from an intercept survey of museumgoers.

Rate the Cleanliness of Your Streets

7.4. The City of New York's photographic standards for rating street cleanliness are available at www.nyc.gov/html/ops/downloads/pdf/scorecard/about_scorecard.pdf. Using these photographic standards, try rating several streets in your area. Rate at least one busy, more commercial street and one quieter, more residential street. If working with a classmate or as part of a team, try rating the same street and comparing your scores. How easy, or difficult, was it to rate the streets? What does the comparison of your scores with those of your classmates tell you about interrater reliability?

Objectives: In this chapter, you will learn a variety of concepts and tools to analyze quantitative data and to interpret that analysis usefully. You will learn about the importance of units and rates, as well as basic descriptive statistics (such as mean and standard deviation) used to summarize distributions. You will also learn about practical significance and effect size, as well as statistical significance, and how these ideas differ. This chapter will also introduce you to correlation and regression analysis (a topic continued in the next chapter). The conceptual and statistical tools of this chapter are essential for analyzing the kinds of descriptive data covered in earlier chapters. They are just as important for understanding the methods discussed later in Part III on causation.

Guessing what's in a gift box resembles the logic of significance testing.

Source: Istockphoto.com

Making Sense of the Numbers

8

Last Weekend I Walked Eight

A good friend comes up to you with a big smile on her face and says: "I feel great—this weekend I walked eight!" You smile back at her, a bit perplexed.

What does she mean? Eight what? Did she walk eight blocks? Eight miles? Eight hours? It's hard to know how to react appropriately without more information—more context. Numbers do not speak for themselves, contrary to the popular saying, but rather require context and interpretation. That is what this chapter is about—making sense of the numbers reported as part of research, from fairly simple numbers such as "eight" to more complex statistics.

We cover making sense of numbers and statistics at this point in the book for a few reasons. After the steps covered in the previous chapters—measuring variables, sampling, and gathering data—the next logical step is to describe the patterns and relationships in the data. Also, certain statistical ideas and techniques are essential background to studies designed to demonstrate causation—the theme of the chapters in Part III.

This chapter does not present a traditional overview of statistics. Rather, it covers various issues and ideas not typically emphasized in a statistics course, such as the distinction between practical and statistical significance, that matter a great deal in understanding real research. So even if you have a background in statistics, we encourage you to read this chapter (although you may wish to skip over some of the more basic topics).

Some people are afraid or intimidated by statistics. If you are one of those people, we have some words of encouragement. First of all, it's not as bad as you probably imagine, particularly once you see in this chapter how to understand and apply statistics. And even if you consider yourself hopelessly math phobic, you don't want to be silenced or cowed by colleagues or adversaries who throw numbers around. A lot of methodologically sloppy research overly impresses people because its statistical facade gives a false impression of scientific rigor. You want to be able to face the numerical results on your own, without fear, and think for yourself about what the results really mean.

I feel great—I walked eight.

Source: © iStockphoto.com/unaemlag.

Units, Rates, and Ratios

In statistics, *variables* describe the attributes or characteristics of individual people, households, geographic areas, or other *units of analysis*. The level of measurement of a variable can be either *quantitative* or *categorical* (*nominal* or *ordinal*)—as explained in Chapter 4. But quantitative variables can appear in many units and in various forms, including counts, percentages (or proportions), rates, risks, or odds.

What Units?

The friend in the opening example said that she "walked eight"—what made this confusing is that the statement lacked **units**. Eight *what,* we need to know. A basic but often overlooked requirement in reporting and reading research is to clearly define the units of measurement. This requirement applies to tables of statistics, graphs and charts, and sentences that mention numerical results.

An example from a research paper illustrates the importance of units. Table 8.1 is an extraction of Table 1 in a paper by Tami Gurley-Calvez and colleagues (Gurley-Calvez, Gilbert, Harper, Marples, & Daly, 2009), showing summary statistics for investors in their sample data. Notice how the authors explain that each variable is in thousands. Without that explanation, it would be impossible to interpret the statistics. However, the authors do not specify that the variables are in thousands of *dollars*. While the latter fact may be obvious since the data are from the United States, it would have been even better to make the currency of dollars explicit, since researchers in other countries might read the table.

Table 8.1   Extraction of Table 1 in Gurley-Calvez et al.

Variable	NMTC Investors 2000	NMTC Investors 2004
Total income (thousands)	580.98	1020.48
Wealth (thousands)	9914.88	14163.43
Home equity (thousands)	39.88	36.09
Note: Table entries are means.		

Even experienced researchers and statisticians can sometimes misinterpret or fail to clarify units. The importance of units cannot be overemphasized.

Rates or Why Counts Often Mislead

Counts—such as the number of murders in a city—are useful facts to know, but as variables in statistical analysis, they often mislead. If we had data on many cities, and also measured the count of pet goldfish in each city, we might be surprised to find that—shocking news indeed—the more pet goldfish, the more murders! In fact, we would likely find quite a strong relationship. But it would be nonsense, of course—big cities have more of everything: murders, pet goldfish, park benches, and so on. Comparing or correlating counts of anything in this way is misleading.

Instead, the comparisons should be made relative to the population. Therefore, it is better to use **rates**, such as *murders per 100,000 residents*. To calculate a rate, you divide the count by the population and then multiply by the base (100,000 in the example of murders just given). Here is the basic formula:

$$\text{Rate} = (\text{Count/Population}) \times \text{Base}.$$

Big cities have more of everything, including pet fish.
Source: © 2009 Jupiterimages Corporation.

For example, in 2008, New York City recorded 522 murders, while neighboring Newark, New Jersey, recorded only

67 murders—but these are counts, not rates, so we can't directly compare them. According to the Census Bureau, there are 8.2 million residents in New York City but only 265,000 residents in Newark. So the murder rates per 100,000 residents in the two cites are as follows:

$$New York: (522/8200000) \times 100000 = 6.4$$

$$Newark: (67/265000) \times 100000 = 25.3$$

These murder rates per 100,000 residents are more comparable—and they tell a much different story than did the counts.

Percentages, such as the percentage of the population owning a pet goldfish, are also rates—goldfish owners per 100 people. (A percentage is just a rate with a base of 100.) With these new variables in hand, our shocking finding of a goldfish–murder link would surely disappear. Box 8.1 provides an example that further illustrates the importance of relevant comparisons.

BOX 8.1
Relevant Comparisons

In "Going Under: A Doctor's Downfall, and a Profession's Struggle With Addiction," Jason Zengerle (2008) makes the case that anesthesiologists have a serious addiction problem. He notes that they account for 13% of physicians being treated for drug addiction.

One might not think that was serious, but Zengerle provides the relevant comparison by noting that only 5% of physicians are anesthesiologists. His evidence is even more striking when he notes that less than 5% of residents are in anesthesia, while more than 33% of residents in drug addiction treatment are in anesthesia.

By finding the right comparison, a share like a third is shown to be enormous. The easiest way to present the comparison would be to describe the rate of serious addiction among anesthesiologists compared with the rate among all doctors or other specialists.

In epidemiology and other areas of health research, rates are often referred to as **risks**—for instance, the risk of being murdered. We can say that the risk of murder in New York City is 6.4 in 100,000, while the risk of murder in Newark is 25.4 in 100,000.

Percent Change and Percentage *Point* Change

Say the poverty rate in a region rose from 10% in 1950 to 20% in 2000. How much would you say poverty had risen? You might be tempted to say, "It went up 10%," but this would be incorrect.

The key is to remember what a **percent change** means—change relative to a base. If you were lucky enough to have a salary of $100,000, and your salary rose by 10%, then your new salary would be $110,000. Here is the math:

$$10\% \text{ Change} = ((\$110,000 - \$100,000)/\$100,000) \times 100.$$

$$\% \text{ Change} = ((\text{New} - \text{Old})/\text{Old}) \times 100.$$

Let's apply the same logic to determine the percent change of the regional poverty rate:

$$\text{Percent change in poverty rate} = ((20\% - 10\%)/(10\%)) \times 100 = 100\% \text{ change.}$$

After all, the poverty rate doubled, right?—in other words, a 100% increase.

What is confusing is that poverty is a proportion, already measured as a percentage. Clearly, the poverty rate rises by 10 in the units it is measured in—percentage points. To make the distinction clear, we say that the poverty rate rose by 10 *percentage points*. The change in a percentage, expressed in its own units, is a **percentage point change**.

The Strangeness of Percent Change on the Return Trip

Suppose sometime in the future, say 2050, the poverty rate in the region above returns to 10%. In that case, the change in the poverty rate between 2000 and 2050 would be a 10 *percentage point* decline—the reverse of the increase between 1950 and 2000. However, measured as a *percent change*, things would look quite different. Between 2000 and 2050, the poverty rate would be cut in half or a 50% reduction:

$$\% \text{ Change} = ((\text{New} - \text{Old})/\text{Old}) \times 100$$
$$= ((10\% - 20\%)/20\%) \times 100$$
$$= -50\%.$$

Going in the reverse direction, the base was higher and so the percent change was lower. When interpreting percent change, always remember the base.

Because the percent change takes on a different value depending on the direction, this definition of percent change can be awkward in some applications. Therefore, sometimes, the midpoint between the new and old is used as a base. For example, in economics, the *midpoint elasticity* is defined with percentages that use the midpoint as a base. Unless otherwise specified, a percent change always takes the old value as a base, but you should be aware of the option of using the midpoint.

Rates of Change and Rates of Change of Rates

How rapidly a social or economic condition, such as births or unemployment, changes over time—its **rate of change**—is frequently of interest to policymakers and others. But it is important to choose an

Odds are familiar to many in gambling, but odds are also used in research.

Source: © 2009 Jupiterimages Corporation.

appropriate unit of time for rates of change. Should we examine change in the rate of births from month to month? Or is a year a more useful window for comparison? A year may be too long, however, for observing changes in other conditions, such as unemployment or crime.

Change over time in the number of new events may be of interest, such as the number of births per year, but as we have just seen, counts can often be deceiving. More births may simply reflect population growth, not a change in the birth rate. So it is often better to consider a percent change over time in a rate, such as a birth rate.

Odds

In some fields, such as public health, odds are commonly understood. But in many other fields, odds appear—well, a bit odd. If we think of one of two outcomes as a "success" and the other as a "failure," then the **odds** of an outcome are defined as follows:

$$\text{Odds} = \text{Successes/Failures}.$$

If three out of every five high school students graduate successfully, then it follows that two of five fail to graduate. We can then say that the odds of graduating are 3/2 or 1.5.

Odds are also commonly used in the context of sports. For example, "What are the odds that the Yankees will beat the Mets?" You might say that the odds are even, or 1 to 1. Or you might say that the odds are 2 to 1 in favor of the Yankees. But these are subjective odds—guesses. In research, odds are calculated from data.

While odds can refer to the ratio of successes to failures, they can also be used to refer to any kind of dichotomous variable. For example, we could refer to the odds of getting a heart attack (vs. not getting a heart attack), the odds of committing a felony, and so on.

It's important not to confuse odds with proportion. For example, the proportion of successes would be the successes divided by the total (both successes and failures). Consider Table 8.2, showing all possible success-failure outcomes in a sample of $n = 5$ events.

Notice that odds less than 1 indicate that a success is less likely than a failure, and odds greater than 1 indicate that a success is more likely than a failure. Both odds and proportions have a lower limit of 0. But proportions have an upper limit of 1.0 (100%), while odds have no upper limit (or infinity ∞).

Prevalence and Incidence

In epidemiology (the study of disease), the number or share of a population that has a particular disease or condition is referred to as **prevalence**. The estimated prevalence of diabetes in U.S. adults

Table 8.2 Odds and Proportions

Successes (A)	Failures (B)	Total (C)	Odds (A/B)	Proportion (A/C)
0	5	5	0.00	.00
1	4	5	0.25	.20
2	3	5	0.67	.40
3	2	5	1.50	.60
4	1	5	4.0	.80
5	0	5	∞	1.00

20 years of age or older, for example, is 23.5 million or 10.7% of this population. This figure refers to all U.S. adults with some form of diabetes, including those who have lived with the disease for many years (National Diabetes Information Clearinghouse, n.d.).

It is also of interest to know the rate at which new cases of a disease appear in a population, which is the **incidence**. The estimated incidence of diabetes in U.S. adults 20 years of age or older in 2007 was 1.6 million new cases or 0.7% of this population.

The terms *prevalence* and *incidence* are sometimes used in other disciplines, for example, the prevalence and incidence of crime victimization. Regardless of the context, it is important not to confuse the two. There are many more people who have been victims of crime at some point in their lives than there are those who are victimized in a given year.

Distributions

Variables are so named because they vary—they take on different values. This variability produces a **distribution**—that is, a pattern of values spread out over the variable's categories or numeric range.

Distribution of a Categorical Variable

We examine the distribution of a categorical variable by counting the number of individuals in each category, or better, by calculating the percentage of individuals in each category. This produces a **frequency distribution** (or *frequencies* for short) like that shown for the race/ethnicity of U.S. teens based on the federal government's Youth Risk Behavior Survey (YRBS) in Table 8.3. The column labeled "valid percent" shows the percentages disregarding the 251 missing individuals for whom race/ethnicity is missing.

Table 8.3   Frequency Distribution of Race/Ethnicity (Youth Risk Behavior Survey)

	Race/Ethnicity		
		Frequency	Percent	Valid Percent
Valid	White	8321	59.3	6.03
	Black or African American	2076	14.8	15.1
	Hispanic/Latino	1184	8.4	8.6
	Multiple—Hispanic	1142	8.1	8.3
	Asian	480	3.4	3.5
	Multiple—Non-Hispanic	345	2.5	2.5
	Am Indian/Alaska Native	135	1.0	1.0
	Native Hawaiian/Other Pacific Islander	108	.8	.8
	Total	13790	98.2	100.0
Missing	System	251	1.8	
Total		14041	100.0	

A **bar chart** can be used to graph the distribution of a categorical variable, as shown in Figure 8.1. Bar charts show how the frequencies differ across categories more clearly than do tables. It is always important to graph your data—this is one of the basic guidelines of statistics.

A **pie chart** can also be used to graph a categorical variable, as demonstrated in Figure 8.2. Although pie charts are popular with novice analysts, most experienced researchers prefer bar charts because they are visually simpler and work better to convey the frequencies. As can be seen from Figure 8.2, pie charts with more than a few categories can get a bit confusing.

Displaying data using graphs helps you visualize your data, perceive patterns, and notice any unusual features. It is therefore an essential preliminary step in any well-done data analysis. Graphs are also very useful for presenting data.

Distribution of a Quantitative Variable

To visualize a quantitative variable, such as years of age or dollars of income, a different graph is needed: a **histogram**. Figure 8.3 is a histogram showing the distribution of the weight of 14-year-olds in kilograms from the YRBS. It shows how the individuals in the data are distributed across equal intervals of weight, in this case 5-kilogram intervals (also called *bins*).

You can see that most of the 14-year-olds weigh between 40 and about 80 kilograms, or approximately 88 to 177 pounds (a kilogram is equivalent to 2.2 pounds). The center of the distribution looks to be about 60 kilograms (121 pounds), but there is quite a spread, particularly at the upper

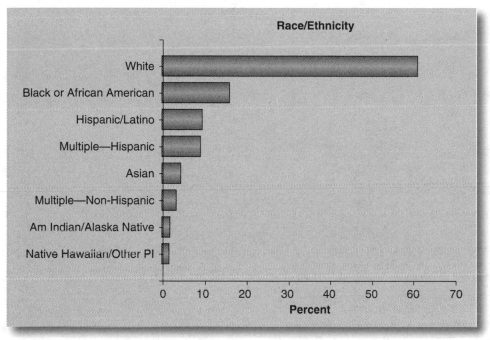

Figure 8.1   Bar Chart of Race/Ethnicity (Youth Risk Behavior Survey)

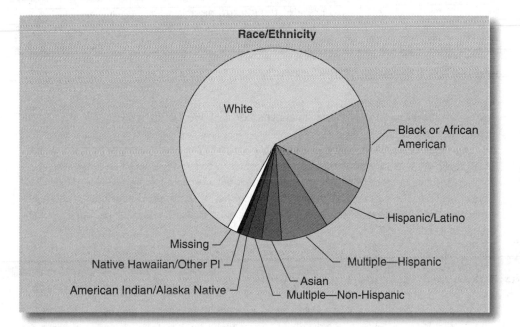

Figure 8.2   Pie Chart of Race/Ethnicity (Youth Risk Behavior Survey)

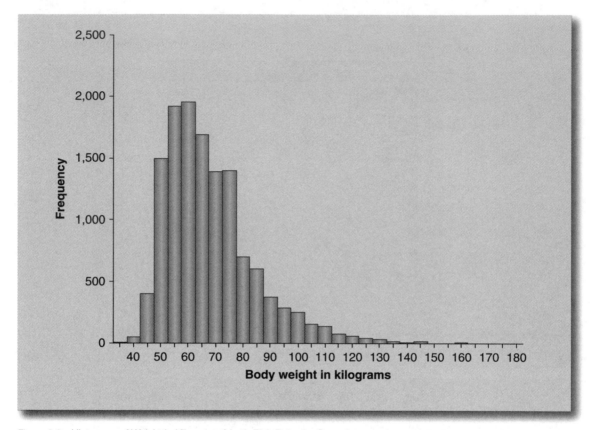

Figure 8.3   Histogram of Weight in Kilograms (Youth Risk Behavior Survey)

end of the distribution (this is referred to as right skewness). We'll review more precise measures of center and spread shortly.

Explaining the variability visible in a distribution is, in an important sense, what much research is all about. We want to know why some 14-year-old kids weigh more while others weigh less. Much of this variability may be attributable to genetic factors, but a fair amount may be the result of behaviors or health habits that could be changed by public policy or some other intervention. Obesity is a growing health problem for young people, so knowing what produces variability in childhood weight can help us address this issue.

Measures of Center: Mean and Median

For quantitative variables, we can calculate summary statistics to represent the center and spread of the distribution. The center of the distribution is important because it is the middle or average— what's typical or expected.

The most common measure of the center of a distribution is the **mean**. The mean is the arithmetic average found by adding up all the values and dividing by the total (see Box 8.2 for the formula). But the mean is not always the best measure of center because it can be influenced by extreme scores (called **outliers**) or by a long tail of scores trailing out in one direction (called **skewness**). In other words, a few very high values have a large influence on the mean.

BOX 8.2
Mean: The Formula

The mean of a variable is simply its total divided by the number of observations. Formally,

$$\bar{x} = \frac{1}{n} \sum_{i=1}^{n} x_i,$$

where x_i refers to the individual observations and n refers to sample size. $\sum$ is the summation symbol and means *add them up*.

An often better measure of center is the **median**—the point that splits the distribution into two equal halves. The median is less influenced by outliers or skewness than the mean. Indeed, we could see skewness in the weight distribution of 14-year-olds. So let's compare the mean and median for the YRBS weight data:

Mean	63.1 kilograms
Median	59.9 kilograms

The mean is drawn up by the right skewness of the distribution, while the median remains closer to the visual center of the distribution. Many economic variables, such as incomes or house prices, are extremely right skewed (a few very rich individuals or very expensive homes stretch out the right tail of the distribution).

When to Use Median? When to Use Mean?

The *New York Times* compared the mean (which they call "average") and median net worth of families in the United States in 2001 and 2004, as shown in Figure 8.4.[1] So how much is the typical American family actually worth? The $400,000 plus mean (average) is misleading because it reflects the large

---

[1]*New York Times*. June 4, 2006. BUSINESS/YOUR MONEY. "Economic View: When Sweet Statistics Clash With a Sour Mood," by Daniel Gross.

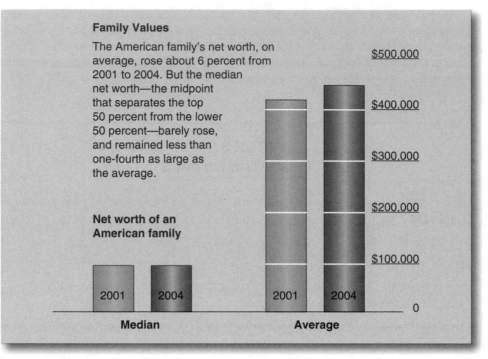

Figure 8.4   Median and Mean (Average) Net Worth of American Families
Source: New York Times

fortunes of a few very wealthy American families. The more modest median at less than $100,000 better represents how much wealth the typical American family truly possesses.

But for other purposes, the mean is quite useful, even when the distribution is skewed. Consider this example: Most people stay in the hospital only a short time, but a small number of people stay for weeks or even months on end. The median length of stay would tell us the experience of a typical patient. But from the perspective of an insurer or government agency that must pay for all hospital stays, the mean is more important. Everyone in the pool needs to contribute enough to cover the total cost, including the few really long hospital stays. If people just paid to cover the median stay, we would fall far short of the contributions needed to break even.

Measures of Spread and Variation

Although not noticed as much, the *spread* of a distribution is just as important or maybe more important than the center.

Standard Deviation

Spread can be measured by the range from minimum to maximum, but the most widely used measure is the **standard deviation**. The standard deviation represents how far the scores are, on average, from the mean. (The formula for the standard deviation is in Box 8.3.) A small standard deviation tells you that, on average, the scores are close to the mean. A large standard deviation tells you that, on average, the scores are far from the mean.

BOX 8.3
Standard Deviation: The Formula

The standard deviation (*SD*) of a variable measures how far each observation is from the mean on average. Formally,

$$SD_x = \sqrt{\frac{1}{n-1}\sum_{i=1}^{n}(x_i - \bar{x})^2},$$

where x_i refers to the individual observations, $\bar{x}$ is the mean, and n refers to sample size. $\sum$ is the summation symbol and means *add them up*.

The mean height of 14-year-olds in the YRBS is 167 centimeters (66 inches), but as expected, there is variability or spread in the heights of the children studied. How far, on average, are these individual heights from the mean? The standard deviation tells us: 9 centimeters (about 3.5 inches).

You can also use the standard deviation as a kind of yardstick to judge how typical, or extreme, a score is against the backdrop of the distribution of all scores. A 14-year-old who stands 1 standard deviation above the mean, or 176 centimeters (69 inches), is tall but not extraordinarily so. In contrast, a child who stands 2 standard deviations above the mean, or 185 centimeters (73 inches), would be highly unusual among 14-year-olds. Thus, within 1 standard deviation is not that far from the average; beyond 2 standard deviations is quite far from the mean.

The square of the standard deviation is the **variance**. Its units are hard to understand (because they are squared units), but the variance turns out to be useful in certain statistical formulas and procedures.

Pay Attention to the Standard Deviation, Not Just the Mean

Let's practice interpreting standard deviations by looking at some results of an international assessment of the reading literacy of 15-year-olds, shown in Table 8.4. Which of these three countries is doing the best job at imparting reading literacy to its young people?

Table 8.4   Literacy Score Means and Standard Deviations for Three Countries

	Mean	Standard Deviation
International average	500	100
New Zealand	529	108
South Korea	525	70
Brazil	396	86

Source: National Center of Education Statistics

Most of us are drawn initially to the means and can see that New Zealand tops the list. But the scores for students in New Zealand have a relatively large standard deviation as well—meaning there is more variation, or dissimilarity, among students. Perhaps the educational system is divided, with some doing exceptionally well, while others are falling short. In contrast, Korea has a mean nearly as large but a much lower standard deviation—meaning its students score more consistently (they are more alike in reading literacy). But consistency is not always a good thing—especially if you are doing poorly, such as Brazil. The key point here is to consider more than just measures of center, like the mean, when interpreting data; think about the standard deviation as well.

Standardized (z) Scores

For educational tests or psychometric scales, which do not have natural units, the standard deviation is used to convert raw scores to **standardized scores** or **z scores**. Standardized or z scores are scores on a variable converted to standard deviation units. Thus, a *z score = 1* means that the individual score is 1 standard deviation above the mean, and a *z score = −1.5* means that the individual score is 1.5 standard deviations below the mean. Here is the formula for a z score:

$$z = \frac{x - \bar{x}}{SD_x}.$$

It says, "Take a given value of x, subtract the mean, and divide by the standard deviation." This formula converts each individual x into standard deviation distances from the mean.

To get rid of the negative numbers, educational testers and others often further transform the z score into something more presentable. In the international literacy example above (Table 8.4), the test scores are transformed to a mean of 500 and a standard deviation of 100. In addition to 500 being a nice, round number to place at the center, very few if any test scores will fall as much as 5 standard deviations from the mean—so no scores for this test will end up with negative values.

Quantiles: Another Way to Measure Spread

The standard deviation is a good measure of spread for symmetric distributions but not highly skewed distributions, such as wealth, income, or length of stay in a hospital, which have a few very high values. Outliers or skewness heavily influence the standard deviation, as they do the mean. In such cases, a measure based on **quantiles** is more useful.

To create quantiles of income in a sample of adults, for example, imagine first lining them up in order from the lowest to the highest income. We can then divide the lineup into equal parts, cutting it in half, which is the median or 50th percentile (a quantile). We could also define the 25th percentile, the income such that 25% of the people have a lower income. Similarly the 75th percentile is the income at which 75% of the people have a lower income. We can measure almost any quantile, although the 25th, 50th, and 75th are most common.

For a skewed distribution, the interquartile range—the difference between the 75th and 25th percentile—can be a better measure of spread. That measure would have the same units as income itself, for example, thousands of dollars in the year 2000. For making comparisons over time or across countries, such units can be awkward. If a unit-free measure is desired, a ratio may be used, such as the ratio of the 90th percentile to the 10th percentile in the income distribution. That measure can be used to compare inequality across countries and over long periods of time.

Coefficient of Variation: A Way to Compare Spread

The standard deviation divided by the mean is referred to as the **coefficient of variation (COV)**. The COV is useful when making comparisons across variables with different scales or units. Consider results on the height and weight of U.S. teenagers from the YRBS, shown in Table 8.5.

Table 8.5   Height and Weight of U.S. Teenagers (Youth Risk Behavior Survey data)

	Minimum	Maximum	Mean	Standard Deviation	Coefficient of Variation (COV)
Q6 Height (in centimeters)	1,270	2,110	1,690	100	0.06
Q7 Weight (in kilograms)	35	181	69	17	0.25

Because height (in centimeters) and weight (in kilograms) are such different units, it's hard to compare them in terms of spread—is there more variation in height or in weight? The COV gives us the answer: There is much more spread or variation in the weight of U.S. teenagers than there is in height.

Relationships Between Categorical Variables

Cross-Tabulation

Cross-tabulation (cross-tabs for short) is the method most often used to describe relationships between categorical variables, either ordinal or nominal. Cross-tabs (also known as two-way tables or contingency tables) are relatively straightforward and can be presented to audiences unfamiliar with statistics. They often appear in news reports of polling results, for example.

But mistakes can be made in presenting and interpreting cross-tabs. One mistake is to focus on counts and not percentages. Say we are interested in teen smoking, and we want to compare rates of teen smoking by race in the United States. Table 8.6 presents the relevant data from the YRBS, but in the form of counts. The counts are useful for some purposes, such as inspecting the size of the sample. But it is quite difficult to compare racial groups from a table of counts alone. Although there are more than twice as many White smokers (2,888) as Hispanic smokers (1,116), there are more Whites overall than Hispanics in the sample—5,644 compared with only 1,806.

Table 8.6   Cross-Tab of Race/Ethnicity by Smoking (Counts Only)

Ever Smoked?	Race/Ethnicity								
	American Indian/ Alaska Native	Asian	Black or African American	Native Hawaiian/ Pacific Islander	White	Hispanic/ Latino	Multiple— Hispanic	Multiple— Non- Hispanic	Total
Yes	194	127	1,449	54	2,888	1,116	1,015	203	7,046
No	90	285	1,347	47	2,756	844	791	169	6,329
Total	284	412	2,796	101	5,644	1,960	1,806	372	13,375

To make a more useful comparison, the *rate* of smoking within each group must be calculated and compared. As Table 8.7 shows, this can be done with *column percentages*—the cell count divided by the *column* total. (For example, the proportion of Asian teenagers who smoke, .308, is calculated from the cell count, 127, divided by the total number of Asian teenagers, 412.) Column percentages allow us to look across the racial groups and see that Hispanic teens smoke at a somewhat higher rate (56.9%) than White teens (51.2%). We can also see that the rate of smoking is highest for American Indians and Alaska Natives and lowest for Asians.

Table 8.7 Cross-Tab of Race/Ethnicity by Smoking (Column Percentages)

Ever Smoked?	Race/Ethnicity								
	Am. Indian/ Alaska Native	Asian	Black or African American	Native Hawaiian/ Pacific Islander	White	Hispanic/ Latino	Multiple— Hispanic	Multiple— Non-Hispanic	Total
Yes	194	127	1,449	54	2,888	1,116	1,015	203	7,046
	68.3%	30.8%	51.8%	53.5%	51.2%	56.9%	56.2%	54.6%	52.7%
No	90	285	1,347	47	2,756	844	791	169	6,329
	31.7%	69.2%	48.2%	46.5%	48.8%	43.1%	43.8%	45.4%	47.3%
Total	284	412	2,796	101	5,644	1,960	1,806	372	13,375
	100.0%	100.0%	100.0%	100.0%	100.0%	100.0%	100.0%	100.0%	100.0%

Not every kind of percentage that a cross-tab can produce, however, provides relevant comparisons. Table 8.8 shows *row percentages*—the cell count divided by the *row* total. This tells us—among smokers, for example—how many are American Indian, Asian, Black, and so on. The share of smokers who are American Indian is small, because the share of teenagers who are American Indian is small. So this is not really helpful for our purposes: What we want to do is to compare *across* racial groups, and row percentages are not helpful for this.

Finally, cross-tabs can be used to produce yet a third type of percentage, *total percentages*—the cell count divided by the *overall total* (13,375 in our example). But this percentage is even less informative about the relationship between smoking and race. (The total percentages, however, can be a useful description of the overall sample.)

To help you clarify the construction of useful cross-tabs, it is sometimes good to follow these guidelines:

- Put the independent variable in the column position
- Put the dependent variable in the row position
- Calculate column percentages

This way of constructing cross-tabs encourages a focus on how the dependent variable changes as you change categories of the independent variable. It is also consistent with the conventions of an X-Y scatterplot for quantitative variables, in which X (the horizontal dimension) is the independent variable and Y (the vertical dimension) is the dependent variable.

Table 8.8   Cross-Tab of Race/Ethnicity by Smoking (Row Percentages)

Ever Smoked?	Race/Ethnicity								
	Am. Indian/ Alaska Native	Asian	Black or African American	Native Hawaiian/ Pacific Islander	White	Hispanic/ Latino	Multiple— Hispanic	Multiple— Non- Hispanic	Total
Yes	194	127	1,449	54	2,888	1,116	1,015	203	7,046
	2.8%	1.8%	20.6%	.8%	41.0%	15.8%	14.4%	2.9%	100.0%
No	90	285	1,347	47	2,756	844	791	169	6,329
	1.4%	4.5%	21.3%	.7%	43.5%	13.3%	12.5%	2.7%	100.0%
Total	284	412	2,796	101	5,644	1,960	1,806	372	13,375
	2.1%	3.1%	20.9%	.8%	42.2%	14.7%	13.5%	2.8%	100.0%

Relative Risks and Odds Ratios: Another Way to Show Relationships in Categorical Data

Although cross-tabs can be used to express a relationship between two *dichotomous* or *dummy* variables, health researchers and others sometimes prefer to use *relative risks* and *odds ratios*. They are not the same thing, and often people mix them up.

Relative Risks

We saw how *rates*—such as murders per 100,000 people—can be directly interpreted as *risks*. Now imagine that we want some way to describe how a rate or risk varies between two groups. Consider the data in Table 8.9 on the survival of male and female passengers on the Titanic.

Table 8.9   Deaths of Male and Female Passengers on the Titanic

	Male	Female	Total
Survived	142	308	450
Died	709	154	863
Total	851	462	1,313
Death rate (died/total)	0.83	0.33	
Relative risk (male rate/female rate)	2.50		

Source: Simon (2008).

The death rate for females is $154/462 = .33$, or 33%. The death rate for males is $709/851 = .83$ or 83%. This is what we would calculate if we were calculating column percentages in a cross-tabulation.

The *relative risk*—sometimes called the *risk ratio*—compares the probability of death in each group. The **relative risk** of death is the ratio of the risk of the two groups, which is $.83/.33 = 2.5$. This tells us that there was a 2.5 greater probability of death for males than for females on the Titanic. In this way, the relative risk describes the relationship between gender and dying on the Titanic, both dichotomous variables.

Odds Ratio (OR)

What were the odds that a female passenger on the Titanic died? We can calculate these odds from Table 8.9: It is the number of females who died divided by the number of females who survived, or $154/308 = 0.5$. For males on the Titanic, the odds of death were $709/142 = 4.99$, or very nearly 5 to 1.

The **odds ratio** (**OR**) compares the relative odds of death in each group. The odds ratio comparing males and females on the Titanic is $4.99/0.50 = 9.98$. There is very nearly a 10-fold greater odds of death for males than for females. Odds ratios like these are particularly common in medicine and epidemiology.

Notice the large difference between the odds ratio and the relative risk. There is a 2.5 times greater relative risk for a male dying on the Titanic compared with a female. However, there is a 10-fold greater odds. Both show that males were much more likely to die, but the odds ratio seems to imply a larger difference.

The problem with odds ratios is that people often implicitly assume that they refer to relative risks, because it is more natural for us to think in terms of risks than odds. When possible, therefore, it is often better to avoid using odds ratios to describe relationships between two dichotomous variables. However, in certain study designs (case-control studies, discussed in Chapter 13) and certain types of analysis (logistic regression, described in Chapter 9), relative risks (and cross-tabs) cannot be calculated.

Adjusted and Standardized Rates: When to Use Them

Many diseases or health conditions get worse with age. So if we are interested in comparing disease rates (or prevalence) across communities or demographic groups, for example, we might prefer to take this fact into account—to use age-adjusted rates

To adjust a rate, R, as though it had a standard distribution among groups (such as age groups), indexed by g: First determine the standard group population shares (e.g., share of the population in each age group), s_g to be used to adjust all the rates. Second, calculate the rate within each group, R_g for every area. Then calculate that area's adjusted rate by weighting the area's group-specific rate by the population in that age group.

$$\text{Adjusted rate} = \sum_g R_g s_g.$$

Rates can also be adjusted through multiple regression, as discussed in Chapter 9. Adjusted rates are particularly common in epidemiology and demography. Rates should be adjusted for any variable whose effect is predictable, well understood, and not of interest in the particular analysis. To learn more about the topics in this section, consult any elementary epidemiology textbook (e.g., Gordis, 2000).

Relationships Between Quantitative Variables: Scatterplots and Correlation

A relationship between two *quantitative variables*—such as education (in years) and income (in dollars)—can be graphed with a *scatterplot* and summarized numerically either by a *correlation* or a *simple regression*.

Scatterplots

Consider Figure 8.5, which shows a **scatterplot** (sometimes called an *X-Y* graph) of the relationship between gross domestic product (GDP) and years of life expectancy in 179 countries (based on data compiled by the United Nations). This relationship is evidently nonlinear (not a straight line). It is

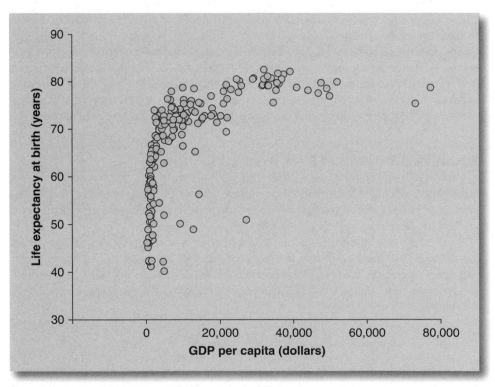

Figure 8.5   Scatterplot of GDP and Life Expectancy in 179 Countries

important to spot this pattern before calculating statistical summaries, because correlation, regression, and many other related techniques assume or are most informative with a linear relationship. Remember: Always begin your analysis by graphing the data.

For some statistical methods, such as regression, it is necessary to *transform* one or more of the variables to coax the data, as it were, into a more linear pattern. For example, if we take the *natural log* of GDP and regraph the data, we get the pattern shown in Figure 8.6, which is much closer to a linear relationship.

Influential observations and outliers are also revealed in scatterplots, and these can have a large influence on the calculation of correlations, regressions, and other numerical summaries of relationship. Again, be sure to graph your data first.

Correlation

Correlation is a measure of the strength and direction of a relationship between two variables. It is typically represented by r, also known as **Pearson r** or the **correlation coefficient**, which ranges from -1 to 1, with 0 meaning no relationship. (The formula for the correlation r is in Box 8.4.) But beyond

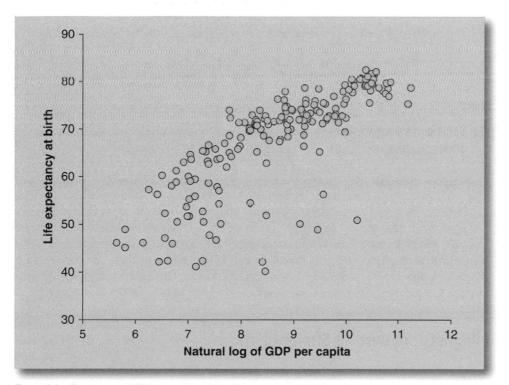

Figure 8.6 Scatterplot of GDP Logged and Life Expectancy in 179 Countries

this, many people struggle with how to interpret the actual magnitude of a correlation. So here are some general guidelines (based on Cohen, 1992):

Correlation r	Size
.10	Small
.30	Moderate
.50	Large

It is also helpful to know this interpretation of a correlation: If a variable (X) changes by 1 standard deviation, the correlation r represents the expected standard deviation change in the other variable (Y). For example, the correlation from Figure 8.3 showing GDP logged and life expectancy is $r = .8$, which is a large correlation. We can interpret this as telling us that a 1 standard deviation increase in GDP logged is associated with a .8 standard deviation change in life expectancy.

BOX 8.4
Correlation: The Formula

The correlation r between two variables (x and y) is calculated with the following formula:

$$r = \frac{1}{n-1} \sum_{i=1}^{n} \left(\frac{x_i - \bar{x}}{SD_x} \right) \left(\frac{y_i - \bar{y}}{SD_y} \right).$$

The basic idea of how correlation is calculated is to first standardize each variable. Specifically, see how far each observation is from its mean and divide by the standard deviation, creating a z score for each observation for both variables. Then the covariation of the z scores is averaged, to see if x and y move together and if so in which direction.

Correlation is a unit-free measure that permits comparisons across completely different types of variables. While these features are strengths for some purposes, they are weaknesses for others. For example, we might want to know not just that education and income are positively correlated but also *how much* (on average) more highly educated individuals earn. In principle, income and education could be just as highly correlated if one more year of education was associated with earnings $10 higher on average as if one more year of education was associated with earnings $10,000 higher on average.

Simple Regression: Best-Fit Straight Line

Simple regression uses a best-fit straight line to describe how one quantitative variable—the *independent variable* (often denoted as X)—predicts another quantitative variable—the *dependent variable*

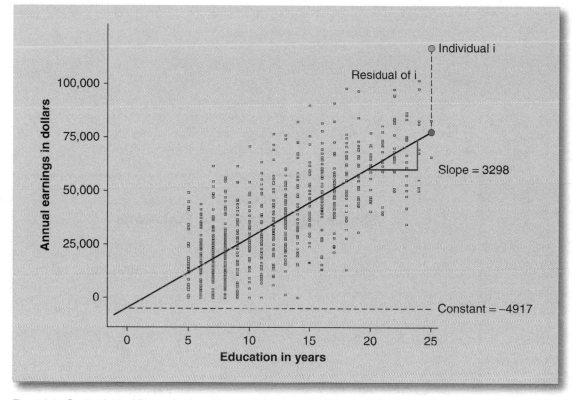

Figure 8.7   Scatterplot and Regression Line Showing the Relationship Between Education and Income

(often denoted as *Y*). *Multiple regression analysis*, with more than one independent variable, will be discussed in Chapter 9. Regression analysis is perhaps the most widely used statistical method in social and policy research.

Consider the relationship between earnings and education, measured in years.[2] Figure 8.7 shows a scatterplot of the data and the regression line fitted from the data.[3] The regression line, like any straight line, is completely described by two numbers: the *slope* and the *intercept*. In regression, the slope is more commonly referred to as the **coefficient of the independent variable** (e.g., education), because it is the number the independent variable is multiplied by. The intercept is more commonly referred to as the **constant**, because its contribution to the dependent variable does not vary as the value of the independent variable changes.

---

[2]We will use simulated data because real world data are a lot messier and thus harder to use for initial teaching.

[3]Experienced readers may be concerned that Earnings are not normally distributed and think that we should log Earnings. However, normality is only important for inference: We can calculate a least squares regression line for any variable.

In this example, the constant is −4,917, and the slope is 3,298. The regression equation, more easily interpreted if the actual variable names are used in place of X and Y, is:

$$\text{Earnings} = -4917 + 3298 \times \text{Educ.}$$

The equations used to determine the coefficient and constant are given in Box 8.5. The constant term is interpreted as *the predicted value of the dependent variable when the independent variable is zero*. In this case, earnings of − \$4,917 are predicted for someone with zero years of education.[4] It is, however, the coefficient that provides information about the magnitude of the relationship.

BOX 8.5
Simple Regression: The Equations

There are data points for N individuals, with the individuals indexed by i. A specific data point has independent variable value, x_i, and dependent variable value, y_i.

$$\text{Coefficient of the independent variable} = \text{Slope} = \quad b = \frac{\sum_{i=1}^{N}(y_i - \bar{y})(x_i - \bar{x})}{\sum_{i=1}^{N}(x_i - \bar{x})^2}.$$

$$\text{Constant} = a = \bar{y} - b\bar{x}.$$

$$\text{Predicted } y = \hat{y}_i = a + bx_i \quad \text{Residual} = \hat{\varepsilon}_i = y_i - \hat{y}_i$$

$$SST = \sum_{i=1}^{N}(y_i - \bar{y})^2 \qquad SSR = \sum_{i=1}^{N}(\hat{y}_i - \bar{y})^2 \qquad SSE = \sum_{i=1}^{N}\hat{\varepsilon}_i^2 = \hat{\sigma}^2.$$

$$R^2 = \frac{SSR}{SST}.$$

Note: SST is the total sum of squares; SSR is the regression sum of squares, the explained variation; and SSE is the error sum of squares (sum of squared residuals).

Interpreting the Regression Coefficient (Slope)

From a policy or practice perspective, the most interesting, bottom-line result of a regression is the coefficient of the independent variable—or the coefficients in a multiple regression. The coefficient

---

[4]See discussion of out-of-sample extrapolation in Chapter 9 to understand why the constant is negative, and how it should be interpreted.

reveals the quantitative influence of the independent variable. But to be useful, a coefficient must be interpreted in terms understandable to the wider world. Technically, the coefficient is interpreted as *the change in the dependent variable associated with a one-unit increase in the independent variable.* In our example, in everyday language, the coefficient informs us that someone with one more year of education is predicted (or expected) to earn $3,298 more. Box 8.6 describes how to systematically interpret a regression coefficient in a manner useful for policy or practice.

BOX 8.6
Steps for Interpreting a Regression Coefficient

1. Identify the independent variable and its units.

   Our example: Education measured in years is the independent variable

2. Describe a one-unit increase in the independent variable in everyday language.

   Our example: One more year of education

3. Identify the dependent variable and its units.

   Our example: Annual earnings measured in dollars is the dependent variable

4. The coefficient is the change in the dependent variable, which is predicted for a one-unit change in the independent variable. Describe that change in everyday language, making the units clear.

   Our example: Those with one more year of education are predicted to have earnings $3,298 higher. In other words, the coefficient predicts an additional $3,298 per year of education.

The Importance of Units in Interpreting Regression Coefficients

Just as the phrase "I walked eight" is useless without knowing the units of eight, so a regression coefficient is useless without knowing its units. In our example, the coefficient is in dollars per year of education—specifically, 3,298 dollars of additional annual income are predicted with an additional year of education.

If earnings had been measured in *thousands of dollars* instead of *dollars*, the coefficient's numerical value would be 3.298. The numerical value of the coefficient would also change if education had been measured in *months* instead of *years*—so the units of the independent variable matter as well. The units of the coefficient are always the units of the dependent variable divided by the units of the independent variable.

We recommend writing the units of the constant and the coefficient when writing their numbers. In our example, the constant is −$4,917, and the coefficient of education is $3,298 per year. To translate this abstraction into a useful form, describe both the independent and dependent variable changes in words understandable to a larger audience. (See Box 8.6 for the systematic approach.)

$$\text{Earnings} = -\$4917 + (\$3298/\text{year}) \times \text{Educ.}$$

Can a Regression Coefficient Be Interpreted As a Causal Effect?

When we interpreted the regression coefficient, we carefully chose the language of expectation or prediction—for example, those with one more year of education are *expected* to (or *predicted* to) earn on average $3,298 more. We took care not to say that one more year of education *causes* (or *results in*) $3,298 more in earnings (on average).

But can a regression coefficient be interpreted as the effect of the independent variable on the dependent variable?

The answer is complex. On the one hand, regression is essentially just another way of representing correlation, and correlation does not prove causation. (We will have much more to say about this in Chapter 10.) Just because education and earnings are correlated does not necessarily mean that more education causes higher earnings.[5]

On the other hand, under some circumstances described in Chapter 11 on control variables—and with much care and many caveats—regression *can* be used to measure a causal effect. Indeed, this is its most common application in social and policy research. The interpretation method of Box 8.6 is particularly useful when making a causal interpretation.

BOX 8.7
Which One Is the Dependent Variable?
Which One Is the Independent Variable?

To help answer the question, the following little model is often quite useful:

$$X \rightarrow Y$$

Here *X is the independent variable,* and *Y is the dependent variable.* Then ask yourself the following:

Which variable is the presumed cause (or predictor)?

Make this the *independent variable—X.*

Which variable is the presumed effect (or the outcome being predicted)?

Make this the *dependent variable—Y.*

This is the variable that *depends* on the other one.

---

[5]In fact, education does have a causal effect on earnings. In the four chapters on causation, we will illustrate how that can be proven.

Changes Versus Levels

Care must be taken not to confuse interpretation of the regression coefficient with interpretation of the whole regression equation. The coefficient provides information about how the dependent variable *changes* when the independent variable *changes*. In our example, the coefficient says that someone with one *more* year of education is predicted to earn $3,298 *more*.

In contrast, the equation as a whole—the constant plus the coefficient multiplied by the *level* of the independent variable—provides information about the *level* of the dependent variable. To illustrate, let's predict the income for someone with 16 years of education:

$$\text{Predicted earnings} = a + b_{educ} \times \text{Educ}$$

$$= -\$4917 + \$3298/\text{year} \times \text{Educ}$$

$$= -\$4917 + \$3298/\text{year} \times 16 \text{ years}$$

$$= \$47,851.$$

Notice how we used the whole regression to predict the *level* of earnings of someone with 16 years of education to be $47,851. The distinction between the *change* represented by the coefficient and the *level* predicted by the whole equation will become important for more advanced forms of analysis covered in later chapters.

R-Squared and Residuals:
How Well Does the Line Fit the Data?

R-squared (defined formally in Box 8.5) expresses the *proportion of the variation in the dependent variable that is explained (or predicted) by variation in the independent variables*. In our example, *R*-squared is .56, so we say that 56% of the variation among people in their earnings can be predicted just by variation in their education. The remaining, unexplained variation is in the error terms—known as the **residuals**.

Here is how to think about residuals: If the data were perfectly predicted by the regression, all the points would lie on the line. In this case, the residuals would all be zero and the *R*-squared would be one, meaning that 100% of the variation in the dependent variable was predicted using variation in the independent variable alone.

But with real data, the regression prediction (the line) does not completely coincide with the actual observed data. Consider the person, individual *i*, shown in Figure 8.7 who has 25 years of education and earns $117,375. The value of earnings predicted by *i*'s education would be $77,533, also marked on the line. The residual is this difference between the actual earnings and the predicted earnings, measured by the vertical distance from the data point to the regression line. The larger the residuals, across all data points, the poorer the fit—the smaller the residuals, the better the fit.

How Is Best Fit Defined?

The equations for the constant and the coefficient come from a criterion called *least squares*, so this form of regression is most correctly called *ordinary least squares* (OLS) regression. OLS regression chooses the constant and coefficient to minimize the sum of the square of the residuals.

While that is a reasonable method, it is clearly not the only one. Why not minimize the sum of the absolute value of residuals? That method would reduce the large influence of outliers in OLS regression analysis. Or why not minimize the horizontal distance from the data to the line? In fact, all these methods and others are both possible and reasonable, but they require a lot of numerical computation and do not have simple formulas. Historically, they were often not possible. While possible now, they are not common and should be reserved for those situations where one wants to minimize the influence of outliers.

For further reading on correlation and regression, consult an introductory statistics book, such as *Statistics* (Friedman, Pisani, & Purves, 2007) or *The Basic Practice of Statistics* (Moore, 2009). For more on regression, consult an introductory econometrics book, such as *Introductory Econometrics: A Modern Approach* (Wooldridge, 2009).

Effect Size and Practical Significance

The numbers that come from analysis and research are meant to inform. Although it may seem obvious, *magnitude*—the size of the number—matters. An effect or difference may be too small to make much difference in the real world—or it may be very large and of crucial practical importance. How can we decide if an effect is large enough to matter?

Effect size

To answer this question, we can use various measures of **effect size**. The *correlation r*, discussed above, is one possible measure of effect size. Another commonly used measure of effect size is the ratio of the effect or difference to the standard deviation. Intuitively, an effect size provides a measure of how big a difference or effect is relative to the ordinary variation that the variable undergoes. Effect size is a way of comparing magnitudes from different variables or different studies.

To illustrate, let's consider the effects of an employment program on the time it takes for participants to find a job and on their starting wage, relative to a control group, as shown in Table 8.10. As these results show, the program has a much larger effect on reducing the days it takes to find a job than on the starting wage.

Practical Significance

Effect size is not the only way of assessing magnitude and sometimes not the best way. Another approach is to look directly at the magnitude of the difference or effect and see what it means when applied practically to the real world. The **practical significance** of a difference or relationship is the

Table 8.10   An Imaginary Employment Program

	(A) Program Group	(B) Control Group	Difference (A − B)	SD	Effect Size (Difference/SD)
Days to find a job	7 days	14 days	− 7 days	10 days	− .70
Starting hourly wage	$12	$11	$1	$5	.20

extent that its magnitude (if true) would be important or relevant in the real world. Practical significance is also referred to as *substantive significance*, or as significance in whatever subject is being examined, such as *clinical* significance, *economic* significance, *policy* significance, and so on (Miller, 2004, 2005).

For example, if a regression revealed that one more year of education was associated with just $1 more in annual earnings, most people would think that this effect is not economically significant. But if a year of education is associated with a boost of $10,000 per year in annual earnings, it's a much different picture. To determine the practical significance of a regression coefficient, interpret it in real-life terms, as described in Box 8.6. Knowing the units is essential for doing this.

Practical Significance Is a Matter of Judgment

Consider another example: If we learn that an antismoking campaign reduces smoking rates by 5 percentage points, that is clearly practically significant. It is a big enough effect that anyone would care. On the other hand, if the campaign reduced smoking rates by 0.5 (one half) of a percentage point, many might decide that this was too small to matter in the practical world.

Still, some people might feel that a .5 percentage point reduction in smoking is practically significant—especially if there are few alternatives with larger effects. Ultimately, practical significance is determined by those applying or using the results, including policymakers, advocates, and program planners, based on their values and judgment.

Inference and the Standard Error

The data in social and policy research often come from a random sample that aims to represent a much larger population, as we saw in Chapter 5. The monthly unemployment statistic in the United States, for example, comes from the Current Population Survey (CPS), a random sample designed to represent the labor force. The sample produces a statistic or *estimate* (such as the proportion unemployed last month) that aims to represent the true population **parameter** (which is unknown). The methods involved in making conclusions about an unknown population parameter, based on a sample estimate, is called **statistical inference**. The next few sections review these methods.

Recall from Chapter 5 how random samples—while being *unbiased*—still tend to produce estimates that can be a bit off the mark from the true population parameter, simply from *sampling variability* alone. And we saw how, if you plotted the estimates from many samples (of the same size from the same population), they would form a *sampling distribution* that tends to be normal (bell-shaped).

The standard deviation of the sampling distribution is called the **standard error** (*SE*) and represents the variability, or sampling error, associated with a given statistic (from a sample of a given size). The magnitude of the standard error depends on two factors: variability and sample size. In fact, the standard error of a mean or proportion can be expressed as follows:

$$SE = \frac{\text{Variability}}{\sqrt{\text{Sample size}}}.$$

If everyone in society had nearly the same incomes, then we would not need much of a sample at all to come up with a very precise estimate of the average income of the population. But if incomes in society vary quite a bit, the standard error of our estimate will be much larger. The sample size is also a factor: The more data we have to make our estimate, the smaller the standard error and thus the more precise it will be. Notice that the sample size is under the square root sign. This means that to cut the standard error in half, we have to quadruple the sample size.

The standard error is quite useful in statistics and appears in various procedures—one of which is confidence intervals.

Confidence Intervals

Confidence intervals (discussed in Chapter 5) provide a range, or boundary, around a sample estimate that, with a given level of confidence, contains the true population parameter. They are best known as "margins of error" from polls reported in the news. Roughly two standard errors on either side of a statistic give us a *95% confidence interval*. Here is the formula:

$$\text{Estimate} \pm 2 \times SE.$$

Although this formula is approximately correct, to get exactly 95% confidence requires exactly 1.96 standard errors[6]. And in some situations, we might want another **level of confidence**, such as 90% or maybe 99%. If we let Z^* represent the precise number of standard errors we need to give us a desired level of confidence, the formula looks like this:

$$\text{Estimate} \pm Z^* \times SE.$$

Thus, to determine the confidence interval, start at the actual statistic estimated from the sample and move out in both directions a certain number (Z^*) of standard errors. To find the 95% confidence interval, as we have seen, Z^* is 1.96 *SEs*. To find the 99% confidence interval, Z^* is 2.58 *SEs*. Notice that to be more confident of capturing the true population parameter, the confidence interval must be wider.

---

[6]The 1.96 value depends on a sufficiently large sample size. With very small samples, the number of standard errors needed for a 95% confidence interval is larger. See Moore (2009) for further details.

Univariate Statistics and Relationships Both Have Confidence Intervals

Margins of error—confidence intervals by another name—get attached to percentages from polls. For example, we hear that the president's job approval rating is 57%—*plus or minus 3 percentage points*. The ±3 percentage points (or just points for short) means that we are 95% confident that the true percentage of the population that approves of the president's job approval (the parameter) lies between 54% and 60%. But confidence intervals (and standard errors) can be attached to a wide range of other statistics, including the following:

- A mean
- A difference in means
- A regression coefficient
- An odds or odds ratio

To illustrate, consider Table 8.11, an extract from a study by the Commissioner and others in the New York City Department of Health (Frieden et al., 2005). The table shows 95% confidence intervals for both proportions (e.g., percentage who smoke every day in 2002) and differences in proportions (e.g., percent change in smoking every day). Thus, we learn that in 2002, we are 95% confident that the percentage of New Yorkers who smoked every day was between 13.6% and 15.4%. We are also 95% confident that the percent change (not percentage point change!) in that smoking rate was a decline of between 17.6% and 3.4%.

Table 8.11   Extract of Table 1 in Frieden et al. (2005)

	Percentage in 2002 (95% CI)	Percentage in 2003 (95% CI)	Percent Change (95% CI)
Smoking every day	14.4 (13.6, 15.4)	12.9 (12.2, 13.6)	−10.5 (−17.6, −3.4)
Smoking some days	7.0 (6.4, 7.7)	6.3 (5.7, 6.8)	−13.1 (−23.7, −1.9)

Indeed, you can attach a confidence interval (and a standard error) to almost any statistic calculated from sample data. Although the calculation details and difficulty vary, the meaning of all confidence intervals remains much the same: We are 95% (or 90% or 99%) confident that the true population parameter lies between the lower and upper limit of the interval.

Confidence Intervals Only Reflect Some Sources of Error

Confidence intervals and standard errors do not reflect all sources of error—only sampling error. But as we've seen in previous chapters, there are many other sources of error in research. Some of the sources of error *NOT* captured in a confidence interval (or margin of error) are as follows:

- Measurement error, from how questions are asked or understood or other errors in measuring process
- Coverage error, from failing to include people or households from the sample
- Nonresponse error, from certain people refusing to participate
- Data processing errors, from handling or manipulating the data
- Causal inference error, from incomplete or erroneous models of the causal relationships between variables (to be discussed in Part III)

Although confidence intervals provide useful information, these other sources of error must be considered as well in judging sample statistics.

Confidence intervals are one form of statistical inference. Another is statistical significance tests, the topic of the next section.

Significance Tests

If you read research articles or reports, you will certainly encounter statistical **significance tests**. They are used to determine, for example, if the effect of a job-training program is **statistically significant** or if the reading ability of boys is "significantly" lower than it is for girls. Academic journals, government agencies, and the courts often demand statistical significance tests as evidence. Significance tests are also widely used as part of the strategies for causation discussed in Part III of the book.

But many people find significance testing strange—and, it turns out, for good reason. Even many academics challenge the logic and value of significance testing, with some going so far to suggest that the procedure be abandoned altogether (Ziliak & McCloskey, 2008).

Although it would be convenient to just go along with the critics and avoid the topic, it is important to first try to understand the logic and interpretation of statistical significance tests.

Falsification and the Logic of Significance Testing

A significance test relies on the logic of falsification—gathering evidence for the existence of something by demonstrating what it is *not*. An analogy of guessing what's inside a gift box helps demonstrate that we actually use this style of reasoning in everyday life.

Imagine that you get a nicely wrapped gift in a box from a friend. You're told not to open the box, but of course you can't help trying to guess what's inside. Say you have several guesses (hypotheses) about what's inside the box: a bicycle, a book, or a box of fancy marshmallows (your friend has funny tastes). Just by observing the size of the box, however, you rule out the bicycle hypothesis—it's just too small, even if the bike were disassembled. So it's *not* a bike. But it could still be a book or a box of marshmallows. Then you pick it up and realize it's much too lightweight to be a book. So you conclude it's *not* a book. You've now got evidence in favor of the marshmallow hypothesis by eliminating other possibilities. Of course, you still can't be sure what really *is* inside the box.

Significance testing (also called **hypothesis testing**) works in a very similar way. An explicit claim about the population, called a **null hypothesis**, is put forward. Then we look at the results from our sample data and ask, "How likely is this sample result, if the null hypothesis about the population were in fact true?" If our sample result would only rarely happen, given the null hypothesis, we reject the null. But if the result is at least somewhat likely, given the null hypothesis, we cannot reject it.

The null hypothesis is typically a statement of *no* difference or *no* relationship. There is *no* difference in the population between boys and girls in reading ability, for example. Or there is *no* relationship in the population between education and income. If we reject the null hypothesis, therefore, we have implicit evidence for what is called the **alternative hypothesis**—the logical compliment of the null. There *is* a difference, or there *is* a relationship.

Notice that significance testing uses an implicit language of double negatives. A *statistically significant difference* between boys and girls means *not no difference*, or a *statistically significant relationship* between education and incomes means *not no relationship*. This is poor English, of course, but it is what significance tests tell us. This implicit double-negative language accounts for part of the struggle people have with interpreting significance tests.

Running a Significance Test

Let's practice significance testing with an example. Suppose we wonder if wages in the U.S. South are lower, on average, than those in other parts of the country. We test this question using a sample taken from the CPS, a random sample survey.[7] The mean wage of respondents in the South is $5.38 per hour, while the mean wage of respondents in the rest of the country is $6.18 per hour, a $0.79 difference.

That answers the question, it would seem. But our data come from a sample, a relatively small sample of $n = 526$ at that (this is actually a random subsample of the CPS—the complete survey is much larger). So perhaps we just got this difference by chance, the luck of the draw as it were, when in reality there is really no regional wage difference in the U.S. population. You should recognize this as a *null hypothesis* of no difference between the South and the rest of the United States.

But how do we tell if the difference in wages evident in our sample is large enough to rule out a null of no difference? The standard error—as a gauge of sampling variability—provides a useful benchmark. We can ask, "Is the observed difference large or small, relative to the standard error?" If the difference is large, relative to the standard error, then it is unlikely to be just a fluke of sampling and we can probably rule out the null of no difference.

To make this idea more formal, we construct what is called a **test statistic**:

$$\text{Test statistic} = (\text{Estimate} - \text{Null})/SE.$$

In our case, the sample estimate of the difference in wages was −$0.79 (or 79 cents *less* in the South than in the rest of the United States). The null hypothesis is no difference—$0.00. The computer finds that the standard error of the difference is $0.34, and so we have

$$\text{Test statistic} = (-0.79 - 0.00)/0.34 = -2.36.$$

---

[7] We use only a small subsample of the CPS, which results in a more interesting statistical significance test than would a larger and more definitive sample.

Statistics and probability theory tell us that this test statistic takes the shape of a *t distribution* (which looks much like a normal distribution). A *t* distribution is a density function that can be used to calculate how likely our estimate is, given the null. The statistical software does the *t* test calculations for us, so we won't worry about the details here (you can find them in any introductory statistics textbook). The computer tells us that a *t* statistic of −2.36 has a probability of .0187 (or 1.87%). This is fairly low, in other words unlikely.

p Values

The probability calculated for a test statistic is called a **p value** for short. Here is its meaning again: *A p value represents the probability of observing our sample estimate (or an estimate further from the null), if the null hypothesis about the population is true.*[8] In our example, the *p* value tells us that in a random sample of $n = 536$, we have a 1.87% chance of observing a difference of $-\$.079$ (or a greater magnitude difference) in wages between the South and the rest of the United States, if in the population there is no regional difference in wages.

When the *p* value is low—as in our example—then we reject the null hypothesis. In other words, it is very unlikely that our sample would give us a difference this large, if there is no difference in the population. So the null must be false. Recall the gift box analogy and the language of double negatives: We demonstrate a difference in wages by showing that there is not no difference.

To repeat: We reject the null hypothesis if the *p* value is low. But how low? One answer is that there are rules of thumb, as well as standards enforced by academic journals, regulatory agencies (such as the Food and Drug Administration), and the courts. The most common **significance level** is *.05* or less. In certain circumstances, other significance levels, such as .01 or .10, are used.

But, in fact, there is no right answer. High standards of proof might be important in some situations, such as testing the safety of new drugs. But in other cases, more flexible standards of proof are appropriate, such as exploring possible risk factors associated with dropping out of high school. You might miss something important if your standards of proof are too high.

Because there is no one right standard, results are often shown indicating different significance levels with asterisks or stars. For example, one star might indicate significance at the 10% level, 2 stars 5%, and 3 stars 1%. To illustrate, consider Table 8.12, an extract from Table VI in Katz, Kling, and Liebman (2001), relating to the Moving to Opportunity experiment, which we will discuss in Chapter 12. The table shows the differences in children's outcomes between families who got housing vouchers to move to a low-poverty neighborhood (treatment group) and those who did not (control group), with stars indicating the level of statistical significance of the difference. We are confident that children in the voucher group differed from children in the control group and had fewer injuries or accidents with a *p* value of less than .05; that they differed in asthma attacks requiring medical attention with a *p* value of less than .10; and that they did not differ significantly (at least at the 10% level) in going to a doctor for immunization (Katz et al., 2001).

---

[8]The phrase "or . . . further from the null" makes this a two-sided hypothesis in which our alternative hypothesis includes both positive and negative differences. It is also possible to have one-sided hypotheses in which only a difference that is larger in magnitude but of the same sign is part of the alternative and used to calculate the *p* value. We do not discuss one-sided hypotheses further. See Friedman et al. (2007), Moore (2009), or any introductory statistics book for more details.

Table 8.12   Extract From Table VI of Katz et al. (2001) on the Moving to Opportunity Experiment

	Control Mean	Experimental-Control Difference
Any injuries or accidents during the past 6 months that required medical attention	.105	− .059 **
Any asthma attacks requiring medical attention	.098	− .051 *
Been to doctor for regular checkup or immunization during the past 6 months	.856	− .043
Note: *p < .10, **p < .05.		

Chi-Square Test of Cross-Tabs

To test whether two categorical variables are related, a **chi-square test** can be used. The test is similar in logic to the usual test statistic but takes a somewhat different form.

The first step is to determine what counts would be expected if there were no relationship between the two variables. In the relationship between smoking and race/ethnicity, for example, if Hispanics are 10% of the population, 10% of the smokers will be Hispanic. The next step is to compare the actual observed counts to what would be expected if there was no relationship (the null hypothesis) in all the cells. The greater the differences, the easier it is to reject the null of no relationship.

The chi-square formula works like this:

- *Step 1:* Find the expected count (expected if no relationship) in each cell in this way: (Row total × Column total)/Table total
- *Step 2:* Calculate the chi-square statistic = $\chi^2 = \Sigma$ (Observed − Expected)^2/Expected
- *Step 3:* Look up the associated p value using a chi-square table or software, with degrees of freedom = (Rows − 1) (Columns − 1)

Most statistical software packages will do all the chi-square calculations for you, so the most important skills are to be able to interpret the p value and the patterns in the data.

Other Test Statistics

t and chi-square are just two of several different test statistics. Others include F and z statistics. And each test statistic can be calculated in a variety of different ways depending on the analysis. For example, the t test can be used to test one mean, a difference in means, and a regression coefficient, to name a few. Table 8.13 shows the most common tests used for some of the most common statistical analyses.

Universality of the p Value

Because the details of statistical significance testing appear in many forms, depending on the data and the question, we recommend that you focus on understanding the null hypothesis and

Table 8.13   Common Statistical Analyses and Their Test Statistics

Analysis	Usual Null Hypothesis	Test Statistic
Comparison of means	Diff = 0, No difference	t statistic
Comparison of proportions	Diff = 0, No difference	z statistic (or chi-square)
Paired sample means	Mean of differences = 0	t statistic
Odds ratio	OR = 1, No difference	Chi-square statistic
Cross-tabulation	No relationship	Chi-square statistic
Regression	Coefficient = 0, No relationship	t statistic
ANOVA	No difference across all means	F statistic

the p value and pay less attention to the magnitudes of t statistics, chi-square statistics, F statistics, and so on. p Values are universal. Once you learn their interpretation—and you know what null hypothesis is being tested—you can make sense of significance testing without knowing the technical details.

Statistical Significance, Practical Significance, and Power

Many people read too much into a significance test. Such tests help us decide if an observed difference or relationship is a fluke or not. But they do not tell us if the magnitude of the difference or relationship is big enough to matter in the real world—if it has *practical significance*. Earlier we discussed practical significance and measures of effect size. Let's see now how statistical significance does not tell us the same thing.

Consider another antismoking campaign, and let's say this time we observe what we consider to be a practically insignificant .1 percentage point reduction in smoking rate, which is nonetheless statistically significant. You might wonder how such a small difference like .1 percentage point could turn out to be statistically significant. It all boils down to small standard errors, most likely stemming from a very large sample size. While a smaller difference is less statistically significant, all else held equal, even a very small difference can be statistically significant if the standard errors are sufficiently smaller still. If the standard error in our smoking rate estimate is .01 percentage points, a difference of .1 percentage points (10 times the standard error) will be statistically significant.

Combinations of Statistical and Practical Significance

To illustrate the possible combinations of statistical and practical significance you may encounter in a study, Table 8.14 presents four fictional examples involving school children and their math scores. The differences in mean test scores between boys and girls and the standard errors of those differences are calculated.[9] The test statistic is then the difference divided by the standard error. Table 8.14 provides the data and calculations.

---

[9]To make things simpler, we will assume that the standard deviation is the same for boys and girls.

Table 8.14   Scenarios for All Possible Combinations of Statistical and Practical Significance

	All Possible Combinations of Statistical and Practical Significance: Four Made-Up Examples Comparing Boys' and Girls' Mean Test Scores			
	A	**B**	**C**	**D**
Sample size	10,000	10,000	9	1,000
Overall mean test score	200	200	200	200
Standard deviation	25	25	100	25
Girls' mean test score	175	199	175	199
Boys' mean test score	225	201	225	201
Δ = Difference in Test Score (Boys' − Girls')	50	2	50	2
Effect size	$= \Delta/SD$ $= 50/25$ $=2$	$=\Delta/SD$ $=2/25$ $=.08$	$=\Delta/SD$ $=50/100$ $=.5$	$=\Delta/SD$ $=2/25$ $=.08$
Practically significant?	Yes	No	Yes (If difference true)	No
Standard error of the difference in test score mean[10]	$=2 \times SD/\sqrt{N}$ $=2 \times 25/\sqrt{10,000}$ $=.5$	$=2 \times SD/\sqrt{N}$ $=2 \times 25/\sqrt{10,000}$ $=.5$	$=2 \times SD/\sqrt{N}$ $=2 \times 100/\sqrt{9}$ $=66.6$	$=2 \times SD/\sqrt{N}$ $=2 \times 25/\sqrt{1,000}$ $=1.58$
t statistic for test of difference	Δ/SE $=50/.5$ $=100$	Δ/SE $=2/.5$ $=4$	Δ/SE $=50/66.6$ $=0.75$	Δ/SE $=2/1.58$ $=1.26$
p value	$p < .0001$	$p < .001$	$p > .40$	$p > .20$
Statistically significant?	Yes	Yes	No	No
Qualitative description	An important difference that's really there	Lots of data make small, unimportant difference statistically significant	Could be large, important difference, but we have no idea. Not enough data to tell	We're sure that there is no difference of a magnitude large enough to matter

[10]The standard error of the difference between two groups with equal standard deviations and equal sample sizes (as in this case) is $2 \times SD/\sqrt{N}$, where N/2 is the sample size of each group.

Column A shows a difference between boys and girls that is both practically and statistically significant. Boys score 50 points higher on average, and there is no possible way that this difference was a fluke of sampling (the *p* value tells us this). Policymakers should take the gender gap seriously and look for ways to address the problem.

In column B, the difference in means between boys and girls is trivial in magnitude, too small to care much about. But the difference is still statistically significant because the standard errors are so small. In other words, the means were measured with tremendous precision, due to the large sample size, so we know that the 2-point difference between boys and girls is not just a sampling fluke. But it is still just a mere 2-point difference, not of much importance in the real world of education policy and practice. Given a large enough sample, almost any difference can become statistically significant.

In column C, the difference between boys' and girls' scores is large. It would be practically significant—if it were an accurate picture of reality. But with data on only nine students and lots of variability (a high standard deviation), the standard errors are high, and the means are not estimated with much precision. Thus, the difference in means might well be just a fluke of sampling due to the very small sample size. There might be something going on here—there may be a gender gap in the scores—but we just do not know. What is needed to make a sound decision is more data.

In column D, the results are neither practically nor statistically significant. It might seem like these results are of little use for policy or practice, but in fact, they provide valuable information. Practically important differences between boys' and girls' test scores have been ruled out. Policymakers would know that they do not need to worry about a gender gap.

The easiest way to see that a practically significant difference has been ruled out is to calculate the confidence intervals. A 95% confidence interval for the 2-point difference in means is roughly $2 \pm 2 \times 1.58 = 2 \pm 3.2 = -1.2$ to 5.2. So we are 95% confident that the true result lies somewhere between boys scoring 1.2 points below and 5.2 points above girls. Provided we don't consider the magnitude of either the upper or lower bounds of the confidence interval to be of a practically important magnitude, we have ruled out practically important results.

Statistically Insignificant Results Can Be Useful

Statistically insignificant results are interesting and informative, provided they come with narrow confidence intervals. If a finding of a difference or an effect would be interesting, the finding of no difference or no effect is also interesting, provided you're *sure* that there really is no difference or no effect.

Unfortunately, it is often hard to publish statistically insignificant results. But it can be done by emphasizing the narrow confidence intervals and how striking and interesting the lack of effect is. In fact, a major problem in the scientific literature is the publication bias toward statistically significant results, which can make it seem like something is effective when it is not. In fact, that tendency undermines the usefulness and accuracy of meta-analysis studies that combine the results from many different articles to produce a more precise result. (Meta-analysis is discussed further in Chapter 5.)

Although our example used a comparison of means (independent samples *t* test), the same ideas apply to all kinds of significance tests, including regression and cross-tabs. For any kind of significance test, pay attention to the magnitude of the effect or effects—not just the *p* value. Just because something is statistically significant does not mean that it is practically significant—its magnitude could be tiny. In these days of explosive quantities of data, this situation is increasingly common.

Box 8.8 summarizes the various possible causes of statistical significance and insignificance and the different kinds of practical conclusions that should be drawn.

BOX 8.8
Sources of Statistical Significance
and of Statistical Insignificance

SOURCES OF STATISTICAL SIGNIFICANCE

1. Large, practically important differences or relationships

   - Large differences swamp standard errors → statistical significance
   - You can conclude that a practically significant difference exists

2. Very small standard errors

   - Usually due to very large sample size
   - Very precise measures
   - Very small, practically insignificant differences can still be large relative to smaller standard errors → statistical significance
   - Beware of statistically significant results that have only trivial or no practical significance

SOURCES OF STATISTICAL INSIGNIFICANCE

1. Large standard errors

   - Usually due to small sample size
   - Even large magnitude differences could be a fluke of who was sampled
   - Be aware that the lack of statistical significance does not necessarily mean that there is no practically significant difference

2. Differences of a very small magnitude

   - With sufficiently narrow confidence intervals, you know that no practically significant difference exists

---

Failing to Recognize a Difference: Type II Errors

Another set of ideas can help sort out the same kind of issues. Think about the example of a new drug being compared with an existing treatment. Two possibilities exist: (1) The new drug is better and

(2) the new drug is not better. Suppose standard policy is to accept the evidence that the drug is better if you can reject the hypothesis of no difference with a p value of .05 or less. In other words, we are willing to accept a 5% risk that we will conclude that the new drug is better when in fact it is not.

This is an example of **Type I error**—the null hypothesis of no difference is in fact true, but we erroneously reject it. Conventional standards for statistical significance limit the probability of a Type I error to 1% or 5% (sometimes even 10% is considered okay, for exploratory studies). The idea is that to accept a new treatment or program as effective, we want to be sure that it really is better.

Unfortunately, the less likely we are to make Type I errors, the more likely we will make another type of error, called a **Type II error**—accepting the null of no difference when in fact it is false and should be rejected (Table 8.15). In the drug testing example, a Type II error would happen if we concluded that the new drug is not effective (we accepted the null) when the new drug is in fact better.

Mathematically, the smaller the likelihood of a Type I error, the larger the likelihood of a Type II error. The only way to reduce the probability of both kinds of errors is to get more data (a larger sample size). But in many situations, gathering more data is expensive. And in others, it is not even possible. For example, think about a series of annual test score results for a given school system or changes in the world population over time. There are only a certain number of years worth of data; we just can't get any more. In such cases, it may be worth accepting a greater risk of Type I error probability to reduce Type II error.

Table 8.15   **Type I and Type II Errors**

	Null Hypothesis Is True	**Alternative Hypothesis Is True**
Accept null hypothesis	Correct decision	Type II error
Reject null hypothesis	Type I error	Correct decision

Power

Another way of looking at this issue is to ask, "How well will the researchers be able to tell if the null is false?" This is referred to as statistical **power**—the ability to recognize that the null is false. Formally, power is defined as

$$\text{Power} = 1 - \text{Probability of a Type II error.}$$

Power is very important, yet it is too often overlooked. That is largely because it is hard to calculate and does not pop out automatically from a statistical software package. To calculate it, one needs to know the true differences and distributions in the population and, of course, we do not (that is why we are doing inference in the first place). Bloom (1995), however, provides useful guidance on how to calculate and report a **minimal detectable effect**, the smallest difference or effect that a particular study has the power to detect (to reject the null hypothesis) at a given level of significance.

You should know a few key points about statistical power. First, the larger the sample size, the more power you will have to detect differences or effects. Second, the stricter the standard of proof—in other words, the lower you set your significance level and thus your probability of Type I error—the less power you will have. In certain circumstances, particularly when you have no control over the sample size, it may be worth accepting a higher p value to get more power. At the very least, power is something to ask about and calculate.

Multiple Comparison Corrections

Sometimes researchers analyze many, many variables looking for differences between two groups, without any hypotheses or theories about why and when there should be differences. They may further try breaking their data into a variety of different subgroups without any particular theory or hypothesis about why some groups might differ but not others. When so many statistical tests are performed, some differences may be statistically significant just by chance. When data are mined in this kind of fashion, without prior hypotheses, a higher bar is needed for statistical significance. In such cases, the p value should be corrected using a **multiple comparison correction**.

There are a number of different approaches to such corrections, including the Bonferroni, Scheffe and more recent methods. There is an extensive technical literature on multiple comparison corrections and the specifics of the corrections (see Howell, 2007, for an introduction to the issue). Moreover, when and even whether specific multiple comparison corrections are desired is disputed (Rothman, 1990). However, understand that if you perform many, many significance tests, without any specific theory, some of them will turn out significant by chance and not due to any real differences. The best approach is to start with substantive hypotheses. After that, exploring data is fine and even valuable, but be aware that the results are only suggestive until tested with new data. This is another version of the point made in Chapter 1 about requiring new data for theories found inductively.

The Debate About Significance Testing

Significance testing is a very rigid either/or approach. As we have seen, it can be misleading if one focuses on statistical significance alone. Confidence intervals are an important complement. One should always examine both the upper and lower bound of a confidence interval and ask if either would be a practically significant effect.

Since significance testing often leads people to just focus on statistical significance and ignore practical significance, some researchers advocate not using significance testing at all. They believe that only confidence intervals should be used, because they combine information on statistical and practical significance in a single range of numbers.

Sample Size Calculations: Getting the Precision You Want

When designing a study, whether a survey or other sort of study, more subjects (larger sample size) are always valuable, because they increase precision. More precision, in turn, means you are more likely to be able to detect statistically significant differences between groups. However, more subjects create more expense. You can estimate how many subjects are needed to get the precision desired through the use of a **sample size calculation**.

Sample size calculations are best illustrated with an example. Suppose you want to estimate a proportion, perhaps to a margin of error (95% confidence interval) of ±2 percentage points. Using the formula from Chapter 5, we can plug the desired margin of error into the margin of error formula:

$$.02 = \text{Margin of error} = 1.96 \times SE = 1.96\sqrt{\frac{P \times (1 - P)}{n}}.$$

This equation could be solved for n, the needed sample size, if only the proportion P were known. Of course, P is not known, since the whole point is to estimate it. However, a worst case, the largest possible sample size, occurs if $P = .5$. Alternatively, an educated guess for P could be made.

Similar methods exist for other statistics and also for tests of relationships. However, sample size calculations always require *assumptions* about unknown parameters. For example, to estimate the sample size needed for a mean, an assumption about the standard deviation must be made. The more complicated the statistic, the more quantities assumptions must be made about.

Adjusting Inference for Clustering and Other Complex Sampling

The basic formulas and methods for all statistical inference, including standard errors, confidence intervals, and significance tests of regression, are ultimately based on simple random sampling. But when using complex sampling methods such as clustering, stratification, oversampling, and multi-stage sampling (discussed in Chapter 5), the usual formulas for confidence intervals, standard errors, and significance tests are not correct. These formulas must be adjusted to take into account the complex nature of the sampling.

The intuition behind the need for adjustment can be made clear with an example. Consider a clustering study in which first schools are sampled and then students are sampled within each school. If there are 1,000 students in the sample, the usual formula for the standard error will be based on having 1,000 independent students. But the students in the same schools are likely to be more similar to one another than to students in another randomly selected school—certainly the same region, perhaps similar socioeconomic background or ethnicity, many of the same teachers, and so on. So all these variables are clustered, and in effect, there are essentially fewer than 1,000 fresh data points. For this reason, standard errors (and thus confidence intervals and significance tests) should be corrected for clustering. Similar intuitions apply for oversampling and stratification.

Unless instructed otherwise, statistical packages assume that data are a simple random sample and use the usual formulas. Some statistical software packages (such as SAS and Stata) contain commands that make these adjustments to the reported standard errors, if the sampling method is entered correctly. An alternative approach is to use resampling methods of calculating standard errors, such as the jackknife or bootstrap method (Mooney & Duval, 1993).

Statistical Software

Various software programs can be used for statistical analysis, including general-purpose spreadsheet programs, such as Excel, as well as specialized statistical software packages.

Spreadsheets

Spreadsheet software, such as Microsoft Excel, provides a number of built-in statistical analysis tools. Excel's statistical analysis tools are organized under an option called the Analysis Toolpak. If your data are quantitative and you do not have missing data, spreadsheets can do a fair amount, from basic descriptive statistics to regressions and significance testing.

But if the data include many categorical variables or missing data, spreadsheets can be somewhat limited. Using a spreadsheet is also more difficult with larger data sets containing many cases and variables. Finally, spreadsheets can be awkward to use for multiple regression with multiple independent variables. In such cases, a full statistical package may be a better choice.

Statistical Packages: SAS, IBM® SPSS®, and Stata

SAS, SPSS, and Stata are the most widely used general-purpose statistical software packages. SAS and SPSS have both been around for decades, and so many people have grown accustomed to using them. Stata is a newer program that has gained in popularity. All these programs do a wide range of descriptive statistics, graphing, data management, regression, and various advanced methods, from specialized regression to factor analysis and multilevel modeling. For most serious data analysts or quantitative researchers, it is important to know one or more of these packages.

Specialized Modeling and Matrix Language Programs

There are specialized programs for structural equation modeling, most notably LISREL, AMOS, and MPLUS. And there are specialized programs for multilevel modeling, such as HLM, MLwiN, and aML.

Some prefer matrix language programs such as S, SPLUS, R, GAUSS, or MATLAB. These programs allow analysts to go beyond the ready-made procedures built into the standard statistical software packages. They also allow for more control over the formulas and estimation methods used in calculating statistics.

Conclusion: Tools for Description and Causation

The tools that we have learned in this chapter are important for describing data. They are also fundamental techniques required for the next part of the book, which deals with causation. But to fully tackle the question of causation, we need to learn about some additional methods that take account of many influences at once—multivariate methods. These are the topic of the next chapter.

EXERCISES

8.1. Below is an excerpt from the variables page of SPSS for a data set.

Name	Label	Values
Pres92	VOTE FOR CLINTON,BUSH,PEROT	{1, BUSH} . . .
Age	AGE OF RESPONDENT	None
Agecat	Age categories	{1, lt 35} . . .
Educ	HIGHEST YEAR OF SCHOOL COMPLETED	None
Degree	RESPONDENT'S HIGHEST DEGREE	{0, lt high school} . . .
Sex	RESPONDENT'S SEX	{1, male}

For each variable, state whether it is quantitative, nominal categorical, or ordinal categorical.

8.2. The following was excerpted from a data set for 1995.

Country	Population in Thousands	Literacy (% People Who Read)	Predominant Religion	Fertility (Average Number of Kids)	Predominant Climate	Daily Calorie Intake
Botswana	1,359	72	Tribal	3.13	Arid	2,375
Brazil	156,600	81	Catholic	5.19	Tropical	2,751
Bulgaria	8,900	93	Orthodox	3.95	Temperate	
Burkina Faso	10,000	15	Animist	4.00	Tropical	2,288

a. What is the unit of analysis (the individual) in this data set?
b. According to this data, in Brazil, how many people can read?
c. Give an example of two variables that could be used for a cross-tabs analysis.
d. Describe how Botswana's literacy rate is different from Burkina Faso's literacy rate as a percentage point difference and two kinds of percent difference. Discuss how such a difference should be reported to be most clear.
e. For each of the following three scatterplots based on the complete data set, state whether you think that the correlation coefficient is most likely to be: close to − 1, negative but close to zero, approximately zero, positive but close to zero, or close to +1. Briefly explain why you made the choice in each case.

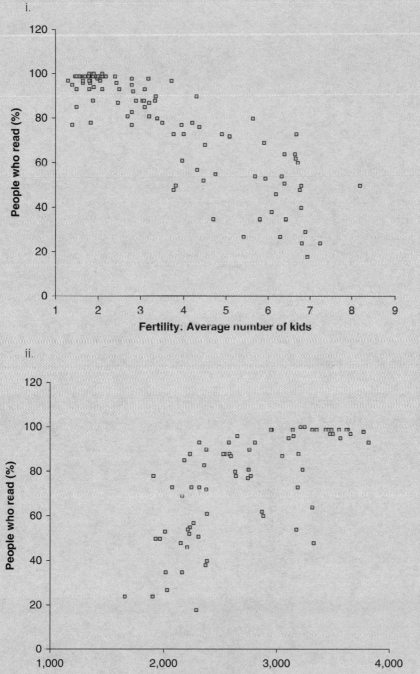

iii.

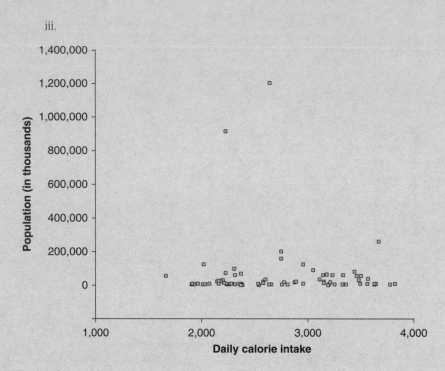

8.3. Use the graph below on the number of homes sold at different prices in several neighborhoods:

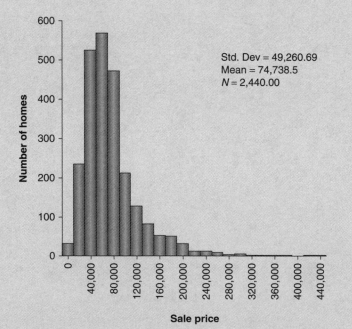

a. Do you think the median is likely to be about the same as the mean or above it or below it? Explain why.

b. In each of the cases below, describe whether the mean or the median would be more relevant and explain why:

   i. The property tax is a percentage of the sale price. Your job is to predict tax revenues.

   ii. Your job is to describe the community to firms trying to decide whether to locate there.

8.4. Using data from employees at a particular firm, a regression was carried out. Salary was measured in dollars per year. Educational level was measured in years of education. Use the resulting SPSS output below to answer questions.

Model Summary

Model	R	R-Square	Adjusted R-Square	Std. Error of the Estimate
1	.661(a)	.436	.435	$12,833.540

Note: Predictors: (Constant), Educational Level (years)

Coefficients(a)

Model		Unstandardized Coefficients		Standardized Coefficients		
		B	Std. Error	Beta	t	Sig.
1	(Constant)	−18331.178	2821.912		−6.496	.000
	Educational level (years)	3909.907	204.547	.661	19.115	.000

Note: Dependent variable: Current salary

a. Interpret the slope term (coefficient of the independent variable). What information does it give you? Make sure to say what units the slope term is in. Comment on and explain any striking features.

b. Interpret the constant term. What information does it give you? Make sure to say what units the constant term is in. Comment on and explain any striking features.

c. Explain the meaning of R-square in general and interpret the R-square result for this regression.

d. Predict the salary level of someone with 12 years of education.

8.5. In a general social survey, the following results were obtained. (RS refers to the respondent to the survey. Mother is the respondent's mother.) Interpret the results of this cross-tabulation.

RS Highest Degree × Mother a College Grad Cross-Tabulation

			Mother a College Grad		
			No	Yes	Total
RS highest degree	Less than HS	Count	211	5	216
		% within Mother a college grad	17.2%	4.0%	16.0%
	High school	Count	673	41	714
		% within Mother a college grad	54.9%	32.8%	52.9%
	Junior college	Count	72	12	84
		% within Mother a college grad	5.9%	9.6%	6.2%
	Bachelor	Count	185	44	229
		% within Mother a college grad	15.1%	35.2%	17.0%
	Graduate	Count	84	23	107
		% within Mother a college grad	6.9%	18.4%	7.9%
Total		Count	1225	125	1350
		% within Mother a college grad	100.0%	100.0%	100.0%

8.6. Incomes for a sample:

$20,000	$100,000	$50,000	$40,000	$190,000

a. What is the median income? Show your work and explain.
b. What is the 25th percentile income? Show your work and explain.
c. Does the following sample have a higher or lower standard deviation than the one above? Explain.

$20,000	$100,000	$50,000	$40,000	$150,000

8.7. Consider a data set of cities. z scores have been calculated for all variables. City ABC has a z score of $-.03$ for its crime rate and a z score of 2.1 for its median house prices.

Is the crime rate of ABC very low, somewhat low, about average, somewhat high, or very high? Are housing prices in ABC very low, somewhat low, about average, somewhat high, or very high? Explain briefly.

8.8. Regressions in Imaginary Worlds: A Thought Experiment

Imagine the following world with very strict laws: Those with an eighth-grade education earn $10,000/annually. For every year of additional education, someone earns $5,000 more. The law does not allow any variation whatsoever. Everyone goes to school until at least eighth grade.

Researchers collect data on years of education and earnings from everyone in this imaginary world. They perform a regression of earnings on education (i.e., earnings is the dependent variable and education is the independent variable) and calculate the correlation between the two variables.

Before continuing, try to answer these questions, explaining your answers:

- What is the correlation coefficient?
- What is the R-squared of the regression?
- What is the regression coefficient of education? (Make sure to state its units.)

Answers:

- If we compare two individuals and one has one more year of education than the other, that person necessarily earns $5,000 more. That is true in absolutely every single instance. So education and earnings are perfectly correlated in lockstep. The correlation is positive, because when education is higher, earnings are higher. Thus, the correlation coefficient is 1.
- If we try to predict earnings using education in a regression, we predict perfectly, because earnings are determined by education and nothing else. So R-squared is 1, because 100% of the variation in earnings is predicted by variation in education.
- The regression coefficient of education is $5,000 per year: For every additional year of education, earnings are $5,000 higher.

8.9. From a random sample of births in three states, the data on birth weight were analyzed. Birth weight is measured in grams.

Descriptives

			Statistic	Std. Error
Birth weight (grams)	Mean		3330.99	1.705
	95% confidence interval for mean	Lower bound	3327.65	
		Upper bound	3334.33	
	Standard deviation		555.899	

    a. Explain how to interpret the 95% confidence interval of the birth weight mean. What does it tell us about births in the three states sampled?

    b. Explain what information the standard deviation provides.

    c. Explain what information the standard error of the mean provides. Explain how it is related to the confidence interval.

    d. Explain how and why the standard error of the mean and the standard deviation are related.

    e. What other factor affects the standard error of the mean? Explain why it does so as intuitively as possible.

    f. What would the 90% confidence interval look like relative to the 95% confidence interval? Explain why.

8.10. A regression of income on years of experience is performed using a sample of people who work in not-for-profits. Income is measured in thousands of dollars and experience is measured in years of experience.

    a. What units is the slope coefficient (the coefficient of years of experience) in?

    b. If the slope coefficient had the value 0.85, what would that tell you?

    c. If the p value associated with the slope coefficient were .03, what would that tell you? Make sure to include the null and alternative hypotheses being tested as part of your explanation. Make sure that you explain what the number .03 actually tells you.

8.11. Data are gathered on 16 students. Half of the students are randomly assigned to a new tutoring program and half have their usual school experience. A study finds that test scores for the tutoring program students are on average 10 points higher than those for the other students. The p value for a test of improvement from the program is 0.3, not significant at even the 10% level.

    a. If mean test scores are 200 and the standard deviation is 40, are these results practically significant, in your opinion? Explain what practical significance means.

    b. Explain what causes this result to be not statistically significant.

    c. Do you conclude that the tutoring program is ineffective because the results are not statistically significant?

Objectives: In this chapter, you will learn statistical tools for analyzing multiple variables at the same time—multivariate statistics. In particular, this chapter will help you understand multiple regression—the most widely used statistical method in social and policy research. You will learn about confidence intervals and significance tests for regression, interaction terms, how categorical variables can be included as independent or dependent variables, and how to transform variables when necessary. And you will learn many other practical tips for doing and interpreting multiple regression. You will also get an overview of other advanced multivariate methods—their basic purposes as well as some of their strengths and weaknesses. Statistical methods have become increasingly sophisticated, but this chapter will help you understand the aims, assumptions, and interpretation of the most widely used multivariate statistics in an intuitive, largely nonmathematical way.

Multivariate analysis considers many variables at the same time.

Source: © 2009 Jupiterimages Corporation.

Making Sense of Multivariate Statistics

9

The real world is more than two dimensional—many factors exert their influence at the same time and in complex ways. Your health, for example, is a result of your age, diet, lifestyle, and family history, as well as the interactions of these influences. In addition, we often observe the real world only indirectly, through multiple indicators. What you call your "health" is really a composite of many things, such as functional ability, blood pressure, cholesterol levels, body weight, even mood, and so on.

This chapter is about statistical methods for dealing with multiple variables at the same time—**multivariate statistics**. It focuses primarily on multiple regression, the most widely used statistical tool for social and policy research. But an overview of other multivariate techniques will appear at the end of the chapter.

This chapter, like the previous chapter, is about tools, rather than about a particular area of research. The tools by themselves cannot answer important policy and practice questions, but answering such questions often requires these tools.

Multiple Regression: The Basics

Most outcomes have many causes—that is the basic idea behind multiple regression. **Multiple regression** predicts or explains a dependent variable (Y) using several independent variables (X_1, X_2, etc.). It is a direct extension of simple regression, explained in the previous chapter, but with two or more (sometimes many more) independent variables:

$$Y = a + b_1X_1 + b_2X_2 + \ldots b_kX_k.$$

In this equation, Y is the dependent variable or outcome and the Xs are the independent variables (1 through k)—also referred to as covariates. The bs represent the coefficients of each independent variable and are of particular interest because they express how the independent variables are related to the dependent variable. (Note that b_1X_1, for example, really means "b_1 times X_1" and is written this way to simplify reading the equation.)

To illustrate, consider the following multiple regression to predict earnings (Y) using years of education (X_1) and years of work experience (X_2):

$$\text{Predicted earnings} = a + b_{Ed} \times \text{Education} + b_{Exp} \times \text{Experience}.$$

$$= -\$6739 + \$3292/\text{year} \times \text{Education} + \$415/\text{year} \times \text{Experience}.$$

This multiple regression was calculated using statistical software and the same (simulated) data used to illustrate simple regression in Chapter 8 (Figure 8.4), but again now we are using more than one independent variable. The *R-squared* turns out to be .57, or 57%.

Let's now consider the interpretation of multiple regression, which in most respects remains analogous to simple regression as discussed in the previous chapter. Thus, in this example we have the following:

- The constant (a) of – $6,739 is the predicted value of the dependent variable when all the independent variables (both education and experience) are 0. Notice that 0 years of education (not even first grade) is not a very meaningful value in a modern society. The constant is mathematically necessary, even if it may lack a social or practical meaning.
- Each slope or coefficient (b) describes how much the dependent variable is predicted to change when the independent variable increases by one unit—*holding all other independent variables constant*. This last part is what makes multiple regression different from simple regression. Thus, $3,292 is the amount of additional earnings predicted for someone with one more year of education but no difference in experience—in other words, holding work experience constant. And $606 is the amount of additional earnings predicted for someone with one more year of experience—holding education constant. Notice that holding constant works both ways (and more, if other variables are included as well).
- *R-squared* is the proportion of variation in the dependent variable explained by variation in *all* the independent variables. Thus, education *and* work experience together explain 57% of the variation in earnings.

We will skip the equations for multiple regression. But if you're interested in the underlying details and formulas, we suggest that you consult the brief book by Lewis-Beck (1980) or Wooldridge (2009). Multiple regression is used for two main purposes:

- First, it can be used to predict a dependent variable using a combination of independent variables. For example, it can be used to predict tax revenues from a combination of economic and demographic variables. As a *best linear predictor,* multiple regression also has value as a description of the data—what variables are jointly related to or associated with tax revenues.
- Second, multiple regression can sometimes be used to estimate whether one variable affects another, causally—and the magnitude of the effect. For example, it is used to estimate the causal effect tobacco taxes have on the rate of smoking, holding other variables constant. This is also referred to as *statistical control.*

Using multiple regression for estimating causal effects can be tricky and involves important logical and conceptual issues, which we cover fully in Chapter 11. So we begin here with multiple regression for prediction as an introduction to the basic statistical issues.

Multiple Regression for Prediction

To predict the earnings of someone with 12 years of education and 10 years of experience, from the equation presented above, simply plug these values into the equation like this:

Predicted earnings $= -\$6739 + (\$3292/\text{year} \times 12 \text{ years}) + (\$415/\text{year} \times 10 \text{ years}) = \$36,915$.

The result says that we predict, based on our data, that someone with 12 years of education and 10 years of work experience would earn $36,915. Box 9.1 outlines the steps involved in doing prediction with regression.

BOX 9.1
Steps for Predicting With Regression

1. Using data and software, find the coefficients $(a, b_1, b_2, \ldots, b_k)$ for the regression equation

$$Y = a + b_1 x_1 + b_2 x_2 + \ldots + b_k x_k.$$

2. Plug in desired values of $x_1, x_2, \ldots, x_k$ into the equation.

3. Calculate the predicted value of Y.

The Danger (and Necessity) of Out-of-Sample Extrapolation

Using regression to make a prediction far from the data used to fit the regression is referred to as **out-of-sample extrapolation**. From our example, we know that one more year of education predicts $3,292 more in earnings, holding experience constant. So would completing as much as 40 years of formal education lead to a *much larger* paycheck?

We need to be careful: The regression equation is fitted using data we have on people who mostly have between at least 8 and not more than about 20 years of education, with no one above 25 years of education. Predicting the income of someone with 40 years of education assumes that the line would fit the same way well beyond the range of the actual data—but we have no evidence that it does. Because the constant is the predicted value of the dependent variable when all the independent variables are 0—which may have little real-world meaning—it is frequently an out-of-sample extrapolation as well.

Unfortunately, the real-world demands of policy and practice frequently require out-of-sample predictions, for example, predicting a decrease in smoking rates from a large increase in tobacco taxes. In such cases, we often want to predict what would happen when variables (such as tobacco taxes) take on values that they have never taken on before. In such cases, there is no alternative to out-of-sample extrapolation. Such extrapolations are more trustworthy to the extent that the following conditions hold: The plugged-in values are not too different from the range of values in the data, the model fits the data well (a high R-squared), and multiple models and varying assumptions give a similar answer. This last point refers to what are known as **robustness** checks, and they are essential to good prediction.

R-Squared and Adjusted R-Squared

In multiple regression, R-squared expresses the variation in the dependent variable explained by *all* the independent variables combined. And as we have just seen, a higher R-squared is generally better for prediction because it means a tighter fit to the data and less error around the line. R-squared, however, does not need to be near perfect to do good prediction—it all depends on the situation and on available data.

Adding a variable to a multiple regression always increases R-squared—at least a little. Even adding a variable that consists entirely of random noise will increase the R-squared, although it does not really contribute any meaningful predictive power. To tell whether a variable really adds predictive power, researchers often use an **adjusted R-squared** instead. It adjusts for the number of independent variables in the multiple regression equation. Technically, adjusted R-squared is an unbiased estimator of the population R-squared—the proportion of the dependent variable variance explained by all the independent variables *in the population.*

All Else Held Constant: A Bit More Mathematics

The equations and proofs behind multiple regression are not our focus here. (There are many excellent treatments, e.g., Wooldridge, 2009.) However, useful insight can be gained by looking intuitively at what all the mathematics behind multiple regression actually accomplishes.

In a simple regression, the variation in the independent variable that is shared with the dependent variable determines the regression coefficient. In our simple regression example, the effect of education on earnings is identified by their shared variation.

In multiple regression, the variation in a given independent variable that it shares with the other independent variables in the equation is removed: It does not count. Only the remaining, unique variation in the independent variable that it shares with the dependent variable produces the regression coefficient. In our example, only variation in education that is uncorrelated with variation in experience contributes to the estimate of the effect of education on earnings.

Venn Diagrams Illustrate Multiple Regression Method

Kennedy (2003) developed the use of Venn diagrams to illustrate how multiple regression works. Venn diagrams illustrating our current earnings and education example are illustrated in Figure 9.1. Each circle represents the variation of that variable. The shaded part illustrates the variation used to calculate the coefficient of education—effectively the data used for the estimation.

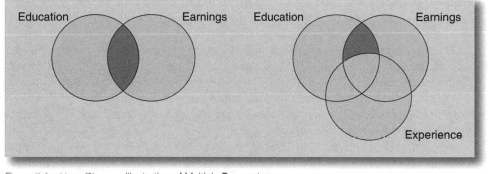

Figure 9.1   Venn Diagram Illustration of Multiple Regression
Source: Adapted from Kennedy (2003).

For the simple regression of Education on Earnings, shown in the left panel, the shaded area is simply the overlap of those two variables. All variation shared by both variables contributes to the coefficient of education estimate. For the multiple regression shown in the right panel, the shaded area is the overlap of Earnings and Education that does not also overlap with Experience. The regression coefficient of Education, b_{Ed}, in this multiple regression is determined by the variation shared by Earnings and Education that is not also shared by Experience.

Multicollinearity

When two variables are perfectly correlated—when they move in perfect lockstep, we cannot tell them (or more precisely their variation) apart. For the statistical purposes of regression, they are essentially the same variable. This is called *perfect collinearity*. In such a case, both variables cannot be used as independent variables in the same multiple regression—we can only use one of them.

Perfect **multicollinearity** occurs when an independent variable is a perfect linear combination of two more of the other independent variables. (Perfect collinearity is just a special case, with only two variables.) In such cases, the variable provides no unique information that cannot be obtained from the other variables. Again, we cannot use all these variables together in the same multiple regression.

When the independent variables are highly correlated, but not perfectly correlated, they may be included in the same equation—but it can make it difficult to estimate the coefficients with precision. This is also known as multicollinearity, and although it is not perfect multicollinearity, it can still cause problems.

When You Can't Disentangle the Independent Variables

An imaginary example might help illustrate multicollinearity. Say we live in a world where aptitude at a young age exactly determines how much education a person receives—the variables aptitude and education, in other words, are perfectly correlated. And say that both variables influence earnings. Now imagine that we want to do a multiple regression to determine the separate effects of both education and aptitude on earnings. How can we disentangle one from the other? We cannot. All that we can know is that education or aptitude, or some combination of the two, increases earnings, but we have no way to assign credit to one variable or the other.

The Venn diagrams, again, help illustrate this. If Education and Aptitude were perfectly correlated, their circles would sit right on top of one another, leaving no area of unique overlap between Education and Earnings. So it would be impossible to estimate coefficients for both. This is an example of perfect multicollinearity. If statistical software were given such data and a command to regress Earnings on both Aptitude and Education, the package would simply drop one of the two independent variables from the equation.

An example of (imperfect) multicollinearity occurs when the variables are strongly (but not perfectly) correlated. Only variation in the independent variable of interest that is not correlated with any other independent variable is used to calculate the coefficient. Again, this can be seen in a Venn diagram, as shown in the right panel of Figure 9.2.

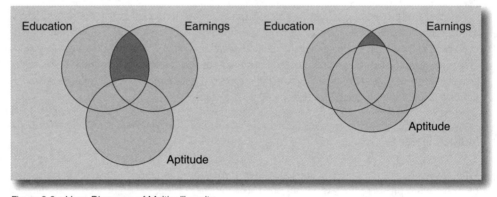

Figure 9.2   Venn Diagrams of Multicollinearity

Source: Adapted from Kennedy (2003).

The more collinear Education and Aptitude are, the smaller the unique overlap area between Earnings and Education, as shown in the right panel of the Figure 9.2. The more multicollinear the independent variables are, in other words, the less information is available to estimate the regression coefficients. As we discuss soon, greater multicollinearity means the regression coefficients will have larger standard errors and thus less precision.

How Many Independent Variables Can One Regression Have?

How many independent variables can one regression have? It depends on many factors, but the most important is how much data there are: The more observations, the more information, and thus the more coefficients that can be estimated. A common rule of thumb is that 1 independent variable can be added for every 10 observations. However, it also depends on the multicollinearity, as just discussed, on how much variation there is in the independent variable, and on other factors. Most critically, it also depends on how precisely you want to estimate the coefficients. Indeed, the question of how many independent variables are possible is best understood as a problem of precision, which will be clearer after inference for regression, which we cover shortly.

Standardized Coefficients:
The Relative Importance of Independent Variables

It can be useful to express the coefficients of a regression in terms of the standard deviations—called standardized coefficients (or beta weights). The interpretation is similar to a correlation: The *predicted number of standard deviations Y changes, given a 1-standard-deviation increase in X*. In simple regression (with only one independent variable), the standardized coefficient is in fact equivalent to the correlation *r*.

In multiple regression, however, the interpretation is a bit different: The *predicted number of standard deviations Y changes, given a 1-standard-deviation increase in X—holding all the other independent variables constant*.

Standardized coefficients are useful because, in the context of multiple regression, they are directly comparable and tell us how important the independent variables are relative to each other. The largest beta weight is thus the most important predictor, the second largest beta the next most important, and so on. Although it depends on many considerations, we can follow these guidelines for judging the magnitude of a standardized coefficient in a multiple regression analysis:

$$beta = .05 \quad \text{Small}$$
$$beta - .15 \quad \text{Moderate}$$
$$beta = .25 \quad \text{Large}$$

Standardized coefficients are particularly useful when the units of independent variable(s) and/or dependent variable have no obvious real-world meaning, as when a variable is an index or scale. For this reason, standardized coefficients are commonly used in disciplines such as psychology that often use multi-item scales.

Inference for Regression

The multiple regression coefficients or slopes (*b*s) are estimates calculated from data, often data from a random sample. And just as a basic mean or proportion from a random sample is an estimate of the *true* mean or proportion in the population—the *parameter*—so too are the regression coefficients (or sample slopes) estimates of the true slopes in the population.

Standard Error of the Coefficient

As estimates of population parameters, multiple regression coefficients can be off the mark because of *sampling variability*. To express this sampling variability, we use *standard errors of the coefficients*. Consider Table 9.1, which shows the influence of homework and TV watching on standardized test

Table 9.1   Regression Results, NELS Subsample of $n = 100$

	b	Std. Error
(Constant)	46.636	2.882
Number of hours spent on homework per week	1.540	.629
Number of hours spent watching TV on weekdays	−.083	.044

Note: Dependent variable is the standardized test score (reading, math) on a 0 to 100 scale.

scores. These results are SPSS output from a random subsample of $n = 100$ students in the National Educational Longitudinal Study (NELS).

The results tell us that we predict 1.54 test points more for a student who spends one more hour on homework. In contrast, for a student who spends one more hour watching TV, we predict a test score .083 lower (a negative slope). These are the estimates or coefficients—the *b*s. The standard errors of these coefficients are also shown—.629 and .044, respectively. These tell us how much sampling error there is in the coefficients.

The bigger the sample size (the more data), the more precise the regression coefficient and thus the smaller the standard errors of the coefficients. This sample size effect is true for any statistic: The more data, the more precision.

Table 9.2 shows a much larger random subsample of $n = 10,000$ students in the NELS. The coefficients change somewhat: They are now 1.457 for homework hours and −.097 for TV-watching hours. But the really big difference is in the standard errors, .062 and .004, respectively. They are now one tenth as large as they were in the previous table, when the sample was only 100. So these coefficient estimates are much more precise than before.

Table 9.2   Regression Results, NELS Subsample of $n = 10,000$

	b	Std. Error
(Constant)	46.184	.278
Number of hours spent on homework per week	1.457	.062
Number of hours spent watching TV on weekdays	−.097	.004

Note: Dependent variable is the standardized test score (reading, math) on a 0 to 100 scale.

Confidence Intervals in Regression

The confidence intervals (CIs) are calculated from standard errors for regression coefficients in the same way as for any other statistics. A 95% CI of the regression coefficient is ±1.96 standard errors.[1]

---

[1]The 1.96 value depends on a sufficiently large sample size. With small samples, you need more than 1.96 standard errors for a 95% confidence interval. See Lewis-Beck (2008) or Wooldridge (2009) for technical details.

Table 9.3 shows the results again for a small subsample of 100 students in the NELS, this time with the confidence intervals. We can interpret these confidence intervals as telling us that, with 95% confidence, the true constant and coefficients (the parameters) lie somewhere between the lower and upper bounds shown in the table.

Table 9.3   Regression Results, NELS Subsample of n = 100, Showing Confidence Intervals

		95% Confidence Interval for b		
	b	Std. Error	Lower Bound	Upper Bound
(Constant)	46.636	2.884	40.919	52.352
Number of hours spent on homework per week	1.540	.629	.295	2.786
Number of hours spent watching TV on weekdays	−.083	.044	−.170	.004

Note: Dependent variable is the standardized test score (reading, math) on a 0 to 100 scale.

Confidence Interval of a Predicted Value

When regression is used for prediction, it is often desirable to have an estimate of the confidence interval of the prediction, also referred to as the prediction error. That prediction has error not only because of the standard errors of the coefficients but also because of the residuals or the error in fit. In fact, the further away from the means of the independent variables, the greater the prediction error, because the fit is not as good. Most statistical packages can calculate prediction errors. Wooldridge (2009) has a good discussion in Chapter 6, Section 4.

Significance Testing in Regression

With multiple regression, there are many coefficients, and many different hypotheses could be tested. However, the most basic test is whether there is a relationship between the dependent variable and the independent variable of interest, holding the other independent variables constant.

In this case, the null hypothesis is that the parameter is 0—no relationship. The formal statistical test is a t test. Most statistical packages produce output that automatically contains t statistics and/or p values associated with that test. Table 9.4 shows the significance test results for the same NELS regression: The t statistic to test the hypothesis that hours spent on homework have no effect (denoted t) is 2.45, and the associated p value is .016.

It may be useful to test null hypotheses other than that the slope is 0. For example, you might wish to test whether the coefficient is significantly larger than some standard of effectiveness. You may wish to test whether two coefficients have the same value or not. Or you may wish to see if a coefficient has changed meaningfully from its previous value when adding another independent

Table 9.4   Regression Results, NELS Subsample of $n = 100$, Showing Significance (t) Tests

	b	Std. Error	t	p Value
(Constant)	46.636	2.884	16.168	.000
Number of hours spent on homework per week	1.540	.629	2.451	.016
Number of hours spent watching TV on weekdays	− .083	.044	− 1.897	.060

Note: Dependent variable is the standardized test score (reading, math) on a 0 to 100 scale.

variable. Remember that the p value given by software corresponds to a test of a null hypothesis of 0 (no relationship in the population); this may—or may not—correspond to the substantive hypothesis you have in mind.

Influences on Inference in Multiple Regression

We saw earlier how a larger sample reduces the standard error and, in turn, narrows the confidence interval and strengthens the significance tests (bigger t statistics). But sample size is not the only factor influencing the standard errors in a regression.

Another important factor is how spread out the data are from the best-fit regression line, which is determined by the size of the residuals and denoted by σ. If the data fit very tightly around the regression line, it is easy to accurately fit the straight line, even without many data points. Thus a poor fit, described by a low R-squared and a high σ, results in higher standard errors. In contrast, a good fit, described by high R-squared and low σ, will result in smaller standard errors.

Another influence on the standard error of the regression coefficient is the amount of variation in the independent variable. If there is little variation, then it is difficult to tell how changing the independent variable changes the dependent variable. In the extreme, imagine trying to determine the effect of TV watching using a sample of students who all spend the exact same number of hours in front of the TV—it's impossible. The more variation there is in the independent variable, the more easily the slope (regression coefficient) can be measured—and thus, the smaller the standard errors.

Multicollinearity also has an important influence on the standard errors. If the independent variables are highly correlated with one another, if their variation overlaps substantially, you have little unique information left over to precisely estimate the regression coefficients (recall Figure 9.2). As a result, the more multicollinearity among the independent variables, the larger the standard errors.

The Effect of Adding Independent Variables on Precision

When researchers use multiple regression for prediction, they sometimes think that more predictors—more independent variables—can only help. But this is not always the case. On the one hand, to the extent that an added variable raises explanatory power, raising the R-squared and reducing the residuals (σ), the standard errors are reduced. So adding variables that do a good job at explaining Y generally helps things. On the other hand, if the newly added independent variable is highly multicollinear with the other independent variables, the standard errors increase (as we just saw), thus making things worse.

Categorical Independent Variables

Regression is an intrinsically quantitative method, yet many plausible independent variables are categorical—such as occupation, race, and gender. So we might like to include them, for example, in a regression analysis of earnings. Fortunately, categorical variables can be turned into *dummy variables*, which can be used as if they were quantitative. Dummy variables were described in Chapter 4, but we will review the idea here.

Dummy Variables

A dummy (or indicator) variable is a variable that is 1 if true and 0 if false. For example, a *female* dummy variable takes on the value of 1 if the individual is a woman and takes on the value of 0 if the individual is a man. A dummy variable can be used in regression as if it were a quantitative variable because order means something: Higher values of the female dummy variable mean more femaleness, as it were. Scale also means something: A one-unit increase means changing from a male to a female.

Any variable that has only two possible values, any dichotomous variable, can be made into a dummy variable. It is arbitrary which of the two possible values defines the dummy variable. For example, a *male* dummy variable could have been chosen instead of the female dummy variable. Whichever category is 0 becomes the *reference category*. For a *female* dummy variable, the reference category is male, and for a *male* dummy variable, the reference category is female.

Returning to the simulated-data example of earnings, a regression of earnings on a female dummy variable results in the following equation:

$$\text{Earnings} = a + b_{\text{fem}} \times \text{Female}$$

$$= \$37314 + -\$5272 \times \text{Female}.$$

The regression reveals that, on average, women earn $5,272 less than men. It also reveals that men earn, on average, $37,314.

If a male dummy variable had been used instead, its coefficient would have been (positive) $5,272, just the negative of the coefficient of the female dummy variable.

Dummy variables are widely used to represent programs or treatments in experimental and quasi experimental studies (covered in Chapters 12 and 13). Some individuals participate in a program or receive a treatment (coded 1), while others—those in the control group—do not (coded 0).

Isn't There a Simpler Way to Estimate Differences in Means?

You might wonder why anyone would bother to do a regression to learn the difference in average earnings between men and women. Why not just calculate the mean of earnings for females and earnings for males and then take the difference? In fact, if that is all you are interested in, then forget the regression and just take a difference in means.

But dummy variables are useful in multiple regressions because most often we want additional independent variables as well. This allows us to learn about how being female predicts earnings, holding constant other variables such as education, experience, occupation, and so on. Such a regression might help us find out how much of the earnings difference between men and women could be attributed to discrimination rather than to differences in background or qualifications. We will learn much more about these ideas in Chapter 11, on observational studies with control variables.

Categorical Variables With More Than Two Possible Values

Of course, many categorical variables that would make good predictors—such as occupation and race—have more than two possible values. Luckily, such categorical variables can still be used as independent variables in regression by creating a set of dummy variables. This is best illustrated with an example.

Consider a race variable with five categories: *White, Black, Hispanic, Asian*, and *Other*. It is possible to create five dummy variables, one for each race category. If an individual is Asian, for example, then the dummy variables White, Black, Hispanic, and Other all have the value of 0, while the dummy variable Asian has the value of 1. (See also Box 9.2.)

To figure out someone's race, however, you would need to know only four of the five possible variables. For example, suppose dummy variables for each status other than White are provided. If the others are all 0, we know that the person must be White. If one of the others is 1, then we know that the value of White must be 0. Therefore, all five variables are perfectly multicollinear.

To include a categorical variable as an independent variable in a regression, simply include all possible dummy variables but one. The omitted category is also referred to as the *reference category*, since all effects are measured relative to that omitted, or reference, category.

Dummy variables needed for regression = Number of categories − 1.

What If Someone Belongs in More Than One Category?

Using our race variable, everyone had to be in one and only one of the five categories. However, in reality, people fall into more than one race category. Hispanics can be Black or White, for example, and some people are of mixed race. In fact, to deal (partially) with this very problem, the U.S. Census Bureau changed its race question, eliminating Hispanic as a race and creating a separate Hispanic variable (Grieco & Cassidy, 2001). Unfortunately, to use a categorical variable in statistical analysis, we must have an *exhaustive and mutually exclusive* list of categories, even if that doesn't fit so well with reality.

BOX 9.2
Representing a Categorical Variable
With More Than Two Categories: Diabetes Example

Diabetes status can be broken into three categories:

- No diabetes
- Type 1 diabetes
- Type 2 diabetes

So it is possible to create three diabetes dummy variables:

Diabetic =	0	if person has diabetes
	1	if person has neither type 1 nor type 2 diabetes
Type 1 =	0	if person has type 1 diabetes
	1	if person does not have type 1 diabetes (person must have either type 2 or no diabetes)
Type 2 =	0	if person has type 2 diabetes
	1	if person does not have type 2 diabetes (person must have either type 1 or no diabetes))

Any two of the three dummy variables could be used in a regression. For example, just type 1 and type 2 could be used. The coefficient of each would then describe the effect of that kind of diabetes compared with not having diabetes (the reference category).

Once we convert our categorical variables of interest into sets of dummy variables, it is possible to include any combination of categorical and quantitative variables we want as independent variables in our regression analysis. The interpretation of the coefficient is then supplemented with the usual modifier, "holding all other independent variables constant."

Interpreting the Coefficient of a Dummy Variable

Box 9.3 lays out the systematic steps for interpreting the coefficient of a dummy variable. The units of the coefficient of any dummy variable are those of the dependent variable. The reference category, however, must be made clear, since it is arbitrary. If we estimate the effect of gender on earnings, we can describe the effect of being female relative to being male, or the effect of being male relative to being female, depending on how we have coded the gender variable.

BOX 9.3
Interpreting the Coefficient of a Dummy Variable

Steps	Example A	Example B
1. Identify the indicator category (coded 1).	*Female* is the indicator category (1)	*Type 1 diabetes* is the indicator category (1)
2. Identify the reference category (the omitted category).	*Male* is the reference category (0)	*Not having diabetes* is the reference category (0) (Another category, *type 2*, is also measured relative to not having diabetes.)
3. A one-unit increase in the independent variable means going from the reference category to the indicator category.	Switching from *male* to *female*	Switching from *no diabetes* to *type 1 diabetes*
4. Identify the dependent variable and its units.	Earnings in dollars	Medical expenditures in dollars
5. The coefficient is the difference on average between the indicator and reference category of the dependent variable.	The earnings difference (in dollars) between females and males (on average)	The medical expenditures difference (in dollars) between type 1 diabetics and nondiabetics (on average)

More categories bring more choices of a reference category, so it is important to choose a reference category that makes interpretation easy and relevant. To illustrate, consider a regression to determine the effect of different levels of education (different degrees) on earnings. One option is to make the reference category high school dropout. In that case, the coefficient of college graduate would reveal the differences in earnings between college graduates and high school dropouts, not the most meaningful contrast. But if we make high school graduate the reference category, the coefficient would reveal the difference in earnings between college graduates and high school graduates—the premium for completing college. And the coefficient of dropout would reveal the penalty for dropping out. It makes more sense to set things up in this way.

Adjusting Rates and Other Variables

In the previous chapter, we described how rates could be adjusted for other variables to focus on relevant variation in an outcome. For example, when comparing prevalence of disease across geographic areas, the prevalence is often adjusted to reflect a standard age distribution. The common epidemiological method was described in Chapter 8, but multiple regression provides a more flexible way of accomplishing the same thing.

Regression adjustment allows quantitative variables to be used as adjusters, not just categorical variables. Also, many combinations of adjusters can be used, not just one or two. And it is not necessary to choose one standard for the adjusters (such as a particular age distribution). Finally, many kinds of dependent variables, not just rates, can be adjusted.

Analysis of Variance (ANOVA)

ANOVA is a statistical method that comes from experimental research (discussed in Chapter 12) and that compares the means of a dependent variable across categories. It is equivalent to a regression with a set of dummy variables representing a single categorical variable, but ANOVA results are presented and interpreted somewhat differently.

First, the statistical significance test that appears in ANOVA (an F test) applies to all the differences between means combined (what researchers call an *omnibus test*), rather than testing each category against a reference group as in regression. However, regression output from statistical software also provides an equivalent F test for the whole regression model. Second, the ANOVA results focus on a comparison of how much of the dependent variable's variation occurs *between* the independent variable categories (and thus is predicted by them) versus how much of the dependent variable's variation occurs *within* the independent variable categories (and thus is not predicted by them). This is related to R-squared in regression, which is the percentage of variation explained or predicted by the model.

ANOVA can be extended to include more than one categorical variable (factor) as well as quantitative variables (covariates). It is then referred to as factorial ANOVA or as *analysis of covariance* (ANCOVA). Because multiple regression can accomplish many of the same aims and is now more familiar to many researchers, you do not see ANOVA or ANCOVA used as much as in the past. But it remains common still in much experimental research in fields such as psychology or medicine.

Interactions in Regression

Sometimes the effect of one variable depends on the value of another. For example, the effect of having diabetes on medical expenditures may depend on whether or not the person also has hypertension. In that case, hypertension is a *moderator* of diabetes, as we defined the term in Chapter 2.

This phenomenon is different from the effect of hypertension itself and can be modeled in regression with an interaction term.

An **interaction variable** is a variable defined as the product of two other variables. For example, we could define an interaction as the product of a dummy variable for diabetes and a dummy variable for hypertension. In this case,

$$\text{Inter} = \text{Hyper} \times \text{Diabetes}.$$

The variable Inter takes on the value 1 for someone who has *both* hypertension and diabetes and takes on the value of 0 for everyone else.

Interaction variables are particularly useful for some kinds of program evaluation analyses, such as difference-in-differences, as described in Chapter 13.

How to Use and Interpret Interaction Variables

Consider predicting an individual's medical expenditures using data on their diabetes and hypertension status. A regression without an interaction would be

$$\text{Exp} = a + b_{diab}\text{Diabetic} + b_{hyper}\text{Hyper}.$$

The coefficient b_{diab} predicts the difference in medical expenditures, for a diabetic relative to a nondiabetic, holding constant hypertension status. And the coefficient b_{hyper} predicts the difference in medical expenditures, for a hypertensive relative to a nonhypertensive, holding constant diabetes status.

With no interaction, however, we cannot detect if the effect of one variable influences the magnitude of the effect of the other. To do that, we include an interaction term:

$$\text{Exp} = a + b_{diab}\text{Diabetic} + b_{hyper}\text{Hyper} + b_{int}\text{Inter}.$$

Now, we need to interpret the coefficient of the interaction. Moreover, once an interaction term is used, the interpretation of the coefficients of the diabetes and hypertension variables (referred to as **main effects**) becomes somewhat more complicated. We describe both below.

Interpreting the Main Effects With Dummy Variable Interactions

Interpretation is most easily explained using a numerical example. Suppose

- $a = \$1,200$
- $b_{diab} = \$1,000$
- $b_{hyper} = \$700$
- $b_{int} = \$1,500$

Using the regression equation, we can see the average expenditures for someone:

without diabetes or hypertension	$= a + b_{diab} \times 0 + b_{hyper} \times 0 + b_{int} \times 0$
	$= a$
	$= \$1200$
with diabetes, without hypertension	$= a + b_{diab} \times 1 + b_{hyper} \times 0 + b_{int} \times 0$
	$= a + b_{diab}$
	$= \$1200 + \$1000$
	$= \$2200$
without diabetes, with hypertension	$= a + b_{diab} \times 0 + b_{hyper} \times 1 + b_{int} \times 0$
	$= a + b_{hyper}$
	$= \$1200 + \$700$
	$= \$1900$
with diabetes, with hypertension	$= a + b_{diab} \times 1 + b_{hyper} \times 1 + b_{int} \times 1$
	$= a + b_{diab} + b_{hyper} + b_{int}$
	$= \$1200 + \$1000 + \$700 + \$1500$
	$= \$4400$

Thus, it can be seen that the coefficient b_{diab} predicts the difference in expenditures for a diabetic relative to a nondiabetic, for someone who is *not* hypertensive (main diabetic effect). The coefficient b_{hyper} predicts the difference in expenditures for a hypertensive relative to a nonhypertensive, for someone who is *not* diabetic (main hypertensive effect). Thus, to interpret the main effect when there is an interaction of two dummy variables, the reference category of both dummy variables must be known.

Interpreting the Coefficient of the Interaction: The Effect on the Effect

Among those who have hypertension, those with diabetes have mean expenditures $4,400 − $1,900 = $2,500 higher. This difference is composed of the $1,000 effect of diabetes among those without hypertension and the additional $1,500 that having hypertension raises the main effect of diabetes. The *interaction* is how much the second disease changes the effect of the first, above its main effect.

It can be interpreted symmetrically. The $1,500 is also the amount that having diabetes raises the main effect of hypertension, from $700 to $700 + $1,500 = $2,200. Among those with hypertension, those with diabetes have average expenditures $2,200 higher. So the coefficient b_{int} predicts the difference in the hypertensive effect between diabetics and nondiabetics; it also predicts the difference in the diabetic effect between hypertensives and nonhypertensives.

Interactions With Quantitative Variables

Thus far, we have illustrated and discussed interactions with dummy variables only. But interactions can also involve quantitative variables. For example, imagine that the effect of age (in years) on medical expenditures depends on whether one has diabetes or not. In that case, we could define an interaction variable, Inter = Diabetic × Age. The interaction variable takes on the value of 0 for everyone who is not diabetic and takes on the value of their age for everyone who is diabetic. The regression equation is as follows:

$$\text{Expenditures} = a + b_{age}\text{Age} + b_{diab}\text{Diabetic} + b_{int}\text{Inter.}$$

In this example, the coefficient b_{age} tells us how much each additional year of age raises medical expenses on average for nondiabetics. The coefficient b_{int} tells us how much *more* an additional year of age raises medical expenses for a diabetic, *above* what an additional year raises expenditures for a nondiabetic. And the coefficient b_{diab} predicts the difference in expenditures for a diabetic relative to a nondiabetic, for someone who is 0 years old. (This can be more intuitively thought of as the constant term in a regression of expenditures on age among those with diabetes.)

Always Include Both Main Effects

When using an interaction variable, it is important always to include both main effects as independent variables in the regression. Even if you think the variable does not have its own main effect on the outcome, leaving it out of the equation risks producing bias. If, for example, age does have its own main effect on expenditures, despite our assumption to the contrary, leaving age out of the equation would then assign the main effect of age to the interaction term.

Functional Form and Transformations in Regression

Simple regression is a best-fit *straight* line. Multiple regression is a multivariate version of the same thing, with every independent variable having a *linear* effect. However, not all relationships are linear. For example, average health expenditures are higher for both low-income and higher-income people but lower for middle-income people—a U-shaped relationship. For another example, the effect of experience on earnings is first very high but then diminishes and eventually flattens out.

Fitting such relationships with an ordinary linear regression is hazardous for several reasons. First, we will often fail to find a nonlinear relationship (such as a U-shaped relationship) if we rely solely on linear regression. Second, even if a relationship is found, a linear regression will be a poor fit for a nonlinear pattern, and our predictions will be off the mark. Third, the formulas for statistical inference in regression are based on having normally distributed errors. Fitting the wrong relationship—often called misspecification—will result in nonnormal errors and thus inaccurate inference formulas.

How to Fit a Curved Relationship

Regression can be used to fit nonlinear relationships by adding a quadratic (squared) or a higher-order polynomial version (such as a cubic) of the independent variable, along with the usual linear term of the variable. For example, it is common to use experience and experience-squared as independent variables in a regression to predict earnings, like this:

$$\text{Earnings} = a + b_{exp}\text{Experience} + b_{sqr}\text{Experience}^2.$$

Say, hypothetically, that $a = \$12,000$, $b_{exp} = \$6,000/\text{year}$, and $b_{sqr} = -\$150/\text{year}^2$. In this case, the negative coefficient of experience-squared captures the diminishing marginal effect of experience. Figure 9.3 shows the same equation graphically. Quadratics can also capture an increasing marginal effect, in which case the coefficient of the squared term would be positive and the line would instead bend upward.

When a quadratic or other polynomial term is included in a regression, the two coefficients must be interpreted together. For example, the effect of an additional year of work experience depends on the level of experience the person starts with. An additional year of experience counts for more early in one's career and less later on.

In addition to polynomials, independent variables may be transformed in a variety of ways, for example, into exponentials. The dependent variable may also be transformed. The transformations chosen can be determined by theory. Or they can be determined by examining the data to determine what fits. Always graph the data, even though multivariate patterns can be hard to discern.

How to Interpret Regression Coefficients When a Variable Is Logged

One particular transformation, the *log*, is extremely common. Variables such as earnings, medical expenditures, and housing prices are often highly skewed, because they can't go below 0, but they have a small number of very high values. To be used in regression, whether as independent or dependent variables, such variables are almost always transformed by taking their natural log.[2]

For example, Figure 8.5 from the previous chapter shows how the relationship between the gross domestic product (GDP) of nations, which is right-skewed, and life expectancy is nonlinear. Figure 8.6 then shows how this relationship can be coaxed into a linear pattern by taking the natural log of GDP.

---

[2]In fact, earnings would essentially never be used in a real regression study. We chose to illustrate regression using earnings, instead of log earnings, because it made it easier to explain how to interpret the coefficient. This decision further forced us to use simulated (made-up) data, because no real earnings data would have behaved well unlogged.

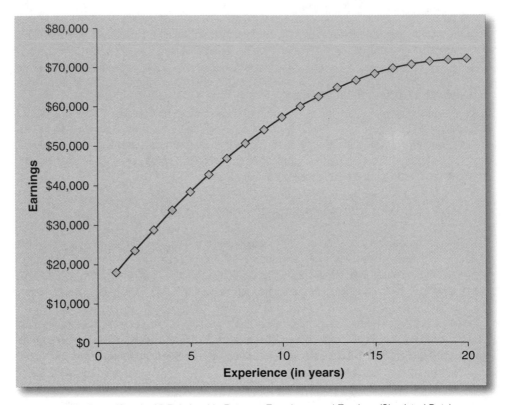

Figure 9.3   Nonlinear (Quadratic) Relationship Between Experience and Earnings (Simulated Data)

Interpreting regression coefficients when the variables have been logged turns out to be fairly simple. The change in a logged variable is just the proportional change in the unlogged variable. Consider a regression with log earnings as the dependent variable and years of education as the independent variable, whose coefficient is .03. That would mean that someone with one more year of education would be predicted to have .03 more earnings proportionally—or 3% more. In other words, take the coefficient, multiply it by 100, and the predicted percent change is given.

Things are even easier when both dependent and independent variables are logged. Consider a regression of log medical expenditures on log length of stay. The coefficient reveals the percent change in medical expenditures due to a 1% change in length of stay. The percent change in one variable due to a 1% change in another is referred to as the *elasticity* and is common in economics.

The Value of Robustness and Transparency

As discussed earlier, out-of-sample extrapolation can be hazardous, although it is often necessary to make such predictions for policy purposes. To further exacerbate the problem, different functional forms can result in quite different out-of-sample extrapolations. If the line is straight, we expect one thing; if it curves down, we might expect something quite different.

Policy-relevant relationships, such as how subsidizing health insurance influences people's decision to obtain coverage, can be modeled in a variety of different but reasonable ways. Such models are often used to predict the effects of a policy, such as a particular health care reform, that represents a large change from the way things are—in other words, out-of-sample extrapolations. As illustrated by Remler, Graff Zivin, and Glied (2004), out-of-sample extrapolations exacerbate the functional form differences, causing predictions from different models to diverge a great deal. In related work, Glied, Remler, and Graff Zivin (2002) propose guidelines for such extrapolations and encourage transparency of methods so that others may duplicate the calculation. Most of all, the robustness of different functional forms and models should be assessed. If the results are robust, they gain credibility. If they are not, then we at least realize our ignorance.

Categorical Variables as Dependent Variables in Regression

Many outcomes or dependent variables of interest in policy and practice are categorical—for example, graduating from high school or not, having a felony conviction or not, or having a disease or not. There are several forms of regression for dummy dependent variables such as these, including the linear probability model, logistic regression, and probit regression. They are similar to regression, although the interpretation of the coefficients can be a bit more difficult.

Linear Probability Model

The most easily interpretable method for doing a multiple regression with a dummy dependent variable is the **linear probability model** (**LPM**). LPM is really just regular regression with the coefficients interpreted as the predicted probability that the dependent variable will occur. For example, let's consider data from the 2007 Youth Risk Behavior Survey (YRBS) on the probability of teenagers being sexually active as predicted by their age (in years) and gender (a dummy variable, with female = 1 and male = 0).

$$\text{Prob(Sexuallyactive)} = a + b_{age}\text{Age} + b_{fem}\text{Female}$$

$$\text{Prob(Sexuallyactive)} = -1.27 + .11 \times \text{Age} - .05 \times \text{Female}.$$

The coefficient $b_{age} = .11$ tells us that each year of age brings with it an 11 percentage point increase in the likelihood of being sexually active, holding gender constant. The coefficient $b_{fem} = -.05$ tells us that, holding age constant, females are 5 percentage points *less* likely on average to be sexually active. (The constant is not meaningful because it refers to a male with 0 years of age.)

Some researchers dismiss LPMs, because the errors are not normally distributed (violating an assumption for inference). However, their results are easily interpretable (as we have just seen), unlike the more rigorous approaches discussed below. LPM requires a large sample and a good fit (high *R*-squared), and relatively few of the predictions should fall outside the 0 to 1 range. To test whether it is okay to use an LPM, its predictions should be examined and also compared with one of the more rigorous methods below.

Logistic and Probit Regression

Two more rigorous regression models for predicting dummy dependent variables are the **logistic** (logit, for short) and probit models, of which logistic is more common. For the logit equation, the log odds of an event are predicted. For the probit, as for the LPM, the probability is predicted. We will not go into any technical details about these methods. However, it is possible to read, even read critically, studies using these methods without understanding their technical complexities. We describe below what you need to know.

Unlike regular ordinary least squares (OLS) or LPM coefficients, the coefficients of logit and probit regressions cannot be interpreted meaningfully without doing some calculations. For logit regressions, the most common calculation converts the coefficients into odds ratios—the kind discussed in Chapter 8.

Consider some logistic regression results from the same YRBS data and variables as before used to predict whether teenagers are likely to be sexually active, based on their age and gender. Logistic regression output provides the odds ratio for Age, which turns out to be 1.62, meaning that the odds of being sexually active, holding gender constant, increases by this amount with each year of age. The odds ratio for Female is .81, meaning that the odds of being sexually active for females, holding age constant, is .81 to 1 (teenage girls are less likely to be sexually active on average than teenage boys). These results parallel those from the LPM.

It is also important to consider how good a fit a logit or probit model is, using one of its goodness-of-fit measures, such as the pseudo *R*-squared (which is similar to *R*-squared in ordinary regression).

Marginal Effects

The effects of independent variables in logit or probit regressions can be described using a **marginal effect** (or incremental effect)—the predicted difference in the probability due to a specified change in the relevant independent variable. Marginal effects may be calculated for probit and logistic regressions using means of the independent variables, but it is better to calculate them for each data point and then average.

What If the Dependent Variable Has More Than Two Categories?

Any categorical variable with more than two categories can be collapsed into a dummy variable. For example, self-reported health status (excellent, good, fair, poor) can be converted into two categories, Poor Health or Not-Poor Health (better than poor health). Therefore, the techniques above, such as the LPM or logistic regression, can be used for such categorical variables. However, collapsing categories often results in the loss of important information, such as differences within the various better-than-poor health categories.

Fortunately, some more advanced regression techniques allow categorical dependent variables with multiple categories. *Ordered logits* allow ordinal categorical variables to be used as dependent variables. *Multinomial logits* (also called *conditional logits*) and *multinomial probits* allow nominal categorical variables to be used as dependent variables.

Beware of Unrealistic Underlying Assumptions

The complexity of the regression methods with dependent categorical variables raises issues beyond just those of interpretation. The underlying equations are based on a variety of assumptions, and those assumptions may not be realistic.

For example, multinomial logit assumes the *independence of irrelevant alternatives* (*IIA*). IIA means that adding another alternative or changing the characteristics of another alternative does not affect the relative odds between the two alternatives considered in a specific multinomial logit equation. This is not true in many cases. A famous illustration shows that the choice between commuting on a blue bus or on a train is unchanged by the addition of a red bus, even though a red bus and a blue bus are obviously close substitutes (McFadden, 1974). Careful nesting of logits can alleviate the IIA problem.

Although you may not know the technicalities and specific assumptions of all these advanced methods, you should expect researchers and analysts to know them. You should also check that they state the assumptions and justify them in the particular application.

Which Statistical Methods Can I Use?

As you have seen, the appropriate statistical method depends on the type and quantity of variables. We have introduced some, although certainly not all, of the most important methods. To help you determine which statistical methods are available in a particular situation, we provide Table 9.5. The columns describe different possible types of dependent variables, while the rows describe different possible types of independent variables. The corresponding cell then provides possible statistical methods. For example, when both the independent and dependent variables are quantitative, ordinary regression may be used.

While this table is a useful guide, the methods above may not always apply. For example, OLS regression is intended for continuous variables—quantitative variables that can take on any value. A count variable (such as the number of jobs someone has held) must be a positive integer (or 0). In many circumstances, OLS regression cannot be used for count data. In the limited dependent variables section below, we discuss some of the circumstances in which another method is required.

Table 9.5 Which Statistical Methods Can I Use?

Independent Variable Type	Dependent Variable Type			
	Quantitative	Dichotomous (Dummy)	Ordinal Categorical	Nominal Categorical
Quantitative	OLS regression	Logit or probit Less rigorous: Linear probability model (LPM)	Ordered logit	Multinomial logit (also known as polychotomous logit)
Dichotomous (Dummy)	(1) z test (comparison of means) (2) OLS regression with single dummy as independent variable	(1) Cross-tabs and χ^2 test if only a single independent variable (no controls) (2) z test (comparison of proportions) (3) Logit or probit with single dummy as independent variable (4) Less rigorous: LPM with single dummy as independent variable	(1) Cross-tabs and χ^2 test if only a single independent variable (no controls) This "wastes" info contained in ordering. (2) Ordered logit with single dummy as independent variable	(1) Cross-tabs and χ^2 test if only a single independent variable (no controls) (2) Multinomial logit with dummy as independent variable
Ordinal Categorical	OLS regression with dummies as independent variables	(1) Cross-tabs and χ^2 test if only a single independent variable (no controls) (2) Logit or probit with dummies as independent variables (3) Less rigorous: LPM with dummies as independent variables	(1) Cross-tabs and χ^2 test if only a single independent variable (no controls) This "wastes" info contained in ordering. (2) Ordered logit with dummies as independent variables	(1) Cross-tabs and χ^2 test if only a single independent variable (no controls) (2) Multinomial logit with dummies as independent variables
Nominal Categorical	OLS regression with dummies as independent variables	(1) Cross-tabs and χ^2 test if only a single independent variable (no controls) (2) Logit or probit with dummies as independent variables (3) Less rigorous: LPM with dummies as independent variables	(1) Cross-tabs and χ^2 test if only a single independent variable (no controls) This "wastes" info contained in ordering. (2) Ordered logit with dummies as independent variables	(1) Cross-tabs and χ^2 test if only a single independent variable (no controls) (2) Multinomial logit with dummies as independent variables

Note: It is possible to create a dichotomous variable from any ordinal or nominal variable by combining categories. However, this throws out information. It may nonetheless be desirable if cell sizes are small.

Other Multivariate Methods

Many research studies use multiple regression in one of the forms we have discussed. However, some studies use other multivariate methods. It is beyond the scope of this book to fully describe all the quantitative analysis methods used in applied social research. However, we can provide a brief lay of the land—a sort of roadmap to some of the most common multivariate methods, along with their basic purposes and a few strengths and weaknesses.

Path Analysis

Often, researchers want to explore a complex set of relationships between many variables, making use of theory that describes and restricts the relationships. **Path analysis** does this by estimating the pattern of relationships between variables in a presumed causal structure.

Path analysis typically begins with a path diagram such as the ones introduced in Chapter 2. The results are presented as path coefficients next to the arrows linking the variables in the path diagram. The numerical estimates typically come from a set of ordinary regressions.

The main strength of path analysis is that it encourages researchers to specify and examine the presumed causal order of variables, in the form of a path diagram, and to empirically estimate both direct as well as indirect effects. This is illustrated in the path diagram of Figure 9.4.

The coefficients on the direct paths from education → earnings, age → earnings, and experience → earnings come from the following standardized regression:

$$\text{Earnings} = .40(\text{Education}) + .10 \times \text{Age} + .30 \times \text{Experience}.$$

The remaining two paths, age → education and age → experience, come from the following simple regressions:

$$\text{Education} = -.20 \times \text{Age}.$$

$$\text{Experience} = .50 \times \text{Age}.$$

In simple regression, these standardized coefficients are equivalent to the correlation r between the variables.

The results of the path analysis help us interpret how age influences earnings. According to these data, age has only a modest *direct* effect on earnings—which would be our conclusion had we used the regression analysis alone. But age has a larger *indirect* effect on earnings through experience, which can be calculated by multiplying the coefficients along the path: $.50 \times .30 = .15$ (older people have more experience, and experience leads to more earnings). The indirect effect of age through education, however, is negative: $-.20 \times .40 = -.08$ (older people tend to be less educated, and education boosts earnings). The *total* effect of age on earnings is composed of the direct effect plus the indirect effects: $.10 + .15 - .08 = .17$. In this way, path analysis helps illuminate indirect effects, in addition to direct effects, and provides a fuller picture of the pattern of relationships among variables.

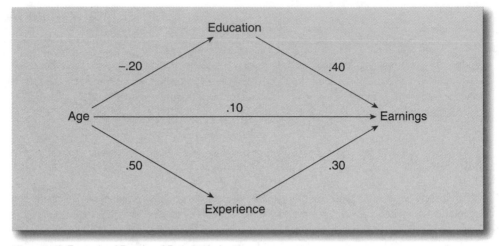

Figure 9.4   Example of Results of Path Analysis

While path analysis' greatest strength is its ability to explore and explain a particular theory, described by a path diagram, its dependence on that theory is also the method's greatest weakness. Path analysis is a structural method: What it can find is dictated by the structure, the path diagram that is assumed to be true.

Factor Analysis

In Chapter 4, on measurement, we saw how many indicators can be combined to create a scale. **Factor analysis** is a multivariate method that helps with this task by empirically grouping many variables (indicators) into a smaller set of underlying *factors*. For this reason, it is sometimes referred to as a *data reduction* method. Because it reduces many overlapping variables into fewer, less overlapping (less correlated) factors, it can help with the multicollinearity problem in regression discussed earlier.

To give an example of factor analysis, say we ask people in a health survey how often they do the following:

1. Walk up several flights of stairs

2. Lift heavy objects

3. Walk several blocks

4. Feel down in the dumps

5. Lack interest in things

6. Find life dull and routine

Although these are six separate variables that we could analyze individually, the first three seem to indicate physical health while the last three seem to reflect emotional health. It might make more sense for us to use just these two dimensions. With factor analysis, we can examine this possibility empirically—as Table 9.6 illustrates.

Table 9.6   Factor Analysis

	Factor 1	Factor 2
Walk up several flights of stairs	.722	.122
Lift heavy objects	.661	.083
Walk several blocks	.698	.100
Feel down in the dumps	.043	.806
Lack interest in things	.102	.786
Find life dull and routine	.097	.749

The numbers shown are **factor loadings**, essentially correlations between the variables and the underlying factors (two in this case). These results show a coherent pattern: The first three variables load highly on factor 1 (see the bolded factor loadings) while the second three variables load highly on factor 2 (again, see bolded factor loadings). Thus, the results support our idea of combining the first three variables into one factor, and the next three into a separate factor. The first factor seems to relate to physical health, while the second factor seems to relate to mental health. In this case, physical health and mental health are *latent variables*, underlying but not directly observable measures (as discussed in Chapter 4).

The above is an example of **exploratory factor analysis**, also known as **principal components analysis**, in which the researcher does not use theory to impose a structure on the factor analysis. Specifically, the researcher lets the computer choose the number of factors and estimate how the items correlate with each factor.

Confirmatory Factor Analysis: Making Use of Theory

Alternatively, researchers can use measurement theory to specify both the number of latent variables (factors) and which variables are related to each latent variable (which variables load onto each factor). This is referred to as **confirmatory factor analysis**, because it uses factor analysis to confirm a particular measurement model. In the above example, the researcher could have specified that two factors, one for physical health and one for mental health, existed and that the first three variables related to the physical health factor and the second three variables related to the mental health factor. The factor analysis would be performed under those restrictions. The data would then serve two purposes: (1) to create the best representation of physical and mental health through the factor loadings, and (2) to test or confirm the measurement model through goodness-of-fit measures. Confirmatory factor analysis is actually a form of structural equation modeling, which we cover next.

Structural Equation Modeling

Structural equation modeling (**SEM**) essentially combines both factor and path analysis into one estimation method. In fact, SEM is the method most often used for confirmatory factor analysis, and some prefer to use SEM in place of regression to estimate ordinary path models. But in its full form, SEM includes both a structural model, as in path analysis, and factors represented by multiple indicators.

SEM has several strengths. First, causal models of latent variables can be explored in a manner that allows the data to be optimized simultaneously for both purposes: causal structure and measurement. Second, by explicitly removing the measurement error from the latent variables, the causal model can be more reliably estimated. Third, as with path models, SEM results show more explicitly how variables are related to each other.

Figure 9.5 shows an example from an SEM study of influences on trust of the civil service across 33 nations (Van Ryzin, 2009). The main outcome, Trust of the civil service, is an observed variable. However, the main hypothesized causes, Government process and Government outcomes, are factors, or latent variables, observed in the real world through their indicators.

In the diagram, observed variables are shown in rectangles with latent variables shown in ovals. The estimates (standardized coefficients in this case) are next to each of the arrows. The structural coefficients are interpreted the same way as path coefficients, and the factor coefficients are equivalent to factor loadings. (The small circles connected to each observed variable represent unique components, and the coefficients next to these small circles are the explained variances.)

As with path analysis and all structural methods, SEM's main weakness is its sensitivity to the theory. This weakness can be somewhat alleviated by testing competing theories, but all the results are driven by strong assumptions about the causal relationships of the variables.

Multilevel Models

Theories and models used to estimate the theories must specify the unit of analysis. Using the example of the determinants of crime, do we model crime on an individual level? A neighborhood level? A city level? A country level? One can imagine influences that work at each of these levels. An individual's family background matters, but so does the degree of order in his or her neighborhood and the job opportunities in his or her city. Moreover, some variables are determined at the higher level by higher-level processes and influenced by what happens at the lower levels.

Multilevel models (also known as *hierarchical linear models*) allow researchers to jointly consider variables measured at different units of analysis, such as how crime at the individual level, order at the neighborhood level, and job opportunities at the city level are jointly determined. Because it allows researchers to consider the influence of context on individuals, multilevel modeling has become especially important in fields such as education, public health, and criminal justice.

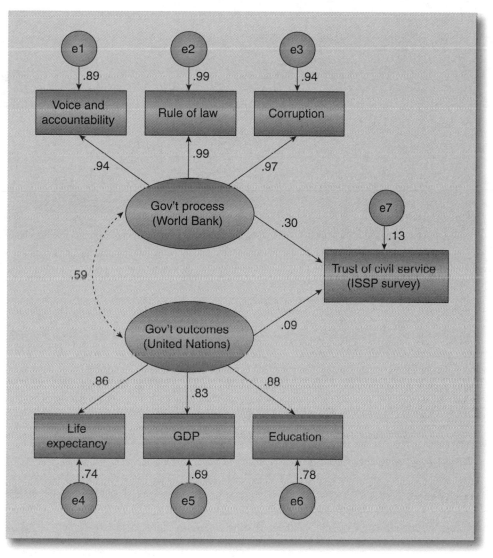

Figure 9.5   Example of Structural Equation Modeling Results

Source: Adapted from Van Ryzin (2009).

Note: ISSP, International Social Survey Program.

Figure 9.6 illustrates a multilevel model using education variables that are measured at the school, classroom, and individual levels. To estimate the model, we might have data, say, on 10 schools, 100 classrooms (10 in each school), and 2,000 students (20 in each classroom). Thus, each variable in the model describes a different unit of analysis, yet we would estimate it all as one model.

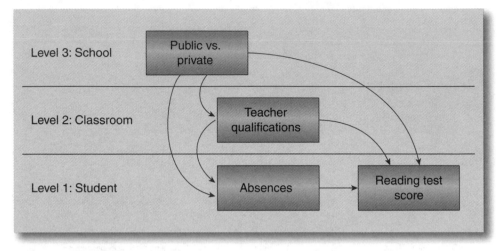

Figure 9.6   Example of Multilevel Model

Source: Leonard, Bourke, and Schofield (2002).

There are variations on multilevel modeling, some of which fall short of full multilevel modeling. For example, we could create a dummy variable for the public-private school status of each student and also assign dummy variables to the qualification levels of their teachers, then run the model as an individual-level regression. But this approach is not as good because it multiplies the observations at a higher level (we have just 100 teachers, not 2,000), distorting the standard errors, and it does not give information on cross-level effects and interactions. See Luke (2004) for more information on the motivations for and detailed methods of multilevel modeling.

Time Series and Forecasting

In time-series data, the variation is over time, rather than being cross-sectional variation. For example, a time series might consist of world population in each year over 20 years. Using regression with time-series data is more difficult than with cross-sectional data—treacherous, even, in some cases.

Time Trends and Correlation Over Time

Over time, the number of computers per capita is rising and the population is growing. If a regression of computers per capita on population were performed using time-series data, it would show a strong relationship. In fact, any time series generally going up (or down) over time would seem strongly related to any series going up (or down) over time. But that could just be the general trend of both. With time-series data that have a trend over time, care must be taken with regressions.

The simplest approach is to include a linear time trend in the regression equation. In this way, the coefficient describes how the deviations from trend of the variables are related. For example, by estimating the regression

$$\text{ComputersPerCap} = a + b_{pop}\text{Population} + b_{trend}\text{Year},$$

the coefficient b_{pop} reveals the extent that variations from trend in the two series are correlated.

But time series is more complicated than most regressions for other reasons. A basic assumption of inference for regression is that the error terms (other factors driving the dependent variable) are independent. In the context of time series, this means that the factors driving the dependent variable in one period are unrelated to the factors driving it in another period.

That is highly unlikely with many sorts of time series. In general, whatever happens at one point in time depends on what happened at earlier points in time. Consequently, lagged (earlier period) variables may need to be included in the regression equations. Time series has its own methods to deal with such correlations over time, known as *autocorrelation*. Wooldridge (2009) offers a good introduction to the basics of time series. These methods are common in finance and macroeconomics.

The growth of a variable is defined as the percentage change over time. For example, the annual population growth in a country could be 1%, meaning that the population increases by 1% over the course of a year. Growth rates must specify the unit of time. Some forms of time-series data, particularly in demography and economics, are best described through growth rates. Therefore, growth rates of variables, rather than levels, are often used as the dependent variables.

Many phenomena vary in a systematic way with the season. For example, hiring regularly slows down around Christmas. To focus on variation driven by other factors or changes that represent "real" changes, such data are often seasonally adjusted. Specifically, the effects of the seasons are estimated using a long time series. The seasonal variation is then predicted and subtracted from the actual data.

Forecasting means using data from time series in the past to predict future values of the dependent variable(s). Forecasting is particularly common in demography and economics. Forecasting is, in some sense, an out-of-sample extrapolation. The further into the future a forecast must go, the more out of sample it must go—and therefore the less confidence we can have in it.

Panel Data Methods

Panel data, described in Chapter 6, often consist of repeated measures of the same variables for the same individuals over time. It thus combines both cross-sectional and time-series variation. A number of special methods exist to make use of these multiple dimensions. One method is known as *fixed effects*.[3] The idea is that there is some particular characteristic (related to the dependent variable) that varies across individuals, is unknown, but does not vary over time. In this case, an individual-specific dummy variable is included in the regression. Essentially, the regression is

---

[3] This refers to the fixed-effects method of econometrics, not the fixed-effects method of experimental analysis and design.

estimated from the relationships between changes over time in individuals' dependent variable and changes in their independent variables. This is discussed further in Chapter 13 on natural and quasi experiments.

Spatial Analysis

Spatial data of many kinds are becoming increasingly available due to geographic information science (GIS). GIS generally refers to a broad set of techniques that range from creating spatial data (e.g., identifying the geographic coordinates for events or calculating distances between features of interest) to creating maps. Spatial analysis builds on GIS, in that spatial data are used with spatial methods.

Spatial methods are typically used to conduct analysis of spatial properties such as identifying spatial patterns in data, for example, clustering of mortality or poverty (Center for Spatially Integrated Social Science, 2009). As for time series that have to be concerned with temporal autocorrelation, care must often be taken with spatial data, because each location is similar to and not independent of nearby locations; this is called spatial autocorrelation. A simple form of spatial analysis uses cross-sectional data where the unit of analysis is a location, perhaps a very finely defined location, with variables, such as mortality, describing the location. One variation is a "hot" or "cold" spot analysis in which one looks for clusters of especially high or low mortality. The Center for Spatially Integrated Social Science provides many references and resources (www.csiss.org).[4]

Limited Dependent Variables

A regular regression implicitly assumes that the dependent variable is a quantitative variable that can take on any value. It can be positive or negative. It is continuous and not restricted to integers or any particular region. A dependent variable that cannot take on all possible values is known as a **limited dependent variable**. We have already examined categorical variables, which are one special kind of limited dependent variable. However, there are other kinds.

Many variables cannot possibly take on values below 0. For example, it is not possible to have a negative weight. These can result in what is called truncated variables. Regression models exist to treat such situations, such as the Tobit model. The Poisson model can be used for dependent variables that are counts—nonnegative integers. In other circumstances, the variable can take on a full range of values, but we cannot observe them, because they are censored. For example, many surveys top-code income, that is, they do not provide measures of income over a certain amount, but simply describe those incomes as top-coded. A closely related case is referred to as *truncated data*, which is essentially sample selection bias, because the sample is truncated in a way that is related to what is being estimated.

There are more advanced methods for dealing with all these problems. They are beyond the scope of this book. (See Wooldridge, 2009, for further treatment.) However, there are two things that you do need to know. First, ignoring such problems, unless their magnitude is small, can be a mistake that

---

[4]We thank Deborah Balk for providing us with information on spatial analysis.

leads to wrong conclusions. Second, the methods that do exist frequently depend on quite a few assumptions. They work by substituting functional forms assumptions to predict data or relationships that are not known. In some cases, the assumptions used are good, but in other cases, they are not.

Survival Analysis

Frequently, researchers want to predict the length of time until some event, such as the length of an unemployment spell (time until a job is found) or how long someone lives (time until death) following treatment of a particular disease. Such analysis is often referred to as **survival analysis,** due to its use in medical research. It is a particularly important form of limited dependent variable. In addition to the natural restrictions to the form the variable can take, data are often censored, because the data collection ends before all individuals reach the event (e.g., death, employment).

More Multivariate Methods Not Covered

We have only been able to give an overview of some of the multivariate methods most commonly used in social and policy research. There are many more, with each field or discipline having its own preferred toolkit of techniques. To understand any of these methods, it helps to focus on the big picture of why the method is needed and what it provides. What questions does the method help answer? What insight does it provide? How does it differ from methods you already know? How is it the same?

Conclusion

Social and policy phenomena are complex and involve many variables. Each variable is related to many other variables like threads in an intricate web. For this reason, analysis of such phenomena frequently requires multivariate techniques. Moreover, many of the multivariate techniques of this chapter become essential tools for getting at causation, discovering what causes what and properly estimating the size of causal effects. But by themselves, these tools and techniques are not sufficient. Theory, careful thought, and additional evidence are required. The next part of the book discusses what else you need to know to investigate and demonstrate causation.

Exercises

9.1. Consider the following simulated results from a multiple regression using state-level data in the United States. The dependent variable is the state's smoking rate (measured as a percentage). The independent variables are the tax on cigarettes, measured in cents per pack, and a dummy variable indicating whether or not the state has a tobacco industry. The results are as follows:

$$\text{smokerate} = 15 - .5 \times \text{cigtax} + 20 \times \text{tobaccoindustry}.$$

Interpret the constant term, the coefficient of cigtax, and the coefficient of tobaccoindustry. Make sure to state the units of each.

9.2. Consider a regression of medical costs on the independent variables type 1 and type 2, described in Box 9.2. The unit of analysis is the patient.

a. What information does the coefficient of type 1 provide? What information does the coefficient of type 2 provide?

b. Suppose that, using data from many patients at many hospitals, the coefficient of type 1 is $300 and the coefficient of type 2 is $150. What is the expenditure difference between type 1 and type 2 diabetes predicted to be?

9.3. These questions continue the imaginary world Exercise 8.8 in Chapter 8.

Imaginary World B: Imagine the following world with very strict laws: Everyone goes to school until at least eighth grade. Earnings are $10,000 for someone with an eighth-grade education and no experience. Each additional year of education increases earnings by $2,000, and each additional year of experience increases earnings by $1,000.

a. Study 1 in Imaginary World B
This study is just like the one done in World A of Question 8 of Chapter 8. Researchers collect data on years of education and earnings from everyone in this imaginary world. They perform a regression of earnings on education (i.e., earnings is the dependent variable and education is the independent variable). Note that the only independent variable is education. They also calculate the correlation between the two variables.

- What is the correlation coefficient (very roughly)? Explain why it has that value.
- What is the R-squared of the regression (very roughly)?[5]

b. Study 2 in Imaginary World B
Now, suppose researchers do a multiple regression of earnings on education and experience.

- What is the R-squared of the regression?
- What is the regression coefficient of education? (Make sure to state its units.)
- What is the regression coefficient of experience?

c. The studies of real-world researchers who want to predict earnings—are they more like Study 1 or Study 2 in Imaginary World B?

---

[5]You may wonder why we don't ask what the coefficient of education is. In fact, more information is required to know that—it depends on whether there is any correlation between education and experience. This issue will be covered in Chapter 11.

PART III

STRATEGIES FOR CAUSATION

Objectives: In this chapter, you will learn that correlation does not imply causation. You will discover other possible causal explanations for a correlation—such as reverse causation and common causes—and see how they can make correlation a biased indicator of the magnitude of a causal effect. Much of the problem arises because real-world programs or treatments—the independent variables of interest—are self-selected and therefore endogenous. Because causation is so difficult to pin down, you will see how it helps to think about it in terms of a counterfactual definition—or what would happen, with and without the cause. Experimentation provides an idealized approach to estimating the counterfactual by imposing treatments from outside—exogenous treatments—and by controlling other variables. But experimentation is not always possible or ethical. This chapter thus provides the theoretical and conceptual tools needed to understand and apply other empirical strategies—covered fully in the chapters that follow—for establishing causation and measuring causal effects.

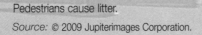

Pedestrians cause litter.

Source: © 2009 Jupiterimages Corporation.

Causation

10

Family Dinners and Teenage Substance Abuse

According to a national survey, teens who have dinner frequently with their families use drugs and alcohol less than teens who do so only infrequently. Teen drug and alcohol abuse is a major public

Family day—a day to eat dinner with your children.

Source: © iStockphoto.com/markchentx.

health issue, so the survey got a lot of attention. The results inspired a public health movement titled *Family Day—A Day to Eat Dinner With Your Children*. Clearly, those behind this movement believe that if they could get parents to spend more time with their teens, by having family dinners, for example, teen drinking and drug usage would decline (see Box 10.1).

BOX 10.1
Children Who Have Frequent Family Dinners Less Likely to Use Marijuana, Tobacco, and Drink Alcohol

NEW YORK, Sept. 15, PRNewswire. From 2003 to 2008 research by the National Center on Addiction and Substance Abuse (CASA) at Columbia University has consistently found that children who have frequent family dinners are less likely to use marijuana, tobacco and drink alcohol. CASA research reveals that compared to children who have frequent family dinners (five or more per week), children who have infrequent family dinners (less than three per week) are two and a half times likelier to have used marijuana and tobacco, and one and a half times likelier to have drunk alcohol.

Ever Used	0–2 Dinners/Week	5–7 Dinners/Week
Alcohol	48%	30%
Tobacco	29%	13%
Marijuana	27%	11%

Teens Who Have Used Substances By Frequency of Family Dinners (Average Over 6 Years: 2003–2008)

Monday, September 22nd will mark CASA's eighth annual 'Family Day—A Day to Eat Dinner with Your Children(™)' celebration. Family Day is a national movement to inform parents that the parental engagement fostered during frequent family dinners is an effective tool to help keep America's children substance free and reminds parents that "Dinner Makes A Difference!" "If you asked me based on CASA's 16 years of intensive examination of substance abuse and addiction in our nation what's the most effective thing we can do to curb this scourge and protect our children, I would say parental engagement. And there is no more effective example of this than frequent family dinners," said Joseph A. Califano, Jr., CASA's chairman and president and former U.S. Secretary of Health, Education, and Welfare. "Years of surveying teens have consistently shown that the more often they have dinner with their parents, the less likely they are to smoke, drink and use drugs."

Source: www.reuters.com/article/pressRelease/idUS183576 + 15-Sep-2008 + PRN20080915.

Correlation Is Not Causation

This national survey showed that time spent at the family dinner table was negatively *correlated* with—or negatively associated with—use of drugs and alcohol. (*Negative* in the sense that the *more* teens eat dinner with their families, the *less* they use drugs and alcohol—as we learned in Chapter 2.) The study treats family dinners as the *independent variable* and drug and alcohol use as the *dependent variable*. After reading these results, we are tempted to conclude that family time around the dinner table *caused* teens to use less alcohol and drugs. We tend to want to jump from correlation to causation.

Regular family dinners might in fact produce less teen drinking and drug use—the relationship could be causal. But there are plausible alternative explanations—which we will look at shortly—for why teens who frequently eat dinner with their families are less likely to use drugs and alcohol. Not all these reasons imply that if you could persuade parents to have more family dinners, teen drug and alcohol usage would decline.

On days when it rains, more people carry umbrellas to work. However, we don't believe that carrying umbrellas causes rain. "Correlation is not causation" is an easy enough caveat to appreciate in nonsense examples such as rain and umbrellas. However, it is much harder to resist jumping to a causal conclusion when the correlation corresponds to what we already believe is true and good. After all, family dinners must produce good things—right? Remaining critical takes work.

To remain critical, we will spell out some possible causal models of the observed correlation, using the method of path diagrams from Chapter 2. We will then begin to learn strategies for empirically identifying causation. Thus, this chapter lays both the conceptual groundwork and the initial empirical framework for causal, as opposed to purely descriptive, research. Subsequent chapters will go deeper into the various statistical strategies and research designs used to get at causation in actual social and policy research.

Possible Explanations of a Correlation

Let's consider some possible explanations, or models, for the correlation between frequency of family dinners and drug use by teens.

Causation and Reverse Causation

To begin with, there is the initial possibility that family time (the independent variable) does, indeed, cause less substance abuse (the dependent variable)—as the press release (Box 10.1) implies. This causal model appears in the upper part of Figure 10.1.

But the causal relationship implied by the press release is only one of several plausible explanations. What if teens who drink, smoke, and use drugs simply want to avoid being detected, so they stay away from home—and avoid the dinner table at night? Surely this is a plausible explanation as well. This possibility—**reverse causation**—is shown in the lower part of Figure 10.1.

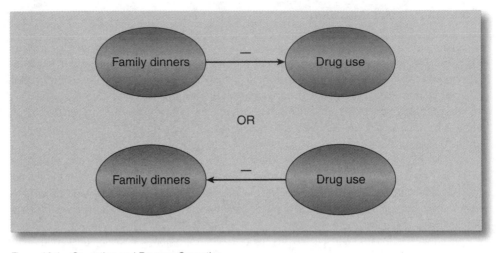

Figure 10.1 Causation and Reverse Causation

When contemplating a correlation that seems to imply causation, ask yourself: Could it work the other way around? Could it be reverse causation?

Common Causes

Another possibility is that psychologically more mature teens—that is, teens who act more grown up and identify more with adults—prefer to spend more time with their parents, and their parents probably prefer to spend more time with them. Such teens also may have a stronger sense of responsibility and perhaps a greater awareness of the negative life consequences of drinking and drugs, factors likely to lead to less use. In other words, a maturity factor might underlie both family dinners and drug use, making them correlated but not causally connected.

We refer to this situation as a **common cause,** and it is depicted in Figure 10.2. Family dinners and drug use are only correlated (represented by the dotted curved line with no arrows) because they both reflect the same common cause, the maturity level of teenagers. Note again that this correlation between family dinners and drug use remains true empirically—however, it is not causation. It is what researchers sometimes call a **spurious relationship**.

Bias From a Common Cause

Now, let's suppose again that family time does have some causal connection with drug use after all—but its influence is mixed up with a common cause. Figure 10.3 shows an example of this, where the psychological maturity of the teen influences both family time and drug use, as before (Figure 10.2), but now, family time does indeed exert some causal influence of its own on drug use.

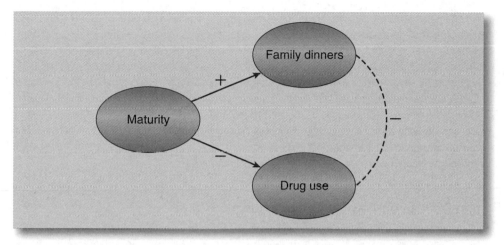

Figure 10.2 Common Cause

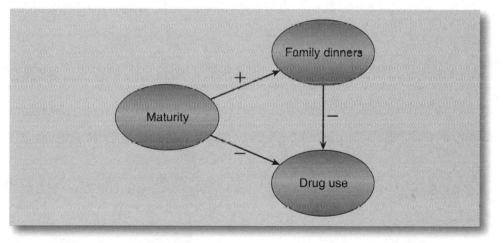

Figure 10.3 Bias From a Common Cause

This pattern of causation is quite common yet tricky, because if we don't take account of the maturity factor, the connection between family time and drug use will appear exaggerated—it will be biased. That's because the influence of maturity flows through and gets mixed up with family time.

Confounding is another common term for this phenomenon—maturity confounds family time and drug use. (We will learn several more commonly used terms for the same phenomenon in Chapter 11.)

The national survey suggests, for example, that marijuana use would drop from 27% to just 11% (a decline of 16 percentage points) if families that failed to eat dinner together frequently just changed their ways—a big effect. We can illustrate the magnitude of the difference: If 1 million families in the United States made this change, we would expect about 160,000 fewer teens to use marijuana.

But is the size of this estimated effect biased? The estimate was based on the assumption that *all* the difference in marijuana use was due to differences in family dinner time. It does not take account of possible common causes, such as the level of maturity of the teenagers (or whether the parents are working long hours, divorced, etc.). We don't want to make the mistake of thinking that some cause will produce a big change in the world when, in fact, it will produce only a small one. Again, knowing the correct *magnitude* of a causal effect is important.

Bias From an Unknown or Complex Common Cause

Bias and confounding can come from an unknown or complex common cause as well. This situation can be represented by a curved, dotted line with arrows connecting the variables, as in Figure 10.4. (A curved line without any arrows just indicates a correlation with no causal implications.) Say drug dealing is more prevalent in urban areas, and thus, teenagers living in urban areas are more likely to be exposed to drugs. And suppose also that families that live in urban areas, as a result of a variety of cultural and lifestyle factors, have less frequent family dinners. Living in urban areas, however, does not *cause* less frequent family dinners, per se. Rather, both urban living and family dinners them- selves have some unknown, complex common causes that lead them to be correlated with each other. We will have more to say about this issue in Chapter 11, but it is important here to note the similarity with Figure 10.3 and to recognize that common causes can still exert bias even when they are not entirely clear or fully understood.

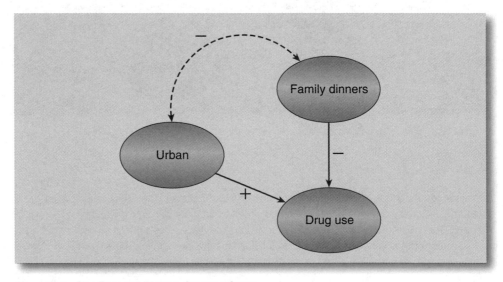

Figure 10.4   Bias From an Unknown Common Cause

Bias From Reverse Causation: Simultaneity Bias

It is also possible that both causation and reverse causation are true at the same time—simultaneously. Suppose, for example, that family dinners really do cause a reduction in teen drug abuse, but that in addition, teens who use drugs do still avoid family dinners. This possibility is shown in Figure 10.5. Once again, the magnitude of the causal effect of family dinners implied by the press release would be biased. In econometrics, this is known as **simultaneity bias** because it stems from causal relationships that simultaneously go in both directions.

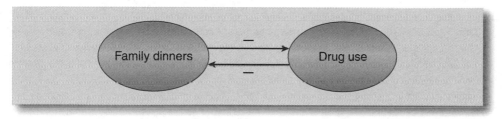

Figure 10.5   Simultaneity Bias

Other Examples of Correlation That Imply Causation

As you can see, trying to decide if a correlation is due to causation—and if so, how much of it is causation—turns out to be more difficult than it at first appears to be. So let's practice these ideas by looking at a few other policy-related examples of correlations that seem to imply causation.

Are Busy Hospitals Better?

Practice, practice, practice if you want to get better at something, so the saying goes—but does this advice apply to hospitals too? Evidence indicates that hospitals performing a higher volume of a given procedure, such as heart valve replacement, do have better outcomes (fewer complications and deaths). As a result, some heart patients decide only to consider high-volume hospitals, and some state governments set volume standards in an effort to reduce risk.

But could this be a case of reverse causation? After all, if a restaurant serves good food, it's more likely to be crowded with happy diners. Perhaps hospitals that do a successful job at

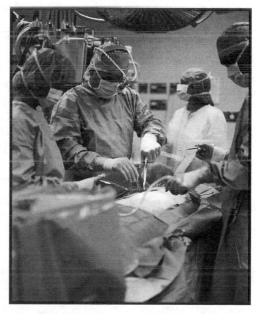

Patients at high-volume hospitals experience better outcomes.

Source: © 2009 Jupiterimages Corporation.

replacing heart valves simply attract more heart patients. Or could the higher-volume, better-outcome relationship reflect a common cause? One possible common cause might be the level of health insurance coverage in the populations served by different hospitals. Hospitals that serve affluent populations, covered by first-rate health insurance, might be more likely to receive referrals for valve replacements than hospitals serving populations with only limited health insurance coverage. Health insurance coverage also helps ensure earlier diagnosis and better postoperative care, resulting in fewer complications and deaths.

Are Organizations With Happy Workers More Successful?

A number of studies of businesses and other organizations find that those with high levels of employee satisfaction are also more successful (as measured by such things as profits or market value) (e.g., Best, 2008). So management gurus urge organizations to do what's needed to make their workers happier. But it could well be that success itself breeds happiness—because of more pay and benefits, fewer layoffs, and less stressed-out bosses. Everybody is in a better mood when the organization is doing well. Common causes are also likely, for example, when a particular industry is in a downturn because of larger-scale changes in the economy, society, or technology. Imagine working at Kodak during the years when consumers all switched to using digital cameras. Such a trend both hurts the firm and discourages the workers.

The Power of a Library Card

Various studies show that students who own library cards read more and perform better on standardized language arts tests (e.g., Whitehead, 2004). So it is not surprising to find some education leaders attempting to boost academic performance by distributing library cards to all students, as the minister of education did in New Brunswick, Canada (Communications New Brunswick, 2004). We are tempted to hope that ownership of a library card itself *causes* kids to read more. But reverse causation is quite likely in this case—the kids who already read a lot are the ones who have the library cards. There could well be common causes at work too, such as parents who value and encourage their children to read *and* own a library card.

There are many correlations in the world, and often they suggest causal relationships that would be useful for policy or practice—but only if they are indeed causal. We want to find ways to reduce drug use, improve patient outcomes, make organizations more productive, and get kids to read. But it is important to understand that causation might flow in the opposite direction. And common causes may be at work behind the scenes, making the correlation a biased if not false indication of causation.

Causal Mechanisms

In Chapter 2, we noted that a key element of a theory is a causal mechanism—some notion of *how* the independent and dependent variables are related. The causal mechanism can be thought of also as the process, or chain of cause-effect linkages, that transmits (mediates) the causal effect.

Furthermore, we modeled this situation by specifying *intervening variables*, or *mediators*, that lie along the causal pathway between the independent and dependent variables.

Returning to our opening example, let's consider a causal mechanism through which family dinners could result in less drinking and drug use. One possibility is that regular family dinners facilitate *communication* between parents and teenagers. As a result, parents better understand the social pressures and day-to-day exposure to drugs faced by their teenagers. Perhaps then, they can find ways to intervene to counteract these influences. And the teenagers learn from their parents during family dinners too, both about the dangers of drug use and about their parents' concern for them. Figure 10.6 shows this mechanism of *communication* in path diagram form as an intervening variable between family dinners and drug use.

We could add additional intervening variables to elaborate the causal mechanism, for example, putting a variable representing parental *intervention efforts* between communication and drug use. Whether to specify an intervening variable, and how many intervening variables are needed to elaborate the causal mechanism, depend on the context. Would this information change the substantive implications of the research? Would it change the way a program is designed? If so, then the intervening variables should be spelled out.

Chance Correlations and Statistical Significance

Correlation between two variables, such as family time and drug use, could occur by chance. In such a case, there may be no causal explanation at all for the correlation—not even a common cause. The two variables just happen to be correlated because of some fluke or coincidence.

For example, in a particular metropolitan area, during a specific period of time, more auto accidents may occur on odd-numbered days of the month than on even-numbered days. This pattern can happen just by chance, and if we were to collect data over the long run (a larger sample size), we might well see

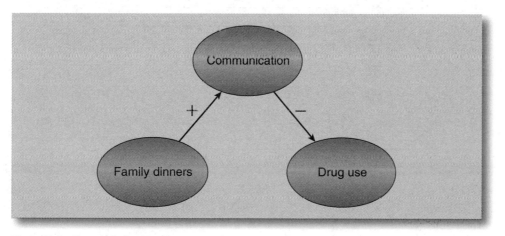

Figure 10.6   Causal Mechanism Shown as an Intervening Variable

that accidents eventually balance out across even and odd days. But in the short run, we might be tempted to jump to an erroneous causal conclusion: Watch out—avoid the roadways on odd-numbered days!

Statistical significance tests, discussed in Chapter 8, can check to see if a difference or correlation is unlikely to be the result of mere chance coincidence. Statistical significance tests can rule out chance as the explanation for a correlation. The size of the correlation and the amount of the available data (sample size) are key factors in gauging statistical significance.

But importantly, just eliminating chance does not prove causation: Alternative explanations—reverse causation or a common cause—could still be responsible for a genuine nonchance correlation. *No statistical significance test on its own can ever prove causation*. It does not matter how fancy or clever the test is. Proving causation requires further reasoning strategies and ways to gather and analyze evidence, which is what this chapter and the others in Part III provide.

Arrows, Arrows Everywhere

Real-world correlations can be due to all the causal pathways discussed so far—causation, reverse causation, common causes (including complex common causes), mechanisms, and even chance—operating at once. Figure 10.7 shows this kind of complex causal model.

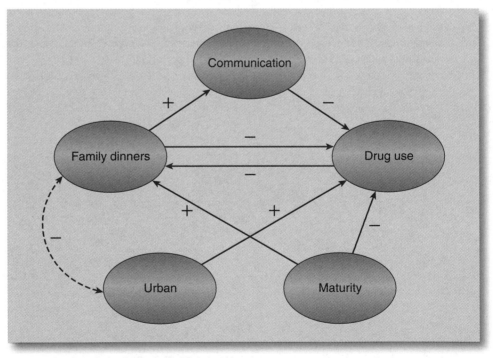

Figure 10.7   Complexity: Many Causal Relationships

Reviews of previous research on the topic of drinking and drug use among teens would undoubtedly add more common causes and more mechanisms. Prior research would also likely give us some sense of the relative importance of different factors. All this reflects the fact that a behavior such as teen substance abuse has complex origins and is mixed up with other things going on in the lives and personalities of teens and their parents. After all, if it were a simple picture, teen drinking and drug use would be an easy social problem to fix.

Why Worry About the Correct Causal Model?

We worry about a correct causal model because it guides the actions we take. If regular family dinners simply and directly influence drug and alcohol use, then encouraging families to spend more time around the dinner table with their kids holds promise as a national prevention strategy. With the help of some clever social marketing consultants, we can fill the airwaves and put up billboards with convincing appeals to families to devote more time and attention to the traditional mealtime (as the program's sponsors indeed have done). As a result, teen drinking and drug use should decrease.

But if it turns out to be a case of reverse causation, then all our time and money spent on boosting the popularity of family dinners would be wasted (at least in terms of doing something about drug and alcohol abuse). This would be like trying to make it rain by handing out umbrellas on the street. Clearly, we need to know in which direction the causal arrow really flows.

Situations of common causes have important practical consequences, too. If family time and drug use are both the effects of some common cause, such as maturity, then we might want to turn our attention to that common cause and ignore family dinner time as the key factor. Or if family time's effect on drug use is real but appears larger than it really is—if it is biased—because of a common cause (even an unknown or complex common cause), we will be misled in our judgments about the importance of promoting family time as a policy lever.

And if family time's influence on drug use works indirectly through some mechanism, such as better communication between parents and teens, then perhaps we can more directly influence drug use by focusing more specifically on the intervening variable(s). Maybe it is not family dinners per se that we should target but any type of activity that encourages communication—going on family outings, sharing hobbies, and so on.

Although theories and path models help us think about complex realities, demonstrating causation requires proof in the form of empirical evidence.

Evidence of Causation: Some Initial Clues

We'll soon have much more to say about evidence for causation, in this chapter as well as in the rest of Part III, but it helps to begin with some initial clues that point to a possible cause-effect relationship. These clues alone are not proof of causation, but they help build a stronger case.

The Cause Happens Before the Effect

The time order of events is very important in establishing cause and effect (Davis, 1985). The national survey looked at families at one point in time—a snapshot of family dinners and teen substance abuse. But which came first? It's hard to tell. Perhaps the families with drug-using kids once had family dinners frequently, but things began to fall apart after the teens got involved in drugs. But if the survey could show that the frequency of family dinners was an established pattern of family behavior, going well back into the child's early years, then the evidence might be more convincing. The frequency of family dinners would then clearly predate the teen's current use of drugs—providing better evidence of causation.

When Is Time Order Misleading? Expectations

Because human beings are intelligent and often try to predict the future, determining the time order of events is not as easy at it might appear. Consider again the example of umbrellas and rain. If you think about it, often, people start carrying umbrellas before the rain arrives. So if we rely just on the naive time order of our everyday observations, we may jump to the conclusion that umbrellas are indeed the cause and rain the effect.

But of course, people carry umbrellas when they expect rain, perhaps because it was forecast by meteorologists or perhaps because they see dark clouds in the morning sky. Meteorological conditions cause rain. These conditions also give us signs in advance that we perceive (such as dark clouds), causing us to expect rain and therefore to carry umbrellas. The meteorological conditions precede and cause rain. They also cause expectations of rain in people, which cause (and precede) umbrella carrying. Thus, meteorological conditions are a common cause of both rain and umbrella carrying and do indeed precede both of them.

Expectations of what will happen in the future play a particularly important role in finance and economics. So before taking time precedence as evidence supporting causation, consider whether human expectations may be at work. And think about possible prior common causes.

The Correlation Appears in Many Different Contexts

Rarely does a correlation from one study, in one particular time and place, provide good evidence of cause and effect. But a correlation that turns up repeatedly, across different contexts, becomes more convincing. Does a volume-outcome relationship appear in studies of different types of surgery? Does it appear in studies in different regions of the country, or even different countries of the world? The more often the correlation appears, in different contexts, the more we begin to suspect causation. This is why *replication*—the repeating of studies in different places—is so important in research.

But, as we will see, biased studies may also be reliably replicated. So replication is a necessary—but not sufficient—condition for causation. (See Box 10.2.)

BOX 10.2
Prominent Epidemiologists Discuss Clues of Causation

When trying to decide if some factor, such as traffic density, secondhand smoke, hormone replacement therapy, or oatmeal consumption contributes to getting a disease, epidemiologists must often rely on the kinds of evidence we discuss, including replication, time precedence, plausible mechanism, magnitude of effect, and the control variables strategy we will look at in Chapter 11.

The highly regarded journal *Science* interviewed many prominent epidemiologists about what constitutes sufficient evidence to infer causation (Taubes & Mann, 1995). While some epidemiologists considered replication a compelling element, David Sackett of Oxford University said, "If there's an inherent bias, it wouldn't make any difference how many times it's replicated. Bias times 12 is still bias" (p. 169).

A Plausible Mechanism and Qualitative Evidence

A *plausible* mechanism for a causal relationship strengthens the case for causation. If a causal relationship has no plausible mechanism, then other forms of evidence, such as replication, tend to be viewed skeptically. For example, without a plausible mechanism through which even or odd days of the month influence traffic fatalities, most people would view that causal hypothesis skeptically.

Evidence for a plausible mechanism further strengthens the case for causation. Qualitative research can often provide evidence of a causal mechanism (as discussed in Chapter 3). Correlations that imply causation—such as the survey suggesting a link between frequent family dinners and teen drug and alcohol use—can gain credibility if confirmed by qualitative research. In a focus group or in-depth interview, will teens say that having family dinners regularly is meaningful to them? Do they report that this plays a role in their decision to use, or not use, drugs and alcohol? Do they talk about what happens during family dinners that influences their thinking? If unbiased qualitative research clearly supports the presumed causal mechanism, we can more easily believe that the statistical correlation reflects a true cause-effect relationship.

There Are No Plausible Alternative Explanations

Determining causation can be viewed as a competition among alternative explanations—which is a lot of what we have been talking about so far in this chapter. But these alternative explanations, too, must be plausible. If we (or our critics) can't come up with any plausible alternative explanations, then the case for a cause-effect relationship gains credibility.

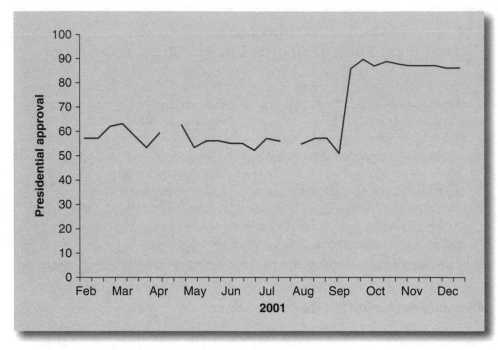

Figure 10.8   U.S. Presidential Approval Before and After 9/11

Source: POLLING REPORT, INC., and polling/sponsoring organizations.

Take the example of presidential approval in the United States following the September 11, 2001, terrorist attacks (see Figure 10.8). President Bush's popularity jumped nearly 30 points just after the attacks occurred. Did the attacks cause U.S. citizens to rally around the president and view him favorably, driving the large and sudden change in public opinion? Is there a plausible alternative explanation for such a large and sudden jump?

On the day of the 9/11 terrorist attacks, President Bush was visiting an elementary school in Florida to promote his new education bill. Perhaps this televised demonstration of his commitment to education, or the popularity of the bill itself, captured the public's imagination at the same moment as the attacks. But this appears highly implausible. Presidential approval does not skyrocket because of a proposed education bill. In fact, it is hard to come up with any plausible event—other than the horrific attacks of 9/11—that could produce such a sudden change in the nation's mood. In this way, the lack of plausible alternative explanations builds the case for causation.

More typically, however, many plausible alternative explanations can be found. And we are often unsure which one represents the truth.

Common Causes Are Accounted for in the Analysis

Evidence for causation gains strength when plausible common causes are taken into account in the analysis (researchers say *controlled for*). Suppose girls read more than boys, and suppose also that more girls own library cards. Then the correlation between owning a library card and reading ability reflects an underlying gender difference, a common cause. But in the analysis of the data, we can address this by looking at the library card → reading relationship separately for boys and for girls. Do *boys* with library cards read more than *boys* without library cards? Do *girls* with library cards read better than *girls* without library cards? If the relationship still holds, separately for girls and boys, then gender is not a common cause—so we eliminate this alternative explanation.

Of course, eliminating one alternative explanation—one possible common cause—still leaves others. What if the parents encourage both reading and owning a library card? We could continue with the same strategy, splitting the kids into a group whose parents encourage reading and a group whose parents don't. The problem now, however, is that this characteristic of parents is more difficult to measure than a clearly observable fact such as the sex of the child. Accounting for a common cause in the analysis only works if we have a measure of that common cause.

We will have much more to say about statistically taking account of common causes—the control variables strategy—in Chapter 11.

Self-Selection and Endogeneity

Why is it so difficult to know which explanations of a correlation are true? Because often our independent variables of interest—such as family time, health care procedure volume, or owning a library card—reflect *choices*. Frequency of family dinners is driven by choices, both the choices of teens and the choices of parents. Factors such as personality, occupation, family history, and so on, influence these choices. Similarly, patients (and doctors acting on their behalf) choose hospitals, and the patients who choose high-volume hospitals may be different (more educated, more urban, better insured, healthier, etc.) than the patients who choose low-volume hospitals.

Much of what we do and value in life focuses on choices: our favorite pastimes, our career choices, deciding where to live, whom to marry, how to spend our free time. We value choice, free will. But human choice and free will complicate our understanding of causal relationships in social and policy research.

Self-Selection

The influence of choices is referred to in research as the **self-selection** problem, and it is ubiquitous. Self-selection happens when the individuals studied, or someone acting on their behalf, choose their category or level of the independent variable of interest.

As a consequence of self-selection, teens who eat dinner often with their families may be different from teens who don't—and the parents may be different, as well. Also, patients in low- and high-volume hospitals may differ in a variety of characteristics—characteristics that also influence their health outcomes. In this way, self-selection introduces many possible common causes into the picture. This makes it quite difficult to attribute any observed difference in the dependent variable—such as substance abuse or health outcomes—solely to the independent variable of interest (family time or health care procedure volume).

To conclude, for example, that the difference in health outcomes between patients in high- and low-volume hospitals truly stems from the hospital volume, and not something else, we would need the patients, doctors, and all other relevant features of the hospitals to be comparable. But, because of self-selection, they are not.

Endogeneity

As it turns out, self-selection is one common source of a more general problem referred to as the **endogeneity** of the independent variable. An **endogenous** independent variable is one whose value is caused by variables or processes that also affect the dependent variable—or by the dependent variable itself. In other words, if there is a common cause—or if there is reverse causation—the independent variable of interest is said to be endogenous.

Endogeneity is often due to self-selection, but it may also be due to other processes. For example, some hospitals may obstruct or even deny care to patients with certain risky conditions or characteristics, giving preference to those patients with the best chance for success. This is a form of *treatment selection*. This positively biased selection is also called *cream skimming*, selecting only those patients who are most likely to thrive after treatment. Thus, various forms of treatment selection, such as cream skimming, are another source of endogeneity in the independent variable—it is a process that introduces common causes, and thus bias, into the picture. (See Box 10.3.)

Various other political, administrative, or cultural processes can likewise bring in common causes. We will have more to say about endogeneity later on in this chapter when we introduce its converse, exogeneity, in more detail.

BOX 10.3
Treatment Selection Bias and Sample Selection Bias

The bias in a causal estimate due to self-selection, cream skimming, and other forms of *treatment selection* can be confused sometimes with the bias from *sample selection*. In discussions of research, "treatment selection bias" sounds quite a lot like "sample selection bias." But these two forms of bias are really quite different.

As we saw in Chapter 5, bias in sampling refers to the way in which reliance on voluntary or convenience samples, or the problems of coverage and nonresponse in random sampling situations, can produce findings that differ systematically from what would be obtained from the entire population of interest. If we only interview households with standard landline telephones, and skip households that use cell phones only, our findings may not represent all households in a community. Or if only people with an interest in the topic of our survey respond, the results may not represent how the less interested nonrespondents feel about the issue. In both cases, there are reasons to suspect *sample selection bias*.

In contrast, the bias we describe in this chapter is bias in an estimate of a causal relationship. As we have seen in this chapter, individuals (or someone acting on their behalf) often select their category or level of the independent variable (such as whether to have family dinners or not) in a way that is somehow related to the dependent variable. Their choice could be due to a common cause, due to a complex common cause, or due to the dependent variable itself (reverse causation). In such cases, treatment selection causes bias in an estimate of a causal relationship and is known as *treatment selection bias*.

The Counterfactual Definition of Causation

We've seen that many things may cause teen drug use, and family dinners may be part of the explanation, all of it, or perhaps none of it. We've learned some concepts that help us think about various alternative explanations, but how do we get to the truth? How can we know the unique, causal effect of family time on drinking and drug use—or whether such effects exist at all? To answer this question, we need to back up a little and think about what it means to say that one thing causes another—that is, what we really mean by **causation**.

Philosophers of science have written volumes on the question of causation, but for practical purposes, we can simply state that a *cause* is something that produces some change—an *effect*—in the world (Blalock, 1961). When the cause is absent, there is no change, no effect. A cause also comes before its effect in time (keeping in mind the problem of expectations discussed earlier). For example, we know that lots of pedestrian traffic on a street produces litter. No pedestrians, no litter. The pedestrians show up before the litter begins to accumulate.

In an important sense, we often identify a cause by observing its effect. More specifically, we compare things as they are with the cause present to things as they are (or would be) absent the cause. The world as it would be without the cause present is referred to as the **counterfactual** (Morgan & Winship, 2007; Pearl, 2000).

The sidewalk without pedestrians—yet with everything else exactly the same (car traffic, store fronts, trees)—is the counterfactual. How much litter would there be with no pedestrians on the street? (Not much, probably.) How much litter is there with many pedestrians? (Quite a lot.) Comparing the counterfactual with observed reality gives us a measure of the *effect* of pedestrians—what the presence of many pedestrians has *caused* to happen. Again, we often know a cause by its effect.

BOX 10.4
Counterfactuals and Potential Outcomes

In the real world, one thing actually happens in a particular case and the other does not. So we can refer to what might have happened but did not as the *counterfactual*. But that language can sometimes be confusing when we are referring to what *might* happen in a future or hypothetical situation. For example, if we are thinking about family dinners in

(Continued)

(Continued)

a particular family next year or family dinners in the abstract, which one, family dinners or no family dinners, is the counterfactual and which one is the "factual"?

To avoid such confusion, Rubin (2005), one of the innovators in this field, uses the term *potential outcomes*. With this term, all possible potential outcomes are treated equivalently. Other important innovators, including Manski (1995) and Heckman (2000), also sometimes use the *potential outcomes* term. However, we use the increasingly common term *counterfactual*, using it to mean simply another potential outcome. See Morgan and Winship (2007) for further discussion of the history and technicalities of the counterfactual.

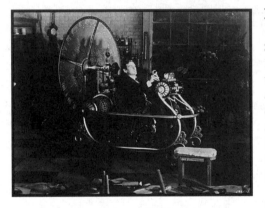

With a time machine, we could observe the counterfactual.

Source: Photobucket.com.

If We Only Had a Time Machine

Strictly speaking, a counterfactual can never be observed. Reality cannot be two things at one time. The same sidewalk, at the same moment in time, cannot both have many pedestrians and none at all. Returning to our example of family time, the counterfactual is also not directly observable. A teenager during a given period of time cannot have both frequent and infrequent family dinners. Yet to really measure the effect of frequent family dinners on a teenager's life, we need to know what his or her life would be like if we took those family dinners away.

A time machine of the kind found in science fiction (such as the one in the picture) would be the ideal instrument for gauging the counterfactual. We could climb into the machine, send ourselves back in time, and then change just one thing or event of interest (the cause). Then we could return to the present to see what had changed (the effect). By comparing two versions of the same moment in time, we could directly observe the counterfactual as well as the factual, and thus understand with certainty the relationship between cause and effect.

Alas, we have no time machines, so we need other devices or strategies to estimate counterfactuals and therefore assess causation. The most effective device researchers rely on is experimentation.

Experimentation and Exogeneity: Making Things Happen

Experimentation refers to the act of manipulating a cause to observe an effect—or, as one philosopher of science puts it, *making things happen* (Woodward, 2003). Experimentation contrasts with passive observation—or just *watching things happen*. Let's consider an example that helps illustrate the contrast between these two approaches to figuring out causation.

Can Exercise Cure Depression?

A counselor at an assisted living community in Arizona is worried: She notices that a resident, Emily, is feeling tired often, staying in bed much of the day, and taking little interest in the people and activities around her. Emily's husband died recently, and her children and grandchildren live far away. The counselor worries that Emily may be depressed (a common mental health problem facing the world's growing elderly population).

People choose to exercise.

Source: © iStockphoto.com/kelvinjay.

Then one spring day, the counselor notices that Emily has signed herself up for the Morning Birds, an exercise club that meets each day for a walk around the grounds. Emily starts getting up in the morning to join the group, and she soon appears much more interested and engaged in her surroundings. The counselor clearly observes a big improvement in Emily's mood. Regular exercise, it seems, has cured Emily of her depression.

In a laboratory in China, some rats in a cage were feeling a bit down as well. They had been subjected to weeks of unpredictable stresses: having their tails held down for 5 minutes, a series of intermittent foot shocks, a swim in cold water, and so on. All these stresses were short in duration, spaced carefully over many hours, and not physically harmful, but they added up to a distinct pattern of what psychologists call learned helplessness—a psychological state very similar to depression in humans. The scientists confirmed the onset of depression in these rats by observing a decrease in their exploratory behavior and a reduction in their consumption of sucrose solution (Zheng et al., 2006).

Observing that the rats had indeed become depressed, the scientists then introduced an exercise wheel into the rats' cage. After a few days with the exercise wheel, the rats began to exhibit increased exploratory behavior and began to consume more sucrose solution, signs that their depression had abated. The scientists concluded that exercise caused a reduction in the depressive symptoms of these rats.

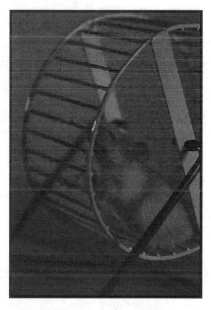

Experimenters give rats an exercise wheel—or take it away.

Source: © 2009 Jupiterimages Corporation.

Why Experimentation Beats Passive Observation

Emily's elevated mood after joining the club should not convince us that exercise relieves depression. She made the choice to begin exercising—so her exposure to exercise was *self-selected* and thus quite likely *endogenous*. Perhaps, Emily started exercising *because* she began feeling better, a case of *reverse causation*. Or perhaps something else—a *common cause*, such as the arrival of the longer, warmer days of spring—influenced both her decision to begin exercising and her rosier outlook.

The rat experiment, however, does provide convincing evidence that exercise alleviates depression. This is because the researchers *made it happen*—they imposed exercise on the rats to observe whether or not it influenced depression (which itself was imposed on the rats at the start of the experiment). We might find the experiment distasteful, even cruel. And we might complain that it is much too artificial to guide policy and practice for the elderly or anyone else suffering from depression (rats are not like people, after all). But the experiment does do a good job of demonstrating cause and effect.

We'll return to the important question of the ethics of experimentation as well as to the issue of limited generalizability. But before that, let's try to understand and appreciate the key features of experimentation that provide good evidence of causation.

Exogeneity: Imposing a Change

Experiments impose different conditions or *treatments*, deliberately independent of and apart from the choices, preferences, or other characteristics of the subjects in the experiment. That is, they make the independent variable **exogenous** instead of endogenous. Exogenous means *from outside*, and it refers to the way scientists manipulate the independent variable, in a planned way, from outside the situation under investigation.

In the rat experiment, the researchers initially deprived the rats of exercise by not providing a wheel in their cage; then later, they introduced it exogenously—from outside. Although the rats chose, in a sense, to run on the wheel (something rats like to do), the rats did not choose to have the wheel placed in their cage in the first place. The scientists did that. Furthermore, the scientists did not give the exercise wheel only to the lively looking rats or to rats that were especially down in the dumps. In an experiment, the treatment is not self-selected, and there is no other type of favoritism or bias shown in assigning the treatment. In this way, an experimental treatment is designed to be truly *exogenous*—it comes completely from outside the system of internal and external factors influencing the outcome.

In Emily's case, as we already noted, the exercising was self-selected and thus endogenous. So a plausible alternative explanation is reverse causation, that the better mood came first before the exercise. But what if, somehow, we could find a way to give Emily's exercising an *exogenous push*—such as that shown in Figure 10.9—manipulating it separately and apart from her mood or anything else happening in her life? If the causal influence really runs in reverse, then an exogenous push will do nothing—the arrow is flowing in the wrong direction for this to cause an improvement in mood. If, however, the causal arrow flows from exercise to mood, then an exogenous push to exercise will in turn affect her mood. Finding a way to make exercise exogenous—perhaps by actively convincing Emily to join the club, rather than waiting for her to voluntarily join—would help *identify* which way the causal arrow truly flows.

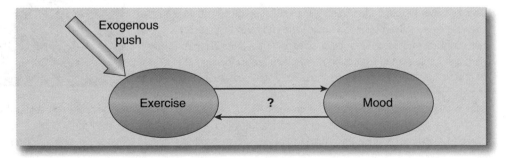

Figure 10.9   Exogenous Push Disentangles Reverse Causation From Causation

Let's consider the same picture in the context of a common cause, such as the arrival of spring weather, as shown in Figure 10.10. Again, if we could find a way to give her exercising an exogenous push—recruit her to the exercise club, rather than wait for her to volunteer—we could learn a lot. If Emily's exercising and her mood only reflect the common cause *weather*, and not a causal effect, then an exogenous push to exercise does nothing. But if the causal arrow flows from exercising to mood, then an exogenous push to exercise will change mood.

However, we need to worry here about the timing of our exogenous push—suppose it coincides still with the arrival of spring? How can we eliminate the change of seasons as a factor, or any other change, for that matter, that may also be influencing Emily's mood? Ideally, we would like to control all such factors—fix them, hold them constant.

Control: Holding Things Constant

Returning to the rat experiment, the impact of exercise on depression was measured by comparing the rats' exploratory behavior and consumption of sucrose solution before and after the introduction of an exercise wheel. For this comparison to lead to a valid causal conclusion, the experimenters had to carefully **control** (or *hold constant*) other possible causes of the change in the rats' behavior. The feeding schedule, the presence of people in the room, the cleaning of cages, the temperature and lighting in the laboratory—all these aspects of the rats' environment had to be exactly the same both before and after the introduction of the exercise wheel. Only by carefully controlling other possible causes could the experimenters attribute the outcome to the treatment and only the treatment.

Contrast this situation with Emily in her retirement community in Arizona. The season was changing, the days growing longer and the weather warmer. Perhaps Emily had some new neighbors who befriended her. Or maybe she changed her medication or diet. In short, the features of Emily's world before and after joining the exercise group were not in any way controlled; they were natural and

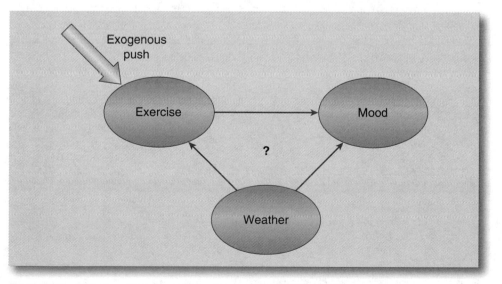

Figure 10.10   Exogenous Push Disentangles Common Cause From Causation

variable. So it is quite difficult to separate out the influence of exercising from everything else that was going on in Emily herself and in her surroundings.

Statistical Control: Holding Things Constant in the Analysis

Researchers who cannot physically hold things constant often attempt to accomplish the next best thing in their analysis—*statistically controlling* other variables. We noted this idea earlier, and it will form the central theme of Chapter 11. Here, it is important simply to distinguish experimental control—physically or materially holding conditions constant—from attempts to hold variables constant in the analysis.

Experimentation: A Review of the Basic Steps

Figure 10.11 summarizes the basic steps in experimentation. First, we measure the dependent variable; then we apply the treatment; and then we observe the dependent variable again. Importantly, the treatment must be exogenous—imposed from outside the situation being studied—not self-selected or otherwise endogenous. In addition, other possible causes of the outcome need to be controlled, held constant, so that only the treatment changes. The outcome at the start provides an estimate of the *counterfactual*—what the outcome would be like at the end of the experiment had the treatment not been applied. Of course, the treatment does get applied, so we don't really know what would have happened had it not been. But we hope that our controls are strong enough that the outcome would, apart from the treatment, remain the same as it was before.

Comparative Experiments

Because it is often difficult to physically hold constant everything that might make a difference, real-world experiments typically compare a treatment group that is exposed to the cause with a control group that is not. The control group gives information on what would have happened to the treatment group had it not gotten the treatment—that is, the counterfactual. We will have much more to say about this comparative design in Chapter 12, on randomized field experiments.

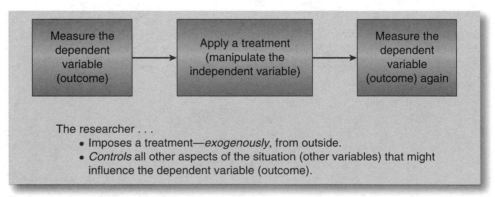

Figure 10.11   The Basic Process of Experimentation

Limited Generalizability of Lab Experiments

Although experimentation provides good evidence of causation, it is often not practical in the real world of policy and practice for a variety of reasons. We first discuss how experimentation can be overly artificial and thus of limited generalizability.

Lab experiments are, almost by definition, artificial. Laboratory scientists create settings, produce stimuli, and confine and manipulate their subjects. This artificiality raises important questions about the results of any lab experiment: Is the experimental setting a good representation of reality? Do things work the same way in the outside world? Can the results be generalized to real people going about their daily lives? Often it's a stretch. Indeed, one of the reasons lab experiments do not appear more often in applied research—even assuming they were practical and ethical—is that we often want to know how things will work in the real world, not in some artificial lab.

So there is a trade-off: good evidence of causation versus realism and the ability to generalize to practical situations. Still, as we will see in the chapters that follow, there are ways to bring elements of the lab experiment into the real world, such as *randomized field experiments* and *quasi experiments*.

Ethical Difficulties Are Inherent in Experimentation

For most of us, images of experimentation are not very happy ones. Indeed, there seems to be something almost sinister about the typical lab experiment—the cold-hearted scientist inflicting painful treatments on innocent beings so as to manipulate some aspect of their health or behavior. The very features of a lab experiment that (as we have been arguing) provide good evidence of causation—exogenous treatment and control—also raise serious ethical issues.

As scientists, we may prefer treatments that cannot be self-selected, but as human beings, we find this notion objectionable. Indeed, we generally value and seek as much freedom (self-selection) as possible in our daily lives. Similarly, strict constraint on a person's environment (control) strikes us as a loss of freedom as well, if not a form of unjustified confinement. Thus, the importance of free choice in ethics directly conflicts with the basic framework of an experiment.

Moreover, the history of experimentation involving both human beings and animals includes many instances of unethical practices, as we discuss in Chapter 14. To prevent unethical experimentation, formal principles have been established, including *informed consent*, *voluntary participation*, *no harm to subjects*, and the notion that the benefits must outweigh the risks of the research. Moreover, as we have already discussed with regard to other forms of research such as surveys and the use of administrative data, all forms of research involving human subjects, not just experimentation in labs, are extensively regulated.

We discuss further both the broader issues and the details of ethics in research in Chapter 14. But it is important here because ethics put many experiments out of bounds, forcing us to look for other methods of determining causation.

Experimentation, Policy, and Practice

By focusing on the logic of laboratory experimentation, we are not recommending its use for applied social research. Indeed, much of the rest of the book is about techniques that can be used in place of traditional experimentation to answer important policy and practice questions. However, a clear understanding of laboratory experiments—particularly the ideas of exogeneity and control—will enable you to develop and evaluate real-world research strategies that address causal questions with other methods.

Conclusion: End of Innocence

This chapter should mark the end of your innocence about correlation implying causation—even (or especially) when the correlation confirms some theory that you believe in. We hope that you will always remain skeptical and alert to alternative theories that might explain the correlation. But you may feel a bit overwhelmed, even discouraged, by now. After all, you probably want to do something about problems such as teen drinking and drug use, or seek to improve health outcomes, or pursue some other important policy or practice goal. But given the fact that it seems that the causal arrows could go in many possible directions, how are you ever supposed to figure out how to make a real difference?

We have provided some initial ideas in this chapter—ideas that will be developed more fully in the chapters that follow. For example, randomized field experiments (Chapter 12) and natural and quasi experiments (Chapter 13) incorporate the key ideas of exogeneity and control to investigate causal relationships. Another idea is to take account of common causes by measuring them and incorporating them into the analysis. This is the strategy of control variables—the topic of the next chapter—perhaps one of the most common types of research applied to public policy and practice.

BOX 10.5
Critical Questions to Ask About Causation

- What is the implied causal relationship in a given study, report, or news item? Which variable is assumed to be the independent variable (cause) and which the dependent variable (effect)?
- Could the implied causal relationship work the other way round—could it be reverse causation? How plausible is this?
- What common causes might be at work behind the scenes? How plausible are these common causes as an alternative explanation of the correlation? How might they bias the reported results?
- Was the independent variable—the assumed cause—self-selected? If so, how might this bias the reported results?
- Did the study acknowledge the possibility of reverse causation or common causes? Were alternative explanations considered?
- Did the study rule out plausible alternative explanations, either by the use of logical argument or by reference to empirical evidence? How convincing are the arguments or evidence?

EXERCISES

Can Computer Skills Help Welfare Recipients Find Work?

10.1. Agency records show that welfare recipients in an economically distressed county who volunteer for a computer skills class are more likely to get off welfare and find a job than other welfare recipients in the county. Did the new computer skills cause this better outcome? What are some alternative causal explanations?

Do Private Schools Prepare Kids Better Than Public Schools?

10.2. Studies of urban education suggest that kids who attend private schools are much more likely to graduate and go on to college than kids who attend public schools. Does this correlation between private schooling and going to college imply causation? What are some alternative causal explanations?

Exogenous or Endogenous?

10.3. See if you can decide:

a. Is a person's level of education endogenous or exogenous to his or her income? Explain why.

b. Is the choice of whether or not to put a child in day care endogenous or exogenous to a child's behavior? Explain why.

c. Is a city's spending (per capita) on police protection endogenous or exogenous to the city's crime rate? Explain why.

d. Are a state's medical malpractice laws endogenous or exogenous to a gynecologist's choice of whether to do a C-section for a particular woman giving birth? Explain why.

Make It Exogenous

10.4. Can you think of a way to use experimentation, or some other approach, to make X exogenous to Y?

a. X = frequency of police patrols; Y = crime rate

b. X = class size; Y = reading test scores

c. X = smoking; Y = lung cancer

d. X = public transportation; Y = amount of driving

e. X = high health insurance deductible; Y = health

Objectives: In this chapter, you will learn how researchers use observational studies not only to describe the world but also to estimate causal effects by employing control variables. You will learn how to identify appropriate and inappropriate control variables. And you will learn to evaluate when the use of control variables is not adequate to determine causal effects. You will learn a straightforward way to implement control variables—stratification. And you will learn a more flexible and effective alternative—multiple regression. Observational studies with control variables are a very widely used method for estimating causal effects in applied research, and so learning about the logic and limitations of this strategy is particularly useful.

How much does education raise earnings?

Source: © iStockphoto.com

Observational Studies With Control Variables

11

Private Versus Public Schools

Do private schools educate children better than public schools? Many people think so, at least as judged by their willingness to pay out of pocket for private education while forgoing free public schools. And we hear increasing calls for the privatization of education, in the form of school vouchers or charter schools, as a solution to educational reform. Much of this enthusiasm for private schools rests on the observation that kids in private schools perform better, at least as measured by the National Assessment of Educational Progress (NAEP). Known as "The Nation's Report Card," the NAEP is a rigorous sample survey of more than 300,000 public and private school children in Grades 4 and 8 in more than 13,000 schools across the United States.

According to the 2003 NAEP, public school fourth graders scored only 216 on a scale of reading ability—but their private school counterparts scored 235. And this 19-point difference is *practically* significant relative to other differences: Over the three decades from 1973 to 2003, the overall progress in reading scores nationwide was only 16 points. But the difference could be due to a variety of common causes of private schooling and test scores. What would a study that accounted for such common causes show?

Observational Studies

The NAEP data are considered an **observational study**. Of course, all research involves observation of some kind, but in an *observational* study, researchers do not attempt to change or manipulate variables to test their effects; they simply observe or measure things as they are in the "natural," unaltered world. In contrast, experiments manipulate or change variables (see Rosenbaum, 2002). In Chapter 10, we discussed lab experiments, and in Chapter 12, we will look at randomized field experiments. But the great majority of social and policy research simply measures or observes behavior as it naturally occurs in society, often using existing government surveys or administrative data.

Do private schools educate kids better than public schools?

Source: © 2009 Jupiterimages Corporation.

Chapter 6 described many of the sources that provide such observational data. Some examples of observational data include the following:

- Telephone surveys that ask about the characteristics, behaviors, or attitudes of a population (such as the Gallup and Pew polls)
- Administrative record data on crimes, hospital admissions, or auto accidents (such as the FBI's *Uniform Crime Reports* or birth and death certificates collected by state governments in the United States)
- Secondary data from large government surveys, such as NAEP, the Current Population Survey (CPS), the National Crime Victimization Survey (NCVS), and many others
- Digital data gathered from consumer transactions, communications, Web searches, and so on

The Gold Standard for Description—but Not for Causal Estimation

For *describing* the world, observational studies are exactly what we need, although subject to all the potential limitations of measurement and sampling we described in earlier chapters. NAEP is often referred to as the "gold standard" for measuring educational performance, and it does an excellent job at *describing* the differences between public and private school students: The 19-point test score gap between public and private schools is a valid description of things as they are in American education. Moreover, describing the world accurately is important: We need an accurate description of a problem before we can even begin to think about how to change it.

However, the policy question here that motivates politicians and parents is a different one: "If students currently in public schools went to private schools, what would happen to *their* test scores?" This is an example of a causal question with a presumed *counterfactual*—what would happen if something were done differently? Unfortunately, as we saw in the previous chapter, answering such a question with an observational study is not so easy. Still, most applied research must rely on observational studies such as the NAEP to answer causal questions. So it becomes essential for you to understand the limitations of such studies—as well as their potential to inform policy and practice.

Limitations of an Observational Study

What are the limitations of observational studies such as the NAEP for answering causal questions? Reflect for a moment on why some students go to public schools and other students go to private schools. The income and wealth of the students' families, the quality of schools where they live, the parents' interest in education, the students' interest in education, the extent of students' behavioral problems, the families' religious traditions—along with a host of other motivations and preferences of the students and their families—will influence that choice.

This is the problem of *self-selection* we learned about in the previous chapter. And schools often select students as well—a form of treatment selection. Together, such mechanisms make the kind of school a child attends *endogenous*—determined by variables or processes that also influence the dependent variable.

In observational studies, as it turns out, the independent variables we are interested in are very often self-selected or otherwise endogenous. Using observational data to answer causal questions requires us to deal with this endogeneity.

Control Variables

To address the problem of endogeneity in observational data, researchers try to make fairer comparisons—apples-to-apples comparisons, as it were. For example, they compare the test scores of private and public school children, adjusting for the effect of other variables such as family income that might influence test scores. Such adjusting variables are called **control variables**.

Controlling for variables can be done with various statistical methods that will be explained later in this chapter. But first, it's important to understand the logic of control variables, without the statistical details, and to see how control variables can change our understanding of a relationship.

How Control Variables Help Disentangle a Causal Effect

The U.S. Department of Education commissioned a study to compare public and private schools, and to do so, the researchers used data from the 2003 NAEP (National Center for Education Statistics, 2006). To make a fair, apples-to-apples comparison, the researchers did not simply compare public and private schools on reading and math scores. Such a comparison would not be fair, because the scores of private school kids do not make a good *counterfactual* for what would happen to the scores of public school kids if they switched to private schools. Instead, the researchers used control variables to make the comparison fairer—and thus create a better estimate of this counterfactual.

For example, it would not be fair to compare students in private schools whose families have a computer in the home with students in public schools whose families do not have a computer in the home. We wouldn't know if the difference in their reading scores was due to the different schools—or due to the computers at home. Thus, one control variable that the researchers used was the presence of a computer in the home.

When added to the analysis of observational data, control variables work by *holding constant*—or *statistically equalizing*—the individuals in terms of the characteristics measured by the control variables. In effect, they allow us to see how test scores differ between public and private school students whose families are identical in terms of having a computer in the home.

Of course, as we saw, public and private school students differ in a variety of ways likely to influence student test scores, beyond just the presence of a computer. The control variables used in the government's study were these:

- Computer in the home
- Eligibility for free lunch (based on family income)
- Participation in Title I (for economically disadvantaged students)
- Number of books in the home
- Gender
- Race-ethnicity
- Student has a disability
- English language learner
- Number of absences

How to Choose Control Variables

Why were these control variables chosen? They represent characteristics of students that differ between public and private schools—differences that the researchers believe may influence reading scores. In other words, these variables represent *common causes* of both school type and reading ability.

For example, private schools (many of which are Catholic schools) might have more girls (because they have more same-sex schools that appeal especially to girls), and girls may read better in fourth grade than boys. If we control for gender, we avoid this problem of comparing public schools with more boys to private schools with more girls. The race-ethnicity variable works the same way. If we control statistically for race-ethnicity, then we make public and private schools equal in terms of their representation of race-ethnic groups. Public schools may serve more students with disabilities (including learning disabilities) and also more English language learners (recent immigrants), both characteristics that might well lead kids to score lower on reading tests. The number of books in the home, as well as the presence of a computer, represent resources for learning and also serve as a proxy for the educational level of the parents. Eligibility for free lunch and participation in Title I (a federal program for economically disadvantaged students) are both indicators of the income or economic status of the students. Number of absences reflects the health of the child but also perhaps the amount of discipline and supervision the child receives at home.[1]

The U.S. Department of Education's study controlled for, or held constant, all these potential common causes in their study.

How Did Control Variables
Change the Estimate of a Causal Effect?

What happened to the public-private school test gap in reading when these common cause variables were controlled or held constant? The difference in average test scores fell to only one tenth of one point, practically zero, and not significant statistically. The control variables wiped out nearly all the original 19-point difference between public and private schools in fourth-grade reading performance.

To put it another way, the government study suggests that the public-private school test gap in reading appears to be due to differences in student characteristics (the control variables)—not something that private schools per se do, such as requiring uniforms, using traditional curricula, teaching values, and so on. The study implies that if you sent the public school students to private schools—the counterfactual—their reading test scores would not improve. The use of control variables gives us a better estimate of this counterfactual, although still not a perfect one. So the message that the pundits took away from the simple observational NAEP data—send the public school kids to private schools and they will read better—was contradicted by this study.

Control variables can be implemented with a variety of statistical methods, ranging from the simple to the very complex. In the next section, we will look at the effect of education on earnings to show how control variables can be applied with a simple statistical method, stratification.

An Empirical Example: Education and Earnings

Education is widely seen as the key to a better job with higher earnings and as a source of national prosperity. As a result, students and their families make real sacrifices to get more education—and governments provide education grants and loans. Many believe that if people can just change one thing about themselves—the amount of education they have—they will produce and earn more. Note again that this implies a counterfactual—how people would be different if they had more education. In other words, education is thought to have a substantial *causal* effect on earnings.

---

[1]Later, we discuss why including the number of absences as a control variable could be problematic.

Let's look at the relationship between education and earnings to see how control variables work in the statistical analysis of real data. The belief that more education will increase earnings is grounded in the observation that generally people with more education do indeed earn more. Data from the National Longitudinal Survey of Youth (NLSY) show that in 2002, those with a college degree or more education earned an average of $61,500 annually, while those with less education earned an average of $29,500, a difference in annual earnings of $32,000 (Table 11.1).[2]

Table 11.1   Average Annual Earnings in 2002, NLSY

No College Degree (B)	College Degree (A)	Difference (A – B) "Effect of College"
$29,500	$61,500	$32,000

But these results do not mean that we can tell a room full of people without college degrees that if they graduated from college, their annual earnings would rise by $32,000, on average. Once again, our observational study is only observing reality as it is now—it is not observing the counterfactual, what would happen if those with less education got more (or those with more got less). The amount of education that someone gets is self-selected and therefore endogenous—affected by variables that might also affect earnings. We'll see this fact illustrated soon, using actual data from the NLSY. But we can use control variables to help us sort things out—to get as close as possible to observing the counterfactual, and thus to make better causal conclusions.

Step 1: Speculate on Common Causes

The first step is to reflect on how people with and without college degrees may differ—and why. We suspect that they differ on average in many ways other than their educational level: their parents' educational levels, their parents' incomes, their interest in and aptitude for learning, and so on. If these same variables also affect the dependent variable—if they are *common causes* of both educational level and earnings—then we should include them in our analysis as control variables.

Let's think about how some of these differences might be common causes of both the level of education and earnings. To begin with, parents with more education could help their children more with their studies or push their children to get more education. So whether or not someone gets a college degree is likely to be partially caused by his or her parents' education level—an example of the independent variable being driven by parents' education. It is also possible that more-educated parents can use their connections and their knowledge of the professional world to help their children get higher-earning jobs. Thus, parental education is a likely *common cause*, a variable that influences both the independent and the dependent variables.

---

[2]All calculations using the NLSY for this chapter were done with the publicly available data, extracted by Jingyun Jiang, whom we thank for her excellent work. The data are described further at www.bls.gov/nls/nlsy79.htm. All calculations are weighted with the cross-sectional weights for 2002 and were performed on a consistent sample with no missing data for any of the variables used in the analysis. Note that the sample with no missing data may not be fully representative if data are not missing at random.

Similarly, people with more interest in and aptitude for learning will not only go further in school, on average, but probably also do more on-the-job learning that helps them advance faster. Thus, aptitude would be a common cause, too. If we thought about it some more, we could probably come up with a variety of other common cause variables. And we should remember that some common causes are complex, not simple one-step relationships. We can use existing theory, common sense, qualitative research, and prior empirical studies to identify these potential common causes. This is the first, and probably most important, step in an observational study with control variables.

Step 2: Look for Differences

The second step is to look at the data to see how groups with different values of the independent variable compare in terms of potential common causes—and proxies for complex common causes. In our example, we examined how individuals with differing amounts of education—those with and without college degrees—differ in ways that might also affect their earnings. The NLSY contains information on the education of the parents, scores on an aptitude test of the person surveyed when he or she was young, and a large variety of variables going back to youth.[3]

Table 11.2 shows this comparison. We see from the table that those with a college degree are less likely to have lived in poverty as children. And they are much more likely to have had mothers with a college degree and also with professional, technical, or managerial work experience. Those with a college degree also had fathers who completed more education. The two groups also differ in terms of race, with more Blacks among the group without a college degree. Notably, those with a college degree had an average aptitude score of 74 points (on a standardized test) at age 14, while those without a college degree had an average score of only 40, a substantial difference. Overall, we see that going well back into their youth, those with college degrees and those without college degrees differed in many ways. When comparing their earnings, we are comparing "apples to oranges," not "apples to apples."

Step 3: Stratify by Control Variables

One of the most striking differences between those with a college degree and those without can be found in their average aptitude scores at age 14. Those with greater academic aptitude would certainly be likely to obtain more education, perhaps because they enjoyed it more or found it easier. Academic aptitude might also make individuals more productive and better paid later in life, regardless of the benefits of schooling.[4] So ideally, we would like to give both groups the same aptitude score.

---

[3]In fact, this is why we use the NLSY data for this chapter. Many other data sets have the education and earnings results, and they are more commonly and easily used to provide results such as those in Table 10.1. However, such data sets, for example, the CPS, do not contain information such as parents' education and therefore do not supply the control variables that we want.

[4]There is a long and controversial literature on the extent to which aptitude tests such as the one used in the NLSY do in fact measure academic aptitude or instead measure other things, such as family socioeconomic background. We do not want to enter into that debate here. For the moment, just assume that the scores measure something, perhaps quality education in early childhood—anything that would also *independently affect earnings*. It does not matter for our purposes here if that something is innate ability, socioeconomic status, the quality of education at earlier ages, or something else altogether.

Table 11.2   People With and Without College Degrees, NLSY 2002

	No College Degree	College Degree
Family in poverty during childhood	15%	8%
Mother has a college degree or higher	5%	25%
Mother is a professional or technical worker	8%	27%
Mother is a manager	4%	8%
Highest grade completed by father	11	14
White	82%	91%
Black	15%	7%
Hispanic	3%	2%
Aptitude score at age 14	40	74
High aptitude score	20%	72%

One way we can do this is to **stratify** the data, also known as *conditioning* (Morgan & Winship, 2007, Chapter 3). Specifically, we break up our data into groups—called *strata*—based on aptitude scores. The variable used to divide up our observations into groups, aptitude score, becomes the control variable. College degree is the independent variable of interest, and earnings is the dependent variable. The stratification of the data into groups based on the control variable allows us to compare the mean earnings of those with different amounts of education, but similar aptitude scores. (The specific control variables technique is *stratified comparison of means*.)

We can do this by identifying a "high aptitude" stratum, defined as those scoring in the top third of all scores. We did this already in Table 11.2, and we see there that among those with college degrees, 72% had high aptitude scores, while among those without college degrees, only 20% did. This is a big difference, as we noted before when looking at the means. Now, we want to control for this difference—hold it constant or condition on it, in other words, equalize people in terms of this key variable.

How Does Controlling for Aptitude Change the Estimated Effect of College?

Table 11.3 shows the mean earnings of those with and without college degrees, but now stratified by higher and lower aptitude. Among those with high aptitude scores, average earnings are $67,600 for college degree holders, compared with $39,800 for non-college degree holders—a difference of $27,800. Among those with lower aptitude scores, average earnings are $45,600 for college degree holders, compared with $26,900 for non-college degree holders—a difference of $18,700.

Compare these college degree "effects" with the effect of $32,000 based on the unstratified data, the same result we had in Table 11.1. Among both high and lower aptitude groups, the gap between

Table 11.3   Mean Earnings by Education, Controlling for Aptitude

	Less Than a College Degree	College Degree or Higher	"Effect" of College Degree
High aptitude scores	$39,800	$67,600	$27,800
Lower aptitude scores	$26,900	$45,600	$18,700
Both groups combined	$29,500	$61,500	$32,000

college and non-college degree holders is smaller than the $32,000 gap we observed initially in our comparison of earnings. So we see that by controlling for aptitude, the magnitude of the effect of getting a college degree has been reduced appreciably.

Omitted Variables Bias

Our initial $32,000 estimate of the causal effect suffered from what researchers call **omitted variable bias**—bias that results when we fail to control for a common cause. Naive interpretation of the unstratified difference in earnings between those with and those without a college degree led us to incorrectly attribute to educational differences some of the earnings differences that were due to differences in *aptitude score*. The naive interpretation got the magnitude of the effect of education wrong.

In Chapter 10, we saw several similar examples of how such naive interpretation of a correlation might get the magnitude of a causal effect wrong, such as the effect of family dinners. But in that chapter we did not learn ways for determining the actual *amount* of such bias. Now, with control variables, we have begun to discover how to figure this out.

Omitted variables go by a variety of names, including **confounder** and *lurking variable*. The different terms are described in Box 11.1.

BOX 11.1
Omitted Variable Bias by Any Other Name

We have seen how an *omitted variable*—in the form of an important common cause left out of a statistical analysis—can produce *omitted variables bias*. Different disciplines use different terms for the same idea. Another commonly used term is *confounder*, and yet another term is *lurking variable*. Others refer to omitted variable bias as *spurious effect*, especially when the true causal effect is zero.

While controlling for aptitude lowers the estimated effect of a college degree, the effect is still substantial. In fact, more sophisticated methods to be covered shortly and in later chapters (including multiple regression and a variety of natural experiments) provide much more compelling evidence that education really does have a substantial causal effect on earnings.[5] Nonetheless, it is important to use the control variables to get the *magnitude* of the effect right.

A control variable can eliminate a relationship, reduce it in magnitude, increase it in magnitude, even reverse the direction of the relationship, or have no effect whatsoever. Any of these are possible when control variables are added into the analysis.

Interactions

So far, we focused on how stratification in Table 11.3 reduced the magnitude of the apparent $32,000 effect of college. However, Table 11.3 also shows that the effect of more education seems to *differ* between the high aptitude score group and the lower aptitude score group. The boost in income from education appears larger among the higher scorers—$27,800—than among the lower scorers—$18,700. This is an example of an *interaction* (or moderator), as described in Chapter 2. Specifically, the effect of the independent variable, education, on income depends on the level of another variable, aptitude.[6]

A Different Choice of Control Variable

Let's see what happens to the education and earnings relationship when we stratify with a different control variable—whether the mother has a college degree or not. The results are shown in Table 11.4. In this case, we see that the apparent "effect" of a college degree, $32,000, was actually slightly strengthened among those with a college graduate mother, to $36,100, although it was weakened among those whose mother lacks a college degree, to $29,300. Once again, there appears to be an interaction: The effects of a college degree differ by mother's education.

Table 11.4　Mean Earnings by Education, Controlling for Mother's Education, NLSY 2002

	Less Than a College Degree	College Degree or Higher	"Effect" of College Degree
Mother college graduate	$34,200	$70,300	$36,100
Mother not college graduate	$29,300	$58,600	$29,300
Both groups combined	$29,500	$61,500	$32,000

---

[5]See Card (1999).

[6]There is a substantial technical literature on different forms that interactions can take, "multiplicative," "additive," and so on. This distinction is not so important for consumers of research. However, whether or not there are interactions *is* important. Always remember that the magnitude of the effect of one variable, such as education, could differ depending on the level of some other variable, such as aptitude test score.

More Than One Control Variable at a Time

So far, we have shown how to control for one variable at a time. We had to choose between aptitude and mother's education. However, based on our theories and our initial examination of how those with and without college degrees differ, we should control for many other variables and we should control for them all at once. After all, we want our groups to be comparable in every way that matters.

Unfortunately, it is difficult to use stratification to control for many variables at once. Suppose that we try to control for both aptitude and mother's education at the same time. We get a table such as Table 11.5, which has two deep layers and in effect involves looking at four different comparisons.

Table 11.5 Mean Earnings by Education, Controlling for Aptitude and Mother's Education

		Less Than a College Degree	College Degree or Higher	"Effect" of College Degree
High aptitude score	Mother college graduate	$40,803	$74,284	$33,481
	Mother not college graduate	$39,753	$64,809	$25,056
Lower aptitude score	Mother college graduate	$29,951	$48,093	$18,142
	Mother not college graduate	$26,761	$45,219	$18,458

Although this table is hard enough to keep in one's head, imagine if we had more than two categories for each of the control variables. Suppose, for example, we had separate categories for high school dropouts and those with graduate degrees, resulting in four education categories. We certainly could (and perhaps should) break up the aptitude variable into more than two categories as well. Next, imagine trying to control for three or four variables at once, rather than just two variables. Suppose, for example, that we wanted to add in childhood poverty status, resulting in even more layering of the cross-tab. You can see how complex and confusing the table would get. And there is another problem with such layering: The amount of data in the cells of the table (cell sizes) would become very small, making it difficult to estimate the many comparisons with any kind of precision.

Fortunately, there is an alternative to stratification that can overcome many of these limitations— the technique of *multiple regression*, which will be covered shortly (and was introduced in Chapter 9). Although multiple regression comes with a bit more technical baggage, the important conceptual issues are the same for stratification and for regression. So before turning to multiple regression, let's consider the important conceptual issue of how to choose control variables.

BOX 11.2
What If the Dependent Variable Is Categorical?

This chapter demonstrates stratification with a quantitative dependent variable— earnings. How can stratification be implemented if the dependent variable is categorical?

(Continued)

(Continued)

For example, suppose we're interested in how one's occupation affects political party affiliation—both categorical variables. The relationship could be examined with a cross-tabulation (and tested with a chi-square test). Suppose the cross-tab reveals that those with administrative jobs are more likely to be Democratic, while those with factory jobs are more likely to be Republican. At first glance, we conclude that occupation affects political party affiliation.

But we also know, from studies of many kinds, that gender has an effect on both occupation and political party affiliation. Gender—another categorical variable—could be a common cause, and so we seek to control for gender in the analysis.

The stratification method still works. Specifically, we can stratify the cross-tabs of occupation and political party by gender, resulting in two separate cross-tabs. To the extent that the occupation-political party relationship is reduced or eliminated, we have observed the effect of controlling for gender. Stratified cross-tabs are also referred to as *layered cross-tabs*.

How to Choose Control Variables

How do you know if your study, or a study you are reading, includes the right control variables? To answer this question, ask yourself first, "Are there any common causes that are not included in the analysis?" If an important common cause is omitted, then we will erroneously attribute its influence to the independent variable of interest: The study will suffer from *omitted variables bias*. If family wealth drives both educational level and getting a high-paying job—and we fail to *control* for family wealth—we will think that simply getting more education will raise income by more than it actually does.

But identifying the right control variables is not an easy task—even for experienced researchers. Perhaps it is best to begin with a few basic precautions:

- Simply "using control variables" of any kind in a study does not mean that the results are therefore correct and unbiased. The study may have used the wrong control variables, or something important may still be missing. Beware of people who assure you that they have "controlled for all the usual variables": There is no such thing as a standard set of control variables (e.g., sex, race, and income) that works for every (or even most) studies.
- Beware at the same time of the "kitchen sink" approach: throwing everything into the analysis as a control variable. As you will see shortly, you can overdo the use of control variables and be just as wrong (biased) in doing so as you would be by omitting an important control variable.

The choice of control variables involves careful thought and, importantly, an understanding of the theory or model of relationships among important variables. As a practical matter, much depends as well on the availability of data—you must have an empirical measure of the common cause variable, or at least a proxy (about which we will have more to say shortly), before you can employ it as a control variable.

The Importance of Using Path Diagrams

It is impossible to determine the relevant control variables simply through empirical methods, without resorting to theory. Only theory can ultimately determine what is and is not a common cause variable. Drawing a path diagram, such as that shown in Figure 11.1, helps us make our theory explicit and find common causes. Specifically, it calls our attention to variables that have arrows leading to both *X* (the independent variable of interest) *and Y* (the dependent variable). The real work of statistical analysis using control variables lies in theorizing and searching through existing knowledge to determine what control variables are truly needed. The importance of this conceptual task cannot be emphasized enough.

There are some practical steps serious analysts take to come up with good ideas for control variables. One is to read a lot about the topic, including scholarly articles as well as newspaper reports, advocacy publications, popular books, and so on. Of course, looking at what other researchers who studied the same topic did, what control variables they employed, is always a useful thing to do—but prior studies may have missed things or done things wrong. Another source of ideas is to talk with experts, advocates, or practitioners who have hands-on knowledge of the problem or program. *Qualitative research*—involving case studies, in-depth interviews, or focus groups—is another important way to generate many useful ideas about what kinds of control variables need to be considered.

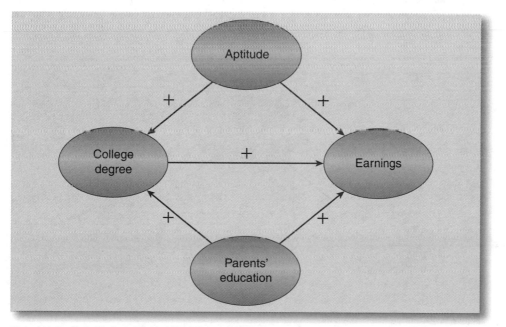

Figure 11.1   Path Diagram Used to Find Common Causes

Finally, exploring the data, looking for patterns of correlation—specifically, variables that empirically correlate with both the independent and the dependent variables of interest—can *suggest* previously unconsidered control variables.

But be careful here: The fact that a variable is empirically related to both the dependent and independent variables does not, in itself, necessarily make it a good candidate for a control variable. It could instead be an *intervening variable*, something along the causal pathway of how the independent variable works, and thus should *not* be controlled for. We discuss this issue next.

Intervening Variables Should Not Be Used as Controls

Suppose, for example, that people with a college degree learn to write better and that writing skills are a key factor in getting a higher paying job. This theory is depicted in Figure 11.2. In that case, writing ability is an *intervening variable,* a *mechanism* through which a college degree raises income. Empirically, writing ability would be correlated with both educational level and income, and thus seem a potential common cause and therefore a potential control variable.

Using an intervening variable such as writing ability as a control variable, however, would be a serious mistake. It could bias the estimate of the effect of having a college degree by taking writing ability completely out of the picture. Rather, we should allow our comparison to include differences in writing ability—because it is precisely such skill gains that result from a college education and that employers reward.

In general, adding an intervening variable as a control variable is a mistake that can lead to misleading causal conclusions. It is sometimes referred to as *overcontrolling*, and it can result in just as much bias as omitting an important common cause.

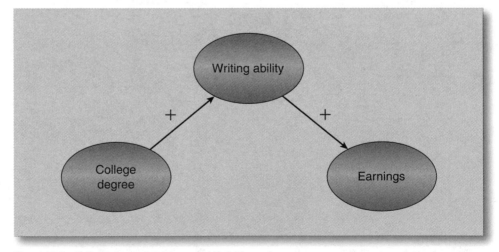

Figure 11.2   Path Diagram of an Intervening Variable

What If a Variable Is Both a Common Cause and an Intervening Variable?

Recall in the study of public and private schools that *daily attendance* was used as a control variable. On the one hand, daily attendance could reflect differences in a student's health or family life, factors that we would want to control for when comparing public and private school students—especially if no direct measures of health or family life are available. On the other hand, daily attendance could be due to school leadership and policies—part of what schools do to provide a good education. If so, attendance would be an intervening variable—something along the causal pathway between type of school and reading ability—part of the causal *mechanism*. In that case, we would not want to control for it. What should we do?

There is no right answer in such situations—much depends on judgment. Whenever a variable could be both a common cause and an intervening variable, a good practice is to show the results both with and without it as a control. Then observe how the results differ and consider what possible reasons might explain the difference. Which theories (and effect magnitudes) are consistent with the difference?

Complex Common Causes and Unexplained Correlations

Sometimes a variable can be correlated with both the independent and dependent variable—but you have no theory or explanation of why this is so. Because of the complexity of many social phenomena, two variables may be related through a chain of causation that runs too deep to be clearly understood. In other words, the correlation may be due to a complex or unknown common cause, as described in the previous chapter.

Consider the variable years of age as a possible control variable in an analysis of the effect of education on earnings. Age could influence both education and earnings directly, due to historical and life experiences, and thus be a common cause. But even if age is not a direct common cause and even if no explicit theories of its effect on education and earnings can be found, age remains a likely complex common cause that should be included as a control variable. Why? Because age is clearly exogenous, it could not possibly be affected by education and thus could not be an intervening variable.[7]

This gives us a clue as to how to proceed: If there is a variable correlated with both independent and dependent variables—*and* it could not possibly be an intervening variable—then it is likely to be a complex common cause and should be considered as a control variable. Unfortunately, the situation is often ambiguous and the decision not so clear-cut. When there is no simple answer, it is often best to do the analysis both with and without the variable as a control.

Causes That Can Be Ignored

Variables that are causes of the dependent variable (*Y*) but not the independent variable of interest (*X*) are not *common* causes and can be omitted without causing bias. Take the example of musical

---

[7]As a practical matter, both age and experience cannot be included because of multicollinearity, discussed in Chapter 9. In fact, in many data sets, experience is not known and is estimated from age and education.

ability and earnings. Say that musical ability in a young person predicts fairly well an individual's chances of having a career as a musician, which probably does not pay very well on average (even including the very few who hit it really big in pop music or entertainment). Thus, musical ability may influence earnings, albeit in a downward direction. Yet musically talented kids may get just as much education, on average, as their less musically talented peers. In this situation, it would do little good to control for musical ability in our analysis of the effect of education on earnings, despite the fact that musical ability predicts earnings.[8]

What about causes that influence *only* the independent variable of interest (X) but not the dependent variable (Y)? To continue with our education and earnings example, if states differ in financial aid laws, then those laws would drive part of the variation in how much education people get while not driving earnings (except through education). Such variables should not be included as control variables. However, as we will see in Chapter 13, these variables will prove valuable for estimating causal effects, through their use as *instrumental variables*.

Choosing Good Control Variables Depends on Your Question

The right choice of control variables depends a great deal on the question you're asking. Consider the case of the effect of race on income. One analysis might want to determine if there is presently racial discrimination in hiring and salaries. To answer this question, one wants to compare people of different races but equal qualifications and productivity on the job. Clearly, level of education, the type of education, work experience, and the type of jobs held in the past are all relevant controls.

However, one might also want to ask whether people of different races enjoy different standards of living for a variety of structural reasons that promote, or discourage, their life chances. These could include the effects of historical discrimination, de facto school segregation, family wealth and connections, cultural norms and expectations, and other structural factors that thereby reduce the level and quality of education someone receives, the jobs he or she seeks, and so on. In that case, education and prior career experiences are probably not valid controls. A different question is being asked here, requiring a different set of control variables.

Unmeasured Variables and Omitted Variables Bias

In real-world quantitative empirical work, measures of all the desired common causes are simply not going to be available. For example, in studies of the effect of education on income, one might want to have a measure of *ambition*, which would presumably affect both educational attainment and earnings. Measures of ambition are not generally found in most surveys or administrative data. When such important common causes are not available in the data, we refer to them as **unmeasured**

---

[8]However, when using multiple regression, under some circumstances including these variables as "controls" (i.e., additional independent variables) can increase the precision of our estimates. Our point here is that omitting them will not cause any *bias*. A researcher might also include them in a multiple regression due to an interest in the effects of these variables themselves or a wish to learn about all of the determinants of earnings. We return to this point later in this chapter.

variables, sometimes known as unobservables (see Box 11.3). The inability to include such unmeasured variables means that the results of the study are, at least to some extent, biased—they suffer from omitted variables bias.

BOX 11.3
Jargon: Unmeasured Variables and *Unobservables*

Researchers frequently refer to variables that they believe to be important but that they do not have in their data as *unobservables*, because the variables are unobservable to the researcher. However, that term implies that the variables are intrinsically unobservable, which may not be the case. By using the term *unmeasured variable*, we hope to suggest that at some point, perhaps in some future study, the potentially important variable could be measured and thus both observed and used as a control variable.

Researchers should try, if only in future studies, to get measures of the unmeasured common causes. Nonetheless, in any given study, it is almost inevitable that some common cause is missing and thus that some omitted variables bias exists. Still, we argue that this bias does not totally undermine observational studies. Rather, studies should acknowledge such biases and assess their potential magnitudes. Identifying influential unmeasured variables also highlights what data should be collected in future studies.

Proxies

One possible way around the problem of unmeasured variables and the resulting omitted variable bias is to find *proxies*, measured variables that stand in for or substitute for the unmeasured variables. Moreover, in working with real data, we often are required to move from our theories about relevant common cause variables—aptitude, family connections, and so on, to variables that we can find in the data.

There are a number of issues to think about here. First, we often cannot get the variable we would really like, and so we have to use a *proxy*, just as we did in Chapter 4, when our focus was on description. Second, we often have to work hard to try to get the variables we want. In our education and earnings example, there are many other—and much better—sources of data, such as the CPS, on education and earnings. However, those data don't contain much information on common cause variables of both education and earnings or even very good proxies for those common cause variables. In contrast, because the NLSY has data going back to respondents' youth, it does have good proxies for common cause variables. Therefore, we used the NLSY, and indeed, such data needs are why the government funds a longitudinal survey—a difficult and expensive task.

Bias in Perspective

Remember that the perfect study does not exist: All studies have their weaknesses. Much can still be learned from observational studies with control variables, despite the fact that there will likely remain some unmeasured variables—and therefore omitted variable bias of some kind. We must always attach caveats to our interpretation of the study. And we must remain aware of the common cause variables that we couldn't get and how they might bias our results.

From Stratification to Multiple Regression

We have illustrated the control variables strategy thus far with stratification because it is a familiar method and relatively straightforward to interpret. But in most social and policy studies, researchers use *multiple regression* (of one kind or another) to implement the control variables strategy. Multiple regression handles several of the important limitations we encountered with stratification, such as needing to use more than one or two control variables at a time and handling quantitative (noncategorical) variables.

Using More Than One (or Two) Control Variables

As we saw, aptitude is only one of the many factors that helped determine how much education individuals get. Whether or not the mother was a college graduate was also influential. Some introspection, and a lot of prior evidence, suggests that indeed many family background and community variables influence education. Thus, all these variables must be controlled for *at the same time*. Stratifying by more than one or two variables soon makes interpretation impossible. Stratification by many variables can also be imprecise because each subgroup or cell in the table contains so little data.

Multiple regression can incorporate many control variables at the same time. In effect, the impact of one independent variable is measured, holding all the control variables constant. In our example, multiple regression can provide the effect of more education while family background, community, and other factors do not change. (Of course, we need data on all the control variables.)

Mathematically, multiple regression treats the independent variable of interest and the control variables in exactly the same way—they are all just independent variables. It is the researcher's choice to focus on learning the causal effect of a single variable. This contrasts with the use of multiple regression purely for prediction or description, as described in Chapter 9.

Control Variables That Are Quantitative

Aptitude score is a quantitative variable. More precisely, aptitude, as measured in the NLSY, is the position of an individual in a distribution of aptitude scores—a percentile—that can take on any value between 0 and 100. To use stratification, to break our data into different aptitude groups, we had to make aptitude into a categorical variable. We created two groups: one with high scores and one with lower scores.

But within the groups we defined as having high and lower scores, aptitude still varies. The supposedly comparable groups created by stratification into two groups are not, in fact, completely comparable in aptitude. To really control for aptitude, the full range of variation in aptitude must be taken into consideration.

And the same point applies to our independent variable of interest: education. We have been focusing on having a college degree or not—but what if we were interested in the effect of years of education (as we will be shortly)? After all, there is a range of educational attainment among those without a college degree, and even those with a college degree can complete different years of education.

Multiple regression is not limited to categorical variables only and thus allows us to include the full range of a variable in our analysis.

Regression: From Description to Causation

As explained in Chapter 8, simple regression uses a best-fit straight line: An *independent variable* (X) predicts a *dependent variable* (Y). Consider the relationship between annual earnings and education, measured in years this time, again using data from the NLSY. Figure 11.3 shows a scatterplot of the data and the regression line fitted from the data,[9] which is described by the slope (or coefficient) and the intercept (or *constant*). In this example, the constant is −$47,113, and the slope is $6,268/year (i.e., $6,268 per year), or, in equation form,

$$\text{Earnings} = -\$47{,}113 + \$6{,}268/\text{year} \times \text{Educ.}$$

The formulas used to determine the coefficient and constant were given in Chapter 8.

(You probably noticed that the data in Figure 11.3 look a bit strange: so many data points at exactly $236,000 of earnings but none above $130,000. The reason is *top-coding*: To protect the privacy of participants in the NLSY, any earnings greater than $130,000 are top-coded at the average of all earnings above that value, $236,000.)

We were careful in Chapter 8 to use regression results such as this only for *prediction* and not as evidence of *causation*. Simple regression—regression with one independent variable (as in this example)—is, after all, essentially another form of correlation. Thus, we were careful not to say, for example, that if someone got 1 more year of education, we would expect that person to earn $6,268 more as a result.

When X Is Exogenous, Regressions Estimate Causal Effects

In many situations, however, we would very much like to use regression to make such counterfactual claims. And we can—when the independent variable is exogenous. If education were exogenously

---

[9] Experienced readers may be concerned that Earnings are not normally distributed and that we should therefore log Earnings. Although we recognize this issue, normality is only essential for inference. A best-fit straight line (least squares regression) can be calculated for any variables, although, of course, the fit may not be as good. But still, we chose to use Earnings, rather than logged earnings, to keep the interpretation as simple as possible.

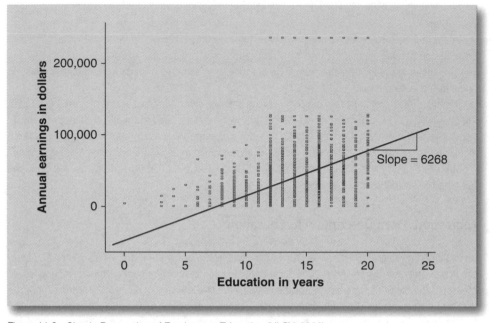

Figure 11.3   Simple Regression of Earnings on Education (NLSY, 2002)

determined, assigned through the toss of a coin and without any self-selection, we could interpret the slope causally. We could honestly tell a large group of people, in other words, that if they all got 1 more year of education, their earnings would rise by an average of $6,268.

Although it is a rare occurrence, every now and then such variables do turn out to be exogenous in the real world. Governments run lotteries to award limited school vouchers or health insurance coverage, for example. We will learn how to identify and use such situations, referred to as *natural experiments,* in Chapter 13. But in most cases, unfortunately, it is extremely unlikely that our independent variable of interest, for example, education, is in fact exogenous. To interpret regression coefficients causally—to tell people how much more they could expect to earn with more education (the counterfactual)—we need to add control variables. And to do that, we need to go beyond simple regression to multiple regression.

Multiple Regression: Brief Overview and Interpretation

Multiple regression predicts or explains a dependent variable (Y) using several independent variables (X_1, X_2, and so on). It is a direct extension of simple regression, but with two or more (sometimes many more) independent variables:

$$Y = a + b_1X_1 + b_2X_2 + \ldots b_kX_k.$$

In this equation, Y is the dependent variable or outcome and the Xs are the independent variables (1 through k). The bs represent the coefficients of all the independent variables and are of particular interest because they express how the independent variables are related to the dependent variable.[10]

When using multiple regression as a control variable method, the dependent variable is regressed on the independent variable of interest (the one whose causal effect we wish to measure) and on the control variables (the other independent variables). (See Box 11.4 for a description of how to run multiple regressions using software.) Continuing with the earlier example, say the dependent variable is *earnings*, the independent variable of interest is *education*, and the control variables are *aptitude at age 14*, *mother's education*, *living in poverty as a child*, and so on.

BOX 11.4
How to Run a Multiple Regression Using Software

You can run multiple regressions using statistical software packages, such as SAS, SPSS, and Stata, described in Chapter 8. It is fairly easy to do. First, the data must be read into the software from the kind of flat file described in Chapter 6. Then, using a point and click menu or a command line in a program, you specify the dependent variable and your selection of independent variables. The software treats the independent variables equally and does not distinguish between the independent variable of interest and the control variables—that is your job as part of the interpretation.

The software then performs the calculations and produces output in the form of a regression table. The regression table typically includes the constant term, the coefficients for each of the independent variables, the associated standard errors and significance tests on the coefficients, the R-squared fit statistic, and various other results. Examples were shown in Chapter 9 with the National Educational Longitudinal Study data.

Multiple regression can also be done with spreadsheet software, such as Excel, although it is somewhat more limited. For example, some spreadsheets will not handle missing values, and the columns representing the independent variables typically must be contiguous in the spreadsheet (requiring cutting and pasting if you want to try out different combinations of independent variables).

The coefficient of the independent variable of interest provides the effect of the independent variable on the dependent variable, with all control variables held constant. In essence, it's like creating individuals who all have the same aptitude, mother's education, poverty background, and so on, but who vary in education. But unlike stratification, where we did this by grouping individuals, with multiple regression, the controls can take on all possible combinations of all possible variables. The effect

---

[10] Recall from Chapter 9 that the coefficients, such as b_i, multiply the independent variables, X_i. Placing them right next to one another implies multiplication.

of education is some kind of average of its effect at all the different control variable values (Morgan & Winship, 2007, chap. 5).

How Multiple Regression
Is Like Stratification: A Graphical Illustration

Figure 11.3 illustrates a simple regression of earnings on education with no controls, Earnings $= a + b_{Ed}$Educ. Because education is not exogenous, however, we cannot interpret b_{Ed} as the causal effect of 1 more year of education, as we would like to. This is the same problem that we had in the naive comparison in Table 11.1, but now we are not just comparing two educational categories—we are looking across all the possible values that the quantitative variable years of education can take on.

Now, we will control for aptitude by stratifying the regression, just as we stratified the comparison of means earlier, using a categorical high aptitude variable indicating the top third of aptitude scores. We will run one regression with the high aptitude portion of the data and another regression with the lower aptitude portion of the data. The two resulting regressions, one for high aptitude and one for lower aptitude, are illustrated in Figure 11.4.

The slopes of the stratified regressions, shown in Figure 11.4, are now $6,876/year for the high aptitude and $3,561/year for the not-high aptitude. The not-high aptitude slope is notably less than the slope of the original unstratified regression, $6,268/year, shown in Figure 11.3. We can see that much of the original apparent effect of education was due to the individuals in the high aptitude group.

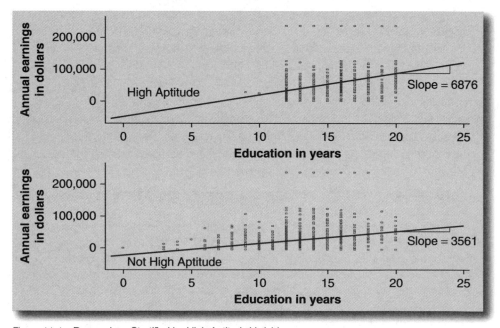

Figure 11.4   Regressions Stratified by High Aptitude Variable

This result is similar to what we saw in Table 11.3, in which controlling for aptitude reduced the initial $32,000 effect to $27,800 for the high aptitude group and to $18,700 for the lower aptitude group. In both cases, stratifying by the aptitude indictor variable dramatically reduced the magnitude of the apparent effect of education on earnings for the lower aptitude group.

Multiple regression is basically the same idea, but it is not mathematically equivalent.[11] Consider the multiple regression equation Earnings = $a + b_{Ed}$Educ + b_{apt}Aptitude. The variable *aptitude* is now a quantitative score, not just two groups defined by having high and low aptitude. The multiple regression works by essentially estimating the effect of education on earnings for many different aptitude levels represented by the quantitative score. So unlike when we stratified, we can now take advantage of the full range of variation in aptitude scores. (We described what multiple regression literally estimates in Chapter 9.)

How do the stratified regressions compare with the multiple regression? The effect of education in the multiple regression, b_{Ed}, depends on the effect of education at many different constant values of aptitude. Very roughly, the effect of education estimated in a multiple regression is some kind of combination of the two b_{Ed}s from the stratified regressions. In fact, putting the quantitative variable *Aptitude* in as a control variable results in an education coefficient of $4,135/year (see Table 11.6).

Specification: How the Choice of Control Variables Influences Regression Results

In multiple regression, the estimated effect of an independent variable of interest depends a great deal on which control variables are used. We illustrate this in Table 11.6, which shows the results with different control variables (or different *specifications*) in adjacent columns—a common method of presenting such results.

Let's begin by considering how these regression results compare with our initial results using stratification. Specification 1 shows the regression estimate of the effect of having a college education on earnings, which is $32,000—the same difference we obtained from stratification. Notice also that the constant is $29,515, which is the average earnings of those without a college degree. The average earnings of those with a college degree is $29,500 + $32,000 = $61,500. Again, this is the same initial result we obtained from stratification (see Table 11.1). But with regression, we can now look at the effect of *years of education*—a variable with more range, more variation. Specification 2 shows this effect, which is $6,268 (p value < .001)[12] more in earnings for each year of education completed. This is the same slope as in Figure 11.3.

Now, we can begin to add control variables. In Specification 3, we include an aptitude score from the person's youth as a control variable. As a result, the coefficient of education becomes $4,135/year, while the coefficient of aptitude itself is $297/point. Thus, aptitude was an omitted variable in the NLSY study,

---

[11] It would be literally equivalent if the test score variable was simply a categorical variable with the two categories of *high test score* and *lower test score* and if there was also an interaction between the high test score variable and Education.

[12] The real NLSY data have skewed earnings data, like almost any real earnings data. Consequently, it would be better to use log earnings as the dependent variable. By using unlogged earnings, we do not fit the data as well, and our inference results, such as p values and standard errors, are not accurate. Almost any published study would use log earnings, but unlogged earnings are easier for explaining concepts, and therefore we use them here. See Chapter 9 for the interpretation of coefficients with logged variables.

Table 11.6   Coefficients in Regressions of Earnings With Various Specifications (NLSY)

	Spec 1	Spec 2	Spec 3	Spec 4	Spec 5	Spec 6
Education (years)		6,268**	4,135**	4,962**	4,042**	4,847**
College graduate or not	32,000**					
Aptitude (AFQT score)			297**		286**	208**
High aptitude				13,027**		
Mother's education (years)					363*	323
Family in poverty						969
Female						−25,735**
Black						−3,447
Mother a manager						2,714
Constant	29,500**	−47,113**	−32,686**	−33,833**	−35,108**	−28,163**

Notes: **$p < .01$; *$p < .05$; dependent variable is dollars of earnings in 2002; AFQT, Armed Forces Qualification Test.

and the coefficient in the simple regression suffered from omitted variables bias. The bias from omitting aptitude is large—controlling for it reduces the education coefficient from $6,268/year to $4,135/year.

These multiple regression results are analogous to Table 11.3, but they make use of the full range of variation of both education and aptitude. To give some sense of what is lost with just stratification, consider what happens when instead of using aptitude itself as a control variable in multiple regression, we use the dummy variable indicating high aptitude scores. In that case, the coefficient of education only drops to $4,962/year, rather than to $4,135/year (Specification 4 of Table 11.6).

Adding More Control Variables

A major advantage of multiple regression over stratification is that many control variables can be used at the same time. What happens if we include both aptitude and mother's education as control variables? Now, the coefficient of education drops a bit more, to $4,042/year (Specification 5). As we saw in stratification, mother's education creates some omitted variables bias, but not nearly as much as aptitude.

With multiple regression, we can add lots of control variables at the same time. Suppose we add controls for mother's education, poverty status of family in youth, gender, race, and mother having a managerial career, arguably all common causes or proxies for complex common causes. The coefficient of education actually climbs back somewhat, to $4,874/year (Specification 6). This illustrates how our estimate of the effect of education on earnings depends, crucially, on the availability and choice of control variables.

What About Unmeasured Variables?

Even if researchers control for every relevant variable they can lay their hands on and even if the full range of variation of the variables is used, multiple regression does *not* solve the problem of *unmeasured variables* and the omitted variables bias it can cause. A multiple regression study is not unbiased just because it has controls—it must have all the relevant common causes as controls and no others. However, multiple regression does provide some tools for investigating the effects of control variables, as we have just seen in the section on adding and removing controls.

To practice these ideas—and to get a better feel for interpreting multiple regression results—we turn next to an example of a pair of published studies in which multiple regression is used to answer a causal question.

The Effect of Breastfeeding on Intelligence: Is There a Causal Connection?

First Studies

The effects of breastfeeding are of substantial medical, public health, and public policy interest. There are highly plausible mechanisms through which breastfeeding could influence an infant's healthy development, and studies support this idea. Interest has grown in demonstrating the long-term effects of breastfeeding on many outcomes, including intelligence. Many of the early studies that related breastfeeding to intelligence were based on naive interpretations of simple associations. Those studies were criticized for not controlling for potential common causes, such as the mother's education. More-educated mothers are more likely to breastfeed, and so the studies could potentially be biased due to the common cause of mother's education.[13]

To address such concerns, Mortensen, Michaelsen, Sanders, and Reinsch (2002) examined the relationship between the duration of breastfeeding and adult intelligence (of the breastfed child), with duration of breastfeeding as the independent variable. The control variables were education and social status of parents; single mother status; mother's height, age, and weight gain during pregnancy; cigarette consumption; number of pregnancies; estimated gestational age; birth weight; birth length; and indexes of pregnancy and delivery complications. Mortensen et al. found that even after adding all these controls, the relationship between breastfeeding duration and adult intelligence was both statistically significant and of reasonable practical magnitude.

Other researchers, however, challenged that result as still suffering from omitted variables bias. To illustrate such bias as well as how to read and interpret a control variables study implemented through multiple regression, we trace in detail a later study by Der, Batty, and Deary (2006) that challenged studies such as those of Mortensen et al. (2002).

Step 1: Speculate on Common Causes

Remember that Step 1 of a control variable study involves using theory, common sense, and other evidence to think of any and all possible common causes. It is important to be aggressive in speculating

---

[13]In medicine and public health, *confounding* is the preferred term for omitted variables bias. See Box 11.1.

about potential bias due to unmeasured variables. Der et al. (2006) thought that the controls used by Mortensen et al. (2002) and others still missed important common causes. In particular, they were familiar with the large literature on the heritability (genetic correlation) of intelligence. Mother's education was probably related but not a sufficient proxy and a different variable.

So Der et al. (2006) decided to do a study that would include the mother's score on an aptitude test (AFQT test) as a control. They used the NLSY, the same data that we have used to illustrate the relationship between education and earnings. Their dependent variables were several different aptitude tests taken by the children at various ages. The main independent variable of interest was whether or not the mother breastfed the child.

Step 2: Examine the Relationship Between the Independent Variable of Interest and Potential Common Causes

Step 2 of a control variable study is to examine the relationships between the independent variable of interest and the potential common causes. Der et al. (2006) do this in Table 1 of their paper, reproduced as Table 11.7. Notice, for example, that the mean AFQT score was about 26 for mothers who did not breastfeed as compared with about 46 for mothers who did. The difference is statistically significant at $p < .001$. (The difference is also presented as an odds ratio, which is common in medical research.) The practical magnitude of the 20-point difference is quite large—it is close to 1 standard deviation. To look at another difference, the poverty rates differ dramatically, with about 36% of families in poverty among not breastfeeding mothers as compared with a poverty rate of about 16% among breastfeeding mothers. Again, the difference is strongly statistically significant. Indeed, all the differences are statistically significant, except for male infant and gestation in weeks. Many of the differences, such as the poverty rate difference, also appear practically significant.

Step 3: Implement Control Variables Through Multiple Regression

The third step of a control variables study is to implement the control variable and observe the effect of the independent variable on the dependent variable, holding constant all the controls.

Whether or not the child was breastfed is a dummy variable. As discussed in Chapter 9, the coefficient of a dummy variable is the difference in the average value of the dependent variable between those with and those without the characteristic. In this case, the coefficient of breastfeeding reveals the difference in average test score between children who were breastfed and those who were not, holding constant all the control variables. Ideally, the coefficient of breastfeeding will reveal the difference between breastfeeding and its counterfactual—the causal effect of breastfeeding.

Der et al. (2006) performed a multiple regression using all the control variables that had statistically significant differences in Table 11.7 but not those with statistically insignificant differences. In contrast to that practice, some researchers believe that all variables theorized to have an effect should be included in the regression, not just those with statistically significant differences or effects. They worry about data mining and its potential to find chance correlations that happen to be in the data.

Table 11.7   Association of Potential Confounders With Breastfeeding

Confounder	Not Breastfed		Breastfed		Odds Ratio* (95% Confidence Interval)	p Value
	Mean (SD) or %	No	Mean (SD) or %	No		
Mother's AFQT score	26.24 (22.33)	3001	46.44 (27.76)	2701	2.30 (2.16 to 2.44)	<0.001
Mother's education	11.50 (2.14)	3119	12.79 (2.48)	2819	1.33 (1.73 to 1.95)	<0.001
Mother's age	23.83 (4.50)	3125	25.79 (4.64)	2823	1.55 (1.47 to 1.64)	<0.001
HOME cognitive stimulation	94.09 (16.62)	2844	100.00 (14.26)	2620	1.59 (1.50 to 1.69)	<0.001
HOME emotional support	96.18 (16.54)	2791	100.67 (14.45)	2601	1.44 (1.36 to 1.52)	<0.001
Gestation (weeks)	39.05 (1.58)	3125	39.01 (1.55)	2823	0.97 (0.93 to 1.03)	0.315
Birth weight (g)	3390 (47)	3125	3470 (47)	2823	1.21 (1.15 to 1.27)	<0.001
Birth order	1.97 (1.07)	3125	1.85 (1.02)	2823	0.90 (0.85 to 0.94)	<0.001
Family in poverty†	36.4%	3103	15.8%	2817	0.33 (0.29 to 0.37)	<0.001
Mother smoked in pregnancy†	35.7%	3129	25.6%	2816	0.62 (0.55 to 0.69)	<0.001
Male infant†	51.7%	3125	50.6%	2823	0.96 (0.87 to 1.06)	0.413
Hispanic††	49.4%	615	50.6%	630	0.72 (0.63 to 0.82)	<0.001
Black††	74.9%	1264	25.1%	423	0.24 (0.21 to 0.27)	<0.001
Not Black/Hispanic††	41.3%	1245	58.7%	1770	1.00	

Source: Der et al. (2006, Table 1).

AFQT = Armed Forces Qualification Test; HOME = home observation of the environment.

†Odds ratios for breastfeeding are per 1 SD of mother's AFQT score education, age, HOME scores, gestation, and birth weight.

††Reference groups are family not in poverty, mother did not smoke in pregnancy, female.

Row percentage.

The multiple regression results are shown in Table 11.8. The four columns, marked PIAT, Math, and so on, refer to four dependent variables—the total (composite) test taken by the children and its individual components. We will focus on the PIAT total for our detailed exploration. The coefficient column (marked *B*) refers to the coefficient of the variable listed. For example, the coefficient of breastfeeding is 0.52, the coefficient of mother's AFQT score is 4.43, and the coefficient of mother smoking during pregnancy is 0.08.

Next to the coefficients, their standard errors are given in parentheses. For example, the standard error of the breastfeeding coefficient is 0.36 and the standard error of the AFQT score coefficient is 0.26. The standard error provides information about the sampling error in the coefficient—information about the lack of precision due to sampling. Next to the coefficients and standard errors are *p* values associated with a test of whether or not the coefficient is 0—no relationship between that variable and the child's intelligence test score.

How to Interpret Multiple Regression Coefficients: Effects of Controls

Next, we practice interpreting multiple regression results by first focusing on the effects of the control variables—effects that are not our main interest. The coefficient of family in poverty is −1.72 points. Remember to pay attention to the units of any coefficient. The coefficient of a dummy variable has the units of the dependent variable—the points of the PIAT test, in this case. The family in poverty coefficient shows that being in poverty lowers a child's score on the PIAT test by 1.72 points, holding constant all the other variables, including breastfeeding. The coefficient of poverty is statistically significant, with a *p* value of $< .001$, ruling out chance as an explanation of the magnitude of the effect. Finally, we should examine the practical significance of the effect of poverty—a 1.72-point decline is not that big relative to a standard deviation of 15 points, but it is not nothing, either. In any multiple regression study, the coefficients of all the control variables should be examined to make sure that their sign and magnitude are plausible.

What of the effect of mother's AFQT score, the variable omitted from prior studies? It was strongly statistically significant ($p < .001$). To interpret its magnitude practically, we need to know that AFQT was measured in terms of its standard deviation.[14] So the coefficient shows that a 1 standard deviation increase in mother's AFQT score results in a 4.43-point increase in her child's PIAT score—almost a third of a standard deviation increase, quite a large effect.

How to Interpret Multiple Regression Coefficients: Effect of Interest

Now, we turn to the coefficient of interest, the coefficient of breastfeeding. Its coefficient is 0.52 points. First, note that it is not statistically significant—the *p* value is .149, well above the conventional threshold of .05. Recalling from Chapter 8 how to interpret a *p* value, we see that there is about a 15% chance that we could have gotten the .52-point effect or something of greater magnitude even

---

[14]The effects of all quantitative (nondummy) variables were measured in terms of standard deviations.

Table 11.8 Mutually Adjusted Effects of Breastfeeding and Confounders on Cognitive Outcomes in 3,161 Mothers, 5,475 Children, and 16,744 Assessments

Confounder	PIAT-Total		Maths*		Reading*			
	B (SE)	p	B (SE)	p	B (SE)	p	B (SE)	p
Breastfeeding	0.52 (0.36)	0.149	0.52 (0.34)	0.150	0.36 (0.37)	0.332	0.52 (0.35)	0.134
Mother's AFQT score	4.43 (0.26)	<0.001	3.87 (0.25)	<0.001	3.77 (0.27)	<0.001	3.97 (0.25)	<0.001
Mother's education	1.03 (0.24)	<0.001	1.10 (0.23)	<0.001	0.96 (0.25)	<0.001	0.62 (0.23)	0.007
Family in poverty	-1.72 (0.41)	<0.001	-0.98 (0.39)	0.012	-1.70 (0.42)	<0.001	-1.82 (0.39)	<0.001
Mother's age	0.98 (0.20)	<0.001	0.72 (0.19)	<0.001	1.05 (0.20)	<0.001	0.69 (0.19)	<0.001
Mother smoked in pregnancy	0.08 (0.38)	0.839	0.37 (0.36)	0.305	-0.11 (0.39)	0.771	0.14 (0.36)	0.694
HOME cognitive stimulation	0.83 (0.10)	<0.001	0.78 (0.12)	<0.001	0.79 (0.11)	<0.001	1.13 (0.12)	<0.001
HOME emotional support	0.17 (0.09)	0.072	0.25 (0.11)	0.020	0.15 (0.10)	0.120	0.14 (0.11)	0.200
Birth weight	0.32 (0.16)	0.047	0.40 (0.15)	0.010	0.20 (0.17)	0.234	0.25 (0.16)	0.113
Birth order	-1.54 (0.18)	<0.001	-0.79 (0.17)	<0.001	-1.47 (0.19)	<0.001	-1.69 (0.18)	<0.001
Hispanic	-0.36 (0.52)	0.494	-1.85 (0.49)	<0.001	0.33 (0.53)	0.534	0.48 (0.49)	0.329
Black	-0.90 (0.50)	0.074	-2.79 (0.47)	<0.001	0.54 (0.52)	0.299	-0.03 (0.48)	0.950

Source: Der et al. (2006, Table 3).

PIAT= Peabody Individual Achievement Test; AFQT = Armed Forces Qualification Test; HOME = home observation for measurement of the environment.

*Individual components of PIAT.

if, in fact, there is no effect of breastfeeding on intelligence. So the estimated breastfeeding effect could be due to simple chance in who got sampled.

Even if a result is not statistically significant, it is important to examine the practical significance of the upper and lower bounds of the confidence intervals. Recall from Chapter 8 that a statistically insignificant result with a small standard error (i.e., a narrow confidence interval) could be quite informative and reveal that the study definitively ruled out a practically significant effect.

A 95% confidence interval is roughly 2 standard errors in either direction from the estimated effect. In this case, we are 95% confident that the effect of breastfeeding on PIAT score is somewhere between $.52 - 2 \times .36 = -0.20$ points and $.52 + 2 \times .36 = 1.24$ points. Compared with the effect of mother's AFQT score or education, the effect of breastfeeding is small in a practical sense. We can conclude that, controlling for mother's AFQT score and the other controls, breastfeeding does not have an effect on intelligence.

Adding and Removing Controls: What Can Be Learned?

Since prior studies that did not have mother's aptitude test score as a control found substantial effects of breastfeeding on intelligence, it is important to understand the relationship between those results and this one. More generally, understanding the mechanism of an effect is valuable. Examining how coefficients change as controls are added and removed can help shed light on this issue.

Table 11.9 shows the coefficient of breastfeeding (and its standard error) from many distinct regressions. The top row, marked *unadjusted*, shows the effect of breastfeeding on test score, without any control variables. The biased naive estimate of the effect of breastfeeding on the PIAT test score is about 4.7 points. The rows beneath the unadjusted effect all show the coefficient of breastfeeding with a different *single* control variable. For example, for the PIAT test, the coefficient of breastfeeding when mother's AFQT score is a control is reduced to 1.30 points. This represents a reduction of 72% relative to the unadjusted coefficient of about 4.7 points. That percent reduction is also shown next to each coefficient and its standard error. The percent effect of mother's AFQT score is greater than that of any other control variable used individually.

The findings of prior studies can be understood by examining the effect of mother's education used as a single control. In that case, the effect of mother's education on PIAT score is estimated to be 2.96 points per year, almost three times its estimated effect when mother's AFQT score is also used as a control. That contrast reveals that AFQT score apparently drives both mother's education and child's aptitude test score.

Notice that in this study, the authors first presented the results with only one control (Der et al., 2006, Table 2) at a time *before* the full results with all the controls. We might wonder why they did that, since a great advantage of multiple regression as a means of implementing control variables is precisely its ability to implement many controls at once, and they had reason to believe that all were important. We can speculate that they probably did this for several reasons. First, they were addressing a literature that had found substantial effects, and they wanted to illustrate that mother's AFQT score was an important variable and that without it, mother's education seemed very important. Second, in the medical and public health literatures, stratification is a common form of control variable analysis, particularly layered cross-tabs, and so they wanted to present evidence in a form

Table 11.9   Effect of Breastfeeding on Cognitive Outcomes, Unadjusted and Adjusted Singly for Each Confounder, in 3,161 Mothers, 5,475 Children, and 16,744 Assessments

	PIAT—Total		Maths*		Reading*		Comprehension*	
	B (SE)	%†	B (SE)	%†	B (SE)	%†	B (SE)	%†
Unadjusted	4.69 (0.38)		4.65 (0.56)		4.09 (0.38)		4.22 (0.36)	
Adjusted for:								
Mother's AFQT score	1.30 (0.36)	72	1.30 (0.34)	72	1.02 (0.37)††	75	1.21 (0.35)	71
Mother's education	2.95 (0.37)	37	3.06 (0.35)	34	2.38 (0.37)	42	2.69 (0.35)	36
Family in poverty	3.94 (0.38)	16	3.96 (0.36)	15	3.30 (0.37)	19	3.46 (0.35)	18
Mother's age	4.29 (0.38)	9	4.18 (0.36)	10	3.64 (0.38)	11	3.96 (0.36)	6
Mother smoked in pregnancy	4.60 (0.38)	2	4.60 (0.36)	1	3.98 (0.38)	3	4.14 (0.36)	2
HOME cognitive stimulation	4.29 (0.37)	8	4.20 (0.35)	10	3.66 (0.37)	10	3.64 (0.35)	14
HOME emotional support	4.57 (0.38)	3	4.47 (0.36)	4	3.96 (0.38)	3	4.06 (0.36)	4
Birth weight	4.60 (0.38)	2	4.52 (0.36)	3	4.02 (0.38)	2	4.15 (0.36)	2
Birth order	4.55 (0.38)	3	4.57 (0.36)	2	3.94 (0.37)	4	4.01 (0.35)	5
Race	3.65 (0.38)	22	3.30 (0.36)	29	3.32 (0.39)	19	3.34 (0.37)	21

Source: Der et al. (2006, Table 2).

Note: All significant at $p < .001$ except where marked.

PIAT = Peabody Individual Achievement Test; AFQT = Armed Forces Qualification Test; HOME = home observation for measurement of the environment.

*Individual components of PIAT.

†Percentage of unadjusted figure.

††$p = 0.006$.

familiar and understandable to their audience. In Chapter 15, we discuss such choices in presenting research results.

Technical Complexities

The actual Der et al. (2006) study differed from the usual straightforward multiple regression study in one respect. The NLSY has multiple observations of the children's test scores, and the researchers wanted to take advantage of the statistical power these observations provided. However, clearly, multiple observations of the same child are not unrelated; they are correlated. Moreover, mothers often had more than one child, and presumably, siblings are correlated. Therefore, the researchers had to use a more advanced technique, in particular, one that adjusted all their standard errors for the various correlations. (This issue was discussed in Chapter 8.)

Notice, however, that it was possible to understand and interpret many of the main results of the paper without knowing anything about this technical complexity. Provided you, as a reader, are able to trust that the authors got their technical details right, you can focus on the part that interests you and make real use of the results. In Chapter 15, we discuss issues such as peer review and journal prestige that can provide assurance that technical matters were probably handled correctly.

Further Topics in Multiple Regression

Now that you've become more familiar with the control variables strategy using multiple regression, there are a few further topics to consider in both interpreting and implementing this approach.

Possible Effects of Adding Control Variables

In the breastfeeding study, adding the mother's AFQT as a control variable *eliminated* the effect of breastfeeding on the child's cognitive outcomes. In the earlier example of earnings and education, controlling for aptitude score *reduced* the magnitude of the effect of education—but did not eliminate it.

Adding control variables can have two other types of effects, although they are less frequent. A control variable could *increase* the magnitude of the effect of the independent variable of interest. Or a control variable could *reverse* the sign or direction of the effect of the independent variable of interest. It all depends on the magnitude and sign of the effect of the control on the independent variable and the magnitude and sign of the effect of the independent variable of interest on the dependent variable. In other words, different patterns of correlation among the key variables can alter the effect control variables have on the estimate of the causal effect.

Interactions, Functional Form, and Categorical Dependent Variables

All the technical extensions to multiple regression, introduced in Chapter 9 when using multiple regression for prediction, apply when the method is used to determine causal effects with control variables. For example, moderation—when the effect of one variable depends on the magnitude of the other variable—is implemented using interaction terms. More flexible functional forms, such as logs and polynomials, can be used. And categorical dependent variables can be accommodated with probit, logistic, linear probability, ordered logit, and other models. Valid causal interpretations depend on the issues described in this chapter, of course, but otherwise, everything carries over from the use of multiple regression purely for description or prediction.

The Decision to Focus on One Causal Effect—and the Confusion It Can Cause

Because estimating causal effects is so difficult, often researchers (particularly in economics and program evaluation) choose to focus their efforts on estimating the effect of just one independent variable. We have already seen several examples of this: the effect of education on earnings, or the effect of breastfeeding on cognitive development. In these studies, the focus is on the independent variable of interest, with the other independent variables selected primarily as control variables that serve to improve the one causal estimate.

Other researchers (in sociology and other fields), tend to focus on as many causes of the dependent variable as they can. For example, they might be interested in multiple factors in a person's life that influence earnings, not just education. Or they might want to develop a causal model of the many influences on the cognitive development of children, not just the effect of breastfeeding. In such studies, most of the independent variables are viewed as causes of interest in their own right, not as control variables. (See Box 11.5 about the use of the term "control variable.") These studies also tend to be interested in comparing the effects of multiple causes, such as how much of an effect breastfeeding has on cognitive development compared with nutrition, early childhood education, parental influences, and so on.

BOX 11.5
When to Call Something a Control Variable

In our main focus on the effect of one independent variable of interest, we referred to the other independent variables as **control variables**. As we use the term, the purpose of a *control variable* is to statistically equalize comparisons across the independent variable of interest. Some researchers often use the term *control variable* to refer to all the independent variables, but we suggest reserving the term *control variable* for a variable used to disentangle the causal effect of the independent variable of interest. In a multi-cause model, use the term *independent variable* for all the causes.

Both types of researchers use multiple regression, and their statistical tables tend to look similar. But they view what they are trying to do with multiple regression very differently, and this sometimes leads to confusion and contention. So it is important to make clear the difference in research questions and in the purposes for using multiple regression. It is also important to understand that both kinds of research can be useful and informative.

When Is Low *R*-Squared a Problem?

As explained in Chapters 8 and 9, the *R*-squared of a regression is the proportion of the variation in the dependent variable that can be predicted by (or "explained by") the independent variables. A low *R*-squared means that many of the important causes of the dependent variable are not in the equation. In doing prediction, the *R*-squared is obviously very important—we want the most accurate prediction possible (although useful predictions can still be made without a high *R*-squared). As the example in Box 11.6 illustrates, actuaries care a lot about whether someone's occupation predicts their use of health care—regardless of whether it is causal. As a result, many people pay a lot of attention to *R*-squared.

BOX 11.6
The Health of Taxi Drivers: Prediction Versus Causation

Some occupations are associated with more health risks.

Source: © 2009 Jupiterimages Corporation.

Actuaries for health insurance companies try to predict individuals' likelihood of being hospitalized, having doctors' visits, and so on, to determine what premiums they should be charged. They use regression models with independent variables such as age, gender, medical history (if available), occupation, and so on.

An actuary might find, for example, that taxi drivers are more likely than those in many other occupations to have heart attacks. This effect could be causal, with a mechanism of taxi driving raising stress and stress causing heart attacks. Alternatively, people could end up driving taxis because they have fewer options and harder past lives, and those fewer options and harder past lives would have made them more prone to heart attacks no matter what their occupation. That alternative would be an example of common cause.

Would the actuary, and the health insurance plan employing the actuary, need to know *why* being a taxi driver predicts having a heart attack? No. Their task is to determine health insurance premiums, and so they only need to predict health care usage in the most accurate and precise way possible. They do not need to know whether a predictor variable is itself causal or really a proxy for some common cause.

Public health officials, in contrast, might care *why* taxi drivers are more prone to heart attacks. Their job is to develop and implement policies to improve the health of the public. If driving a taxi is truly responsible for making someone more likely to have a heart attack, a public health official might want to change aspects of their working conditions, such as the length of shifts. On the other hand, if driving a taxi is just a proxy for what drives heart attacks, then public health officials might want to focus on those other causes to see if they could perhaps change them.

Both public health policy and insurance premiums are determined, in part, by multiple regression models such as the ones we have described. But the very different purposes mean that they should be interpreted and applied in different ways.

But when using multiple regression to get at causation, R-squared itself is not all that important. The focus is instead on the coefficient of the independent variable of interest, including both its statistical and practical significance. Even in a regression with a low R-squared, such statistical and practical significance is still quite possible. Many dependent variables in social and policy research—variables such as earnings, cognitive development, or consumption of health care—have multiple and varied causes. Most of these causes are out of the reach of policy and practice. If a variable that can be influenced by policy or practice has a statistical and practical effect, it is important to know that—even if the variable does not explain all that much total variation in the outcome.

Of course, if the goal is to understand and demonstrate as many causes of the dependent variable as possible, R-squared matters. Once again, much depends on the aims of the study and the reasons for using multiple regression.

Software Doesn't Know the Difference, but You Should

Whether multiple regression is being used for prediction, description, disentangling a single causal effect, or estimating many causal effects together, the multiple regression commands in the statistical software are the same. The software just asks for the dependent variable and the independent variables. The calculations the software performs do not depend on the purpose. However, how a researcher should choose those independent variables—and how multiple regression results should be interpreted—depend very much on what the purpose is.

The proliferation, advanced capabilities, and ease of use of both computers and software today make it easy to run regressions. However, just as one needs to be very careful about the quality and meaning of the data, one needs to be careful about the choice of control variables and the interpretation of the results.

Control Variables in Perspective

The really hard work of the control variable method lies not in the technicalities of the different statistical methods. Rather, it lies in figuring out what common cause variables have been left out—the inevitable unmeasured variables—and in searching for the best possible proxies for those omitted unmeasured variables. It lies in determining whether a potential control variable is an intervening variable. Where there is ambiguity about whether something is a common cause or an intervening variable or in situations where it can play both roles, the best course is to do the analysis both with and without the variable as a control. The control variables method is not a simple recipe with every step spelled out.

Observational studies with control variables are the most widely used method for estimating causal effects in applied social research. However, as we have seen, the method has drawbacks. Control variables cannot solve the problem of reverse causation. And often, important common causes are unmeasured, leading to omitted variables bias. Data with measures of every relevant common cause are often not available. Sometimes observational data, even if used in the best possible control variables study, cannot provide convincing causal effect estimates. The next chapter describes randomized experiments, which do provide convincing causal effect estimates, although they have other weaknesses.

BOX 11.7
Critical Questions to Ask About
Observational Studies With Control Variables

- Does the study use control variables, or does it rely on simple differences or correlations to infer causation?

(Continued)

(Continued)

- Does the study implement control variables using stratification or some form of multiple regression? Keep in mind that using regression to implement the control variables strategy can involve probit, logistic, linear probability, ordered logit, and other varieties of regression models.
- What control variables does the study employ—and why were they selected? Is there an explicit theory, or rationale, given for picking the control variables? Are intervening variables mistakenly used as controls?
- Are important common cause variables included as control variables? What important common cause variables are omitted? What bias (sign and magnitude) might result from omitting these common cause variables?
- Is the study focused on estimating the effect of one main independent variable of interest? Or is the study focused on explaining the dependent variable as a result of many causes? Is the study clear about this distinction in its choice and interpretation of variables?
- After adjusting for the control variables, how large were the reported effects in practical or policy terms? Beware of "statistically significant" effects that turn out, on closer inspection, to be only trivial differences, in policy or practice terms.

EXERCISES

Education and Earnings Continued

11.1. Think of some other common causes of education and earnings in the real world—other than those mentioned in this chapter. What bias results from their omission?

Thinking About Important Control Variables to Include

11.2. Following are some possible relationships that we might find in observational data that come, say, from a sample survey of U.S. adults:

  a. Computer skills → Earnings
  b. Exercise → Diabetes
  c. Marital status → Happiness

  Given that these simple relationships come from observational data, and that we are interested in getting at the true causal effects, what control variables would we need?

Think about likely common causes of both variables, and be careful not to pick intervening variables.

Bias in Your Field

11.3. Think of an outcome (Y) of interest in your field of interest. Think of a particular cause (X) of the outcome that is observed in ordinary observational data but that might be changeable through policy or practice changes. Draw the basic $X \rightarrow Y$ causal diagram, substituting in the names of your variables.

- What relationship would you expect from the simple regression or association? Would it be positive or negative, and how strong would it be?
- Think of any relevant common causes. What would happen to the estimated relationship if they were added as controls?
- Could you get real-world measures of these common causes? What about proxies?
- Is reverse causation a potential issue?

Part-Time Faculty and Graduation Rates

11.4. Studies show that colleges that make greater use of part-time faculty have lower graduation rates.

   a. Describe a common cause theory that *both* explains the correlation described above *and* does *not* imply that part-time faculty cause lower graduation rates. Use a path diagram as well as a brief description in words.
   b. Does your theory reveal a control variable that could be used to create more convincing evidence of a causal effect—an estimate with less bias? If so, explain why and how you could do such a control variable study. If not, explain why not and what kind of theory you would need to help you find a control variable.
   c. Describe a reverse causation theory that *both* explains the correlation described above *and* does *not* imply that part-time faculty cause lower graduation rates. Use a path diagram as well as a brief description in words. Can you find a control variable to eliminate the bias of the reverse causation theory?

Why Did They Do That?

11.5. Find an article in your field or on a topic of interest to you—an article that involves observational data and control variables. (A great many studies in social and policy research are of this type, so you should be able to find one in most issues of a research journal.) Find the main table in the article that shows the stratification or multiple regression results.

Which variable is the independent variable of interest? Which variables are the control variables? Why did the researchers choose the control variables that they did? Are there any important variables missing—in other words, is there possible omitted variables bias?

Teenage Pregnancy and Earnings (Advanced Question)

11.6. Imagine trying to do a control variables study with observational data to determine the effect of teenage pregnancy on earnings in middle age. Consider the issue of whether education is an appropriate control variable.[15]

    a. Could education be an intervening variable? Describe a theory consistent with that.

    b. Could education be a common cause? Describe a theory consistent with that.

    c. Consider how having longitudinal data on education at different points in time might help decide how to use education as a control variable.

    d. Could education be a complex common cause, perhaps a proxy for interest in or aptitude for education? Describe a theory consistent with that. What would that theory imply about using education as a control variable?

    e. If you could have any variables you liked in a long-term longitudinal data set such as the NLSY, what variables would you want to deal with the complex common cause problem just suggested?

---

[15]We thank Sanders Korenman for this example.

Objectives: This chapter introduces you to the randomized field experiment—the "gold standard" in social and policy research for demonstrating causation. You will learn the logic and structure of a randomized field experiment, in particular, how it creates statistically equivalent groups and eliminates bias from common causes and reverse causation. And you will understand how random assignment—the key feature of such experiments—differs from random sampling (covered in Chapter 5). You will become aware of the limited generalizability of many randomized field experiments as well as appreciate the practical and ethical limitations of such studies. And you will learn various experimental designs and become aware of issues that arise in the analysis of experimental data. Despite important advantages, the randomized field experiment is not always the best design for research.

A randomized field experiment looked at the effect of welfare time limits on employment

Source: © Nubar Alexanian.

Randomized Field Experiments

12

Time Limits on Welfare

Aid to Families with Dependent Children (AFDC) began in the 1930s under the New Deal as America's welfare program for poor widows. But it came under increasing criticism in the postwar decades for creating disincentives to work and, according to some, discouraging marriage (only single-parent families were eligible for AFDC). By the 1990s, many advocated time limits on the receipt of welfare to prevent it from being seen as a way of life and to encourage recipients to find and keep a job. But advocates for the poor and others warned that time limits would remove a vital safety net for struggling families and punish them unfairly for employment problems beyond their control. Time limits on welfare have been very controversial.

How could this debate be informed by research? Evidence from government surveys suggests that families who stay on welfare for a short time are more likely to find jobs and earn better wages, compared with long-term welfare families. But this could be a case of reverse causation: Finding a good job causes families to leave welfare, not the other way around. Or it could reflect a common cause, such as motivation, which might make people both less likely to stay on welfare and more successful in the job market. And even the clever use of control variables—the strategy discussed in the previous chapter—does not deal with reverse causation and unmeasured common causes, such as motivation.

What we would prefer is more solid evidence of causation—the kind of evidence that controlled laboratory experiments (such as the ones we saw in Chapter 10) give us. But how can you get such evidence outside the laboratory—in the real world of public policy and programs? One important strategy is the randomized field experiment. Randomized field experiments are increasingly demanded these days for purposes of policymaking and program evaluation. However, they have some drawbacks and are far from the last word on a controversial topic such as time-limited welfare.

Florida's Family Transition Program:
A Randomized Field Experiment

The State of Florida's Family Transition Program (FTP) is a randomized field experiment to evaluate time limits on welfare (Bloom et al., 2000). The program was implemented in Escambia County, in the panhandle section of the state, around Pensacola. Let's use this example to examine the various components of a randomized field experiment, as diagrammed in Figure 12.1.

Beginning in 1994, welfare recipients who lived in the county were assigned to either the treatment group or the control group—randomly, by the flip of the coin, as it were (more on this later). This method of assigning treatment is the defining feature of a **randomized experiment**. **Randomized field experiments** are randomized experiments conducted in an actual social or policy setting—the *field*. Randomized experiments are also known as **randomized controlled trials** (RCTs), or in medicine as *clinical trials*.

The **control group** was enrolled in the usual AFDC program, while the **treatment group** was enrolled in the new FTP. The control group is also known as the *control condition*, or, in medicine, the **placebo** group. It serves to estimate the counterfactual—what would have happened to the treatment group had they not gotten the treatment.

The FTP program—the **treatment**—imposed a time limit on welfare payments of 24 months (in any 60-month period). But it also included an array of incentives (such as an earned income disregard) and services (such as child care) to encourage recipients to find and keep jobs. Therefore, the treatment comprises *all* these features—everything that differs from the usual AFDC available to the control group.

Since welfare benefits apply not only to mothers but their children as well, it is *families* that were randomized. Therefore, families were the **experimental units** or **subjects**, the units randomized to the treatment and control conditions. Thus, both mother and child *outcomes* could be (and were) measured and assessed.

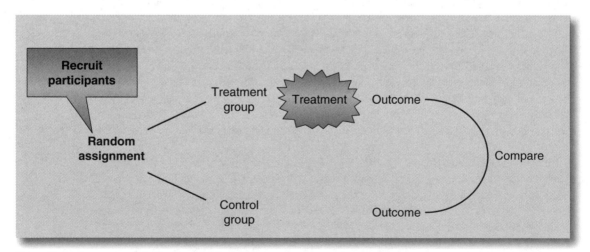

Figure 12.1   Components of a Randomized Experiment

The outcomes of particular interest in the evaluation of FTP are mothers' employment, mothers' earnings, and children's school performance. These outcomes are then compared across treatment and control groups. How much did the mothers in the experimental group earn relative to the control group? How did children of FTP families perform in school, relative to children of families getting the usual AFDC? We will look at what the data have to say shortly. But first, let's examine more closely why the comparisons set up by a randomized experiment such as FTP provide such convincing evidence of causation.

Random Assignment: Creating Statistical Equivalence

Recall from Chapter 9 that in a controlled laboratory setting, we establish two key conditions that allow us to answer causal questions—exogeneity and control. In a randomized experiment, **random assignment** is used to provide, or withhold, the treatment following a procedure similar to flipping a coin. The treatment is not self-selected, targeted to the needy, or based on any individual characteristics that could influence the outcome later on. In this way, random assignment ensures that the treatment is exogenous.

In a laboratory setting, other variables that might affect the outcome are controlled—physically held constant. But in most real-world social, medical, or policy settings, it is impossible to hold constant all the various factors that might influence an outcome such as the earnings of mothers or the performance of children in school. Indeed, that is why we used control variables in the previous chapter. Randomization addresses this problem too, not by physically holding things constant or by employing control variables, but by producing **statistical equivalence**.

Think of statistical equivalence this way: Ideally, we want to compare apples with apples. But if we cannot find identical fruits for both baskets, we can at least ensure that we have essentially the same *mix* of fruits in each basket. Provided there are enough pieces of fruit (sample size)—and that they were all well mixed together ahead of time (random assignment)—the two baskets of fruit will be statistically equivalent. Because the control group is statistically equivalent to the treatment group, it can be used to estimate the counterfactual.

Random Assignment in Practice

Let's look more closely at how random assignment is used to make the FTP treatment group and AFDC control group statistically equivalent.

After completing some initial paperwork on families, but before placing them in a program, welfare caseworkers in Pensacola called the Manpower Demonstration Research Corporation (MDRC), the research organization managing the evaluation (see Box 12.1). MDRC used a computer to randomly assign the families to either FTP (the treatment group) or AFDC (the control group). The caseworkers then completed the enrollment process into the appropriate program. MDRC could have used the flip of an ordinary coin to do the random assignment, but a computer routine makes the process more structured, more easily traceable, and less susceptible to conscious or unconscious tampering. Table 12.1 demonstrates how random assignment using a computerized random number generator is done.

BOX 12.1
Manpower Demonstration Research Corporation (MDRC)

MDRC is an influential policy research organization known for its use of randomized field experiments to evaluate public programs, including Florida's Family Transition Program. Here is what they say about themselves on their Web site, www.mdrc.org:

... Created in 1974 by the Ford Foundation and a group of federal agencies, MDRC is best known for mounting large-scale evaluations of real-world policies and programs targeted to low-income people. We helped pioneer the use of random assignment—the same highly reliable methodology that is used to test new medicines—in the evaluation of such policies and programs. In some cases, we work with others to design pathbreaking initiatives and then subject those initiatives to rigorous testing. In other cases, we conduct careful evaluations of programs designed and operated by government agencies or others.

Over the years, MDRC has brought its unique approach to an ever-growing range of policy areas and target populations. Once known primarily for evaluations of state welfare-to-work programs, today MDRC is also studying public school reforms, employment programs for ex-prisoners and people with disabilities, and programs to help low-income people succeed in college. We have worked in nearly every state and most major cities; we also helped create a sister organization in Canada and are currently managing a large project in the United Kingdom with British partners ...

Working in fields where emotion and ideology often dominate public debates, MDRC is seen as a source of objective, unbiased evidence. From welfare policy to high school reform, MDRC's research has frequently helped to shape legislation, program design, and operational practices across the country.

Source: MRDC, www.mdrc.org/about_what_is_mdrc.htm.

Table 12.1 shows the name of the applicant and the date and time the caseworker called MDRC.[1] At the time of the call, the random number was picked by the computer from all possible numbers between 0 and 100, with each number having an equal probability of selection. The preestablished rule for assignment was that random numbers less than 50 were assigned to AFDC, while random numbers equal to or greater than 50 were assigned to FTP. Thus, the first two applicants were assigned to AFDC, the next four applicants were assigned to FTP, and the last applicant shown was assigned to AFDC.

Although there may be short-run imbalances in the assignment of treatment and control group members, over the long run, as this process of random assignment continues and the sample size becomes large enough, the number of applicants in each group will be approximately the same. In

---

[1]These are artificial data but based generally on the procedures used in the FTP evaluation, as described in Bloom et al. (2000).

Table 12.1   Random Assignment

Applicant Name	Date/Time of Call	Random Number	Assignment
P. Jones	3/21/94 9:10 AM	38.2	AFDC
J. Aristide	3/21/94 11:45 AM	10.1	AFDC
K. Smith	3/21/94 2:20 PM	59.6	FTP
B. Thomas	3/22/94 10:05 AM	89.9	FTP
L. Sanchez	3/22/94 12:00 PM	88.5	FTP
N. Allen	3/23/94 9:55 AM	95.8	FTP
C. Fernandez	3/23/94 1:15 PM	1.4	AFDC

Pensacola, a total of 2,817 families were randomly assigned in this way, and 1,405 ended up in FTP and 1,412 in AFDC.

Notice that it takes deliberation and discipline to do proper random assignment—*random* in the context of a randomized field experiment does not mean haphazard or lackadaisical.

Statistical Equivalence: A Look at the Data

What does random assignment, so deliberately done, actually achieve? Notice that the values of the random numbers become the sole basis for assigning a family to the FTP treatment or to the AFDC control condition, and the values are generated entirely by chance selection. The values selected, therefore, are not related in any way to the characteristics of the applicant families. Compared with those assigned low random numbers, families assigned high random numbers are not any younger or older, more or less educated, smaller or larger, and so on.

One way to look at what random assignment achieves is to compare the means of the treatment and control groups formed by use of the random variable, before the start of the program. Table 12.2 does this for three relevant variables: education, age, and work experience.[2]

Table 12.2   Comparing means

	Treatment	Control
Education (years)	11.6	11.5
Age (years)	34.5	34.7
Work experience (years)	7.7	8.0

Note:*p < .05.

_____

[2]These results are not from the actual FTP evaluation but rather based on real data from another survey. For purposes of this numerical example, the survey respondents were assigned to a treatment group and a control group using a random number.

The differences in means between the treatment and control groups are trivial. In fact, they are only random differences, as confirmed by statistical significance tests (indicated by the lack of stars in Table 12.2). So we say that the two groups are *statistically equivalent*, that is, equivalent within the bounds of what differences might arise just by chance.

Table 12.3 is a matrix of correlation coefficients that illustrates this same point another way. Recall from Chapter 8 that correlation coefficients range from −1 to +1 and indicate the direction and strength of a statistical relationship. A correlation coefficient of zero indicates no relationship. The correlations between the random number and the other variables are all very close to zero, indicating no relationship. Thus, the random number is only very weakly (randomly) correlated with the variables education, age, and work experience. In contrast, education is negatively related to age (older people did not get as much education as younger people generally do these days) and positively related to work experience. Indeed, all the variables other than the random number have statistically significant (starred) relationships with each other. Provided the number of subjects is large enough so that any chance differences average out, randomized assignment ensures statistical equivalence.

Table 12.3   Correlations Among Variables

	Random Number	**Education**	**Age**	**Work Experience**
Random number	1.00	0.01	−0.01	−0.02
Education	0.01	1.00	−0.11*	0.34*
Age	−0.01	−0.11*	1.00	0.25*
Work experience	−0.02	0.34*	0.25*	1.00

Note: *$p < .05$.

Why Random Assignment Is Better Than Matching or Control Variables

We want this kind of statistical equivalence not only for variables that we have measured, such as education, age, and work experience, but also for important characteristics that are not measured, such as having neighbors with good job connections or being highly motivated. Fortunately, because FTP used random assignment, the near-zero correlations and the trivial differences in means happen not just with these three variables (education, age, and work experience) but also with any other variables or characteristics we might think of. It applies to characteristics that are easy to record, such as the number of children in the family, as well as those that are more elusive or difficult to measure, such as personality or motivation. Whatever it is, the random number will be uncorrelated with it (or nearly so), and the means for the treatment and control groups created by use of the random number will be the same, except for chance differences.

This fact, statistical equivalence on *all* variables, is what makes random assignment better than *matching* or pairing units based only on observed similarities—and better than using control variables. No matter how careful or detailed the matching—or how sophisticated the control variables—there is always the possibility that some unmeasured difference or common cause lurks beneath the surface and may bias the results later on. Random assignment statistically equalizes the groups across all possible variables—measured, unmeasured, and even unimagined alike.

Many, including organizations such as the Coalition for Evidence-Based Policy (described in their own words in Box 12.2) advocate wider use of randomized field experiments because of their superior evidence of causation.

BOX 12.2
The Coalition for Evidence-Based Policy

The Coalition for Evidence-Based Policy is a nonprofit organization that promotes the use of randomized experiments to evaluate social programs. Here is what they say about themselves on their Web site, www.coalition4evidence.org:

> The Coalition is a nonprofit, nonpartisan organization, whose mission is to increase government effectiveness through rigorous evidence about what works. In the field of medicine, public policies based on scientifically-rigorous evidence have produced extraordinary advances in health over the past 50 years. By contrast, in most areas of social policy—such as education, poverty reduction, crime and justice, and substance abuse prevention—government programs often are implemented with little regard to evidence, costing billions of dollars yet failing to address critical needs of our society. However, rigorous studies have identified a few highly-effective social interventions, suggesting that a concerted government strategy to build the number of these proven interventions, and spur their widespread use, could bring rapid progress to social policy similar to that which transformed medicine.

> The Coalition advocates many types of research to identify the most promising social interventions. However, a central theme of our advocacy, consistent with a recent National Academy of Sciences recommendation, is that evidence of effectiveness generally cannot be considered definitive without ultimate confirmation in well-conducted randomized controlled trials.

Source: The Coalition for Evidence-Based Policy (2009).

Findings: What Happened in Pensacola

We've seen how random assignment makes families in the FTP treatment and AFDC control groups statistically equivalent. If we left well enough alone, yet followed the families over time, we would logically expect much the same outcome from both groups—jobs, births, divorces, whatever it is we're interested in. But of course, we don't leave things alone: We expose one group to the new FTP program and the other to the old AFDC program. Since this difference in treatments is the only variable that systematically distinguishes the two groups, any difference in outcomes can be attributed to the treatment and the treatment alone.

So let's look now at what actually happened to the 2,817 families in the Pensacola area that were randomly assigned to the FTP treatment (the new time-limited welfare program) or the AFDC control condition. Were the outcomes the same or not? After 4 years, only 6% of families in the FTP treatment ended up receiving welfare on a long-term basis, compared with 17% in the AFDC control group. Families in the FTP treatment group had more earnings earlier on in the study period, although by the end of the 4 years, the two groups had about the same earnings. There was little difference between the groups in material hardship, with both groups reporting frequent difficulties paying bills and buying food and other necessities. As for the children, there were no real differences between the treatment and control group in the children's educational performance at the elementary levels. At the upper grade levels, however, the children in the FTP treatment group actually performed somewhat worse in school than did those in the AFDC control group. The researchers speculated that the increased maternal employment associated with FTP might have had negative consequences for some of the older children. (Speculation such as this can be addressed with qualitative research, as we discuss later.)

The Logic of Randomized Experiments: Another Look

A randomized experiment seeks to isolate the causal relationship between one explanatory variable, the treatment (X), and one or more response variable, or outcome (Y). If we were to draw a model of just this relationship, it would look like this:

$$\text{Treatment} \rightarrow \text{Outcome}$$

or

$$X \rightarrow Y$$

But what about all the other multifarious, real-world chains of cause and effect that produce a complex outcome such as employment? Indeed, all the intricate personal and situational causes of employment do still come into play—one's education, age, work experience, motivation, the local job market, and so on. But because of random assignment, as we have just seen, the treatment itself is not related to any of these other factors. The treatment cuts through this tangle of nonexperimental influences as a light beam cuts through a driving rain. Figure 12.2 provides a visual image, a path model, of what a randomized experiment achieves.

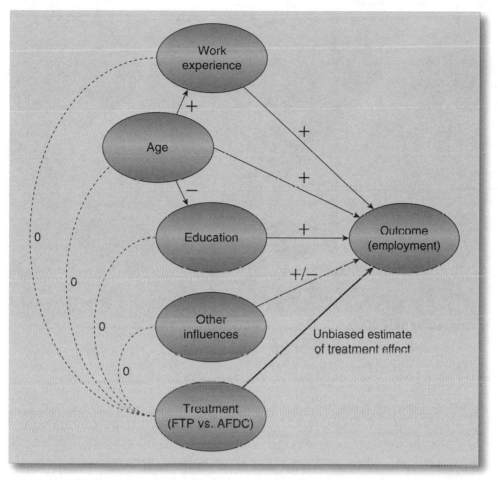

Figure 12.2   Path Model of the FTP Experiment

All the other variables and influences are still there in Figure 12.2, and they still have their relationships with employment (the outcome) and each other. The experiment doesn't change any of this. But the treatment variable, as the dotted lines and 0 correlations indicate, is not related to any of these other variables or influences. It operates alone and apart.

As a result, the link between the treatment and outcome emerges as an unbiased—in the sense of unconfounded with any other variable or influence—estimate of the effect of the treatment, and the treatment alone, on the outcome.

So variable X, the treatment, is known to be independent from and uncorrelated with all other variables causing Y—in other words, it is *exogenous*.

Take another brief example: A student's performance on a test is produced by a process or system (which we could represent by a model) that includes the influence of parents, siblings, peers, innate

Many causes influence how well a student does on a test.

Source: © iStockphoto.com/scottdunlap.

ability, sleep and eating habits, and all the other factors that go into how well a student performs on a given day when he or she takes a test. If we want to know the true effect, for example, of class size as a factor, we want class size to be exogenous—to come from outside this messy tangle of other variables and relationships that influence the student's reading performance. Assigning class size randomly to students ensures this: It imposes a given class size on students from outside—from above as it were—regardless of the other characteristics or influences exerting themselves on the student. Thus, class size randomly assigned is exogenous.

Statistical Significance of an Experimental Result

Statistical significance tests—such as a *t* test for the difference between two means (discussed in Chapter 8)—has a special meaning in the context of a randomized experiment. Let's say we observe that a result, average reading test score, appears higher in the treatment group than in the control group—like this:

Treatment group mean = 223

Control group mean = 216

There are four possible explanations—and only four—for this result:

1. The treatment caused the outcome.

2. The outcome caused the treatment (reverse causation).

3. Something else, correlated with the treatment (a common cause), caused the outcome.

4. The outcome just happened by chance.

In a randomized experiment, the researcher's ability to impose a treatment, exogenously, eliminates Number 2 as an explanation. And the statistical equivalence produced by random assignment, as we have just seen, eliminates Number 3 as a possible explanation.

Still, just by chance, random assignment might have produced an unhappy result—a chance difference in the means, which is Explanation 4. So we apply a significance test and ask, "Is the difference in means larger than we would expect, just from the luck of the draw (random assignment)?" If it is a larger-than-chance difference—if the result is statistically significant—then we can reject Number 4 as an explanation. And so the winner is . . . Number 1, the treatment caused the difference.

One important lesson here is that statistical significance tests cannot prove causation on their own; to do so, they must be considered together with the overall design of the study, such as a randomized experiment. Statistical significance tests used in nonexperimental studies to estimate causal effects must be interpreted with caution.

Do the Results Have Practical or Policy Significance?

Beware of statistically significant *yet practically trivial* treatment effects. With a large enough treatment and control group, even minor differences in means can turn out to be statistically significant. And because the result comes from a randomized experiment, we know the treatment caused the difference. So it can happen that a randomized experiment gives us strong evidence that the treatment caused a tiny effect. Always look carefully at the size, or magnitude, of the reported treatment effect—not just its statistical significance.

Generalizability of Randomized Experiments

Although randomized experiments provide convincing evidence of cause and effect, this often comes at a price: limited generalizability. We will look at some of the reasons for this trade-off. At the outset, however, it is important to understand the basic difference between random assignment and random sampling.

Random Assignment Versus Random Sampling

Randomized experiments demonstrate causation primarily through the device of *random assignment*, as we have seen. However, random assignment to a treatment or control group is not at all the same thing as *random sampling*—and it is critical to distinguish the two.

Random sampling, discussed in Chapter 5, uses chance to select a sample of units from a larger population, as when telephone numbers are dialed at random to conduct an opinion poll. Using relatively small samples of large populations, random sampling enables accurate *descriptions* of the population, including accurate descriptions of the correlations within those populations. As we have seen, random *sampling* by itself, however, does nothing to help establish a cause-effect relationship between variables.

Limits of Random Sampling Revisited: The Current Population Survey

The Current Population Survey (CPS), which involves a scientifically conducted random sample of about 60,000 households in all 50 states in the United States, shows convincingly that owning a computer is strongly associated with greater employment and earnings. Does this prove that computer ownership *causes* greater earnings? Not really. It could be that having a job gives people the extra income to afford a computer (reverse causation), not the other way around. Maybe those who own computers are more comfortable with and good at technology, and it is this talent that causes their higher employment and earnings along with their ownership of a computer (common cause). Maybe those who don't own computers simply tend to be older people who did not grow up with computer technology, and older people are less likely to be working and earning high incomes (another common cause).

The CPS is one of the most important and most rigorous random sample surveys of the United States, but it still provides us only with evidence of correlation—not causation. To try to disentangle the causal effect of computer ownership on earnings, we could use the control variables approach from Chapter 11, first speculating on and looking for evidence of common causes and then including relevant control variables in a multiple regression. However, the effect we estimate from control variables could still be biased due to reverse causation and unmeasured common causes. To get really convincing evidence of whether and how much computer ownership causally influences people's ability to work and earn money, we would need to set up a randomized experiment that uses random *assignment*. We could randomly assign people to a treatment group that gets a free computer, let's say, and a control group that does not. We could then follow up after some time and compare their earnings.

The Limited Settings of Randomized Field Experiments

Because they take place in the real world of policy and programs, randomized field experiments are more realistic than small-scale, highly artificial laboratory experiments. But because of the challenges and constraints of experimenting in the real world, they can still have limited generalizability.

Geographic Limitations

The Pensacola time-limited welfare experiment provided rigorous evidence of cause and effect—but only for welfare applicants in Escambia County, Florida. The researchers make a case that Escambia County is fairly typical of Florida counties. But how would such a policy work in a different part of the country, say, in a northern big city or a western rural area? The Pensacola experiment cannot directly answer these questions because its findings are limited in space.

The fact that experiments require a great deal of planning and close control often means that they must be confined to one small area or location. Only the most expensive social experiments—such as the RAND Health Insurance Experiment (see Box 12.3) or the more recent Moving to Opportunity (see Box 12.7) housing voucher experiment—can afford to operate in multiple locations. And even these experiments include only a handful of locations. In contrast, many (though certainly not all) observational studies involve large probability samples representing large national or even international populations.

BOX 12.3
The RAND Health Insurance Experiment

The RAND Health Insurance Experiment (HIE) was a 15-year, multimillion-dollar randomized field experiment. Results of the study helped make the cash copayment to visit a doctor nearly universal. To this day, its results are used as inputs for virtually any projection of the effects of a change in health insurance policy. Here is the RAND Corporation's own description of the HIE:

In the early 1970s, financing and the impact of cost sharing took center stage in the national health care debate. At the time, the debate focused on free, universal health care and whether the benefits would justify the costs. To inform this debate, an interdisciplinary team of RAND researchers designed and carried out the HIE, one of the largest and most comprehensive social science experiments ever performed in the United States.

The HIE posed three basic questions:

- How does cost sharing or membership in an HMO affect use of health services compared with free care?
- How does cost sharing or membership in an HMO affect appropriateness and quality of care received?
- What are the consequences for health?

The HIE was a large-scale, randomized experiment conducted between 1971 and 1982. For the study, RAND recruited 2,750 families encompassing more than 7,700 individuals, all of whom were less than 65 years of age. They were chosen from six sites across the United States to provide a regional and urban/rural balance. Participants were randomly assigned to one of five types of health insurance plans created specifically for the experiment.

Source: RAND Corporation (n.d.). See Newhouse (1993) for further information.

Limitations in Time

The period of the FTP experiment, the mid-1990s, had a fairly strong labor market. Indeed, the majority of families in the AFDC control group left welfare and found jobs during the study period. What would the effects of time limits look like in a weaker labor market, say, during a severe recession? The Pensacola experiment cannot directly answer this question because its findings are limited in time. For programs and outcomes of social relevance, effects may vary over time in important ways.

Randomized field experiments can sometimes take quite a long time to plan and implement, with final results arriving many years after the study was initially commissioned to answer a policy or practice issue. In this way, randomized field experiments can have limited generalizability to more immediate policy or practice debates. In contrast, the use of observational data from existing government and other surveys typically provides much faster results (although with less certainty about causation).

Volunteers and Generalizability

Many randomized experiments rely on volunteers. For ethical reasons, most clinical trials in medicine obtain their subjects by recruiting informed volunteers from a hospital or its surrounding community. (See the Johns Hopkins advertisement below.) Volunteers may be quite different from those who do not volunteer. They may suffer more from the ailment being treated; they may have stronger financial

Advertisement to recruit volunteers for an experiment.

Source: Craigslist.org

or other motivations to join the experiment; and they may trust more in doctors and modern medicine. The effectiveness of the treatment in a group of volunteers, therefore, may be quite different from its effectiveness in a group of nonvolunteers.

Volunteering makes the participants in a randomized experiment different from what random sampling would provide. Volunteers could differ in systematic ways that influence the effect of the treatment and hence the generalizability of the experimental results to a broader population. Even if those who volunteer look like the population on observable characteristics, such as age or education, they might be different in unobservable ways relevant to the outcome of the study. The results of an experiment thus generalize only to the people or other units like those that volunteered.

For example, think about a randomized field experiment to evaluate the effect of a substance abuse treatment program. Individuals who are utterly unmotivated to kick the habit might refuse to participate, while those who genuinely want to stop using drugs are likely to volunteer. In this case, the experiment would estimate the effect of the program on *drug users already motivated to quit*. Results would not generalize to the population of drug users at large.[3]

The Ideal Study: Random Sampling, Then Random Assignment

In an ideal world, researchers would first randomly *sample* subjects from a population of interest (say, all welfare-eligible families in the United States). They would then randomly *assign* the individuals in the sample to a treatment group and control group, apply (or withhold) the treatment, and observe the outcome. The estimated cause-effect relationship would then be generalizable to the whole population from which the sample came, and we would have the best of all possible studies: solid causal evidence (thanks to random *assignment*) and wide generalizability (thanks to random *sampling*).

But imagine how difficult it would be to keep track of several hundred or more treatment and control group members scattered across nearly as many cities and towns, not to mention how difficult it would be to provide each one with a uniform program or other treatment. Unless the treatment is very simple to administer, such as providing different versions of a questionnaire to survey respondents in a split-ballot experiment (see Box 12.4), doing random sampling and then random assignment are not feasible for most policies or programs of interest.

BOX 12.4
Split-Ballot Experiments in Survey Research

Split-ballot experiments in survey research are one of the few types of studies that use both *random sampling* and *random assignment*. They begin with a random (probability) *sample* of respondents, using survey sampling methods, then randomly *assign* respondents to different versions of a question. The aim is to test the effect of wording or other aspects of asking a question on survey results. Here is an example:

(Continued)

---

[3]Thanks to Katherine E. Harris for suggesting this example.

(Continued)

An experimental comparison of question forms used to reduce vote overreporting.

Via telephone, a national probability sample of 1464 respondents randomly received one of three question versions of a voter turnout question in the months of December, January, and February, following the November 1998 Congressional elections in the United States. The long version form contained memory cueing techniques and face-saving response options, the short form, modeled after the 2000 American National Election Studies (ANES) question, included only the face-saving response options, and the standard form, modeled after ANES questions used before 2000, included neither. The long form led to significantly lower reported turnout in comparison to both the short and standard forms, indicating that the long form successfully reduced vote overreporting in comparison to the other question versions.

Split-ballot studies such as this are used for finding new and better ways to ask survey questions, especially when respondents are prone to overreport socially desirable behaviors (such as voting or exercising) or underreport socially undesirable behaviors (such as drug use or domestic violence).

Source: Belli, Moore, and VanHoewyk (2006).

However, an NSF-funded program called Time-Sharing Experiments for the Social Sciences (TESS) has tried to increase the use of such random assignment experiments implemented on random samples of broad populations (See Box 12.5). One of the goals of the program is to increase the generalizability of randomized experiments, particularly for topics in which a convenience sample (most often, undergraduate students at university campuses) may be inadequate or misleading.

BOX 12.5
Randomized Experiments on Random Samples

Time-Sharing Experiments for the Social Sciences (TESS) is an NSF infrastructure project that offers researchers opportunities to test their experimental ideas on large, diverse, randomly selected subject populations. Investigators submit proposals for experimental studies, and TESS fields selected proposals on a random sample of the

United States population using the Internet. TESS thereby allows investigators to capture the internal validity of experiments while realizing the benefits of contact with large, diverse populations of research participants.

Source: http://tess.experimentcentral.org (n.d.).

Generalizability of the Treatment

Frequently, experiments involve model programs that are carefully administered by motivated staff and funders. When the program gets taken to scale, moving out of the "hothouse," as it were, often subtle yet important changes occur that may alter the effectiveness of the program. The staff administering the program may care less about clients than during the experimental period. The procedures of the program may become more confusing and bureaucratic. Even important features of the program—such as the amount of funding for services—may change. Because of the possibility of such changes, the treatment itself in a randomized field experiment may not generalize to how it would operate as a full-scale program.

In sum, most randomized experiments rely on volunteers, occur in limited locations, and involve treatments that may not match full-scale programs. Therefore, randomized field experiments often do not generalize perfectly to the real world of policy and programs.

Variations on the Design of Experiments

So far, we have considered a randomized experiment that looks a certain way—one treatment group, one control group, and a comparison of outcomes. But there are variations on the design of such experiments, so that randomized experiments can appear different and more complex than Figure 12.1 suggests.

Arms in an Experiment

To begin with, there can be more than one treatment condition, as well as more than one control condition, sometimes referred to as **arms of an experiment**. The basic randomized experiment we have been considering has just two arms, but a randomized experiment may have three or more arms. The RAND Health Insurance Experiment (see Box 12.3), one of the largest policy experiments ever, had at least five main arms, including four cost-sharing health insurance plans and one free plan, although minor variations in the four cost-sharing plans actually resulted in a total of up to 14 arms (13 cost-sharing plans and one free plan). The MTO housing voucher experiment (see Box 12.7) had three arms: housing vouchers with a mobility requirement (that families move to low-poverty census tracts), ordinary housing vouchers (without a mobility requirement), and a control group that received no vouchers.

Factors in an Experiment

So far, we have focused on experiments examining the effect of a single independent variable. Some experiments try to examine the effect of more than one independent variable, called **factors**, and how they interact with one another. These are referred to as **factorial designs**. The simplest and most common is a two-factor design in which two independent variables each take on two possible values, in all possible combinations, resulting in four arms. For example, a public health experiment in Indonesia (Lind et al., 2004) examined the effects of iron and zinc supplements on the development of infants, randomizing subjects to one of four conditions:

Arm 1: 10 mg iron

Arm 2: 10 mg zinc

Arm 3: 10 mg iron and 10 mg zinc

Arm 4: Placebo (no iron, no zinc)

The iron supplement constitutes the first factor, the zinc supplement is the second factor, and the combined supplement tests the *interaction* of the two factors, all of which are compared with the control condition (placebo). This particular study found that although both iron and zinc were beneficial, the interaction of the two supplements did little to further improve the physical or cognitive development of young children in Indonesia.

Sometimes experiments test more than two factors, although the sample size must be quite large to do this. Even with a 2 × 2 factorial design, the sample size needed to test the interaction is usually much larger than to test the single treatments.

Heterogeneous Treatment Effects

We have been referring to *the* treatment effect, using the singular. However, it is reasonable to expect that different people respond differently to time limits on welfare, housing vouchers, or any other treatment—something researchers call **heterogeneous treatment effects**. Time limits may have different effects for mothers with young children than for mothers with teenagers. Time limits might differently affect someone with a self-reliant personality from someone who prefers structure and authority. In a randomized experiment, what we really estimate is an *average treatment effect* among all those who participate in the study.

For observable characteristics, such as gender, it is possible to use the data to see how treatment effects differ between groups that vary in that characteristic. For example, the Moving to Opportunity study looked at the effect on boys and on girls separately. They found that moving to a higher income neighborhood improved educational outcomes for girls but worsened them for boys. Of course, subgroups have smaller sample sizes and therefore less statistical precision.

The effects of treatment also probably differ among some subgroups that we are unable to identify. For example, the effects of job training or welfare time limits might be different depending on the motivation of the participants. But if we lack a measure of motivation, we are unable to see how treatment effectiveness varies with motivation and are forced to average over subjects with different motivation levels.

Human Artifacts in Experiments

People will be people—and this adds another layer of complexity to field experiments. People can figure out what the experiment is about, and what the researcher expects of them. They can imagine what the effects of the treatment will do to them—and even convince themselves that it is happening. Researchers themselves can let their expectations cloud their observations, measurements, and data analysis. All these *human artifacts* make doing a randomized experiment more difficult than it appears on paper (Rosnow & Rosenthal, 1997).

Placebo Effect and Blinding

The most important of these human artifacts is the so-called **placebo effect**—the fact that people often respond to any kind of treatment, even a completely phony or useless one. This is similar to the **Hawthorne effect**, a less precise term that refers to various effects produced by participants' awareness of the experimental situation, particularly the effect of researchers' attention (Draper, 2008).

For example, if we were to give you a sugar pill (without mentioning that it was only a sugar pill) and tell you that the pill was designed to make people mentally more alert while learning complex material such as research methods—it might actually work. You might feel more alert, read more carefully, and get more out of this book. But this effect would be entirely due to your belief in the power of the pill—not anything in the pill itself.

Blind experiments correct this problem by keeping subjects ignorant of which group they are in. This typically involves giving a *placebo* to the control group—a lack of treatment masquerading as a treatment. Therefore, both treatment and control groups are subject to the placebo effect and the control group makes a valid counterfactual to the treatment group.

Subjects can also respond to their desire to satisfy the researchers' expectations, a problem, given that the researchers often expect or hope that the treatment group will perform better. This weakness can be addressed through **double-blind experiments**, in which the research workers who interact with the subjects, or make measurements, are also ignorant about which group the subjects are in.

The Difficulty of Placebos in Social Policy Experiments

Giving the control group a placebo is practical for drug studies but more difficult for many social programs. After all, people know whether or not they went through a job training program, received a housing voucher, or obtained free health insurance. Thus, the placebo effect is a real issue in many randomized social or policy experiments.

For example, consider the results of the famous Perry Preschool Study (see Box 12.6), which is widely cited as evidence for the long-term benefits of early childhood education. The experiment evaluated a model preschool program in Ypsilanti, Michigan, and the research team followed up with 58 kids in the treatment group and 65 in the control group for an unusually long time, well into their adulthood. Interestingly, although the initial effects on IQ and achievement tests had mostly leveled off by second grade, the researchers began to discover large differences by adolescence and into adulthood. The treatment group was more likely to graduate from high school, go to college, earn more income, own a house, and stay out of prison.

But why this delayed reaction? As the treatment group matured into adulthood, they were regularly contacted and interviewed by the research team and even the media, heightening their awareness of their special status as Perry Preschool Graduates. They might have come to view themselves as special and to be aware that the researchers and others in society had high expectations of them. Perhaps these expectations encouraged them to finish school, go to college, buy a house, and so on. Or perhaps the effects of high-quality preschool are indeed latent for a time, only to emerge with force later on in life. But the placebo effect possibility at least deserves careful consideration in such social policy experiments.

BOX 12.6
The Perry Preschool Study

The High/Scope Perry Preschool Project is one of the longest running randomized field experiments to test a public policy or program. It involved 123 African American children from Ypsilanti, Michigan, identified in the 1960s as being at high risk for school failure and related problems. Here is how the HighScope Educational Research Foundation, the organization that ran the experiment, describes it:

> From 1962–1967, at ages 3 and 4, the subjects were randomly divided into a program group that received a high-quality preschool program based on High/Scope's participatory learning approach and a comparison group who received no preschool program. In the study's most recent phase, 97% of the study participants still living were interviewed at age 40. Additional data were gathered from the subjects' school, social services, and arrest records.

> The study found that adults at age 40 who had the preschool program had higher earnings, were more likely to hold a job, had committed fewer crimes, and were more likely to have graduated from high school than adults who did not have preschool.

Source: HighScope Educational Research Foundation (2005).

Unobtrusive or Nonreactive Measures

Randomized experiments confront the problem that the situation under study must be manipulated or disturbed to be observed. Thus, not even the control group, strictly speaking, represents a purely natural condition. Still, we use the control group as a *counterfactual* estimate—what would have happened in the absence of treatment. But, in actual fact, we are unable to measure what would have happened without recruitment, informed consent, measurement, and all the rest of the experiences the treatment and control group go through to be part of the study.

Because of this dilemma, researchers often prefer **unobtrusive** or **nonreactive measures**—measures that occur naturally or routinely, or otherwise do not disturb the subjects in an experiment (Webb, Campbell, Schwartz, & Sechrest, 1999). In a school-based experiment, for example, the usual tests given each year to all students would be a kind of unobtrusive measure, since they are not imposed by the experimenters.

We should point out, however, that the need for unobtrusive or nonreactive measures arises in nonexperimental research as well, including purely descriptive studies of people's attitudes or behaviors. For example, say we are trying to measure the food intake of a sample of adults and ask them to save duplicate servings of what they eat in bags for laboratory analysis (a method sometimes used to study food intake). The act of saving duplicate servings in bags, however, is quite likely to alter what people eat—it is an obtrusive, reactive method that makes people much more self-conscious of the type and quantity of food they consume.

Contamination

In a randomized experiment, the researcher controls what treatment the subjects are exposed to—at least, in theory. In practice, however, the control group may gain access or exposure to the treatment, either intentionally or unintentionally. For example, in an experimental evaluation of a new curriculum, the teachers in the control group might find out about the new curriculum, from casual conversation or observation, and decide to try some of the methods or materials themselves. This is one example of **contamination**—something happens that messes up the integrity and logic of the experiment.

Cluster Randomization

To prevent leakage of the treatment to the control group, and resulting contamination, randomization is sometimes done at the group or cluster level, rather than at the individual level. For example, schools could be randomized to the new curriculum to keep people in the treatment and control group isolated from each other. This is referred to as **cluster randomization** and is illustrated in Figure 12.3. As the figure shows, clustering results in randomizing fewer, larger aggregate units to the treatment and control conditions. The cost of such clustering is less statistical power—less statistical equivalence from randomization—even though it helps prevent contamination. If there are only a few aggregate units to randomly assign (as the four clusters shown in the simplified Figure 12.3), cluster randomization turns into more of a quasi experiment (discussed in Chapter 13).

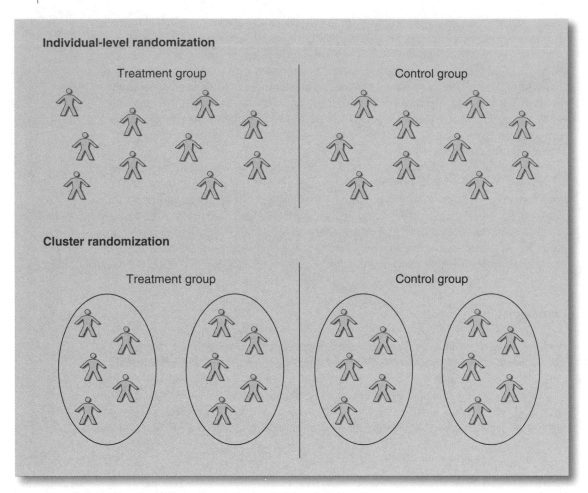

Figure 12.3   Individual-Level and Cluster Randomization (Random Assignment)

Demoralization and Rivalry

The members of the control group may feel neglected and left out because they are not getting the promising new treatment. They could become *demoralized* and take a turn for the worse (worse than they would have been had they not been involved in the experiment to begin with). If so, the treatment would seem more effective than it really is.

Alternately, the control group may engage in *competitive rivalry*, as when the teachers of classes designated as the control group try extra hard to teach their kids to read so that they don't fall behind those classes that received the special, model reading curriculum.

Both phenomena make the experience of the control different in the experimental setting than it would be in the real, unmanipulated world.

Noncompliance

Another problem can occur when the treatment group fails to fully comply with the treatment. For example, they may grow weary of the side effects of a medication and begin to stop taking it, or they may fail to complete a training program. In this case, the treatment whose effect is being measured is not the one intended or advertised.

Often with real-world programs or treatments, the best we can do is to offer or make it available—we can't force people to comply. As a result, what we may want to estimate after all is the effect of simply providing treatment, not necessarily having it taken up. We will have more to say about this issue shortly when we discuss the analysis of data from randomized experiments.

Attrition

Another problem with randomized experiments in the real world is **attrition**—participants dropping out from the experiment. For example, members of the control group lose interest in the experiment (after all, they are not getting the fancy new treatment, so why continue?). If those who drop out are systematically different from those who do not drop out, the study results may be biased. Researchers can examine empirically whether those who drop out differ in measured variables from those who did not. If they do, methods exist to lessen the bias. Of course, those who drop out could also differ in unmeasured ways.

If there is no final outcome data for those who drop out, attrition bias due to unmeasured differences is extremely difficult to avoid. However, if some outcome or proxy outcome can be found, then the bias can be reduced by simply comparing everyone in the treatment group, dropout or not, with everyone in the control group. We will cover this approach in more detail shortly.

Analysis of Randomized Experiments

The analysis of data from a randomized experiment, in contrast to observational data, is fairly straightforward, for the most part. It does not usually require theorizing about and modeling common causes (as we did in the previous chapter), because a well-done randomized experiment statistically equalizes groups on all variables (measured and unmeasured). Therefore, the analysis of randomized experiments generally does not require control variables or multiple regression.

With just one treatment group and one control group, an experiment can be analyzed simply by comparing means (with a two-sample t test of significance) or proportions (with a two-sample z test for proportions or a chi-square test). ANOVA (analysis of variance, discussed in Chapter 8) can be used to compare three or more group means across all arms of an experiment as well as to examine interactions (Brown & Melamed, 1990). Equivalently, ordinary regression with treatment dummy variables can also be used instead of t tests or ANOVA.

But because experiments do not always turn out as planned, complexities can crop up sometimes in the analysis of randomized experiments (Bloom, 2005). We review some of these below.

Balancing and the Occasional Need for Control Variables

In a randomized experiment, it can happen that an important influence on the outcome cannot be *balanced* in the arms because the sample size is too small. Balancing refers to equalization of common causes in the arms of an experiment so that the treatment and control groups are equivalent in all relevant ways. In medicine, for example, randomized experiments generally have the sample size chosen to ensure precision for medical outcomes, but researchers sometimes want to analyze financial outcomes, such as cost, also. Because costs and their causes (e.g., length of stay in the hospital) are often very skewed, the treatment and control arms may not be statistically equalized for those variables; thus, the use of certain control variables may be appropriate.

When control variables are needed to analyze an experiment, researchers will often use ANCOVA (analysis of covariance) as the statistical technique, or equivalently, multiple regression. However, such situations are rare: Generally, randomized experiments do not require control variables.

Sample Size and Minimal Detectable Effects

When conducting a randomized experiment, the analysis should be planned in advance to ensure an adequate sample size. Sample size refers to the number of units or subjects in the treatment and control groups. Clustering reduces the effective sample size because the clusters (e.g., classrooms) are randomized, not the individuals within clusters (e.g., students). Additional arms in an experiment also reduce the effective sample size because the units or subjects must be divided across multiple treatment groups. Sample size matters: You do not want to waste the time, effort and money required to conduct a randomized experiment only to end up with insufficient precision to draw useful conclusions.

Sample size calculations, such as the ones described in Chapter 8, always require assumptions, such as assumptions about the variances of key variables. However, for experiments, one must also specify the desired **minimal detectable effect**—the smallest effect that would still have practical significance. The smaller this desired minimal detectable effect, the more precision and therefore the larger the sample size needed to detect it. Bloom (1995) provides a useful approach to these issues.

Intent to Treat Analysis

As we have seen, units or subjects in a randomized experiment sometimes drop out of the study (attrition) or fail to comply or take up the treatment. What if these people experience systematically different outcomes from those who remain in the study and comply fully with the treatment? If we simply remove the dropouts or noncompliers from our analysis, we could bias the estimated treatment effects.

The safest method for dealing with either attrition or noncompliance is referred to as **intent to treat (ITT)**. Specifically, everyone is kept in their original randomized group—treatment or control. The ITT effect is the difference in outcome between the originally assigned groups, regardless of whether they were exposed to the treatment. ITT avoids all self-selection problems—whether due to noncompliance or attrition.

ITT works well for noncompliance. However, for attrition, final outcomes may not be collected for those who leave, and it may be impossible to calculate an ITT estimate. To the extent that ITT can be calculated, however, it is often the most relevant effect to estimate because, as we noted earlier in this chapter, often in the real world we can only offer treatments—not force people to use them.

Nonetheless, policymakers and researchers sometimes would like to know the actual effect of treatment itself. An example will make this clearer.

Treatment of the Treated in Moving to Opportunity

Moving to Opportunity (MTO) is a randomized experiment in which low-income families in the treatment group were given vouchers usable only in low-poverty neighborhoods and counseling to help them find housing in those neighborhoods (Ludwig et al., 2008; Orr et al., 2003). MTO is described further in Box 12.7. Still, slightly less than half of those in the treatment group in fact moved to low-poverty neighborhoods. In the jargon of medical RCTs, slightly less than half "complied," although their lack of compliance may have been due to factors beyond their control.

Although the ITT estimate is useful, the researchers (Ludwig et al., 2008) decided that

for both scientific reasons (to understand the direct causal effect of location on outcomes) and policy reasons (to allow extrapolation to other mobility programs and settings where compliance rates may be different), it would be desirable to have an estimate of the impact of moving per se. (pp. 152–153)

Therefore, the researchers also estimated what is referred to as the **treatment of the treated (TOT)**—an estimate of the effect of the treatment on those who were actually exposed to it.

To understand TOT, we must first consider several categories of subjects, as illustrated in Table 12.4. Within those families in the treatment group (those given vouchers for low-poverty neighborhoods) in the first column, some moved (the compliers) and some did not (the noncompliers). And evidence shows that compliers and noncompliers differ in ways that may influence the outcome.

Because the control group was created through randomization, it also contains two subgroups that are statistically equivalent to the treatment subgroups: would-be compliers and would-be noncompliers. They are equivalent on average to the corresponding treatment subgroups, subject only to small statistical fluctuations. In a randomized experiment, the control group implements the counterfactual— what would have happened to the treatment group if it had not had the treatment. The same is true of these subgroups.

For the TOT estimator, we would like to know the difference in outcomes between the treatment group compliers (Subgroup A) and the control group would-be compliers (Subgroup B). Our only problem is that we cannot observe the control group would-be compliers (Subgroup B) because we don't know which of the families not offered vouchers would have in fact used them, had they been given the chance.

To calculate the TOT estimator, therefore, we must make some assumptions: First, being placed in the treatment group has no effect on noncompliers. Second, being in the control group has no effect on anyone, neither would-be compliers nor would-be noncompliers. In other words, we assume

Table 12.4   Subgroups in Moving to Opportunity for TOT Calculation

	Treatment Group	Control Group
Compliers	A Moved to low-poverty neighborhood using voucher. Only group affected by experiment	B Would have moved to low-poverty neighborhood if given voucher but not given voucher. No effect of experiment assumed
Noncompliers	C Did not move to low-poverty neighborhood despite having voucher. No effect of experiment assumed	D Would not have moved to low-poverty neighborhood if given voucher or not given voucher. No effect of experiment assumed

no human artifacts of being in an experiment. With these assumptions, *among those who would not comply*, the effect of being in the treatment group relative to the control group is zero, because neither subgroup is affected in any way.

Consequently, the entire ITT effect is driven by the difference between the treatment and control groups *among those who would comply*. From that we know that

$$ITT = \text{Share compliers} \times TOT.$$

The share of compliers (a proportion) is known from the experimental group, and it must be the same in the control group, due to randomization. Thus, the TOT effect is simply ITT effect divided by the share of compliers:

$$TOT = ITT/\text{Share compliers}.$$

The TOT is larger than the ITT because, though all the ITT effect was due only to the compliers, the effect was attributed to the larger group of both compliers and noncompliers. (See Ludwig et al., 2008, pp. 152–154, and Orr et al., 2003, Appendix B, for further discussion.)

Because somewhat less than half of those offered vouchers in fact moved to low-poverty neighborhoods, the difference between the ITT and TOT estimates was large in the MTO evaluation. For example, using the ITT estimator, parents given vouchers to move to a low-poverty neighborhood had a psychological distress measure of 0.1 standard deviations lower than those not given vouchers. But using the TOT estimator, those who moved had a psychological distress measure of 0.2 standard deviations lower than those who did not move, among those who would move if given vouchers (Ludwig et al., 2008, p. 163). The TOT estimate is twice the ITT estimate because only about half of those given vouchers "complied"—moved to a low-poverty neighborhood.

BOX 12.7
The Moving to Opportunity Demonstration

In the 1990s, the U.S. Department of Housing and Urban Development (HUD) conducted a large-scale randomized field experiment called Moving to Opportunity for Fair Housing (MTO). MTO examined the issue of how poor families living in housing projects run by the local public housing authority (PHA) could benefit from housing vouchers and counseling that allowed them to move to low-poverty neighborhoods with better schools, safety, and public services. Here is HUD's description of the experimental design of MTO:

> Five public housing authorities (Baltimore, Boston, Chicago, Los Angeles, and New York City) administer HUD contracts under this 10-year demonstration. Within the PHAs, randomly selected experimental groups of households with children receive housing counseling and vouchers that must be used in areas with less than 10 percent poverty. Families chosen for the experimental group receive tenant-based Section 8 rental assistance that helps pay their rent, as well as housing counseling to help them find and successfully use housing in low-poverty areas. Two control groups are included to test the effects of the program: one group already receiving Section 8 assistance and another just coming into the Section 8 program.

Source: U.S. Department of Housing and Urban Development (n.d.).

See Orr et al. (2003) for a complete description of the experiment. See Ludwig et al. (2008) for more recent results, citations to other MTO results, and valuable discussion of what can and cannot be learned from randomized experiments.

Qualitative Methods and Experiments

Randomized field experiments generally fall into the category of quantitative research, but there are important ways in which qualitative research can help inform both the design and the interpretation of a randomized field experiment.

Before an experiment is implemented, exploratory qualitative research can inform the study's design, including the choice of variables for which quantitative data are gathered and identification of appropriate sites or locations for the field experiment. As an experiment is implemented, qualitative methods can help discover contamination or human artifacts of the field experiment. And both during and after implementation, qualitative methods can help reveal the possible mechanisms or processes that produced the observed outcome, particularly if the experiment results in a somewhat unexpected outcome.

For example, as part of the MTO evaluation, HUD commissioned a series of exploratory studies, many of which used qualitative methods. These explorations suggested that the vouchers provided to the treatment group might be influencing family health, safety, delinquency patterns, and educational outcomes but perhaps not employment or economic status.

Qualitative research also helped later on, when preliminary statistical analysis showed few if any of the expected educational benefits of residential relocation of the treatment group. Qualitative researchers, who spent time interviewing families in their homes and communities after relocation, observed that although the families had relocated to lower poverty neighborhoods, many continued to send their children to the same schools that they attended when they lived in public housing (Ferryman, Briggs, Popkin, & Rendón, 2008). This was due in part to friendship patterns and social connections that tied families to their old neighborhood. It was also due to the simple fact that the families with vouchers did not move all that far away to begin with. (There were lower poverty neighborhoods near the old public housing neighborhoods, and most families preferred this option to relocating to a more distant suburban area outside the city.) Other qualitative research revealed the mechanism behind why relocated families did not find better jobs than control families (Turney, Clampet-Lundquist, Edin, Kling, & Duncan, 2006). These sorts of insights, visible to qualitative researchers on the ground, helped HUD to interpret what turned out to be complex and somewhat unexpected statistical findings from this large randomized field experiment.

Conclusion

Randomized experiments, including randomized field experiments and clinical trials, are considered the "gold standard" for demonstrating cause-effect relationships. They work by using random assignment to create statistically equivalent treatment and control groups, removing any potential bias from common-cause variables—both measured and unmeasured. In this way, randomized field experiments offer a major advantage over observational studies with control variables, which can only take into account measured common causes.

But randomized field experiments have important limitations as well. They often have limited generalizability, either because of their reliance on volunteers, their focus on small areas or populations, or their use of specialized treatments that do not resemble full-scale programs. And randomized field experiments can break down due to contamination, attrition, human artifacts, and other problems that occur in the field. Finally, it is not always possible to implement full random assignment for various ethical, political, or practical reasons.

The next chapter looks at studies that attempt to preserve some of the strengths of a randomized field experiment in the face of real-world constraints—hybrid studies known as natural experiments or quasi experiments.

BOX 12.8
Critical Questions to
Ask About a Randomized Field Experiment

- Was it a true randomized experiment—in other words, were the treatment and control groups formed by random assignment? Look closely: Often things don't quite turn out as planned. How might shortcomings in random assignment bias the results?
- Did people (or other units in the experiment such as families, classrooms, organizations) remain in the experiment, or did some drop out or leave? If so, how might this affect the results of the experiment?
- Was the treatment implemented as planned? And did all of those in the treatment group actually receive the treatment? How might problems in administering the treatment, or failure of participants to take up the treatment, bias the results?
- Was there anything unusual about the treatment? Was the staff especially motivated? Were the services especially well funded? How similar, or different, was the treatment, in comparison with other programs like it?
- Is the placebo effect a possible explanation of the results? Was the treatment group aware of the researchers' expectations, and if so, could this have influenced the treatment group's behavior?
- Where was the experiment conducted, when, and who participated? How generalizable are the study's findings to other places, programs, or people?
- How large were the reported treatment effects, in substantive or policy terms? Beware of "statistically significant" treatment effects that turn out, on closer inspection, to be only trivial differences in policy terms or in the lives of participants.

Exercises

Statistical Equivalence: Seeing Is Believing

12.1. Take an ordinary deck of 52 playing cards, shuffle the cards well, and deal them into two piles of 26. Notice that you have *randomly assigned* the cards to two groups. Now, count the number of red cards in each group. Is it exactly 13, or a little less or more? Reshuffle the deck and repeat (or have different groups or individuals in class doing this at the same time). Average the results together.

a. How does this card game illustrate the idea of *statistical equivalence*?

b. Why isn't the result exactly 13 red cards after each shuffle? How does this shed light on the use of a significance test in a randomized experiment?

Random Assignment Versus Random Sampling

12.2. Below are several examples of research. For each one, decide if it involves random assignment or random sampling.

a. A law center selects 900 civil court records at random from the archive to investigate the effect of having, versus not having, legal representation (a lawyer) on the outcome of the case.

b. A university recruits drug users and divides them, randomly, into two groups to test the effectiveness of a new prevention therapy.

c. A government statistical agency takes a probability sample of the nation's public school students, then randomly administers two different versions of a reading test to compare their difficulty.

Treatment for Alcoholism

12.3. A large randomized field experiment of treatment for alcoholics was conducted with 10,000 subjects. They were randomized to either an intensive short-term inpatient treatment program or a less intensive long-term outpatient treatment program with equal total costs. The main outcome measure is long-term (5-year) sobriety. Results showed that 35% of those in the inpatient program remained sober for 5 years, while 55% of those in the outpatient program remained sober for 5 years.

a. The p value associated with a test of the difference between the programs was less than .001. What is the statistical significance of these results?

b. What is the practical significance of these results?

c. The study was performed according to standard ethical principles of informed consent: Subjects were fully informed about what the study would entail and voluntarily chose to participate. What kinds of alcoholics would agree to participate in the experiment? What kinds would not?

d. Someone reading this impressive study concludes that long-term sobriety rates of *all* alcoholics would be 20 percentage points higher if *all* alcoholics received long-term outpatient treatment than if all alcoholics received short-term inpatient treatment. Do you think this conclusion is valid? Explain.

e. The study as described does not shed light on why the outpatient program had better results—the mechanism. Describe how the use of one qualitative method (e.g., open-ended interviews, structured interviews, focus groups, observation) during the experiment could have shed light on this issue. Briefly describe which method you think would be best and why.

Randomized Experiment in Your Field

12.4. Search one of the major journals in your field of interest for an example of a published study that is a randomized experiment. Read the abstract carefully, as well as other sections of the article as required. Then answer the following questions:

a. How did you know that it was a randomized experiment? What term was used to describe the study—clinical trial, randomized controlled trial, etc.?

b. How many arms were there in the experiment? How many factors?

c. How were subjects recruited into the experiment? How might this have affected the generalizability of the results?

d. Was there any contamination or attrition? How might this bias the results?

Objectives: In this chapter, you will learn about natural and quasi experiments—studies that approximate some, but not all, of the advantageous features of a true randomized experiment. Much applied policy research and program evaluation relies on natural or quasi experiments, in large part because true randomized experiments are often impractical or unethical. It is therefore important to know how to identify the various types of natural and quasi experiments that appear most commonly— such as difference-in-differences or interrupted time-series—and to appreciate their strengths and weaknesses. It is also important to be alert to opportunities to design or administer programs in ways that help create strong quasi experiments to better inform policy and management.

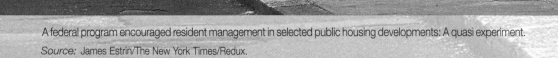

A federal program encouraged resident management in selected public housing developments: A quasi experiment.

Source: James Estrin/The New York Times/Redux.

13

Natural and Quasi Experiments

A Casino Benefits the Mental Health of Cherokee Children

Jane Costello, a mental health researcher, was at work on a long-term study of psychiatric symptoms of children in rural North Carolina, about a quarter of them from a Cherokee reservation. Midway through the study, the Cherokees opened a casino on the reservation, providing profit-sharing payments to reservation families—suddenly lifting them out of poverty. Unexpectedly, Costello and her fellow researchers found themselves with a unique opportunity to observe the causal effect of ending poverty on the mental health of children (Costello, Compton, Keeler, & Angold, 2003).[1]

Costello's results showed that among the children lifted out of poverty by the casino payments, conduct and oppositional disorders improved substantially, yet anxiety and depression did not. Poverty causes (at least in part) conduct and oppositional disorders, Costello and her colleagues could conclude, but not anxiety or depression. This was an interesting finding with important public health and social policy implications.

Researchers had long observed the correlation between poverty and poor mental health, among both children and adults, but they didn't know if poverty caused psychiatric problems (and which ones), if psychiatric problems caused low income, or if other factors caused both. But in Costello's study, the change in income came from a completely outside (exogenous) source, the new casino. This created a *natural experiment* in which additional income was suddenly added to a poor community, independent of the efforts and characteristics of the families, allowing a clearer look at the pure effect of poverty on the mental health of the children.

Revenues from a casino lifted Cherokee families out of poverty: a natural experiment.
Source: Arkansas Democrat-Gazette.

---

[1]Accounts of this work have also appeared in the general media, including O'Connor (2003).

What Are Natural and Quasi Experiments?

Natural and quasi experiments are terms applied to a wide variety of studies that resemble the randomized field experiments we discussed in the previous chapter but that lack the researcher control or random assignment characteristic of a true experiment. They come in many forms, including before-after comparisons, cross-sectional comparisons of treated and untreated groups, or a combination of before-after and group-to-group comparisons (known as difference-in-differences), as will be explained later in this chapter.

Natural and quasi experiments are important for several reasons. First, because of practical or ethical constraints, randomized experiments are often not possible in social and policy research. Second, because of these constraints, a great many policy studies or program evaluations end up being natural or quasi experiments—so you will likely encounter these types of studies frequently in practice and in the literature. Third, natural or quasi experiments can be carried out on a larger scale or in more realistic settings more often than randomized experiments, enhancing their generalizability and relevance for policy or management decisions. And finally, practitioners can carry out these kinds of studies more easily in their own programs or organizations.

But it is important to point out that these advantages come at a price: Natural and quasi experiments typically exhibit more weaknesses than randomized experiments in terms of demonstrating causation. Understanding these weaknesses, as well as what makes for a strong natural or quasi experiment, is an important theme of this chapter.

Natural Experiments: Taking Advantage of Exogenous Events

In a **natural experiment**, the treatment (the independent variable of interest) varies through some naturally occurring or unplanned event that happens to be exogenous to the outcome (the dependent variable of interest). The Cherokee casino is a natural experiment: It provided an exogenous boost to family incomes on the reservation, an increase that was independent of the habits, motivations, dispositions, or other factors that could also influence the mental health of children. In other words, the families on the reservation did not *self-select* into behavior (such as getting a college degree) that resulted in their higher income—the boost in income just happened, like winning the lottery.

Another key to a natural experiment is the ability to make comparisons—either over time or to a group that did not get the treatment. In the Casino study, the researchers began collecting data before the casino opened (they happened to be tracking mental health problems for other purposes). Therefore, they had a *before* measure (or *pretest*) of mental health to compare with mental health *after* the casino opened (a *posttest*). This before or pretest measure provides an estimate of the *counterfactual:* What would have been the mental health status of the children had the casino not opened. By comparing the change, the researchers were able to infer the causal effect of income on mental health.

Moreover, the researchers also gathered data on families not living on the Cherokee reservation and thus not eligible for the sudden additional income from the casino. This unexposed *comparison group* also provides an estimate of the counterfactual. The researchers compared the mental health of reservation children whose families got the income boost with similar poor children who did not. The difference revealed the effect of the income on mental health.

Combing both the before-after comparison with a comparison group, unexposed to the treatment, adds extra strength to a study—as we'll see later on in this chapter.

What's "Natural" About a Natural Experiment?

The word "natural" in the term *natural experiment* requires some explanation. Sometimes a natural experiment does involve a truly natural event—such as a hurricane or a heat wave. But often the event is "natural" in the sense that it was not planned or intended to influence the outcome of interest. The Cherokee casino was certainly not a natural event like a flood, and it involved a good amount of financial and architectural planning. But the casino was *not* planned or intended as a treatment for the mental health of children—the outcome of interest (dependent variable) in Costello's study. Thus the casino opening can be considered a "natural" experiment *with respect to* children's mental health.

Most Observational Studies Are Not Natural Experiments

Researchers do not create natural experiments—they find them, as Costello and her colleagues did. In this way, natural experiments resemble observational studies—studies in which the world is observed as is, without any attempt to manipulate or change it (as we saw in Chapter 10). However, most observational studies are *not* natural experiments. Finding a good natural experiment is a bit like finding a nugget of gold in a creek bed. It happens sometimes, but there are a lot more ordinary pebbles in the creek than gold nuggets.

How does a natural experiment differ, then, from an observational study? As we saw in Chapters 10 and 11, the treatments (or independent variables of interest) in most observational studies suffer from self-selection and endogeneity. In observational studies, people select treatments for themselves based on their own motivations or interests, such as choosing to get a college degree. Or others select treatments for them based on merit or need, such as determining that a family is needy enough to qualify for a government benefit.

In a natural experiment, some chance event helps ensure that treatment selection is *not* related to relevant individual characteristics or needs. For example, *all* Cherokee families received higher income because of the casino, not just those in which the parents worked harder, got more education, or had a special need for income support. Thus, in a natural experiment, instead of the usual self-selection or other treatment selection bias that generally occurs, something happens that mimics the exogeneity of a randomized experiment.

Examples of Natural Experiments

To get a better feel for how to recognize a natural experiment, it helps to briefly look at a few more examples.

Does noise inhibit learning? Psychologists Arlene Bronzaft and Dennis McCarthy were able to investigate the impact of noise on learning by finding a New York City elementary school built close

Some elevated trains pass close by schools: a natural experiment.

Source: © iStockphoto.com/Terraxplorer.

The Olympics stopped traffic in Atlanta: a natural experiment.

Source: AFP/Getty Image.

to an elevated subway line. The train, which passed at regular intervals throughout the day, ran close by one side of the school building but not the other. Teachers were assigned to classrooms and children to teachers in a fairly random way at the start of each school year. This resulted in a strong natural experiment involving a treatment group of students on the noisy side of the school and a comparison group on the quiet side. Bronzaft and McCarthy (1975) found that "the mean reading scores of classes on the noisy side tended to lag three to four months (based on a 10-month school year) behind their quiet side matches" (p. 517). This study led to efforts by transportation officials to implement noise abatement programs on elevated train tracks near schools.

Does car traffic cause childhood asthma? Public health researcher Michael Friedman and colleagues took advantage of the 1996 Summer Olympics in Atlanta to study the impact of traffic patterns on asthma. During the 17 days of the Olympic Games, the City of Atlanta implemented an alternative transportation plan that greatly restricted cars in favor of buses and other forms of mass transit. Using pediatric medical records for the periods before, during, and after the Olympics, the study found a 40% decline in the rate of childhood asthma emergencies and hospitalizations during the Olympics. This natural experiment provides fairly good evidence of the causal impact of traffic on asthma because of the abrupt, exogenous nature of this one-time alteration in Atlanta's transportation patterns. According to Friedman, Powell, Hutwagner, Graham, and Teague (2001): "These data provide support for efforts to reduce air pollution and improve health via reductions in motor vehicle traffic" (p. 897). Clearly, it would be hard to imagine how the same hypotheses could be tested using a traditional randomized experiment on something so massive as the traffic patterns of a major metropolitan area.

We will look shortly at what specific features make some natural experiments stronger or weaker, with respect to their causal evidence. But because these features are also relevant to quasi experiments, we turn now to defining quasi experiments and considering some examples.

Quasi Experiments: Evaluating Intentional or Planned Treatments

Very often, treatments that influence outcomes don't just happen naturally—they are implemented precisely to influence outcomes. And because the treatment must be allocated based on technical or political considerations, or because evaluation of the program occurs after important funding and targeting decisions have already been made, the researcher cannot randomly assign people or other units to treatment and control groups. Here is where we find **quasi experiments**—studies of planned or intentional treatments that resemble randomized field experiments but lack full random assignment.

To understand the features of a quasi experiment, it is helpful to consider a real example.

Letting Residents Run Public Housing

In the 1990s, the U.S. Department of Housing and Urban Development (HUD) implemented a grant program to encourage resident management of low-income public housing projects (see Van Ryzin, 1996). Inspired by earlier, spontaneous efforts by residents who organized to improve life in troubled public housing projects, HUD implemented a program of grants and technical assistance to selected housing projects in 11 cities nationwide to establish resident management corporations (RMCs). These nonprofit RMCs, controlled and staffed by residents, managed the housing projects and initiated activities aimed at long-standing community issues such as crime, vandalism, and unemployment.

Selected is the critical word—the HUD-funded projects were not just any housing projects but ones that thought themselves, or were judged by HUD, to be good candidates for the program. Technical and political considerations also played a role in project selection. Thus the treatment (the award of HUD funding) was not randomly assigned.

To evaluate the effectiveness of the program, a set of similar housing projects in the same cities but that did not receive the HUD grants were identified as a comparison group.

The term **comparison group** is often used in the context of quasi experiments rather than *control group*, the term used in randomized experiments, to highlight the lack of random assignment. (However, researchers do not always obey this distinction, so still look closely at how the assignment was done.) Surveys and other data were collected on the families living in the treatment and comparison groups to measure the possible effects of resident management on maintenance conditions, security, economic well-being, and residential quality of life.

The housing projects were not randomly selected to receive the HUD grants, and families were not randomly assigned to live in the different public housing projects. That would not be practical—or ethical. However, by finding housing projects in the same cities that were similar in their population and architectural characteristics to the ones that received the HUD grants, the hope was that they could provide a reasonably valid comparison. But because treatment assignment depended in part on the history and motivation of the resident leaders who applied to participate in the program, and on HUD's administrative selection criteria for awarding grants, HUD's evaluation is best described as a weak quasi experiment.

Some Other Examples of Quasi Experiments

Again, it helps to get a feel for quasi experiments by considering a few more examples. Notice how the treatments are intentional, with respect to the outcome of interest, and that these studies have comparison groups—although these are often existing groups, not randomly formed control groups.

Encouraging Kids to Walk to School. Rosie McKee and colleagues evaluated a physical fitness program that encouraged kids in Scotland to walk to school (McKee, Mutrie, Crawford, & Green, 2007). The program involved active travel as part of the curriculum, and it provided interactive travel-planning resources for children and their families to use at home. The school that received the program was compared with another nearby school that did not. Both schools had similar socioeconomic and demographic profiles—but of course children were not randomly assigned to their school. Surveys and the mapping of travel routes were used to measure walking to school, both before and after the invention. The treatment school students increased their average distance walking to school by over eight times and experienced a correspondingly large reduction in their average daily distance driving to school. The comparison school had only a very minor change during the year in average walking and driving distances.

Cracking Down on Gun Dealers. Daniel Webster and colleagues evaluated efforts by three cities—Chicago, Detroit, and Gary—to use undercover stings along with lawsuits to shut down gun dealers suspected of selling illegal firearms to criminals (Webster, Bulzacchelli, Zeoli, & Vernick, 2006). Comparison cities were identified that were similar in size and demographics but were not at the time engaged in an aggressive crackdown on gun dealers. Webster and colleagues found an abrupt reduction of new guns in the hands of arrested criminals in Chicago, some reduction of new guns in Detroit, and not much of a change in Gary. The percentage of new guns changed little over the same period in the comparison cities. The authors concluded,

> The announcement of police stings and lawsuits against suspect gun dealers appeared to have reduced the supply of new guns to criminals in Chicago significantly, and may have contributed to beneficial effects in Detroit. Given the important role that gun stores play in supplying guns to criminals in the US, further efforts of this type are warranted and should be evaluated. (p. 225)

Programs aim to get more kids to walk to school.
Source: © 2009 Jupiterimages Corporation.

Why Distinguish Quasi Experiments From Natural Experiments?

Cracking down on illegal gun sales.
Source: © iStockphoto.com/shapecharge.

Not everyone defines the terms *natural experiment* and *quasi experiment* as we do here. (See Box 13.1 for the origins of both terms.) For example, some refer to natural experiments as a form of quasi experiment or even call their study a "naturally occurring quasi experiment." Others consider the terms *natural* and *quasi experiment* interchangeable—with both referring to any study that falls short of a true randomized experiment.

But we believe that it is important to distinguish quasi experiments from natural experiments because—in a quasi experiment—the program or treatment is consciously implemented to produce some change in the world. This fact alerts us to opportunities to exert

---

BOX 13.1
Origins of the Terms Natural Experiment and Quasi Experiment

Campbell and Stanley coined the term *quasi experiment* in an influential chapter on education evaluation (Campbell & Stanley, 1963). The term quickly caught on and now appears widely not only in education but in criminal justice, public administration, social work, public health, and other fields. In a successor book, the authors Shadish, Cook, and Campbell (2002) define a quasi experiment as an experiment that "lack[s] random assignment . . . but that otherwise [has] similar purposes and structural attributes to randomized experiments" (p. 104).

The term *natural experiment* evolved later than the term *quasi experiment* and is more popular among economists, who often do not do any kind of experimentation, even a weak quasi experiment (Rosenzweig & Wolpin, 2000). However, economists have long paid attention to the idea of exogeneity and thus are alert to situations in which it naturally occurs.

---

policy or administrative control over the assignment of treatments (programs, benefits, or services) in a way that generates more valid causal evaluations.

Below are some ways this can be done as part of program planning and implementation:

- Provide the treatment to some, but not all, eligible recipients to have a comparison group. Although this raises important ethical issues, often a program must operate with limited resources anyway and cannot serve everyone in all places at all times.
- If program resources are scarce and must be rationed, assign the treatment randomly if at all possible—or at least in some way that is fairly exogenous to the outcome. Again, this may not be possible ethically or politically, but it is important to point out that random assignment is in many situations a fair way to ration limited resources.
- If you can't randomly assign *individuals*, at least look for opportunities to randomly or otherwise exogenously assign the treatment to *groups* (such as schools) or geographic areas (such as neighborhoods). Randomly assigning the program at the level of a group or geographic area—even if the program involves relatively few groups or areas—still makes the treatment at least somewhat exogenous.
- If the treatment is a full-coverage or universal program, try to control the timing of program implementation, so that the treatment begins earlier with some participants or in some settings, and later in others. If such variation in the timing of implementation is exogenous to the outcome, then it can be used to estimate a causal effect.
- Finally, it is very important to think ahead and gather outcome measures *before*, as well as after, the start of the program. This is often straightforward with administrative record data or existing performance measures, which tend to get collected on an ongoing basis anyway but should be considered also with surveys and other forms of original data collection designed to evaluate specific outcomes.

Some time ago, Campbell (1969) introduced the notion of the "experimenting society" in which policies and programs are designed to provide more solid knowledge of causation—of what works. And increasingly today, we see pressure in many fields for "evidence-based" programs and management practices—reflecting a demand for greater rigor in assessing what works. While the limitations of randomized field experiment (as discussed in Chapter 12) often prevent experimentation in the traditional sense, we should remain aware of the potential to design and implement programs in ways that allow for at least the best possible quasi experiments.

The recent tradition of natural experiments in economics also suggests that researchers need to be on the lookout for strong natural experiments that provide opportunities for good causal evidence by mimicking true random assignment. A good example is Oregon's health insurance lottery (see Box 13.2), which rationed free health insurance to 3,000 people using a random lottery system because of state budget constraints.

BOX 13.2
Oregon's Health Insurance Lottery

When health economist Katherine Baicker heard about the planned lottery for health insurance coverage (below), she realized that she had found a great natural experiment that was "the chance of a lifetime" (Lacy, 2009).

March 7, 2008—This week Oregon state will begin conducting a lottery with the prize being free health care, reports the Associated Press. Over 80,000 people have signed up to participate since January, although only 3,000 will make the cut and receive coverage under the Oregon Health Plan's standard benefit program.

At its peak in 1995 the Oregon Health Plan covered 132,000 Oregonians, but due to a recession and the budget cuts that followed, the program was closed to newcomers in 2004. Only recently has the state managed to find the money to enroll 3,000 new members. According to the Oregon Department of Human Services, there are an estimated 600,000 people in the state who are uninsured.

BOX 13.3
A Decision Tree for Categorizing Studies

In previous chapters, we've looked at observational studies (Chapter 11) and contrasted these with randomized experiments (Chapter 12). In this chapter, we've added natural and quasi experiments to the picture—making the landscape a bit more complex. So to review and clarify these various types of studies, Figure 13.1 provides a decision tree that can be used to help sort out these distinctions.

Beginning at the top of the tree in Figure 13.1, we ask if the treatment (or independent variable) happens naturally, or is it intentional or planned? Recall that, although most social, political, or economic activities are planned in one sense, we are talking here about treatments that are planned or intended to influence the outcome that the study looks at. Casinos are planned—but they are not planned or intended to improve children's mental health.

Consider the left branch—a naturally occurring (unplanned) treatment. Here we need to ask if the treatment (or independent variable) is self-selected, as it most often is, or is it exogenous? Most things in the world are not random (exogenous)—how much education someone gets, exercising, having dinner with the family, and so on. All these things are driven by characteristics that in turn drive other things too. Thus, most studies under this branch turn out to be *observational studies*.

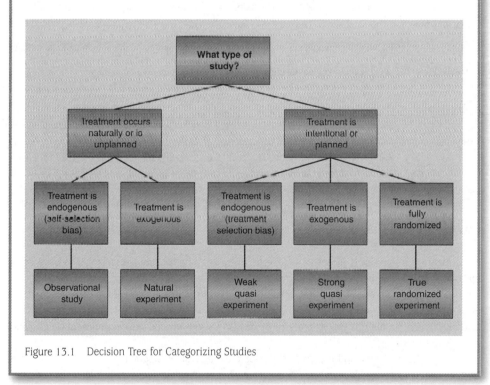

Figure 13.1   Decision Tree for Categorizing Studies

But as we've just seen, sometimes researchers get lucky and a naturally occurring event turns out to be exogenous. A new casino suddenly raises family income in a community in ways unrelated to family motivations or characteristics, or the Olympics arrives and suddenly puts a halt to all car traffic in the city. These kinds of "naturally" occurring, exogenous events produce *natural experiments*.

Moving over to the right branch, we have treatments that are planned to produce some outcome that is the focus of the study. There are three options here. The best causal evidence comes, of course, from a *randomized experiment* in which the treatment is assigned randomly to individuals. Close, but not as good, is when the treatment is exogenous—perhaps the treatment is assigned randomly at some higher level or grouping, or the treatment assignment occurs in some other way that is largely unrelated to relevant characteristics. This situation makes for a *strong quasi experiment*. Finally, there may be a program or treatment designed to produce an outcome that is the focus of the study, but still the program is self-selected or administered in ways that create bias. For example, people maybe volunteer for the treatment or ethical considerations based on need may dictate who gets into the program. This situation is best described as a *weak quasi experiment*.

Internal Validity of Natural and Quasi Experiments

Internal validity is a term researchers use to talk about the strength of causal evidence provided by various types of natural and quasi experiments, as well as traditional randomized experiments. A study that provides convincing, unambiguous evidence of cause and effect is said to have "good internal validity." Randomized experiments, for example, generally have very good internal validity. We will now look more closely at how to judge the internal validity of a given natural or quasi experiment—a somewhat more complex matter.

Exogeneity and Comparability

For a natural or quasi experiment to be able to reveal genuine causal effects—for it to have good internal validity—two basic conditions are needed. First, the treatment or independent variable of interest must be *exogenous*. In other words, the variation in the independent variable can't be driven by anything related to the outcome. This might happen naturally, as in the case of the Cherokee casino (a natural experiment), or by design, as in a randomized experiment or a strong quasi experiment.

Second, the treatment and comparison groups must be truly *comparable*—or homogenous—the same in all relevant ways. For *measured* characteristics, the researcher can simply look at the available data to see how equivalent the treatment and comparison groups appear to be. For *unmeasured* characteristics, we cannot tell so easily and so must try to reason or guess if important unseen differences might lie beneath the surface.

Theory of the Independent Variable

To judge the internal validity of a natural or quasi experiment—to assess the likely degree to which the treatment is exogenous and the groups are comparable—it is important to have a theory of how individuals got to be in the treatment versus the comparison group. In short, we need a theory of what drives the *independent variable*. In a true randomized experiment, the theory is a simple one: Units were randomly assigned to treatment and control groups by a flip of the coin, a randomly generated number, or similar means. In a natural or quasi experiment, the theory is often more complex.

For example, did energetic, engaged, or politically connected tenant leaders in a housing project help secure the HUD grant? Such leaders might also help keep crime down anyway, with or without the help of the program. For another example, perhaps the families on the reservation lobbied for a casino because the stress of family life, including behavioral problems of children, made them desperate for the extra income. In both cases, the treatment and comparison groups differ in ways related to the outcome. By learning what drove the independent variable, we understand how our groups might not be comparable in relevant ways.

Thus, two kinds of theory are important in research:

1. A theory about what factors affect the *dependent variable* (outcome)
2. A theory about what factors drive the *independent variable* (treatment)

In Chapter 2, we talked mostly about the first type of theory—a theory of factors that influence or cause a particular outcome. The second type of theory aims at explaining how people or other units got into the treatment group in the first place.

A good theory of the independent variable is developed in the same ways as any good theory: through qualitative research (such as interviews), imagination, prior experience, the foundational ideas or assumptions of your discipline, and so on. Aggressive speculation is one of the most important tools. Think hard—use your imagination. Speculate on all the possible reasons the independent variable can take on the values that it does. Even if you can't gather evidence, common sense and informal observation can be used to evaluate your theory.

Nothing's Perfect

The goal here is not necessarily perfection—much can be learned from studies that have some weaknesses, as indeed all studies have. Few real-world natural or quasi experiments will have perfect exogeneity and comparability (homogeneity). There is a continuum along both these dimensions. The validity of the causal conclusions drawn must be assessed on a case-by-case basis.

Generalizability of Natural and Quasi Experiments

The generalizability—or *external validity*—of quasi experiments and natural experiments often turns out to be better than in randomized field experiments, despite the fact that quasi experiments typically provide weaker evidence of causation (*internal validity*). This is because quasi and natural experiments involve real-world programs or interventions operating at scale, as it were, in contrast to many random-ized experiments that involve somewhat artificial treatments on a relatively small group of volunteers.

But it all depends, of course, on the details of the particular study. There have been a few large-scale randomized experiments, such as the RAND Health Insurance Experiment or the Moving to Opportunity Demonstration (discussed in Chapter 12), that were nationwide in scope and involved multiple cities and thousands of participants. And there have been many small-scale natural or quasi experiments with only limited generalizability, such as the natural experiment in one New York City public school that studied the effects on learning of elevated train noise. Still, natural and quasi experiments typically occur in real-world settings that more closely resemble the actual contexts and constraints faced by policymakers and practitioners.

A key issue is how well the study's setting and participants reflect a broader population of interest. For example, in the Cherokee casino study, the participants in the study came from a unique Native American community in a rural area. Would the effect of income on mental health be the same in a population of poor Whites in Appalachia, or low-income African American populations living in the inner city of Chicago or Los Angeles? In the HUD study, the resident management program in fact targeted mostly big-city public housing authorities, often with a history of severe management prob-lems. We might wonder: Are the results of this HUD evaluation generalizable to all types of housing authorities, particularly the smaller authorities that do not share the characteristics and management problems of the large, urban housing authorities?

Generalizability of the Treatment Effect

In a randomized experiment, each and every individual is randomly assigned to treatment and con-trol groups. Thus, the effect of the treatment applies to the entire study group, at least on average (because of heterogeneous treatment effects), and in turn applies to whatever larger population the study subjects represent.

But in some natural and quasi experiments, the treatment applies only to some—not all—of those in the treatment group. In the Cherokee casino study, for example, the researchers were especially interested in how being lifted out of poverty—crossing the official poverty line from poor to not poor—influenced mental health. Indeed, much of their data analysis focused on this exogenous change in poverty status. But this change did not happen for those Cherokee families with incomes already above the poverty line before the casino opened. Thus, the treatment effect of a natural or quasi experiment only generalizes to those who were exogenously affected. We will have more to say about this issue in the context of discussing the strategies of instrumental variables and regression discontinuity later on in this chapter.

Having defined natural and quasi experiments and considered some of the issues they raise regarding evidence of causation (internal validity) and generalizability (external validity), we turn next to a more detailed look at the various *types* of natural and quasi experimental studies.

Types of Natural and Quasi Experimental Studies

You can find many varieties of natural and quasi experiments—indeed, clever researchers keep com-ing up with new variations. Shadish et al. (2002), for example, identify at least 18 different quasi experimental designs. In this section, we will look in more detail at those natural and quasi experiments most frequently employed in social and policy research.

Before-After Studies

In the natural experiment from Atlanta described earlier, researchers measured childhood asthma rates *before* the Olympics and compared them with the asthma rates *after* the opening ceremony, when car traffic was drastically curtailed throughout the metropolitan area. There was no comparison group, just a single group (the population of Atlanta) compared at two points in time. Figure 13.2 shows the outlines of this **before-after study**, which is also called a *one-group pretest-posttest* design (or just a *pre-post comparison*).

In the Atlanta study, for example, asthma events (acute care cases) declined from a mean of 4.2 daily cases before the Olympics to only 2.5 daily cases during the Olympics (a practically and statistically quite significant difference), based on administrative data from the Georgia Medicaid claims file.

Weaknesses of Before-After Studies

Although before-after studies are intuitive, they have several inherent weaknesses. Because natural and quasi experiments are not conducted in a lab, researchers do not have the ability to hold all relevant surroundings constant—the world goes on. Campbell and Stanley (1963) referred to this as *history*. The economy, the weather, social trends, political crises—all sorts of events can happen

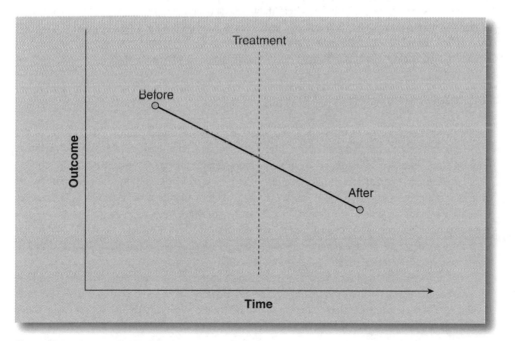

Figure 13.2 Before-After Study

around the time of the treatment, and some of these events could also influence the outcome. This greatly complicates efforts to attribute observed outcome change to the treatment alone.

In the Atlanta study, for example, changes in the weather and other asthma triggers might have coincided with the Olympics, raising doubts about whether the alteration in traffic patterns alone caused all the observed drop in asthma. For this reason, the researchers measured temperature, humidity, barometric pressure, and mold counts during the study period. As it turned out, none of these potential alternative explanations changed in a statistically significant way over the study period.

This suggests a strategy to strengthen the internal validity of a before-after study: Think carefully about what might both influence the outcome *and* coincide with the timing of the treatment—and then find a way to measure it. To the extent plausible alternative explanations can be eliminated in this way, the causal evidence in favor of the treatment gains credibility.

In addition to coinciding external events, people or groups often experience internal changes over time. Second graders, for example, learn to read better by the end of the school year—in part just because they have matured socially and cognitively. New employees in an organization gradually learn how to do their jobs better, so their productivity grows over time. Campbell and Stanley (1963) refer to this as *maturation*. Internal, maturational changes can also bias a before-after study. But they are often difficult to observe and distinguish from the treatment itself.

Thus, many things can drive change over time. A simple before-after comparison largely *assumes* that the change in the dependent variable is due to change in the independent variable, the change in treatment. But this may not be the case.

Statistical Analysis of Before-After Studies

The statistical analysis of a before-after study is usually straightforward: a basic comparison of means or proportions and an appropriate significance test of the difference. If repeated measurements are made on the same individuals, a *gain-score* or *paired sample* approach can be used to increase statistical precision (the ability to detect a statistically significant effect).

Interrupted Time Series

A before-after comparison is much improved when multiple measurements, or a *time series*, of the outcome can be gathered both before and after the treatment. This design is referred to as an **interrupted time series**—a series of periodic measurements interrupted in the middle by the treatment.

For example, Andreas Muller (2004) studied the repeal of Florida's motorcycle helmet law by tracking monthly motorcycle fatalities for several years before and after the law's repeal. Because of Florida's steady population growth and other factors, motorcycle registrations, traffic volume, and motor vehicle fatalities had all been gradually increasing before the helmet law was revoked, although at a very modest rate. But the number of motorcycle fatalities jumped suddenly and quite visibly in the period after the repeal of the helmet law in July 2000.

Such time-series studies are often done with a single aggregate measure repeated over time, as is the case with the Florida study of motorcycle fatalities. However, time-series studies can also be done with panel data—repeated measurements of many individuals over time. We discuss panel data later on in this chapter.

Advantages of Interrupted Time Series

The big advantage of an interrupted time-series study is that it helps answer the question of what the trend in the outcome variable looked like before the intervention. Was there a directional trend (up or down) anyway, or was the trend fairly flat?

Figure 13.3 illustrates the point: Situation A is one in which the higher scores on the outcome after the treatment are clearly part of a more general upward trend over time. In contrast, Situation B is one in which the higher outcome scores after the treatment indicate a marked change from the previous trend. Situation A indicates no causal effect, while Situation B suggests causation. And the evidence from situation B provides much better evidence of causation than a basic before-after comparison of only two point estimates. Of course, it is still possible in Situation B that something else affecting the outcome happened at the very same time as the treatment. But because this is less plausible than Situation A (an existing trend), the evidence of causation in Situation B is much stronger.

Statistical Analysis of Interrupted Time Series

Statistically, an interrupted time series can be analyzed in various ways. For example, ordinary regression analysis can be used with an equation like the following:

$$\text{Outcome} = a + b_{\text{Treat}}\text{Treatment} + b_{\text{Time}}\text{Time} + b_{\text{Inter}}(\text{Treatment} \times \text{Time}).$$

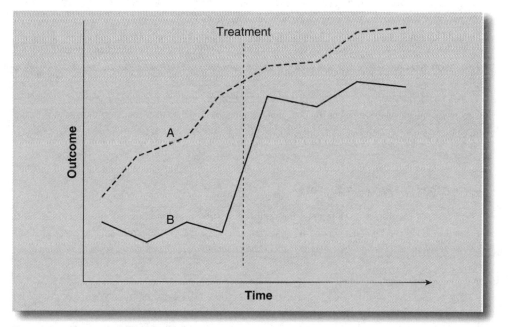

Figure 13.3   Interrupted Time Series

- The treatment dummy variable (Treatment) is coded 0 for the time periods before the interruption and 1 for the periods after. Its coefficient, b_{Treat}, describes the change in the dependent variable (presumably) due to the treatment.
- The time trend variable (Time) is coded 0, 1, 2, 3, and so on for each time period in the series. Its coefficient, b_{Time}, captures the general linear trend over time.
- The final variable is an interaction of the time trend and treatment variables (Treatment × Time). Its coefficient, b_{Inter}, captures any change in the slope of the line due to the treatment or that might be concurrent with the interruption.

For more details on this kind of regression analysis, see McDowall, McCleary, Meidinger, and Hay (1980) or Mohr (1995). However, time-series analysis can be complicated because what happens in one period may be driven by what happened earlier (autocorrelation, discussed in Chapter 9). Consequently, more specialized versions of regression and other time-series methods are often used (Ostrom, 1990). But a picture of the data can tell us a great deal: In most cases, a treatment effect that is large enough to have practical significance (as opposed to just statistical significance) is clearly visible from simply the plotted time series.

Cross-Sectional Comparisons

Before-after studies and interrupted time series make use of variation over time—*longitudinal* variation. But many natural and quasi experiments make use of *cross-sectional* comparisons—comparing two groups, only one of which received the treatment. Such a study is also referred to as a *static group comparison* or a *posttest-only design with nonequivalent groups*.

HUD's evaluation of resident management of public housing is an example of a cross-sectional comparison. The survey that measured the quality of life in the treatment and comparison buildings was conducted only after HUD awarded the grants and the program took effect. Figure 13.4 shows this design schematically.

The key to the internal validity of such a quasi experiment is the comparability of the groups. Were they really the same, in terms of the outcome variable, before the treatment was introduced? Could there be some difference between the groups—other than exposure to the treatment—that explains the observed treatment effect?

Was the HUD Program Effective?

Table 13.1 illustrates the difference between the treatment and comparison groups in the HUD evaluation on three outcomes: building maintenance, security, and tenants satisfaction with their housing. All these outcomes come from the survey, so they are based on residents' judgments of conditions *after* the program's implementation, and each is measured from 0 (lowest possible score) to 100 (highest possible score).

The results show that residents in the treatment group judge building maintenance and security as better on average than do residents in the control group, and the RMC treatment group also appears more satisfied with its housing. The difference in security, however, is relatively small in

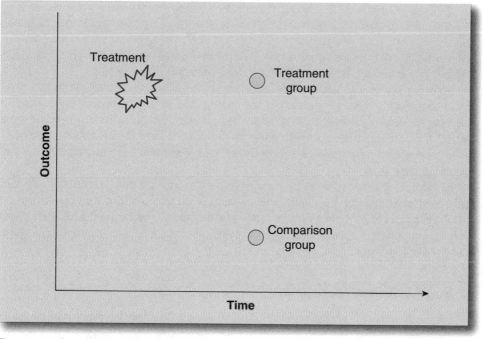

Figure 13.4　Cross-Sectional Comparison

Table 13.1　Judging Outcomes (All Scores are 0 to 100 Indexes)

	RMC (Treatment) Group	Comparison Group
Building maintenance index	63.3*	50.2
Security index	49.5	46.2
Housing satisfaction index	47.0*	38.8

Note: *Significantly different from the comparison group (at $p < .05$ level).

substantive terms and not statistically significant. Still, it does seem from these outcome measures that conditions overall are better for residents in the RMC treatment group.

If the two groups were truly identical in all ways other than the RMC program, then these differences would give us an unbiased estimate of the treatment effect. This is a big "if," however. Recall that the buildings applied to HUD to participate in the program, and HUD selected worthy applicants for funding—so both self-selection and administrative selection processes could make the treatment group different from the comparison group.

One way to address this question is to compare measured characteristics of the groups using available data, as Table 13.2 illustrates. We can see that the two groups appear roughly similar, although the RMC group is slightly better educated and older; has higher income; has more females, more non-Whites and Hispanics; and is more likely to have married members. The differences in age, income, gender, Hispanic ethnicity, and marital status are statistically significant.

Moreover, unmeasured characteristics—not captured by the survey or other available data sources—could be relevant to outcomes such as building maintenance, security, or housing satisfaction. For example, the resident-managed buildings might have dynamic resident leaders, or a tight-knit group of neighbors who already got along well and helped each other. Because these kinds of characteristics were not measured in the survey, we cannot check if the two sets of housing projects are truly comparable in these ways.

Randomized experiments were so convincing precisely because the treatment and control groups were comparable in terms of both measured *and* unmeasured characteristics. If it turns out that the treatment and comparison groups are not comparable in some way relevant to the outcomes, which remains a possibility in a natural or quasi experiment, our conclusions about the effect of the treatment will be less certain.

Not All Differences Are Important

We should emphasize here that it is *not* important that the treatment and comparison groups be equivalent in ways that have nothing to do with the outcome. For example, if one public housing project has blue trim on its windows and doors and another has red trim, provided trim color does not affect security or other outcomes of interest (as we assume it does not), the variable trim color will not matter.

Statistical Analysis of a Cross-Sectional Comparison

The basic statistical analysis for this type of study starts with a comparison of means or proportions, as we saw in Table 13.1. But because group differences on other variables may well exist, as we saw in Table 13.2, the analysis should include *control variables* that attempt to capture the relevant group differences that may influence the outcome. In an important sense, the analysis closely resembles the control variable strategy discussed in Chapter 11 for observational studies.

Table 13.2   Judging Comparability

	RMC (Treatment) Group	Comparison Group
Age of householder	49.2*	43.6
Size of household (persons)	3.0	2.9
Education (in years)	10.5	10.3

	RMC (Treatment) Group	Comparison Group
Household income (in dollars)	$6,223*	$5,021
Male	15%*	26%
Non-White	98%	95%
Hispanic	6%*	20%
Married	10%*	4%

Note: *Significantly different from the comparison group (at $p < .05$ level).

Matching

One strategy researchers often use to construct comparable groups is **matching**—either at a group or individual level. The idea of matching is to find individuals who are as close as possible to those in the treatment group, so they can be used to estimate the counterfactual.

In the HUD study, 11 comparison buildings were matched to the 11 treatment buildings in terms of location (city), architecture, and general demographic characteristics. This is an illustration of *group-level or aggregate matching*, and it is a strategy often used to produce a degree of similarity between treatment and comparison groups. Sometimes, just one comparison group is matched to one treatment group, as in the walking-to-school study in Scotland. In that quasi experiment, a nearby school with similar characteristics was selected as a match for the school that introduced the walking promotion program. Group-level matching is imprecise because of all the unique characteristics that often crop up *within* groups.

How to Match Individuals

Some studies attempt to match at an individual level, which is more precise but also more complicated to carry out. This involves sorting individuals in the treatment group into categories, for example, based on age and gender, and then selecting or recruiting individuals for the comparison group in like proportion. The table below illustrates the idea:

	Treatment Group		Comparison Group	
	Male	Female	Male	Female
Graduate	2	5	??	??
Undergraduate	3	10	??	??

Let's say that the treatment group has been formed already by 20 volunteer participants who signed up for a stress reduction program at a university at the approach of final exam week. The program involves a 2-hour workshop run by a counselor, along with materials and exercises the students use later on their own. We seek a comparison group to evaluate the program.

Because the self-selected treatment group is composed largely of females and undergraduate students, we would want our comparison group to match our treatment group on these variables. Thus, we would recruit individuals for the comparison group using quotas established by the cells in the treatment group table—filling up the corresponding cells in our comparison group table with equal proportions of male and female, graduate and undergraduate students.

Because this is a small-sample situation, there are evident limits to how many variables we can use here to match on. With a larger number of individuals in the program, it would be possible to match on more variables. But even with a larger sample, researchers cannot come close to matching on everything they might want to. Imagine wanting to match 4 levels of education, 4 types of marital status, 5 race/ethnic groups, and 10 age groups—hardly an unreasonable level of demographic detail. That generates 4 × 4 × 5 × 10 or 800 distinct cells (types of individuals). Obviously, matching at that level of detail with enough individuals in each cell is impossible for all but the very largest studies. Consequently, matching cannot be done at the level of precision researchers might hope for. For example, researchers might want to match age at a fine-grained level but only be able to match at a few broad categories. Nor can researchers match on the number of variables they would like.

Propensity Score Matching

To permit matching along many variables, and allow finely grained categories for each variable, **propensity score matching** was developed (Rosenbaum & Rubin, 1985). It employs multivariate statistics to match along many variables at the same time. For example, we might have administrative data on college students—including their exact age, gender, major, year in college, GPA (grade point average), and so on—and use these data to estimate a statistical equation that predicts volunteering for a stress reduction program. The resulting equation produces a predicted probability (propensity) of being a volunteer. Those with high propensity scores but who did *not* volunteer for the program are used to create the comparison group.

The Problem of Regression to the Mean in Matching

Researchers will sometimes match using an earlier measure of the outcome (or dependent variable). All variables move up and down due to random events—measurement error. For example, a child who had an unusually low test score (for that child) in one year is likely to move back toward his or her average the next, while a student with an unusually high score in one year is likely to score lower next time. This effect is known as *regression to the mean*, and it can complicate and even bias a study that uses matching of prior dependent variable values.

Say, for example, that we wish to compare students in a failing school with those in a successful school, before and after a state takeover of the failing school. And suppose, we match the highest-scoring kids from the failing school to the lowest-scoring kids from the successful school (before the state takeover) because this produces what seem to be comparable groups. Because of regression to the mean, however, the high-scoring kids in the failing school are likely to score lower the next year—and the low-scoring kids in the successful school will score higher the next year. The means of the two groups will be pulled apart, due to regression to their respective means, making the failing school look worse.

Weaknesses of Matching Studies

A researcher can only match on variables that are measured and available. If there are important unmeasured variables, in particular common causes, then the conclusions from a matching study can still be biased. This is the same problem we encountered with the strategy of control variables in Chapter 11—not being able to measure and thus take into account important common cause variables.

Even a propensity score matching method cannot make up for important unmeasured variables. Indeed, propensity score matching can exacerbate the problem in some circumstances. For example, if an individual seems exactly like the kind of person who would volunteer for the stress reduction program—has a high propensity to volunteer, in other words—but he or she does not volunteer, then he or she may be different in some important, unmeasured way that affects the outcome.

Case-Control Studies

In a **case-control study**, individuals who experience an outcome, such as a particular injury, are compared with other individuals who did not experience this same outcome (Gordis, 2000). Those with the injury are referred to as **cases**, while those without it are referred to as **controls**. The two groups are then examined to see if they differ in selected independent variable(s) of interest. If so, then the differing independent variables are taken to be risk factors—perhaps causes—of the outcome. It helps to consider a real example.

What Kind of Intersections Increases Pedestrian Fatalities?

Thousands of older pedestrians are killed by cars each year, so it is important to know how to design intersections better to reduce the risk of injury and death to a growing elderly population. With this aim in mind, Thomas Koepsell and colleagues (2002) conducted a case-control study involving

Can intersections be designed better to protect pedestrians?

Source: © 2009 Jupiterimages Corporation.

282 intersections in six cities at which older pedestrians had been hit by a car. They compared these 282 *cases* with a matching set of *controls*—nearby intersections with similar physical and traffic characteristics. They then compared the intersections in terms of the presence of cross-walk markings, traffic signals, and stop signs—in other words, they searched for various causes or treatments. "Almost all of the excess risk," they found, "was . . . associated with marked crosswalks at sites with no traffic signal or stop sign" (p. 2136). The marked crosswalks apparently encouraged older pedestrians to enter the street, but without the protection of a stop sign or traffic light to restrain oncoming cars. This may seem like an obvious finding, but not obvious enough apparently to prevent the construction of several hundred such intersections in the first place.

Notice that the outcome—an older person being struck by a car—is known in advance, and it defines the cases. The cause (or treatment) is unknown; it is what the researchers look for. This is much different from matching in a natural or quasi experiment in which the presence of the treatment defines the treatment group, its absence defines the comparison (control) group, and the researchers look for a difference in outcome.

Weaknesses of Case-Control Studies

In a case-control study, the outcome of interest is often rare, and so studies typically start with an available set of cases, such as the intersections with pedestrian fatalities. While cases may be from a clearly defined population, such as all intersections in six cities, often they are not. For example, cases might be all patients with a rare disease at a hospital that has expertise in treating that disease, and so the population from which they are drawn is unclear. When cases are not drawn from a clearly defined population, generalization is difficult.

Controls are supposed to be comparable with the cases, ideally drawn from the same population. In the intersection fatality study, the controls were selected among intersections in the same cities, using individual matching. In particular, each intersection with a fatality—each case—was matched with a no fatality intersection using specific traffic and physical variables. Controls may also be selected through frequency matching so that the overall distribution of characteristics of the case and control groups match. Controls may not be matched at all but simply drawn randomly from the source population (when known). Finally, controls may simply be a convenience sample whose comparability is unclear. The quality of a case-control study rests critically on how the controls are chosen.

When controls are selected through matching, the matching variables must be chosen carefully. The goal is to make cases and controls comparable in variables that might affect the outcome—except the independent variables of interest to be explored. Moreover, variables along the causal pathway from the potential causes must not be used for matching. That is like controlling for a variable along the causal pathway and could cover up a real effect. For example, consider a case-control study to learn what causes people to commit felonies and whether having a father who is a felon increases that risk. We might consider selecting controls (nonfelons) with matching education levels, but that could be a mistake, because education might be a consequence of having a father who is a felon and part of the mechanism of becoming a felon. The selection of controls must be independent of the potential causes or risk factors (also known as exposures in epidemiology).

Unfortunately, researchers may not always know what should be a matching variable and what should be allowed as a possible independent variable of interest—a risk factor. They use theory and prior evidence to guide those choices, but they cannot know for sure that the right matching variables have been used. Matching on exogenous variables, however, is generally safe.

Case-control studies cannot provide the actual prevalence (or means) of any outcomes or the size of a treatment effect. Case-control studies only provide odds ratios (and measures calculated from them). For example, the study above revealed the ratio of the odds of injury at a marked crosswalk to the odds of injury without a marked crosswalk. (See Chapter 8 for a review of odds ratios.) That is extremely valuable information, but it does not provide information on how common such injuries are in general. Nor does it provide information on how many injuries will be avoided by redesigning crosswalks. Nonetheless, case studies are a very valuable form of study, as we discuss next.

Strengths of Case-Control Studies

Case-control studies provide one of the only ways—frequently the *only* way—to study outcomes that occur only rarely in a population. Other methods, such as observational studies or experiments, will not have enough cases of the outcome to provide statistically significant results—or possibly any results at all. For this reason, case-control studies are common in epidemiology for studying the causes of various diseases, traumas, or other relatively rare health outcomes. Case-control studies are also useful in criminal justice, such as studying the risk factors associated with employees who commit embezzlement or any other area of policy or management research where outcomes are rare. Case-control studies are also useful for outcomes that occur a long time after their causes.

Prospective and Retrospective Studies

As we have seen, some studies are *longitudinal* (such as before-after studies or interrupted time series), while others rely on *cross-sectional* comparisons. Longitudinal studies are distinguished primarily by the fact that measurements occur over time, whereas cross-sectional studies gather data at one point in time.

The distinction can get a bit confusing, however, because some studies involve a cross-sectional *analysis* of longitudinal data. For example, we may analyze the cross-sectional difference in fifth-grade test scores for students who did, or did not, have intensive preschooling many years earlier—in other words, a study of a long-term effect. Box 13.4 explains this issue, which is often a source of confusion when researchers from different disciplines use the term longitudinal.

> ## BOX 13.4
> ## Cross-Sectional Analysis of Longitudinal Data
>
> A *cross-sectional analysis* can be done on longitudinal data, although this idea may seem counterintuitive at first glance. For example, say we have standardized test scores (Y) from a group of fifth graders tested this year. And say we also have records of whether they did, or did not, participate in an intensive preschool program (X) offered by the school 6 years ago on a voluntary basis. Thus, X (the preschool program) predates Y (the fifth-grade test) by 6 years, so the data are longitudinal in a sense. The data could even have come from a truly longitudinal study that followed the children since preschool. But in our analysis, we still basically compare the mean scores of those who did, and those who did not, participate in intensive preschool at one point in time (with appropriate control variables, of course).

In a truly longitudinal *analysis*, in contrast, the statistical analysis makes explicit use of changes over time in the measured variables. An example of this kind of analysis is a difference-in-differences study, including *panel data* analysis, discussed a bit later on in this chapter.

But there is another important issue in thinking about the time dimension of research. In some studies, the researchers look ahead—**prospective studies**, they are called—and take steps to track and measure a cohort of people over time in order to observe what happens to them. For example, a study published in the *New England Journal of Medicine* (Yanovski et al., 2000) investigated weight gain from holiday eating by following a convenience sample of 195 adults and weighing them regularly before, during, and after the U.S. holiday season (which runs from Thanksgiving through New Year's Day). They found no weight gain during the months leading up to the holidays, a weight gain during the holidays, and yet no significant weight loss during the months after the holidays— suggesting that holiday eating may have longer-term effects on weight gain.

Contrast this with the study we saw earlier about the Atlanta Olympics and the effect of automobile traffic on asthma. In that study, the researchers looked backward in time—a **retrospective study**—and reconstructed past trends in childhood asthma events using administrative record data. The logic of the analysis, however, was much the same as the holiday weight gain study: a comparison of the period before, during, and after the treatment (independent variable of interest).

Many case-control studies are retrospective, in large part because they focus on rare outcomes that cannot be observed often enough when prospectively tracking a cohort of people, even a very large cohort. Many natural experiments turn out to be retrospective as well because researchers only discover them after the fact. Some epidemiologists and others argue that prospective studies are better at accounting for confounding and alternative explanations, in part because the time order of events can be more clearly determined. But much depends on the available data, as well as the logic and thoroughness of the analysis. There can be quite convincing retrospective case-control studies and natural experiments, as well as prospective studies with dubious findings because of self-selection, attrition, or other sources of bias.

Difference-in-Differences Strategy

As we've seen, both before-after comparisons and cross-sectional comparisons have weakness in terms of internal validity—that is, providing a convincing demonstration of causation. By putting them together—having two before-after comparisons, one for the treatment and another for the comparison group—we create a much stronger study: a **difference-in-differences** study. The study gets its name from the fact that it compares the *difference* between two before-after *differences*. Some refer to this study as a *pre-post study with a comparison group*.

We highlight the difference-in-differences strategy here because it is quite feasible in real-world policy or practice settings, it can be understood by a wide audience, and it provides fairly good evidence of causation. Of course, certain conditions must be met for good evidence of causation. These conditions, as well as an understanding of the difference-in-differences in general, are best understood through a real example.

Do Parental Notification Laws Reduce Teenage Abortions and Births?

Researchers Colman, Joyce, and Kaestner (2008) used a difference-in-differences strategy to investigate the effect of a Texas parental notification law on abortion and birth rates. The 1999 law required

Parental notification laws are part of the abortion controversy.

Source: Alex Wong/Getty Images News.

Table 13.3   Abortion Rates for Texas Residents Aged 17 and 18 Who Conceived

	1999[a]	2000	Difference
Treatment group Texas teens who conceived at 17	18.7	15.3	−3.4
Comparison group Texas teens who conceived at 18	28.3	26.9	−1.5
Difference in differences	\multicolumn{3}{c}{−3.4 − (−1.5) = −1.91**}		

Note: Abortion rates are defined as the number of abortions per 1,000 age-specific female population.

a. 1999 refers to the period August 1, 1998, to July 31, 1999—before the parental notification law came into effect.

**Significant at 5%.

Source: Adapted from Colman et al. (2008).

that parents of a pregnant girl younger than 18 years be notified before an abortion. Before the law, no parental notification was required.

We could just consider what happened before and after the law was implemented (a before-after study). But both abortion and birth rates for teenagers have been steadily declining, due to broader social changes. It would be helpful to have a comparison group, unexposed to the law, to capture this trend (and thus, better estimate a counterfactual). So Colman et al. (2008) compared Texas teenagers who conceived at age 17 with Texas teenagers who conceived at age 18. The 18-year-olds were only slightly older, yet not legally subject to the state's parental notification laws.

Table 13.3, adapted from the study, shows the number of abortions per 1,000 female population in the two age groups, before and after the notification law change. We see that among 18-year-olds, abortion rates fell by 1.5 abortions per 1,000, while among 17-year-olds, abortion rates dropped by 3.4 abortions per 1,000. The difference in the differences is −1.91. The conclusion is that, compared with what abortion rates would have been (the counterfactual), parental notification laws reduced abortions among teenage girls by 1.91 per 1,000.

Table 13.4 shows a similar analysis of birth rates. Among the 18-year-olds, birth rates fell by 2.76 per 1,000 more than they did among 17-year-olds. The conclusion here is that, compared with what they would have been (the counterfactual), the parental notification law caused a 2.76 per 1,000 rise in teenage births. Thus, these two tables show that the law reduced abortions at the same time that it increased births to 17-year-olds in Texas.

What Does a Difference-in-Differences Study Assume?

Ideally, in a difference-in-differences study, the treatment and comparison groups are as similar as possible, except for being exposed to the treatment. But the strategy can work well even when the two groups are not a perfect match. Girls who conceive at age 17 and those who conceive at age 18 differ in many ways other than being subject to the parental notification law. One obvious difference, shown in the table, is that abortion and birth rates are higher for the older girls. So 18-year-olds are not the perfect comparison group. But such dissimilarities, even in the outcomes of interest such as abortion

Table 13.4   Birth Rates for Texas Residents Aged 17 and 18 Who Conceived

	1999[a]	2000	Difference
Treatment group Texas teens who conceived at 17	86.0	85.8	− 0.1
Comparison group Texas teens who conceived at 18	116.8	113.9	− 2.9
Difference in differences	− 0.1 − (− 2.9) = 2.76*		

Note: Birth rates are defined as the number of births per 1,000 age-specific female population.

a. 1999 refers to the period August 1, 1998, to July 31, 1999—before the parental notification law came into effect.

*Significant at 10%.

Source: Adapted from Colman et al. (2008).

and birth rates, do not necessarily undermine a difference-in-differences study. What really matters is whether the underlying *change* or *trend* would have been the same, in the absence of the treatment.

This crucial assumption of equal change or parallel trends in a difference-in-differences study is illustrated in Figure 13.5. The usual, cross-sectional estimate of the difference between the groups is A − B. The difference-in-difference strategy uses the A − C comparison, which is an improvement. But notice that we assume that the initial difference in levels—represented by B − C—remains constant over time. In other words, a difference-in-differences study assumes that the change over time in the comparison group is the same change that would have happened to the treatment group, if they had not gotten the treatment (the counterfactual).

Abortion rates and birth rates were trending down anyway in Texas. But did they trend down faster for one age group than another? If so, this would undermine the study's conclusions. If not, then the comparison between 17-year-olds and 18-year-olds remains valid.

Researchers sometimes find that although the time trends are not similar across the groups, the proportional changes in the trends are comparable. This often happens in cases when the initial levels of the two groups are quite different. In such situations, researchers will take log transformations of the variables and do a difference-in-differences on the log transformed dependent variables. (In fact, Colman and colleagues, 2008, also did that analysis, just to be sure.) Moreover, when the treatment and comparison groups differ a great deal in initial level, assuming that their logs have the same trend can be as problematic as assuming that their levels have the same trend.

In real-world applied social policy research, the perfect comparison group is rarely available. The authors of the abortion study might have compared Texas with another similar state that did not pass a parental notification law, focusing on just 17-year-olds in the two states. But the detailed data necessary for such a study are not gathered in most states.[2] Moreover, such a comparison group would not

---

[2] In fact, these researchers and others did studies using other states for the comparison group, but other states did not have detailed data on birth dates and conception dates. So those other studies had to look at age at delivery, resulting in somewhat misleading results. See Colman et al. (2008). Since ages of conception are very private data, they were, of course, subject to intense confidentiality restrictions and human subjects oversight. The researchers got the data stripped on all personal identification but nonetheless had to keep them very secure.

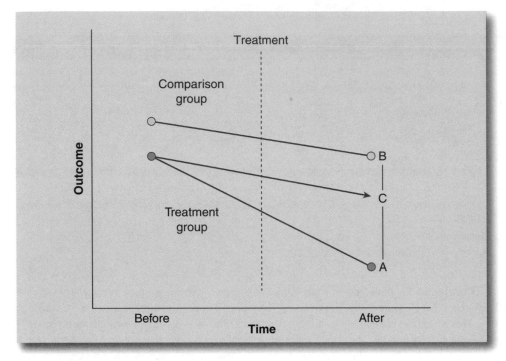

Figure 13.5   Difference-in-Differences Assumptions

be perfect either: states have different demographic characteristics, birth and abortion rates, and trends. The choice of 18-year-olds in the same state, although not perfect, was still a good one for this study.

Retrospective Pretests and Other Retrospective Variables

A difference-in-differences study is usually longitudinal, requiring a before-after measurement of some kind. But it is possible to take advantage of the strengths of the difference-in-differences approach in a purely cross-sectional study by using a *retrospective pretest*. A retrospective pretest is typically a question in a survey that asks about an outcome in the past. For example, in an evaluation of a drug abuse prevention program—in which we are using a cross-sectional survey to compare participants in the program with a comparison group—we can ask both groups to recall their level of drug use several years ago. Then we can calculate the change in drug use, from then until now, in both groups and use a difference-in-differences analysis. In this way, the retrospective pretest provides cross-sectional data that can be analyzed with a difference-in-differences.

Difference-in-Differences in a Regression Framework

The analysis of a difference-in-differences study can also be performed in a regression framework, which offers some advantages. Here is how it works: A dummy variable is constructed for whether or not the individual is in the treatment group, denoted below as Rx. Another dummy variable is constructed for whether or not it is the postperiod, denoted as Post. Finally, an interaction variable is constructed as the product of those two variables, denoted as Rx × Post.

A regression is run with the model:

$$Y = a + b_{Rx}Rx + b_{post}Post + b_{int}(Post \times Rx),$$

where

- b_{Rx} reveals the difference in outcome (Y) between treatment and comparison during the preperiod. This is what is assumed constant over time.
- b_{post} reveals the difference in outcome (Y) between postperiod and preperiod for the comparison group. This is the trend that is assumed to be the same for both groups.
- b_{int} reveals the difference in difference in outcome (Y)—how much more (or less) the treatment group changes than the comparison group, or the presumed causal effect of the treatment.

This regression-based approach to difference-in-differences is identical to the straightforward comparisons of means discussed previously. However, the regression approach can be extended to include control variables that capture important differences between the treatment and control groups. These control variables can be denoted as Cont.

$$Y = a + b_{Rx}Rx + b_{Post}Post + b_{int}(Post \times Rx) + b_{cont}Cont.$$

Control variables allow the researcher to account for relevant factors that are changing differently in the two groups, allowing the assumption that the treatment group would have had the same change or trend, absent the treatment, to be somewhat relaxed (only unmeasured differences between the two groups need to be assumed to be constant).

Panel Data for Difference in Differences

The difference-in-differences studies that we have considered so far made use of just one change over time and at a group level. However, with *panel data*—that is, repeated measurements on the same individuals over several time periods—it is possible to consider many individual changes and pool their effects. In essence, panel data allow for many differences in differences over time for each individual in the study. The individuals may be people or households, but panel data can also represent schools, organizations, neighborhoods, cities, states, or even nations over time.

Consider the example of marriage and the earnings of men. Studies have shown that married men earn more on average than unmarried men. Is the effect causal? Does marriage cause men to take work more seriously and thus earn more? Or are men who earn more just more likely to get married?

Korenman and Neumark (1991) examined this question in an article titled "Does Marriage Make Men More Productive?" They employed panel data that followed men for several years and observed their marital status, wages, and other variables. Their analysis looked at how much men's wages changed when they married (or divorced) and compared those changes with what occurred when their marital status did

Does marriage lead men to earn more?

Source: © iStockphoto.com/TriggerPhoto.

not change. Thus, changes in wages associated with changes in marital status were employed to *identify* the effect of marital status on wages.

Panel data provide the following advantages in a difference-in-differences study:

- Repeated observations over time of the same individuals
- More periods of time
- More possible independent variable values
- More individuals
- Other control variables

More generally, a panel difference-in-differences study measures the correlation of changes in the independent variable for specific individuals with changes in the dependent variable for the same individual. It makes use of within-subject variation, as distinct from between-subject variation. Each subject acts as his or her own control, in some sense.

What Do Panel Difference-in-Differences Studies Assume?

A study such as the one by Korenman and Neumark (1991) uses *fixed effects*—specifically, a method in which each individual has a dummy variable—to capture individual differences. But this assumes that any differences between men relevant to both their wages and their marital status remain constant over time. For example, if emotional stability is an unmeasured common cause that affects both wages and marriage, the method implicitly assumes that emotional stability remains constant over the study. But of course this may not be true—emotional stability may also change over time, potentially resulting in bias.

In this fixed-effects panel study, only those who change their marital status provide information about the effect of marriage on wages. These "changers," in other words, are used to identify the effect of marriage on wages. To illustrate, Table 13.5 shows how the marital status of five men, labeled A through E, changes over time. We see that Men A and C provide no information whatsoever, because their marital status doesn't change in the study period. Man B provides information only in the transition from Year 2 to Year 3. Man D provides information in the transitions between Years 1 and 2 and Years 4 and 5. Man E provides information from the transition between Years 4 and 5. The estimate of the marriage effect is based only on the changes in wages that are associated with these individuals' changes in marriage status.

Weaknesses of Panel Difference-in-Differences Studies

Panel difference-in-differences studies offer many advantages, but they also have limitations. One relates to generalizability: It is difficult to determine what population the study's findings apply to. As we've seen, the identification strategy relies on "changers," such as men who marry and divorce, to calculate a treatment effect. Men who stay single and men who stay married do not come into the picture. Also, men who change marital status more often contribute more to the effect. But such men may not be typical, and therefore, the estimated treatment effect may not generalize to all or even most men.

The fact that only changers contribute to the estimation also reduces the share of the sample that contributes to the analysis, sometimes dramatically. So what seems like a large sample over many years becomes effectively only a small sample when the focus is on only those individuals who change their status. This makes it much harder to obtain statistically significant results. The reliance on changers also means that coding errors can have a large influence. An error in marital status for 1 year will add a lot of error.

Another weakness with such panel studies is that the time scale might not be sufficient for all the independent variables to affect the dependent variable. Using longer time lags can deal with this, but that brings its own problems.

Finally, the biggest issue is the potential endogeneity of the changes, making whatever idiosyncratic factors drive men's earnings not constant over time and related to both the independent and dependent variables. Is the *change* in marital status endogenous? Are changes in independent variable caused by changes in some other factor that also affects the dependent variable—a common cause? For example, do women choose to marry men whose wages appear likely to rise? Are changes in the independent variable caused by changes in the dependent variable—reverse causation? For example, do men wait to propose until their earnings start to increase?

Instrumental Variables and Regression Discontinuity

Estimating the quantitative magnitude of a causal effect is an important goal, especially in research for policy or practice. When the treatment group represents a program—a complete package, as it were—natural and quasi experiments directly estimate the magnitude of the causal effect. In the HUD study, for example, the treatment group represents buildings run by resident-controlled nonprofit corporations, a novel approach to public housing management. In other studies, however, the treatment-control distinction serves as a device (an *instrument*) for manipulating an underlying variable of interest. (Note that this kind of instrument is not the same as an instrument of measurement, such as a survey.)

Table 13.5   Panel Data on Men Marrying Over Time

Man	Year 1	Year 2	Year 3	Year 4	Year 5
A	Married	Married	Married	Married	Married
B	Single	Single	Married	Married	Married
C	Single	Single	Single	Single	Single
D	Single	Married	Married	Married	Single
E	Single	Single	Single	Single	Married

Instrumental Variables

When the treatment/control group distinction works as a device to manipulate an underlying variable—and when that underlying variable can also be measured directly—researchers sometimes use an extension of the natural experiment method known as **instrumental variables (IV)** (Angrist & Krueger, 2001). An **instrument** is a variable that causes the independent variable to change but does not affect the outcome in any way, other than through the independent variable.

In the elevated train noise study, researchers compared student outcomes between the different sides of the school and did not estimate the effect of noise itself. However, side of the school could have served as an instrument for noise, because the side of the school caused noise to vary but was itself unrelated to student learning. But researchers would have needed measures of noise exposure over the school year to estimate the effect of noise by using side of school as an instrument. Technically, if we want to learn the causal effect of X on Y, but X is endogenous to Y, we look for an instrument Z. For Z to be a valid instrument, it must be related to X and exogenous to Y.

The method of instrumental variables is best illustrated with an example.

Maternal Smoking, Cigarette Taxes, and Birth Weight

Mothers who smoke while pregnant reduce the birth weight of their babies. Of course, mothers who smoke while pregnant may differ from mothers who don't smoke in ways likely to affect their babies. In other words, smoking is likely endogenous to birth weight. Evans and Ringel (1999) estimate the effect of maternal smoking on birth weight, using cigarette taxes as an instrument.

Whether or not people smoke is affected by cigarette taxes. Cigarette taxes vary across states and have varied over time. Therefore, some of the variation in maternal smoking is driven by variation in cigarette taxes. That variation, and only that variation, in maternal smoking is used to estimate the effect of maternal smoking on birth weight. In this way, common causes of both maternal smoking and birth weight are excluded from the estimate. Box 13.5 provides a helpful way to identify a valid instrumental variable.

BOX 13.5
How to Determine if an Instrument Is Valid

One of the best ways to determine a valid instrumental variable is to say aloud: "Z only affects Y through its effect on X"—but substitute the variables names for X, Y, and Z. For example, "Cigarette taxes only affect birth weight through their effect on maternal smoking." Sounds reasonable, right?[3] If it does not, then Z is not likely to be a valid instrumental variable. Here are the steps:

---

[3]One of us (DR) thanks Joshua Angrist for teaching her this "trick" in graduate school.

- State the outcome or dependent variable of interest, Y.
- State the independent variable of interest, X.
- Find the candidate instrument Z.
- Does Z affect X in a fairly substantial manner?
  - If not, it can't be a good instrument.
- Does Z affect Y in any way other than through X?
  - If so, it is not a valid instrument.

Generalizability of IV Studies

IV estimates may not generalize to the entire study population. Consider the maternal smoking study. Perhaps some mothers are determined to smoke and will smoke no matter how high cigarette taxes go. Other mothers would never smoke and the level of cigarette taxes is irrelevant to them. Only mothers whose smoking status is affected by cigarette taxes, the instrument, will contribute to the estimate of the effect of smoking on birth weight. Thus, the generalizability of the estimate is reduced and often unclear.[4]

This reduced and ambiguous generalizability was also a feature of the panel difference-in-differences study and, it turns out, many natural experiments. IV studies are simply a specific way to use natural experiments.

Regression Discontinuity

Suppose that students are accepted into a compensatory program only if they score below a certain threshold on a standardized test. Students just above the threshold are presumably very similar but not exposed to the program. Intuitively, the effect of the program on an outcome could be determined by comparing the two groups on either side of the cut point. If they experience very different outcomes, this would suggest a large treatment effect; a small difference would suggest little effect.

This is the essential logic of a **regression discontinuity** study—a study that applies when assignment to the treatment is based on a cut point for a single quantitative assignment variable.

Regression discontinuity studies are analyzed, as the name suggests, in a regression framework:

$$\text{Outcome} = b_0 + b_{\text{Assign}}\text{Assignment} + b_{\text{Treat}}\text{Treatment} + b_{\text{Inter}}(\text{Treatment} \times \text{Assignment}).$$

Assignment is the quantitative variable whose scores alone determine assignment to the treatment group. Its coefficient, b_{Assign}, captures the effect of the variable that is used to determine assignment.

---

[4]An IV estimate is referred to, in the technical literature, as a *local average treatment effect* because it is an average among only the "local" group affected by the instrument (Imbens & Angrist, 1994). See Harris and Remler (1998) for a relatively accessible treatment of the generalizability of instrumental variables estimates.

For example, it could be the ordinary effect of the standardized test used for admission. *Treatment* is a dummy variable coded 1 if the individual is in the treatment group and 0 if the individual is in the comparison group. If the treatment itself has an effect, we expect to see it in its coefficient, b_{Treat}. The interaction term (Treatment × Assignment) can be included if the analyst expects the treatment to change the effect of the assigning variable, not just a change in the level. For example, if a program not only improves student performance but also increases the effect of standardized test scores, there would be an interaction. It is also possible to add further controls or use a more flexible functional form for the effect of the assignment variable.

Napoli and Hiltner (1993) used a regression discontinuity design to evaluate a developmental reading program for community college students. Students were assigned to the program based strictly on having a score below 80 on a reading comprehension test. The researchers then examined the effect of the program on the students' later GPAs. The results, presented in Figure 13.6, suggest that the program was effective. Notice how the regression line for those in the developmental reading program appears higher, shifted up, at the cut point (the slope also appears to be a bit flatter). This finding provides evidence that GPAs of students in the program were higher than they would have otherwise been (if we projected the line for the nondevelopmental comparison group back across the cut point).

A regression discontinuity is an especially strong quasi experiment, although it applies only in rather specific circumstances.

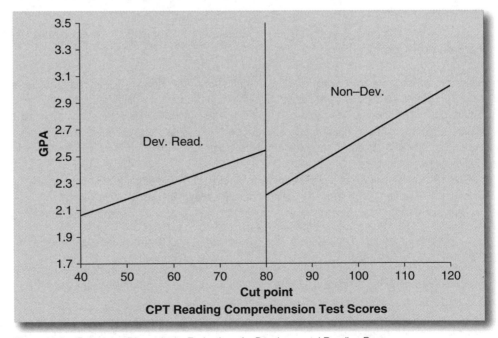

Figure 13.6   Regression Discontinuity Evaluation of a Developmental Reading Program

Source: Napoli and Hiltner (1993).

Conclusion

Searching for and Creating Exogeneity

Natural and quasi experiments are widely used to estimate causal effects in social and policy research. They are usually more generalizable than randomized experiments, often less costly, and frequently more feasible. And they can provide much more convincing causal estimates than do observational studies with control variables. It is not surprising that the many variants of natural and quasi experiments have come to dominant cutting-edge causal research.

In assessing the validity of a natural or quasi experiment, understanding what drove the treatment or independent variable is critical. We encourage you to always be on the lookout for events that could be natural experiments. And we encourage you to try to shape the implementation of programs in ways that allow for strong natural or quasi experiments. In this way, social and policy research will have more valid and generalizable estimates of important causal effects.

Estimating Causal Effects in Perspective: A Wrap-Up to Part III

Research in the aid of policy and practice must often focus on causal effects. Yet resources are limited. To choose the most cost-effective programs, we need to know how truly effective a program really will be. As we showed in the first chapter of Part III on Causation (Chapter 10), estimating causal effects in applied social areas is difficult. In the real world, most variables whose effects we would like to know are endogenous. (For further reading and more advanced treatments, see Angrist & Pischke, 2009; Langbein & Felbinger, 2006; Morgan & Winship, 2007.)

There are three basic approaches. The first is to use observational data with control variables, as we demonstrated in Chapter 11. To the extent that common causes of both outcome and independent variables are measured, their effect can be removed and the true causal effect isolated. However, the bias of any unmeasured common causes persists—and it is almost impossible to get all the relevant common causes. Moreover, the problem of reverse causation cannot be addressed simply with control variables.

The second approach is randomized experiments, which we covered in Chapter 12. Randomized experiments use random assignment to make the treatment or independent variable exogenous and, therefore, do a great job of estimating causal effects. However, they are expensive, sometimes unethical or impractical, and often so artificial or dependent on self-selected volunteers that generalizability is poor.

The third method is natural and quasi experiments, the topic of this chapter. These are not one method but rather a large collection of methods in which exogeneity is found or created but in a form that falls short of a true randomized experiment. These methods are often a researcher's best shot at getting a fairly good estimate of a causal effect. Therefore, as we have urged, researchers should always be on the lookout for natural experiments or opportunities to create strong quasi experiments.

When searching for research that is useful for policy and practice, we hope that you will be cognizant of the weaknesses of the various types of studies used to estimate causal effects. Yet, at the same time, we would caution you not to be too dismissive—most studies have their strengths too. Through a variety of studies, each with different strengths and weaknesses, it is possible to learn a great deal about what causes what—and how large the effect is. We hope that the various research examples we provided illustrate how much we can learn with the limited tools we have.

BOX 13.6
Critical Questions to Ask About
Natural and Quasi Experiments

- Is the study a natural experiment, a quasi experiment, or neither (such as an observational study)? Is the treatment intentional or planned (with respect to the outcome), or not?
- What kind of natural or quasi experiment is it? Think about the possibilities: a before-after study, an interrupted time series, a cross-sectional comparison, a case-control or matching study, a difference-in-differences study, and so on.
- What kind of variation in the treatment (independent variable of interest) is being used to estimate its effect on the dependent variable? Can you describe in everyday language how the treatment effect is being "identified" or traced out?
- What drove the treatment variation used in the estimation? Was it exogenous to the outcome?
- How comparable is the comparison group (or whatever constitutes the counterfactual, such as before period)?
- Who was affected by the variation used in the estimation? What population does that generalize to?

EXERCISES

Family Income and Child Mental Health

13.1. Think of a variety of different causal pathways that could explain the correlation between the family income of a child and that child's mental health. Include examples of mechanisms (intervening variables) for causation, common causes, and reverse causation.

    a. Draw path diagrams to illustrate.

    b. What counterfactual question would you like to be able to answer to address the causal question of the effect of poverty on mental health?

c. Describe a randomized experiment that could be used to answer this question that meets ethical standards.

d. Compare the validity of the causal conclusions of the Casino natural experiment with that of the randomized experiment.

e. Compare the generalizability of the Casino natural experiment with that of the randomized experiment.

Noise, Student Learning, and Diligent Teachers

13.2. Recall the Bronzaft and McCarthy (1975) study of how train noise affected student learning. How might a conscientious teacher respond to the noise? Might such a teacher aggressively pursue a classroom on the less noisy side of the building? If so, how might that affect your conclusions from this study? Explain.

HMOs and Medical Care Usage

13.3. Suppose two manufacturing companies merge and one company switches to the more restrictive health insurance options (only closed panel HMOs) of the other company.

a. Explain why this provides a natural experiment that could be used to evaluate the effects of closed panel HMOs on medical care usage.

b. Describe the data that you would want to collect for such a study.

c. Describe how you would analyze the data.

d. Discuss the validity of the causal conclusions. What weaknesses are there?

e. Discuss the generalizability of the study.

Evaluating Transit System Changes

Excerpts from an Op-Ed contribution from the *New York Times* Sunday City section, by E. S. Savas (2007):

Transit officials are decentralizing the subway system to improve service, cleanliness and on-time performance by appointing individual managers for each of the 24 lines. . . .

The authority plans to start with the No. 7 and L lines and evaluate the pilot program by surveying riders after about three months. This implies only modest goals, as that time is too short for major improvements.

Moreover, more money and manpower are to be allocated to those lines, making it impossible to figure out whether any improvements result from better management or more spending. The plan seems loaded to elicit favorable comments in the short term from riders on those particular lines, which unlike the other 22 lines are isolated: they have separate tracks. . . . (www.nytimes.com/2007/12/16/opinion/nyregionopinions/16CIsavas.html)

13.4. Evaluators of the present plan could use a difference-in-differences framework to evaluate the impact of their decentralization program. Savas notes three problems that undermine the ability of such an evaluation to allow generalizations to the long-term effects of creating individual managers for each of the 24 lines.

 a. Briefly describe the difference-in-differences framework that could be used to do an evaluation of the decentralization program.
 b. Explain the three problems Savas describes. Explain how they would undermine the desired generalization from your difference-in-differences study.

PART IV

APPLICATIONS

Objectives: In this chapter, you will learn about how research fits into the broader political context and the policymaking process, including the pathways through which research influences policy and practice as well as the barriers to its effective use and influence. You will also find out about how research is produced, including the different sources of research funding and the types of institutions that conduct research. And—although you have been exposed to research ethics throughout this book—you will learn more in this chapter about the history of research ethics and the formal rules and procedures that have been established to protect participants in research. Finally, you will be introduced to other ethical dilemmas and ethical issues involved in applying research to policy and practice.

Politics shapes research in many ways.

Source: © 2009 Jupiterimages Corporation.

The Politics, Production, and Ethics of Research

14

Risking Your Baby's Health

A television advertisement by the National Breastfeeding Campaign, sponsored by the U.S. Department of Health and Human Services and a group called the Ad Council, shows images of two pregnant women in a log rolling competition. "You'd never take risks before your baby is born," the ad says. "Why start after?" (U.S. Department of Health and Human Services, 2009). The message clearly suggests that bottle-feeding your baby, instead of breastfeeding, represents a serious risk to your baby's health and well-being. But how good is the research evidence about the benefits of breastfeeding? Is the evidence strong enough to justify a government-funded national campaign using this kind of scare tactic? And what would be the potential health risks if we waited for more or better evidence and did nothing to promote breastfeeding?

There is a large literature on the relationship between breastfeeding and a variety of health and other early childhood outcomes, including stomach and respiratory infections, asthma, obesity, diabetes, and cognitive development. Many (although certainly not all) of the associations between breastfeeding and these outcomes were shown to be statistically significant, and some were large enough to be practically significant as well. But nearly all the studies were observational, and the independent variable of interest, breastfeeding, is likely to be endogenous with respect to many of these outcomes. For example, better educated and higher income mothers tend to breastfeed more, and of course they also have more financial and other resources to devote to the care and upbringing of their young children. Even accounting for income and education, mothers who breastfeed may devote more time and effort in other ways to improving their children's nutrition, health care,

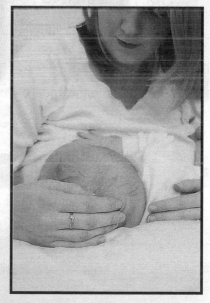

Are mothers who don't breastfeed risking their babies' health?

Source: iStockphoto.com/hidesy.

and early education. So the causal evidence from observational studies alone remains weak—but there was little else available when the campaign was launched.

Does evidence for making policy need to be not just statistically significant and practically significant but also clearly causal? Should the threshold of evidence be higher to employ scare tactics like those in the National Breastfeeding Campaign ad? Does the public need to be made aware of the caveats and limitations of the research used to set this policy or make these kinds of recommendations? And if so, how should this be done? How does the difficulty of doing randomized experiments with complex, personal behaviors such as breastfeeding affect the standard of evidence required to take action? These are the difficult questions that arise when using research to make policy or inform practice.

The National Breastfeeding Campaign also highlights how culture and values interact with research. Wolf (2007) contends that the weakness of the causal evidence of breastfeeding effects was ignored in this case because breastfeeding fits well with a culture of "total motherhood" in our society, particularly among the well educated. Culture and politics shape research at all levels and stages: what research is done and what research is not done; which research results are ignored, and which results are promoted.

In this chapter, we will look at the complex role of research in the political and policymaking process. We will also learn about the institutions that support and conduct research. And we will examine more closely the ethics of conducting research.

From Research to Policy

As a way to begin thinking about how research influences policy and practice, let's initially consider a kind of rational model of analyzing and making public policy.

Rational Model of Policy

Weimer and Vining (1999) describe the steps of a rational model of policy analysis in which research plays a central role. To evaluate alternative solutions, they explain, the policy analyst must "[predict] impacts of alternatives" by "identifying and organizing relevant data, theories and facts" (p. 257). Weimer and Vining also stress the importance of *cost-benefit analysis* (CBA) to make the best use of limited resources, and they point out that research *evidence* about comparative effectiveness is needed to do CBA. Further illustrating how important they consider research to be in policymaking, they provide an appendix that describes how to conduct focused secondary and (to a lesser extent) primary research. For example, they suggest looking for a past natural experiment (not their term) that raised parking fees to help predict the effects of proposed changes.

This kind of rational ideal of the role of research in the policymaking process is a useful place to start because it raises several important issues and questions—even before bringing politics, interests, values, and other real-world complexities into the picture.

Statistical Significance

To become a basis for a policy or administrative action, most would agree that the evidence should be statistically significant—not just a one-off fluke. But as we discussed in Chapter 8, the reality is more complex. First, we don't want to treat a p value of .05 as some magical mark to be applied too rigidly. In some contexts, p values of .10 or perhaps more can be enough evidence to act. Remember also that statistical power is important as well: We don't want to miss out on policies that work because we have too small a sample size or too tough a standard for our p values. In other cases, we might want to be very sure that a program or intervention works and therefore require a lower p value, despite the lower power that it implies. Statistical significance should always be considered, but thoughtfully. And it should be considered in combination with practical significance, discussed next, for example, by the use of confidence intervals in addition to (or even in place of) significance tests.

Practical Significance

We have stressed the importance of presenting and understanding causal effects in terms that allow them to be practically evaluated. Is the magnitude of the effect big enough to be worth implementing? This is the question of practical, as opposed to purely statistical, significance. Measures of effect size are sometimes used to evaluate practical significance, but this is still only a first step. A program with a small effect size might be worth implementing—if it still beats the alternatives or it is combating an important problem.

Evidence of Causation

One of the most difficult challenges involved in making policy or taking administrative action based on research is determining if the evidence of causation is good enough. Statistical and even practical significance alone can never establish causation. Therefore, before implementing a program to achieve a desired outcome, we need to establish that an effect is actually causal and that our estimate of the magnitude of the effect is not biased.

But good causal estimates are very hard to get, as we have seen in previous chapters. On real-world topics, policymakers and practitioners will almost always have to act before or without getting definitive causal evidence.

For example, when the National Breastfeeding Campaign was initially launched, evidence of the causal effect of breastfeeding on child outcomes was not strong, yet some evidence pointed to possibly big effects. Public health practitioners decided to promote a policy based on statistical and practical significance, because they believed it to be valuable and they could not wait for conclusive causal evidence that might never come. Since then, yet more evidence has emerged, although the results are still not clear and continue to be debated (see Box 14.1). The real world cannot always wait for definitive evidence, and sometimes a clear answer will never emerge.

BOX 14.1
The Effects of Breastfeeding: Many Studies

The National Breastfeeding Campaign began in 2003 (as the National Breastfeeding Awareness Campaign) without the benefit of many recent studies of the effects of breast-feeding. Breastfeeding was associated in observational data with many good outcomes for children. Some outcomes had highly plausible mechanisms, while others did not. Many studies with control variables had been performed before the campaign was launched, but important unmeasured variables were still unaccounted for. In Chapter 11, we discussed at length the Der et al. (2006) study that eliminated the effect of breast-feeding on child cognitive skills by adding mother's own aptitude as a control variable. We have already discussed the possible weaknesses of observational studies, even those with control variables.

The best new evidence comes from results of a cluster-randomized experiment. Kramer and colleagues (2001b) designed a study that randomized maternal hospitals and associated polyclinics in Belarus to either a breastfeeding promotion arm or a con-trol group. Mothers in the breastfeeding promotion arm did in fact breastfeed more often and longer, allowing the researchers to measure a causal effect of breastfeeding on a long list of child outcomes. To date, the evidence is mixed: Some outcomes (e.g., respiratory infections, asthma, obesity, dental cavities) show no effect, while others (cognitive skills, infant gastrointestinal infections, atopic eczema) do (Kramer et al., 2001a, 2001b; Kramer, Aboud, et al., 2009; Kramer, Matush, et al., 2007; Kramer, Matush, et al., 2009; Kramer, Vanilovich, et al., 2007).

Moreover, cluster-randomized designs result in weaker evidence of causation than an ordinary randomized trial. Consequently, both significant and insignificant outcomes carry caveats or have been challenged. For example, the finding of no effect on asthma was challenged because the cluster design made the two arms somewhat unbalanced. In particular, the treatment arm had a higher family history of allergies and asthma, rais-ing the possibility that the treatment arm was at an initial disadvantage (Mamabear, 2007). The effects on cognitive skills, which were strongly practically significant, may have been due to the fact that the researchers doing the assessments were not blinded and knew whether the children had been in the treatment or control arm (Kramer, Aboud, et al., 2009). The lack of blinding is an inevitable consequence of the cluster design, which created clustered measurement and therefore measurement errors cor-related with treatment assignment (Kramer, Martin, et al., 2009). Other challenges could include the generalizability of the results to both poorer and richer countries and the legitimacy of statistical significance tests for so many outcomes in one trial, although the outcomes were specified before the experiment began. Of course, such challenges in no way invalidate the research, but they illustrate how hard it is to do definitive research even with a rigorous research design.

Recent new natural experiment studies have also emerged. Two studies make use of differences between siblings in breastfeeding, based on the idea that all other factors driving outcomes are the same among siblings and so the effect of breastfeeding can be isolated (Evenhouse & Reilly, 2005; Rees & Sabia, 2009). Together they show substantial effects on physical health, mental health, cognitive skills, and education but also suggest that most observational estimates are biased. As in most natural experiments, the premise that all other relevant factors are the same among siblings could be challenged, since one wonders why one sibling was breastfed and not the other. Baker and Milligan (2008) use the natural experiment of an increase in mandated maternity leave in Canada that raised breastfeeding. They found no effects on most child health measures. This study, too, could be challenged for several reasons, particularly that a government maternity leave policy had only a small effect on Canadian mothers' breastfeeding.

These many recent breastfeeding articles illustrate two important points. First, real-world policy decisions must often be made with incomplete evidence. Second, evidence is often contradictory.

How Many Studies?

Replication is a central principle of research. It inhibits researchers from cherry-picking, or manipulating their results, helping to ensure that the evidence is more trustworthy. But replication of the same or similar studies is often not enough to provide evidence to justify action. Instead, having different kinds of studies helps because of the various strengths and weaknesses of, for example, observational studies in comparison with natural or quasi experiments.

Consider again the example in Chapter 1 about the effects of divorce on children. Many observational studies showed that divorce is associated with poor outcomes for children but provided little evidence that divorce caused those outcomes. Gruber (2004) used the natural experiments of states changing their divorce laws at different times to provide stronger evidence of causation—but only of no-fault divorce and only on limited outcomes. Collectively, however, the studies made the case that divorce could causally affect many of the correlated outcomes, including hard-to-measure psychological ones not in the Gruber study.

Dealing With Uncertainty, Costs, and Benefits

In applying research to make policy, two kinds of uncertainty must be considered. First, wide confidence intervals mean that we don't know whether there is a difference or not. Second, lack of good causal evidence means that we don't know whether, or the extent to which, a difference reflects a causal effect. As we saw in Chapter 10 in the opening example about family dinners and drug use, there often can be alternative theories that might explain a relationship or difference—meaning there is uncertainty as to which causal explanation represents the truth.

What do we do when we don't know? Obviously, looking for more evidence is a good choice. But what to do while we wait? And what if there is no doable study that can answer the question?

Because policy must be made without perfect research, the available evidence must be weighed against other factors. The cost of acting, including, but certainly not limited to, the financial cost, is a central consideration. If a program is financially cheap, not time-consuming, and carries few risks or side effects, then it is probably worth implementing even if the evidence is weak. Programs with much higher costs, in money, time, risk, or anything else, require stronger evidence of their benefits.

Consider again an individual mother deciding whether or not to breastfeed. If she can breastfeed with little financial or mental health cost, then it makes good sense. Why not? It could be highly beneficial or at least somewhat beneficial. For those mothers who find other benefits of breastfeeding, such as bonding, the decision is clear. But what about mothers—for example, working mothers or single mothers with other children to care for—who may suffer financial costs or stress by trying to breastfeed? How big do the benefits have to be and how good does the evidence need to be for them? And how much of the evidence should they know? Few mothers will read even a small part of the voluminous research literature. They depend on government agencies and other groups to inform them. We return later to the difficult ethical questions this raises for those in charge of informing the public.

Pathways of Influence

Having considered issues that arise even when following a rational ideal of policymaking, we now turn to the ways research actually does influence policy. We will start off with some of the official pathways of influence.

Official Pathways

The use of research is procedurally, and sometimes even legislatively, built into the policymaking process. For example, the government sometimes requires, as part of legislation, evaluation of a program, particularly a new or controversial program. For example, the U.S. Congress mandated an evaluation of the State Children's Health Insurance Program. The U.S. Department of Health and Human Services oversaw the contract to researchers from Mathematica and the Urban Institute, highly regarded research organizations, who published a final report to Congress (Wooldridge, Kenney, & Trenholm, 2005).

Many government agencies conduct both research and analysis ranging from performance measurement through extensive analysis by teams of experienced full-time researchers. Some specialized agencies, such as the Government Accountability Office, are specifically charged with doing independent research and analysis. And many agencies responsible for data gathering, such as the Bureau of the Census and the Bureau of Labor Statistics, do methodological research to sustain their data gathering and other, substantive research. Many of these and other government agencies have scientific advisory boards to ensure that their research and analyses are well done. Examples include the Census Advisory Committee on Agriculture Research and the African Development Foundation Advisory Council, among many others.

The various National Academies of Science also collect and synthesize research to play a role in the policy process. For example, the Institute of Medicine conducted a 3-year study on the lack of health insurance and its implications. Six subcommittees produced a report each, synthesizing research on topics such as societal costs of uninsured populations (Institute of Medicine Committee on the Consequences of Uninsurance, 2003). To ensure balance, all subcommittees contained experts with a variety of disciplinary backgrounds and political affiliations.

"Like Water Falling on Limestone"

For much research, the pathway to policy is slow, indirect, and erratic. Walt (1994) (quoting Bulmer quoting Thomas) said that "the pattern of influence [of research on policy] can be likened to water falling on limestone: The water is absorbed, but there is no knowing what route it will take . . . or where it will come out." The idea is that a lot of knowledge is produced and eventually, some of it gets used.

Many researchers are also teachers at universities, and as such they train their students about bodies of research in their fields of expertise. Eventually, some of those students become legislative staff, advisers, heads of agencies, and so on, where the research they learned as students influences their actions.

Some research does influence policy through this route, but often, nonresearchers play a more active role. That role can be illustrated with the example of taxing cigarettes.

High Cigarette Taxes: The Power of Ideas and of Advocacy[1]

Starting in the early 1980s, university researchers published papers on how sensitive cigarette consumption is to the price of cigarettes (e.g., Lewit & Coate, 1982). The research happened to come out at a time when government revenues were particularly needed and public opinion was turning against smoking. The research was picked up and promoted by various antismoking advocates, in both the United States and Canada. The Canadian advocates succeeded first in getting higher cigarette taxes, and rates of smoking in the country began to fall (confirming the causal predictions of the academic studies). Advocates in the United States then pushed for higher cigarette taxes in California and other states and, eventually, at the federal level as well.

The cigarette tax example illustrates how advocacy groups and think tanks pick up on research findings and try to inform a much broader public of their significance. For that process to succeed, the research must strike some chord and fit in with the values or politics of the moment. The luck of timing can also influence whether someone decides to champion the research in the first place. But to be credible, the research has to be methodologically sound so that it stands up to scrutiny and convinces those who are not already committed to the issue.

---

[1]This section is based on Kennedy School of Government (1993).

Politics and Other Barriers

We have discussed what research ought to influence policy and how research often does influence policy, both directly and indirectly. But valuable research often fails to influence policy. We now turn to the barriers research faces in influencing policy.

Time and Timeliness

Policy is often made quickly, in response to pressing practical or political circumstances that cannot wait. Unfortunately, the research process is often slow, and policymakers have no choice but to form policy without research or with ambiguous research.

Certain forms of research, such as randomized field experiments with long-term outcomes, can be extremely slow. For example, final results from the Moving to Opportunity experiment took 15 years from the time the study was initiated (and even more time since it was a glimmer in someone's eye). Besharov (2009) lists that example and many others when describing how high-quality evidence from randomized field trials often arrives after policies have already been made and formulated. Consequently, he also advocates research studies that can be done comparatively quickly, even if the evidence produced is not as definitive.

Cultural and Moral Values

Sometimes, research does not influence policy because attitudes toward the policy are driven by cultural and moral values and not by evidence. For example, some individuals may oppose educating teenagers about birth control because they feel that it is simply wrong. In that case, their policy positions do not depend on the results of studies comparing the effects of different forms of sex education on teenage pregnancy and sexually transmitted diseases. The death penalty provides another example: Many people are simply opposed to the idea on moral grounds, regardless of whatever evidence there might be regarding the deterrent effect of the death penalty on murder rates.

Researchers should understand that individuals' and societies' values can legitimately trump research when making policy. The democratic process must work out conflicts about values. The role of research is to provide information. The mechanisms through which values can legitimately affect the policy process and restrict the influence of research are many: legal mandates, rights, and fairness procedures (Pannell & Roberts, 2009).

But we should distinguish values about what ought to be from potentially false beliefs about what is. If political positions are based on false beliefs about what is, then ideally, research could play a role. Unfortunately, people may not be open to evidence that contradicts what they believe. In the sex education example, one can believe that educating teenagers about birth control is wrong and oppose it on moral grounds. It is a different matter to refuse to consider evidence that educating teenagers about birth control reduces teen pregnancies.

Distrust of Researchers

Sometimes research cannot influence policy because the public or politicians do not trust researchers. They believe that the research results are driven by the values and biases of the researchers—and sometimes they are right. Values certainly shape the questions that researchers ask and often shape which results researchers pay attention to and which they ignore. And unfortunately, a few researchers sometimes deliberately manipulate or suppress research to support their agenda. Ethics dictate that researchers try their best to be open-minded and react to research results based on the quality of the evidence.

Politics and Interest Groups[2]

Interest groups support policies that benefit them, even if research shows that the policies are inefficient or ineffective. Politicians support policies that benefit their own constituencies or political interests as well. And frequently, interest groups successfully make politicians' interests coincide with their own. In such situations, all these groups may ignore, suppress, or distort research to pursue their own objectives.

But beyond such self-interest, some believe that politics has a life of its own, independent of interests, and that research has a very limited role to play. For example, Stone (1997) describes politics as a paradox in which causes are really more about stories that groups agree on than real causes that research could prove or disprove. Kingdon (1995) describes a similar view but with more of a role for research, in which the political process of creating policy is a soup with three separate ingredients: problems, policies, and politics. These ingredients can be combined or separated as circumstances vary. For example, the policy of public transport was first put forward to combat the problem of congestion, then the energy crisis, and most recently, global warming. Politics determines which problems get attention, which policies get paired with which problems, which policies get implemented, and how and when. Within this theory, research can play a role by finding new problems and policies.

A Failure to Move From Research to Policy: The U.S. Poverty Definition

As the emphasis on research and evidence has grown, measurement, particularly performance measurement, has grown in importance. Therefore, performance measures influence the careers of politicians and senior managers, leading them to not care so much about accurate measurement or the substance of what is supposed to be measured but simply about making their numbers.

In the television series *The Wire,* this tendency was both dramatized and satirized by showing politicians and government officials doctoring both crime and education statistics, "juking the stats," so that success could be claimed (Sheehan & Sweeney, 2009, p. 3). Even when government officials do not try to doctor measures, they may be reluctant to improve their accuracy if it could make things look worse on their watch. This is one of the reasons that the U.S. poverty measure, widely viewed as seriously flawed, has remained as it is for so long.

---

[2]We thank Karl Kronebusch for his help with this section.

In Chapter 4, we described the shortcomings in the official U.S. poverty measure, and we saw that two main problems stood out. First, the income or resources counted in the measure of poverty do not include any in-kind benefits, such as food stamps, public housing, or tax credits (such as the Earned Income Tax Credit). Second, the income threshold was based on three times a basic expenditure on food in 1966, updated for inflation. Since the relative price of food has dropped while the relative prices of other essentials, such as housing, have risen, this threshold is now considered inadequate for essentials or, at the very least, calculated in an arbitrary way unrelated to the prices of essentials. Some have referred to the poverty data as "nonsensical numbers" (Blank, 2008).

And yet, despite fairly widespread agreement that the official poverty measure is flawed, it has proven difficult to change it, and (as of this writing) it has not been changed. Rebecca Blank, an economist, has had extensive involvement in political efforts to reform the poverty measure, including being on the Council of Economic Advisers to the Clinton administration during its failed attempts to reform the measure. In her 2007 address to the Association for Public Policy Analysis and Management (APPAM), she described the political barriers (Blank, 2008).

First, according to Blank, many benefits are tied to the poverty definition. Consequently, a major reform could increase the number of people entitled to benefits, resulting in either a major increase in expenditures or an outcry of unjustly denied benefits. No politician wants to have such budgetary or public opinion difficulties.

Even if the new poverty definition were calibrated to keep the poverty rate constant, the distribution of beneficiaries would change, with some losing benefits while others gained. For example, the recommendations of an expert panel on how to reform the poverty measure would result in more working families being identified as "poor" and fewer families with large in-kind benefits being deemed poor. And, as Blank (2008) notes,

> Both increases and decreases in the number of poor among a group could provoke concern...
> What President wants to announce that poverty has gone up on his watch? But decreases in poverty counts...[appear] to minimize economic need among groups that . . . garner political attention. (p. 241)

Second, a variety of other government programs allocate funds in ways tied to poverty rates, such as mandates that Medicaid cover pregnant women with incomes up to 133% of the poverty level. If the poverty level were changed, many other funding formulas would need to be redone, opening up new political fights.

Third, the main group that was interested in having accurate measures of poverty consisted of economists and statisticians; it was not a major political interest group. Without politically influential groups that can fight for a reformed poverty measure, the costs of reform loomed too large.

How Can Research Have More Influence?

We have described many barriers to research influencing policy, including time, cultural values, and politics. Is there a way to legitimately increase the influence of research? Walt (1994) suggests that researchers need to better understand power and the political process so that information can be strategically deployed to target audiences in the most effective way. He suggests paying attention to timing and making greater efforts with communication. Pannell and Roberts (2009) echo those suggestions and add others, stating that researchers should try harder to "understand the policy-maker's perspective, practice excellent communication, be solution oriented, find a champion, avoid appearances of vested interest, and be simple, patient, persistent, resilient, responsive and timely." Thus, researchers can and should try harder to make their research known and relevant. But policymakers and administrators also need to make efforts to find and interpret research findings that relate to their areas of policy and practice.

We turn next to the production of research, including research funding and institutions, and how these forces shape the priorities and activities of researchers.

The Production of Research

In addition to being a method of inquiry, research is also a major social and economic activity involving billions in spending and employing many thousands of people. The various sources of research funding, as well as the different kinds of research institutions, are important components of a complete understanding and interpretation of research.

Who Funds Research?

Various government agencies, foundations, and private companies fund research around the globe. In the United States, for example, basic science research is funded by the National Science Foundation (NSF), which spends more than $6 billion annually (NSF, 2009). Basic biomedical research is funded by the National Institutes of Health (NIH), which spends about $30 billion each year (NIH, 2009). These agencies also fund some policy research as well as basic research. For example, the NIH includes the National Institute of Mental Health and Substance Abuse (NIMHSA), which does research on many social and policy issues. And the NSF includes a social science section that funds some applied social research. But other government agencies fund most of the applied research. For example, the Institute of Educational Sciences within the U.S. Department of Education sponsors research on education and learning. The Justice Department, the Environmental Protection Agency, the Labor Department, the Department of Transportation, the Department of Housing and Urban Development, the Department of Homeland Security, and the Department of Agriculture, to name a few, all sponsor research and evaluations of new or existing programs or issues, either to respond to a congressional mandate or for their own strategic management purposes. The U.S. Bureau of the Census (housed in the U.S. Department of Commerce) spends about $7 billion collecting and disseminating social and demographic data of various kinds. In addition, state and local governments support applied research related to their own policy priorities and concerns.

Private foundations also spend a significant amount of money to support research of various kinds. The Gates Foundation, the Ford Foundation, the Robert Wood Johnson Foundation, the Andrew Mellon Foundation, the MacArthur Foundation, and many others provide a total of billions in research funding in many areas, including public health, education, criminal justice, and policy research. There are also nonprofit, fund-raising, and advocacy organizations that support research on specific issues or diseases, such as the American Cancer Society, the American Heart Association, the American Foundation for the Blind, and the Public Health Foundation, again just to name a few.

We have been listing mostly U.S. sources of funding, but of course, governments and private foundations in many other countries around the world spend considerable resources on research as well.

Requests for Proposals (RFPs)

When government agencies, foundations, or other funders have research they wish to commission or support, they often put out **requests for proposals** (**RFPs**). These describe the aims of the research funding program, including what research questions the funders want answered and, sometimes, the preferred methodology of the proposed research. The RFPs also describe the amount of time and money available. Researchers apply for funding by submitting proposals that describe their research plans as well as their qualifications and experience. Typically, governments and foundations establish committees—often made up of other researchers in the field (peers)—to review, rate, and rank the proposals and decide which ones will receive funding awards.

Competitive funding awards tend to go to well-defined research questions with a high likelihood of success. This makes it hard, sometimes, for researchers to do more innovative, risky research. Indeed, some researchers complain that to win a grant they must have already done most of the work, demonstrating the potential success.

Unfunded Research

Although external funding is essential for many studies, not all research depends on it. Sometimes research can be relatively inexpensive, for example, when a sole researcher analyzes publicly available data sets using desktop software. Such research is often (but not always) **unfunded**, meaning that no specific grant or contract was provided to support it. College and university professors, who also devote time to teaching and administrative activities, do most of this kind of unfunded research. Strictly speaking, of course, the institutions that employ these professors and provide them with salaries, office space, technology, libraries, and other resources provide important internal, indirect funding.

Some organizations, particularly government agencies, think tanks, interest groups, and international agencies, have staff researchers. These researchers may occasionally compete for external grants and contracts, but much of the research they do is part of their ordinary job duties.

How Time and Cost Shape Research

Research, like all human endeavors, is shaped by constraints of time and cost. For example, a long and expensive randomized experiment might provide a really definitive answer to a particular question, but if no one is willing to fund it (internally or externally), then the research won't be done. And researchers are limited by their other obligations. If a research project would take 50 hours a week, over several years, a professor who teaches six classes a year won't do that research project and will choose a less time-consuming one.

Sometimes, researchers or observers feel that it is bad that time and cost constraints shape research, but these constraints are legitimate. Resources, including an individual's time, always have other uses—"opportunity costs," in the jargon of economists. A particular piece of research should only be done if its expected value is greater than the next best use of the time and other resources.

However, some constraints are a bit artificial. Young researchers at colleges and universities often hope to get tenure, a strong form of job security. To do so, they must have a substantial body of published work by the time they are up for tenure, which is usually less than 7 years after starting as an assistant professor. Projects that require a long start-up and a long data-gathering stage, such as a prospective longitudinal study, are generally avoided by untenured professors. Even tenured faculty and researchers in nonacademic settings have time deadlines—periods of time during which a substantial amount of work is expected to be completed.

All funders of research—government agencies, not-for-profit organizations, and private companies—seek value for money. They have their own budget constraints. Therefore, large-scale, long-term, or labor-intensive research is difficult to fund. Time and cost constraints inevitably affect both choice of research question and choice of research methods.

Where Is Research Conducted?

Social and policy research is conducted in a variety of institutional and organizational settings. Understanding these settings is important, because they shape the focus and methods of a study—and determine what questions researchers ask, or ignore.

Universities and Colleges

Doing research, both basic and applied, is essential to the mission of most universities and colleges. Even colleges that once only focused on teaching now also emphasize research. Still, only a few hundred of the several thousand higher education institutions in the United States are considered research universities with high levels of research activity, according to the Carnegie classification (Carnegie Foundation for the Advancement of Teaching, 2009). These universities emphasize the training of doctoral students, and they tend to require less teaching—and more research—from their faculties. But good research also comes from many smaller, more specialized colleges and universities as well.

The quantity and quality of research have become major criteria in the hiring and promotion of university faculty and in the awarding of tenure. Thus, university and college professors have a major incentive to produce research and to demonstrate its quality by publishing their work in top-rated journals or books. This incentive leads to much good and useful research, but it can also lead to the proliferation of what sometimes seems to be rather restricted, highly specialized, and even arcane research that only relates to fairly narrow academic questions or concerns.

The professional schools—such as schools of public affairs, education, public health, or criminal justice—generally focus more on applied research, while arts and sciences departments (sociology, economics, psychology, etc.) do more basic research. But this division is far from universal, and much applied social research is done in arts and sciences departments.

Government

Some research is performed at government research institutes. In the United States, the NIH and the Centers for Disease Control and Prevention (CDC) are important examples, although less social research is conducted in government institutes than biological or physical science research. In continental Europe, government research institutes play a relatively larger role in the production of research than in the United States.

In the United States, many government agencies whose primary role is not research nonetheless conduct significant amounts of research. A particularly striking example is the Federal Reserve (central bank), but the Department of Agriculture, the Census Bureau, and many other administrative agencies produce research. Obviously, the research is applied and meant to serve the needs of the agency. The research is typically conducted within units devoted to policy analysis or program evaluation.

Think Tanks

Research is also done in foundations and think tanks, which are not-for-profit organizations with some kind of public interest mission. Some prominent public policy think tanks include the Brookings Institution, the American Enterprise Institute, the Heritage Foundation, the Aspen Institute, the Council on Foreign Relations, the Center on Budget and Policy Priorities, the Economic Policy Institute, and the Hoover Institution, among many others. Some of these think tanks are associated with certain political or ideological perspectives. The Heritage Foundation, for example, is a conservative think tank, while the Center on Budget and Policy Priorities is a liberal think tank.

Contract Research Organizations

Policy research is often produced under government contract by organizations such as the RAND Corporation, the Urban Institute, the Research Triangle Institute (RTI), Mathematica Policy Research, the Manpower Demonstration Research Corporation (MDRC), Abt Associates Inc., Westat, Inc., and others. These organizations may be not-for-profit or for-profit entities. They tend to be quite large and to have the technical capability as well as the organizational capacity to carry out large, complex research projects, including large national surveys or major randomized policy experiments.

There are also research companies that focus more on serving the private sector, such as polling and market research firms. Some examples include Gallup, Harris Interactive, Ipsos, Edison Media Research, and Knowledge Networks.

Advocacy Organizations

Advocacy organizations are primarily consumers of research, secondarily commissioners of research, and only thirdly conductors of research. However, they do often have their own in-house researchers.

The lines between think tanks, contract research organizations, and advocacy organizations are often not clear. They depend roughly on the extent to which the organization has a clearly defined mission for which it fund-raises relative to the extent that it just seeks to earn revenue by doing research. But some organizations are often put in more than one category. For example, the Urban Institute is both a think tank and a contract research organization.

The growing accessibility of data and computers makes performing research within reach of far more organizations of all kinds than was once possible.

Research Cultures and Disciplines

Researchers have a culture of their own, just as all occupations do. Researchers tend to value insight and even cleverness. An article that is widely read becomes a status symbol, as are publications in prestigious journals, invitations to speak at important conferences and seminars, and so on. While money has some status, status among researchers is more divorced from money than in many other professions.

The culture of researchers is also fragmented. Particular disciplines have their own cultures. For example, economists are known for their aggressive questioning in seminars. Applied social research cultures are also defined by the policy domain or content of study, so that education research and health services research have specific cultures. And the different settings have their own cultures. In research organizations supported by external funding, the culture values the ability to bring in grants. In academic settings, publication in highly ranked journals is paramount.

In addition to having their own cultures, disciplines have their own theories and tools that shape how specific questions are framed and answered—and even shape which questions are asked and which ones are ignored. Consider this humorous metaphor:

One night someone sees a friend looking around under a lamppost.

"What are you looking for?" the first friend asks.

"My keys," the searching friend says.

"Did you lose them here beneath the lamppost?"

"No. But this is where the light is."

Researchers address questions that they have tools to address, often neglecting more important questions. Like the man who lost his keys, they look where they have light, even if it is not where the keys are. Disciplines all have their own methodological tools, their own kinds of light. So they address questions that can be answered with the tools commonly used in their discipline—even if these are not the most important questions. And they address questions with the tools commonly used in their discipline—even if those tools may not be the best ones for the question at hand.

Ethics of Research

Although we have brought up ethical issues throughout this book, we will look now more closely at the topic of ethics in the conduct of research. Let's begin with an example of a researcher's lapse of ethical judgment.

Restaurant managers did not consent to be research subjects.

Source: © 2009 Jupiterimages Corporation.

Poisoned by New York's Best Restaurants

In an effort to study how firms deal with disgruntled customers, a professor at Columbia University sent the same letter of complaint to 240 fine restaurants in New York City. In the letter, he explained how he had just dined at the restaurant with his wife, a special anniversary dinner, only to spend the night suffering from the symptoms of food poisoning. "Our special romantic evening became reduced to my wife watching me curl up in the fetal position on the tiled floor of our bathroom between rounds of throwing up," the letter complained (*The Michigan Daily*, 2001). The restaurateurs who received the letters were dismayed and distraught, believing that they had somehow committed a grave error that might ruin their reputations and put them out of business. When they found out later that they had been deceived as part of a study, they were outraged at the researcher and the university (and later even tried suing for damages).

History of Human Subjects Abuses in Research

The history of research involving human beings includes many instances of unethical practices, some much more harmful than the bogus food poisoning letters. Early medical experiments were performed on prisoners or residents of poorhouses, often without their knowledge or consent. The Nazis became infamous, during the Nuremburg trials, as revelations unfolded about their inhumane medical experiments on Jews imprisoned in concentration camps during World War II.

In the United States, the U.S. Public Health Service ran the notorious Tuskegee syphilis study from the 1930s through as late as the early 1970s. In that study, researchers recruited African American subjects (mostly poor sharecroppers) with late-stage syphilis into the study and then followed them for many years to observe the consequences of the disease. The participants were never treated for the disease, not even after penicillin was discovered in 1947 as way to treat syphilis. Many of those in the Tuskegee study suffered painful and debilitating symptoms and eventually died from the disease (Jones, 1993).

Ethical concerns have been raised by research in the social sciences as well, particularly with regard to social experiments. In Stanley Milgram's (1974) obedience-to-authority studies of the 1960s, subjects were asked by an authority to give (phony) electrical shocks to another individual sitting behind a two-way glass. Some subjects complied with the request to the point of administering what they believed were fatal shocks to an actor behind the glass—a disturbing experience for someone who simply agreed to participate in a campus psychology experiment. These experiments became notorious symbols of the ethical problems that can arise in social experiments.

Principles of Ethical Research Emerge

Formal principles began to be established in response to these events. The Nuremburg Code of 1947, stemming from the trial verdict, outlined various principles of ethical conduct in research, among them

- Informed consent
- Voluntary participation
- No harm to subjects

- Beneficence (the notion that research should potentially benefit subjects and that these potential benefits must outweigh the risks)

The principles have become the foundation of contemporary research ethics in most countries around the world.

The outrage in the United States over the Tuskegee syphilis study eventually led to the *Belmont Report* of 1979, which provided the framework for the current federal government ethics regulations (known as 45 C.F.R. Part 46). These regulations require the establishment of **institutional review boards (IRBs)** composed of scientists and laypeople that must review and approve the ethics of federally funded research.

The IRB Process

Almost every university, college, hospital, health agency, school system, and research organization now has an IRB. If the organization receives federal money of any kind, then 45 C.F.R. Part 46 requiring an IRB applies. If you are doing research in one of these settings, you will likely need to get IRB approval for your study, even if it is unfunded. Even student research comes under the IRBs.

Although researchers like to complain about the process, IRBs play an important role in contemporary research and not only help protect human subjects who participate in studies but also help prevent researchers from making mistakes. The professor who conducted the restaurant study, for example, did not go to his IRB—and it got him into a lot of trouble.

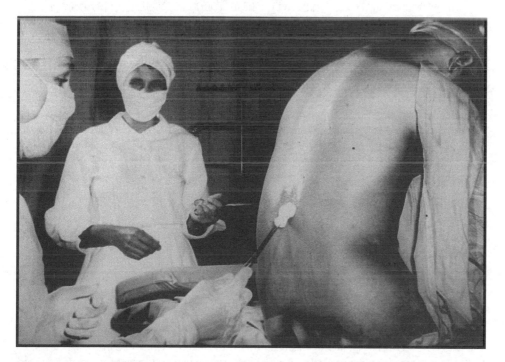

Photograph from the Tuskegee syphilis study.

Source: © Laura Noel/Corbis.

The first step is to be aware of the process—find out about your institution's IRB and its policies. Many IRBs provide training in human subjects protection that you can attend. As *principal investigator* (the lead person on a study), or as a member of a research team, you will then need to become certified in the protection of human subjects. You become certified by completing training and by passing a test about research ethics and related federal rules.

When submitting your study plan to the IRB, you will need to complete a form and provide a narrative describing your study, including procedures for recruiting participants and obtaining their consent as well as the details of the research design, measurement instruments, qualitative methods, and data management procedures that will be used in your study.

Your study will fall into one of the following three categories of review, depending on the level of risk to human subjects:

- *Exempt review*—meaning there is only minimal risk to human subjects and the study meets certain other requirements (such as research using educational tests, surveys, existing data, or observations of public behavior). Much (although not all) observational, social science studies fall into this category.
- *Expedited review*—the study presents only minimal risks, but it does not meet the exempt requirements. Often, these are experimental or medical studies in which the treatments, or measurements, pose no more than minimal risks.
- *Full IRB review*—the study does not qualify for either exempt or expedited review, often because there is more than a minimal risk to subjects, or because the subjects are children, prisoners, pregnant women, cognitively impaired persons, or another of several specially protected groups. This category includes most of the many clinical trials used in testing new drugs or potentially risky medical procedures as well as psychological experiments that cause discomfort or potential harm (such as sleep deprivation studies) or involve deception. The full IRB meets to discuss these studies before granting approval.

You must obtain IRB approval before beginning your research, report any adverse events that occur during the study (such as any complaints from or injuries to participants), and file a final report to the IRB at the end of your study. Nobody likes doing paperwork, and the IRB can seem bureaucratic sometimes, but the importance of its role as a representative of the rights and interests of the people who participate in research is undeniable.

Ethical Dilemmas in Research

Research ethics, like life in general, are often complex and unclear—not a matter of simple right and wrong. Thus, researchers face some ethical dilemmas.

Sham Surgery

Consider the issue of sham surgery (Gerber & Patashnik, 2006). When people receive a treatment of any kind, they experience the placebo effect: The expectation of benefit in fact causes a benefit. The placebo effect is not limited to pills and, in fact, the placebo effect of surgery appears to be higher. In that case, a randomized trial of any surgery, even one that does not actually do anything, would show a positive effect, because those receiving surgery would get a placebo effect while those in the control group would not. As a result, some have pushed for those in the control arm of a surgical intervention to receive sham surgery so that they won't know which arm they are in. Others find this process ethically unacceptable. Surgery always carries some risks, although they can be quite small. How can people be subjected to those risks with no prospect of individual benefit but only benefit to the wider public? On the other hand, under some circumstances, sham surgery may be the only way to demonstrate that a procedure believed to be effective is in fact not effective.

More generally, randomized experiments provide the best evidence of causation and thus are of great value to policymakers and the public. But randomized experiments make the choice of treatment insensitive to the desires of and best wishes of the individuals participating. Regulations about informed consent and no harm done reduce the dilemma but do not eliminate it.

Ethics of Research Dissemination and Presentation

A lot of attention has gone to the ethics of how to conduct research involving human subjects, but less attention has gone to the ethics of research presentation and dissemination. These are also important ethical areas.

We saw at the beginning of this chapter that when the National Breastfeeding Campaign was started in 2003, evidence that the measured effects of breastfeeding were causal was fairly limited, but the campaign was not presented as such (Wolf, 2007). Because causal evidence is so hard to obtain, public health officials and others in charge of disseminating research do face a genuine problem. The epidemiology and public health literatures illustrate how researchers have struggled with these issues (e.g., Sandman, 1991, and other citations in Wolf, 2007).

But the ethical dilemmas are not limited to public health. Researchers and those who use research in all applied areas, including criminal justice, housing, education, and others, must decide how to present research, as well as when and how to disseminate it. Clearly, manipulating or cherry-picking results is unethical. But how much ambiguity and complexity should be presented? Some summary and simplification are essential, and knowing when to draw the line can be difficult.

Life-Saving Research, Limited Access, and Peer Review

Much valuable, and even life-saving, research is published in journals that are not freely available without purchasing a subscription. When such research could benefit people, is it unethical to limit its availability? For this reason, certain articles, particularly in medical journals, are published with open access.

A similar issue arises when apparently life-saving research is subject to a lengthy peer-review process. On the one hand, peer review is used to provide support that apparent research results are really true and is needed to protect the public against false claims. On the other hand, its length of time can mean that those who might benefit remain in ignorance while the review process continues. Ethics dictate that the review process should be sensitive to those issues.

That Ethical State of Mind

Research ethics are not only—and not primarily—about jumping through the hoops required by regulations and IRBs. Ethics imply an effort to pay attention to ethical issues—to pay attention to the harms and benefits to people, to equity issues among people, to the autonomy and liberty of people.

Such attention should be paid even to research that is not subject to IRB approval, such as research done internally within an organization or for purely management purposes.

Conclusion

In this chapter, you have learned how research fits into the broader political context and the policy-making process, including the pathways to as well as barriers against research influencing policy and practice. You also found out about how research is produced, including the different sources of research funding and the types of institutions that conduct research. And you learned more about the history of research ethics and the formal rules and procedures that have been established to protect participants in research.

This chapter may have discouraged some of you who hope to use research to improve policy. But realize that the world of policy and practice must take into account a wide array of influences and interests and that research-based knowledge is only a part of the picture. A few helpful lessons, however, did emerge in this chapter: the importance of selecting good research questions and communicating clearly and effectively. The next chapter discusses both of these skills in more detail as well as the skill of finding relevant research on a topic of interest.

EXERCISES

Research in the Policy Process

14.1. Pick a policy issue that is currently being debated in the news or in your field of study. How does research form part of the policy debate? What advocates, or sides of the debate, are promoting research findings? What other considerations, including values and political interests, also matter in the debate?

Public Information Campaigns Based on Research

14.2. Find a recent public information campaign to change a behavior, similar to the National Breastfeeding Campaign. What body of research lies behind the campaign? (You may find a summary and references on the Web site of the organization sponsoring the campaign.) Does the research being cited meet the standards of statistical significance, practical significance, and evidence of causation?

Where Does Research Come From?

14.3. Look at a journal in your field or area of interest. (If you are not aware of them, we list some in Chapter 15.) Pick out a few articles. Answer the following questions:

- Where was the research done? At a university or a college? If so, what kind of school or department? Or was the research done by a government agency, think tank, or contract research organization?
- Was the research funded, or unfunded? (All external funding should be acknowledged in research articles, sometimes in the footnotes or acknowledgments.) How costly and time-consuming do you think the research was to complete?

Ethical Issues In Your Own Research

14.4. Think about a simple piece of research you might do involving, say, a small survey of people in your community or workplace. What ethical issues would you need to consider? How would you ensure informed consent, voluntary participation, no harm to subjects, and beneficence?

An Alternative to the Food-Poisoning Ruse

14.5. Recall the business school professor who wrote to many of New York's best restaurants stating (falsely) that he had gotten food poisoning from their restaurant. Describe the ethical problems with this research. Can you think of a more ethical way to examine the research question of how firms deal with disgruntled customers? How well would this new, more ethical research answer the question?

Objectives: This chapter will help you find studies on a topic of interest in research journals, government reports, books, and other electronic and print sources. You will also learn about how to develop and focus a research question, one of the most important skills in doing primary research. The chapter also provides some guidance for how to present and write about your own research. Doing good research is important, of course, but it is just as important to communicate research clearly and effectively to various audiences that can use it to decide policy or improve practice.

Research can be found in many sources.
Source: Istockphoto.com.

How to Find, Focus, and Present Research

15

We have given lots of examples of research in this book, and we have covered ways to understand and assess various research strategies. But we have not said much about where to find a study (or studies) on a topic of interest to you. This chapter introduces you to the various outlets where research is published or presented and to some tools for finding relevant studies.

In addition to finding research, some of you will need to do your own research, as part of your academic studies or your professional work. To do this, you must develop and focus on your own question that can be answered with research. It is trickier to do this than it might seem. This chapter provides some guidelines to help you come up with a clear, focused, and doable research topic.

And if you do your own research, you will need to tell others about it, either in a presentation or in a written report. There are standard formats for presenting or writing about research that you need to be aware of, as well as good practices for creating tables and figures to display your results. The last sections of this chapter cover the presentation of research.

Where to Find Research

To read or hear research on a topic of interest, you must first find it—in journals, books, reports, conference presentations and proceedings, and other outlets. So let's begin by considering the major outlets for publishing, presenting, and disseminating research.

Journals

You are likely to find much of the available research on a given topic in **journals**, which are published periodically (quarterly, semimonthly, monthly, or even weekly). This might seem to make the task of finding research seem somewhat manageable—until you realize the sheer number of journals now in existence. One estimate came up with more than 40,000 academic or scholarly journals worldwide, including more than 20,000 peer-reviewed journals (Tenopir, 2004).

Journals are organized by traditional academic disciplines (e.g., economics, psychology, sociology, political science), by applied fields or practice areas (e.g., public administration, public health, education, criminal justice, social work), or by topic area (e.g., traffic safety, personnel administration, drug abuse, early childhood education). Thus, one of the challenges in finding relevant research on a topic of interest is to recognize that it may appear in any one of these types of journals.

A search on the topic of "teenage pregnancy," for example, will turn up articles in journals of public health, family planning, child development, obstetrics and gynecology, sociology, law, psychology, pediatrics, and political economy. Teenage pregnancy is a multifaceted problem, so it makes sense in many ways that research on this topic would appear in so many different types of journals. So when searching for research, be open to searching in journals outside of just one or two fields.

Peer Review and Prestige

If an article is peer reviewed, outside experts—called **reviewers** or **referees**—evaluate the quality and value of a research paper before it is accepted for publication. Reviewers are generally experts in the specific topic of the article, not just any researcher in the general field. Peer review is considered the main guarantor of research quality and integrity. But it is far from perfect. Reviewers cannot redo the analysis and must take the researchers' word on the details of the study. Groups of experts can also collectively fail to see a particular research weakness, with such weaknesses even becoming standard practice. Nonetheless, experienced outside reviewers devote many hours of careful thought to the papers they review and provide the bedrock of quality control in academic journals.

Some journals are very prestigious, with many researchers submitting papers to them in hopes of being published. These first-tier journals typically are known for having a rigorous and demanding review process and for accepting only a small fraction of submitted articles for publication. Articles published in these top-tier journals tend to be of higher quality, although you should always judge for yourself. Table 15.1 gives a few examples of top journals in selected fields (there are too many fields, and too many highly ranked journals, to list them all).

Table 15.1 is just a sampling of the top few in each field—there are many prestigious, selective journals in these fields—especially the larger ones (e.g., economics or psychology). But there are also many other, less selective journals that accept a much higher percentage of the papers submitted for publication. Some journals are less prestigious simply because they are more specialized or narrow in focus, yet they contain useful studies that are well done.

Although you should always judge for yourself, knowing the prestige factor of a journal gives at least a preliminary indication of the quality of the articles it contains and of the research methodology on which they are based. One place to find out about the prestige of journals is at www.eigenfactor.org, a Web site that maps and scores the influence of many journals based on an analysis of citations. *Ulrich's Periodicals Directory* is another, with extensive information about journals with small circulation.

Table 15.1   Some Top Journals by Selected Fields

Field	Top Five Journals by 2006 Article Influence (AI) Score (Excludes Review Journals)
Criminology	*Criminology/Punishment and Society/Journal of Research in Crime and Delinquency/Sexual Abuse/Journal of Quantitative Criminology*
Education	*Scientific Studies of Reading/Educational Evaluation and Policy Analysis/American Educational Research Journal/Harvard Educational Review/Journal of Research in Science Teaching*
Economics	*Quarterly Journal of Economics/Journal of Economic Literature/Journal of Political Economy/ Econometrica/Journal of Financial Economics*
Health policy and services	*Milbank Quarterly/Medical Care/Journal of Health Economics/Health Affairs/Health Services Research*
Planning and development	*World Bank Economic Review/Studies in Comparative International Development/Research Policy/World Development/Journal of Rural Studies*
Political science	*American Political Science Review/American Journal of Political Science/Comparative Political Studies/ Political Analysis/Journal of Conflict Resolution*
Psychology, applied	*Journal of Applied Psychology/Journal of Organizational Behavior/Personnel Psychology/Organizational Behavior and Human Decision Processes/Journal of Organizational Behavior*
Public administration	*Philosophy and Public Affairs/Journal of Policy Analysis and Management/Journal of Public Administration Research and Theory/Public Administration/Public Administration Review*
Public health	*American Journal of Epidemiology/Prevention Science/Journal of Health and Social Behavior/Medical Care/International Journal of Epidemiology*
Social work	*Child Maltreatment/American Journal of Community Psychology/Social Service Review/Journal of Community Psychology/Children and Youth Services Review*
Sociology	*American Sociological Review/American Journal of Sociology/Social Forces/Economy and Society/Social Problems*

Source: www.eigenfactor.org (accessed July 1, 2009).

Types of Journal Articles

Journals focus primarily on peer-reviewed **original research articles**, which are reports of primary research. Most original research articles are primarily or exclusively empirical, but some are entirely theoretical. Journals also contain other kinds of scholarly articles. **Review articles** discuss many research studies, synthesizing the results and reaching broader conclusions. A review article is a good place to start when exploring a new topic. Review articles may or may not be peer reviewed, and some journals specialize in review articles. **Book reviews** also appear in journals, and they are not peer reviewed. Some applied journals also contain comments or opinion essays that are not peer reviewed and contain little or no primary research. Some journals act more like professional magazines, publishing only essays or opinion articles and not original studies. The fact that it is called a "journal" does not necessarily mean that it contains peer-reviewed research; sometimes you have to look closely at the editorial statement (near the title page or at the end of the issue) or visit the journal's Web page to find out for sure.

Open-Access and e-Journals

Most journals are commercially published and require a paid subscription, either to receive the journal in the mail or to gain access to it online. Often, subscription to a journal accompanies membership in a professional association. For example, members of the American Society for Public Administration receive *Public Administration Review*. Universities as well as other organizations often subscribe to full-text journal databases that may give you access to commercially published journals if you are affiliated with the subscribing institution.

But with the possibilities of the Internet, there is now a movement toward "open access" or "e" journals—journals published entirely online and open to free public use. There is a Directory of Open Access Journals, at www.doaj.org, that lists about 5,000 online journals (as of February 2010). Many open-access journals aim to serve readers in parts of the world beyond the United States and Europe, especially developing countries, and many open-access journals are published in languages other than English. Thus, open-access journals fill a need for research in parts of the world, as well as within small institutions, that cannot afford commercially published journals.

Books

In some fields—such as history, anthropology, and qualitative sociology—books are the preferred format for the publication of important primary research. Books are the main form of publishing in-depth case studies, ethnographies, and historical studies. But in many other fields, including applied social and policy research, books serve another purpose. For researchers in these fields, books provide a medium to summarize a line of research and make it accessible to a more general audience. Like review articles, such books are a good place to start secondary research on a new topic.

Attending Conferences and Seminars

Research is often disseminated at research conferences or seminars. Each year, thousands of conferences are held all around the world in many fields and on various special research topics or issues. Governments sponsor research conferences to promote knowledge and inform practice. And professional associations hold research conferences for their members. Universities often have seminar series, some of which are open to the public. So there are many opportunities to hear and learn about research firsthand. A research conference is a bit like a menu tasting: You get to try little bits of research and see what you like. If you find a study interesting, you can ask the researcher for the paper or find the researcher's published work.

Because it typically takes a year or more after a research paper is written before it is reviewed, revised, and available in the pages of a journal, conferences and seminars provide early access to research findings. Some conferences publish some or all of the studies presented in the form of *proceedings* of a research conference or post papers presented on a conference Web site. The practice varies by discipline, and accessing proceedings is sometimes difficult if you are not registered for the conference or a member of the sponsoring agency.

Reports

Government agencies, think tanks, advocacy groups, and other organizations put out many research reports. Most such reports are not peer reviewed, although some government reports go through an advisory board or other review process. Check to see if the report was reviewed, and by whom. With nongovernmental research reports, much depends on the aims and qualifications of the sponsoring organization. Does the organization have a reputation for producing honest, impartial information? Does it have an advocacy agenda, or even an axe to grind? It is also important to look at the qualifications of the researcher or consultant who produced the report. Organizations often hire someone to do the research and write the report, and some hired researchers are more independent than others. In general, it is more difficult to trust the findings of a research report that has not been peer reviewed. If the methodology remains solid, however, the results may still be useful.

Working Papers

Various academic departments, institutes, and organizations publish **working papers**—research papers that are, in a sense, works in progress. One of the most influential in policy research is the working papers of the National Bureau of Economic Research, available at www.nber.org. Many other research organizations post working papers on their Web sites. We suggest that you regularly consult the Web sites of research organizations in your area. Another good source is the Social Science Research Network, available at www.ssrn.com, which publishes working papers and also abstracts of published papers on a wide range of topics.

In some disciplines, work-in-progress manuscripts are distributed even more informally, accompanying a seminar or simply on the researcher's Web page. Working papers can be spread in increasingly diverse ways, including electronic newsletters, blogs, and social networking sites. Such papers have not undergone peer review and should be treated as preliminary (often authors explicitly caution against using or citing the paper). But they do provide a very up-to-date picture of what is happening in a field.

How to Search for Studies

Having reviewed the various outlets for publication and dissemination of research, we turn now to the tools available to help you search for and retrieve studies.

Google Scholar

We begin with Google—the search tool people use for just about everything these days. Google Scholar (beta) is Google's search engine designed especially for research journals, books, and reports (see Box 15.1). It works very well for finding relevant research on most topics, although it has some gaps and should not be considered a compete listing. There are many other important abstract and full-text databases to consider as well in your search—which we will discuss shortly. But Google Scholar is certainly a good, readily available place to start.

BOX 15.1
About Google Scholar

WHAT IS GOOGLE SCHOLAR?

Google Scholar provides a simple way to broadly search for scholarly literature. From one place, you can search across many disciplines and sources: peer-reviewed papers, theses, books, abstracts and articles, from academic publishers, professional societies, preprint repositories, universities and other scholarly organizations. Google Scholar helps you identify the most relevant research across the world of scholarly research.

FEATURES OF GOOGLE SCHOLAR

- **Search** diverse sources from one convenient place
- **Find** papers, abstracts and citations
- **Locate** the complete paper through your library or on the web
- **Learn** about key papers in any area of research

HOW ARE ARTICLES RANKED?

Google Scholar aims to sort articles the way researchers do, weighing the full text of each article, the author, the publication in which the article appears, and how often the piece has been cited in other scholarly literature. The most relevant results will always appear on the first page.

Source: www.scholar.google.com.

Conducting a search using the basic form of Google Scholar is just like conducting a search with any other search engine: Keywords are entered and the search engine's algorithms find relevant information. And just like using other search engines, specific words can be excluded (using -), whole phrases can be searched by putting the phrases in quotes (" "), fragments can be searched using the wildcard (*), and either of two or any of several words can be searched using "OR." Google Scholar can also be used in "advanced scholar search" mode, which provides more search options tailored to scholarly fields and topics.

Electronic Resources: Indexes, Full-Text Databases, and Aggregators

Beyond Google, there are many important electronic resources: databases of research abstracts, often called indexes, databases of full-text articles and reports, and databases that combine both. Very recently, electronic access to books has started to become available. And sometimes a library will combine all the electronic databases to which it has access to form an *aggregator*. Because of all the innovation and mergers, the general term *electronic resources* is used to refer to all these new tools for finding research.

To search electronic resources, one must specify some or all of the available *fields*, which are specific types of information. Available fields generally include author, title, year of publication, language, type of publication, source, and so on. Such searches are more specific than those of a typical search engine where the keyword's role is not specified.

Although the lines between databases are blurring due to aggregators and mergers, we will discuss the different types of databases and provide some examples. We begin with those sponsored by government or nonprofit organizations that are freely available to the public.

ERIC (Education Resources Information Center; U.S. Department of Education) at www.eric .ed.gov: An online, digital library of education research and information, including full-text publications from the U.S. government and other sources.

GPO Access (U.S. Government Printing Office) at www.gpoaccess.gov: Provides free electronic access to most U.S. government reports and publications.

JSTOR at www.jstor.org: A nonprofit organization that archives full-text scholarly articles across the humanities, social sciences, and sciences. (JSTOR does not include articles published in the last 3 to 5 years.)

NCJRS (National Criminal Justice Reference Service; U.S. Department of Justice) at www.ncjrs.gov: A federally funded resource offering access to publications on justice, crime, public safety, substance abuse, and related issues.

PubMed Central (National Institutes of Health) at www.pubmedcentral.nih.gov: A free digital archive of journal literature in the biomedical and life sciences.

Major international organizations, such as the United Nations, the World Bank, the World Health Organization, and the Organization for Economic Cooperation and Development provide some (though not all) of their books and periodicals online for free public use.

In addition to these government and nonprofit databases, a number of commercial services compile research literature across many journals—and even compile across multiple bibliographic databases. These services include EBSCO, IngentaConnect, OCLS, Ovid, ProQuest, and others. These commercial services require subscription, which is typically done through universities or other institutions and made available to affiliated students or employees. Although they are all very comprehensive in their content, and there is some overlap in coverage, no one service provides access to all the published studies and articles that are available. The electronic publishing industry is evolving and changing rapidly, with companies merging or forming alliances and new companies entering the field.

The broad reach of many of these electronic resources, both public and private, is obviously of tremendous value. However, sometimes it is also useful to use a more specific resource, such as Econlit, that includes more specialized or low-circulation journals that represent a particular field or disciplinary perspective.

Portals and Library Services

Technology and practice in finding research is evolving rapidly, and so some of what we discuss here may have changed when you read this. You can discover recent approaches to finding research through the first screen in your library's catalog or information center, also known as its portal. All universities and many research organizations, large commercial and not-for-profit organizations, and public libraries have services that help you conduct a search, such as *Ask a Librarian* or *Text a Librarian*.

Wikipedia

In a very short period of time, *Wikipedia,* an online encyclopedia that can be edited by anyone, has emerged as a remarkable resource. Its content continues to grow rapidly and is generally very up to date, if often uneven in its coverage and quality. Box 15.2 contains Wikipedia's own description of itself.

While anyone can edit Wikipedia, its policy is that all statements should be backed up with good sources and citations. Various editors search pages to note where citations or sources are needed and to remove biased or unsupported information. Wikipedia benefits from the so-called wisdom of crowds in which the aggregated contributions of many people increase accuracy. (James Surowiecki coined the term in 2004.) In the context of Wikipedia, the idea is that false or dubious information, as well as important omissions, are spotted and fixed by the many Wikipedia users all over the world. Nonetheless, the open nature of Wikipedia means that it can contain unreliable and even false information. To address these concerns, Wikipedia's policies remain in rapid flux, with some increasing restrictions on the open editing policy.

Despite the potential problems, we recommend Wikipedia as a place to start secondary research, particularly due to its extensive and up-to-date coverage. But it is *only* a place to start. You should move on to sources of information cited in the Wikipedia article you are reading and eventually reach primary research articles. And you should also use other initial entry points to a subject, such as a scholarly index search, as described earlier.

BOX 15.2
What Is Wikipedia?

WHAT IS WIKIPEDIA?

Wikipedia is a free encyclopedia, written collaboratively by its readers. It is a special type of website designed to make collaboration easy, called a wiki. Many people are constantly improving Wikipedia, making thousands of changes per hour. All of these changes are recorded in article histories and recent changes. For a more detailed account of the project, see About Wikipedia.

HOW CAN I CONTRIBUTE?

Don't be afraid to edit—anyone can edit almost any page, and we encourage you to **be bold**! Find something that can be improved and make it better—for example, spelling, grammar, rewriting for readability, or removing unconstructive edits. If you wish to add new facts, please provide references so they may be verified, or suggest them on the article's discussion page. Changes to controversial topics and Wikipedia's main pages should usually be discussed first.

Remember—you can't break Wikipedia; all edits can be reversed, fixed or improved later. So go ahead, edit an article and help make Wikipedia the best information source on the Internet!

Source: http://en.wikipedia.org/wiki/Wikipedia:Introduction.

Browsing and Following Citation Trails

Once you have found a few relevant research studies or overviews through the various means described above, you should look at the reference lists at the end of the articles for more ideas about articles or other publications to search out. Following a trail of citations in this way can be a very effective approach to finding research of interest. *One hint:* Begin with the newest articles first, as these will have the most up-to-date reference lists.

Browsing bookshelves provides another useful approach. Not so long ago, researchers and others looking to find published research browsed library stacks of books and journals, searching for research. With so many resources available electronically, and some only published online, this kind of physical browsing has become much less common. It is, however, still valuable at times to go into the stacks (especially when searching for older books or journal volumes).

Bibliographic Citation Software

As you search for studies, it is a good idea to keep track of the references you find with **bibliographic citation software**, also known as reference management software. Such software will not only make it easy to collect and remember references but will also make it much easier to add references to your finished paper—and change the reference format to meet the requirements of various journals. Examples of bibliographic citation software include EndNote, RefWorks, Zotero, and others. Zotero is free, works inside Mozilla Firefox, and is capable of capturing not only bibliographic information from Web sites but many other forms of Web content as well (see www.zotero.org). No doubt these products and others will continue to evolve.

We have tried to be up to date in this section on how to search for research, but technology and practice in these areas are evolving rapidly. You should consult your library or information center, as well as colleagues, about new resources and practices.

Thus far, we've focused on how to find research done by others. Sometimes you do this just to gain knowledge about an issue, but often reviewing the literature is part of preparing to do your own research. The next section deals with how you go from a general interest in an issue or problem to focusing on a clear, relevant, and original question that can be answered with your own research.

How to Focus Your Own Research Question

Much of this book has been about the strategies used to answer research questions—but where do these questions come from in the first place? We answered this question initially in Chapter 1, so we will recap some of what we said there. But we will also add some additional, more practical advice on how to focus and frame your own research question.

Different Kinds of Researchers

How to focus and frame a research question depends in part on both the reason for doing the research and the experience of the researcher. Therefore, we give somewhat different kinds of advice to different kinds of researchers. We first provide advice to those just beginning to do research, perhaps doing a research project for a course, or those just starting a master's thesis or doctoral dissertation. Following that, we provide further advice that is relevant to all researchers. We then turn to specific advice for active practitioners and policymakers whose work has provided them with a focused practice or policy question that they must turn into an answerable research question. Finally, we address specific concerns of more experienced researchers who seek to find the answerable research questions most useful to their area of investigation.

For Those Getting Started: Topics, Questions, and Problems

In *The Craft of Research*, Booth, Colomb, and Williams (2008) provide a helpful framework for focusing a research question, composed of topics, questions, and problems. Although their framework stems from teaching students to do research papers in the humanities, it applies broadly and can help focus a question in social and policy research as well.

We start initially with a general *topic* of interest—for example, protecting the environment. Topics come from what we read, the work we do, our curiosity, or the communities in which we are involved. But to do research on this topic, we must translate it into a more specific research question that we can answer with evidence. It helps to begin by narrowing the topic itself, say from the broad notion of *protecting the environment* to the more specific activity of *recycling garbage*. We might narrow it further by specifying the geographic scope of the topic: *recycling garbage in Columbus, Ohio*. Narrowing a topic places it within reach of our ability to investigate it with the tools and resources we have at our disposal.

The next step is to turn this topic into a *question*. Booth et al. (2008) suggest that you first write down lots of possible questions before picking one (or two) to focus on. Do people in Columbus like to recycle their garbage? How much do they know about recycling? How regularly do they recycle? What kinds of garbage do or don't they recycle? What influences how often people in Columbus recycle? What inhibits or prevents recycling? And so on. Review the questions and select the one or two that most interest you.

The final step is to identify the *problem* your selected question helps resolve—its significance. The problem is your answer to the ubiquitous "So what?" question that readers and audiences will demand of you and your research. In applied social or policy research, the problem is often a practical one, while in more basic or academic research it may be a more conceptual or theoretical problem. To identify the problem, it helps to complete this sentence: I am seeking to answer my question, *in order to (or so that)* . . .

Putting these pieces together, you have the following framework for focusing your research question and clarifying its significance (adapted from Booth et al., 2008):

General topic: I am interested in environmental protection.

> *Specific topic:* I will focus on garbage recycling in Columbus, Ohio.

>> *Question:* How much do people in Columbus, Ohio, know about recycling?

>>> *Problem (significance):* So that the local government and advocacy groups can more effectively educate the public and encourage recycling

Using this framework provides a general way to test out your research question, well before planning your study. You can iterate up and down the chain. Perhaps you developed a specific question but then decided it did not address an important enough problem. In that case, you can return to the question or specific topic stage. And you can repeat the whole process several times—with various topics, questions, and problems—until you find your research question.

Make Your Question Positive, Not Normative

We saw in Chapter 1 that research questions are positive—about how the world really is, and not normative—about how we want the world to be. But doing research does not imply giving up your values—indeed, your choice of a topic or issue to study most likely reflects your values, interests, and experiences. Still, your research question should be framed as a positive one. We said this already in Chapter 1, but let's now see more concretely what this means.

Say you care a great deal about the environment and that you want more people to recycle. So you come up with a research question such as this: *Why don't people in Columbus, Ohio, care more about the environment and try harder to recycle their garbage?* This question, however, implies a normative framework (that people *should* care about the environment and *should* recycle). We might well agree with these values, but a researchable question needs to be more positive—for example, *How much do people care about the environment? How often do they recycle? And does caring about the environment influence people's willingness to recycle?* These questions get at the same basic issue, but they are more positive, less normative. As you begin to focus your research question, therefore, keep this distinction in mind as you compose your question.

Know If Your Question Is Descriptive or Causal

Throughout this book, we have made a distinction between descriptive research (that answers "what is" questions) and causal research (that answers "what if" questions). We view this distinction as fundamental to understanding research. When coming up with your own research question, you must be clear about this distinction as well. Do you want a *description* of recycling in Columbus, Ohio— *what is* the level of recycled garbage in the city? Or do you want a *causal explanation* of recycling— *what if* citizens had more knowledge, would the level of recycled garbage increase? These are two very different kinds of questions, requiring different research strategies. So it is important to clarify which type of question, descriptive or causal, will be the focus of your study.

Distinguish the Question You Want to Answer From the Question You Can Answer

Once you have focused and framed a research question—say, *What is the level of knowledge of recycling in Columbus, Ohio?*—you will need to think about how to implement it. For example, in the recycling study, you would need to find a sampling frame for the population of residents of Columbus. You might decide to use a telephone survey. But that would mean missing those with cell phones only, who might be systematically younger and more aware of environmental issues. You would also need to decide what the concept "knowledge of recycling" means: Knowing the local recycling rules? Knowing what materials can be recycled, or what materials cannot? Knowing how the community benefits from its recycling program? And once that is decided, you would need to develop or find a measurement instrument and devise procedures to implement the survey. For other kinds of research studies, you might need to focus on issues such as whether interview questions can be ethically asked; what secondary data sets might be available; whether proxies for important control variables are available; whether what you thought was a natural experiment really is exogenous. In other words, you would focus on the issues we have covered in much of this book.

Once you specify somewhat how to implement a research question, you become aware of the weaknesses of your study, the kinds of weaknesses we described in earlier chapters. At this stage, you should determine the ways and extent to which the research question you can answer falls short of the question you want to answer. We discussed this distinction briefly in Chapter 1, but after reading more about the different types of studies and their strengths and weaknesses throughout this book, you are now in a better position to apply it.

Once you know the actual research question you can answer, you should return to the "so what?" question—how useful will the answer to your question be? If the answer will be so full of holes as to be of little value, you should return to an earlier stage in the process of focusing a research question. To develop a useful *and* doable research question, you usually have to iterate several times. But remember, all research has weaknesses, and you should not judge too harshly, particularly if you are just starting off.

For the Applied Researcher Given a Policy or Practice Question to Answer

Practitioners and policymakers are often given a quite specific question and asked to answer it through research. Clearly, they do not need to go through quite the same topic-questions-problem process outlined above. But they still need to develop a doable research question that, as much as possible, answers the practice or policy question given to them. For example, an analyst working in a child services agency might be asked to determine whether a new procedure for responding to first-time child abuse reports does a better job of accurately assessing whether abuse is taking place than established procedure. How can this practitioner-researcher turn this important question of practice into doable research?

Much of what we already said about formulating research questions applies equally well to this situation. First, the practitioner-researcher must construct a *positive* research question. Sometimes, the question provided is a "should" question, such as "should we keep the new procedure?" But "should" questions depend on values as well as on the consequences of the new procedure. The values part should be separated from the factual, research question. Second, the practitioner-researcher should determine if the question is descriptive or causal. In this case, the question is causal—the *effect* of the new procedure. Unfortunately, as we have seen in previous chapters, getting a definitive causal answer is difficult. If the agency implemented the new policy all at once, and there is no comparison group, it will not be possible to disentangle the effect of the new procedure from other changes in the program and its context. The practitioner-researcher must simply do his or her best in the ways we have described in Chapter 13.

The inability to definitively determine causation is just one of many examples of how doable research questions often fall short of the policy or practice questions to which we seek answers. Another shortfall often occurs in attempts at measurement: how to measure whether "abuse is taking place," for example. There may be no fully accurate measure, and so we turn to the best possible proxy. If a case that was deemed to have no abuse subsequently became a clear abuse case, the mistake is clear. And if a case was deemed to be likely abuse and then found not to be so, that is also a mistake. But mistakes may never be detected. The researcher-practitioner must determine how long to wait to uncover mistakes and thus how long to wait to find study outcomes. In the meantime, he or she might need to compromise even more, looking at more easily available measures such as the share of cases determined to warrant further investigation. But then the researcher-practitioner must make clear that these are at best rough indicators of accuracy.

As this example demonstrates, real-world practice questions are often challenging to address through research. Yet practitioner-researchers on the ground typically have far fewer resources available than researchers in universities and other research organizations. In this example, the researcher-practitioner might only have time to look at a small sample of cases. Practitioner-researchers must do their best. But they should be honest and clearly describe how the questions they can answer differ from the practice questions they were given. Pretending to have better answers will only make the decision-making process less effective.

For Experienced Researchers:
Finding an Important (but Doable) Question

Next, we offer advice to more experienced researchers who get to choose their own research questions to contribute to a policy or practice area. For example, a researcher might be interested in promoting child welfare. How can such a researcher develop a doable research question that can promote child welfare as much as possible? The first step is to find an important policy or practice question—one whose answer is useful in the long or short term.

A good place to start is with the questions policymakers and practitioners have but that require more research than they can do themselves. What do they want to know? Consider our previous example, in which the practitioner had trouble determining the relative accuracy of new procedures to evaluate child abuse reports. Unlike the practitioner, a researcher (working with practitioners) might be able to do a quasi experiment with long-term longitudinal follow-up to evaluate different procedures. Consider another example from Chapter 1: interest in whether divorce has negative impacts on children. Real-world legal, political, cultural, and even personal discussions illustrate how many people want to know the answer to this question. To find such questions, read trade journals and newspapers, talk to those working in the area, and generally read and listen to what they want to know.

But you should not stop with what those in the field want to know, because sometimes they cannot see the forest for the trees. Spend a lot of time thinking theoretically, drawing path diagrams, and speculating. What could be causing what? Why do couples get divorced? What happens to them and their children after they get divorced? What would happen if they did not divorce? Why do some stay in bad marriages? And so on. Such thinking can result in new questions that someone should be asking but no one is.

Once you have found all these valuable questions, try to turn them into doable research questions. That process is much like what we have just described, although past research experience obviously helps a great deal. But there are a few points to add. First, although dedicated researchers have more time, and in some cases more funds than practitioner-researchers, dedicated researchers also face time as well as cost limitations. And as we discussed in the previous chapter, timeliness matters for influencing policy.

Second, pay particular attention to the important questions that people have had trouble answering. What kinds of new measures would help, if only they were available? What kinds of natural experiments would provide needed causal evidence? In this way, you can be on the lookout for opportunities, if and when they arise, to answer previously unanswered questions.

Finally, don't let the ideal of the perfect research study become the enemy of doing good research. Scheiber (2007), writing for a general audience, complained that economists have become too focused on finding really good natural experiments that definitively determine causal effects, "crowd[ing] out some of the truly deep questions we rely on economists to answer." Unfortunately, journal and grant reviewers sometimes favor research that definitively answers a less important question over research that only partially or imperfectly answers a more important question. It is another feature of the "lamppost problem"—only looking where the light is—that we described in Chapter 14.

How to Write and Present Research

To be useful to others, your research must be communicated in the form of a written report or a presentation. Care and effort need to go into the report, because people only know about research through what you write or say about it. So it is important to allow sufficient time and resources for this stage of the research project.

The Importance of Rewriting

Research is often complicated. Therefore, writing and speaking clearly about it is not an easy task. It takes practice—even for those with a lot of experience. It is important not to put off writing until the end, but rather to begin writing as you conduct your research. The process of writing itself will help you clarify your ideas and may reveal flaws in your thinking and in the design of your research. In your initial writing up of your research methods, you may discover alternatives to or variations on your original research plans.

Writing must be good on several levels: overall conceptual organization of the entire piece, including major headings and subheadings; the order of paragraphs within headings; the order of sentences within paragraphs; the structure of sentences; and the choice of specific words. Of course, these different levels can be worked on in different drafts. This is not the place for a detailed discussion of writing, other than to emphasize its importance. You can consult any of the excellent resources on how to do serious, nonfiction writing, such as Joseph M. Williams's *Style: Toward Clarity and Grace* (1995).

Know Your Audience

What makes a good article or presentation depends on who will read or hear it. What is clear to some may be utterly confusing to others. Therefore, when writing, always keep in mind your audience—the people who will read about and use your research. If yours is an academic study, the audience will likely be other researchers or students in the field. This audience will want more information on prior research related to your study, the conceptual or theoretical problem in the field that your study addresses, and the methodological details of importance to the field.

But if yours is an applied study, the audience will likely include policymakers, program managers, funders, advocates, or other nonresearchers. Because this audience is more diverse, you should avoid jargon and technical language, provide background on the social problem or policy the study addresses, and highlight findings with implications for policy and practice. Too many researchers develop the habit of writing in an obtuse, passive-voiced, jargon-heavy style that is inaccessible to practitioners—and, indeed, to many academic audiences as well. It is important to know not only how to do research but how to write and talk about it in a clear, accessible style.

As much as possible, try out your writing or presentation on a target audience. Give drafts of your writing to others for feedback, or practice giving your presentations to a friend or colleague. You will learn a lot in this way about how to match your writing to your audience.

We turn next to the organization of a research report or article.

Organization of a Research Report

There is a standard six-part organization for writing or presenting research: Give an abstract, provide the context, state the objectives (hypotheses), describe the methods, present the findings, and discuss conclusions or implications. Although there is some variation by discipline and some variation by the type of study, most research articles or reports follow this organization. We review each of these parts in turn.

Abstract: The Essentials in Brief

It helps to write this first part of the manuscript last—but you should not overlook the importance of an abstract. As mentioned earlier, readers of research often search and assess studies based solely on abstracts. Indeed, databases of abstracts exist for this purpose (such as the Applied Social Sciences Index and Abstracts). An unclear, inaccurate, or poorly written abstract hurts the chances that your study will be found and read by its intended audience.

Context: Giving the Necessary Background

Although you are immersed in the problems and issues that motivated your research, your audience may not be. And even if most people have heard something about a major social problem, such as drug trafficking on the U.S.-Mexico border or AIDS in Africa, they probably do not know the actual trends or scope of the problem. So it is necessary to give your audience sufficient context to fully appreciate your research.

What is the problem or issue your research addresses—what is its main outcome of interest?

Where is the problem happening—is it local, regional, national, or international?

How big is the problem—how many people are affected? Is the problem getting better or worse?

What are the political or policy responses to the problem?

What prior research has been done—what have been the main findings of prior research?

What conceptual or theoretical problems surround the topic of your study?

In a paper with a very extensive theoretical analysis preceding an empirical analysis, the paper may have a separate theory section, rather than simply presenting the context. Some articles contain a section that is purely a review of the existing academic literature, and those articles may or may not contain an additional context section.

Objectives: Stating the Aims and Hypotheses

Having given the context, the next step in writing or presenting research is to clearly state your objectives. What exactly is the research question your study aims to answer? What specific hypotheses will you test? This section can and often should be concise.

Methods: Explaining How the Study Was Conducted

Novice writers and presenters of research tend to skip over the methods and jump to the findings. But it will be difficult for an audience to make sense of findings, even simple charts, without knowing how the study was conducted. Also, much of the validity of a study—its integrity and worth—lies in the logic and quality of its methodology. Indeed, that has been our theme throughout much of this book. Thus, it is very important to clearly explain *how* the study was conducted. This includes the following points:

- What is the setting of the study—what locations or institutions were included? When were the data collected?
- Who are the participants in the study—how were they sampled or recruited? Is the entire sample included in the study or a subsample with particular characteristics?
- What is the key outcome measure (dependent variable), and what are the other variables? How were these variables measured? What are the units?
- What is the design of the study—is it a survey, an experiment, a natural or quasi experiment (and if so, what kind), a qualitative study, an analysis of secondary data?
- How were the data analyzed? What calculations were performed? Were further approximations or assumptions made?

When the analysis of data is fairly involved, the methods section may be broken into separate "data" and "analysis" sections, or even multiple analyses sections.

The methods section should not present or discuss findings—you must hold off on this for the time being. However, it is appropriate to present basic descriptive statistics for your variables—such as the range, mean, and standard deviation. A table of descriptive statistics can serve as a concise way of defining and describing your variables—but not in an article in which the main results are descriptive statistics. Presenting baseline comparisons may be appropriate in some studies, for example, to show that treatment and control groups are indeed comparable—or if not, how they differ (and thus what control variables need to be taken into account).

Results: Presenting the Findings

In this section, you present your findings in the form of narrative, tables, or figures. Focus in this section on *presenting* the findings and interpreting them in straightforward ways, not on drawing conclusions—that is the work of the final section. The reason for this is that your audience must first grasp *what* you found before they can fully appreciate its implications. For example, in this section, you should present treatment effects directly provided from the analysis and interpret those findings in understandable units and contexts, but you should not compare the effects to those of other programs. Those comparisons belong in the final section.

Introduce tables and figures and explain what they show. Even assuming that the tables and figures are clearly labeled and largely self-explanatory, as they should be, the text or presentation should still walk the audience through each table and figure. Beyond orienting the reader or audience to what they are looking at, the text or presentation should call attention to overall patterns as well as any unusual values or outliers. The direction as well as the magnitude of key relationships or effects should be described. Results should be presented in such a way that readers can place them in a relevant context.

Conclusions: Providing Interpretations and Implications

In this final section, you make interpretations and conclusions based on your findings as well as discuss policy or practice implications. If your aim was to test specific hypotheses or predictions, did your findings support or refute those hypotheses? How strong was the evidence? If the research question was more descriptive or exploratory, what is your interpretation of the main findings? What insights do your findings provide?

An important part of this section is to acknowledge and discuss methodological *limitations* and how they might have influenced the results. Were there difficulties in measuring some of the variables? Are there variables that could not be measured but that might have been important? Were there limitations in the sampling or selection of participants? If the study was an experiment, was there any contamination or problem in administering the treatment? If it was a natural or quasi experiment, how comparable were the groups and how exogenous was the treatment? Acknowledging and discussing such limitations helps your audience judge the meaning and implications of your research, and also it is the ethical thing to do.

This section should also describe how your results add to the existing knowledge base. Return to the issues in the broader context and focus on any policy or practice implications. What has been learned from the study? How should the results alter policy or practice? Do these results suggest other research?

Writing About Numbers

Most of us have had plenty of experience with writing since grade school, but we may not have written very much about numbers. And research, particularly quantitative research, requires us to write a lot about numbers. Some advice can help with this task.

To begin with, it's important to realize that written prose is often not the most efficient or effective way to present numerical information. Especially if there are lots of numbers to present, tables or figures often work much better. Then you can save your prose writing (or oral presentation) for a discussion of what is in the tables or figures, pointing out the patterns or highlights but not giving all the numbers in the text.

But when presenting or discussing just a few numbers, it may help to include them in your written or spoken sentences or paragraphs. How should you do this?

In her comprehensive books on writing about numbers, Jane Miller (2004, 2005) suggests these seven principles for good quantitative writing:

1. Establish the context for the number (the who, what, when, and where) as well as the units the number is in (dollars of annual income, years of age, etc.)

   For example, don't just write, *The income of the state was 58,000.*

   Instead, provide the relevant context: *According to data compiled by the U.S. Census Bureau, the median annual income of households in California in 2007 was 58,000 dollars, 8,000 dollars above the median for all U.S. households.*

2. Use examples, analogies, or comparisons to help your audience interpret the number

   For example, don't just write, *California's unemployment rate was 12.2% in August.*

   Instead, use a comparison to give the number more meaning: *California's unemployment rate was 12.2% in August, the highest level seen since the end of the Great Depression.*

3. Select the right tool to present the numbers—text, tables, or figures (charts).

   We will have more to say about this shortly, but consider this example of a sentence that tries to give too much numerical information (better suited to a table): *California is the most populous state in the United States, with 36.8 million residents, followed by Texas with 24.3 million residents, New York with 19.5 million, Florida with 18.3 million, Illinois with 12.9 million, Pennsylvania with 12.4 million, Ohio with 11.5 million, and Michigan with 10.0 million.*

4. Define your terms, and avoid research or professional jargon (especially for a more general audience).

   Avoid writing like this: *According to our OLS model, state public educational spending has a significant positive coefficient on NAEP math scores, controlling for student SES and demographic variables.*

   Instead, help your audience by spelling out acronyms and using more ordinary language: *Using regression analysis to adjust for the socioeconomic and demographic characteristics of students, we found that states that spend more on public education have higher average math scores on the National Assessment of Education Progress.*

5. Interpret numbers in the text—numbers do not speak for themselves.

   To continue with a previous example, do not just write, *California's unemployment rate was 12.2% in August.*

   Instead, help your audience interpret this number: *California's unemployment rate was 12.2% in August, up from 11.9% in July, and representing 2.2 million state residents who are now unemployed. This is the highest rate of unemployment seen in California since the end of the Great Depression.*

6. Specify the direction and magnitude of a relationship.

   It is not enough just to write, *Our analysis suggests that education spending by the states is related to average math scores on the National Assessment of Educational Progress.*

   Instead, specify the direction and help the reader understand the magnitude of the relationship: *Our analysis suggests that an additional 1,000 dollars per pupil in state spending on education is associated with a 10-point advantage in average math scores on the National Assessment of Educational Progress, which has a 0 to 500 scale.*

7. Summarize patterns in the data.

   When numbers appear in tables or figures, as we will soon see, it becomes important to use the text to summarize the patterns in the data—Is there a trend or relationship? Are there outliers? What is the overall message to take away from the numbers?

Miller (2005) recommends paying special attention to writing about causality (i.e., causation), statistical significance, and substantive significance (i.e., practical significance). We agree. Be sure to explain whether the numbers aim to estimate a causal relationship or simply describe an association. If a causal relationship is the focus, be sure to explain the causal mechanism—the causal theory of the relationship. And be sure to consider the strength of the causal evidence. For example, in an observational study, judge the plausibility of reverse causation or whether important common causes have not been controlled for. As the author of the study, you've given these issues much more thought than an initial reader (or hopefully so), and you should share your considerations and interpretations with your reader.

When writing about statistical significance tests, be sure to understand what they mean in a given context and not overinterpret them (readers tend to do this enough as it is). In most cases, statistical significance tests simply rule out chance as an explanation of an observed difference or relationship; they do not prove causation or even that an effect is important. Miller (2005) suggests that, for non-technical audiences, significance tests should be used simply to decide which results to present and discuss. More technical audiences, however, will want to know details such as the standard errors and p values.

Last, and perhaps most important, be sure to discuss the policy or practical significance of the results—how large is the effect, and what does it mean, in the real world? To do this, the results must be presented in a way that allows interpretation in a real-world context. For example, a logistic regression coefficient has no meaning to most readers and can only be interpreted if converted to an odds ratio or marginal effect.

Tables and Figures

As we noted earlier, prose is often not the best way of communicating numbers—especially when you have lots of numbers to present. Tables and figures (charts or graphs) often help organize or display data more efficiently and effectively. A table gives exact numerical values and organizes the numbers into columns and rows so that the reader can find and compare them more easily. A figure presents the data in the form of a graph or chart that displays the overall pattern visually, typically using bars, lines, or other graphical symbols. But figures do not convey precise values.

We will provide some specific tips on producing good tables and figures shortly. But first, there are a couple of guidelines that apply to both tables and figures:

- *Make your table or figure largely self-explanatory.* Give your table or figure to friends or colleagues to test this out. Can they make sense of what it says on their own? How much additional explanation is required before the meaning comes into focus? How could you incorporate this additional information into the title, headings, or notes to the table or figure to make it more self-explanatory?
- *Number your tables and figures* in the order in which they are mentioned in the text. Some tables or figures require more explanation and discussion than others, but you must always reference a table or figure in the text of the paper. As Table 1 shows, . . . for example.
- *Title your table or figure carefully and completely.* Novice writers or presenters frequently make the mistake of giving their table a vague title or no title at all (just "Table 1," for example). Often, it is better to err on the side of a longer, more descriptive title than a short, cryptic one. With survey data, it can help to use some version of the wording of the question in the title.
- *Avoid just cutting and pasting the tables and figures* from statistical software packages (such as SPSS, Stata, or SAS). Consider reformatting, or even re-creating the table or figure, using a spreadsheet or specialized graphing software to make it more presentable. Statistical software packages increasingly have commands capable of producing tables and figures suitable for publication, but you must use the specialized commands and features and not the standard output.

Let's turn now to more specific advice and examples, beginning with tables.

Tips for Creating Good Tables

When you need to present more than a few numbers, or to compare numbers across groups or categories, you will likely need to prepare a table. Tables are also useful for presenting multivariate results such as coefficients and related statistics from a multiple regression analysis.

A good table requires careful and creative editing and formatting. Include only the essential information your audience needs to make sense of the results—do not overload the table with nonessential numerical detail. The aim should be to make the table as clear and simple as possible so that your readers can make sense of it.

The information for your table will most often come from statistical software, but don't just cut and paste software output into your report or presentation. Table 15.2 shows raw output in SPSS using data from the 2005 World Values Survey, and you can see that it is not that easily interpreted. You will need to reformat this output, cutting extraneous numbers and clarifying the labeling and formatting of the table.

Table 15.2   Unformatted Computer Output (From SPSS)

V248 Are you the chief wage earner in your house * V235 Sex Crosstabulation

			V235 Sex		Total
			1 male	2 female	
V248 Are you the chief wage earner in your house	1 yes	Count	17371	7299	24670
		% within V235 Sex	66.5%	28.2%	47.4%
	2 no	Count	8750	18626	27376
		% within V235 Sex	33.5%	71.8%	52.6%
Total		Count	26121	25925	52046
		% within V235 Sex	100.0%	100.0%	100.0%

Table 15.3 presents the same results in a cleaner, simpler format that audiences can more readily read. Notice that only the column percentages were included because these provided the meaningful results to be interpreted. Counts do not mean very much when the data are from a sample. When presenting any results, particularly complex ones, think about what points are to be made and construct the table layout to facilitate the audience's understanding of those points. It takes some time, effort, and practice to make good tables.

Good resources for advice on preparing tables include the style guides put out by the American Psychological Association (2009), the American Medical Association (JAMA & Archives Journals, 2007), and the University of Chicago (2003), as well as the books by Jane Miller (2004, 2005) and Booth et al. (2008).

Table 15.3   Reformatted Table Using Clearer, Simpler Layout

Are you the chief wage earner in your house?	Male	Female	Total
Yes	66.5 %	28.2 %	47.4 %
No	33.5 %	71.8 %	52.6 %
Total	100.0 %	100.0 %	100.0 %

Note: N = 52,046 respondents in 57 countries.

Source: World Values Survey (2005).

Tips for Creating Good Figures

Figures are typically graphs or charts that use bars, lines, or other graphical symbols to show your data. Figures work better than tables at presenting the overall pattern in the data, but they do not work as well for conveying precise numerical values. Because figures allow for many options of scale, shape, color, and other stylistic elements, they can require more time and effort to produce.

Again, the aim is to keep the figure clear and as simple as possible so that your audience can make sense of it. Avoid distracting colors, textures, and chart junk (such as pictures or symbols) that add little to an understanding of the data.

As with tables, the information for the chart will most often come from statistical software, but again, do not just take what the computer spits out and paste it into your report or presentation. Figure 15.1, for example, shows a simple bar chart from SPSS using 2005 World Values Survey data. By devoting some effort at reformatting, this figure can be made much clearer and simpler, as shown in Figure 15.2. The rotation of the axis provides more space for the full value labels, and the categories are reordered by frequency (rather than just by accepting the order of categories in the raw output). These kinds of changes will help your audience more readily grasp the meaning of your data.

The science and art of graphing data is a big topic that we can only touch on here. Excellent resources for developing this important skill include Tufte's (2001) *The Visual Display of Quantitative Information*, Cleveland's (1994) *The Elements of Graphing Data*, and Henry's (1994) *Graphing Data*.

How to Write About Qualitative Research

Writing about qualitative research is different in many ways. The information you will be presenting comes mostly in the form of language, texts, images, and qualitative observations of behavior, not numbers or statistics. And it is not possible to write about all the information gathered from in-depth interviews or case studies—there is just too much of it, in most cases. Writing about qualitative research, therefore, requires you to make many subtle decisions about what and how to present.

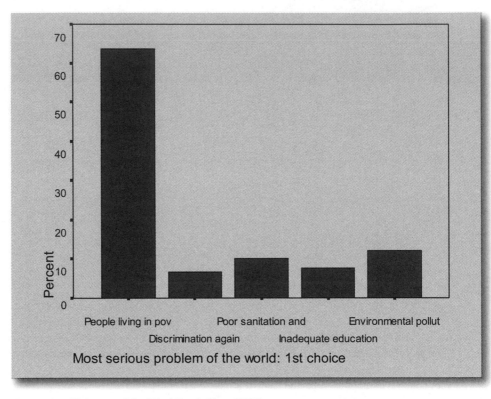

Figure 15.1   Unformatted Statistical Graph (From SPSS)

In his book on qualitative inquiry, Creswell (2006) identifies several rhetorical issues to consider in the writing of a qualitative research report:

- *Reflexivity and representation:* Who are you, as the researcher-writer, and what is your relationship to the participants? How does your perspective, either as an outsider or an insider (say, in the case of full participation), influence your interpretation of the data? Because qualitative research and analysis are inherently more subjective, it is important to reflect on your own perspective in your writing.
- *Audience:* For whom are you writing this report? We discussed this issue earlier with respect to how much technical detail or terminology to use in writing about numbers, but the issue is a bit different in qualitative research. An important point here is to provide your audience with enough information on the context, background, and culture of participants to fully interpret the qualitative evidence.
- *Encoding:* What language or style will you use in your report? This issue is related to the audience question, but it refers more specifically to the style of presentation. Will you write in an informal, journalistic style or a more formal, academic manner? Will you write with a focus on conceptual or theoretical ideas, or with more attention to public policy or practice implications?

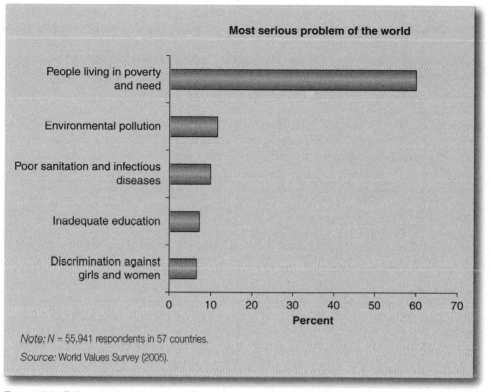

Figure 15.2 Reformatted and Annotated Graph to Improve Presentation

- *Quotes:* What quotes or other examples of your data will you present? You can use extended quotes or dialogue (e.g., from an in-depth interview), or embed shorter quotes that appear in your own narrative interpretation. It is always important to frame the quote in sufficient context about the participant and the situation for it to make sense to your readers. It is also important to give a sense of how representative, or unique, the quote is in relation to all the data (which you are not quoting).

Although writing about qualitative research presents unique challenges, you should be aware that the general standards for presenting research still apply. In particular, you still must tell your audience about the methodology of your study: How many people did you interview or observe? How did you choose (sample) the people or settings in the study? Whom did you leave out, or who did not agree to participate? What questions did you ask or issues did you focus on? What instruments (such as interview guides, observation forms, and audio or video recorders) did you use? How many visits did you make, and how much time did you spend in the setting? How did you summarize or reduce the qualitative data (e.g., by coding, content analysis, or using qualitative software)? Journal editors and reviewers, policymakers, funders, and other readers of your report will expect and deserve answers to these basic methodological questions.

If you coded and content-analyzed your qualitative data, most likely you will have some numerical tables or figures in your report as well. For example, you may want to show the overall frequency of codes, or you may count codes across settings or analytical categories. To this extent, the prior advice about preparing good tables and charts still applies. Be sure to give quotes or other evidence of the actual content and meaning of codes, however, as the code labels alone are often ambiguous and too abstract.

Finally, many studies these days involve *mixed methods*, with both qualitative and quantitative findings to report. You will then need to blend the approaches and advice we have suggested thus far. If initial qualitative methods (such as focus groups) were used to develop a later quantitative effort (such as a survey), it is helpful to present and interpret them in this sequence. The same applies, of course, to qualitative investigation that comes after quantitative findings (such as follow-up interviews with survey respondents). If the qualitative and quantitative methods ran concurrently, however, you should describe each method separately but perhaps interpret them in a more integrated manner (Creswell, 2006).

Presenting: How It Is and Is Not Like Writing

Most of our suggestions about how to write about research apply equally to oral presentations. But presentations do bring up a few special issues. Unlike readers of an article, those listening to and watching a presentation cannot go back and reread if they missed something, and they cannot go more slowly (or quickly) than the presenter does. So pacing is critical. And because of that, knowing what your audience will, or will not, understand becomes especially important. Also, most oral presentations are much shorter, in terms of the number of words, than a written report and somewhat less formal in style. So a presentation must be much more concise and often less technical. One advantage of a presentation, however, is that the audience may ask questions and engage in a dialogue with the researcher.

Most presenters today accompany their talk with some kind of slide show, such as PowerPoint or PDF slides. You should put enough—but not too much—information into your slides. Figures and tables belong in slides, but be aware that tables with too many numerical details are difficult for an audience to read on a screen and make sense of. Figures often work better if you have a choice. Background or commentary are often more effective when they simply come from the speaker—so don't overly script yourself or bore your audience with too many talking points on slides.

BOX 15.3
Where and How to Publish Your Research

You may well want to publish your research, typically in a research journal in your field or practice area. Earlier in this chapter, we discussed the variety of research journals in existence, and in Chapter 14, we discussed the peer-review process that your paper will most likely need to go through. To get ideas for possible journals for your study, you can use electronic resources or ask colleagues for suggestions. See which journals you cited in your review of prior research, as they are likely to be interested in your study as well. To decide if a particular journal is a good fit, skim several issues to see if the journal publishes articles similar to yours in topic and method. Read the journal's mission statement to see if your article fits what they are looking for. Consider also the readership of the journal, the audience that you want most to see your study. Fit is the first hurdle to getting your paper accepted.

But the prestige and selectiveness of the journal is, of course, another important factor in getting your study published. Be aware that the peer-review process can take a very long time, depending on both the discipline and the particular journal. The process is never less than a month; 3 to 6 months is fairly fast; and a year or more is not uncommon. If time is critical, you will want to think hard before submitting to a highly selective journal. Ask more experienced colleagues if they think your work has a chance. If not, it is perhaps better to look elsewhere. But you could always take a chance, if time is not an issue for you, as the reviewers of more selective journals often provide very good feedback.

Once you've identified a journal, get the submission guidelines from the journal's Web site and follow them carefully. Make sure that your manuscript is in good shape and that it has been reviewed and carefully proofread by you and your colleagues.

Finally, the reviewers will nearly always request revisions. Pay careful attention to what the reviewers have to say and be responsive. Avoid being defensive, and appreciate that the reviews you receive represent an especially useful opportunity to improve the final analysis, interpretation, and presentation of your research. In addition to revisions to the paper itself, be sure to communicate what changes you have made clearly and fully to both the editor and the reviewers as well as to explain any revisions that you were unable or unwilling to make.

If your article is accepted, you will be asked to review and respond to page proofs and queries from the copy editor. Then, eventually, your article will appear in print.

Conclusion

In this chapter, you have learned where to find research of interest to you, either as part of a background review of the literature or to learn about an issue. You have also picked up some tips about how to identify and focus a research question of your own that you can answer with research. And we covered some issues related to writing up or presenting your research to others. These are all important how-to skills, and in the end, they require practice to master. So we encourage you to get out there and find studies to read or talks to attend, develop interesting research questions to investigate, and write up or present the results of your own research activities.

In doing all this, we encourage you to keep in mind the broad issues and ideas that we have covered in previous chapters on the strategies for description and for assertions about causation. You will find that understanding the logic and limitations of research methods helps a great deal in reading studies of interest to you, focusing your research question, and presenting your own research. The more you grasp the big picture, the better able you will be to do these tasks.

EXERCISES

Find a Research Article of Interest

15.1. Think of a topic of interest and search for recent research papers about it using some of the search tools discussed in this chapter. After examining paper titles, authors, and abstracts, pick one of particular interest. Which search methods were most useful? How did the abstract influence which paper you settled on? How did the writing and presentation quality influence your choice? What other factors influenced your choice?

Changing Technology of Searching

15.2. Using whatever knowledge you have about libraries and technology in the past, think about what your search experience above would have been like had you been searching in 1980, 1990, and even 2000. It might help to interview someone who was studying or doing research at the time.

Parts of a Research Article

15.3. Using a research article that you find, identify the parts of the research article. Are they the same as the standard six parts outlined in this chapter? If not, in what way do they vary? What do you learn in each part?

Tables and Figures

15.4. Find a research article that presents quantitative research in tables and figures. What tables and figures does the paper use? Could they be largely understood on their own? Why or why not? Could the results have been presented more clearly another way?

Writing About Numbers

15.5. Again find and read a research article of interest, one with numerical results. Do you think that the text should have contained more or less discussion of the quantitative results? If there are statistical significance tests, how are the results presented (stars, p values, other methods)? Is the practical significance of the results discussed, either explicitly or implicitly?

Publishing Your Research

15.6. Find the Web site of a journal in your field or practice area that is of interest to you. Look for the editorial aims or mission statement and read the guidelines for submitting to the journal. What would you need to do, or change, about your own paper or project to submit it to the journal?

Glossary

Activities: Training, counseling, marketing, and other tasks that make up the work of implementing a program and that are described in implementation-oriented logic models.

Adjusted *R*-Squared: An adjusted version of *R*-squared that takes into consideration the number of independent variables. Technically, an unbiased estimator of the population *R*-squared—the proportion of the dependent variable variance explained by all the independent variables *in the population*.

Aggregate Data: Data summarized as a mean, proportion, count, or other statistic at a higher unit of analysis, such as a geographic area or institutional unit (such as a school). Contrasted with *microdata*.

Aggregation Problem: The fact that relationships that hold at one unit of analysis may not hold at more aggregated levels.

Alternative Hypothesis: A negation of the null hypothesis; usually the hypothesis researchers would like to test but cannot do so directly.

ANOVA: A statistical analysis that compares the means across groups, normally used in analysis of experimental data.

Applied Research: Pursuit of knowledge to help in some practical problem or need.

Arms of an Experiment: The groups in an experiment that are each exposed to different treatments or control conditions.

Attrition: The problem of participants dropping out of a study.

Audit Studies: A form of randomized experiment in which matched pairs of race-discordant auditors apply for a job, loan, or other services to test for race discrimination.

Bar Chart: A graph for displaying categorical data with bars representing each category.

Basic Research: Pursuit of basic scientific knowledge that has no immediate practical application.

Before-After Study: Study that compares outcomes before and after a treatment occurs to determine the treatment's effect.

Beneficence: Ethical research norm that dictates that people who participate in research are not harmed and that they should benefit from the research.

Bias: Systematic error in a measure or causal effect.

Bibliographic Citation Software: Software that stores all the fields of references, enabling management, easy insertion into articles, and changing of reference format.

Blind Experiments: Experiments in which subjects do not know if they are in the treatment or control group. See also *double-blind experiments*.

Book Reviews: Articles in scholarly journals that review books but do not contain original research and are not peer reviewed.

Case (in a Case-Control Study): Those with a condition (often rare) in a case-control study.

Case-Control Study: A study in which individuals who experience an outcome, such as a particular disease or injury (the cases), are compared with other, similar individuals who did not experience this same outcome (the controls).

Case Study: Research that focuses on a single complex case, applying multiple qualitative and sometimes quantitative methods.

Categorical Variables: Variables that refer to categories and not to an actual quantity.

Causal Mechanism: Causal process or sequence of events that produces a causal effect.

Causal Relationship: A relationship (correlation or association) due to causation. When one variable changes, another one changes as a consequence.

Causal Research: Research to answer "what if?" questions. Contrasts with *descriptive research*.

Causation: When change in one variable produces change in another variable.

Census: Every member of a population. Contrasts with a *sample*.

Chi-Square Test: Statistical test most commonly employed to see if two categorical variables are related.

Closed-Ended Question: Question that may be answered only with a limited set of predetermined response categories.

Cluster Randomization: Randomization of convenient and natural clusters of individuals (e.g., classrooms) rather than randomization of individuals (e.g., students).

Cluster Sampling: A probability sampling method in which more aggregated units (clusters) are sampled before sampling individuals.

Codebook: Documentation that describes the layout of a data file and how data were collected, coded, and weighted.

Coding: The process of tagging or organizing qualitative data using a system of categories or codes.

Code-Recode Reliability: The consistency of coding qualitative data.

Coefficient of the Independent Variable (in Regression): The number that multiplies a given independent variable in a regression. Also known as the *slope*.

Coefficient of Variation: A measure of spread equal to the standard deviation divided by the mean.

Cognitive Pretesting: Survey questionnaire development stage in which the wording and meaning of the questionnaire are probed carefully through a process of debriefing respondents right after completing the questionnaire or interview or by having them "talk aloud" as they complete the questionnaire.

Common Cause: A variable that is a cause of both the presumed dependent variable (or outcome) and the presumed independent variable (or cause).

Comparison Group: Group in a quasi experiment that does not receive the treatment and implements the counterfactual. Similar to a control group but not created through randomization.

Complete Observer: Researcher in participant observation who attempts to remain unobtrusive and does not interview or engage with people in the setting.

Complete Participant: Role of a researcher in a participant observation study involving full or complete participation.

Complex Survey Sampling: Probability sampling methods that are more complex than simple random sampling, such as cluster sampling, stratified sampling, and disproportionate sampling.

Computer-Assisted Personal Interviewing (CAPI): In-person interviewing done on a computer so that software controls the flow of questions and data are entered in electronic form.

Computer-Assisted Self-Interviewing (CASI): Interview provided to subjects on a computer so that software controls the flow of questions and data are entered in electronic form.

Computer-Assisted Telephone Interviewing (CATI): Telephone interviewing done on a computer so that software controls the flow of questions and data are entered in electronic form.

Conceptualization: Stage in measurement process in which the construct (or concept) to be measured is carefully and fully defined.

Concurrent Validity: The extent to which a measure concurs or agrees with other established classifications or test scores.

Confidence Interval: A range of values in which we have a defined level of confidence (e.g., 95%) that the true value of the statistic being estimated lies.

Confirmatory Factor Analysis: Factor analysis in which theory is used to impose both the number of factors and which variables load onto each factor.

Confounder: Another term for common cause (or omitted variable), a confounder is a variable that causes (directly or indirectly) both the dependent variable and the independent variable of interest and leads to bias. See *common cause* and *omitted variable bias*.

Confounding: When the causal relationship is biased due to a common cause that is not accounted for. Another term for *omitted variable bias*.

Constant (in Regression): The predicted value of the dependent variable when the independent variables are zero in a regression. Also known as the *intercept*.

Construct (or Trait): The concept or trait that a measure is trying to capture.

Construct Validity: The extent to which a measure behaves in a statistical model in a way that would be expected, based on theory and prior research.

Contact Rate: Share who are reached from those sampled from the sampling frame.

Contamination: Something happens that interferes with the integrity and logic of the experiment, such as when the treatment (or elements of the treatment) is taken up by the control group.

Content Analysis: The analysis of the content of qualitative data, such as texts or images, usually involving a process of coding.

Content Validity: How well a measure captures all the important dimensions of a construct.

Contextual Variables: Higher level or more aggregate variables in a multilevel analysis.

Control: Holding constant factors that could affect an outcome.

Control Group: Group that does not receive the treatment being tested in a randomized or quasi experiment.

Control Variable: A variable representing a common cause that is used to stratify or statistically adjust the data to better estimate the causal effect with observational data.

Convenience Sample: A nonprobability sample that was chosen for convenience and that may be biased.

Convergent Validity: The extent to which a measure correlates with other closely related measures in the same data set.

Cooperation Rate: Share who cooperate with a survey request from among those contacted. See also *contact rate* and *response rate*.

Correlation: A measure of the strength and direction of a relationship between two variables.

Correlation Coefficient: The expected standard deviation change in one variable if the other variable changes by 1 standard deviation. Also known as *Pearson r* or simply *r*.

Cost-Effectiveness: The outcome obtained by a program relative to its cost.

Counterfactual: The world as it would be without the cause present but everything else the same.

Coverage Bias: Bias in survey that occurs when members of the sampling frame are systematically different from the target population in a way related to the measures.

Criterion-Related Validity: The extent to which a measure relates, empirically, to various criteria that can demonstrate its validity.

Critical Pragmatism: An approach to research that seeks feasible methods and practical knowledge to help improve some problem or condition in the world.

Cronbach's Alpha: The average of all possible split-half correlations; a measure of the internal reliability of a multi-item scale.

Cross-Sectional Data: Measurements of many individuals, organizations, or places at a single point in time.

Cross-Sectional Variation: Variation across individuals, organizations, or places at a single point in time.

Cross-Tabulation: Method to describe the relationship between two categorical variables.

Data: Unprocessed or aggregated observations—raw data.

Deduction: A process of scientific reasoning in which theories lead to hypotheses (predictions) that are compared with data (observation).

Dependent Variable: The effect, outcome, prediction, or response from a cause or independent variable—the variable the researcher is trying to explain.

Descriptive Research: Research to describe how the world is. Contrasts with *causal research*.

Design Effect: The loss of precision due to a particular complex survey sampling design. See also *effective sample size*.

Difference-in-Differences: A study that compares the difference between the before-after differences of a treatment and comparison group.

Dimension: A facet of a multifaceted construct, also called a *domain*.

Discriminant Validity: Extent to which a measure is independent of (not correlated with) other measures in the same data set that it does not logically relate to.

Disproportionate Sampling: A variation on stratified sampling in which some strata are sampled at different rates. Also called *oversampling*.

Distribution: The pattern of values spread out over a variable's categories or numeric range, illustrating which values are taken on and how often.

Double-Blind Experiment: Experiment in which both the subjects and the research workers who interact with the subjects, or make measurements, do not know who was assigned to the treatment or control groups.

Domain: A facet of a multifaceted construct, also called a *dimension*.

Dummy Variable: Categorical variable that has only two values 0 and 1, where 1 indicates being in the category named by the variable and 0 indicates not being in it. Also called *indicator variable*.

Ecological Data: Another term for *aggregated data*.

Ecological Fallacy: A directional relationship that appears at an aggregated level but does not exist, or is reversed, at the individual level.

Effect Size: A standardized way of measuring the effect of a treatment, usually the ratio of the effect or difference to the standard deviation.

Effective Sample Size: The comparable sample size from a simple random sample; it expresses the design effect (often a loss) due to complex sampling.

Endogeneity: Phenomenon that occurs when the independent variable *is* caused by variables or processes that also affect the dependent variable—or by the dependent variable itself.

Endogenous: Condition of independent variable of interest that occurs when it *is* caused by variables or processes that also affect the dependent variable—or by the dependent variable itself.

Epistemologies: Theories of knowledge, or ways of knowing.

Ethnography: Qualitative research method to describe and understand the culture of a group of people, often using participant observation.

Exogeneity: Phenomenon that occurs when the independent variable of interest is *not* caused by variables or processes that also affect the dependent variable—or by the dependent variable itself.

Exogenous: Condition of the independent variable of interest when it is *not* caused by variables or processes that also affect the dependent variable—or by the dependent variable itself.

Experimental Unit: The units, such as individuals or families, assigned to the treatment and control groups in a study.

Experimentation: The act of manipulating a treatment (presumed cause) to observe an effect—a causal effect.

Exploratory Factor Analysis: Factor analysis in which the number of factors and how items correlate with factors are discovered by the procedure rather than specified in advance by the researcher.

External Validity: The extent to which the results generalize to a wider group or reality, external to the study. Another term for *generalizability*.

Face Validity: On the face of it, how well a measure captures what it is supposed to measure—the extent to which a measure makes intuitive sense.

Factor Analysis: Multivariate method that groups many variables (indicators) into a smaller set of clusters or underlying factors.

Factorial Design: Experimental design that allows for the estimation of two or more treatment effects, along with interaction effects, through arms representing all possible combinations of treatments.

Factor Loadings: Correlations between the observed variables and the underlying and unobserved factors.

Factors (in an Experiment): The independent variables tested in an experiment, which can have main effects as well as interaction effects.

Field Pretesting: Survey development stage in which the complete survey procedures—the contact procedures, the finalized questionnaire or interview, the technology, and any follow-up procedures—are tested on a small test sample of the population.

Flat-File: Two-dimensional data structure generally used by statistical software with variables represented in columns and rows representing the unit of analysis.

Focus Group: A qualitative group interviewing procedure that involves typically 6 to 12 participants, seated around a table, and a moderator who asks questions and guides the discussion.

Forecasting: Using data from times series in the past to predict future values of the dependent variable(s).

Frequency Distribution: The distribution of a categorical variable showing the count or percentage in each category.

Generalizability: The extent to which the results of a study project to a wider group or context of interest.

Grounded Theory: A theory that emerges from observations made in a qualitative study and is grounded in the specific setting.

Group Self-Administered Surveys: Mode of survey research in which self-administered questionnaires are distributed in group settings.

Hawthorne Effect: Effect of being studied on the participants in a study.

Heterogeneous Treatment Effects: Treatment effects that vary systematically with the characteristics of individuals.

Hierarchical Models: Models that describe relationships between variables at different units of analysis. Also known as *multilevel models*.

Histogram: A graph showing the distribution of a quantitative variable.

Household Interview Survey: Survey conducted by visiting and interviewing people in their homes.

Hypothesis: A prediction of what will happen if a theory is correct.

Hypothesis Test: A test to see if a result is unlikely due to chance. Used to test whether groups are really different. See *significance test*.

Incidence: The rate at which new cases of a disease or condition appear in a population.

Independent Variable: The variable whose effect is of interest—the cause, the explanatory variable, the treatment, or the predictor.

Index: A composite measure composed of multiple items, which may be selected for different reasons.

Indicator: Some observable measure that reveals information about a factor or latent trait.

Induction: A process of scientific reasoning in which systematic observation leads to the development of theory and hypotheses.

Inference: Using samples to learn about the population, or using evidence to identify a causal relationship.

Inputs: The financial, human, and material resources required by the program described in more implementation-oriented logic models.

Institutional Review Board (IRB): Board that reviews research to ensure that it meets the required ethical guidelines.

Instrument (of Measurement): Tools that help measure something, such as a survey instrument.

Instrument (of Instrumental Variables): A variable that causes the independent variable to change but does not affect the outcome in any way, other than through the independent variable.

Instrumental Variables (IV): A method that estimates a causal effect through the use of a variable that causes the independent variable to change but does not affect the outcome in any way, other than through the independent variable.

Intent to Treat (ITT): Analysis of randomized experiments in which everyone is kept in their original randomized group—treatment or control—irrespective of compliance or attrition.

Interaction: Situation when two variables each affect the magnitude of the effect of the other on the dependent variable.

Interaction Variable: A variable defined as the product of two other variables, usually used to empirically measure an interaction.

Intercept Interview Survey: Mode of survey research in which people are stopped (intercepted) in public places and asked questions.

Intercoder Reliability: Consistency with which codes are applied to qualitative data.

Internal Validity: Strength of causal evidence provided by a study.

Internet Access Panels: Large e-mail lists of respondents who opt in (sign up) to participate in online surveys on various topics.

Internet Survey: Mode of survey research that uses web-based forms or questionnaires to gather responses. See *Web survey* or *online survey*.

Interrater Reliability: How similar the scores of different raters or interviewers are when they measure the same person or object.

Interrupted Time Series: A study that uses a series of periodic measurements interrupted in the middle by the treatment.

Intersubjectivity: The notion that language allows us to stand in someone else's shoes and see the world from their perspective.

Interval Measure: A quantitative measure in which the size of a difference—an interval—has meaning, but there is no meaningful zero. Contrasts with *ratio measure*.

Intervening Variable: A variable along a causal pathway. Also known as a *mediator*.

Interview Guide: A set of open-ended questions, sometimes accompanied by probes, that help guide or structure the discussion in a semistructured interview.

Intraclass Correlation: Similarity of elements within a cluster. Also referred to as *rho*—the rate of homogeneity.

Journal: Publications, published periodically, which contain research and scholarship, usually peer reviewed.

Justice (In research ethics): Requires consideration of equity among subjects and fairness in regard to who becomes a research subject.

Latent Construct: A construct or trait that is not directly observable.

Level of Confidence: The area—usually 95%—of the sampling distribution that is the basis for a confidence interval.

Level of Measurement: The distinction between quantitative and categorical variables, or "ladder of measurement": nominal, ordinal, interval, and ratio.

Likert Scale: A scale made up of multiple items, usually using an agree-disagree response format.

Limited Dependent Variable: A dependent variable that cannot take on all possible values.

Linear Probability Model: Ordinary least squares regression model in which dependent variable is a dummy variable and predicted values of the dependent variable are interpreted as probabilities.

Logic Model: Model (usually diagram) that communicates the underlying theory or mechanism of how a program will work.

Logistic Regression: Model predicting the log odds of an event.

Longitudinal Data: Data gathered over time.

Longitudinal Variation: Variation over time.

Mail Self-Administered Survey: Mode of survey research in which forms are mailed to respondents along with instructions to complete and return the forms.

Main Effect: The effect of an independent variable on a dependent variable, before or without its moderation by another variable (interaction).

Manifest Construct: A construct or trait that is directly observable. Contrasts with a *latent construct*.

Marginal Effect: The predicted difference in the probability due to a specified change in the relevant independent variable.

Margin of Error: The amount added to the point estimate in both directions to create the confidence interval.

Matching: A study in which individuals in the comparison group are chosen so that the values of their matching variables are as close as possible to those in the treatment group.

Mean: Average of a quantitative variable—the sum of all observations divided by the number of observations.

Measure: The score or result produced by a measurement process.

Measurement: The process of systematically observing some feature or characteristic of the world and then recording it in the form of a number or category.

Measurement Error: Errors in a measure or how it differs from the true construct to be measured. Consists of *noise* and *bias*.

Mechanism: Detailed causal process that produces an outcome.

Median: The value at the point that splits the distribution into two halves, the 50th percentile in the distribution of a quantitative variable.

Mediator: A variable along a causal pathway. Also known as an *intervening variable*.

Meta-Analysis: A method for pooling together multiple smaller studies to get a much bigger, combined study.

Microdata: Data at its most basic level of observation—or unit of analysis—often of individual people or households. Contrasted with *aggregated data*.

Middle Range Theory: A logical description of how a particular corner or aspect of the world works. Contrasts with paradigms or grand theories of society.

Minimal Detectable Effect: The smallest effect that would still have statistical significance in a study with a particular sample size and design, often chosen to perform sample size calculations.

Mixed-Methods Studies: Research approach that combines both quantitative and qualitative research techniques.

Model: A diagram or equation or other representation that serves to articulate and communicate a theory.

Moderator: The person who guides a focus group. Also called a *facilitator*.

Moderator's Guide: A script for the facilitator or moderator of a focus group, containing open-ended questions and sometimes accompanied by probes, that helps guide or structure the discussion.

Moderator Variable: A variable that changes the magnitude of the effect of another variable. See *interaction*.

Modifiable Variable (or Factor): An independent variable of interest that can be changed, or influenced, by policy or practice.

Multicollinearity: Phenomenon in which an independent variable is a linear combination of two more of the other independent variables.

Multilevel (or Hierarchical) Data: Data that combine variables with different unit of analysis.

Multilevel Models: Models that describe relationships between variables at different units of analysis. Also known as *hierarchical models*.

Multistage Sampling: A probability sampling method in which more aggregated units (clusters) are sampled and then sampling occurs within the aggregates.

Multiple Comparison Correction: Correction applied to a single statistical significance measure, when it is one of many statistical tests, because one of the many tests could be significant by chance.

Multiple Regression: The best linear predictor of a dependent variable using more than one independent variable.

Multivariate Statistics: Statistics examining the relationships between multiple (more than two) variables at the same time.

Mystery Shopping Method: Participant observation method in which a researcher plays the role of a customer to experience service quality.

Natural Experiment: Situation in which the treatment (the independent variable of interest) varies through some naturally occurring or unplanned event that happens to be exogenous to the outcome (the dependent variable of interest).

Negative (–) Relationship: Relationship in which the two related variables move in the opposite direction.

Nomological Validity: The extent to which a measure behaves as it should in a system or network of other variables.

Noise: Random measurement error.

Nominal Categorical Variables: Categorical variables that have no intrinsic order.

Nonidentifiable: Not containing information that identifies who an individual is or enables identification through indirect means.

Nonmodifiable Variable: An independent variable of interest that cannot be changed or influenced by policy or practice.

Nonreactive Measures: Measures that occur naturally or routinely or otherwise do not disturb the subjects in an experiment.

Nonresponse Bias: Bias in survey results that occurs when those who do not respond are systematically different from those who do respond in a way related to the measures.

Normal Distribution: A theoretical distribution that is bell-shaped, symmetrical, and has many useful properties in statistics.

Normative Research: Research that deals explicitly with values, or norms, for how people or institutions should behave. Contrasts with *positive research*.

Null Hypothesis: In hypothesis testing, the hypothesis that is directly tested, typically resulting in no difference or no effect.

Observational Study: Study in which researchers do not attempt to change or manipulate variables to test their effects; they simply observe or measure things as they are in the natural, unaltered world.

Observed Sample: The actual data available in the sample, equal to the true sample minus those who could not be reached and those who did not agree to participate.

Observer as Participant: Researcher in participant observation who visits the setting, typically only on one of just a few occasions, to conduct interviews with people and make observations.

Odds: For an outcome that has only two possibilities, the ratio of one outcome (e.g., success) to the other possible outcome (e.g., failure).

Odds Ratio (OR): Ratio of the odds of an outcome for one group to the odds of the outcome for another group.

Omitted Variable Bias: When the causal relationship is biased due to a common cause, including a complex common cause, that is not accounted for.

Online Data Analysis Tool: Software that allows users to directly analyze public data on the Web.

Online Survey: Mode of survey research that uses Web-based forms or questionnaires to gather responses. See *Internet survey* or *Web survey*.

Open-Ended Question: A question that cannot be answered with a limited set of possible answers and gives the person answering the opportunity to choose what information to provide.

Operationalization: The process of devising or identifying an empirical measure.

Ordinal Categorical Variables: Categorical variables that can be put in a meaningful order.

Original Research Article: First published report of primary research in a journal.

Out-of-Sample Extrapolation: Making a prediction using a fitted model (particularly regression) far from the data used to fit the model.

Outcome: The response of interest to a program. See also *dependent variable*.

Outliers: Extreme scores or observations that stand out in a distribution.

Outputs: Immediate products of these activities, such as people trained, brochures distributed, or citations issued, described in implementation-oriented logic models.

Oversampling: A variation on stratified sampling in which some strata are sampled with probability greater than their population share. Also called *disproportionate sampling*.

p Value: The probability of observing our sample estimate (or one more extreme) if the null hypothesis about the population is true.

Panel Data: Repeated measures on the same individuals (or group or entity) over time.

Panel Survey: Survey in which the same respondents are tracked and repeatedly surveyed over time, sometimes over many years. See *panel data*.

Parallel Forms Reliability: The extent to which two forms of a test or measure are really the same.

Parameter: The characteristic or feature of a population that a researcher is trying to estimate.

Participant as Observer: Researcher in a participant observation who spends significant time in the setting, joining in important activities or events, but does not assume an actual role as such.

Participant Observation: A qualitative research method in which the researcher participates in and observes his or her subjects.

Path Analysis: Method that estimates the pattern of relationships between variables in a presumed causal structure.

Path Diagram: A diagram showing causal relationships (represented by arrows) between variables (represented by circles). See *path model*.

Path Model: A model showing causal relationships between variables. See *path diagram*.

Pearson r: The expected standard deviation change in one variable if the other variable changes by 1 standard deviation. It is the most common measure of correlation. Also referred to as the *correlation coefficient*.

Peer Review: Process in which studies or proposals are reviewed and approved (or rejected) by a group of peers—other researchers in the same field—who render a judgment on the methodology and worth of the paper or proposal.

Percent Change: Change relative to the starting base, expressed as percentage.

Percentage Point Change: The change of a variable measured in its own units when it is a percentage. Contrasted with *percent change*.

Performance Measurement: The use of measurement for administrative purposes or leadership strategy.

Pie Chart: A graph showing percentages among categories, shown as segments of a circle.

Placebo: An inert treatment provided to a control group in an experiment so that the experiment can be blind.

Placebo Effect: The fact that people often respond to any kind of treatment, even a completely phony or useless one.

Population of Interest: The population the study aims to investigate.

Pooled Cross Sections: Repeated independent cross sections over time.

Positive Research: Research that aims to describe the world objectively and without making value judgments. Contrasts with *normative research*.

Positive (+) Relationship: Relationship in which the two related variables move in the same direction.

Poststratification Adjustment: Adjustment of sample statistics to ensure that each stratum's share of the sample represents its share in the population. Used to correct samples that do not reflect the characteristics of the population. Also called *poststratification weighting*.

Poststratification Weighting: Adjustment of sample statistics to ensure that each stratum's share of the sample represents its share in the population. Used to correct samples that do not reflect the characteristics of the population. Also called *poststratification adjustment*.

Practical Significance: The extent to which an effect or relationship's magnitude (if true) would be important or relevant in the real world.

Predictive Validity: The extent to which a measure predicts logically related outcomes or behaviors in the future.

Prevalence: The number or share of the population that has a particular disease or condition.

Primary Data: Collecting new *data* to provide a description or explanation of the world.

Primary Research: The original collection or analysis of data to answer a new research question or to produce new knowledge.

Principal Components Analysis: Factor analysis in which the researcher does not use theory to impose a structure but lets the computer choose the number of factors and estimate how the items correlate with each factor. See *exploratory factor analysis*.

Probability Sample: Sample chosen based on probability, at random on some level, which makes the sample representative.

Propensity Score Matching: A matching method that employs multivariate statistics to match along many variables at the same time.

Propensity to Respond: Likelihood of responding to a survey or survey question.

Proportion: The share of a population with some characteristic, usually expressed as a decimal fraction.

Prospective Cohort: Group of study subjects followed longitudinally over time. See also *panel study*.

Prospective Study: Studies in which subjects are followed over time to observe what happens to them. See also *prospective cohort* and *panel study*.

Protocols: Carefully specified procedures for using the instruments properly in measurement.

Power: In statistics, the ability to recognize that the null hypothesis is false.

Proxy: A measure that substitutes for another unavailable measure.

Proxy Reporting: Situation in a survey in which a person who responds provides information about someone else.

Proxy Respondent: A person who responds to a survey providing information about someone else.

Public Use Microdata: Individual-level data collected and made available to the public.

Purposive Sampling: Subjects or cases of research are chosen for a purpose, not to provide a sample that is representative of a population, for qualitative research.

Qualitative Data: The raw data from qualitative research, which can take the form of field notes, interview transcriptions, video or audio recordings, or documents, among others.

Qualitative Data Analysis: The organization and interpretation of qualitative data, which may or may not be aided with software.

Qualitative Research: Research that involves language, images, and other forms of expressing meaning that researchers then interpret—research that does not involve numbers or quantification.

Quantile: Points taken at regular intervals (such as every quarter or tenth) in a distribution.

Quantitative Data: Information that is recorded, coded, and stored in numerical form.

Quantitative Research: Any research involving the statistical analysis of quantitative data—including both quantitative and categorical variables.

Quantitative Variables: Variables that take the forms of numbers that refer to actual quantities of something.

Quasi Experiment: Studies of planned or intentional treatments that resemble randomized field experiments but lack full random assignment.

Rate: Share of a population with a particular characteristic, which is expressed relative to some base size population.

Rate of Change: How rapidly a variable changes.

Random Assignment: Experimental design in which the one who receives the treatment under investigation and the one who is in the control group are determined randomly.

Random Digit Dialing (RDD): A telephone survey method that gives both listed and unlisted numbers an equal chance of being selected by replacing random digits at the ends of listed residential telephone numbers.

Randomized Controlled Trial (RCT): Experiment in which subjects are randomly assigned to conditions (or treatments) in order to test causal relationships. See *randomized experiment*.

Randomized Experiment: Experiment in which subjects are randomly assigned to conditions (or treatments) to test for causal relationships.

Randomized Field Experiment: A randomized experiment conducted in an actual social or policy setting—the *field*.

Random Measurement Error: Errors—deviations from the true construct in a measure—that are not systematic and average out to zero. Also called *noise*.

Random Sample: A subset of a population (sample) chosen at random.

Random Sampling (or Probability Sampling): Choosing from the sampling frame at random.

Ratio Measure: A quantitative measure in which there is a meaningful zero and the size of a difference, an interval, has meaning. Contrasts with *interval measure*.

Referee: Expert on the topic of a research article submitted to a peer-reviewed journal, who carefully evaluates the quality and importance of the research. Also known as a *reviewer*.

Regression: A best linear predictor of a dependent variable from independent variable(s).

Regression Discontinuity: A regression analysis study in which the assignment to treatment is based on a cut point for a single quantitative assignment variable.

Relational Database: Database structure composed of various tables of information that are linked and work together.

Relationship: How the variation of two different variables are related.

Relative Risk: Ratio of the risk of two groups.

Reliability: Consistency of a measure.

Replication: Repeating a study with a different sample, in a different place, time period, or policy context, or with a different study design.

Requests for Proposals (RFPs): Notices distributed by government agencies, foundations, or other funders providing notification of and describing research they wish to commission or support.

Research Personnel: The technicians, interviewers, trained observers, and other personnel who implement research protocols.

Residual: The error in a regression—the difference between the actual value of the dependent variable and the predicted value.

Respect for Persons (In research ethics): Dictates that people used as the subjects of research provide informed consent and are not coerced into participating in research.

Respondent-Driven Sampling: Method of sampling based on respondent contacts, like snowball sampling, but with a statistical foundation.

Response Rate: Share who respond to a survey from among those sampled from a sampling frame.

Retrospective Study: Study in which researchers find subjects and then gather data about them earlier in time.

Reverse Causation: Situation when the presumed dependent variable (or outcome) is actually the cause of the presumed independent variable (or cause).

Reviewer: Expert on the topic of a research article submitted to a peer-reviewed journal, who carefully evaluates the quality and importance of the research. Also known as a *referee*.

Review Article: A type of article in a scholarly journal that discusses many research studies, synthesizing the results and reaching broader conclusions.

Risk: Share of a population with a particular condition or disease, which is expressed relative to some base size population. See *rate*.

R-Squared: In a regression, the proportion of the variation in the dependent variable predicted by variation in the independent variables.

Sample: A subset of people or elements selected from a population.

Sample Size Calculation: A calculation done before a study or survey to determine the sample size needed to get a certain level of precision or to be able to detect certain differences.

Sampling: Process of selecting people or elements from a population for inclusion in a research study.

Sampling Distribution: The distribution of statistics estimated from many repeated samples.

Sampling Error: Error in sample statistics due to random chance of who ends up in a sample.

Sampling Frame: The list of enumeration of the population from which the sample is taken.

Sampling Variability: Variability in sample statistics, across different samples, due to random chance of who ends up in a sample.

Scale: A composite measure composed of multiple items, which are correlated with each other and thought to reflect a single latent construct.

Scatterplot: A graph illustrating the values two quantitative variables take on in data.

Scientific Method: A way of knowing that is based on systematic observation, logical explanation, prediction, openness, and skepticism.

Secondary Data: Data collected by others, such as existing government surveys, administrative records, or transcripts.

Secondary Research: The search for published sources describing the results of research or information provided by others.

Secret (or Mystery) Shopping Method: Participant observation method in which a researcher plays the role of a customer to experience service quality.

Self-Reporting: When survey respondents are asked to report their own behaviors or characteristics.

Self-Selection: Phenomenon when the individuals studied, or someone acting on their behalf, choose their category or level of the independent variable of interest.

Semistructured Interview: A qualitative research method that involves interviewing with an interview guide, including a planned set of open-ended questions.

Significance Level: The standard against which the p value is compared to determine statistical significance: If the p value is less than the significance level, the result is deemed statistically significant.

Significance Test: A test to see if a result is unlikely due to chance. Used to test whether groups are really different. See *hypothesis test*.

Simple Random Sampling: Selecting of people (or elements) from a population in such a way that each individual has an equal chance, or probability, of selection.

Simple Regression: A best-fit straight line for describing how one quantitative variable—the independent variable—predicts another quantitative variable—the dependent variable.

Simultaneity Bias: Bias in an estimate of a causal effect due to reverse causation.

Skewness: Characteristic of a distribution that is not symmetrical and has one tail longer than the other.

Snowball Sampling: Method of sampling or finding study subjects in which interviewees are asked to refer people they know to the researcher for inclusion in the sample. See also *respondent-driven sampling*.

Split-Half Reliability: A measure of reliability of a composite measure such as a scale based on dividing the items randomly into two halves and then looking at the correlation between the two halves.

Spurious Relationship: When two correlated variables are presumed to be causally related but in fact are not and the correlation is entirely due to a common cause.

Spurious Correlation: When two correlated variables are presumed to be causally related but in fact are not, and the correlation is entirely due to a common cause.

Standard Deviation: Common measure of variability of a quantitative variable.

Standard Error: The precision of the estimate—how good a job we expect it to do, on average.

Standardized Score: A variable converted to standard deviation units and shifted to mean zero. Also known as a *z score*.

Statistical Equivalence: The result of random assignment, it refers to the fact that the treatment and control groups in a randomized experiment are equivalent, *on average*, on all variables.

Statistical Inference: Formal procedure that uses facts about the sampling distribution of statistics from a sample to infer the unknown parameters of a population.

Statistical Significance: The extent to which a difference or a relationship exists, judged against the likelihood that it would happen just by chance alone. See *p value*.

Strata: Exhaustive and mutually exclusive subgroups of a target population.

Stratified Sampling: Probability sampling method in which a sample is drawn separately from each group—each stratum—and the population is divided into exhaustive and mutually exclusive strata.

Stratify: To break the data into exhaustive and mutually exclusive groups.

Structural Equation Modeling (SEM): Multivariate method for estimating models in which observed indicators represent latent variables and also latent variables are related to each other in a presumed causal (structural) manner similar to path analysis.

Structuralists: Researchers who insist that social research start with strong theories and test these with empirical predictions (deduction).

Subject: The units, such as individuals or families, studied in an experiment. See *experimental unit*.

Survival Analysis: Method to predict the length of time until some event.

Systematic Measurement Error (or Bias): Errors—or deviations from the true construct in a measure that are systematic and do not average out to zero. Also called *bias*.

Systematic Sampling: Probability sampling method in which individuals or elements are sampled at even intervals—every kth individual for some integer k.

Tailored Design Method: Method for conducting self-administered mail surveys, which emphasizes the importance of all components of the mail survey, including the initial contacting materials, the survey layout and design, the timing and tone of the follow-up requests, and the use of multiple contacts and modes of communication.

Telephone Interview Survey: Survey conducted by telephone, usually based on random digit dialing.

Test-Retest Reliability: An approach to determining reliability based on measuring the same thing twice.

Test Statistic: A statistic used for significance testing (or hypothesis testing), calculated using data.

Theoretical Sampling: Sampling in which people or cases are chosen to generate theory, and the number of people or cases is necessarily limited, for qualitative research. It does not produce a representative sample. See also *purposive sampling*.

Theory: A logical description of how a particular corner or aspect of the world works.

Time Series: Completely aggregated or single-measure data over time.

Trained Observation: A method of data collection that involves training research workers to systematically observe and record conditions or behaviors, typically using an observation rating form.

Trait: Concept, construct, or characteristic of which the measurement is sought.

Treatment: The program whose effect is of interest—the cause, the independent variable, the explanatory variable, or the predictor.

Treatment Group: Group in a randomized experiment that is assigned to receive the treatment under investigation.

Treatment of the Treated (TOT): An analysis of a randomized experiment that provides an estimate of the effect of the treatment on those who were actually exposed to it.

Triangulation: The use of multiple methods or analyses to confirm a finding.

True Sample: All the people or elements originally selected from the sampling frame, regardless of whether they are contacted or respond.

Type I Error: The rejection of a true null hypothesis.

Type II Error: The acceptance of a false null hypothesis.

Unfunded Research: Research with no specific grant or contract to support it.

Unobtrusive Measures: Measures that occur naturally or routinely, or otherwise do not disturb the subjects in an experiment.

Unit of Analysis: The objects, individuals, or things described by the variables or theory.

Unit of Measurement: The units that define the numbers in quantitative variables—how many of what that numbers refer to. Also referred to as simply *units*.

Units: The precise meaning of the numbers in quantitative variables—how many of what the numbers refer to. Also referred to as *units of measurement*.

Universe: The population the study aims to investigate. See *population of interest*.

Unmeasured Variables: Variables that are not measured in the current data, particularly common causes that cause omitted variable bias because they are not used as control variables.

Unstructured Interview: A qualitative research method that involves interviewing with no predetermined set of questions.

Validity (of a measure): How well a measure represents the construct of interest.

Variable: Something that can take on different values or different attributes.

Variance: A measure of spread of a quantitative variable, the square of the standard deviation.

Voluntary Sample: A sample consisting of volunteers.

Volunteer Bias: Bias in a study that occurs when volunteers differ from a more representative sample of the population in ways that influence the findings of the study.

Web Survey: Mode of survey research that uses Web-based forms or questionnaires to gather responses. See *Internet survey or online survey.*

Weighting: A procedure for giving some individuals in the data more, or less, weight in the analysis. Often required when disproportionate or complex sampling is used.

Working Paper: A scholarly article that has not been published and may be still in progress.

z Score: A variable converted to standard deviation units and shifted to mean zero. See also *standardized scores*.

References

Abraham, Jean, Roger Feldman, & Caroline Carlin. (2004). Understanding employee awareness of health care quality information: How can employers benefit? *Health Services Research, 39,* 1799–1816.

Abrams, Laura S., Sarah K. Shannon, & Cindy Sangalang. (2008). Transition services for incarcerated youth: A mixed methods evaluation study. *Children and Youth Services Review, 30*(5), 522–535.

Agence France Press. (2008). *Eurozone unemployment rate remains at record low 7.2 percent.* Retrieved February 10, 2008, from http://afp.google.com/article/ALeqM5jKGho5clytOpivWnaKM_LGOxoYoA

Agresti, Alan. (2007). *An introduction to categorical data analysis* (2nd ed.). Hoboken, NJ: Wiley-Interscience.

Allen, Arthur. (2007). Vaccines and autism? In *Vaccine: The controversial story of medicine's greatest lifesaver.* New York: W. W. Norton.

Allen, Mary J., & Wendy M. Yen. (1979). *Introduction to measurement theory.* Belmont, CA: Wadsworth.

American Psychological Association. (2009). *Publication manual of the American Psychological Association* (6th ed.). Washington, DC: Author.

Angrist, Joshua D., & Alan B. Krueger. (2001). Instrumental variables and the search for identification: From supply and demand to natural experiments. *Journal of Economic Perspectives, 15*(4), 69–85.

Angrist, Joshua, & Jorn-Stefan Pischke. (2009). *Mostly harmless econometrics.* Princeton, NJ: Princeton University Press.

Associated Press. (2008). *Poll finds support for teacher raises.* Retrieved February 7, 2008, from www.kten.com/Global/story.asp?S=7836551

Baker, Michael, & Kevin Milligan. (2008). Maternal employment, breastfeeding, and health: Evidence from mandated maternity leave. *Journal of Health Economics, 27,* 871–887.

Belli, Robert F., Sean E. Moore, & John VanHoewyk. (2006). An experimental comparison of question forms used to reduce vote overreporting. *Electoral Studies, 25*(4), 751–759.

Bernard, H. Russell. (1996). Qualitative data, qualitative analysis. *Cultural Anthropology Methods Journal, 8*(1), 9–11.

Besharov, Doug. (2009). Presidential address: From great society to continuous improvement government: Shifting from "does it work?" to "what would make it better?" *Journal of Policy Analysis and Management, 28*(2), 199–220.

Best, Roger. (2008). *Employee satisfaction, firm value and firm productivity* (Working Paper). Warrensburg: University of Central Missouri, Department of Economics & Finance. Retrieved January 25, 2009, from http://ideas.repec.org/p/umn/wpaper/0806.html

Blalock, Hubert M. (1961). *Causal inferences in nonexperimental research.* New York: W. W. Norton.

Blank, Rebecca M. (2008, Spring). Presidential address: How to improve poverty measurement in the United States. *Journal of Policy Analysis and Management, 27*(2), 233–254.

Bloom, Dan, Richard Hendra, James J. Kemple, Pamela Morris, Susan Scrivener, & Nandita Verma (with Diana Adams-Ciardullo, David Seith, & Johanna Walter). (2000). *The family transition program: Final report on Florida's initial time-limited welfare program.* New York: Manpower Demonstration Research Corporation. Retrieved November 3, 2009, from www.mdrc.org/publications/20/overview.html

Bloom, Howard S. (1995). Minimum detectable effects: A simple way to report the statistical power of experimental designs. *Evaluation Review, 19*(5), 547–556.

Bloom, Howard S. (Ed.). (2005). *Learning more from social experiments.* New York: Russell Sage Foundation.

Bloomberg Press. (2008). *U.S. Michigan consumer sentiment index falls in June*. Retrieved September 15, 2008, from www.bloomberg.com/apps/news?pid = 20601103&refer = news&sid = aQAIoSZDtBuo

Blundell, Richard, & Thomas M. Stoker. (2005). Heterogeneity and aggregation. *Journal of Economic Literature, 43*(2), 347–391.

Booth, Wayne C., Gregory G. Colomb, & Joseph M. Williams. (2008). *The craft of research* (3rd ed.). Chicago: University of Chicago Press.

Bradburn, Norman M., Seymour Sudman, & Brian Wansink. (2004). *Asking questions: The definitive guide to questionnaire design—For market research, political polls, and social and health questionnaires*. San Francisco: Jossey-Bass.

Braunsberger, Karin, Hans Wybenga, & Roger Gates. (2007). A comparison of reliability between telephone and Web-based surveys. *Journal of Business Research, 60*(7), 758–764.

Bronzaft, Arline L., & Dennis P. McCarthy. (1975). The effect of elevated train noise on reading ability. *Environment and Behavior, 7*(4), 517–527.

Brown, Steven R., & Lawrence E. Melamed. (1990). *Experimental design and analysis*. Newbury Park, CA: Sage.

Burnham, Gilbert, Riyadh Lafta, Shannon Doocy, & Les Roberts. (2006). Mortality after the 2003 invasion of Iraq: A cross-sectional cluster sample survey. *Lancet, 368,* 1421–1428.

Campbell, Donald. T. (1969). Reforms as experiments. *American Psychologist, 24*(4), 409–429.

Campbell, Donald T., & Julian Stanley. (1963). *Experimental and quasi-experimental designs for research* (1st ed.). Belmont, CA: Wadsworth.

Card, David. (1999). The causal effect of education on earnings. In O. Ashenfelter & D. Card (Eds.), *Handbook of labor economics* (Vol. 3A, pp. 1801–1863). Amsterdam: Elsevier.

Carmines, Edward G., & Richard A. Zeller. (1979). *Reliability and validity assessment*. Newbury Park, CA: Sage.

Carnegie Foundation for the Advancement of Teaching. (2009). *Basic classification tables*. Stanford, CA: Author. Retrieved November 4, 2009, from www.carnegiefoundation.org/classifications/index.asp?key = 805

CBS News. (2005). *Poll: Katrina response inadequate, public says response to Katrina too slow; confidence in Bush drops*. Retrieved February 19, 2008, from www.cbsnews.com/stories/2005/09/08/opinion/polls/main824591_page2.shtml

Center for Spatially Integrated Social Science. (2009). Retrieved August 11, 2009, from www.csiss.org/

Centers for Disease Control and Prevention. (2008). *BRFSS: Summary data quality reports—Technical information and data*. Retrieved May 28, 2008, from www.cdc.gov/brfss/technical_infodata/quality.htm

Centers for Disease Control and Prevention. (2009a). *Malaria facts: CDC malaria*. Retrieved March 17, 2009, from www.cdc.gov/malaria/facts.htm

Centers for Disease Control and Prevention. (2009b). *NHANES dietary Web tutorial: Dietary data overview: History of dietary data collection*. Retrieved November 10, 2009, from www.cdc.gov/nchs/tutorials/dietary/SurveyOrientation/SurveyDesign/Info1.htm

Centers for Disease Control and Prevention, Division for Heart Disease and Stroke Prevention. (n.d.). *State program, evaluation guides: Developing and using a logic model*. Atlanta, GA: Author. Retrieved May 5, 2009, from www.cdc.gov/DHDSP/state_program/evaluation_guides/logic_model.htm

China launches nationwide AIDS prevention program. (n.d.). Retrieved July 23, 2009, from www.chinadaily.com.cn/china/2008–03/28/content_6574756.htm

Christensen, Michael C., & Remler, Dahlia K. (2009). Information and communications technology in U.S. health care: Why is adoption so slow and is slower better? *Journal of Health Politics Policy and Law, 34*(6), 1011–1034.

City of New York. (2008). *Mayor's office of operations: Scorecard*. Retrieved November 10, 2008, from www.nyc.gov/html/ops/html/scorecard/scorecard.shtml

Cleveland, William S. (1994). *The elements of graphing data* (2nd ed.). Lafayette, IN: Hobart Press.

The Coalition for Evidence-Based Policy. (2009). *Increasing government effectiveness through rigorous evidence about "What Works."* Retrieved November 11, 2009, from http://coalition4evidence.org/wordpress

Cohen, Jacob. (1992). A power primer. *Psychological Bulletin, 112*(1), 155–159.

Colman, Silvie, Ted Joyce, & Robert Kaestner. (2008). Misclassification bias and the estimated effect of parental involvement laws on adolescents' reproductive outcomes. *American Journal of Public Health, 98*(10), 1881–1885.

Communications New Brunswick. (2004, March 25). *Minister unveils literacy initiative as part of Quality Learning Agenda.* Fredericton, New Brunswick, Canada: Author. Retrieved January 25, 2009, from www.gnb.ca/cnb/news/edu/2004e0357ed.htm

Converse, Jean M., & Stanley Presser. (1986). *Survey questions: Handcrafting the standardized questionnaire.* Beverly Hills, CA: Sage.

Cook, Royer F., Alan D. Bernstein, Thadeus L. Arrington, & Christine M. Andrews. (1997). Assessing drug use in the workplace: A comparison of self-report, urinalysis, and hair analysis. In Lana Harrison & Arthur Hughes (Eds.), *NIDA research monograph: Vol. 167. The validity of self-reported drug use: Improving the accuracy of survey estimates* (HIH Publication No. 97–4147). Rockville, MD: National Institute on Drug Abuse.

Costello, E. Jane., Scott N. Compton, Gordon Keeler, & Adrian Angold. (2003, October). Relationships between poverty and psychopathology: A natural experiment. *Journal of the American Medical Association, 290*(15), 2023–2028.

Creswell, John W. (2006). *Qualitative inquiry and research design: Choosing among five approaches* (2nd ed.). Thousand Oaks, CA: Sage.

Creswell, John W., & Vicki L. Plano Clark. (2006). *Designing and conducting mixed methods research* (1st ed.). Thousand Oaks, CA: Sage.

Davis, James A. (1985). *The logic of causal order.* Newbury Park, CA: Sage.

Davis, John M., Nancy Chen, & Ira D. Glick. (2003, June). A meta-analysis of the efficacy of second-generation antipsychotics. *Archives of General Psychiatry, 60*(6), 553–564.

Davies, Huw T. O., Sandra M. Nutley, & Peter C. Smith. (2000). *What works? Evidence-based policy and practice in public services.* Bristol, UK: Policy Press.

Der, Geoff, G. David Batty, & Ian J. Deary. (2006). Effect of breast feeding on intelligence in children: Prospective study, sibling pairs analysis, and meta-analysis. *British Medical Journal, 333*(7575), 945–955.

Dillman, Don A. (2007). *Mail and Internet surveys: The tailored design method. 2007 update.* Hoboken, NJ: Wiley.

Draper, Steven W. (2008). *The Hawthorne, Pygmalion, Placebo and other expectation effects: Some notes.* Retrieved February 12, 2009, from www.psy.gla.ac.uk/~steve/hawth.html

Duncan, Otis Dudley. (1984). *Notes on social measurement: Historical and critical.* New York: Russell Sage Foundation.

European Commission. (2007). *The European Emergency Number 112.* Retrieved February 18, 2008, from http://ec.europa.eu/public_opinion/flash/fl_228_sum_en.pdf2

European Social Survey. (n.d.). *ESS1-2e02 variable documentation list.* Retrieved December 20, 2007, from www.europeansocialsurvey.org

Evans, William N., & Jeanne Ringel (1999, April). Can higher cigarette taxes improve birth outcomes? *Journal of Public Economics, 72*(1), 135–154.

Evenhouse, Erik, & Siobhan Reilly. (2005). Improved estimates of the benefits of breastfeeding using sibling comparisons to reduce selection bias. *Health Services Research, 40*(6 Pt. 1), 1781–1802.

Ferryman, Kadija S., Xavier de Souza Briggs, Susan J. Popkin, & María Rendón. (2008). *Do better neighborhoods for MTO families mean better schools?* (Metropolitan Housing and Communities Center Policy Brief No. 3). Washington, DC: Urban Institute Press.

Fetterman, David M., Shakeh Kaftarian, & Abraham Wandersman. (1995). *Empowerment evaluation: Knowledge and tools for self-assessment and accountability* (1st ed.). Thousand Oaks, CA: Sage.

Fisher, Gorden M. (1992). The development and history of the poverty thresholds. *Social Security Bulletin, 55*(4), 3–14. Retrieved November 4, 2009, from www.ssa.gov/history/fisheronpoverty.html

Fowler, Floyd J. (1995). *Improving survey questions: Design and evaluation.* Thousand Oaks, CA: Sage.

Fowler, Floyd J. (2008). *Survey research methods* (4th ed.). Thousand Oaks, CA: Sage.

Frattaroli, Shannon, & Stephen P. Teret. (2006). Understanding and informing policy implementation: A case study of the domestic violence provisions of the Maryland Gun Violence Act. *Evaluation Review, 30*(3), 347–360.

Frieden, Thomas R., Farzad Mostashari, Bonnie D. Kerker, Nancy Miller, Anjum Hajat, & Martin Frankel. (2005). Adult tobacco use levels after intensive tobacco control measures: New York City, 2002–2003. *American Journal of Public Health, 95*(6), 1016–1023.

Friedman, David, Robert Pisani, & Roger Purves. (2007). *Statistics* (4th ed.). New York: W. W. Norton.

Friedman, Michael S., Kenneth E. Powell, Lori Hutwagner, LeRoy M. Graham, & W. Gerald Teague. (2001). Impact of changes in transportation and commuting behaviors during the 1996 Summer Olympic Games in Atlanta on air quality and childhood asthma. *Journal of the American Medical Association, 285*(7), 897–905.

Fund for the City of New York. (2008). ComNET. Retrieved November 10, 2008, from www.fcny.org/cmgp/comnet.htm

George, Alexander L., & Andrew Bennett. (2005). *Case studies and theory development in the social sciences.* Cambridge, MA: MIT Press.

Gerber, Alan S., & Eric M. Patashnik. (2006). *Sham surgery: The problem of inadequate medical evidence* (Working Paper). Charlottesville: Miller Center of the University of Virginia. Retrieved October 6, 2009, from http://millercenter.org/scripps/archive/colloquia/detail/1959

Glaser, Barney G., & Anselm Strauss. (1967). *The discovery of grounded theory: Strategies for qualitative research.* Piscataway, NJ: Aldine Transaction.

Glied, Sherry, Dahlia Remler, & Joshua Graff Zivin. (2002, December). Inside the sausage factory: Understanding and improving estimates of the effects of health insurance expansion proposals using a reference case approach. *Milbank Quarterly, 80*(4), 602–636.

Gold, Raymond L. (1958, March). Roles in sociological field observations. *Social Forces, 36*(3), 217–223.

Gordis, Leon. (2000). *Epidemiology* (2nd ed.). Philadelphia: W. B. Saunders.

Gray-Little, Bernadette, Valerie S. L. Williams, & Timothy D. Hancock. (1997). An item response theory analysis of the Rosenberg Self-Esteem Scale. *Personality and Social Psychology Bulletin, 23*(5), 443–451.

Grazer, Frederick M., & Rohrich H. de Jong. (2000). Fatal outcomes from liposuction: Census survey of cosmetic surgeons. *Plastic and Reconstructive Surgery, 105*(1), 436.

Grieco, Elizabeth M., & Rachel C. Cassidy. (2001). *Overview of race and Hispanic origin: Census 2000 brief* (Census Report CENSUS-C2KBR/01–1). Washington, DC: U.S. Census Bureau. Retrieved November 3, 2009, from www.census.gov

Groves, Robert M. (2006). Nonresponse rates and nonresponse bias in household surveys [Special issue]. *Public Opinion Quarterly, 70*(5), 646–675.

Groves, Robert M., Floyd J. Fowler Jr., Mick P. Couper, & James M. Lepkowski. (2004). *Survey methodology.* Malden, MA: Wiley-Interscience.

Gruber, Jonathan. (2004). Is making divorce easier bad for children? The long-run implications of unilateral divorce. *Journal of Labor Economics, 22*(4), 799–833.

Gurley-Calvez, Tami, Thomas J. Gilbert, Katherine Harper, Donald J. Marples, & Kevin Daly. (2009). Do tax incentives affect investment? An analysis of the new markets tax credit. *Public Finance Review, 37,* 371.

Harpster, Tracy, Susan H. Adams, & John P. Jarvis. (2009). Analyzing 911 homicide calls for indicators of guilt or innocence: An exploratory analysis. *Homicide Studies, 13*(1), 69–93.

Harris Interactive. (2008). *The Harris Poll: Majority in U.S. favors stricter gun control but gun control is not likely to be much of an issue in upcoming presidential election.* Retrieved March 19, 2008, from www.harrisinteractive.com/harris_poll/index.asp?PID=471

Harris, Katherine M., & Dahlia K. Remler. (1998). Who is the marginal patient? Understanding instrumental variables estimates of treatment effects. *Health Services Research, 31*(5 Pt. 1), 1337–1360.

Hatry, Harry P. (2007). *Performance measurement: Getting results* (2nd ed.). Washington, DC: Urban Institute Press.

Heckman, James J. (2000). Causal parameters and policy analysis in economics: Twentieth century retrospective. *Quarterly Journal of Economics, 115,* 45–97.

Henry, Gary T. (1990). *Practical sampling.* Newbury Park, CA: Sage.

Henry, Gary T. (1994). *Graphing data: Techniques for display and analysis* (Illustrated ed.). Thousand Oaks, CA: Sage.

Herman, Dena R., Gail G. Harrison, Abdelmonem A. Afifi, & Eloise Jenks. (2008). Effect of a targeted subsidy on intake of fruits and vegetables among low-income women in the special supplemental nutrition program for women, infants, and children. *American Journal of Public Health, 98*(1), 98–105.

HighScope Educational Research Foundation. (2005). *HighScope Perry preschool study lifetime effects: The HighScope Perry preschool study through age 40.* Retrieved November 22, 2009, from www.highscope.org/Content.asp?ContentId=219

Hillier, Sharon, Cyrus Cooper, Sam Kellingray, Graham Russell, Herbert Hughes, & David Coggon. (2000). Fluoride in drinking water and risk of hip fracture in the UK: A case-control study. *Lancet, 355*(9200), 265–269.

Holzer, Marc, & Kaifeng Yang. (2004). Performance measurement and improvement: An assessment of the state of the art. *International Review of Administrative Sciences, 70*(1), 15–31.

Howell, David C. (2007). Multiple comparisons among treatment means. In D. C. Howell (Ed.), *Statistical methods for psychology* (6th ed., chap. 12). Belmont, CA: Thomson Wadsworth.

Huurre, Taina, Hanna Junkkari, & Hillevi Aro. (2006). Long-term psychosocial effects of parental divorce: A follow-up study from adolescence to adulthood. *European Archives of Psychiatry and Clinical Neuroscience, 256*(4), 256–263.

Iezzoni, Lisa. (2002). Using administrative data to study persons with disabilities. *Milbank Quarterly, 80*(2), 347–379.

Imbens, Guido W., & Joshua D. Angrist. (1994). Identification and estimation of local average treatment effects. *Econometrica, 62*(2), 467–475.

Institute of Medicine Committee of the Consequences of Uninsurance. (2003). *Hidden costs, value lost: Uninsurance in America.* Washington, DC: Institute of Medicine.

Intergovernmental Panel on Climate Change. (2007). *Climate change 2007: Synthesis report.* Retrieved July 14, 2009, from www.ipcc.ch/publications_and_data/publications_ipcc_fourth_assessment_report_synthesis_report.htm

The Internet Party: Second Amendment. (2008). Retrieved March 19, 2008, from www.theinternetparty.org/comments/index.php?cid=pol20051201000

Jacobsen, Steven J., Jack Goldberg, Toni P. Miles, Jacob A. Brody, William Stiers, & Alfred A. Rimm. (1990). Regional variation in the incidence of hip fracture: US white women aged 65 years and older. *Journal of the American Medical Association, 264*(4), 500.

Jackson Public Schools. (2004). *Class-size reduction grant program.* Retrieved October 22, 2004, from www.jackson.k12.ms.us/departments/curriculum/class_reduction/class_reduction.htm

JAMA & Archives Journals. (2007). *AMA manual of style: A guide for authors and editors* (10th ed.). New York: Oxford University Press.

Jones, James H. (1993). *Bad blood: The Tuskegee Syphilis experiment.* New York: Free Press of Simon & Schuster.

Jorgensen, Danny L. (1989). *Participant observation: A methodology for human studies.* Newbury Park, CA: Sage.

Kalton, Graham. (1983). *Introduction to survey sampling.* Newbury Park, CA: Sage.

Katz, Lawrence F., Jeffrey R. Kling, & Jeffrey B. Liebman. (2001). Moving to opportunity in Boston: Early results of a randomized mobility experiment. *Quarterly Journal of Economics, 116,* 607–654.

Kennedy, Peter. (2003). *A guide to econometrics* (5th ed.). Cambridge, MA: MIT Press.

Kennedy School of Government. (1993). *From research to policy: The cigarette excise tax* (Kennedy School of Government Case C16-93-1233.0). Cambridge, MA: Harvard University Press.

Kiecolt, K. Jill, & Laura E. Nathan. (1985). *Secondary analysis of survey data.* Beverly Hills, CA: Sage.

King, Gary, Robert O. Keohane, & Sidney Verba. (1994). *Designing social inquiry*. Mahwah, NJ: Princeton University Press.

Kingdon, John W. (1995). *Agendas, alternatives, and public policies* (2nd ed.). New York: HarperCollins.

Kirby, Douglas. (2007). *Emerging answers 2007: Research finding on programs to reduce teen pregnancy and sexually transmitted diseases*. Washington, DC: The National Campaign to Prevent Teen and Unplanned Pregnancy. Retrieved September 20, 2009, from www.thenationalcampaign.org/EA2007/EA2007_sum.pdf

Koepsell, Thomas, Lon McCloskey, Marsha Wolf, Anne Vernez Moudon, David Buchner, Jess Kraus, et al. (2002). Crosswalk markings and the risk of pedestrian-motor vehicle collisions in older pedestrians. *Journal of the American Medical Association, 288*(17), 2136–2143.

Korenman, Sanders, & David Neumark. (1991). Does marriage make men more productive? *Journal of Human Resources, 26*(2), 282–307.

Kramer, Fredrica D., Kenneth Finegold, & Daniel Kuehn. (2008, April). *Understanding the consequences of Hurricane Katrina for ACF service populations: A feasibility assessment of study approaches*. Washington, DC: Urban Institute Press.

Kramer, Michael S., Frances Aboud, Elena Miranova, Irina Vanilovich, Robert W. Platt, Lidia Matush, et al. (2009). Breastfeeding and child cognitive development: New evidence from a large randomized trial. *Archives of General Psychiatry, 65*(5), 578–584.

Kramer, Michael S., B. Chalmers, E. D. Hodnett, Z. Sevkovskaya, I. Dzikovich, S. Shapiro, et al. for the PROBIT Study Group. (2001a). A breastfeeding intervention increased breastfeeding and reduced GI tract infections and atopic eczema. *Evidence-Based Nursing, 4,* 106.

Kramer, Michael S., B. Chalmers, E. D. Hodnett, Z. Sevkovskaya, I. Dzikovich, S. Shapiro, et al. for the PROBIT Study Group. (2001b). A Promotion of Breastfeeding Intervention Trial (PROBIT): A randomized trial in the Republic of Belarus. *Journal of the American Medical Association, 285*(4), 413–420.

Kramer, Michael S., Richard M. Martin, Jonathan A. C. Sterne, Stanley Shapiro, Mourad Dahhou, & Robert W. Platt. (2009). The double jeopardy of clustered measurement and cluster randomization. *British Medical Journal, 339,* b2900.

Kramer, Michael S., Lidia Matush, Irina Vanilovich, Robert Platt, Natalia Bogdanovich, Zinaida Sevkovskaya, et al. (2007). Effect of prolonged and exclusive breastfeeding on risk of allergy and asthma: Cluster randomised trial. *British Medical Journal, 335*(7624), 815–820.

Kramer, Michael S., Lidia Matush, Irina Vanliovich, Robert W. Platt, Natalia Bogdanovich, Zinaida Sevovskaya, et al. (2009). A randomized breast-feeding promotion intervention did not reduce child obesity in Belarus. *Journal of Nutrition, 139*(2), 417S–421S.

Kramer, Michael S., Irina Vanilovich, Lidia Matush, Natalia Bogdanovich, X. Zhang, Gyorgy Shishko, G., et al. (2007). The effect of prolonged and exclusive breast-feeding on dental caries in early school-age children. *Caries Research, 41*(6), 484–488.

Lacy, Rebecca. (2009, April 23). Are people with health insurance healthier than those without? *The Oregonian*. Retrieved September 20, 2009, from www.oregonlive.com/news/index.ssf/2009/04/oregon_health_study_tries_to_d.htm

Lamont, Michele, & P. White. (Eds.). (2005). *Workshop on interdisciplinary standards for systematic qualitative research: Report*. Washington, DC: National Science Foundation. Retrieved August 17, 2009, from www.nsf.gov/sbe/ses/soc/ISSQR_workshop_rpt.pdf

de Lancer Julnes, Patria, & Marc Holzer. (2008). *Performance measurement: Building theory, improving practice*. Armonk, NY: M. E. Sharpe.

Langbein, Laura, & Claire Felbinger. (2006). *Public program evaluation: A statistical guide*. Armonk, NY: M. E. Sharpe.

Layard, Richard. (2005). *Happiness: Lessons from a new science*. New York: Penguin Books.

Lemert, Charles. (2004). *Social theory: The multicultural and classic readings* (3rd ed.). Nashville, TN: Westview Press.

Leonard, Carl, Sid Bourke, & Neville Schofield. (2002, December). *Student quality of school life: A multilevel analysis*. Paper presented at the Annual Conference of the Australian Association for Research in Education, Brisbane, Queensland, Australia. Retrieved August 11, 2009, from www.aare.edu.au/02pap/le002063.htm

Lewis-Beck, Michael S. (1980). *Applied regression: An introduction*. Beverly Hills, CA: Sage.

Lewit, Eugene M., & Coate, Douglas. (1982). The potential for using excise taxes to reduce smoking. *Journal of Health Economics, 1,* 121–145.

Lincoln, Yvonna, & Egon G. Guba. (1985). *Naturalistic inquiry*. Beverly Hills, CA: Sage.

Lind, Torbjorn, Bo Lonnerdal, Hans Stenlund, Indira L. Gamayanti, Djauhar Ismail, Rosadi Seswandhana, et al. (2004). A community-based randomized controlled trial of iron and zinc supplementation in Indonesian infants: effects on growth and development. *American Journal of Clinical Nutrition, 80*(3), 729–736.

Lipsey, Mark W., & David B. Wilson. (2001). *Practical meta-analysis*. Thousand Oaks, CA: Sage.

Lohr, Sharon L. (1999). *Sampling design and analysis*. Pacific Grove, CA: Duxbury Press.

Ludwig, Jens, Jeffrey B. Liebman, Jeffrey R. Kling, Greg J. Duncan, Lawrence F. Katz, Ronald C. Kessler, et al. (2008). What can we learn about neighborhood effects from the moving to opportunity experiment? *American Journal of Sociology, 114*(1), 144–188.

Luhrmann, Tanya Marie. (2008). The street will drive you crazy: Why homeless psychotic women in the institutional circuit in the United States often say no to offers of help. *American Journal of Psychiatry, 165*(1), 15–20.

Luke, Douglas A. (2004). *Multilevel modeling* (1st ed.). Thousand Oaks, CA: Sage.

Malhotra, Neil, & Jon A. Krosnick. (2007). The effect of survey mode and sampling on inferences about political attitudes and behavior: Comparing the 2000 and 2004 ANES to Internet surveys with nonprobability samples. *Political Analysis, 15*(3), 286–323.

Mamabear. (2007). *Feeling a little paranoid? You will after this* [Blog entry]. San Antonio, TX: The International Breastfeeding Symbol. Retrieved November 4, 2009, from http://www.breastfeedingsymbol.org/2007/09/24/feeling-a-little-paranoid-you-will-after-reading-this/

Manski, Charles F. (1995). *Identification problems in the social sciences*. Cambridge, MA: Harvard University Press.

McDowall, David, Richard McCleary, Errol E. Meidinger, & Richard A. Hay. (1980). *Interrupted time series analysis* (1st ed.). Beverly Hills, CA: Sage.

McFadden, Daniel. (1974). The measurement of urban travel demand. *Journal of Public Economics, 3,* 303–328.

McGonagle, Katherine A., & Robert F. Schoeni. (2006). *The panel study of income dynamics: Overview and summary of scientific contributions after nearly 40 years*. Ann Arbor: University of Michigan, Institute for Social Research.

McIntyre, Alice. (2007). *Participatory action research* (1st ed.). Thousand Oaks, CA: Sage.

McIver, John P., & Edward G. Carmines. (1981). *Unidimensional scaling*. Beverly Hills, CA: Sage.

McKee, Rosie, Nanette Mutrie, Fiona Crawford, & Brian Green. (2007). Promoting walking to school: Results of a quasi-experimental trial. *Journal of Epidemiology and Community Health, 61*(9), 818–823.

Mead, Margaret. (1971). *Coming of age in Samoa*. New York: Harper Perennial.

Merton, Robert K. (1967). *On theoretical sociology*. New York: Free Press.

The Michigan Daily. (2001, September 9). *Columbia prof. fabricates food poisoning complaints for study*. Retrieved November 25, 2009, from www.michigandaily.com/content/columbia-prof-fabricates-food-poisoning-complaints-study

Miguel-Tobal, Juan José, Antonio Cano Vindel, Iciar Iruarrízaga, Héctor González Ordi, & Sandro Galea. (2005). Psychopathological repercussions of the March 11 terrorist attacks in Madrid. *Psychology in Spain, 9,* 75–80.

Miles, Matthew B., & Michael Huberman. (1994). *Qualitative data analysis: An expanded sourcebook* (2nd ed.). Thousand Oaks, CA: Sage.

Milgram, S. (1974). *Obedience to authority: An experimental view*. New York: HarperCollins.

Miller, D. W. (2001, February 9). Poking holes in the theory of "Broken Windows." *The Chronicle of Higher Education*.

Miller, Jane E. (2004). *The Chicago guide to writing about numbers*. Chicago: University of Chicago Press.

Miller, Jane E. (2005). *The Chicago guide to writing about multivariate analysis*. Chicago: University of Chicago Press.

Miller, N., Verhoef, M., & Cardwell, K. (2008). Rural parents' perspectives about information on child immunization. *International Electronic Journal of Rural and Remote Health Research, Education, Policy and Practice, 863*. Retrieved May 28, 2009, from www.rrh.org.au/articles/subviewnthamer.asp?ArticleID = 863

Mills, Mary Alice, Donald Edmondson, & Crystal L. Park. (2007, April). Trauma and stress response among Hurricane Katrina evacuees. *American Journal of Public Health, 97*(1), S116–S123.

Mohr, Lawrence B. (1995). *Impact analysis for program evaluation*. Thousand Oaks, CA: Sage.

Moldova. (2009, October 30). In *Wikipedia, The Free Encyclopedia*. Retrieved November 1, 2009, from http://en.wikipedia.org/w/index.php?title = Moldova&oldid = 322953548

Mooney, Christopher Z., & Robert D. Duval. (1993). *Bootstrapping: A nonparametric approach to statistical inference*. Newbury Park, CA: Sage.

Moore, David S. (2009). *The basic practice of statistics* (5th ed.). New York: W. H. Freeman.

Morgan, Stephen L., & Christopher Winship. (2007). *Counterfactuals and causal inference: Methods and principle for social research*. Cambridge, UK: Cambridge University Press.

Mortensen, Erik Lykke, Kim Fleischer Michaelsen, Stephanie Sanders, & June Machover Reinsch. (2002). The association between duration of breastfeeding and adult intelligence. *Journal of the American Medical Association, 287*(18), 2365–2946.

MSNBC News Report. (2007, November 1). *Sixty-seven percent of parents support giving contraceptives to teenagers*. Retrieved November 12, 2009, from http://msnbcmedia2.msn.com/i/msnbc/Components/ArtAndPhotoFronts/HEALTH/071101/AP_BIRTH_CONTROL.gif

Muller, Andreas. (2004). Florida's motorcycle helmet law repeal and fatality rates. *American Journal of Public Health, 94*(4), 556–558.

Nagourney, Adam, & Megan Thee-Brenan. (2009, April 6). Outlook on economy is brightening, poll finds. *New York Times*. Retrieved May 27, 2009, from www.nytimes.com/2009/04/07/us/politics/07poll.html

Napoli, Anthony R., & George J. Hiltner III. (1993). An evaluation of developmental reading instruction. *Journal of Developmental Education, 17*(1), 14.

National Center for Educational Statistics. (2006). *Comparing private and public schools using hierarchical linear modeling* (NCES 2006–461). Washington, DC: U.S. Department of Education.

National Center for Health Statistics. (2007). *FASTATS: Illegal drug use*. Atlanta, GA: Centers for Disease Control and Prevention. Retrieved November 27, 2007, from www.cdc.gov/nchs/fastats/druguse.htm

National Diabetes Information Clearinghouse, National Institutes of Health. (n.d.). *National Diabetes Statistics, 2007: General Information*. Bethesda, MD: Author. Retrieved June 16, 2009, from http://diabetes.niddk.nih.gov/DM/PUBS/statistics/#y_people

National Institutes of Health. (2009). *The NIH Almanac: Appropriations*. Retrieved November 25, 2009, from www.nih.gov/about/almanac/appropriations/part2.htm

National Science Foundation. (2009). *NSF congressional highlight: Congress passes FY09 omnibus bill*. Arlington, VA: Author. Retrieved October 5, 2009, from www.nsf.gov/about/congress/111/highlights/cu09_0310.jsp

Newhouse, Joseph P., & The Insurance Experiment Group. (1993). *Free for all: Lessons from the RAND health insurance experiment*. Cambridge, MA: Harvard University Press.

New York Times. (2009). How the poll was conducted: NYTimes.com. Retrieved November 10, 2009, from www.nytimes.com/2009/11/02/technology/02mbox.html?_r = 1

O'Connor, A. (2003, October 21). Rise in income improves children's behavior. *New York Times*. Retrieved November 27, 2009, from www.nytimes.com/2003/10/21/health/rise-in-income-improves-children-s-behavior.html?scp = 1&sq = O%E2%80%99Connor,%20A.%20(2003,%20October%2021).%20Rise%20in%20income%20improves%20children%E2%80%99s%20behavior.%20New%20York%20Times&st = cse

OECD. Stat Extracts ALFS Summary tables. (2008). Retrieved February 10, 2008, from http://stats.oecd.org/WBOS/default.aspx?DatasetCode = ALFS_SUMTAB

Orr, Larry, Judith D. Feins, Robin Jacob, Erik Beecroft, Lisa Sanbonmatsu, Lawrence Katz, et al. (2003). *Moving to opportunity for fair housing demonstration project. Interim impacts evaluation.* Washington, DC: U.S. Department of Housing and Urban Development.

Ostrom, Charles W. (1990). *Time series analysis: Regression techniques* (2nd ed.). Newbury Park, CA: Sage.

Pannell, David J., & Anna M. Roberts. (2009). Conducting and delivering integrated research to influence land-use policy: Salinity policy in Australia. *Environmental Science and Policy.* Retrieved November 27, 2009, from www.sciencedirect.com/science?_ob = ArticleURL&_udi = B6VP6-4VDSJTG-2&_user = 10&_rdoc = 1&_fmt = &_orig = search&_sort = d&_docanchor = &view = c&_searchStrId = 1112684737&_rerunOrigin = google&_acct = C000050221&_version = 1&_urlVersion – 0&_userid = 10&md5 = 270d0ea80bf195080a9cfb4efac1b257

Patton, Michael Quinn. (2002). *Qualitative research and evaluation methods* (3rd ed.). Thousand Oaks, CA: Sage.

Pearl, Judea. (2000). *Causality: Models, reasoning and inference.* Cambridge, UK: Cambridge University Press.

Peffley, Mark, & Jon Hurwitz. (2007, October). Persuasion and resistance: Race and the death penalty in America. *American Journal of Political Science, 51*(4), 996–1012.

Petrella, Margaret, Lee Biernbaum, & Jane Lappin. (2007). *Exploring a new congestion pricing concept: Focus group findings from Northern Virginia and Philadelphia.* Cambridge, MA: Volpe Center, U.S. Department of Transportation.

Poister, Theodore H. (2003). *Measuring performance in public and nonprofit organizations* (1st ed.). San Francisco: Jossey-Bass.

PollingReport.com. (2008). *Direction of the country, Associated Press-Ipsos poll.* Retrieved September 15, 2008, from www.pollingreport.com/right.htm

PollingReport.com. (2009). *Terrorism.* Retrieved November 10, 2009, from www.pollingreport.com/terror.htm

Project on Human Development in Chicago Neighborhoods. (2008). *Systematic social observation.* Retrieved September 10, 2008, from www.icpsr.umich.edu/PHDCN/descriptions/sso.html

RAND Corporation. (n.d.). *The Health Insurance Experiment: A classic RAND study speaks to the current health care reform debate.* Retrieved November 22, 2009, from www.rand.org/pubs/research_briefs/RB9174/index1.html

Rees, Daniel I., & Joseph J. Sabia. (2009). The effect of breast feeding on educational attainment: Evidence from sibling data. *Journal of Human Capital, 3*(1), 43–72.

Remler, Dahlia K., Joshua Graff Zivin, & Sherry A. Glied. (2004). Modeling health insurance expansions: Effect of alternate approaches. *Journal of Policy Analysis and Management, 23*(2), 291–314.

Roberts, Les, Riyadh Lafta, Richard Garfield, Jamal Khudhairi, & Gilbert Burnham. (2004). Mortality before and after the 2003 invasion of Iraq: Cluster sample survey. *Lancet, 364,* 1857–1864.

Robinson, William S. (1950). Ecological correlations and the behavior of individuals. *American Sociological Review, 15*(3), 351–357.

Rosenbaum, Paul R. (2002). *Observational studies* (2nd ed.). New York: Springer.

Rosenbaum, Paul R., & Donald B. Rubin. (1985). Constructing a control group using multivariate matched sampling methods that incorporate the propensity score. *The American Statistician, 39*(1), 33.

Rosenberg, Morris. (1965). *Society and the adolescent self-image.* Princeton, NJ: Princeton University Press.

Rosenzweig, Mark R., & Kenneth I. Wolpin. (2000). Natural "Natural Experiments" in economics. *Journal of Economic Literature, 38*(4), 827–874.

Rosnow, Ralph L., & Robert Rosenthal. (1997). *People studying people: Artifacts and ethics in behavioral research.* New York: W. H. Freeman.

Rossi, Peter H., Mark W. Lipsey, & Howard E. Freeman. (2003). *Evaluation: A systematic approach* (7th ed.). Thousand Oaks, CA: Sage.

Rothman, Kenneth. (1990). No adjustments are needed for multiple comparisons. *Epidemiology 1*(1), 43–46. Retrieved November 4, 2009, from www.jstor.org/stable/20065622

Rubin, Donald B. (2005). Causal inference using potential outcomes: Design, modeling, decisions. *Journal of the American Statistical Association, 100,* 322–331.

Sampson, Robert J., & Stephen W. Raudenbush. (1999). Systematic social observation of public spaces: A new look at disorder in urban neighborhoods. *American Journal of Sociology, 105*(3), 603–651.

Savas, E. S. (2007). *Slow train to better service*. Retrieved November 22, 2009, from www.nytimes.com/2007/12/16/opinion/nyregionopinions/16CIsavas.html

Scheiber, Noam. (2007, April 2). Freaks and geeks: How Freakanomics is ruining the dismal science. *The New Republic*. Retrieved November 28, 2009, from www.tnr.com/article/freaks-and-geeks-how-freakonomics-ruining-the-dismal-science?page=0,0

Schemo, Diana Jean, & Ford Fessenden. (2003, December 3). A miracle revisited: Measuring success; gains in Houston schools: How real are they? *New York Times*. Retrieved November 28, 2009, from www.nytimes.com/2003/12/03/us/a-miracle-revisited-measuring-success-gains-in-houston-schools-how-real-are-they.html?scp=1&sq=gains+in+Houston+schools%3A+How+real+are+they%3F+&st=nyt

Schmitz, Connie C., & Beverly A. Parsons. (1999). *Everything you wanted to know about logic models but were afraid to ask*. Boulder, CO: InSites. Retrieved November 4, 2009, from www.insites.org/documents/logmod.htm

Schwartz, J. (1994, January). Air pollution and daily mortality: A review and meta analysis. *Environmental Research, 64*(1), 36–52.

Seron, Carroll, Van Ryzin, Gregg, & Frankel, Martin. (2001). Impact of legal counsel on outcomes for poor tenants in New York City's housing court: Results of a randomized experiment. *Law & Society Review, 35,* 419.

Shadish, William R., Thomas D. Cook, & Donald T. Campbell. (2002). *Experimental and quasi-experimental designs for generalized causal inference*. Boston: Houghton Mifflin.

Sheard, Laura, & Charlotte Tompkins. (2008). Contradictions and misperceptions: An exploration of injecting practice, cleanliness, risk, and partnership in the lives of women drug users. *Qualitative Health Research, 18*(11), 1536–1547.

Sheehan, Helena, & Sheamus Sweeney. (2009). The Wire and the world: Narrative and metanarrative. *Jump Cut: A Review of Contemporary Media, 51*. Retrieved October 8, 2009, from www.ejumpcut.org/currentissue/

Simon, Steve. (2008). *Odds ratio vs. relative risk*. Retrieved June 17, 2009, from www.childrensmercy.org/stats/journal/oddsratio.asp

Small, Mario Luis. (2005). Lost in translation: How not to make qualitative research more scientific. In *Workshop on interdisciplinary standards for systematic qualitative research* (Appendix 6, pp. 165–171). Retrieved August 17, 2009, from www.nsf.gov/sbe/ses/soc/ISSQR_workshop_rpt.pdf

Smith, Robert. (2005). *Mexican New York: Transnational lives of new immigrants*. Berkeley: University of California Press.

Spector, Paul. (1992). *Summated rating scale construction: An introduction*. Newbury Park, CA: Sage.

Stone, Deborah. (1997). *Policy paradox: The art of political decision making*. New York: W. W. Norton.

Stringer, Ernest T. (2007). *Action research* (3rd ed.). Thousand Oaks, CA: Sage.

Struyk, Michael, & Raymond J. Fix. (1993). *Clear and convincing evidence: Measurement of discrimination in America*. Lanham, MD: University Press of America.

Surowiecki, James. (2004). *The wisdom of crowds: Why the many are smarter than the few and how collective wisdom shapes business, economies, societies and nations*. New York: Doubleday of Random House.

Taubes, Gary, & Charles C. Mann. (1995). Epidemiology faces its limits. *Science, 269*(5221), 164–169.

Tenopir, Carol. (2004, February 1). Online databases—Online scholarly journals: How many? *Library Journal*. Retrieved June 29, 2009, from www.libraryjournal.com/article/CA374956.html

Time-Sharing Experiments for the Social Sciences. (n.d.). *Welcome*. Retrieved November 11, 2009, from http://tess.experimentcentral.org

Treloar, Carla, Becky Laybutt, Marianne Jauncey, Ingrid van Beek, Michael Lodge, Grant Malpas, et al. (2008). Broadening discussions of "safe" in hepatitis C prevention: A close-up of swabbing in an analysis of video recordings of injecting practice. *International Journal of Drug Policy, 19*(1), 59–65.

Trochim, William. (2001). *The research methods knowledge base*. Cincinnati, OH: Atomic Dog.

Tufte, Edward R. (2001). *The visual display of quantitative information* (2nd ed.). Cheshire, CT: Graphics Press.

Turner, Charles F., Leighton Ku, Susan M. Rogers, Laura D. Lindberg, Joseph H. Pleck, & Freya L. Sonenstein. (1998). Adolescent sexual behavior, drug use, and violence: Increased reporting with computer survey technology. *Science, 280*(5365), 867–873.

Turney, Kristin, Susan Clampet-Lundquist, Kathryn Edin, Jeffery R. Kling, & Greg J. Duncan. (2006). Neighborhood effects on barriers to employment: Results from a randomized housing mobility experiment in Baltimore. In G. Burtless & J. R. Pack (Eds.), *Brookings-Wharton papers on urban affairs* (pp. 137–187). Washington, DC: Brookings Institution Press.

University of Chicago. (2003). *The Chicago manual of style* (15th ed.). Chicago: University of Chicago Press.

United States Elections Project. (2008). Retrieved February 7, 2008, from http://elections.gmu.edu/Voter_Turnout_2006.htm

U.S. Bureau of Justice Statistics. (2008). *Crime and justice data online.* Retrieved August 13, 2008, from http://bjsdata.ojp.usdoj.gov/dataonline/index.cfm

U.S. Census Bureau. (2008). Oklahoma QuickFacts from the US Census Bureau. Retrieved February 7, 2008, from http://quickfacts.census.gov/qfd/states/40000.html

U.S. Census Bureau. (2009a). *Annual survey of manufactures: How the data are collected.* Retrieved November 10, 2009, from www.census.gov/manufacturing/asm/how_the_data_are_collected/index.html

U.S. Census Bureau. (2009b). *The 2009 statistical abstracts. Incomes, expenditures, poverty and wealth* (Table 687). Retrieved November 10, 2009, from www.census.gov/compendia/statab/tables/09s0687.pdf

U.S. Census Bureau. (2009c). *The 2009 statistical abstracts. Law enforcement, courts, & prisons: Crimes and crime rates.* Retrieved November 10, 2009, from www.census.gov/compendia/statab/tables/09s0301.pdf

U.S. Department of Health and Human Services. (2009). *Women's Health.gov. Ad Council Materials.* Retrieved November 25, 2009, from www.womenshealth.gov/breastfeeding/programs/nbc/adcouncil/#b

U.S. Department of Housing and Urban Development. (n.d.). *Moving to opportunity for fair housing.* Retrieved November 22, 2009, from www.hud.gov/progdesc/mto.cfm

U.S. Department of Labor, Bureau of Labor Statistics. (2009). *News: The employment situation – August 2008.* Retrieved September 15, 2008, from www.bls.gov/news.release/archives/empsit_09052008.pdf

U.S. Federal Bureau of Investigation. (2008). *Forcible rape: Crime in the United States 2006.* Retrieved January 22, 2008, from www.fbi.gov/ucr/cius2006/offenses/violent_crime/forcible_rape.html

U.S. Global Change Research Program. (2009). *Global climate change impacts in the United States.* Washington, DC: Author. Retrieved July 14, 2009, from www.globalchange.gov/usimpacts

USA Today. (2008). Quick question: How many firearms do you own? *On Deadline: USATODAY.com.* Retrieved April 20, 2009, from http://blogs.usatoday.com/ondeadline/2008/06/quick-question.html

Valverde, Maria de la Luz, & Hassan Tajalli. (2006). *The City of Austin citizen survey 2006.* Retrieved November 10, 2009, from www.ci.austin.tx.us/budget/06-07/downloads/citizensurvey2006.pdf

Van Ryzin, Gregg G. (1996). The impact of resident management on residents' satisfaction with public housing: A process analysis of quasi-experimental data. *Evaluation Review, 20*(4), 485–506.

Van Ryzin, Gregg G. (2008). Validity of an on-line panel approach to citizen surveys. *Public Performance & Management Review, 32*(2), 236–262.

Van Ryzin, Gregg G. (2009, October 1–3). *Outcomes, process, and citizens' trust of the civil service.* Paper presented at the 2009 conference of the Public Management Research Association, Columbus, Ohio.

W. K. Kellogg Foundation. (2004). *Logic model development guide.* Retrieved November 4, 2009, from www.wkkf.org/Pubs/Tools/Evaluation/Pub3669.pdf

Walt, Gill. (1994). How far does research influence policy? *European Journal of Public Health, 4,* 233–235.

Wasunna, Beatrice, Dejan Zurovac, Catherine A. Goodman, & Robert W. Snow. (2008). Why don't health workers prescribe ACT? A qualitative study of factors affecting the prescription of artemether-lumefantrine. *Malaria Journal, 7*(1), 29.

Webb, Eugene J., Donald T. Campbell, Richard D. Schwartz, & Lee Sechrest. (1999). *Unobtrusive measures* (Rev. ed.). Thousand Oaks, CA: Sage.

Webb, Theresa, Lucille Jenkins, Nickolas Browne, Abdelmonen A. Afifi, & Jess Kraus. (2007). Violent entertainment pitched to adolescents: An analysis of PG-13 films. *Pediatrics, 119*(6), e1219–e1229.

Webster, Daniel W., Maria T. Bulzacchelli, April M. Zeoli, & Jon S. Vernick. (2006). Effects of undercover police stings of gun dealers on the supply of new guns to criminals. *Injury Prevention, 12*(4), 225–230.

Weimer, David L., & Aidan R. Vining. (1999). *Policy analysis concepts and practice* (3rd ed.). Upper Saddle River, NJ: Prentice Hall.

Weiss, Carol H. (1997). *Evaluation* (2nd ed.). Upper Saddle River, NJ: Prentice Hall.

Weiss, Robert S. (1994). *Learning from strangers: The art and method of qualitative interview studies.* New York: Free Press of Simon & Schuster.

Whitehead, Nicole. (2004). The effects of increased access to books on student reading using the public library. *Reading Improvement, 41*(3), 165.

Williams, Joseph M. (1995). *Style: Toward clarity and grace.* Chicago: University of Chicago Press.

Wilson, James Q., & George L. Kelling. (1982, March). Broken windows. *The Atlantic Monthly.* Retrieved May 27, 2009, from www.theatlantic.com/doc/print/198203/broken-windows

Wolf, Joan B. (2007). Is breast really best? Risk and total motherhood in the national breastfeeding awareness campaign. *Journal of Health Politics, Policy and Law, 32*(4), 595–635.

Woodward, James. (2003). *Making things happen: A theory of causal explanation.* Oxford, UK: Oxford University Press.

Wooldridge, Jeffrey. (2009). *Introductory econometrics: A modern approach* (4th ed.). Florence, KY: SouthWestern Cengage Learning.

Wooldridge, Judith, Genevieve Kenney, & Christopher Trenholm (with Lisa Dubay, Ian Hill, Myoung Kim, Lorenzo Moreno, Anna Sommers, & Stephen Zuckerman). (2005). *Congressionally mandated evaluation of the state children's health insurance program* (Final Report to Congress). Cambridge, MA/Washington, DC: Mathematica Policy Research/Urban Institute Press.

World Health Organization. (2009). *Malaria fact sheet.* Retrieved March 18, 2009, from www.who.int/mediacentre/factsheets/fs094/en/index.html

World Values Survey. (2005). Retrieved November 25, 2009, from www.worldvaluessurvey.org/

Yanovski, Jack A., Susan Z. Yanovski, Kara N. Sovik, Tuc T. Nguyen, Patrick M. O'Neil, & Nancy G. Sebring. (2000). A prospective study of holiday weight gain. *New England Journal of Medicine, 342*(12), 861–867.

Yin, Robert K. (2008). *Case study research: Design and methods* (4th ed.). Thousand Oaks, CA: Sage.

Zengerle, Jason. (2008, December 31). Going under: A doctor's downfall, and a profession's struggle with addiction. *The New Republic,* p. 21.

Zheng, Hang, Yanyou Liu, Wei Li, Bo Yang, Dengbang Chen, Xiaojia Wang, et al. (2006). Beneficial effects of exercise and its molecular mechanisms on depression in rats. *Behavioural Brain Research, 168*(1), 47–55.

Ziliak, Stephen T., & Deirdre N. McCloskey. (2008). *The cult of statistical significance.* Ann Arbor: University of Michigan.

Index

Supporting researchers for more than 40 years

Research methods have always been at the core of SAGE's publishing program. Founder Sara Miller McCune published SAGE's first methods book, *Public Policy Evaluation*, in 1970. Soon after, she launched the *Quantitative Applications in the Social Sciences* series—affectionately known as the "little green books."

Always at the forefront of developing and supporting new approaches in methods, SAGE published early groundbreaking texts and journals in the fields of qualitative methods and evaluation.

Today, more than 40 years and two million little green books later, SAGE continues to push the boundaries with a growing list of more than 1,200 research methods books, journals, and reference works across the social, behavioral, and health sciences. Its imprints—Pine Forge Press, home of innovative textbooks in sociology, and Corwin, publisher of PreK–12 resources for teachers and administrators—broaden SAGE's range of offerings in methods. SAGE further extended its impact in 2008 when it acquired CQ Press and its best-selling and highly respected political science research methods list.

From qualitative, quantitative, and mixed methods to evaluation, SAGE is the essential resource for academics and practitioners looking for the latest methods by leading scholars.

For more information, visit **www.sagepub.com**.